The Royal Cookery Book

LONDON: PRINTED BY
SPOTTISWOODE AND CO., NEW-STREET SQUARE
AND PARLIAMENT STREET

THE
ROYAL COOKERY BOOK

(LE LIVRE DE CUISINE)

BY

JULES GOUFFÉ

CHEF DE CUISINE OF THE PARIS JOCKEY CLUB

TRANSLATED FROM THE FRENCH AND ADAPTED FOR ENGLISH USE

BY

ALPHONSE GOUFFÉ

HEAD PASTRY-COOK TO HER MAJESTY THE QUEEN

COMPRISING

DOMESTIC AND HIGH-CLASS COOKERY

ILLUSTRATED WITH ONE HUNDRED AND SIXTY-ONE WOODCUTS FROM
DRAWINGS FROM NATURE BY E. RONJAT

NEW EDITION

LONDON
SAMPSON LOW, SON, AND MARSTON
CROWN BUILDINGS, 188 FLEET STREET
1869

TRANSLATOR'S PREFACE

THE UNPRECEDENTED SUCCESS of the *Livre de Cuisine* in France has led to its reproduction in England; and the publishers trust that a work which, on its first appearance, was so favourably received will be equally appreciated by the English public.

Whilst adhering, as near as possible, to the text of the original, I have endeavoured to adapt the recipes to the capabilities and requirements of English households.

The great number of technicalities which must abound in a work of this kind render it a difficult task to retain in a translation the clearness of the original.

I have striven to give the recipes in a simple and comprehensive manner, and I have never introduced a French word where I have been able to find an effective substitute in the English language.

I must except, of course, all the terms belonging to that special culinary nomenclature which I have been compelled to adopt; although all of French origin, most of these have now, by their constant recurrence, become household words in England.

With the hope that the merits of the work have not suffered at my hands, I will only add, that to the author alone will be due whatever favour the book may meet with in this country.

THE TRANSLATOR.

LONDON: *May* 1868.

PREFACE

It was after much deliberation that I decided upon writing the book which I now publish. The chief cause of my hesitation for so many years was, I will frankly own it, the perfect uselessness of such Cookery Books as have hitherto been published, which, in the majority of cases, have been servile copies one of the other,—repeating the same recipes, with the same vagueness, and often the same mistakes,—following all one routine, and falling into the same errors, without precising in their formulæ either weight, measure, quantity, or length of time in cooking,—rather lowering our profession, than exalting it :—in a word, guides which were of help to none : neither to those who knew, nor to those who wished to learn ; neither to the professional or the amateur.

Have I done better? Have I had at last the satisfaction of *realising the Cookery Book* universally required ?

The public will judge ; all I can say is, that I have done otherwise than had hitherto been attempted.

In Cookery Books generally there is confusion between Domestic and High-Class Cookery, between the simplest dishes and those of the most complex description ; thence an unfortunate jumble, sufficient to account for the little progress made hitherto in the study and practice of culinary art.

For instance, what can be more irrational than to give recipes for *Bisques*, *Suprèmes*, &c., intermixed with those of Haricot Mutton, Stewed Rabbit, or Veal, and such elementary dishes of Domestic Cookery? What more likely to produce confusion, and prevent masters or servants understanding anything?

The dimensions of this work have allowed me to give a complete treatise of Cookery. Separating what to my mind cannot conveniently go together, I have divided the work into two quite distinct Parts,—the First, treating of Domestic Cookery, the Second of the Higher Class Cookery. These two branches undoubtedly correspond and complete one another, as I will frequently show ; but it is nevertheless true that, for all practical purposes, they form two different subjects.

Every one will admit that the duties of a Plain Cook are very different to those of a *Chef* in a large establishment.

The First Part will, therefore, treat of the so-called *Domestic* or *Household Cookery*, free from complications of any kind on the score of execution or expense. It will be seen that I have spared none of the minutest particulars or most definite instructions, in order to bring this First Part within the comprehension of beginners.

I have constantly kept in view the leading principle of this work (a principle which, I trust, may, even on that score alone, give it a value of its own)—namely, to give in these Domestic Recipes *the most exact quantities*. Nothing has been explained or taught in ordinary Cookery, if one treats only of approximate quantities, or proceeds by arbitrary data of weight, measure, or of length of time to be devoted to each operation.

I have not written down a single one of my elementary directions without having continually my eye on the clock, and my hand on the scales. I must at once add, that one is not required, in practice, to refer constantly to such punctilious admeasurement, as soon as one has become a perfect practitioner ; but, when it is a question of laying down rules for persons without any prior knowledge, I maintain that one cannot be too careful : it is the only way to put an end to those approximations and doubts which still beset the steps of the inexperienced, even in the simplest operations, and which account for so many people eating indifferent meals at home, and complaining, with reason, of the little progress made hitherto in Domestic Cookery.

In the Second Part, I have represented High-Class Cookery, with all its developments and improvements. I think I have omitted nothing. I have, however, avoided with the greatest care all such pompous or bizarre nomenclature, all such silly ·*chàrlatanisme* of unknown dishes, which go to fill up so many books, and only represent, in a word, show dishes of which

none partake, or· else old friends under new names.
And why should I not also add that I have been led
to write this Cookery Book by the pressing solicita-
tions of many of my younger *confrères*, who are good
enough to refer occasionally to me for advice?

They bade me remember that, by my personal position and the circumstances of my life, I was in Cookery,
at once, the man of the past and the man of the
present,—of every day fare and of extra occasions,—and
competent, by the very fact, to write, upon the *ensemble* and the details of our profession, useful and in-
structive things, which had not been said before.

A cook from my earliest years, I have seen, noticed,
and practised much in all ways.

I have had opportunities of studying closely the
modus operandi of our old authorities, whose names
and fame it would be wrong to let die: foremost
among these stand Loyer, the man who, to my. mind,
was the most expert in dishing up; Drouhat, as good
a manager as he was good cook; Léchard, practising
all branches with the same ability; Bernard, so well
known for the delicate minuteness of his work;
Tortez, whose unfailing energy was equal to all emer-
gencies. I was, besides, employed, for seven consecutive
years, as cook and pastrycook, under the illustrious
Carême; I have striven to benefit as much as possible
by his excellent precepts and his great traditions,
which it would be well to see revived in our day.

The remembrance of bygone times has never made
me unjust to the present; I am not of those who
declare that French Cookery—that part of our natio-

nality of which we are with reason proud—is declining, and will never rise again ; good and true things never die ; there may be times of weakness, but, with work, intelligence, and goodwill, sooner or later there is a recovery. I maintain that never was it so possible to do well—nay, very well—as now.

Full of this conviction and of the continual progress of which Cookery is susceptible, as well in its simpler as in its higher walks, not a day passes without my seeking and working amongst young practitioners already celebrated, who witness enough, by their talent and well-earned fame, that the young school has in no wise degenerated from the old. In the first rank I must name Messrs. Paul Pasquier, Charles and Léon Canivet, Paul Dessoliers, Got (now Chief Pastrycook to the Emperor of the French), Bernard, jun., Madelain (*Chef* to the Duke of Buccleuch), Amédée Bain (·*Chef* to the Dowager Queen of Spain), Cogerie, &c. Many of them call themselves my pupils ; they must allow me to give them no other name than that of *confrère* and friend.

I owe them a number of excellent recipes, that I have only had to copy literally ; all those that I have named, and more particularly Messrs. Amédée Bain and Charles Canivet, my special *collaborateurs*, have greatly assisted me, by their active and devoted co-operation, in the execution of this long and difficult task, completed among our daily work, on our stoves,—the Cookery Book's true place.

Amongst other helpers I must also mention my two brothers, Alphonse Gouffé (Head Pastry Cook to the

a 2

Queen of England for the last twenty-eight years), and
Hippolyte Gouffé (*Chef* for the last twenty-five years
to the Count André Schouvalloff, in Russia).   The information which they have supplied me with from
abroad has been of great assistance to me; it is not
only as a brother that I thank them, but as a cook
doing justice to their acknowledged merit.

In a word I may sum up—it is by using it that
the Cookery Book must be judged.

If, owing to the improvements and rules I recommend, I learn that, between now and a few years
hence, every one eats of the best according to his
means; that, on the one hand, Domestic Cookery is
carried on with care, economy, and comfort; and, on
the other hand, the Higher Cookery is practised with
that tastefulness and *éclat* which an age of refinement
and luxury such as ours demands—then I shall have
attained the object I had in view; I shall be fully
satisfied with the result, and well rewarded for my
labour.

JULES GOUFFÉ.

PARIS: *July* 15, 1867.

THE TABLE LAID—THE SOUP SERVED

ILLUSTRATIONS OF THE BOOK

I THINK IT NECESSARY to explain the special object of the Woodcuts illustrating the text.

I will not dwell on their artistic value, nor on the merit of those draughtsmen and engravers who have given me their help ; but will merely mention that, although they are undoubtedly a very great addition to the appearance of the work, they were not introduced merely on that account, but also materially to assist the culinary teaching, which has been my first object in writing the book.

In dishing up, for instance, where theory is of so little use, I have not hesitated to represent separately all the component parts of removes, *entreés*, &c., so that the cook may understand them in their details and *ensemble*.

This has seemed to me preferable to representing, without any explanation of their details, large show dishes, of so complicated a nature, that a mere drawing of them would be more likely to discourage than enlighten beginners. It will be seen that I do not employ illustrations for the higher class of cookery only; many will be found explaining the simplest processes of domestic cookery ;—these will prove specially useful.

I think this way of completing recipes by sketches will be of great advantage to young practitioners desirous to learn, not by routine, as has been done so long, but by joining to the mere manual part, observation, study, science, and taste, without which there can be no good cook.

CAULIFLOWER

CONTENTS

—•◦•—

PART THE FIRST

HOUSEHOLD COOKERY

PART THE SECOND

HIGH-CLASS COOKERY

PART THE FIRST

HOUSEHOLD COOKERY

KITCHEN UTENSILS

PRELIMINARY OBSERVATIONS

UNDER this heading I have collected a number of precepts and elementary principles, which I consider the very bases of domestic and high-class cookery. I must bespeak for this Chapter the best attention of those of my readers who wish to study the practice of cookery from its starting point. Plain cooks will find here some very essential directions, which I would also recommend masters and mistresses making themselves acquainted with, if they care about their table being provided for in a suitable manner.

The following short list of the subjects of these Preliminary Observations will at once show their importance :—

1st. *Terms used in Cookery.*—Explaining what is understood by these, I shall endeavour to give them their proper value, whilst avoiding, as much as possible, those technicalities which only obscure the meaning.

2nd. *Kitchen Arrangements.*—It is self-evident that to work to advantage a proper *locale* is required. I make a great point of a clean and well kept kitchen ; on this head I shall enter into minute particulars, which it will be to the interest of all —masters and servants—to bear in mind.

3rd. *Kitchen Appointments.*—I give as complete a list as possible of the sundry utensils and appliances which a kitchen should contain; as well as some indications respecting firing, according to the degree of heat required for different operations.

4th. *Purveying.*—Conveying a few hints on marketing and selecting.

5th. *Spices and Herbs.*—Explaining their use and the manner of preparing them; in each recipe I quote exact quantities, as I have done throughout the work.

6th. *Table Arrangements and Serving.*—I conclude by indicating the way of serving meals properly—both from the kitchen and in the dining-room. I believe that in studying these preliminaries, with care and intelligence, bearing them in mind, and applying them when at work, the progress in cookery will be rapid, and the tedious time of apprenticeship considerably curtailed.

KITCHEN BELLOWS

I

TERMS USED IN COOKERY

I head this Chapter thus, more in deference to the generally adopted custom, than from my own convictions. For there are no, properly so-called, *Cookery terms* now: modern cookery, following the progress of the age, is natural and simple, and should be expressed in terms understood by all. If certain technicalities, now mostly obsolete, had formerly crept in, there is no advantage in perpetuating them; as, barring a very few exceptions, the things they represent can be expressed just as well in the ordinary phraseology. It will, therefore, be rather of cookery *operations*, than *terms*, that I shall have to treat of here; it is essential to have, at least, an exact notion of the former, before entering into further details of the culinary art.

To blanch is to parboil, or scald in water, for a determined length of time, certain vegetables, with a view to remove their acrid flavour—calves' heads and feet are similarly blanched, to soften them and facilitate their trimming.

To braize is to cook meat slowly in a closed stewpan, adapted to hold live coals on its cover.

To clarify — this applies to the operation of clearing, or freeing of foreign bodies, jellies, gravies, broths and butter. Jellies are clarified with egg; gravies and broths are clarified, with meat, and butter, by melting on a slow fire and straining through a cloth; it is then used in many cooking operations.

To cool is to pour cold water over vegetables, &c., after blanching, to preserve their colour.

To glaze is to paint with a brush, dipped in thick gravy, called *glaze*, larded meats, roasts, hams, and *sautés*.

This term is also applied to the sugaring over of fritters, pancakes, and cakes.

To moisten is to add sufficient liquid in a stewpan for stewing.

To reduce is to boil broth down to a glaze, gradually slackening the heat.

To sauter is to fry with little butter over a brisk fire.

To score is to make cross incisions on fish or vegetables, to facilitate cooking.

To singe is to pass plucked fowls or game over a flame—a spirit lamp is very handy for this.

To trim is to cut away those portions of a fowl or piece of meat which spoil its appearance.

To truss is to tie a fowl, or game, together with string, passed through it in such way as to prevent its getting out of the shape given to it, either for roasting or boiling.

To turn is to cut vegetables or fruit, for garnishes, into the shape of corks, balls, pears, &c.

II

KITCHEN ARRANGEMENTS

The very first consideration under this head is—that a kitchen should be as large and as well ventilated as possible; well supplied with all the necessary utensils and appliances. Those who wish to live well should study the comfort of their servants, by making such arrangements as will ensure satisfactory results. Unfortunately, even in some of the wealthiest houses, where luxury and comfort have been so much studied, the kitchen is often that part which is most neglected, and where the simplest teachings of experience and notions of progress have been discarded ; there is certainly much here that calls for amendment. However, as in this First Part we are treating of Domestic Cookery, we must be content with ordinary kitchens, as they are found in most houses of the middle classes. We will not deny that in many, even high-priced houses, the kitchens will be found deficient in size, light, and accommodation ; and that this is an evil: but, an intelligent cook should, by care, goodwill, and dexterity, strive, even under such disadvantages, to arrive at good results. In our profession one must often be content with things as one finds them : there are not many such kitchens as those of Chantilly and Ferrières ; but I maintain that, even in very small ones, good, nay excellent, things may be made. I mention this mainly for beginners, who should not be discouraged on finding themselves called upon to work in unsuitable *locales* ; they must learn to make the best of them ; improvements in kitchen arrangements being, unfortunately, but matter of slow progress. As an example of the practical philosophy requisite in such a case, I will instance what happened to one of my most intimate friends, who, on being called to Baron D——'s château at Argenteuil, found on his arrival that he was expected to make two large *pièces montées* and an *entrée*, with no better accommodation than was offered by a narrow passage ; and with no other appliances than a hanging shelf and a marble slab let into the wall. Without either baking-sheets or tins, it was necessary to bake the *pâte d'office* in the dripping-pan, which fortunately was of copper, and had but recently been tinned ; our friend discovered a perfect treasure in such a strait in the shape of two japanned iron trays, which, after their varnish had been burnt off, he papered and used as baking-sheets, for puff paste and cakes for garnishes. In spite of all, and of being obliged to dish up on the swinging shelf, he not only creditably accomplished his task, but received such praise, as other cooks, provided with all the requisite appliances, might not have obtained. By mentioning this fact I do not intend to advocate bad kitchens, but to show that much may be done in an inconvenient *locale* ; the more inconvenient a kitchen may be, the more need for cleanliness, carefulness, and for plentiful and good utensils to simplify one's work.

Cleanliness! cleanliness!—the great essential in all cooking operations—should, I maintain at the risk of being thought over particular, be written in large capitals on the door of every kitchen, large or small ;—a kitchen may be small, badly arranged and lighted ; but it should never, on any plea, be dirty.

I will mention the principal points to observe to secure this desideratum; not fearing to enter into details which will only appear minute to those without experience, and who cannot imagine that, in many cases, failure is attributable to a want of attention to cleanliness. Nothing more than a dirty saucepan will often be sufficient to spoil the effect of a whole dinner! I would therefore recommend:

That the floor of every kitchen be scoured at least once a week with plenty of water; then sprinkled with sawdust, to be changed daily.

Let the sink be scoured daily with soft soap and boiling water, then well rinsed.

Iron stoves should be washed, scraped, and black-leaded every evening.

Charcoal stoves should be brushed when in use, and whitened at night.

When the day's work is done, open all windows to dispel unpleasant smells; when the fires are out, a kitchen should be as free from smell as the dining-room.

All kitchen utensils should be examined daily, and every article, such as copper saucepans, beginning to redden, should be retinned. I do not like the plan of having a general retinning at certain fixed intervals; but think it preferable to send each article as it requires it. Everyone knows the unwholesomeness of insufficiently tinned saucepans; moreover, no cooking can be done satisfactorily in them; they will give a bad colour to whatever is cooked in them, consommés, sauces, jellies, &c. Besides attending to their tinning, saucepans cannot be kept too clean; they should be washed, scoured with fine sand and well rinsed each time they are used.

The washing of many things in the same water should be carefully avoided; the greasiness that this engenders adds much to the labour of cleaning.

I think it quite right that saucepans should be bright and polished, and am one of the first to admire the shining rows of saucepans in a kitchen; but the cleanliness of the inside must not be sacrificed to the brightness which strikes the eye. That such may be the case I have often experienced. In the kitchen of one of our great houses, I was once asked to make a sauce, and had to have *eleven* saucepans taken down, without finding one fit to use. I was at last obliged to have one cleaned before me, and then I found that the tin was nearly worn off; one might judge of the state of the remainder by this specimen. This lesson was taken to heart; having been in the same kitchen many times since, I have always found the utensils everything that could be wished.

III

KITCHEN APPOINTMENTS

Let every kitchen, large or small, be provided with the best possible utensils; this is a rule which any sensible person, even if entirely wanting in practical knowledge of our profession, must admit; for it is unreasonable to expect cooking to be well done without the necessary implements. Therefore, I have thought the following good advice to give to every housekeeper, even to the one who looks the closest to expense: 'Let your kitchen contain every requisite; you will find it to your advantage, both as regards economy and successful results; moreover, buy at the best shops and of the best.' The old adage that 'Nothing is so dear as cheapness,' applies very generally to all provisioning.

I give herewith a list of appointments for a good middle-class kitchen, in character with the recipes comprised in the First Part of this work. It will be observed that in naming the articles, I also explain their use, and, as far as possible, how to employ them; this will not, I think, be uncalled-for, as many beginners are unable to guess the object of articles often seen in kitchens.

KITCHEN UTENSILS

2 copper stock-pots—a 2-gallon one for making 1 gallon of broth, and a gallon one for ordinary use, to make 2 quarts of broth.

1 broth skimmer

1 tinned copper slice, for boiled meat, vegetables, &c.

1 soup ladle.

2 gravy spoons, to dish up stews and take off fat.

10 sizes of copper stewpans, from 4 to 12 inches diameter—each stewpan provided with its lid.

3 *sauté*-pans with covers, 8, 10, and 12 inches diameter.

1 oval pan, 12 inches long by 8 inches and 7 inches deep, with its drainer—this is used for all braizes, hams, fillets of beef, veal cushions, and even sometimes for fish.

1 glazing stewpan and cover, 8 inches diameter, 5 inches deep.
1 turbot kettle with drainer, 18 inches by 10.

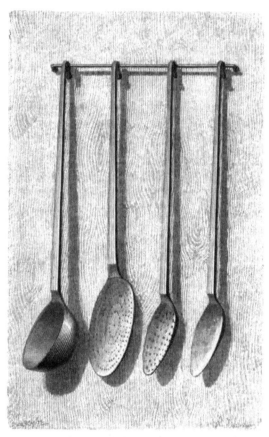

SPOONS AND SKIMMERS

1 fish kettle with drainer, 22 inches by 7.
1 plain mould for *Charlottes, timbales,* and rice cakes.
1 cylinder mould for *aspics,* jellies, and creams.
1 pie mould.
2 open tart moulds.

I do not give the dimensions of the preceding moulds,—they must be selected to suit one's requirements.

c

2 baking-sheets, 12 inches by 8.

4 copper baking-sheets, from 6 to 12 inches diameter.

LARGE COPPER COLANDER

These sheets can be used for baking pastry, and also for pressing,—as we shall see under the paragraphs *Galantine*, Breasts of Mutton, Braized Cutlets, &c.

1 blanching pan, 12 inches diameter, 8 inches deep.

1 copper preserving pan, 12 inches diameter, 6 inches deep.

1 copper skimmer, for preserves.

2 untinned copper sugar-boilers, one 4 inches and the other 8 inches diameter, for *compôtes*, syrups, sugar for glazing, &c.

1 copper egg bowl and whisk.

1 large tinned copper colander, 8 inches diameter, for stews, blanching, &c.

1 medium colander, 5 inches diameter, for draining, and parsley frying.

3 oval tinned copper dishes, for *gratins*, one 12 inches by 7 ; one 10 inches by 8; one 16 inches by 9.

These dishes have no handles.

OVAL DISH FOR GRATINS

1 sheet iron cover with turned-up edges, to hold live coals to brown *gratins*, &c.

1 tinned copper frying kettle, 13 inches by 10, and 4 inches deep; this should have a handle at each end.

1 smaller frying kettle, 9 inches by 6, and 5 inches deep.

2 untinned iron frying-pans, one 8 inches diameter, the other 6 inches; the smaller should be kept specially for omelets.

2 iron gridirons, one 8 inches, the other 12 inches.

POINTED GRAVY STRAINER

1 wire frying-basket, used to prevent what is frying from catching at the bottom of the kettle, and also to facilitate the removal, at one operation, of the things fried; this is very useful in the case of fritters, croquets, &c.

2 tin colanders, 5 and 4 inches diameter; these colanders having very fine holes, are, in moderate households, substituted for tammy cloth.

6 wooden spoons of different sizes.

1 tinned wire sieve for *purées*.

BOX OF LARDING NEEDLES

1 hard-wood *pureé*-presser, to rub forcemeat and *purées* through the sieve.

1 large daubing needle for larding large braizes.

1 medium larding needle for similar use.

1 box of 12 larding needles, for fillets of beef, veal cushions, sweetbreads, fillets of venison, &c.

2 steel trussing needles, 6 and 8 inches long.
1 cutlet bat.

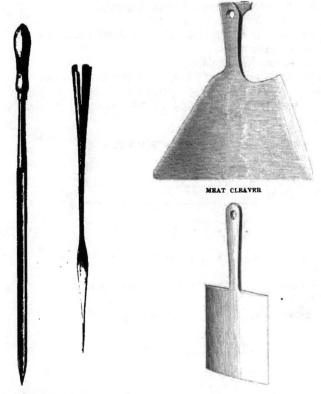

MEAT CLEAVER

LARGE AND MEDIUM LARDING NEEDLE   CUTLET BAT.

1 meat cleaver.
2 mincing knives for forcemeat, vegetables, &c.
1 meat saw.

TRUSSING NEEDLES

1 marble mortar, 10 inches diameter, 7 inches deep, with hard-wood pestle; this is indispensable in a kitchen, to pound forcemeat, *godiveaux, quenelles, purées,* &c.

1 rolling pin, 18 inches long by 2 inches diameter.

1 tin sugar dredger, for sweets, cakes, &c.

2 boxes of cutters, one of plain, the other of fluted; these are used for patties, *vôl-au-vent,* &c.

1 box of long cutters for vegetables.

1 syrup gauge and tall testing glass, to determine the quantities of sugar in *compôtes,* jellies, and preserves. The gauge is ascertained to be correct by plunging in cold water, where it should register zero.

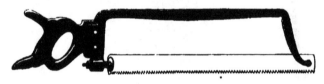

MEAT SAW

2 chopping-boards, 18 inches by 12 by 2.

1 wooden block.

1 set of scales and weights, capable of weighing up to 28 lbs.

12 sizes of basins.

6 common dishes; 10, 12, and 14 inches long.

KITCHEN KNIVES

1 beech-wood kitchen table, with drawers.
1 filter.
2 tin funnels.
3 kitchen knives.
2 pastry knives.
12 diaper cloths for straining *consommés* and jellies; these take the place of silk sieves, which are so expensive and of little wear.

MEAT SAFE, TO FIT A WINDOW

1 meat safe. I annex two illustrations of small handy safes; things should be allowed to become perfectly cold before being put in a safe.

1 clock; this is indispensable in a kitchen, to ensure regularity in cooking and punctuality in serving.

1 spirit lamp: in kitchens that have no charcoal stoves this is used for singeing poultry, &c.

1 quart measure
1 pint „
1 halfpint „
1 gill „

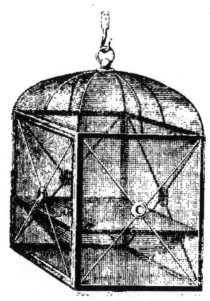

HANGING SAFE

Remarks on Kitchen Utensils

I recommend copper saucepans, although not to the entire exclusion of tinned iron articles, which, if cheaper, do not last so long or answer as well as copper saucepans, stewpans, and glazing pans. Such utensils as stock-pots, braizing-pans and fish-kettles are, however, just as good when made of tinned iron.

The foregoing list of kitchen articles, which I consider indispensable for the use of an average household, is not in excess of what will be required to cook for two persons, and is equal to providing for twelve,—a figure I have not wished to exceed, in order to stay within the limits of domestic cookery. I need not add that this list can be modified according to circumstances: for instance, in households where there are never more than two, or four, or six, to provide for, the first and second sizes of stock-pots and stewpans would alone be necessary; also, where no preserves are made at home, the preserving pan and skimmer would be superfluous. Without wishing to swell the estimates —my constant object having been, in this First Part, to study

economy — I, would still suggest that, however unnecessary it
may be to provide things in excess of one's own requirements,
there are but few households where there is not, now and
then, an extra dinner party, and that it is advisable that every
household should possess the things needful to meet these
occurrences.

Everyone knows from experience the unpleasantness of wanting, in the busy hour of preparation for a dinner, such and
such indispensable articles, which the cook asks for in vain, and
which the mistress bitterly regrets not including, from the first,
in her household-fittings.

I would also point out that, in the matter of stewpans,
gridirons, frying-pans, &c., there is generally a double advantage
in choosing large in preference to smaller articles; for, in the
first place, it is easier to work satisfactorily in large quantities;
and it is also often preferable to make dishes sufficient for four
or five persons, even if there be only two to partake of them.
Time and fuel are saved thereby, and the evil of shortness of
supply thus avoided. Taken as a whole, the expense of fitting
up a kitchen properly is, after all, but very trifling; good utensils,
carefully bought and well looked after, will last a whole life-
time: the first cost is, therefore, the only consideration. It is at
all events a satisfaction to know, that, if your meals are badly
served, the fault does not lie in a short-sighted curtailment of
appliances.

KITCHEN STOVES AND RANGES

Of these the most general are — the old-fashioned Charcoal
Stove and the patent Kitchener. A charcoal stove should have
three firing holes; one 7 inches square, and the two others 6
inches square. These will suffice for the whole cookery treated
of in the First Part of this work. The main point is to well fill
the largest hole, in such a way as to set boiling stock-pot, blanch-
ings, vegetables, &c. The two other openings are used—the one
for simmering braizes, and the other for several purposes where
little heat is generally required. Round one of the openings a
stock-pot and three saucepans will simmer at once, provided a
brisk fire is kept up, and fresh fuel constantly added in the
centre without disturbing the saucepans. The cook should so
manage that the larger opening should be always in use for
those things which require brisk cooking, and which should

IMPROVED STOVE.

D

follow one another in uninterrupted succession, so as to avoid loss of fuel.

Coal is used in the kitchener, which consists of a plate of iron heated by a covered fire below. The opening is fitted with one or two removable iron rings, which serve to graduate the heat: when a very brisk fire is required they are taken out. Upon the hot plate, saucepans and stock-pots are arranged, according to the heat they require. The oven, which is below the plate on one side of the fire, is used for glazing, bruizes, *entremets*, pastry, and *gratins*.

Both stove and kitchener have their special advantages: the charcoal stove certainly facilitates the giving a greater finish to dishes; whilst the kitchener, by its oven, allows of baking *gratins*, *soufflés*, and pastry, none of which can be attempted with the former. The main point is to know how to use both equally well, and to be doubly careful in undertaking those operations for which either the one or the other is less adapted; as, in the question of *locale*, I will repeat that one must know how in cookery to overcome difficulties.

I have met in a private household with an improved stove which appeared to me to combine the advantages of stove and kitchener: I will give a description of it herewith. I do not wish to recommend it to the exclusion of all others, particularly as I always advise that use should be made of the stoves and kitcheners such as they are found; but anyone having to get one constructed could not do better than adopt this one.

SECTION OF IMPROVED ROASTING APPARATUS

This stove (*vide* woodcut, page 17) being built of brick, with an iron plate on the top only, the extreme heat attending kitcheners is avoided. It is so arranged as to burn wood or coal. The iron plate only extends over the fire hole and oven. It is of sufficient size for ordinary cooking. Beyond this hot plate there is an opening on the left for burning charcoal, where sauces, *liaisons, caramels*, and things requiring a moderate heat, may be cooked.

While speaking of stoves and firing I will most particularly recommend gas stoves, which can be used with so much advantage where a steady and even degree of heat is required. I am surprised this invention has not become more general, and its utility, in so many operations, recognised. The gas stove, moreover, takes very little room; a consideration not to be overlooked in many kitchens. Besides stoves, a kitchen, unprovided with an open range, should contain a roasting and broiling apparatus ; namely, an open grate fixed in the wall, with a roasting-jack and screen attached. This arrangement is particularly adapted to small kitchens.

In kitchens where neither charcoal, or gas stove, or kitchener, is to be found, the common open range is a fair substitute. The top of the oven will be the best place for slow cooking, and the oven itself will be used as in the case of a kitchener.

KITCHEN FIRES AND FUEL

There are, in cookery parlance, several descriptions of fires suited to the different cooking operations. I think it will be useful, without entering here into details as to duration of cooking, for this will be specified in each recipe, to give a general idea of these different fires. They may be separated into three distinct kinds :—

1st. *Stock-pot fire:* very slow and continuous : this will be enlarged upon in paragraph *Pot-au-feu.*

2nd. *Broiling fire:* which should be very equal ; *i. e.* with the fuel thoroughly lighted in all parts.

3rd. *Roasting fire:* a bright steady fire, which should never be allowed to get low.

On the stove corner is an expression continually recurring in explaining cooking operations: as I shall make use of it often, I think it necessary that its meaning should be thoroughly understood.

When we speak of a stewpan being put *on the stove corner*,

it is to convey that a slow fire is required, so that its contents should be kept simmering only. Ebullition will then only take place on one side of the stewpan : with a sauce, for example, a few air bubbles will alone rise on the side next the fire. With charcoal stoves this is easy to manage, as the stewpan may be put on the angle of the opening : thus, with a 10-inch stewpan, only about four inches should be on the fire : if this latter is too brisk, it should be partly covered with ashes. But with coal fires, either in kitcheners or open ranges, this operation becomes more difficult ; even the expression *on the stove corner* is inappropriate : the stewpans should then, however, be arranged on the hot plate, or the hob, in such a way that boiling shall only take place on one side.

REMARKS ON BOILING AND REDUCING

Upon these two operations I may make the following remarks, gathered from my personal experience.

To cook satisfactorily by boiling, a slow and steady fire should be kept up. Do not expect to hasten the cooking by indiscriminately heaping up the fuel. Once the boiling point reached, all excess of heat is wasted : you will lose the benefit of a progressive cooking without expediting it.

To reduce, on the contrary, a brisk fire producing quick evaporation is indispensable. A glaze, or sauce, reduced too slowly will lose at once in appearance and flavour.

IV

PROVISIONING

It is quite evident that, without good materials, the greatest cook in the world will never produce anything palatable. Too great a care cannot, therefore, be paid to one's provisioning and marketing : this alone is a study of itself, to be mastered, as other branches of the culinary art, by experience and practice.

I must limit my remarks here to certain general notions upon the art of choosing and buying. I shall have to recur in greater detail on the outward appearance of meat, fish, game, and vegetables, when treating of each in their respective chapters.

As first hints, or fundamental rules, for inexperienced buyers, I will only say : —

Before making your purchases, learn, first of all, the ruling prices of those things you require, which you can easily do by enquiring at different shops.

Never bind yourself to any special tradesman. Do not give your custom, nor your whole confidence, to one individual. Rely rather upon your own judgment and observation, than upon a tradesman's word, however trustworthy he may be.

Whenever any article is pressed upon you, be more particularly on your guard : there are very few tradesmen who can resist the temptation of palming off, at all hazard, any remaining fish, game, or meat of questionable freshness.

Be on good terms with all tradespeople, without becoming intimate with any. It is very seldom that a too great familiarity does not, in the long run, result in some unfair advantage being taken of the purchaser.

The following are a few elementary principles which it will be well to be guided by in the selection of provisions :—

BUTCHER'S MEAT

Beef should be chosen of a bright red colour, with light yellow fat, approaching the hue of fresh butter. If the beef should be hard and firm to the touch, with flaccid and little fat, of a brown and dull colour, these are sure indications of inferior quality.

As complement to what concerns beef, we represent beef kidney of superior and inferior qualities.

Veal should be chosen of a light colour, with very white and transparent fat. Avoid lean veal of a reddish tint, and the kidney of which is surrounded by red-looking fat.

Prime mutton is known by the same signs as good beef, viz. a bright red colour, freedom from gristle, and very white and transparent fat.

Inferior mutton is of a dull red colour, with yellow and opaque fat.

POULTRY

In the first place, poultry should be selected very tender, particularly when not in season, from the 1st of December to the 1st of May. Spring chickens begin in May, but at any time they should be carefully examined before buying. A tender chicken is known by the size of its feet and neck; a young fowl always has large feet and knee-joints : these characteristics disappear with age. A tough fowl has a thin neck and feet, and the flesh of the thigh has a slight violet tinge.

After examining these external signs, the flesh of the pinion and breast should be tried : if tender in both these places, the chicken can be used with confidence.

Never use Old Fowls

I call particular attention to this principle, which I consider a very important one—Never use an old fowl in cookery. Whichever way you dress it, it will never be good. It is a great mistake to recommend, as in many Cookery Books, the putting of an old hen in the stock-pot. Instead of improving the broth, it can do nothing but impart to it the unpleasant flavour of the hen-house. It is also a mistake to expect to make a good *daube* with an old goose or turkey ; nothing but a bad result will be obtained. It is well, however, to distinguish between hard, but young, poultry and the toughness of an old fowl. With the former something may be done, by means indicated in the Chapter specially devoted to Poultry ; but with the old and tough birds, I repeat most emphatically, nothing, absolutely nothing, can be done.

A good turkey will be recognised by the whiteness of the flesh and fat. Beware of those with long hairs, and whose flesh, on the legs and back, is of a violet tinge.

To select a goose, try the flesh of the pinion and break off the lower part of the beak, which should break easily : the fat should be light coloured and transparent. Ducks are chosen in the same way.

Pigeons should have fillets of a light red colour ; when old, these darken to blackish violet, and the legs get thin.

FISH

A fresh fish is recognisable by the redness of the gills, the brightness of the eyes, and the firmness of the flesh.

It is not enough to be guided by the smell : it may have laid days on ice without acquiring any noticeable smell, but the flesh in such a case will be dull and flaccid, and care should be taken not to employ fish in that condition.

It should be borne in mind that fish will lose in quality in the spawning season; this should regulate one's purchases.

My remarks on old poultry apply even more particularly to old fish, which should never, on any consideration, appear on the table.

GAME

Old hares should be discarded, they can be turned to no good account; leverets and young hares alone should be bought; you can tell a tender hare by the ease with which the fore-paw may be broken, by its large knees and short stumpy neck.

Good wild rabbits are known by the same indications.

Pheasants should be selected with the spur but little developed; the tenderness of the bird is known by trying the flesh of the pinion.

Woodcocks are also tried by pinching the pinion and breast.

Similarly with respect to wild ducks, teal, widgeon, and other water-fowl.

Partridges are also tested in the same way; their age can be ascertained by examining the long feathers of the wing,—round at the tip in an old bird, and pointed in a young.

VEGETABLES

The first consideration in the purchase of vegetables is to have due regard to the variations of taste and appearance which the same vegetables undergo in different seasons; spring carrots, for instance, are very different to those of autumn and winter. I will, at the proper place, state when each species of vegetables is in season; this should regulate their employment.

GROCERIES, ETC.

As to all articles to be had from the Grocer's, the Oilman, and Dairyman, I would more than ever recommend that none but the best be bought; this is sure in the end to prove more satisfactory and economical.

An inferior quality of oil, used in cookery, will spoil the sauce or whatever else it may be added to; the same with butter, which should always be selected of the freshest and best.

A small quantity of sweet butter will improve any preparation where it is required; whereas, with bad butter, the result will be exactly the reverse : the more you add of it, the worse will your dish become.

Never buy butter without carefully smelling and tasting it; these two tests are indispensable. If you have any doubts as to its freshness, do not on any account buy it, but try elsewhere ; it is an invariable rule that ' no good cookery is to be done with questionable butter.'

Never employ eggs without examining them carefully, not only when buying them but also when they are broken.

An egg may appear perfectly good, and still have an unpleasant damp-straw flavour, which is sufficient to spoil a whole dish. Eggs should be broken, one after the other, and none put into the basin until their freshness has been ascertained.

With respect to bacon, one should likewise be very particular in selecting none but what is very white, with the least gristle possible, and quite fresh, and free from rustiness.

Fresh pork should be of a light brownish hue, and free from any inequalities of colour.

V

SPICES AND AROMATIC HERBS

Spices and herbs for seasoning come among the necessaries of a kitchen.

The following should be always at hand :—

Salt,	Olive oil,
Pepper—ground and whole,	Plain white vinegar,
Nutmeg,	Tarragon vinegar,
Cloves,	Chili vinegar,
Thyme,	Cinnamon,
Bay leaf,	Vanilla,
Garlic,	Flour—best whites,
Mustard,	Orange-flower water,
French mustard,	Loaf sugar,
Cayenne pepper,	*Caramel*,
Chilies,	Mixed spices.

SPICES

Under this general name is designated a mixture of certain herbs and spices, much employed as a seasoning of, for instance, cold dishes, *galantine*, pies, &c.

The best way to have these spices good is to prepare them one's self. The following are the proportions for ordinary cookery :

Place in a paper bag :

¼ oz. of thyme,	⅛ oz. of marjoram,
¼ oz. of bay-leaf,	⅛ oz. of rosemary ;

Put the bag into the hot screen until the herbs are quite dry ; mix in a mortar, with :

½ oz. of nutmeg,	¼ oz. of whole pepper,
½ oz. of cloves,	⅛ oz. of cayenne pepper ;

Pound the whole, and pass through a hair sieve ;

Keep these mixed spices in a dry and well-corked bottle. These spices are used either alone or with salt added ; the proportion for mixing with salt is 1 oz. of the mixture to 4 oz. of fine salt.

In conforming to these proportions, a good seasoning will be secured. It is easy to perceive all the advantage of having such a mixture ready prepared, together with definite instructions as to the proper quantities required for different seasonings. As an instance of the employment of the mixture in practice, I will at once mention that 1 oz. of the spiced salt just referred to will be the quantity required to season 3 lbs. of *galantine* forcemeat.

FAGGOT, OR BOUQUET GARNI

Under this name is known a mixture of parsley, thyme, and bay-leaf ; it is of general use for seasoning, and generally composed thus :

1 oz. of parsley, say a small handful,

$\frac{1}{16}$ oz. of thyme, say a sprig,

$\frac{1}{16}$ oz. of bay-leaf, say one bay-leaf ;

The parsley should be first washed ; the thyme and bay-leaf placed in the midst of it, and the extremities of the parsley folded down to enclose the two former ; it should then be tied round with string, and trimmed so that none of the outside leaves break off in the liquid. A properly made faggot should be 3 inches long.

PINCH OF SALT OR PEPPER

The expressions *pinch* and *small pinch* of salt and pepper will, at every moment, recur to convey a notion of determined quantities, which it is important to specify accurately, if one is to

E

proceed with certainty. The scales are of course the best criterion of quantities; they are of frequent assistance, but, in the hurry of work, to have continual recourse to them is impracticable.

It will, therefore, be necessary for everyone to ascertain the capacity of one's fingers by weighing what they can hold; thus it will be found that, in taking a pinch of salt or pepper, such or such definite weight is taken.

I have adopted $\frac{1}{4}$ oz. as the weight of a *pinch* and $\frac{1}{16}$ oz. as that of the *small pinch*. Whenever I shall have in the text to use the words *pinch* and *small pinch*, an exact idea will thus be had of their equivalent in weight.

Average Weight of Vegetables (of those used in the Pot-au-Feu)

An average sized carrot	weighs	5	oz.	
,, ,, onion	,,	4	oz.	
,, ,, leek	,,	$1\frac{1}{2}$	oz. when peeled	
,, ,, head of celery	,,	$1\frac{1}{2}$	oz.	
A large shalot	,,	$\frac{3}{8}$	oz.	
A clove of garlic	,,	$\frac{1}{4}$	oz.	

It is as well to accustom one's self as much as possible to tell by sight the weight of these several vegetables, as well as of all other articles of constant use, so as to avoid continually referring to the scales.

VI

TABLE ARRANGEMENTS AND SERVING

The table arrangements, concerning more immediately the *maître d'hotel*, can hardly find their place in a Cookery Book, which it is desirable to keep to its own subject, already in itself sufficiently extensive; and even less so when it treats of Domestic Cookery. Ordinary serving merely consists in putting the dishes on the table in succession—often the order in which they are to come is fixed by the mistress of the house.

The details of cloth-laying are so well known that to specify them here would be to presuppose a too great degree of ignorance on the part of my readers.

As to the sending up from the kitchen, I will merely recall to all cooks a great practical principle which they should never lose sight of: namely, that it is always better to be in advance in the preparation of any meal, rather than behindhand. It is always easy to proceed slower, when one finds oneself ready too soon; but when you are compelled to hurry things for want of time, there is every probability of doing badly, and it is rare that some part of the meal should not suffer. It is a mistake to suppose that a well-dressed meal will be sufficient to cause its want of punctuality to be forgiven. How many times have I seen excellent dinners, both as regards choice and execution, badly received, and fail on account of the time which the famished and impatient guests had been kept waiting, and who felt on that account aggrieved and indisposed to acknowledge its merits! An unpunctual cook will never be a true cook, to my mind.

STOCK-POTS

CHAPTER I

POT-AU-FEU, OR BEEF BROTH

BEEF BROTH is the soul of domestic cookery; it constitutes the most nutritious part of daily food. Besides being extensively served as soup, it is also the basis of numerous preparations : such as stews, sauces, *purées*, &c.

It is undoubtedly the best of broths; ranking far above other sorts, such as chicken, vegetable, fish, and game broths. To make a good *pot-au-feu* has always appeared to me to be one of those elementary and fundamental operations which should be made clear to everybody when treating of domestic cookery.

Here, less than ever, shall I shrink from giving the most minute details, even at the risk of appearing prolix, to those who do not take into account the inexperience of a beginner; my object, before all, is to enable such a one to be sure of success at the first trial, if the recipes are followed to the letter.

STOCK-POTS

The two stock-pots in most general use are, a tinned iron one, and a tinned copper one; these are the best, being more easily cleaned—a consideration of great moment; the quality of the broth depending upon the cleanliness of the pot—two other very general stock-pots, one of cast iron, and the other of earthenware, are, on that very account, to be discarded.

COPPER STOCK-POT

INGREDIENTS OF A GOOD SOUP

I make a distinction between a *pot-au-feu* for every-day use and one for extra occasions.

For the first, or small *pot-au-feu*, take :

1½ lb. of beef (leg or shoulder parts),
¼ lb. of bone (about the quantity included in that weight of meat),
3½ quarts of water,
1 oz. of salt,
1 middle-sized carrot, say 5 oz.,
1 large onion, say 5 oz. with a clove stuck in it,
3 leeks, say about 7 oz.,
½ head of celery, say ½ oz.,
1 middle-sized turnip, say 5 oz.,
1 small parsnip, say 1 oz. ;

Garlic is sometimes added ; I do not recommend it, it imparts too strong a flavour to the broth, which would, for instance, make it unsuitable for the use of sick people.

For the larger *pot-au-feu* take :

3 lbs. of beef,
1 lb. of bone,
5½ quarts of water,
2 oz. of salt,
2 carrots, say 10 oz.,
2 large onions, say 10 oz.,
6 leeks, say 14 oz.,
1 head of celery, say 1 oz.,
2 turnips, say 10 oz.,
1 parsnip, say 2 oz.,
2 cloves in the onion.

It may be asked, whether the small *pot-au-feu*, which I call small with reason, answers the purpose of a small family of moderate means?

In this First Part, I have always had in view the requirements of persons of very moderate incomes. The soup produced under this recipe will be found amply sufficient for four or five persons; if there be only two to partake of it, the remainder will not on that account be lost, as it will do for a second time; it will also be useful to have at hand, to add to the sauce when warming up the beef.

THE MEAT FOR SOUP

The pieces of beef best adapted for broth are: all the different parts of the leg, extending from the shin, and including the rump; the upper parts of the shoulder, known as gravy beef, are also very generally employed—besides producing a good broth they make a good *bouilli*. Nevertheless, it is admitted that the upper parts of the leg produce a more nourishing broth than the shoulder. Ribs of beef are also used for broth; they leave a good eating meat, but are not fleshy enough to give a savoury broth.

In instances where the *bouilli* is not required, shin alone is sometimes used; but I do not recommend it, as that part, containing more gelatinous than nutritious substance, does not make a good broth. It is, however, well to add about a pound of shin when the rump or ribs are used, for it will increase the strength of the broth, whilst the latter will, when boiled, make good removes.

Perfect freshness of the meat is indispensable; a dried-up piece of beef would not make good broth, or leave a good *bouilli*.

MODE OF PREPARATION

The first requisite is a good slow fire: feed your stove well with charcoal, so as not to have to replenish it for three hours; and, when you *do* have to renew the fire, be careful not to hurry the boiling, which should always proceed slowly. Do not close the pot hermetically, as this would prevent the broth being clear.

After boning the beef, tie it round with string, to keep it together, and in shape;

Break the bones with the cleaver; put the pieces in the pot first, then the meat over them;

Add 3½ quarts of cold filtered water, and 1 oz. of salt, for the small pot ; or, 5½ quarts of water, and 2 oz. of salt, for the large one ;

Put the pot on the fire.   When nearly boiling, skim, and add ½ gill of cold water for the small pot, or 1 gill for the large one, to accelerate the rising of the scum.   Repeating this operation about three times will secure a clear and limpid appearance to the broth ; add then the vegetables indicated above, and, as soon as boiling recommences, remove the pot to the stove corner, as directed in the ' Preliminary Observations ;' let it remain there simmering for four or five hours, according to the quantity. The fire should be kept steady all the time, so that a slight but continual ebullition take place.

When the broth is done, take out the meat, and put it on a dish ; taste the broth, and, if any additional salt be required, add it,—but only at the last moment, when the soup is poured in the tureen, it being best to keep the stock of light seasoning, as this will always increase in warming up and reducing for sauces.

SKIMMING THE FAT

Freeing the broth from fat is one of the essential points to be observed for its preservation ; it should be done, with a spoon, whilst the pot is boiling, on the stove corner.   The fat can be made useful for frying purposes by clarifying it on a slow fire for about an hour, and then straining through the pointed gravy strainer (*vide* page 11).

REMARKS ON THE VEGETABLES FOR POT-AU-FEU

The vegetables add amazingly to the flavour of the broth ; but they should not remain in the pot a minute longer than necessary to be well cooked, as they will otherwise absorb some of the flavour of the broth, a fact easily proved by tasting them when they have thus been allowed to linger in the broth after their proper cooking.   It will then be found that they have taken much of the richness of the broth, of course to the latter's detriment.

In spring and summer, vegetables, being tender, cook more rapidly ; it is, therefore, necessary to make proper allowance for the difference of seasons.

It is generally required, with reason, that broth should be of a rich golden colour ; although not really better on that account, it pleases the eye—always a desirable end in cookery. The essential point in colouring broth is not to alter its flavour ; I therefore advise those who value its quality never to use burnt onions, carrots, or similar ingredients, which only impart an acrid and disagreeable taste.

The only innocuous colouring substance is *caramel*, or burnt sugar, prepared in the following manner : put in a copper pan ½ lb. of pounded sugar ; stir it over the fire, with a wooden spoon ; when the sugar is thoroughly melted, keep it boiling very slowly, for a quarter of an hour, leaving the spoon in to stir occasionally. When the sugar attains a very dark brown colour, add 1 quart of cold water ; boil, for twenty minutes, on the stove corner ; let cool, strain, and keep ready for use, in well corked—and perfectly clean—bottles.

Good *caramel* should be of a dark brown colour ; if allowed to boil too quickly, it will become black, and impart a bad colour.

With this *caramel*, colour the broth only in the soup-tureen when wanted ; it is better to keep the stock of its natural colour for *poulette* sauce, *blanquettes*, &c. It is always easy at any time to add the colouring to it.

PRESERVATION OF THE BROTH

The first requisite, in order to preserve broth, is to clear it entirely of fat, and strain it carefully ; let it cool thoroughly before putting it away, and keep it in a cool place, without covering it.

In winter, it will keep sweet for two or three days.

In summer, it is necessary to boil it up daily, and put it by, in a very clean vessel.

ON PROLONGED COOKING

With reference to *pot-au-feu*, and broth, I have often been asked the following question :

' Would not seven or eight hours' boiling produce a broth of more savour and better quality than five hours' ? ' to which I answer : 'By no means ; after a certain time, when the meat is thoroughly cooked, it has parted with all its nutritive principles and flavour ; and leaving it in the broth after that will rather tend to deteriorate than improve it ; thus, to produce good broth, the meat should be done to a nicety—neither too much nor too little.

I indicate five hours' boiling for the larger *pot-au-feu*,—but it must be understood, that this is not an invariable rule ; I have given the average time required, but it of course depends on the age and quality of the meat ; to ascertain when the meat is cooked, try it, after four or five hours' boiling, with a trussing needle ; if this goes in easily, the beef is cooked, and the broth has arrived at perfection ;—further boiling will but spoil it.

SEASONING BOX

F

SOUP TUREEN AND ACCESSORIES.

CHAPTER II

SOUPS

It is needless to insist on the importance of a good soup, which is rightly considered as the *ouverture* to a good dinner.

I give the recipes of twenty or twenty-five soups, which I have chosen amongst those most in use.

I might have extended the list by adding some more *recherché* or of more ambitious name; but these are naturally included in the Second Part of the book, which treats of high-class cookery; as for the unknown or unusual soups, of which nobody ever partakes, there is no room for them in either Part of this work. The recipes here given, with their explanatory details, will, I have no doubt, be found amply sufficient for the ordinary purposes of domestic cookery.

I

MEAT SOUPS

BREAD SOUP*

This soup, although very plain and simple, demands much care; and I will here protest at once against the too generally spread

* The recipes of the different soups are calculated for four persons.

idea that every day cookery does not require the best attention ; it is quite the reverse, preparations recurring so often should
be the most carefully attended to ; for, in their case, failure is
without excuse.

We left the broth boiling, and free from grease (*vide Pot-
au-Feu*, page 31); then should the soup be served.

For four persons : take about 1 quart of broth, and 2 oz.
of bread (French rolls); slice to a thickness of a quarter of an
inch ; and dry the slices in the oven to expel all moisture liable
to impair the flavour of the broth; put the slices in the soup-
tureen; pour the broth over; and serve. The vegetables taken
out of the broth should be put on a dish, and handed round
with the soup.

BROTH À LA MINUTE,
OR QUICK METHOD OF PRODUCING GOOD BROTH

I give this recipe in the Domestic Cookery, although it is not
an economical way of preparing broth; but it may be found very
useful in cases of illness, when the question of economy is quite
of secondary importance.

To produce broth quickly, take :

    1 lb. of lean beef,

    half of a hen, boned ;

Pound together in a mortar; add $\frac{1}{4}$ oz. of salt; put in a stewpan, with $2\frac{1}{2}$ pints of water; and stir over the fire, till boiling;
then add carrots, onions, leeks, and celery, the whole cut fine;
boil, for half an hour; strain ; and serve.

VERMICELLI SOUP

Use none but pastes of the first quality,—the Italian are
considered the best ;

Blanch 2 oz. of vermicelli, for five minutes, in a quart of water,
to which a small pinch of salt has been added ; cool, and drain
in a colander ;

Pour the vermicelli into a quart of boiling broth ; stir, with a
spoon, to prevent it getting lumpy ; simmer, for five minutes, on
the stove corner; skim ; and serve.

All pastes for soups, without distinction : *pâtes d'Italie*, maccaroni, *nouilles, lazagues*, &c., are prepared in the same way.

With all these soups you may serve a plateful of grated
Parmesan cheese.

TAPIOCA SOUP

West Indian tapioca is the best.

Boil 2½ pints of broth ;

Throw 1½ oz. of tapioca in it,—being careful to stir all the time, to keep it smooth ; put the stewpan, closely shut, to simmer for twenty minutes on the stove corner ; skim; and serve.

RICE SOUP

Carolina rice is the best.

Wash 1¼ oz. of rice, in cold water, three times ;

Blanch, for a couple of minutes, in a quart of water ; cool, and drain.

Put the rice into 2½ pints of boiling broth ; place the stewpan to simmer, for half an hour, on the stove corner ; skim ; and serve.

SEMOLINA SOUP

Great care is required in the selection of semolina, as it is often damaged by damp or dust,—and in this state would spoil any broth.

Drop 2 oz. of semolina into 2½ pints of boiling broth ; keep stirring ; then cover the stewpan, and let simmer, for half an hour ; skim ; and serve.

SOUP MITONNÉE, OR SOAKED-BREAD SOUP

Put in a stewpan, with 2½ pints of broth, 2 oz. of bread, broken, not cut,—as cut bread does not mix so easily ; simmer for twenty minutes, whilst stirring with a wooden spoon. When the whole of the bread has been reduced to a pulp, and the soup is thick enough, serve.

CABBAGE SOUP

Cabbage soup can be made in all seasons.

Take, preferably, a Savoy cabbage ; trim off the outside leaves, —which are generally hard ;

Cut it in quarters ;

Wash, in plenty of water ;

Blanch the cabbage, and ½lb. of streaky bacon together, for ten minutes, in boiling water ; steep, for half an hour, in plenty of cold water ;—by this process cabbage and bacon will have become more digestible ;

Drain the cabbage; press the water out; and season each piece with a pinch of salt, and a light sprinkling of pepper; take:

A *bouquet garni* (or faggot);
A small carrot, say 4 oz.,
An onion, say 4 oz., with 2 cloves stuck in it;

Put the quarters of cabbage in a 4-quart stewpan, with the faggot, carrot, and onion; over these place:

1lb. of brisket of beef,
and the bacon;

Add 3 quarts of water; boil; skim carefully; and leave the stewpan, for three hours, simmering on the stove corner;

Take out the meat, bacon, and vegetables;

Cut the cabbage in pieces, and put in the tureen with 1 oz. of sliced rolls; pour over the broth; and serve.

CABBAGE-LETTUCE SOUP

This is also a soup for all seasons.

Trim half a dozen cabbage-lettuces (say 8 oz.), removing the hard outside leaves.

Blanch, in boiling water, for ten minutes; cool, and press out all the water; sprinkle with pepper and salt;

Put the lettuces in an 8-inch stewpan;

Add 3 gills of good broth;

Simmer, till the broth is quite reduced.

Be careful that the lettuce does not adhere to the stewpan, —which will undoubtedly happen if the fire be too fierce.

Add 1 quart of broth; when boiling remove to the stove corner to simmer, for ten minutes;

Put 1½ oz. of sliced roll in the soup-tureen;

Skim the soup; pour it in on the bread; and serve.

II

SOUPS MAIGRES (WITHOUT MEAT)

JULIENNE SOUP

Julienne is only in season for nine months of the year;— in January, February, and March, such vegetables as carrots, turnips, and leeks, are tough and stringy.

INGREDIENTS

1 good-sized carrot, say 4 oz.,
1 turnip, say 4 oz.,
1 leek, say 2 oz.,
1 small onion, say 2 oz.,
¼ head of celery, say ½ oz.,
¼ of a Savoy cabbage, say 1 oz.,
1 cabbage-lettuce, say ½ oz.,
12 leaves of sorrel, say ½ oz.,
a few leaves of chervil, say ½ oz. ;

Scrape the carrots, and turnips ;

Clean the leek, celery, onion, and cabbage ;

Wash and dry each vegetable ;

Cut them in thin shreds, 1 inch in length and ⅛ inch thick ; put in an 8-inch stewpan, with ¼ lb. of butter ;

Stir, over a brisk fire, till slightly brown ;

Add : 2½ pints of water (or, preferably, the liquor of boiled peas, beans, or lentils); 2 pinches of salt ; and 2 small pinches of pepper ;

Boil three hours on the stove corner, with a slow fire, to avoid too much reducing.

Half an hour before serving add the sorrel, lettuce, and, lastly, the chervil ; skim ; and serve.

Julienne is generally served up plain, but sometimes a few sippets of bread are added.

The compressed vegetables which are sold for *Julienne*, having lost much of their flavour by the drying process, are never equal to fresh vegetables, even when these are out of season.

Julienne is also prepared in the same way with broth, instead of water, allowance being made for the difference of seasoning.

ONION SOUP

Peel 2 good-sized onions (say 7 oz.), cut them, in halves and then crosswise, in thin shreds ;

Blanch, in boiling water, for five minutes, to remove their acrid flavour ;

Put in a 6-inch stewpan, with 1½ oz. of butter ;

Stir over a brisk fire, and, when the onion becomes of a light brown colour, add a tablespoonful of flour, say 1 oz. ;

Keep on the fire for two minutes longer ;

Add : 1 quart of water ; 2 pinches of salt ; and 2 small ones of pepper ;

Stir till boiling ;

Simmer, for five minutes, on the stove corner ; taste the seasoning ;

Put in the soup-tureen 2 oz. of sliced dried roll, and 1 oz. of butter ; pour in the soup, stirring gently with a spoon to dissolve the butter.

Serve.

ONION SOUP THICKENED WITH EGG

Onion soup is also made, thickened with yolks of egg.

Prepare the soup as above ;

Put 3 yolks of egg in a basin, with 1 oz. of fresh butter ; mix with a few spoonfuls of the soup ;

Stir with the spoon, to mix thoroughly ; pour into the soup-tureen whilst stirring the soup.

This operation requires to be done quickly, and at the moment of serving.

SORREL SOUP

Pick, and wash :

¼lb. of sorrel,

a handful of chervil, say 1 oz.

1 cabbage-lettuce, say 2 oz. ;

Shred the whole ;

Put in a stewpan with 1 oz. of butter, 3 pinches of salt, and a small pinch of pepper ;

Stir over the fire, with a wooden spoon, till the vegetables are melted down ;

After five minutes, add ½ oz. of flour ;

After five minutes more, add 1 quart of water ; keep stirring all the time, to prevent the flour getting lumpy ;

Simmer for fifteen minutes, on the stove corner ;

Break 2 eggs in a basin ; beat them up as for omelet ; and add 2 oz. of fresh butter :

Take the soup off the fire, and add 1 gill of it to the egg ; stir, to melt the butter ; pour in another gill of soup ;

Put 2 oz. of sliced dried roll in the tureen ; pour the soup on the bread ; then add the *liaison*, namely, the eggs that you have mixed with some of the broth ; stir well ; and serve.

Observation.—I recommend that the eggs be thoroughly

beaten, in order to prevent the whites' poaching in lumps in the boiling soup.

In the months of September, October, and November, sorrel is extremely acid; in those months half the quantity indicated will therefore be found sufficient.

LEEK SOUP

This is only good when leeks are young; it is therefore unadvisable to make it in March and April.

Trim and wash 6 good-sized leeks (say 7 oz.); cut them in strips, 1 inch long, and ½ inch thick;

Fry them, in ½ oz. of butter, till they take a slight brown colour;

Add: 1 quart of water; 3 pinches of salt; and 2 small pinches of pepper;

Boil, and put on the stove corner to simmer, for twenty minutes;

Put 1½ oz. of sliced French roll in the soup-tureen;

Break 2 yolks of egg in a basin, for the *liaison*;

Moisten the latter with 1 gill of cold milk; add 1 oz. of fresh butter; and mix.

Pour the soup on the bread in the tureen;

Pour in the mixture of egg with one hand, whilst stirring round the soup with a spoon with the other.

When the butter is completely melted, serve.

POTATO AND LEEK SOUP

Trim and wash 3 good-sized leeks, say 4 oz., as above;

Fry, moisten, and season, as for leek soup;

Add ¼ lb. of good mealy potatoes, peeled, and washed, and cut in large pieces;

Boil gently, till the potatoes are done to a *purée*;

Add: 1 oz. of bread, cut in thin slices; and 1½ oz. of fresh butter;

Stir up, till the butter is melted; and serve.

PURÉE OF LENTILS SOUP

Pick 1 pint of good new yellow lentils;

Wash them in lukewarm water; put them in a stewpan, with:

    3 pints of water,

    1 small onion, say 1 oz.,

a sprig of celery, say $\frac{1}{4}$ oz.,
half a small carrot, say 1 oz.,
$\frac{1}{4}$ oz. of salt;
Boil; then allow to simmer till the lentils are cooked (which you can ascertain by pressing one between the fingers, when it should bruise easily).

SIEVE FOR PURÉES

To accelerate the cooking, pour in, every half hour, a quarter of a tumbler of cold water, starting the boiling again after adding the cold water.

(It was formerly usual to soak dry vegetables for *purées* for twenty-four hours; but the addition of cold water whilst boiling renders this operation unnecessary.)

The lentils being well done, drain them in a colander;

Reserve the liquor;

Pass the lentils through a wire sieve on to a dish placed underneath, to receive the *purée*;

Moisten, now and then, with some of the liquor, to facilitate the passing of the *purée*.

When done, put the *purée* in a stewpan, and moisten with as much of the broth as required for soup;

Boil and simmer for half an hour, stirring with a wooden spoon to prevent adhesion to the bottom of the stewpan;

Put $\frac{1}{2}$ oz. of sliced bread in the soup-tureen;

Add 2 oz. of fresh butter;

Pour in the soup, stirring to melt the butter;

Serve.

G

PURÉE OF WHITE HARICOT BEANS SOUP

Pick 1 pint of new white Soissons haricot beans, and proceed as for the *Purée* of Lentils.

PURÉE OF RED HARICOT BEANS SOUP

Pick 1 pint of red haricot beans, and proceed as directed for the *Purée* of Lentils (*vide* page 41).

PURÉE OF SPLIT PEAS SOUP

Pick 1 pint of very green split peas ;
Wash them, and put in a stewpan with :
   6 pints of water,
   ¼ oz. of salt, only ;
Then proceed as for *Purée* of Lentils (*vide* page 41).

Observation.—All these *purées maigres* may be modified by substituting good broth to water in their preparation—always bearing in mind, to make about a quart of soup for four persons.

PUMPKIN SOUP

This is in season from October to February.
Take 2 lbs. of yellow pumpkin ;
Take out the seeds, and pare off ¼ inch of the rind ;
Cut it in pieces 1½ inch square ; put in a stewpan, with :

1 oz. of butter,	1 oz. of sugar,
1 pinch of salt,	½ pint of water ;

Simmer for an hour and a half, and drain in a colander ;
Put back in the stewpan, and add 1½ pint of boiled milk—otherwise, if unboiled, the milk is liable to curdle ;
Boil for a minute, and pour in the soup-tureen, in which ½ oz. of bread has been sliced ;
Serve.

Observations on Purée *Soups*

Notwithstanding all the care taken in ascertaining the exact proportions required for these operations, it may happen that they will not answer in all cases—some dry vegetables requiring more moisture than others ; it will be easy to meet such cases, by adding a little more water, or broth, if the *purée* be too thick.

RICE AND BARLEY FOR PURÉE SOUPS

Rice and barley are frequently used, instead of bread, with these soups.

1 oz. of rice will be the requisite quantity for soup for four.

Wash the rice, in cold water;

Put, in a small stewpan, with ½ pint of water: ½ oz. of butter, and a pinch of salt;

In twenty minutes the rice should be done;

Mix with the *purée*, adding another ½ oz. of fresh butter in the soup tureen;

Stir; and serve.

Barley is prepared in the same way.

Moisten 1 oz. of barley, with 1½ pint of water; add ¼ oz. of salt; and boil, for an hour and a half, on a very slow fire;

Drain well in the colander;

Mix the *purée* and barley in the soup-tureen, adding ½ oz. of fresh butter; stir until the butter is melted; and serve.

SORREL SOUP, WITH RICE

Take:

    2 handfuls of sorrel, say 2 oz.,

    2 cabbage-lettuces, say 2 oz.,

    1 handful of chervil, say 1 oz.;

Pick, wash, and chop, as for sorrel soup;

Put in a 2-quart stewpan, with:

    ½ oz. of butter,

    ¼ oz. of salt,

    a small pinch of pepper;

Stir over the fire for ten minutes;

Add 3½ pints of water;

Simmer for fifteen minutes on the stove corner;

Add 2 oz. of well-washed rice;

Stir with the spoon, and boil gently for half an hour;

Add, when serving, another oz. of fresh butter;

Stir; and serve.

This soup may be made in the same way with vermicelli or any other paste.

RICE MILK SOUP

Blanch, in plenty of water, 2½ oz. of best Carolina rice;

Cool with plenty of cold water, and drain;

Boil 3 pints of milk, in a 2-quart stewpan;

Mix the rice in the milk, and stir on the fire till boiling;

Add a lump of sugar, and a small pinch of salt, say ¼ oz. of each;

Boil gently for half an hour; serve.

Observation.—I indicate purposely very small quantities of sugar and salt; they are both indispensable in rice milk, but, of course, taste must regulate the preponderance of one or the other.

In case the rice is preferred rather underdone, twenty minutes' boiling would be sufficient.

All milk soups—vermicelli, semolina, tapioca, &c.—are prepared in the same way.

THICK MILK, OR BOUILLIE

Put, in a quart stewpan:

1 oz. of best flour,

1 dessert spoonful of sugar, say ¼ oz.,

a small pinch of salt;

Mix gradually to a smooth paste, with a pint of milk;

Stir on the fire, with a wooden spoon, till boiling; if too thick, add a little more milk;

After boiling slowly for a quarter of an hour, the *bouillie* should be thick enough to coat the spoon.

Some flours thickening more than others, it is difficult to indicate absolute quantities; but, a little practice will soon show when more or less milk is required.

Use none but the best flour, as it will always produce a more digestible article, specially adapted for infants.

BREAD PANADA SOUP

Put, in a 2-quart stewpan, 3 pints of water, with:

2 oz. of bread, broken in pieces,

1 pinch of salt,

½ oz. of butter;

Place on a sharp fire; stir with a wooden spoon—to prevent adhesion to the stewpan;

Boil for twenty minutes, stirring all the while;

Mix in a basin 4 yolks of egg, with ½ gill of milk;

Add 1 oz. of fresh butter;

Put the soup in the tureen;

Pour in the *liaison*, stirring all the while ;
Serve.

Observation.—Should the panada be too thick, add a small quantity of milk.

Use of Butter in Maigres Soups

I will end this Chapter with a general precept relating to the use of butter in all the preceding soups.   It should be borne in mind that the butter required for *maigres* soups must be added at two different times, *Julienne* excepted, which, requiring no *liaison*, the whole of the butter is put in at once.

The first quantity of butter, which goes to fry the vegetables, should be small, as it adds very little to the flavour, which is mainly imparted by the second quantity, or uncooked butter, put in the tureen with the *liaison*.   This butter, being only melted, retains a freshness of taste, destroyed, in the other part, by the action of the fire.

BROTH BASIN

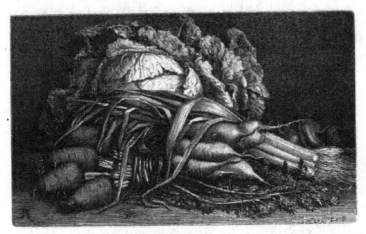

VEGETABLES

CHAPTER III

GARNISHES, LIAISONS OR THICKENINGS, SAUCES IN GENERAL USE

IT WILL, perhaps, appear strange to see introduced, in this First Part, a Chapter on Garnishes, which are generally supposed to belong to the higher class of cookery.

I would remark that, although they certainly play an important part in the latter class, where I will not fail to give them due importance, there is also, in household cookery, a *specialité* of garnishes which it is necessary to know : it is these that form the subject of this Chapter.

The garnishes for domestic cookery consist principally of vegetables cooked with the meat, and which are served round it.

With respect to the sauces, as with the soups, I shall restrict myself to indicating those in most general use ; making a point of giving these in all their details, rather than attempting to describe a greater number of—mostly useless and impracticable—sauces, beyond the limits of domestic cookery. I add to the recipes of garnishes and sauces, those of *liaisons* (or thickenings), which I consider as their complement.

This Chapter will lead us to the *entrées* of meat, fish, and poultry, for all of which a previous knowledge of sauces will be necessary.

I

GARNISHES

TURNED MUSHROOMS

Mushrooms are used, both for garnishes and sauces.

Forced mushrooms must be white, full, and firm.

For the garnish of a dish for four persons, take 1 pottle of moderate-sized mushrooms, or buttons.

Cut away the gritty part near the stalk, and throw the mushrooms in a basin of cold water, rince them well, and drain them on a cloth. They should not be allowed to remain long in water, as their taste and appearance would suffer thereby.

FLUTED KNIFE

Put, in a quart stewpan, a tablespoonful of lemon-juice, the same quantity of water, and a pinch of salt.

Turn each mushroom; that is, separate the button part from the stalk; hold it in the four fingers of the left hand, and, with a small knife in your right, cut the skin all round.

It is not necessary to peel mushrooms; but by the process of turning them they will more readily absorb the lemon-juice, which makes them white.

When turned put them in the stewpan with the lemon juice, and toss them to impregnate them with the liquid.

Put on a sharp fire, with 1 oz. of butter; boil for five minutes, tossing them occasionally; then pour them out into a basin; cover it with a round of paper,—to keep the moisture in, and preserve them white.

When so prepared, they are ready for use, for garnishes and sauces.

The mushroom trimmings should be kept carefully for the purpose mentioned further on.

Remark.—The object of the lemon-juice is to keep the mushrooms white; for those who dislike the acidity imparted by the lemon, it will be necessary to steep the mushrooms afterwards, for a quarter of an hour, in lukewarm water, with a pinch of salt added. The liquor in which the mushrooms have been boiled should be preserved, as it is very useful in all sauces.

POSITION OF THE HANDS IN TURNING MUSHROOMS

FINES HERBES,
OR CHOPPED HERBS FOR GARNISHES AND SAUCES

I designate, under the name of *fines herbes* for garnishes and sauces, the mixture hitherto known under the ambitious name of *d'Uxelles*, a term totally out of place in unpretentious cookery. I have, therefore, preferred a plainer name, indicating the same thing.

After turning the mushrooms, as explained in the preceding article, chop all the trimmings very fine; squeeze the water out of them, in the corner of a cloth.

Chop the same quantity of parsley, previously washed and dried in a cloth; add about half the quantity of chopped shalot, also well washed and drained; say about 2 oz. of shalot to 4 oz. of mushrooms and 4 oz. of parsley.

Put, in a stewpan, the shalot first; with:

$\frac{1}{2}$ oz. of butter,
1 pinch of salt,
1 pinch of pepper;

Put on the fire, stirring with a spoon for five minutes;
Add the mushrooms and parsley;
Boil for five minutes more;
Pour in a basin; cover with a round of buttered paper, to prevent drying.

These *fines herbes* are used for *gratins, barigoules, papillotes*, also for Sharp and Italian Sauce.

The trimmings of mushrooms must be prepared as *fines herbes* immediately after turning the mushrooms; if kept, they become black, and lose their flavour.

STEWED MUSHROOMS FOR GARNISH

Take 1 pottle of mushrooms; clean, and wash them, as explained in the preceding article (*vide* page 47); slice the buttons, and the stalks, about the thickness of $\frac{1}{4}$ inch;

Put 4 oz. of butter in the frying-pan;

When the butter is hot, without acquiring any colour, throw the mushrooms in it, with 2 pinches of salt, and 2 small pinches of pepper; toss them, for four minutes;

Sprinkle them with 1 oz. of flour, as a thickening; toss again, for a minute;

Moisten with 1 gill of broth;

Add 1 tablespoonful of chopped parsley, and 1 shalot, also chopped, and well washed.

Mushrooms prepared in this way should be of a light brown colour.

CARROTS

Carrots can be used all the year round for garnishes.

The season for new carrots is from the beginning of May to the end of July.

Take 40 spring carrots, as near the same size as possible, —to ensure even cooking;

Turn them to a pear shape;

Wash, drain, and put in a 2-quart stewpan, with :

$\frac{1}{2}$ pint of broth,

a teaspoonful of salt, say $\frac{1}{4}$ oz.,

a teaspoonful of sugar, say $\frac{1}{4}$ oz.

Put on a sharp fire, for twenty minutes—keeping the cover on the stewpan.

That length of time should be sufficient to cook the carrots, and reduce the broth.

If the broth does not reduce quickly enough, uncover the stewpan, to accelerate the reduction.

Keep the carrots ready for garnishes, when wanted.

H

After the month of July, when carrots are too large to be used whole, cut them, in cork-shaped pieces, 2 inches long and 1 inch diameter.

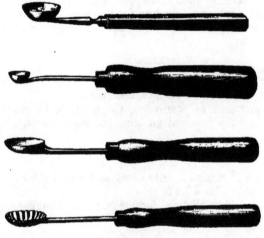

VEGETABLE SCOOPS

Wash, drain, and put in a stewpan, as before stated, with:
  3 gills of broth,
  a teaspoonful of salt, say $\frac{1}{4}$ oz.,
  a teaspoonful of sugar, say $\frac{1}{4}$ oz. ;
Put on a moderate fire, for half an hour, with the cover on ; taking it off, if the reduction of the broth is too slow.

LONG, OR VEGETABLE, CUTTER BOX

This process it is advisable to follow from the end of July to the end of September.

Winter carrots are prepared in the same way, but require to be blanched in boiling water, then drained, and moistened with 1½ pint of broth, and left to simmer, for two hours, on a slow fire, as their greater toughness requires slower and longer cooking.

TURNIPS

The season for turnips is from May to the end of February. Choose them very white, smooth, and sound.

They are prepared for garnishes, either white or coloured, according as they are required for large braizes or stews.

WHITE TURNIP GARNISH

Cut 40 pieces of turnip, 2 inches long and 1 inch thick;
Pare the outside with a knife;
Wash, drain, and blanch them, for five minutes, in boiling water;
Put them in a 2-quart stewpan with :

    ½ pint of broth,
    1 gill of water,
    a teaspoonful of salt, say ¼ oz.,
    a teaspoonful of sugar, say ¼ oz. ;

Stew, on a slow fire, for twenty minutes ;
Try, with a trussing needle, to ascertain whether cooked ;
Take off the fire, and leave in the stewpan, to be drained when wanted.

BROWN TURNIP GARNISH

For this preparation wash, drain, and blanch the turnips, as aforesaid ;
Put 1 oz. of butter, to melt in a frying-pan ;
When the butter is hot, without colouring, put in the turnips, and toss them for eight or ten minutes, to give them a light brown colour ;—always taking care to regulate the length of time of cooking by the degree of tenderness of the vegetables ;
Drain them, and, when added to stews, they will complete their proper cooking.

ONIONS

Onion garnish can be used all the year round.
There are three different ways of preparing onions ; namely :

White: for fricassee of chicken, or *blanquette* of veal;

Coloured brown: for stews, jugged hare, stewed eels, rabbits, &c.;

Glazed: for garnishing beef.

WHITE ONION GARNISH

Choose 20 large button onions;

Cut a thin slice off both extremities;

Blanch, in a quart of boiling water, for ten minutes;

Drain, and cool; peel off the yellow and the first white skins;

Put the onions in a quart stewpan, with:

    1½ pint of water,

    a teaspoonful of salt, say ¼ oz.,

    a teaspoonful of sugar, say ¼ oz.;

Boil very gently till cooked, which you can ascertain by trying them with the trussing needle;

Drain, and put the onions in the fricassee, five minutes before serving.

COLOURED ONION GARNISH

Prepare and blanch the onions, as in the preceding paragraph;

Fry them, with a little butter and sugar, until they are slightly browned.

Drain, and mix in the stew, where they will finish cooking.

GLAZED ONIONS

Pick a dozen large-sized onions; cut off the two extremities;

Blanch, for twenty minutes, in plenty of boiling water;

Drain, and cool;

Peel off the two first skins, and remove the middle, with a vegetable cutter of a quarter of an inch diameter;

Spread 1 oz. of butter in a *sauté*-pan;

Arrange the onions, side by side, to fill up the pan;

Put 2 small pinches of pounded sugar in the hole made in the middle of each onion;

Put on a fire, sharp enough to give the onions a slight colour, without burning the butter;

Keep turning them, to colour both sides alike; then add a sufficient quantity of broth, to cover them;

Put to glaze, by covering the *sauté*-pan with a sheet-iron cover, containing live charcoal on the top, till the broth reduces and forms a glaze;—be careful to baste the onions with the liquor every ten minutes, to ensure an equal glazing.

Keep warm, till required to garnish.

POTATOES

The kinds of potatoes to which I would give the preference for garnishes are : the *Vitelotte*, or French kidney, and the Dutch, as they do not break in cooking ; for *purée*, or mashed potatoes, the Regents are undoubtedly the best.

Potatoes for garnish may be divided into three kinds :—

Plain boiled potatoes ; mostly used with fish, and all kinds of meat.

Potatoes *sautés*, or tossed in butter; for garnish of fillet of beef.

Fried potatoes ; for beefsteaks, steaks, chops, &c.

PLAIN BOILED POTATOES

Pick 20 middle-sized potatoes; peel them, to the shape of an egg;

Wash, and drain them ; put them, in a 2-quart stewpan, with a quart of water, and 1 teaspoonful (say $\frac{1}{4}$ oz.) of salt ;

Boil for fifteen minutes, when they will be nearly done ; drain the water, and cover the stewpan closely, and set on the hob, for five minutes, to steam.

VEGETABLE KNIFE

POTATOES SAUTÉS, OR TOSSED IN BUTTER

Shape the potatoes as above ; wash, and dry them in a cloth ;

Put $\frac{1}{2}$ oz. of butter in a *sauté*-pan, large enough to allow the potatoes to lay clear of one another ;

Melt the butter over the fire, without colouring, and, when hot, put in the potatoes whole, and toss them, every two or three minutes, till done of a light brown colour ;—they should be served immediately they are done.

FRIED POTATOES

Peel 6 large potatoes, and slice them, to a thickness of an eighth of an inch; wash, and drain them in a cloth;

Melt your frying fat over a brisk fire, and throw the potatoes in; stir with the skimmer occasionally, to secure an even cooking; eight or ten minutes' frying will suffice;

Drain them, on a wire sieve, and sprinkle with salt;

Serve.

When potatoes are required very crisp, let them fry four or five minutes longer.

WHITE HARICOT BEANS

Boil 1 pint of white haricot beans, as previously described for *Purée* Soups (*vide* page 42).

When done, drain them and put them in a 2-quart stewpan; add: 1 gill of broth; ¼ lb. of butter; 1 tablespoonful of chopped parsley; 1 pinch of salt; and 2 small pinches of pepper;

Toss up till the butter is melted;—the heat of the beans will be sufficient to do this; serve.

LENTILS

Same process as for haricot beans.

CAULIFLOWERS

Cauliflowers are to be had good in all seasons.

Choose them very white, firm, and small-grained—extreme whiteness is an indication of freshness and quality.

Pick one, or two, cauliflowers, according to their size; cut the stalk, and divide the cauliflower in quarters; pare away the tough skin round the stalk;

Throw the pieces in a large basin of cold water, adding ½ gill of vinegar;—by this means any caterpillar, or insect, they may contain will be sure to come out;

Blanch, in 2 quarts of boiling water, for five minutes, to render more digestible; cool, and drain; then boil again, in 2 quarts of water, with ½ oz. of salt.

You can ascertain whether the cauliflowers are done by taking a small piece between the fingers, when it should give way easily, although still retaining a certain firmness.

As cauliflowers will continue cooking whilst left in the water in the stewpan, it is important to take them off the fire before they are quite done.

SAUERKRAUT

Choose your sauerkraut white, and fresh-looking.

It is used both with and without being blanched. I prefer the first mode; and, while admitting that it loses some of its flavour in the blanching process, this is amply compensated by its thereby becoming more wholesome and digestible.

Take 2 lbs. of sauerkraut; blanch, in boiling water, for ten minutes; cool, drain, and press the water well out;

Put it in a 4-quart stewpan;

Add: 1 quart of broth; 1 pint of the fat, skimmed off the top of the stock-pot; and a pinch of pepper;

Simmer, on a very slow fire, for eight hours,—the stewpan all the time hermetically closed;

Pour out in a basin, and cover with a round of paper, ready to be warmed for use, if not used at once.

BRUSSELS SPROUTS

The season for Brussels sprouts is from November to the end of February.

Select them green, sound, and without any yellow leaves.

Take about 1 lb. of Brussels sprouts; cut the stalks; and pare the few outside leaves;

Wash, drain, and boil, for a quarter of an hour, in 4 quarts of water, with $\frac{1}{2}$ oz. of salt;

Drain them on a clean cloth; melt $\frac{1}{2}$ oz. of butter in a frying-pan, and toss the sprouts for a couple of minutes, sprinkling them with a little salt, and grated nutmeg; serve.

SPINACH

Spinach is obtainable nearly the whole year; but, in the very warm months, and also during prolonged frosty weather, it becomes scarce, and reaches a price which renders it too expensive for the purposes of domestic cookery.

Pick about 3 lbs. of spinach;—taking off the stalks, and any straw or weed which might be amongst it;

Wash it in plenty of water; drain in a colander; then put in a 4-quart saucepan of boiling water with ½ oz. of salt; boil for five minutes; cool thoroughly, in plenty of water—as otherwise it will assume a yellow colour;

Press all the water out; spread the spinach out on the chopping-board, and turn it over carefully with a knife, to be quite sure that it is perfectly cleansed; then chop it very fine with the chopping knife, and put it on a clean dish;

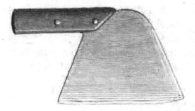

CHOPPING KNIFE

Put 1 oz. of butter in a 2-quart stewpan, together with 1 oz. of flour; stir over the fire for three minutes; then add the spinach, and stir again for about five minutes; add 2 pinches of salt, and 3 gills of broth (at three separate operations), stirring all the time;

When ready to serve, add another oz. of butter, and a small pinch of grated nutmeg;

When this last quantity of butter is melted and mixed, the spinach is ready to be served.

ENDIVES

The season when endives are cheap is from June to January. Choose 12 heads of endive, as yellow and fresh as possible;

Trim them, by taking off the outside leaves, and cutting off the green tips; then cut the stalk, to loosen all the leaves; open them, to see if there should be any caterpillar or other insect hidden within;

Wash, drain, and boil as for spinach,—but, instead of five minutes, boil for twenty-five, endives requiring much longer cooking.

Cool them well, drain, and press the water out with the hands; then put on the board, and chop fine.

For the preparation and addition of butter, flour, salt, and broth, proceed as in the case of spinach.

SORREL

The season for sorrel is from the 1st of May till the end of October.

Take 3 lbs. of sorrel,—the fresher and greener the better;

Pick the sorrel, by taking away the stalks; wash in plenty of water; drain, and put in a 4-quart stewpan, with 2 pinches of salt, and 1 quart of water;

Put on the fire for fifteen minutes, stirring with a wooden spoon, to prevent its catching;

Drain on a wire sieve;

When well drained, put on the chopping-board; clear it of straws, &c., as with spinach (*vide* page 56); chop, for twenty minutes;

Put, in a 2-quart stewpan:

    1½ oz. of butter,

    1 oz. of flour;

Stir, over the fire, for three minutes;

Put in the sorrel with 2 gills of broth—one at once, the second ten minutes afterwards; stir on the fire, for twenty minutes;

Break 3 eggs in a basin; add ½ gill of milk;

Beat well together, and pour into the sorrel, stirring briskly over the fire, for five minutes. It is then ready for garnishes.

FRIED PARSLEY

Fried parsley is generally used as a garnish for fried dishes: such as fish, croquets, rissoles, &c.

Pick a good handful of parsley (say 2 oz.), leaving the stalks two inches long;

Wash, drain, and dry with a cloth;

Put the parsley in the frying basket; dip it in the hot fat; let it fry for forty seconds, stirring with a spoon, to cook it evenly.

Drain, and keep hot, to use when wanted.

CAULIFLOWER

1

II

LIAISONS

The different processes of thickening soups and sauces are called *liaisons*.

I explain those most frequently used in ordinary cookery, thinking it preferable to give them a separate Chapter to themselves, preceding the one on Sauces, which will thereby become more intelligible.

LIAISON À L'ALLEMANDE

The thickening known as *Liaison à l'Allemande* is composed of flour, diluted in water, milk, or broth, according to the nature of the dish for which it is required. It produces a yellowish-white coloured sauce.

Mix the flour smooth, with one of the above-mentioned liquids;

Strain through the pointed strainer; then, with one hand, pour the *liaison* into the preparation requiring it, whilst stirring with the other.

I shall fix the exact quantities of this *liaison* when explaining the different recipes requiring it.

POSITION OF HANDS MIXING THE LIAISON

Observation.—Do not mistake the *Liaison à l'Allemande* for the *Allemande Sauce*—one of the principal sauces of high-class cookery.

I have adopted this title, *Liaison à l'Allemande*, because it represents an effective substitute to the *Allemande Sauce*; equally useful in many ways, and possessing, besides, the advantages of economy, and facility of preparation, specially required in the sort of cookery at present under our notice.

LIAISON AU ROUX

Roux itself is made of butter and flour.

Melt ½ lb. of butter; add 1 lb. of flour; mix well, and leave on a slow fire, stirring occasionally till it becomes of a light mahogany colour.

When cool, it may be kept in the larder, ready for use.

The *liaison* is made by pouring the broth into the stewpan containing the *roux*, and stirring, till it boils.

It may be mixed with either hot or cold broth :

If mixed cold, stir over the fire till boiling;

If mixed hot, moisten with the broth, by degrees, and off the fire, to prevent lumping.

LIAISON OF EGG

This *liaison* is used for soups, *poulettes*, fricassee of chicken, &c.

The first care is to take the sauce off the fire two minutes before adding the *liaison*.

This partial cooling is absolutely necessary to prevent the eggs from curdling.

The *liaison* is made by mixing part of the sauce with the yolks of egg (previously beaten), in a basin; then, pouring into the remainder of the sauce, and stirring on the fire till near boiling.

LIAISON OF BLOOD

This is used with game or poultry; the blood should be added in the same way as the yolks of egg, in the preceding recipe.

LIAISON OF BUTTER

That quantity of cold butter which is added to soups and sauces when taken off the fire, before serving, constitutes what is called the *liaison of butter*.

I will repeat the remark made at the paragraph Soups (*vide* page 45)—*never* add this fresh butter till the last minute: for, if boiled, the flavour is quite altered, and the butter lost.

LIAISON OF BUTTER AND CREAM

This *liaison* is mostly used for soups; it is made by mixing the cold butter and cream in the tureen; the soup is then poured in, and stirred, till the butter is melted.

For sauces and vegetables: pour the *liaison* into the stewpan containing them; stir, till well mixed; and serve.

III

PLAIN SAUCES

MELTED BUTTER, OR WHITE SAUCE*

Observation.—I have often heard mistresses complain that the preparation of melted butter failed more frequently than any other operation. This has much astonished me, as no sauce is easier to make; and, without flattering myself, I think I can say, that success is certain, if the recipe I subjoin be followed literally.

Take:

3 oz. of butter,	1 pinch of salt,
1 oz. of flour,	1 small pinch of pepper;
½ pint of warm water,	

Put in a quart stewpan, first:

    1 oz. of butter,
    1 oz. of flour;

Mix the butter and flour to a paste;

Add the pepper, and salt, and ½ pint of warm water;

* The quantities are given for four persons.

Stir over the fire, with a wooden spoon, till boiling ;—the sauce should then be thick enough to coat the spoon.

Then add the 2 oz. of remaining butter, cut in pieces to accelerate its melting ; take off the fire ; and stir, till melted.

The sauce is then ready ;—the foregoing quantities should produce about 1 pint of melted butter.

Observation.—In case the melted butter should be too thick, which is quite possible, some flours requiring more moisture than others, add ½ a gill or so of water, according to circumstances, before putting in the cold butter.

Cause of Failure in the Preparation of Melted Butter.

As shown above, the great point for melted butter is, as soon as it has come to the boil, to take it off the fire, and add to it the cold butter which gives it its flavour.

Why is it so often bad? how is it that, in many families, melted butter is brought to table, bearing a pasty or starchlike appearance, and with no other flavour than that of flour and water?

My answer is : That the quantity of flour used has been too much in excess of the quantity of butter; and has destroyed the flavour; often, also, the fault lies in mixing, at once, the whole of the butter with the flour ; producing thereby those tasteless and pasty sauces with reason condemned. I have often seen melted butter prepared in this way, with an extravagant quantity of butter, while half, properly used, would have been quite sufficient to produce a good sauce.

If the sauce be too thick, add one or two tablespoonfuls of water; if, on the contrary, it is too thin, mix a tablespoonful of flour with ½ oz. of cold butter; take the sauce off the fire; allow it to cool for three minutes; add the mixture of flour and butter; and stir off the fire ; when melted, put the sauce over the fire again, till just boiling; then add the remainder of the butter as aforesaid.

The most essential, in fact, indispensable requisite is, that the flour and butter should be of the very best; otherwise, good melted butter is unobtainable, whatever recipe be followed.

Bad flour will not thicken properly,—thence the non-success of the sauce.

Butter, unless of good quality, and very fresh, can impart no pleasant flavour, nor consequently produce a good sauce.

Melted butter is sometimes preferred slightly acid : in this case, add a few drops of vinegar, previously reduced; or a little lemon-juice, to the sauce, in the sauce-boat, when about serving.

DUTCH SAUCE, OR SAUCE HOLLANDAISE

Take 4 oz. of the freshest butter ;

First reduce, in a quart stewpan, 2 tablespoonfuls of vinegar, seasoned with 1 pinch of salt, and 1 small pinch of *mignonnette* pepper ;* when reduced to a teaspoonful, take it off the fire ; add 2 tablespoonfuls of cold water, and 2 yolks of egg, well freed from white; replace on the fire for a minute, stirring well, with a wooden spoon; avoid boiling; take off the fire, and add the sixth part of the cold butter, and stir till melted ; then put again on the fire for a minute, and add another sixth part of the butter ; repeat this process until all the butter is used, mixing occasionally a tablespoonful of cold water, to prevent the sauce getting too thick or curdling.

Season according to taste ; and serve.

Observation.—It is often the case that flour, potato-flour, or even melted butter, is mixed with Dutch Sauce; these additions, whilst needlessly increasing the work, only tend to destroy the character of the sauce, which should have no other bases than yolk of egg and butter.

To epicures, well-made *Hollandaise* is the first of white sauces.

MAÎTRE D'HÔTEL BUTTER

To make *maître d'hôtel* sufficient for two beefsteaks or two mackerel, take :

6 oz. of butter,

1 oz. of parsley—picked, washed, and chopped ;

It is necessary to wash the parsley twice: first, whole in plenty of water; and, when chopped, put it in the corner of a cloth, dip it in cold water, and wring the water out.

I recommend this second washing, to diminish the acrid taste which all parsley has, particularly in autumn and winter.

Put, in a basin : the butter, chopped parsley, 2 pinches of salt, 2 small pinches of pepper, and a tablespoonful of lemon-juice ;

---

* White pepper coarsely ground and sifted.

Mix near the fire, till the butter becomes of the consistence of thick cream; then keep ready for use;—avoid melting it, as it would turn oily.

MAÎTRE D'HÔTEL SAUCE

Take 5 oz. of *maître d'hôtel* butter, prepared as above ;

Put, in a quart stewpan : a gill of melted butter (*vide* Melted Butter, page 60), diluted with a gill of water ; boil for three minutes ; then add the *maître d'hôtel* butter, and take off the fire ; stir, till well melted.

BUTTER MELTED

Butter melted, used mostly with boiled fish, *à la Hollandaise*, is prepared in the following way ; take :

½ lb. of butter,	2 small pinches of pepper,
2 pinches of salt,	2 tablespoonfuls of lemon-juice ;

Put the butter and seasoning in the stewpan, and stir over the fire with a wooden spoon. When the butter is half melted, take off the fire, and continue stirring till quite melted. If this is done, the freshness of flavour, and creamy appearance of the butter, will be retained ;—they would be lost, if entirely melted on the fire.

BEURRE NOIR, OR BROWNED BUTTER

Cut up 10 oz. of butter ; put in the frying-pan over the fire ; cook till it acquires a dark brown colour, without being burnt ; take off the fire to cool ;

Put, in a quart stewpan :

3 tablespoonfuls of vinegar,

2 small pinches of pepper ;

Reduce one-third ; take off the fire ;

When the butter is cooled, strain through the pointed strainer, into the stewpan containing the vinegar, and warm up for use, without boiling.

It is necessary that the butter should be cooled before mixing, —as, otherwise, it would probably froth over the stewpan.

An inferior quality of butter is good enough for this preparation ; as the prolonged cooking destroys its taste, and, with better butter, the result would be the same, with additional expense.

SHARP SAUCE, OR SAUCE PIQUANTE

To make sufficient sauce for about 1 lb. of *bouilli* beef, take :

1 pint of broth,
4 shalots, say ½ oz.,
1 oz. of butter,
1 oz. of flour,
1 tablespoonful of chopped parsley, as for *maître d'hôtel*
(*vide* page 62),
1 tablespoonful of chopped gherkins,
4 tablespoonfuls of vinegar ;

Pick the shalots, and chop and wash them, as the parsley for *maître d'hôtel* ;

Put in a quart stewpan, with the butter and vinegar ;

Put on the fire, and stir, with a wooden spoon, till the vinegar is reduced,—which is indicated by the butter becoming clear.

The vinegar is to impart the necessary sharpness ; but, if it were not reduced, it would prevent the flour and butter from mixing properly.

When the shalot has absorbed all the vinegar, mix the flour with the butter, and stir for four minutes ; then add the pint of broth, 2 small pinches of pepper, and a few drops of *caramel* for colouring ;

Boil for a quarter of an hour ;

Add the chopped gherkins, and parsley; boil; skim; and serve.

Observation.—I do not mention any extra seasoning,—as that must be regulated by the saltness of the broth, and, if necessary, is to be added before serving.

ITALIAN SAUCE

For same quantity as Sharp Sauce, take :

3 gills of broth,	1 oz. of flour,
1 gill of white French wine,	1 oz. of butter,

3 tablespoonfuls of *fines herbes* for sauces (*vide* Garnishes ;
     Fines Herbes, for Sauces, page 48).

Reduce, in a small stewpan, the gill of white wine to half the quantity, adding 2 small pinches of salt, and the same quantity of pepper ;

Make a *roux* (*vide* page 59) with the butter and flour ;

Stir for three minutes over the fire ;

Moisten with the 3 gills of broth, and the reduced wine (*vide*, for mixing hot or cold, the observation at the paragraph *Liaison au Roux*, page 59);

Boil for fifteen minutes;

Add the 3 table-spoonfuls of *fines herbes*;

Skim; and serve.

POIVRADE SAUCE

Take:

1 pint of broth,	4 cloves,
1 oz. of butter,	1 handful of picked parsley,
1 oz. of flour,	say 1 oz.,
1 gill of vinegar,	2 onions, sliced, say 2 oz.,
3 shalots, say $\frac{1}{2}$ oz.,	1 small carrot, sliced, say 1 oz.,
1 sprig of thyme,	1 teaspoonful of *mignonnette*
2 bay leaves	pepper, say $\frac{1}{4}$ oz.;

Put in a quart stewpan all the above-named ingredients, —except the flour, butter, and broth;

Boil, till the vinegar is reduced to half the quantity;

Add the broth;

Boil, and put on the stove corner.

Take another quart stewpan; mix the butter and flour for *roux*; stir for three minutes over the fire; add the contents of the first stewpan by degrees,—mixing well all the time, to prevent lumping;

Boil, and stir again for twenty minutes; add a few drops of *caramel*; strain through the pointed strainer;

Skim; and serve.

To salt: take into account, as usual, the seasoning of the broth.

POULETTE SAUCE

Take:

1 pint of broth,	1 oz. of butter,
1 oz. of flour,	2 yolks of egg;

Make a *roux* with the flour and 3 parts of the butter; stir over the fire for three minutes; add the pint of broth; stir for a quarter of an hour; thicken with the 2 yolks of egg, and the fourth part of the butter (*vide Liaison* of Egg, page 59).

Strain through the pointed strainer; season; and serve.

Observation.—Mushrooms are generally used in *Poulette* Sauce. Care should be taken that some of the liquor they have been

K

boiled in be added to the sauce, with the broth,—as it greatly improves the flavour.

Sometimes chopped parsley is introduced. I simply indicate this addition, which may be omitted, if unsuitable to taste.

OYSTER SAUCE

Take 1½ dozen of oysters; open them carefully, and put them in a stewpan, to boil, in their own liquor, for two minutes; drain them, and strain the liquor;

Mix 1 oz. of butter, and 1 oz. of flour, to a smooth paste; add the liquor, and enough milk, to make a pint altogether; stir over the fire till boiling; add 1 oz. of butter; stir off the fire till melted; beard the oysters; put them in the sauce, to warm— but, not to boil; and serve.

TOMATO SAUCE

Tomato Sauce is made either with fresh or preserved tomatoes. The season for fresh tomatoes is from June till the end of October. They can be had almost all the year; but, out of these months they are too expensive;—consequently, unsuitable for domestic use.

Choose a dozen bright red tomatoes (say 2 lbs.); cut away the stalks; cut each tomato in two; press out the seeds, and water; and put them in a 2-quart stewpan, with:

1 faggot,	2 gills of water,
2 pinches of salt,	1 small pinch of pepper;

Put on the fire, the stewpan well covered; boil for forty minutes, stirring with a wooden spoon every five minutes, to prevent the tomatoes catching; press through a wire sieve;

Make a *roux* in a quart stewpan, with 1 oz. of butter and ½ oz. of flour; stir over the fire for three minutes; remove the stewpan from the fire, and mix the *purée* of tomatoes by small quantities, stirring well all the time; add 2 gills of broth, and boil again, for twenty minutes.

If the sauce be too thick: mix one or part of a gill of broth.

When preserved tomatoes are used, proceed in the same way, adding the preserved tomatoes from the bottle, instead of the *purée* of fresh tomatoes; mix, with the *roux*, and broth; taste; and serve, as before.

COLD SAUCES

WHITE MAYONNAISE SAUCE

Put, in a small basin : the yolk of 1 egg, well freed from white ; 1 pinch of salt ; and a small pinch of pepper ; stir with a wooden spoon, and pour in, by drops at first, then by teaspoonfuls, about 4 oz. of oil,—being careful to mix the oil well before adding any more ; at every eighth teaspoonful of oil, add 1 teaspoonful of vinegar, till all the oil is used ; taste the seasoning ; and serve.

Mayonnaise should, as a rule, be of rather high seasoning.

GREEN MAYONNAISE SAUCE

Prepare a white *mayonnaise*, as just indicated ;

Chop 3 tablespoonfuls of *ravigote*, i.e. a mixture of chervil, tarragon, cress, and burnet ;—if tarragon is scarce, chervil alone, with a tablespoonful of tarragon vinegar added to the sauce, will do as well.

Mix the herbs, in the sauce ; and serve.

REMOULADE SAUCE

Same process as for White *Mayonnaise* Sauce ; add :

    1 tablespoonful of chopped capers,
    1 tablespoonful of chopped gherkins,
    3 shalots, say $\frac{1}{2}$ oz., chopped, and washed,
    2 anchovies, well cleaned and chopped,
    1 tablespoonful of French mustard ;

Mix, in the sauce ; and serve.   .

TARTAR SAUCE

Prepare White *Mayonnaise* Sauce (as above); add :

    1 tablespoonful of dry mustard,
    3 shalots, say $\frac{1}{2}$ oz., chopped fine, and well washed,
    6 gherkins, say $\frac{1}{2}$ oz., also chopped fine,
    1 tablespoonful of *ravigote* (chervil, tarragon, and burnet, chopped),

1 teaspoonful of Chili vinegar,
.   or, 1 small pinch of Cayenne pepper ;
Mix all together ; and serve.

HOUSEHOLD GRAVY

I have made it a rule, in this First Part, to avoid everything
trenching on high-class cookery, which I have sought to keep
quite distinct ; but, still, this is no reason why I should not
indicate here what I think will tend to improve domestic
cookery.

When, within the limits of domestic expenditure, it is possible
to produce a good and useful element of food, I feel bound to
describe it ; bearing in mind, what I stated in the Preface,—that
my object has been to help all to eat of the best, according to
their means.

I trust, therefore, that the following recipe, for the preparation
of a good economical gravy, will be welcome ;—it will enable
the plain cook to substitute it without too great disadvantage
to the reduced glaze, one of the mainstays of more elaborate
cookery.

Preparation

To make 3 pints of gravy :
Take 2 lbs. of lean fillet, or leg, of veal ;
Bone, and tie with string as beef for *pot-au-feu* (*vide* page 30) ;
put the veal in a 2-quart stewpan, with $\frac{1}{2}$ pint of water ; put on
a slow fire, to reduce gently, till a light brown glaze forms at the
bottom of the stewpan ; turn the piece of veal, to colour it evenly ;
add : 3 pints of water ; $\frac{1}{2}$ oz. of salt ; a little pepper ; a faggot ;
1 carrot (say 4 oz.) ; 1 onion (say 4 oz.), with two cloves stuck
in it.

As soon as ebullition takes place, put on the stove corner
to simmer, for an hour ; keep the cover only three parts over the
stewpan ; be careful to simmer only,—as quick boiling would
certainly prevent the gravy being clear.

Strain the broth, through a perfectly clean lawn sieve, or broth
napkin ; free it carefully of grease, and put by, till wanted.

Take the piece of veal out of the stewpan ; put it on a dish ;
sprinkle with salt, and make use of it for *blanquette*, or serve
with Italian or Sharp Sauce, &c.

If the gravy is required set to a jelly for cold dishes, cook in

the same manner, adding a calf's foot before boiling; at the end
of an hour, take out the piece of veal, as indicated; but the calf's
foot should be left in to boil till quite tender; strain the gravy
through the sieve or napkin; skim carefully all the fat, and put
in a cool place, to set to a jelly.

Put the calf's foot on a dish, bone it, sprinkle with salt, and
press it, namely, place it between two baking-sheets (*vide*
Kitchen Utensils, page 10), with a 4 lbs. weight on the top, until
cold,—when pressed thus it may be warmed with *Poulette* Sauce
or *Marinade.*

Observation.—A mere glance at this recipe will show that this
Household Gravy is really, what I have given it out to be,—namely
easy of preparation and economical (for I indicate the way of
making use of the meat employed to produce it). Even those
little acquainted with cookery details will easily understand the
benefit to be derived from having such gravy at hand,—either
to take the place of broth, when one is short of it, or to add
that to the flavour of dishes which broth alone cannot impart.
Often a few spoonfuls of this gravy, well prepared, will give to
sauces that richness and aroma, so desirable to obtain, even in
the simplest dishes of domestic cookery.

If you happen to have any spare trimmings of fillet of beef,
of the neck or loin of veal, or mutton, I recommend adding
them to the gravy; they can but improve the quality,—provided
always that they are perfectly sweet. I do not, however, advise
putting in the stewpan *anything* you may have, such as leg of
mutton,—chop or chicken-bones,—as indicated in many Cookery
Books.

I cannot too strongly condemn such notions, equally opposed
to cleanliness and to the success of the operation. Any bones,
thus added, are more likely to impart a stale and greasy flavour
to the gravy, than to improve it in any way.

It is, therefore, best to use, as indicated, none but uncooked
meat, perfectly clean, fresh, and sound.

EGGS IN A BASKET

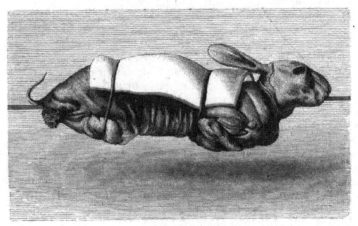

HARE ON THE SPIT

CHAPTER IV

ROASTING, BROILING, FRYING, BREADING

WITHOUT exactly pretending to write a graduated course of cookery, I am desirous that those who wish to learn from this book should understand the progression I have followed, particularly in the domestic recipes. I therefore open at once the subjects of Roasting, Broiling, and Frying; because I think it more reasonable to place them at the beginning, rather than at the end, of the book, in company with the Chapter of Sweets, as has hitherto been the practice.

I fancy that it is impossible to learn too soon what roasting, broiling, and frying mean; this knowledge, with that of sauces, treated of in the last Chapter, are the A B C of all cookery.

ROASTING

The first consideration to roast properly, is to have a well and evenly lighted fire, which should never be allowed to get low, but must constantly be replenished with coals, added in such a way as not to deaden it. It stands to reason that, if the fire is not kept up, no stated length of time can be fixed for cooking.

Avoid all draughts between the fire and screen ;—a joint subjected to such a draught would take much longer to cook.

To roast the following joints the time required will be :

For a piece of beef, weighing 7 lbs., an hour and three quarters;

For a leg of mutton, weighing 7 lbs., an hour and a half ;

For a neck or loin of veal, weighing 3 lbs., fifty minutes ;

For a neck or loin of pork, weighing 3 lbs., fifty minutes ;

For a turkey, weighing about 8½ lbs., an hour and three quarters ;

For a small turkey, weighing about 3½ lbs., forty-five minutes;

For a goose, weighing about 6 lbs., an hour and a half ;

For a capon, weighing about 4 lbs., fifty minutes ;

For a fowl, weighing about 3 lbs., half an hour ;

For a pigeon, a quarter of an hour ;

For a pheasant, thirty-five minutes ;

For a partridge, or woodcock, a quarter of an hour ;

For larks, six minutes, before a brisk fire ;

For a duck, a quarter of an hour ;

The same time for a wild duck ;

For a leveret, half an hour ;

For a hare's back, half an hour ;

For a small wild rabbit, a quarter of an hour.

The fire should be thoroughly lighted before the roast is put before it ; put 2 gills of broth in the dripping-pan for basting ; large joints, poultry, and game, should be basted five or six times during cooking ; partridges and small game, three times.

I need not point out that these rules of time required for cooking, will of course be modified by circumstances : there are different natures and qualities of meat, which cook more or less rapidly. It will always be necessary to ascertain whether a joint is done, before taking it off the spit ; the easiest way to find this out is, in the case of meat, to press the fleshiest parts with the finger ; in the case of poultry and game, the flesh of the leg should be tested—if the cooking is perfect, both will give way to the finger ; if not, there will be a certain degree of resistance.

BROILING

To broil with charcoal : make a layer of charcoal, cinders, and lighted embers, covering a surface extending 2 inches beyond the edges of the horizontal gridiron. The thickness of lighted coal should be 1½ inch for a brisk fire, and 1 inch for a slow fire; in either case, the embers should be thoroughly and equally lighted ; and not, in parts dead and at others burning brightly. It is a mistake to seek to economise fuel in broiling: the result will most probably be,—inefficient cooking, and, perhaps, entire spoiling of the meat.

HORIZONTAL GRIDIRON

It is general to set up the gridiron, as indicated, on a cast-iron slab, or on the plate covering the stove.

A rump steak, trimmed, weighing 1½ lb., will require eight to ten minutes, according to thickness, to broil on a brisk fire ;

A fillet steak, trimmed, weighing 7 oz., will require seven minutes to broil on a brisk fire ;

A mutton chop, trimmed, weighing on the average 5 oz., will require six minutes to broil on a brisk fire ;

A bread-crumbed mutton cutlet should be broiled on a slow fire, and left one minute longer ;

A sheep's kidney will require four minutes to broil on a brisk fire ;

A veal chop, trimmed, weighing 7 oz., will require nine minutes to broil on a brisk fire ;

A pork chop of the same weight will require the same time ;

A bread-crumbed veal or pork cutlet should be broiled on a slow fire, and left on two minutes longer.

FRYING

Fat is the best for frying ; the light-coloured dripping of roast meat and the fat taken off broth are to be preferred. These failing, beef suet, chopped fine, and melted down on a slow fire, without browning, will do very well; when the bottom of the stew-pan can be seen through the suet, it is sufficiently melted. Let it cool for a quarter of an hour, and strain through the pointed gravy strainer,—to do this, while too hot, would be likely to melt the strainer.

When butter is used for frying, it requires special care, and, on account of its heating quicker than fat, calls for a slow fire.

FRYING-KETTLE AND DRAINER

Oil may also be used for frying, but requires careful handling,—it should be warmed first, for at least twenty-five minutes, on a very slow fire, so as to prevent its rising and boiling over. Lard is also extensively employed; but I am no advocate for it,—as it always leaves an unpleasant coating of fat on whatever is fried in it.

Fat may be kept in use for frying until it assumes a dark brown colour, which is a sign of its uselessness,—for then it will no longer fry well, and will impart a bad colour and unpleasant taste.

Instructions for Frying

Use the frying-kettle and drainer described in the Kitchen Utensils (*vide* page 11; never more than half fill the kettle with fat,—in order to avoid its boiling over.

The fat should vary in heat according to the nature of the things to be fried; too great a degree of heat should be avoided

L

in all cases. This excessive heat is indicated by the smoke rising from the kettle.

The different degrees of heat may be determined by throwing into the fat a small piece of crumb of bread of the size of a nut; if it fizzes and produces, at once, large air bubbles, the fat has reached that degree of heat which we shall designate as *hot fat*.

For *warm fat*, the piece of bread should produce very small air bubbles, accompanied by scarcely any fizzing.

Should too many things be put in the frying-kettle together, they will be badly fried; for instance : if five whiting were put in together in a kettle only large enough for three, there would not be sufficient heat to cook them properly. In such a case, the fish should be taken out when three parts done ; the fat then made *very* hot, and three whiting put in again for two minutes ; when these are taken out, the other two should be put in, for the same length of time ; this will remedy the evil of crowding too many fish in the kettle at once.

Fried things should be of a light golden brown colour, crisp, and free from fat.

FRYING BATTER

Frying batter is used for meat, fish, and sweet dishes. To make it : $4\frac{1}{2}$ oz. of flour, 2 eggs, and 2 tablespoonfuls of oil, will be required.

Sift the flour, through a sieve, into a basin ;

Make a hole in the centre, and pour in 1 gill of water ;

Add a small pinch of salt, the 2 yolks of egg (reserving the whites for whipping), and the 2 spoonfuls of oil ;

Work into a smooth paste, thick enough to cover the spoon with a coating of about $\frac{1}{8}$ of an inch ;—should it be too thick, a gill, or half a gill, of water may be added.

Twenty minutes before using the batter, add the whites of egg, well whisked, and put by for frying purposes.

BREADINGS AND RASPINGS

For breading, use beaten eggs, oil, and the crumb of stale bread. Put the bread in a cloth, of which take up the four corners in one hand, and, with the other, rub the bread to break it up small, then pass it through a wire sieve, dry in the oven, and put by, in a closed box, for use. For breading, the eggs should be well beaten and mixed together; to 3 eggs, add 1 tablespoonful of oil, 1 tablespoonful of water, a pinch of salt, and a small pinch of pepper. The water is added to prevent the breading being too thick.

Raspings are made with crusts of bread, baked to a bright golden colour, then crushed with a rolling-pin, or in a mortar; passed through a wire sieve, and put by, in a box, for use.

ROAST PARTRIDGE

HORS-D'ŒUVRE

CHAPTER V

HORS-D'ŒUVRE IN GENERAL USE

In this Chapter I give a selected list of the *hors-d'œuvre* most in use in ordinary households ; it may be objected, that these belong rather to the *maître d'hôtel's* department, than to the cook's ; but this will not be the case in smaller establishments, where the plain cook will have to attend to these, in addition to her ordinary work ; this list of *hors-d'œuvre* has therefore appeared to me to have its proper place in domestic cookery.

It is customary to dish up *hors-d'œuvre* in small oval dishes or flat boats.

RADISHES

These are to be had the whole year ; they should be chosen of a light red colour, small, and sound ; hollow radishes are large and of a dark red. Radishes are prepared for table by cutting the leaves to a length of $1\frac{1}{2}$ inch ; scraping off the outer skin ;

washing them in plenty of water, and dressing them, in a boat, with a little cold water.

BUTTER, AS HORS-D'ŒUVRE

Butter is served as *hors-d'œuvre*, in very cold water; either in pats, or scraped up into the shape of shells.

GHERKINS

Should be firm, and green, and served in a boat, with vinegar.

LYONS, BOLOGNA, OR GERMAN SAUSAGE

To serve these sausages as *hors-d'œuvre*, slice them in rounds, about ⅛ inch thick; remove the skin; and dish up, with parsley.

OLIVES

Choose these firm and green,—the *picholine* are the best.

Should the olives be too salt, steep them in water for an hour; then serve them, in a boat, with cold water.

Olives that return from table should be put back in the bottle with salted water,—being careful that none remain uncovered, else they will turn black.

ANCHOVIES

Eight anchovies will be sufficient for a small boat.

The best come from Nice; they should be small and plump, with white scales; the pickle should be of a dark red colour.

Steep the anchovies two hours, in cold water, and open them; if they are sufficiently soaked, they will open easily without breaking.

Take out the backbone; scale, and wash them; and dry, on a cloth.

Trim the anchovies on both sides, so as to take off the small bones; put them in a boat; cover them with oil; and serve.

SARDINES

Take eight sardines out of the tin box; wipe them slightly, with a cloth; put them in a boat; garnish, with chopped parsley and capers; cover with oil,—but on no account using that out of the box.

PICKLED HERRINGS

Take three pickled herrings; put them in a boat; and add oil, parsley, and capers.

PICKLED OYSTERS

Take a dozen and a half of pickled oysters, out of a barrel; put them in a boat; strain the pickle through a cloth; and pour over the oysters; sprinkle with chopped parsley; and serve.

MIXED PICKLES

These are put in a boat,—taking advantage of their different colours, to arrange them tastefully.

CUCUMBER

This is in season from the middle of April to the end of September.

Choose a green cucumber; cut it in four equal lengths, and peel the green skin; these pieces, sliced very thin, should be put in a basin, with ½ oz. of salt; and allowed to remain four hours to pickle; then drained well, and seasoned as salad, with oil, vinegar, and pepper, adding a tablespoonful of chopped *ravigote* (for *ravigote*, vide *Mayonnaise* Sauce, page 67).

RAW ARTICHOKES À LA POIVRADE

Choose six very green and tender artichokes, about 2 inches diameter; cut off the bottom leaves, and the tips of the other leaves;

Put the artichokes in cold water, with a little vinegar—to prevent their turning black;

When required for use, drain them, and put in a dish, with a little cold water;

A seasoning of vinegar, oil, pepper, and salt, should be served, in a boat, with the artichokes.

BLACK RADISH

Choose a radish with a smooth black skin, and very white and sound internally; peel and slice it; put in a basin, with ½ oz. of salt, for six hours, to pickle; drain well; and serve, in a boat.

This is the ordinary way of dressing black radish; but it is sometimes seasoned like salad.

MELON

BOILED BEEF, GARNISHED WITH VEGETABLES

CHAPTER VI

BEEF

BOUILLI BEEF

This domestic *bouilli*, or boiled beef, has, on account of its want of savour, and uninviting aspect and taste, been much decried —I must confess, with some reason, particularly when unfairly brought into comparison with more elaborate dishes. Meat, which has been boiled for broth, must be expected to have lost some of its qualities; but, such as it is, *bouilli* represents a standard dish, which will ever hold its own in domestic cookery. The main thing is to present it, at once, in a profitable and a palatable shape; and the talent of a plain cook will rest in making the most of this *bouilli*, both *au naturel* and dressed in different ways.

As soon as the broth is made, the beef should be taken out, and placed on a dish, to send to table; remembering to remove the string with which it has been tied.

BOUILLI GARNISH

I should always recommend garnishing round any beef intended for serving;—it will make it more welcome, and is advisable even on economical grounds. I would hardly advocate the old-fashioned parsley garnishing, which has no practical use, as it cannot be eaten, and is always removed for carving. In domestic cookery, it is preferable to keep to the useful and tangible, rather than to the ornamental; it is therefore best, as garnishing to *bouilli* beef, to use none but, simply—but carefully—prepared vegetables, such as I have indicated at the Chapter on Garnishes.

Thus: potatoes fried whole in butter, glazed onions, carrots, turnips, mushrooms, cauliflowers, Brussels sprouts

All these, according to seasons, make an excellent garnish for the beef of the *pot-au-feu*.

The woodcut on the preceding page will show how a plain piece of boiled meat can assume an inviting appearance, by the mere tasteful arrangement of the garnishing.

MIROTON OF BEEF

Cut 1½ lb. of cold boiled beef into slices about ¼ inch thick, removing the outside, which may be dry, and all the fat; set the slices in the smallest of the oval copper pans for *gratins* (*vide* Kitchen Utensils, page 10); sprinkle, with 1 pinch of salt, and 2 small pinches of pepper.

Prepare 1 lb. of onions as for Onion Soup (*vide* Onion Soup, page 38); when the onions are of a light brown colour, sprinkle them with 1 oz. of flour, 1 pinch of salt, and 2 small pinches of pepper; and let them cook five minutes longer;

Take off the fire; add 1 pint of broth, and stir well on the fire for twenty minutes; add 1 teaspoonful of mixed mustard, and half a teaspoonful of *caramel*; pour the onions on the slices of beef; bake in a slow oven, for twenty minutes; and serve, in the pan used for cooking.

BOUILLI, WITH SHARP SAUCE OR SAUCE PIQUANTE

Slice the same quantity of beef as for a *Miroton* (*vide* preceding recipe); set the slices in a *gratin*-pan; moisten with 1 gill of broth; and put in the oven for fifteen minutes;

Pour 1 pint of Sharp Sauce (*vide* page 64) over the beef; and serve.

M

BOUILLI, WITH TOMATO SAUCE

Slice the beef, and warm it in the oven, as above; take 1 pint of Tomato Sauce (*vide* page 66).

Pour on the slices; and serve.

BOUILLI, WITH ITALIAN SAUCE

Slice the beef, and warm it, as above (*vide* page 81).

Pour over 1 pint of Italian Sauce (*vide* page 64); and serve.

BOUILLI, AU GRATIN

Slice the beef, as previously directed; set it in the *gratin*-pan, and pour over 1 pint of Italian Sauce; cover with fine raspings; warm in the oven; and salamander.

BOUILLI, WITH PARSLEY

Cut the beef in slices as before; put 4 oz. of butter, to melt in a frying-pan; place the slices in the pan,—avoiding their being one over the other; sprinkle with 1 pinch of salt, and 2 small pinches of pepper;

After five minutes' frying, turn the slices over, and let them fry five minutes longer; sprinkle again with salt and pepper; take out on a dish; add 2 tablespoonfuls of vinegar to the butter in the pan; boil one minute, and pour on the beef; strew with half a tablespoonful of chopped parsley; and serve.

BOUILLI, WITH POTATOES

Take 1½ lb. of beef; cut it into pieces 1½ inch square,—removing all dry and fat parts;

Take 4 oz. of streaky bacon; remove the rind, and cut the bacon in pieces 1½ inch square; fry, with 1 oz. of butter, in a 2-quart stewpan; when it is brown, add:

1 quart of water,
1 faggot,   1 medium-sized onion,
1 lb. of potatoes, peeled and cut in squares, like the beef;
Boil for fifteen minutes;

Add the pieces of beef, and boil gently for ten minutes;

When the potatoes are done, take out the faggot, and taste,
—the saltness given by the bacon will then be appreciated, and
more salt added, if necessary ;

Dish up; and serve.

MINCED BOUILLI

Prepare 1½ lb. of beef, by removing all gristle, fat, and dried
parts ; chop fine.

Stir 1 oz. of flour, and 1 oz. of butter, in a stewpan, and cook
for three minutes ; take off the fire ; add 1 pint of broth, 2 pinches
of salt, and 1 small pinch of pepper ; mix for two minutes, and put
on the fire ; stir for ten minutes ; then add the beef together
with 1 tablespoonful of chopped parsley ; stir again for two or
three minutes.

Should the mince be too thick, add a gill, or half a gill, of
broth.

This mince may be made with Italian or Tomato Sauces, to
which, when warmed, the beef should be added as above, stirred
on the fire for five minutes ; and served.

BOUILLI CROQUETS

Chop 1½ lb. of beef, very fine ;

Make 1 pint of *Poulette* Sauce (*vide* page 65), in a 2-quart
stewpan ; reduce it to ½ pint ; thicken with 3 yolks of egg ;
put the chopped beef in the sauce ; add 1 tablespoonful of
chopped parsley, 1 pinch of salt, and 2 small pinches of pepper ;
mix well together, with a wooden spoon ; and spread out on a
dish, to a thickness of 1½ inch ; let it get firm, and cold ; then
divide into sixteen equal parts.

Strew a board with bread-crumbs (*vide* Breading, page 74)
about $\frac{1}{16}$ of an inch in thickness, put the sixteen parts of mince
thereon, leaving a space of two inches between each ; cover them
with a similar thickness of bread-crumbs ; roll each part into the
shape of a cork, making them as near the same size as possible.

Beat the three remaining whites of egg for one minute, so as
to mix, but not froth, them ; add :

1 small pinch of pepper,	1 tablespoonful of oil,
2 pinches of salt,	1 tablespoonful of water ;

Dip the croquets in this mixture ; roll them in the bread-
crumbs ; and set them on a plate.

Twenty minutes before serving have some hot fat (*vide* page 73); arrange the croquets in the frying-basket, and put them

CROQUETS

into the fat to fry; when they are nearly fried, move them gently, with a slice, to ensure their colouring evenly.

When they are of a light brown colour and crisp, they are done; sprinkle them with salt, dish up, garnish with parsley; and serve (*vide* woodcut).

SALAD OF BOUILLI

Cut up 1½ lb. of cold boiled beef in small dice, removing all gristle and fat; put in a salad bowl, with:

1 gill of cold broth,	2 pinches of salt,
2 tablespoonfuls of vinegar,	2 small pinches of pepper;

Let it pickle for two hours;

Before serving, add:
  4 tablespoonfuls of oil,
  2 tablespoonfuls of chopped *ravigote*, and seasoning, if required.

If liked, onions and shalots may be added to this salad.

HOT BEEF À LA MODE

Take 4½ lbs. of thick flank of beef; 10 oz. of fat bacon (cut off the rind, and put it aside to blanch); cut the bacon into strips ½ inch thick, and sprinkle them with pepper;

Lard the beef, in the grain of the meat; and tie it up with string, as for *pot-au-feu*;

Put into a stewpan, with:

1 pint of French white wine,	1½ pint of broth,
1 gill of brandy,	1 pint of water,

2 calf's feet, which have been blanched and boned; also, the blanched rind of bacon;

Put on the fire, and add 1 oz. of salt; boil and skim as for *pot-au-feu*; then add:

3 carrots, say 1 lb.,	3 cloves,
1 onion,	1 faggot,

2 small pinches of pepper;

Put to simmer, in a closed stewpan, for four hours and a half, on the stove corner; try the beef; and, when done, take it out, together with the calf's feet and carrots; keep hot, till serving.

Strain the gravy through the pointed gravy strainer; take off all the fat, and reduce it one-fourth; untie the beef; put it on a dish, and garnish it round with the calf's feet, each cut into 8 pieces, with the carrots cut to the shape of corks, and 10 glazed onions (*vide* page 52).

Pour the gravy over all, and, should there be too much, reserve it for the next day;

Taste for seasoning;—*à la mode* beef should be full flavoured. A clove of garlic is sometimes added; I mention it, although it is not essential,—at the same time I would recommend, before using it, that the mistress's taste be consulted.

COLD BEEF À LA MODE

Cold beef *à la mode* for luncheons should be prepared as directed in the preceding recipe: put in a basin together with the calf's feet, vegetables and the gravy, which will set to a jelly.

When ready to serve, turn out of the basin on to a dish; the beef *à la mode* will then present its proper appearance.

Remarks on Beef à la Mode

Beef *à la mode* is a dish so general and popular, in domestic cookery, that I will recapitulate the main points of its preparation, to allow of their being followed with all confidence.

The most important consideration, after the selection of the meat, is its proper cooking, which should be carried on very slowly ;—this is the great secret of success.

Beef à la mode cooked too quickly will infallibly produce a white, watery, and insipid gravy, such as is met with in so many households, where proper regard is not paid to these simple practical details.

The gravy should be red, rather thick, and of a certain gelatinous consistence, full of that nourishing savour of braized meat, and vegetables stewed in gravy, which is the distinctive character of this dish.

It is unnecessary to cook and flavour the carrots with spices before putting them with the meat; this would entail extra trouble, perfectly useless in the ordinary course.

Cook the carrots in the gravy, adding to the meat as directed, and they will be of a good colour, and full of that savoury flavour which is so highly prized by connoisseurs.

As in the case of all other braizes, I recommend that the pieces of meat should, for beef à la mode, be chosen rather too big than too small.

A slow cooking will always answer better when applied to large rather than small joints. Braized meats, particularly with gravy set to a jelly, can easily supply two meals.

It is, therefore, better, in my opinion, to eat twice of a good thing, rather than, by curtailing the quantity to that barely sufficient for one meal, run the risk of getting a badly cooked dish by adding to the difficulty of preparation.

BRAIZED RIB OF BEEF

Take a rib of beef, weighing 4½ lbs. ; cut very short; take out the chine bone, leaving only the rib; tie with string, as for *pot-au-feu* ; and put in a stewpan that will just hold it.

Add :

2 pints of broth,	1 onion, say 4 oz.,
1 gill of brandy,	1 clove,
1 oz. of salt,	1 faggot,
2 small pinches of pepper,	1 carrot, say 4 oz. ;

Cover the stewpan, and boil slowly for two hours.

Ascertain if the meat is cooked by trying it with a trussing-needle ; take it out, and put it on a dish, and keep warm.

Strain the gravy through the pointed gravy strainer, and, after taking off the fat, reduce it one half; pour it over the meat; and serve.

Rib of beef is frequently garnished with maccaroni, *nouilles*, or such of the vegetables as are indicated in Chapter III., under Garnishes.

BULLOCK'S HEART À LA MODE

Take a very fresh and fat bullock's heart; cut it nearly through lengthwise; open and wash well, to clear it of blood; and dry with a cloth.

Lard as for beef *à la mode*; cook, garnish, and season, also in precisely the same manner.

BRAIZED RIB OF BEEF, WITH GARNISH

FRESH OX TONGUE

Steep the tongue in cold water for one hour, previously trimming the root; put the tongue, with 4 quarts of water, into a 6-quart pot, with:

1½ oz. of salt,	2 faggots,
3 small pinches of pepper,	2 cloves;
1 onion, say 4 oz.,	

Boil for three hours; ascertain whether it is cooked, and take off the fire; strip off the white skin, and put the tongue on a dish.

Beef tongue is served *au gratin* with Sharp, Italian, or Tomato sauce.

The liquor in which the tongue has been boiled can be used for vegetable soups instead of—and in preference to—water.

OX PALATES

Take 3 ox palates; blanch them, for ten minutes; cool, drain, and scrape them, carefully; cut in two pieces, and put in a 2-quart stewpan with :

1½ pint of broth,	1 faggot,
1 gill of fat, or clean dripping,	1 onion, say 4 oz.,
1 oz. of salt,	1 clove ;

Boil slowly, for three hours ;

Drain the palates on a cloth—carefully removing any remaining fat ;

Dress on a dish, in a circle ; and serve.

Palates are served *à la Poulette, au Gratin*, or with Italian sauce (*vide* pages 46 and 60).

STEWED OX TAIL

Take 1 ox tail; disjoint, and cut it into pieces 2 inches long; blanch, for twenty minutes; then steep in cold water, for an hour ;

Drain, and wipe the pieces of tail ; put them in a gallon stewpan, with 5 pints of broth ; as soon as it comes to the boil skim carefully, and add :

    2 onions, say 8 oz.,
    3 carrots, say 1 lb., turned to the shape of corks,
    3 cloves,
    2 faggots (of course it is understood that when 2 faggots
        are mentioned the quantity of herbs used for 1 faggot is
        merely doubled) ;
    2 pinches of salt,
    2 small pinches of pepper ;

Put it on the stove corner to simmer till the tail is tender ; —it will take about three hours and a half;

Drain the contents of the stewpan in a large colander ; wipe the pieces of tail, and put them in a 2-quart stewpan ;

Put the carrots in another stewpan holding 1 quart ; take off all the fat from the liquor, and reduce it one half; then, with it, moisten the tail and carrots in their respective stewpans ;

Warm; pile up the tail in a dish; pour over the gravy; and serve; garnish with the carrots and 10 glazed onions (*vide* page 52).

FRIED OX TAIL

To fry ox tail it should be prepared as in the preceding paragraph; then bread-crumbed; fried in hot fat, to a light brown colour; and served with Tomato Sauce.

Ox tail is generally fried to warm up any that has been left.

STEWED TRIPE À LA MODE DE CAEN

Take 2 lbs. of white and well-cleansed tripe; cut it into 3-inch squares; blanch five minutes; and drain in a colander;

Take 8 oz. of streaky bacon, and, after taking off the rind, cut it into pieces 1 inch thick;

Bone a calf's foot; cut it into six pieces; and blanch with the rind of bacon;

Put the tripe, calf's foot, and bacon, well mixed together, in a 4-quart stock-pot, with:

2 quarts of broth,	3 pinches of salt,
3 onions, say 10 oz.,	4 small pinches of pepper,
1 double faggot,	1 gill of brandy;
3 cloves,	

Cover the pot close; when it has boiled, let it simmer very gently three hours; when ready to serve, take out the onions and faggot, and skim off the fat;

Pour into a deep dish; and serve.

TRIPE À LA LYONNAISE

Cut 1 lb. of tripe in pieces, 2 inches long, $\frac{1}{2}$ inch thick; put them, on a brisk fire, in a *sauté*-pan, with:

2 oz. of butter,	2 pinches of salt,
2 oz. of oil,	2 small pinches of pepper;

The tripe when cooked should be crisp, and of a light brown colour;

Fry 6 onions (say $1\frac{1}{4}$ lb.), prepared as for Onion Soup, in a frying-pan with 2 oz. of oil;—when fried, the onions should be of a reddish brown colour, as for a *Miroton*;

Put the tripe into the frying-pan with the onions ;

Add a tablespoonful of chopped parsley and one tablespoonful of vinegar ; warm all together one minute; and serve.

BEEF KIDNEY SAUTÉ

Take a piece of beef kidney; cut in two lengthwise ; then cut each piece across in slices ⅛ inch thick ;

Put 4 oz. of butter in a *sauté*-pan ; when well melted, add the slices of kidney, with 2 pinches of salt, and 2 small pinches of pepper ; shake the pan every minute—to ensure equal cooking ; after six minutes' frying, drain the kidney ;

Put in a quart stewpan :

3 gills of French white wine,
1 pinch of salt,
1 small pinch of pepper ;

And reduce it one fourth ;

Put the kidney back into the pan ; sprinkle with 1 oz. of flour ; let it warm two minutes ; then add the reduced wine, 1 gill of water, and 1 gill of broth ; boil one minute ; throw in a tablespoonful of chopped parsley ; put in a dish ; and serve.

Beef kidney can also be *sauté* in the following way :

Without draining from the butter, or previously boiling the wine, sprinkle with the flour, moisten with 2 gills of wine, and 1 gill of broth ; boil one minute, and take out the kidney ; boil the gravy four minutes more ; put in a tablespoonful of chopped parsley ; pour over the kidney ; and serve.

This is a quicker way than the first, but that is its only advantage ; the wine, not being boiled, tends to give the kidney an acid flavour—to be avoided, if possible.

ROAST RIB OF BEEF

Take a rib of beef, cut and trimmed as for Braized Rib of Beef (*vide* page 86);

Roast one hour, before a moderate and even fire ;

Strain the gravy out of the dripping-pan ; take off the fat ; pour over the meat; and serve.

General Remarks on Roast Meat

I do not advise flavouring the meat in any way before roasting ; the only preparation allowable is to oil it slightly, if it has to be kept any time before cooking ; and this is only done with a view to its preservation—not to impart any flavour.

Butcher's meat needs no other flavour than its own : anything in the way of improvement thereon will only spoil it. The main point, to have meat at its best, is to cook it neither too fresh nor high.

ROAST SIRLOIN OF BEEF

The sirloin is the part of loin with the fillet attached.

Tie the flap end underneath, and put on the spit. A piece of sirloin weighing 7 lbs. will take an hour and three quarters' roasting.

ROAST FILLET OF BEEF

Take 3½ lbs. of fillet of beef; lard with fat bacon, cut in lengths of ¼ inch in thickness; choose the bacon white, and very fresh ;—a single piece of rank flavour will spoil the whole fillet ;

Put on the spit, and roast for forty minutes, basting frequently ;

Strain the gravy, and take off the fat; pour over the meat; and serve.

Sharp, Italian, or Tomato Sauces are generally served in a sauce boat with fillet of beef.

RIB-STEAK WITH POTATOES

Cut a steak ½ inch thick from between two ribs ;

Remove all gristle and fat ; trim it to a pear shape; and sprinkle on both sides with salt and pepper ;

Oil it—to prevent the outside hardening ;

Broil twelve minutes, over a moderate and even fire ;

Put 4 oz. of *maître d'hôtel* butter (*vide* page 62) on a dish ; lay the steak on it ; and garnish with fried potatoes.

Sharp, Tomato, and Italian Sauces are also often served with this steak.

FILLET-STEAK WITH POTATOES

This steak should be taken from across the fillet, in slices 1½ inch thick, slightly flattened with the bat, and trimmed to an oval shape, oiled as above, and sprinkled with salt and pepper.

Broil eight minutes, over a moderate and even fire; put on a dish with 2 oz. of *maître d'hôtel* butter; garnish with fried potatoes; and serve.

It will be understood that I recommend oiling the meat to facilitate cooking, not to give it any particular flavour.

RUMP-STEAK À L'ANGLAISE

Proceed as above.

This steak, cut from the rump, is generally served quite plain, with gravy, instead of *maître d'hôtel*, but Oyster Sauce (*vide* page 66) is occasionally served with it.

STEAK WITH ANCHOVY BUTTER

For an ordinary-sized steak, take one large anchovy, which should be well washed, and dried, and pounded on a board, with the back of a knife,—the mortar is not required for so small a quantity. Mix the anchovy with 1½ oz. of butter, and pass through a hair sieve; put it on a warm dish; lay the steak on the anchovy butter; and serve.

FILLET OF BEEF SAUTÉ, WITH MUSHROOMS

Cut the fillet, as indicated for Fillet Steak with Potatoes (*vide* page 91); sprinkle with salt, and pepper;

Put ½ oz. of butter in a small *sauté*-pan; put in the fillet, and let it cook, four minutes each side, on a brisk fire—(be careful that the butter does not burn); take out the meat, and put ¼ oz. of flour in the pan; stir one minute, with a wooden spoon; pour in 1 gill of broth, and the liquor in which the mushrooms, prepared for garnish, have been boiled;

Strain into a small stewpan, through the pointed gravy strainer;

Take ½ pottle of mushrooms, prepared as indicated in Garnishes; and warm them in the sauce;

Put the slices of fillet on a dish; garnish with the mushrooms; pour over the sauce; and serve.

FILLET OF BEEF WITH OLIVES

Proceed as directed above.

Take 24 large and round olives; stone them, and blanch, in

boiling water, for five minutes; dry in a cloth; put the olives in the sauce, to warm for two minutes; garnish round the slices of fillet; and serve.

It will be well to use the Household Gravy (*vide* page 68), instead of broth, for the sauce for this fillet.

Remarks on Sautés

For *sautés*, the fire should be brisk; so that the meat may retain its juices in cooking; and become of a light golden colour, which could not be accomplished on a slow fire. Care must, however, be taken that the butter does not burn; as this would give the gravy a bad flavour.

COLLOPS OF FILLET OF BEEF WITH SHARP SAUCE

These collops are generally made to warm up cold roast fillet.

. Cut in very thin collops, and warm in some Sharp Sauce (*vide* page 64), without boiling.

Should roasted meat be allowed to boil in warming, it will harden, and lose its savour.

I do not specify the quantity of sauce, as it will be determined by the quantity of meat to be used.

MIROTON OF BEEF

CALF'S HEAD AND FEET

CHAPTER VII

VEAL

ROAST VEAL

THE pieces of veal used for roasting are: the neck, loin, and chump end of the loin;—never buy any but very white veal with clear, transparent fat.

For roast neck of veal: take about 4 lbs. of the neck; saw off the chine bone; and shorten the rib bones to half their length—that is, leaving the bones about 2 inches long. Roll the flap underneath, and tie round with string; put on the spit, to roast, before a moderate fire, for an hour and a half; sprinkle with salt, five minutes before taking off the spit;

Strain and skim the fat off the gravy; pour over the meat, and serve.

For roast loin of veal: take about 4 lbs. of the part including the kidney;

Trim off some of the fat, and saw off the chine bone; then roll the flap underneath, enclosing the kidney;

Tie with string; put on the spit to roast, before a moderate fire, for two hours,—basting every quarter of an hour; take the meat off the spit, sprinkle with salt, and put it on a dish;

Strain and skim the fat off the gravy; pour over the meat; and serve.

For roast chump end of loin: take a piece of about 4 lbs.; bone it entirely; tie it with string, to keep it in shape; and proceed in the same manner as for neck and loin.

ROAST CHUMP END OF LOIN OF VEAL

BLANQUETTE OF VEAL

Breast of veal is generally used for *blanquette*. Cut about 3 lbs. of breast of veal, into pieces 2½ inches square, and put in a 2-quart stewpan;

Cover the meat entirely with water; add 3 pinches of salt, and 3 small pinches of pepper;

Boil, and skim; add:

    2 onions, say 8 oz.,

    3 cloves,

    1 double faggot;

Simmer gently, for an hour;

When the veal is done, drain in a colander; clean each piece, and put them in a 2-quart stewpan;

In another 2-quart stewpan, mix 1 oz. of butter, and 1 oz. of flour; stir over the fire for four minutes; take off the fire, and add all the liquor drained from the veal; reduce for twenty minutes, stirring all the time; thicken with 3 yolks of egg (*vide*

Liaison with Egg, page 59); strain through the pointed gravy strainer, into the stewpan containing the veal;

Boil for a minute; add a tablespoonful of chopped parsley; mix; and serve.

Blanquette is also prepared with the remains of roast veal.

Cut the veal in slices, 1½ inch long, and ¼ inch thick, trimming off all the brown;

Warm gently in 1 pint of *Poulette* Sauce (*vide Poulette* Sauce, page 65);—avoid boiling, which would harden the veal; add half a tablespoonful of chopped parsley; and serve.

VEAL À LA BOURGEOISE

This is prepared with a *noix* or cushion of veal.*

Take a *noix* of veal, of about 3 lbs.; lard it with fat bacon, as Beef *à la Mode* (*vide* Beef *à la Mode*, page 84);

Tie with string, and put it in a 4-quart stewpan; moisten with 2 quarts of broth;

Add: 1 calf's foot, previously boned and blanched, and the rind of the bacon, also blanched;

Boil and skim; add:

3 carrots, say ¾ lb.,	1 double faggot,
3 onions, say 10 oz.,	2 pinches of salt,
3 cloves,	2 small pinches of pepper;

Simmer for three hours;—the stewpan three parts covered.

Twenty minutes before serving, put some live coals on the cover of the stewpan, to glaze the meat, basting five or six times, with the gravy;

Try with a trussing-needle, to make sure that the veal is done; drain it; and put it on a dish;

Strain the gravy through the pointed gravy strainer; skim off the fat, and reduce it one half; add a teaspoonful of *caramel*, to colour it.

Cut the carrots in equal-sized cork-shaped pieces; untie the veal; put it on a dish; garnish round with the carrots, and 10 glazed onions; pour a part of the gravy on the veal, reserving the rest to set to a jelly.

COLD VEAL À LA BOURGEOISE

The foregoing preparation is also served cold; prepare it a day before it is wanted, and put it in a basin, with the gravy,

---

* This cushion or *noix* is the part of the leg of veal covered by the udder.

which will set to a jelly; when required, turn it out of the basin on a dish; and serve.

Observation.—Veal *à la Bourgeoise* is, like Beef *à la Mode*, one of the stock dishes of ordinary cookery, which one should make sure of always preparing successfully. I repeat what I have said often before;—the main point of the process is the slow simmering; the richness of the gravy, one of the most essential conditions, is obtained by the reducing which I have indicated; it ensures against thick and tasteless sauces, and secures a full-flavoured gravy.

BRAIZED LOIN OF VEAL

Take 4 lbs. of loin of veal; bone, and tie it round with string;

Put in a stewpan, with 1 oz. of butter; fry lightly, till the meat is slightly and evenly coloured;

Pour in 1 quart of broth; then add:

1 carrot, say 4 oz.,	1 faggot,
1 onion, say 4 oz.,	2 pinches of salt,
2 cloves stuck in it,	1 small pinch of pepper;

Simmer on a very slow fire, for an hour and three quarters, —keeping the stewpan half covered;

Take out the meat, and keep it warm;

Strain the gravy, through the pointed strainer; skim off the fat; and reduce one half;

Untie the veal; put it on a dish; pour the gravy over; and serve.

With braized loin of veal: sorrel, endive or spinach, is served.

FRICANDEAU OF VEAL

Take 3 lbs. of the fleshy part of the fillet of veal; bone, trim, and lard the outside with thin strips of bacon.

Put, in the glazing stewpan (*vide* Kitchen Utensils, page 9), the trimmings of the meat:

2 oz. of sliced carrot,	1 pinch of salt,
2 oz. of sliced onion,	1 pinch of pepper;

Then lay the *fricandeau* on the top; add ½ pint of broth; boil till the broth is reduced, and becomes thick, and yellow; then add 1½ pint more broth, and simmer for an hour and a quarter,—the stewpan half covered; then close the stewpan, and

o

put some live coals on the top; baste the *fricandeau*, with the gravy, every four minutes, till it is sufficiently glazed; take out the *fricandeau*, and put it on a dish.

FRICANDEAU

Strain the gravy, through the pointed strainer; skim off the fat, and pour over the meat, and serve.   Served plain thus, this preparation is known as *Fricandeau with Gravy*, but it is most generally served with sorrel.   Put the sorrel on a dish, then lay the *fricandeau* on it, and pour in the gravy (prepare the sorrel as directed in Garnishes, page 57).

Fricandeau is also served with endive or spinach (*vide* Endive and Spinach Garnish, pages 55, 56).

BROILED VEAL CUTLETS

A veal cutlet, trimmed, weighs between 7 and 8 oz.; it is cut from the neck of veal.

Trim it, and flatten it with the cutlet bat; take off the chine bone, gristle, and skin;

Before broiling, sprinkle the cutlet with salt, and pepper, on both sides; then oil it slightly (*vide* Broiling, page 71); broil for eight minutes; and serve.

BREAD-CRUMBED VEAL CUTLETS

To bread-crumb, dip the cutlets in butter melted, and proceed as indicated at paragraph Breading, page 74;

Broil on a moderate fire, for ten minutes;

Put on the dish, with 1 gill of warm Household Gravy (*vide* page 68); and serve.

VEAL CUTLETS WITH SHARP SAUCE

Prepare the cutlets as above, either plain or bread-crumbed put them on the dish, with Sharp Sauce.

1 gill of sauce per cutlet is sufficient.

VEAL CUTLETS WITH MAÎTRE D'HÔTEL BUTTER

Same preparation as the above (*vide* Plain Broiled Veal Cutlets), adding the *maître d'hôtel* butter under the cutlets when serving.

1½ oz. of *maître d'hôtel* butter is sufficient for each cutlet.

VEAL CUTLETS WITH TOMATO SAUCE

Prepare plain or bread-crumbed broiled cutlets, and add 1 gill of Tomato Sauce per cutlet (*vide* Tomato Sauce, page 66).

VEAL CUTLETS WITH MUSHROOMS

Prepare plain or bread-crumbed broiled cutlets (*vide* page 98).

For every two cutlets, prepare half a pottle of mushrooms, as directed at the paragraph Mushrooms for Garnish (*vide* page 47);

Sprinkle the cutlets with a little salt and pepper; put them in the small *sauté*-pan, with ½ oz. of butter;

Fry for twelve minutes, turning them at the end of six minutes,—to ensure even cooking;

Put the cutlets on a plate;

Add, in the *sauté*-pan, ¼ oz. of flour; stir over the fire, for two minutes;

Pour in ½ pint of broth, and the liquor of the mushrooms, prepared for garnish;

Stir, and boil for five minutes more;

Strain through the pointed strainer, into a stewpan;

Warm the mushrooms in the sauce for three or four minutes; put the cutlets on a dish, with the mushrooms round; and serve.

SAUTÉ-PAN (*vide* page 8)

o 2

VEAL CHOP WITH CARROTS

Take a large neck chop, weighing about 1 lb. ; saw off the chine bone ;

Fry in a *sauté*-pan, with 1 oz. of butter, for about five minutes each side ; add 1 pint of broth ;

Boil, and take off the fire ; strain the gravy through the pointed strainer ;

Wash the *sauté*-pan ; put the chop in again with the gravy ; and :

> 20 pieces of carrot, cut to a cork shape,
> 1 onion, say 4 oz., with two cloves stuck in it,
> 2 pinches of salt,
> 2 small pinches of pepper ;

Put on the fire, and simmer, very gently, for an hour ;

When the carrots are sufficiently done, the meat will also be cooked ;

Put the chop on a dish, with the carrots round it ;

Strain the gravy over ; and serve.

VEAL CUTLETS EN PAPILLOTES

Trim and flatten the cutlets as for Broiling (*vide* page 98).

Put them in the *sauté*-pan with 1 oz. of butter ; fry for twelve minutes, turning at the end of six minutes to cook them evenly ; when done, take them out, and put them on a plate ;

Put 1 oz. of flour in the *sauté*-pan ; stir over the fire for two minutes ; add 1 pint of broth ; boil five minutes ; then strain through the pointed gravy strainer.

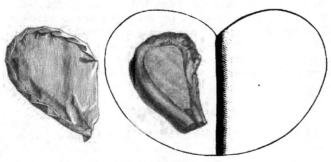

VEAL CUTLET EN PAPILLOTE

Clean the *sauté*-pan ; put the sauce in again, and boil to reduce to half the quantity ; add 3 tablespoonfuls of *fines herbes* (*vide Fines Herbes* for Sauces, page 48) ; reduce five minutes more.

For each cutlet take a sheet of stiff white paper, and cut it ac-cording to woodcut, large enough to leave a margin of $1\frac{1}{2}$ inch round the cutlet ; oil the paper, and lay on it, first : a thin slice of fat bacon, cut in the shape of the lean part of the cutlet ; put on the bacon : a tablespoonful of the sauce ; then, the cutlet itself ; another spoonful of sauce ; and, lastly, a slice of bacon similar to the first.

Fold the paper, and double down the edges all round, as shown in the woodcut.

A quarter of an hour before serving, put the *papillotes* on the gridiron, and broil over a very slow fire for eight minutes, on one side, and seven minutes the other ; put on a dish ; and serve.

SCOLLOPS OF VEAL WITH FINES HERBES

Take about 2 lbs. of fillet of veal ; trim off bone, gristle, fat, and skin ; and cut in scollops, $\frac{1}{2}$ inch thick, and 2 inches in width ; flatten them with the bat ; butter the *sauté*-pan thickly ; season with a pinch of salt, and two small pinches of pepper ; set the scollops in the pan side by side ; sprinkle with pepper and salt, and fry on a brisk fire for four minutes each side ; take out the scollops, and put them on a plate ;

Put a tablespoonful of flour in the *sauté*-pan ; stir, with a wooden spoon, for one minute ; add 3 gills of broth ; and boil for five minutes ;

Add the gravy which has drained into the plate from the scollops ;

Pile up the scollops on a dish ; put the sauce over the fire ; and, when boiling, add 1 oz. of butter cut in pieces, and a table-spoonful of chopped parsley ; stir with the spoon to mix the butter ; pour the sauce over the scollops ; and serve.

These scollops are also served with Italian Sauce (*vide* page 64) ;—1 pint of the sauce is sufficient for the above quantity.

TENDONS OF VEAL À LA PROVENÇALE

Take 2 lbs. of breast of veal, and cut it in pieces 2 inches square ;

Slice 2 onions, say 8 oz., as for Onion Soup ; to which add

half a bay leaf, a sprig of thyme, and a clove of garlic—all cut fine ;

Put 4 oz. of salad oil in a 3-quart stewpan ; and add : the meat, onions, thyme, bay leaf, garlic ; 2 pinches of salt ; and 4 small pinches of pepper ;

Put the stewpan on a slow fire, with a little lighted charcoal on the cover ; simmer for two hours, stirring frequently with the spoon ; add ½ pint of broth ; and 2 tablespoonfuls of coarsely chopped parsley ; boil for five minutes ;

Pile the *tendons* up on a dish ; pour the sauce over ; and serve.

Observation.—It should be borne in mind that *Provençale* Sauce is served without taking off the fat. The garlic intro- duced is the special characteristic of the sauce—but it may be dispensed with when very objectionable.

SWEETBREADS WITH GRAVY, ENDIVE, SORREL, OR TOMATO SAUCE

Take 2 perfectly fresh heart sweetbreads ; steep them in cold water for four hours, changing the water occasionally ; blanch them in 1 quart of cold water ; put them on the fire, and as soon as they become firm and round without being hard, which would prevent larding them, cool them thoroughly ; drain on a cloth, and press them between two baking-sheets with a 4 lbs. weight on the top ; lard them as for *Fricandeau,* page 98.

Put the sweetbreads in a small *sauté*-pan with ½ pint of strong broth, slightly coloured with half a teaspoonful of *caramel* ; sprinkle with a pinch of salt ; reduce the broth till it thickens ; then add ½ pint more broth ; cover the pan with live coal on the glazing cover ; baste the sweetbreads frequently with the gravy to glaze them ; when of a light brown colour, they are done ; trim the under part of the sweetbreads ; put them on a dish ; pour the gravy over them ; and serve.

Observation.—If the gravy is too much reduced, add ½ gill of broth, and boil again till of a proper consistence.

For sweetbreads with endive, sorrel, spinach, or Tomato Sauce, half the quantity of each indicated in the Chapter on Garnishes will be sufficient.

CALF'S HEAD AU NATUREL

Take a white calf's head, in size in accordance with the number of guests ; cut it in two, and bone it entirely ; put the brains to steep in cold water ; put the tongue by ;

Blanch the head for ten minutes in boiling water; drain and cool it well; cut each half of the head in four pieces; keeping the ear piece square, to facilitate the dishing up.

Prepare a white braize as follows :—

Take ¼ lb. of beef suet, chopped very fine; melt over the fire; when clear, add : ¼ lb. of flour, 1 gallon of water, 2 sliced onions (say 4 oz.), 1 double faggot, 3 cloves, 1 clove of garlic, ½ gill of vinegar, 1½ oz. of salt, ½ oz. of pepper; stir over the fire, and, when boiling, put in the pieces of head and the tongue;

Boil for two hours and a half on the stove corner, putting a round of paper over to prevent the pieces floating on the top of the braize from getting black;—the stewpan should be only three parts covered.

When the head is cooked, which you ascertain by trying it with the finger, remove the white skin from the tongue; cut the latter in half, lengthwise, without separating it altogether; drain, and dish up on an oval dish, on a napkin; the ears at each end, the four other pieces in the centre; the tongue laid on the top, and upon it the brains; garnish with parsley; and serve, hot.

Calf's Head *au Naturel* is eaten with oil and vinegar; serve with it, on a plate, chopped onion and parsley (well washed), and capers.

Preparation of the Brains

Steep them in cold water for an hour; then pick all the skinny particles from the surface,—being careful not to bruise the brains; when very clean and white, put them in a stewpan with 1 quart of water, ½ oz. of salt, and ½ gill of vinegar, and boil gently for twenty-eight minutes.

CALF'S HEAD WITH POOR MAN'S SAUCE

Prepare, and dish up a calf's head as aforesaid.

For Poor Man's Sauce, put in a quart stewpan 3 shalots, well chopped and washed, and ½ gill of vinegar; boil until entirely reduced; then strain into the stewpan 1 pint of the calf's head braize; boil for five minutes; add a tablespoonful of chopped parsley; taste for seasoning; and serve, in a sauceboat.

CALF'S HEAD WITH POULETTE SAUCE

Blanch half of a calf's head; cut it in pieces 1½ inch square; boil as directed for Calf's Head *au Naturel*; when done, drain it, and take 1½ pint of *Poulette* Sauce (*vide* page 65); add to it a tablespoonful of chopped tarragon; put the pieces of calf's head in the warm sauce; dish up; and serve.

MARINADED CALF'S HEAD

Cut, in 1½ inch pieces, half of a calf's head, previously blanched and boiled as before; put it in a basin to pickle for an hour, with:

| 1 pinch of salt, | 1 small pinch of pepper, |
| 1 tablespoonful of oil, | 2 tablespoonfuls of vinegar; |

Stir occasionally, to season evenly; twenty-five minutes before serving, drain the pieces; prepare 1½ pint of frying batter (*vide* Frying Batter, page 74).

Warm some fat in the frying kettle; dip each piece of head in the batter, and fry in the hot fat; keep moving with the skimmer till they are of a light brown;

Drain the pieces on a cloth; sprinkle them with salt; dish them up on a napkin; garnish with fried parsley; and serve. Send a boat of Tomato Sauce separately.

CALF'S TONGUE AU GRATIN

Trim a calf's tongue; blanch, boil, and prepare it for *gratin*, as *Bouilli au Gratin* (*vide* page 82). Calf's tongue is also served plain-boiled; with Italian, Sharp, or Tomato Sauce;— 1 pint of either for a tongue.

CALF'S LIGHTS

Cut ½ lb. of streaky bacon into small squares; fry them in a 4-quart stewpan, with 2 oz. of butter, and, when brown, put on a plate.

Cut 2 lbs. of calf's lights into pieces 3 inches square; fry, without burning, in the same stewpan, till of a rich brown; dredge over them 1½ oz. of flour; stir three minutes; then add:

1 pint of broth,
½ pint of French white wine,
1 pint of water,
and the liquor of a pottle of turned mushrooms;

Stir till boiling; then put in:

2 pinches of salt,   1 onion with 2 cloves stuck
2 small pinches of pepper,   in it,
1 faggot,   and the fried bacon;

Simmer an hour and a half,—the stewpan not quite closed;
fry 20 large button onions in the frying-pan; then put them in
the stew, and boil for another half-hour; take out the faggot,
onion, and cloves; put the mushrooms in; taste the seasoning,
which should be highly flavoured; put on a dish; garnish round
with the onions and mushrooms; pour the sauce over; and
serve.

CALF'S FEET WITH POULETTE SAUCE

Take 2 calf's feet; remove the large bone, and blanch and
boil the feet as directed for Calf's Head; when this is done, take
out with care all remaining bones; press the feet between two
baking-sheets, with a 2 lbs. weight on the top, till thoroughly
cold;

Cut each foot in 8 equal pieces; warm $1\frac{1}{2}$ pint of *Poulette*
Sauce; put the pieces in; boil for two minutes; and serve.

FRIED CALF'S FEET

Boil and prepare 2 calf's feet as in the preceding recipe; fry
in the same way as Marinaded Calf's Head (*vide* page 104);
serve with fried parsley and *Poivrade* Sauce, in a boat. Calf's
feet may also be served prepared in halves, bread-crumbed, and
broiled on a slow fire, with Tartar Sauce, in a sauce boat.

CALF'S BRAINS EN MATELOTTE

Clean, steep, and boil a set of calf's brains, as indicated in the
Preparation of Calf's Brains (*vide* page 103); after boiling, steep
the brains in hot water, with a little salt in it, to remove the
acidity of the vinegar;

Peel and blanch 20 button onions; fry them in $\frac{1}{2}$ oz. of
butter; when of a light brown colour, stir in $\frac{1}{2}$ oz. of flour for
three minutes; then add: $\frac{1}{2}$ pint of broth, and 1 gill of French
red wine; 1 pinch of salt, and 1 small pinch of pepper; simmer
on a slow fire, for half an hour;

Pick, wash, and cut in pieces, 1 pottle of mushrooms; throw
them into the sauce, and boil for eight minutes; drain the
brains; put them on a warm dish; garnish round with the
onions and mushrooms; pour over the sauce; and serve.

P

CALF'S BRAINS WITH BROWN BUTTER

Prepare the brains as above.

Take ½ pint of brown butter (*vide* page 63) ;

Drain the brains ; put in a dish ; pour over the butter, and garnish with fried parsley.

Calf's brains are also served with Tomato Sauce, or garnished with onions, or mushrooms ; also fried, and, occasionally, cold, with oil and vinegar.

BROILED VEAL KIDNEY WITH MAÎTRE D'HOTEL BUTTER

Cut a veal kidney lengthwise, in two pieces ; flatten it slightly with the bat ; season with salt and pepper ; dip each piece in butter ; bread-crumb them, and broil on an even fire, four minutes each side ;

Make 2 oz. of *maître d'hôtel* butter (*vide* page 62) ; put it on a dish, the pieces of kidney over it ; and serve.

Same process of preparation, and same sauce, as for Beef Kidney (*vide* page 90).

STEWED CALF'S LIVER

Take 2 lbs. of fresh and white calf's liver ; lard it through with strips of fat bacon, two inches long ; season with salt and pepper ; put it in a 3-quart stewpan, with 4 oz. of butter, and fry it ;—being particular in turning it, to secure an even colour ; then take the liver out of the stewpan, and mix 1 oz. of flour to the butter ; stir over the fire for four minutes ; and add :

1 pint of water,	1 onion with 2 cloves stuck
1 pint of French white	in it,
wine,	2 pinches of salt,
1 faggot,	2 small pinches of pepper ;

Stir till boiling ; put the liver in again, with 20 pieces of carrot, cut to a cork shape ; simmer very slowly—the stewpan only three parts covered ; after two hours, put in 10 large button onions, previously fried ; simmer for another hour ; put the liver on a dish ;

Pour the sauce through a colander ; skim the fat off ; and if there be too much sauce, reduce it on a sharp fire for five minutes ; take out the faggot, onion, and cloves ; garnish the liver with the carrots and onions ; pour over the sauce ; and serve.

CALF'S LIVER SAUTÉ À L'ITALIENNE

Cut 2 lbs. of calf's liver lengthwise, in slices ½ inch thick; season both sides with pepper and salt, and flour them; melt ¼ lb. of butter in a *sauté*-pan; when the butter is hot, put the slices of liver in, and fry for three minutes on one side; turn them, and fry them three minutes more on the other side—six minutes in all for cooking; take the slices out, and keep them warm; put, in the *sauté*-pan: 1 oz. of flour, 1 shalot, chopped fine and washed, ½ pottle of chopped mushrooms; stir over the fire, and moisten with ½ pint of French white wine, and ½ pint of broth; reduce for ten minutes;

Dish the slices in a circle on the dish;

Add a tablespoonful of chopped parsley to the sauce, and pour the latter over the liver;—if the sauce is too thin, reduce it; if too thick, add a little broth.

CALF'S LIVER SAUTÉ À LA LYONNAISE

Cut the liver in slices, as in the preceding recipe; season, flour, and fry in the same way;

Take the slices out of the *sauté*-pan on to a dish;

Put 1 oz. of butter, 1 onion (say 4 oz.), chopped very fine, and well washed, into the *sauté*-pan; stir on the fire for three minutes;

Dish up the liver, and pour the onion and butter over it; and serve.

Send a lemon on a plate with it.

CALF'S LIVER SAUTÉ À LA MÉNAGÈRE

Cut 2 lbs. of calf's liver, in pieces 2 inches square and ½ inch thick; melt ½ lb. of butter in the frying-pan; when hot, put the liver in; add 3 pinches of salt, and 3 small pinches of pepper; fry for six minutes—tossing it up all the time, to ensure even cooking; strew the liver with 1 oz. of flour, 1 shalot, chopped fine, and washed, and a tablespoonful of chopped parsley; moisten with ½ pint of French wine, red or white, and ½ pint of broth; stir till boiling; and serve.

STUFFED SHOULDER OF VEAL

I advise dressing a whole shoulder, because it is occasionally useful to have large joints; besides which, this will make a first-rate dish for picnics.

Take a shoulder of veal, weighing about 8 lbs., without the knuckle; bone it entirely, without piercing the skin; spread it on the table, the skin downwards; pare off some of the meat from the thickest parts, to leave it of an even thickness;

Add to these trimmings, 2 lbs. of fillet of veal, and 2 lbs. of fat bacon; season with 2 oz. of mixed salt, pepper, and grated nutmeg; chop the whole together, and pound for ten minutes in the mortar; cut ½ lb. of fat bacon in large dice (reserve the rind, to blanch with the calf's feet), and mix it with the force-meat; sprinkle over the shoulder 2 pinches of salt, and 3 small pinches of pepper; spread the forcemeat on the shoulder, about 3 inches thick; fold the shoulder over, to enclose the forcemeat, and roll it up in a cloth, to keep the shape; tie both ends with string; tie also two pieces of string across, to prevent its bulging out, when boiling.

Put in the oval stewpan: 4 quarts of water; 1 gill of brandy; 3 calf's feet, previously boned and blanched; the rind of the bacon, also blanched; the bones broken in pieces; 2 carrots (say 8 oz.); 3 onions (say 10 oz.); 3 cloves ; 1 double faggot; 2 oz. of salt; ¼ oz. of pepper; put on the fire; boil, skim, and simmer for four hours; then take off the fire; drain the shoulder, untie it, take off the cloth, and put the shoulder on a baking sheet; rinse the cloth in hot water, and retie the shoulder in it as before boiling; press it between two baking sheets, with a 4 lbs. weight on the top; when cold untie, and put it on a dish; strain the liquor through a clean napkin; clear it of all fat, and let it cool in a basin, to set to a jelly, to garnish the stuffed shoulder.*

* Remember to press the calf's feet used, in the same way as directed for Calf's Feet à la Poulette (vide page 105), and to warm, and serve them with Poulette Sauce, or fried next day.

CALF'S BRAINS

LEG OF MUTTON.

CHAPTER VIII

MUTTON

ROAST LEG OF MUTTON

TAKE A 6 lbs. leg of mutton ; saw off the shank bone 1½ inch below the knuckle ; put it on the spit to roast, before an even fire, for an hour and a half ; put 2 gills of broth in the dripping-pan, as indicated at the Chapter on Roasting (*vide* page 70), and baste well during cooking ; sprinkle with 2 pinches of salt, five minutes before taking from the fire ; put the mutton on a dish, with a paper frill round the knuckle bone ; skim the fat from the gravy ; strain, through the pointed gravy strainer; pour over the meat ; and serve.

With roast leg of mutton : white haricot beans, maccaroni, *purée* of haricot beans, or endive, are frequently served, either under the meat, or in a separate dish.

SEVEN HOURS' LEG OF MUTTON

It is a mistake to imagine, that the long cooking required for braizing will make a hard leg of mutton tender ;—for braizing, as for roasting, the best meat alone should be used.

Take a leg of mutton, weighing about 6 lbs. ; saw off the

shank bone, as for roasting; bone the leg—that is, detach the meat from the thigh bone; then saw it off at the knuckle joint, without splitting the skin;

Take 8 oz. of fat bacon, removing the rind, and cut it into pieces 2 inches long, ½ inch thick; season with 1 pinch of salt, and 2 small pinches of pepper; lard the leg of mutton inside, being careful not to pierce through the skin; and tie as for *pot-au-feu.*

Put the mutton in the oval pan for braizes, with 4 oz. of butter, and fry till of a light brown; add :

1 quart of broth,	1 pinch of salt,
3 carrots, say 14 oz.,	2 small pinches of pepper ;

When it comes to the boil, simmer very gently for three hours; then turn the mutton; add 6 large onions, and ½ gill of brandy; simmer for an hour and a half more, making four hours and a half's cooking,—during the whole of which, live coal should be kept on the cover of the pan;

When cooked, there should remain about 1 pint of gravy in the pan ;

Put the mutton on a dish, with a paper frill round the knuckle; garnish round with the carrots, cut to the shape of corks, and the onions; strain the gravy; pour over the meat; and serve.

BRAIZED LEG OF MUTTON

Take a leg of mutton, of the same weight as above; bone, season, and prepare it, as in the preceding recipe; put it in the braizing pan; with:

> 2 calf's feet, boned and blanched as for Beef *à la Mode* (*vide* page 85),
> 1 quart of water,
> 1 quart of broth,
> ½ gill of brandy,
> 1 onion, with 3 cloves stuck in it,
> 1 small carrot, say 4 oz.,
> 2 pinches of salt,
> 2 small pinches of pepper ;

Boil, skim, and let it simmer slowly three hours, with live coals on the top of the pan ;

Take out the meat; strain the gravy; reduce 1 pint of it to ½ pint; pour over the meat; and serve.

The remaining gravy may be used for haricots *à la Bretonne*, endive, spinach, glazed onions, &c.

MINCED MUTTON

This mince is generally made with cold roast mutton.

Remove all gristle, fat, and skin, from the meat; mince it fine; mix it with Italian Sauce, and warm together without boiling.

For 1 lb. of the mince, take 1 pint of sauce.

The mince may be garnished with sippets of fried bread, or poached eggs.

MUTTON CROQUETS

Proceed as for Beef Croquets (*vide* page 83).

MUTTON COLLOPS WITH SHARP SAUCE

These collops are generally made with cold roast mutton.

Cut the meat in thin collops, and warm in the sauce, without boiling (*vide* Beef Collops, page 93)..

STUFFED SHOULDER OF MUTTON

Bone a shoulder of mutton, without breaking the skin; spread it open on the table, and sprinkle with salt and pepper;

Take ½ lb. of lean pork, and ½ lb. of bacon, to prepare some forcemeat, as for Stuffed Shoulder of Veal (*vide* page 108); stuff the shoulder with the forcemeat; sprinkle with salt and pepper, and sew it up in a round shape, with the trussing needle, and fine string; put it in a 4-quart stewpan with 2 oz. of butter, on a brisk fire, for a quarter of an hour,—turning it after eight minutes; pour in ½ gill of brandy, and 1 quart of water; boil and skim; then add:

1 small carrot, say 4 oz.,	1 oz. of salt,
1 onion, say 4 oz., with	1 small pinch of pepper,
2 cloves stuck in it,	1 faggot;

Without quite closing the stewpan, simmer for an hour and a half, after which put some live coals on the cover; baste the meat with the gravy, five or six times; and let it glaze for half an hour;

Take out the meat; strain, and skim the fat from the gravy; and reduce it one half;

Untie the meat; put it on a dish; pour over the gravy; and serve; garnish round with glazed onions, or turnips, or mushrooms *sautés*.

STEWED MUTTON WITH VEGETABLES

Take 2 lbs. of breast, or neck, of mutton; take off the outer skin, and cut into pieces 2 inches square; put these in a gallon stewpan, with 4 oz. of butter, 4 pinches of salt, and 3 small pinches of pepper; fry for a quarter of an hour, on a brisk fire,—so that the meat may retain its juices, without, however, burning the butter.

The quality of the stew depends, in a great measure, on this frying process;—the pieces of meat should not be laid one over the other in the stewpan;

Dredge 1 oz. of flour over the pieces, and brown for four minutes; add 1 quart of water, and stir till it boils; drain the contents of the stewpan, through a large colander, into a basin;

Remove any lumps of flour which may adhere to the meat; rinse the stewpan; put back the pieces in it, and pour back the gravy through the pointed gravy strainer; put on the fire, to simmer for an hour, with 1 faggot, and 1 onion, with 2 cloves stuck in it; cut 1 lb. of turnips into the shape of corks, and peel 10 large button onions; fry both in a frying-pan, with 1 oz. of butter, till they are of a bright brown, and put them in the stew, when it has already cooked for an hour. Half an hour before serving, put in 15 small potatoes, and taste the stew for seasoning.

Two hours and a half are generally required to cook the above quantities; but the length of time will, of course, depend on the tenderness of the mutton.

Take out the faggot, and the onion with the cloves; clear of fat; and serve.

Observation.—In summer, when vegetables are young, the onions and turnips should only be added at the same time as the potatoes.

BRAIZED FILLET OF MUTTON

Take 3 lbs. of a loin of mutton; bone, without separating the under fillet; take off the outer skin, and bind the meat round with string, with the flap turned underneath.

Fry the mutton in a stewpan, with ½ oz. of butter,—turning, to ensure an even colour; add:

1 pint of water,	1 faggot,
1 onion, with 2 cloves	2 pinches of salt,
stuck in it,	2 small pinches of pepper;

Simmer for one hour, on a slow fire, in a covered stewpan; then put some live coals on the top, and cook for three quarters of an hour; baste the meat with the gravy, every ten minutes, to glaze it. Take out the fillet; untie, and put it on a dish; strain the gravy, reduce it one half; pour it over the meat; garnish with 1 lb. of turnips, prepared as indicated for Garnish (page 51); and serve.

ROAST FILLET OF MUTTON

Bone, and tie a piece of loin, as above,—the same weight will require thirty minutes' roasting; take off the spit; untie it; strain, and skim the fat off the gravy; pour over the meat; and serve.

BROILED MUTTON CUTLETS

Take the best end of a neck of mutton, which will give seven chops; saw about 4 inches off the end of the upper rib-bones; the piece thus trimmed off is used for broiled breast of mutton. Saw off the chine bone; and cut the seven chops, clearing of meat an inch of the end of each bone; flatten then with the bat; remove the gristle from round the lean; and pare away the meat and skin from the inside of the bone;—this is to give the cutlets the requisite shape. Sprinkle the cutlets on each side with 2 pinches of salt, and 1 small pinch of pepper; oil them

MUTTON CUTLETS

Q

slightly (*vide* Broiling, page 71); put them on a gridiron over a brisk fire, and cook them four minutes on one side, three minutes on the other; dish up in a circle; and serve.

MUTTON CUTLETS BREAD-CRUMBED

Prepare the cutlets as above; and season, with salt and pepper;

Melt about 1 oz. of butter, in the small *sauté*-pan; dip each cutlet in the butter; then strew it with bread-crumbs (*vide* Breading, page 74); put the cutlets on the gridiron, over a slow and even fire; cook on each side four minutes; dish up in a circle; and serve.

MUTTON CUTLETS SAUTÉS WITH GRAVY AND VEGETABLES

Prepare as for broiled cutlets; season with pepper and salt on each side; butter the *sauté*-pan, and set the cutlets in it;—avoid their overlapping each other; let them fry eight minutes, turning after four minutes; dish them in a circle; and serve.

The Household Gravy may be served with these cutlets; warm 1 gill, and put in the dish.

All vegetable garnishes, as well as Tomato, Italian, or Sharp Sauce, may also be served.

BREAST OF MUTTON BRAIZED, BREADED, AND BROILED

The object of this dish is generally to use the upper rib-bones sawn off the neck, when cutlets have been cut, although of course breasts of mutton can be bought separately.

Take a piece weighing about 1½lb.; the following are two ways of cooking it:

Either in the *pot-au-feu*; tie it up like the beef; put it in the stock-pot; and boil till the bones can be taken out easily;

Or, if you are not making *pot-au-feu*, put the mutton in a 3-quart stewpan, with:

the trimmings and bones,	1 small carrot, say 4 oz.,
2 quarts of water,	3 pinches of salt,
1 faggot,	3 small pinches of pepper,
1 onion, with 2 cloves stuck in it;	

Boil, and skim; then simmer till the bones come out easily;

drain on a dish; untie the mutton; draw out the bones; and sprinkle the mutton with salt; press it between two baking tins, with a weight on the top; when quite cold, cut it in six equal parts;

Melt 1 oz. of butter in a *sauté*-pan; dip the pieces in the butter; then strew them with bread-crumbs, and broil like the breaded cutlets.

Breast of mutton is served either with Tomato or Sharp Sauce, endive, or spinach.

BROILED KIDNEYS

Take six kidneys;

Cut them open from the rounded part, without separating them; peel off the skin; put a metal or wooden skewer through them; sprinkle with salt and pepper; oil slightly; and broil on a brisk fire, three minutes on each side; take them off the fire, and put on a dish—the hollow side uppermost;

Take 4 oz. of *Maître d'Hôtel* Butter; divide into six parts; and put one on each kidney; and serve.

BREADED KIDNEYS

To bread-crumb kidneys: proceed as directed for Mutton Cutlets; broil on a skewer, as above; and serve.

KIDNEYS SAUTÉS

Proceed as for Beef Kidney (*vide* Beef Kidney *Sauté*, page 90).

SHEEP'S FEET OR TROTTERS WITH POULETTE SAUCE

Take 8 feet; remove the wool from the hoof; singe, and put them in a 3-quart stewpan; blanch, for five minutes, in boiling water; cool and bone them, by holding the foot in the left hand, and giving the bone a sharp twist with the right;

Cut 1 inch off the end of the foot, including the hoof; make some white braize as for Calf's Head (*vide* page 103); put the feet in it to boil, for three hours and a half; when done they should be tender; drain, and put them in 1 pint of *Poulette* Sauce, prepared as for Calf's Head (*vide* page 103); add 1 pottle of turned mushrooms.

MARINADED SHEEP'S TROTTERS

Singe, blanch, bone, and boil the feet as before; drain and marinade them; then fry in the same way as Marinaded Calf's Head (*vide* page 104).

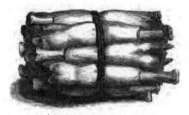

SHEEP'S TROTTERS

FRICASSEE OF CHICKEN

CHAPTER IX

POULTRY

FRICASSEE OF CHICKEN

Pick, draw, and singe a chicken, weighing about 3 lbs.,—this will be sufficient for four or five persons.

To cut it up: place it on a table with its head towards you; make an incision from the point of the breast bone to the wing joint, on both sides; turn the chicken, and make two other incisions to separate the legs from the body; cut off the neck, the pinions at the second joint, and the feet at the first joint; take off the wings and legs; separate the breast from the back, and cut each across in two pieces, then trim them neatly,—keeping the skin on each piece.

Steep the pieces in cold water one hour; drain, and put them in a 3-quart stewpan with:

1 quart of water,	2 small pinches of pepper,
1 onion, say 4 oz., with	1 faggot,
1 clove stuck in it,	2 pinches of salt;

Boil, and skim; then simmer on the stove corner for half an hour—the stewpan not quite closed;

When the chicken is done, drain in a colander, and cool it for five minutes in water;

Reserve the broth in which it has been boiled;

Put 3 oz. of butter, and 3 oz. of flour, in a 2-quart stewpan ; stir over the fire for five minutes, without browning; add the broth and the liquor of a pottle of mushrooms (prepared as indicated page 47); when the sauce comes to the boil, let it simmer for half an hour ;

Put the pieces of chicken into a *sauté*-pan ; strain over them ½ pint of the sauce ; and warm on a slow fire ;

Thicken the remainder of the sauce with the yolks of 4 eggs and 1 oz. of butter, as described at Thickening with Egg (*vide* page 59); then strain through the pointed gravy strainer, and add the mushrooms ;

Dish up the chicken in the following way :

Put the two pieces of the back in the centre; on them lay across, one above the other, first the feet, then the two pieces of neck, and lastly the two pinions ; against each side of the square thus formed, lay the two legs and wings ; and on the top put the two pieces of the breast ;

Pour over the sauce ; and garnish with the mushrooms (*vide* woodcut, page 117).

Four fine crayfish at the corners will much improve the appearance of this dish.

Croûtons, button onions, or artichoke bottoms, may also be used as a garnish for Fricassee of Chicken.

Remarks on Fricassee of Chicken

Fricassee of chicken is deservedly held to be one of the very best dishes of domestic—as well as of higher-class—cookery. A too careful attention cannot, therefore, be given to the several elements of success; firstly, to the selection of the chicken, which should always be very fresh and tender ; secondly, to the time to be given for cooking, which should be limited simply to that necessary to boil the chicken thoroughly. It is a mistake to imagine that to keep the fricassee long on the fire will improve it ;—once cooked, further boiling will only spoil it, and destroy the flavour.

Lastly, the eggs and butter for the *liaison* should be of the choicest.

Such are the main points to bear in mind; thus, if the different ingredients are carefully selected, and the length of time specified for cooking strictly adhered to, I will venture to predict an invariably successful result in the preparation of a dish both choice and profitable, and which, notwithstanding all the innovations of modern culinary art, still remains one of the best examples of old French cookery.

CHICKEN À LA BONNE FEMME

Pick, draw, singe, and cut up a chicken as for Fricassee (*vide* page 117).

Put, in a 3-quart stewpan :

    1 sliced carrot, say 4 oz.,
    1 sliced onion, say 4 oz.,
    6 oz. of butter ;

Fry five minutes, stirring with a wooden spoon; put in the pieces of chicken, 3 pinches of salt, and 2 small pinches of pepper ; fry five minutes, still stirring ; add 2 oz. of flour, and fry three minutes more ; then put in 1½ pint of broth, and 4 oz. of picked tomatoes broken in pieces ; stir till boiling, then simmer twenty minutes ; add 1 pottle of mushrooms, in slices ½ inch thick ; and one tablespoonful of coarsely chopped parsley ; boil, for ten minutes ; taste ; dish up in the same way as Fricassee of Chicken ; and serve.

CHICKEN À LA MARENGO

Prepare a chicken as for Fricassee (*vide* page 117).

Set the pieces of chicken in a *sauté*-pan, so that they do not overlap one another, with :

1 gill of oil,	2 shalots, say ½ oz. whole,
3 pinches of salt,	1 bay leaf,
2 small pinches of pepper,	1 sprig of thyme,
1 clove of garlic, say ¼ oz. whole,	1 bunch of parsley, say 1 oz.;

Fry twenty-five minutes, till the chicken is done ; take it out, and keep warm on a dish ;

Stir 1 oz. of flour into the pan ; fry four minutes, and add 1 pint of broth ; boil ten minutes, still stirring ; strain, through the pointed gravy strainer ; dish up the chicken as for Fricassee ; pour over the sauce ; and serve.

Observation.—The fat is not taken off the sauce of Chicken à la Marengo.

Mushrooms may be added as a garnish.

CHICKEN SAUTÉ WITH MUSHROOMS

Cut up the chicken as for Fricassee (*vide* page 117);

Butter a *sauté*-pan with 1 oz. of butter, and set the pieces of chicken in it; sprinkle with 3 pinches of salt, and 2 small pinches of pepper; cook for twenty-five minutes; when done, take out the chicken, and keep hot on a dish;

Stir into the pan 1 oz. of flour, for three minutes; then add 1 pint of broth, and the liquor in which the mushrooms have been boiled; stir ten minutes; strain, through the pointed strainer, into a quart stewpan; put in 1 pottle of turned mushrooms (*vide* Garnishes, page 47), to warm;

Dish up the chicken as for Fricassee (*vide* page 117); garnish with the mushrooms; pour over the sauce; and serve.

BOILED CHICKEN WITH ROCK SALT

Pick, draw, and singe a chicken, weighing about 3 lbs.; truss it as for boiling; and put it in a stewpan, with:

1 pint of broth,	1 faggot,
1 onion with 2 cloves stuck	2 pinches of salt,
in it,	2 small pinches of pepper;

Wrap the chicken in a sheet of buttered paper, to keep it white; and close the stewpan; boil gently half an hour, turning the chicken at the end of fifteen minutes; when done, drain and strain the gravy, through the pointed strainer, into a small stewpan, adding 12 drops of *caramel* to it; reduce for ten minutes;

Untie the chicken; put it on a dish; pour over the gravy, and place a teaspoonful of rock salt on the breast.

BOILED CHICKEN WITH TARRAGON

Prepare and cook a chicken, as directed in the preceding recipe; add ½ oz. of tarragon to the seasoning; reduce the gravy five minutes; strain, skim, and put a tablespoonful of coarsely chopped tarragon in it;

Place the chicken on a dish; pour over the gravy; and serve.

BOILED CHICKEN WITH TOMATO SAUCE

Prepare and cook a chicken, as described for Chicken with Rock Salt (as above).

Take 1½ pint of Tomato Sauce (*vide* page 66); pour over the chicken; and serve.

CHICKEN WITH RICE

Prepare a chicken, as indicated for Chicken with Rock Salt (*vide* page 120); boil gently fifteen minutes, and take out the faggot, onion, &c.;

Add 6 oz. of well-washed rice; boil half an hour; take out the chicken; mix the rice and the gravy, well together; put in a dish, with the chicken on it; pour over 1 gill of Household Gravy (*vide* page 68); and serve.

CHICKEN WITH POULETTE SAUCE

Prepare and cook a chicken, as described for Chicken with Rock Salt (*vide* page 120);

Take 1 pint of *Poulette* Sauce (*vide* page 65), and 1 pottle of turned mushrooms (*vide* page 47);

Put the chicken on a dish; pour over the sauce, so as entirely to cover it; garnish round with the mushrooms; and serve.

ROAST FOWL

Pick, draw, singe, and truss a fowl for roasting; cook thirty-five minutes before a bright fire; when done, untie, and put it on a dish;

Strain, and free the gravy from fat; pour it under the chicken; garnish round with watercresses; and serve.

MARINADED FOWL

Fowl is generally marinaded, to make use of any remaining roast fowl.

Take, say, half a fowl; cut it in pieces, about 2 inches long, and 1½ inch broad; marinade them in a basin, with: 2 table-spoonfuls of vinegar; 1 pinch of salt, and 1 small pinch of pepper; let them soak two hours; then drain.

Warm 2 lbs. of fat in the small frying-kettle; dip each piece of fowl in some frying batter (*vide* page 74), and fry as indicated, page 73; dish up the pieces on a napkin, on a dish; and garnish with fried parsley.

Tomato Sauce is served with the fowl in a boat.

R

MAYONNAISE OF FOWL

Cut the cold fowl in pieces, and marinade as above ; dish them up, and pour 3 gills of White *Mayonnaise* Sauce (*vide* page 67) over the chicken ; garnish round with hard-boiled eggs, cut in quarters, and the hearts of a few cabbage lettuces (*vide* woodcut below).

DUCK WITH TURNIPS

When choosing ducks, bear in mind my general remarks on poultry, and never select any but young and tender ones.

Pick, draw, singe, and truss a duck as for roasting ; put it in a stewpan, with 1 oz. of butter, 2 pinches of salt, and 1 small pinch of pepper ; fry for ten minutes, turning it to ensure an even colouring ; take it out of the stewpan, and put it on a dish ;

Then put in the stewpan, 1½ oz. of flour ; stir three minutes ; and add 1¼ pint of broth ; boil for five minutes, and strain through the pointed strainer ;

Clean the stewpan, and put in the duck and the sauce, with 1 faggot, and 1 onion, with 2 cloves in it ; simmer on a slow fire, three quarters of an hour ; then add ¾ lb. of turnips, prepared for garnish (*vide* page 51) ; when these are done, take out the onion and faggot ; untie the duck, and put it on a dish ; garnish round with the turnips ; free the gravy from fat ; pour over the duck ; and serve.

MAYONNAISE OF FOWL

DUCK WITH GREEN PEAS

Prepare a duck, and fry slightly, as above;

Blanch ½ lb. of streaky bacon; remove the rind, and cut the bacon in 1½ inch squares; then fry these in a stewpan, with 1 oz. of butter, till of a light brown; dredge in 1 oz. of flour, and stir over the fire three minutes, with a wooden spoon; add:

1 pint of broth,	1 faggot,
1 onion, with 2 cloves	1 pinch of salt,
stuck in it,	2 small pinches of pepper;

Stir till boiling, then put in the duck, and a quart of green peas; simmer one hour and a quarter,—the stewpan three parts covered only. When the duck is done, take out the onion and faggot; free the peas from fat; put them on a dish, with the pieces of bacon; untie the duck; put it on the peas; pour over the gravy; and serve.

Observation.—Middle-sized peas should be used for garnish, —as the smaller ones, if used for this purpose, would be done to a pulp, and the larger ones are only good for *purées*.

DUCK WITH OLIVES

Prepare and cook a duck as indicated for Duck with Turnips (*vide* page 122); make the same gravy;

Take 40 olives (prepared as for Fillet of Beef with Olives, *vide* page 92); boil for five minutes, in the gravy;

Untie the duck, and put it on a dish; garnish round with the olives; free the gravy from all fat; pour it over the duck; and serve.

ROAST DUCK

A particularly tender duck should be procured for roasting.

Stuff the duck with stuffing, prepared as follows:

Take 4 onions, say 1 lb., cut in slices, with 24 sage leaves; blanch both for five minutes; drain, and chop them fine; put in a stewpan, with 1 oz. of butter, 2 pinches of salt, and 2 small pinches of pepper; simmer gently for ten minutes, stirring with the wooden spoon; add a handful of bread-crumbs, and stir for two minutes more; the stuffing is then ready for use; truss the duck; and put it down to roast, before a very brisk fire, for sixteen minutes.

R 2

Roast duck should be sent to table rather underdone. Remove the string; pour the gravy under the duck; and serve.

If not stuffed, a garnish of watercresses is sometimes served round roast duck.

PIGEONS

Three kinds of pigeons are used for the table : house, wood and rock pigeons.

House pigeons are the best; their finer quality will amply compensate for their greater cost.

Wood pigeons should only be used for roasting, and when very young.

Rock pigeons are smaller, and not so good in quality as house pigeons.

STEWED PIGEONS

Draw, and singe, two house pigeons;

Cut off the heads, and necks;

Put back the livers in the inside of the birds, and truss them with the legs inward;

After removing the rind from ½ lb. of streaky bacon, blanch it in boiling water, and cut it into 1½ inch squares; fry it in a stewpan, with 1 oz. of butter, till of a light brown; then take it out;

Put the pigeons in the same stewpan, and fry till they assume a light brown colour; take them out, and put them aside on a plate, together with the bacon. Make a *roux* with 1 oz. of flour, and the butter in the stewpan; moisten with 1 pint of broth, and the liquor in which a pottle of turned mushrooms has been boiled; season with 1 pinch of salt, and 2 small pinches of pepper; stir over the fire, till boiling; strain, through the pointed strainer;

Rinse out the stewpan, and put in the pigeons with the gravy, 1 faggot, the bacon, and 20 button onions, previously blanched, picked, and fried, as for Onions for Garnish (*vide* page 51).

Simmer twenty-five minutes; add the mushrooms; and cook five minutes more;

When the pigeons are done, remove the string, and put them on a dish; take out the faggot; skim the fat off the gravy; pour the gravy over the pigeons; garnish round with the bacon, onions, and mushrooms; and serve.

STEWED PIGEONS WITH GREEN PEAS

Prepare and cook two pigeons, as above;

Make the same sauce,—but, instead of onions and mushrooms, put in 1 quart of green peas, 1 faggot, and the same quantity of bacon as mentioned above;

Simmer slowly half an hour; when done, untie the pigeons; take out the faggot; skim the fat off the peas, and put them on a dish with the bacon; place the pigeons on them; and serve.

PIGEONS À LA CRAPAUDINE

Cut two pigeons lengthwise, under the breast, turning them over as indicated in woodcut, page 128; flatten with the cutlet bat; and season with 1 pinch of salt, and two small pinches of pepper;

Fry the pigeons in a *sauté*-pan, with 1 oz. of butter, for fifteen minutes; then press them between two baking tins, with a 2 lbs. weight on the top;

Put 1 oz. of washed and chopped shalot, in the butter left in the *sauté*-pan; stir over the fire two minutes, and add ½ pint of broth, or Household Gravy (*vide* page 68), with 2 small pinches of pepper; reduce one half; skim off the fat; and strain the gravy through the pointed strainer, into a small stewpan;

Melt ½ oz. of butter; dip in the pieces of pigeon, then bread-crumb them (*vide* Breading, page 74); broil them, over a slow fire, five minutes on each side; warm the gravy; pour it in a dish; put the pigeons on it; and serve.

Send a lemon on a plate to table with these pigeons.

ROAST PIGEONS

Draw and singe three pigeons.

Cut off the heads, and necks, and the toes at the first joint; truss for roasting.

Tie a slice of fat bacon, 3½ inches long, by 2½ inches, and ¼ inch thick, over the breast of each bird; put them down before a brisk fire, and roast for fifteen minutes; when done, take off the spit, untie, and put them on a dish; replace the slice of bacon on the breast; pour over the gravy; garnish round with watercresses; and serve.

ROAST TURKEY

Take a small hen turkey, weighing about 4 lbs.; truss it for roasting; put it before an even fire, and roast one hour; take off the spit, untie and put it on a dish; pour the gravy under the bird; garnish with watercresses; and serve.

A roast turkey, when done to perfection, should be of an even golden colour, with the skin rather loose on the flesh.

Croquets may be made of any remaining cold roast turkey; it may also be warmed up *en poulette*, or dressed cold with *Mayonnaise* Sauce.

ROAST TURKEY STUFFED WITH CHESTNUTS

Trim, free from gristle, and chop 10 oz. of fillet of veal, and 1 lb. of fat bacon; season with 1 oz. of spiced salt (*vide* Spices and Herbs, page 24).

While chopping, moisten with 1 gill of broth; put the forcemeat in a mortar, and pound it for ten minutes; put it in a basin, and add 40 chestnuts, previously slowly roasted and peeled;

Draw and truss a turkey, as in the preceding recipe; when cutting off the neck, leave as much of the crop skin as possible; stuff the turkey, with the forcemeat and chestnuts;

Roast it, before an even but moderate fire, for an hour and forty minutes; take it off the spit; untie; and put it on a dish;

Free the gravy from all grease; pour it under the turkey; and serve.

TURKEY GIBLETS WITH TURNIPS

Take a set of turkey giblets; blanch, in boiling water, two minutes; singe, and cleanse them carefully;

Cut the neck in four equal parts; the gizzard in four pieces; the pinions and legs each in two pieces;

After removing the rind of ½ lb. of streaky bacon, cut it in pieces 1½ inch long, 1 inch thick; fry these in a stewpan, with 1 oz. of butter; when slightly brown, take them out; put the giblets in the same stewpan; fry and cook them in the same way as Stewed Mutton (*vide* page 112); add the bacon, and 1 lb. of turnips, cut to the shape of corks, and ten large button onions; fry these to a red brown, with 1 oz. of butter;

Peel 15 potatoes to an egg shape, and add them to the stew half an hour before serving; add the liver only ten minutes before serving;

Boil one hour and a half;

Take out the faggot, and skim off the fat

Put the legs, gizzard, liver, and head, in the centre of a dish with the pieces of neck round them, and the pinions on the top; pour over the gravy, and vegetables; and serve.

ROAST GOOSE

Take a goose weighing about 6 lbs.; pick, draw, singe, stuff (*vide* Stuffing for Roast Duck, page 123), and truss it for roasting;

Roast one hour and a quarter, before a moderate and even fire;

Sprinkle it with a little salt; and, when done, take it off the spit; remove the string, and put the goose on a dish; strain, and skim off all the fat from the gravy; pour it on the dish; and serve.

Goose dripping should be kept to add to sauerkraut, cabbage, onion, or leek soups, &c.

GOOSE STUFFED WITH CHESTNUTS

Proceed as for Turkey Stuffed with Chestnuts (*vide* page 126).

GOOSE WITH SAUERKRAUT

Pick, draw, singe, and truss a goose for boiling; and put it in a stewpan, with: 4 lbs. of sauerkraut, prepared as indicated in

GOOSE WITH SAUERKRAUT

garnishes (page 55); ½ lb. of streaky bacon, and ½ lb. of un-cooked Bologna sausage; 1 onion, and 2 cloves stuck in it;

Simmer two hours; take out the bacon and sausage as soon as they are done;

Cut the sausage in slices ¼ inch thick; take the rind off the bacon, and cut it in slices 1½ inch long, 1 inch broad, and ¼ inch thick; and put by to keep warm till wanted.

When the goose is done, remove the string; strain, and press the sauerkraut in a colander; put it on a dish, and place the goose on it; garnish round with the bacon and sausage.

PIGEON À LA CRAPAUDINE

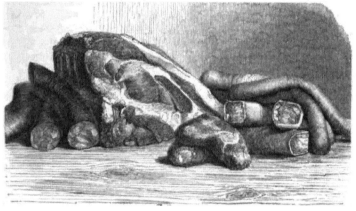

PORK

CHAPTER X

PORK

I WILL only include under this heading, the recipes which are properly of the cook's department, without touching at all upon those preparations which belong to the pork-butcher's business. Some treatises of cookery, which boast of aiming at simplicity and practicability, give recipes for sausages, stuffed tongues, &c., which can of course be of no use, as it is acknowledged that these things are not made at home, but are bought ready prepared. This only serves to increase the bulk of books with useless matter, taking the room of more necessary knowledge. What is more important to learn is: which parts of pork are used in home preparation, and how to cook well that which is bought ready dressed of the pork-butcher's; and the selection of which demands the greatest care.

ROAST LOIN OF PORK

Take 4 lbs. of loin of pork,—the flesh of a delicate and even colour; trim the fat, leaving it only $\frac{1}{4}$ inch thick; saw off the

s

chine bone; rub ¼ lb. of coarse salt into the pork; put it in a
basin to pickle for two hours, turning it over frequently; wipe
it well, and put it on the spit, to roast before a moderate fire
for an hour and a quarter; take it off the spit; put on the dish;
strain, and skim the fat off the gravy; pour it over the pork;
and serve.

ROAST LOIN OF PORK WITH SAUCE ROBERT

Prepare the pork as in the preceding recipe; put it in a
stewpan, with:
    ¼ oz. of butter,
    2 pinches of salt,
    2 small pinches of pepper;
Fry it on both sides till of a light brown colour; add:
    ½ pint of broth,
    ½ pint of French white wine,
    1 faggot,
    1 onion, with two cloves stuck in it;
Close the stewpan, and put to simmer for two hours; basting
the pork every half hour.

For the *Sauce Robert*, peel three onions (say 10 oz.), slicing
off both ends; cut them in ¼ inch dice; put them in a quart
stewpan, with 1 oz. of butter; fry till slightly browned; add
1 oz. of flour; stir with the wooden spoon over the fire for two
minutes; take off the fire, and pour in 3 gills of broth, with 1
pinch of salt, and 2 small pinches of pepper; boil for ten
minutes, stirring all the time. When the pork is done, pour out
the gravy; strain, and skim it, and add it to the sauce; reduce
for five minutes; pour the sauce into the dish; lay the pork
over it; and serve.

Observation.—A tablespoonful of French mustard is often
added to the *Sauce Robert*; but as many persons object (to my
idea with reason) to warmed mustard, this should remain a
question of taste.

PORK CHOPS WITH SHARP SAUCE

Take two bones of neck of pork; cut and trim, as directed
for Veal Cutlets Broiled (*vide* page 98);
    Melt 1 oz. of butter in a *sauté*-pan;
    Sprinkle each chop, on both sides, with 2 pinches of salt, and
2 small pinches of pepper; put them in the *sauté*-pan; fry for

twenty minutes, ten minutes each side; dish them up; pour over 3 gills of Sharp Sauce (*vide* page 64); and serve.

PORK CHOPS BREAD-CRUMBED AND BROILED

Trim the chops, as in the preceding recipe; season with salt and pepper;

Melt 1 oz. of butter in a *sauté*-pan; dip each chop in it, and bread-crumb them (*vide* page 74); broil for twelve minutes, six minutes each side;

Warm 2 gills of Household Gravy; put the chops on the dish, the gravy under; and serve.

With these, Tomato or Italian Sauce is frequently served.

PORK KIDNEYS SAUTÉS

Cut a kidney in slices ¼ inch thick, and proceed as with Beef Kidney (*vide* page 90).

PIG'S FEET À LA ST. MENEHOULD

Procure two large pig's feet; pickle them in salt brine for a week; wash them, and boil them gently for three hours, in a quart of broth, together with:

| 1 carrot, say 4 oz., | 1 faggot, |
| 1 onion, say 4 oz., | 2 oz. of celery; |

When done, cut them in two, lengthwise; remove the large bone; press the feet between two baking sheets, till cold; season with pepper and salt; dip them in butter, melted; and bread-crumb them;

Broil on a moderate fire, turning them twice, till of a nice yellow colour; serve, very hot.

BROILED SAUSAGES

Prick the sausages with a trussing needle, on both sides, to prevent their bursting; broil them, over a moderate fire, for six minutes, turning them after three minutes; serve them on a very hot dish.

s 2

SAUSAGES WITH MASHED POTATOES

Broil the sausages, as in the preceding recipe, and dish them up with mashed potatoes, or *purée* of haricot beans, peas, or lentils; these *purées* are prepared as for Soups (*vide* page 40, and following); add ¼ lb. of butter to the mashed potatoes, or the *purée*, before serving.

Put the mashed potatoes, or *purée*, on a dish, and the sausages round it; pour over 1 gill of Household Gravy; and serve.

SAUSAGES WITH WHITE WINE

Take 6 sausages; put them in a *sauté*-pan, with 2 gills of French white wine, and 2 small pinches of pepper; cover the *sauté*-pan, and boil for eight minutes; take the sausages out, and add 1 gill of *Poulette* Sauce (*vide* page 65), to the wine in the *sauté*-pan; reduce for four minutes; take off the fire, and add 1 oz. of fresh butter, and a tablespoonful of chopped parsley; stir till the butter is melted; put the sausages on a dish; pour the sauce over; and serve.

FLAT SAUSAGES OR CRÉPINETTES

Take 1 lb. of fresh pork, half lean, and half fat; chop it moderately fine with the chopping knife; season with ¼ oz. of salt, 1 pinch of pepper, a small sprig of thyme, and ¼ of a bay leaf, chopped very fine; separate this meat into eight equal portions; roll each to a flat oval shape, and wrap it in pig's caul; when ready, broil the sausages on each side for six minutes; serve, very hot.

FLAT SAUSAGES, OR CRÉPINETTES, WITH RICE AND TOMATO SAUCE

For four *crépinettes*, take:

¼ lb. of well-washed rice,	1 small pinch of pepper,
1 pint of broth,	½ an onion, say 2 oz. ;
1 pinch of salt,	

Boil; then simmer, for twenty minutes,—the stewpan closely covered; stir the rice with the spoon; put it on a dish, and place the sausages, previously broiled, on it; pour over 3 gills of Tomato Sauce (*vide* page 66).

BLACK PUDDING

Take 1½ pint of pig's blood; add to it ½ pint of boiled cream; 1 lb. of the inside fat of the pig, cut into small dice; cut 3 onions, also in dice, and fry them in 2 oz. of butter, till of a yellow colour; season with ½ oz. of salt, 1 small pinch of pepper, a little grated nutmeg; a sprig of thyme, and ½ a bay leaf, chopped very fine; mix all well together, and fill the skins, previously well cleansed and washed, with this mixture, taking care not to have the skins too full, to allow of tying them with string into 5-inch lengths; when thus tied, put them in a large stewpan of boiling water, without boiling them, and let them remain therein till set firm; take them out, and hang them to cool.

When wanted, they should be cut into lengths; well scored with a knife, to prevent breaking; and broiled on a moderate fire for about ten minutes, turning them round after five minutes' broiling; then served, very hot.

SAUERKRAUT WITH SAUSAGES

Prepare 2 lbs. of sauerkraut, as directed, page 55; put it in a 4-quart stewpan; add: ½ lb. of well-washed streaky bacon; ½ lb. of Bologna sausage; 6 pork sausages; 1 onion, with 2 cloves stuck in it; and 1 faggot;

Boil all together; take out, first, the sausages, as they require less cooking; then the Bologna sausage; and, lastly, the bacon, when done; drain the sauerkraut; put it on a dish;

Cut the Bologna sausage in pieces ¼ inch thick; trim the bacon, and cut it in slices;

Garnish round the sauerkraut with the pieces of bacon and Bologna sausage, and lay the sausages on the top; serve hot.

KNUCKLE OF HAM

PARTRIDGES WITH CABBAGE

CHAPTER XI

GAME

ROAST ROEBUCK

TAKE a leg of roebuck, weighing about 5 lbs.; saw off the bone below the knuckle; strip about 4 square inches off the top skin of the joint, and lard this part with shreds of bacon as for *Fricandeau* (*vide* page 97).

Roebuck is served fresh, or marinaded.

To roast it fresh: first wrap it in buttered paper, keeping both ends open; put it on the spit, and roast for fifty minutes, before an even fire; ten minutes before it is cooked, take off the paper, and sprinkle the joint with 2 pinches of salt; take off the spit; put on a dish, with a paper frill round the knuckle, and serve with *Poivrade* Sauce in a boat (*vide* page 65).

Leg of roebuck marinaded is prepared and larded as above; make a marinade as follows: take

1 carrot, say 4 oz.,	1 sprig of thyme,
2 onions, say 8 oz.,	2 shalots, say 1 oz., whole,
2 bay leaves,	1 oz. of parsley ;

Put these ingredients in a 4-quart stewpan, with 1 oz. of butter, and fry for five minutes; then add:

1 pint of vinegar,	1¼ oz. of salt,
1 quart of water,	½ oz. of pepper;

Boil; then simmer on the stove corner for half an hour; strain into a basin, large enough to hold the leg of roebuck, which should be put to marinade in the liquor for two days;

An hour before serving, take it out of the marinade; wrap it up in buttered paper, as in the preceding recipe, and roast it, for fifty minutes, before a steady fire;

Serve with *Poivrade* Sauce, prepared in the following manner:

Boil, and strain through a cloth, 1 quart of the marinade; make a *roux* in a 2-quart stewpan, with 1¼ oz. of butter, and 1½ oz. of flour; stir over the fire for two minutes; then take off the fire, and mix with the marinade; reduce to 1½ pint, add a few drops of *caramel* to colour; taste the seasoning; strain through the pointed strainer; and serve in a boat;

Currant jelly is also served in a boat, with roast leg of roebuck.

Observation.—Leg of roebuck can be kept in the marinade in a cold place, for eight or ten days.

MINCED ROEBUCK

The remains of the leg can be served minced with *Poivrade* Sauce.

Cut the meat as directed for Minced Leg of Mutton (*vide* page 111).

ROAST HARE

Take a young hare; skin, empty, and wash it, keeping the blood in a small basin; cut it in two under the shoulders; reserve the forepart for stewing;

Prepare the hind part of the hare for roasting, by crossing the hind legs, that is, passing one through the other; roll the skin round on each side, and secure it with wooden skewers; hold the loin and legs over a charcoal fire for a minute, to set the flesh, and facilitate larding; lard the fillets, and thick part of the legs, as directed for *Fricandeau* (*vide* page 97); put on the spit, and cover with buttered paper, doubled over the fillets; put down to roast, before a steady fire, for thirty minutes, making the fire brisker on the side of the legs; untie the paper, to colour the larded part; take off the spit, and put on a dish, with the gravy;

Have a pint of *Poivrade* Sauce, and thicken it, when boiling, with the blood you have reserved, as indicated at Thickening with Blood (*vide* page 59);

Serve the sauce in a boat.

STEWED HARE

Take, and cut in 2-inch pieces, the fore part of the hare remaining from the preceding operation; cut, also, $\frac{3}{4}$ lb. of lean streaky bacon in 1-inch dice; blanch the bacon for five minutes in boiling water; drain, and fry it in a 3-quart stewpan, with 1 oz. of butter; when fried yellow, take it out on a plate;

Put the pieces of hare in the stewpan, and fry them for ten minutes; dredge over 2 oz. of flour, and stir for two minutes; add 1 pint of red French wine, and 1 pint of broth; boil, and stir for five minutes; then strain through the colander; rinse the stewpan, put the pieces of hare back into it, after cleaning them, and strain the sauce in, through the pointed gravy strainer; add: a faggot; the bacon; 1 pinch of salt, and 3 small pinches of pepper; cover the stewpan, and simmer on the stove corner for twenty minutes; add 20 button onions, previously fried in butter, and simmer again till the onions are done; five minutes before serving, add a pottle of mushrooms, prepared as indicated page 47; take the faggot out; skim off the fat; dish up the pieces of hare, with the sauce and garnishes round; and serve.

ROAST RABBIT

Skin a rabbit; cut the hind legs, above the knuckle joint, the fore legs, at the first joint;

Empty, clean, and truss it; the hind legs crossed, and the head secured by a string passing between the shoulders; cover the back with a layer, or slice, of fat bacon; put on the spit, and roast for twenty-five minutes, before a good fire; take it up, untie, put it on a dish, and serve with $\frac{1}{2}$ pint of *Poivrade* Sauce, in a boat.

Observation.—I do not give the weight of hare, or rabbit; convinced that, if young, they will be cooked in the time I mention.

STEWED RABBIT

Skin, empty, and wash a rabbit; cut it in 2-inch pieces; cut also ½ lb. of lean streaky bacon in pieces 1½ inch by 1 inch; blanch, drain, and fry the bacon with 1 oz. of butter; when yellow, take it out on a plate; put the pieces of rabbit in the stewpan; fry them for ten minutes; dredge in 1 oz. of flour, and stir over the fire for two minutes; add:

> 3 gills of broth,   2 small pinches of
> 3 gills of French red wine,   pepper,
> 1 pinch of salt,   1 faggot,
> 15 button onions, previously fried in the frying pan, and the pieces of bacon;

Simmer, for twenty minutes, in the covered stewpan; add half a pottle of mushrooms; boil for five minutes more; take out the faggot; dish up; and serve.

RABBIT SAUTÉ

Skin, empty, and cut a rabbit in pieces as directed for Stewed Rabbit, in preceding recipe;

Put, in a *sauté*-pan:

> 1 oz. of butter,   2 small pinches of
> 3 tablespoonfuls of oil,   spices,
> 2 pinches of salt,   1 small pinch of grate
> 2 small pinches of pepper,   nutmeg;

Melt the butter, and put the rabbit in the *sauté*-pan; stir over a brisk fire for twenty minutes; then take out the rabbit on a dish, and put 1 oz. of flour into the *sauté*-pan; stir over the fire for a minute; add 2 gills of French white wine, and 1 gill of broth; boil for five minutes, and strain the sauce through the pointed strainer; clean the *sauté*-pan, and put in it the rabbit and the sauce; add ½ oz. of shalot, chopped and well-washed, and a tablespoonful of chopped parsley; put on the fire, and, when boiling, take out the rabbit; dish it up; and serve, with the sauce.

Observation.—I must repeat the recommendation I have made,—always to avoid boiling *sautés*, as it would make the meat hard.

T

ROAST PARTRIDGE

Pick, draw, and singe a partridge as directed for Roast Fowl
(*vide* page 121); cover it over with a slice of fat bacon, 3½ inches
long, 2½ inches wide, and ¼ inch thick; tie it on the partridge;
put on the spit, and roast for sixteen minutes before a good fire;
take off the spit; untie the string; dish up with a little gravy,
and garnish with watercresses; and serve.

STEWED PARTRIDGES WITH CABBAGE

It is often thought that old and tough birds are good enough
to dress as stewed partridges;—this is a great mistake. I can
but repeat my remarks on old poultry and game;—they must be
absolutely discarded in all cookery.

Pick, draw, singe, and truss two partridges, with the legs
tucked in as for boiling; insert a few strips of fat bacon in the
breast, cutting off the outside ends;

Cut a good Savoy cabbage in quarters; blanch it, steep it in
cold water for an hour; cut the stalks off; press all the water
out, and put them in a 4-quart stewpan; bury the partridges in
the cabbage, and add:

½ lb. of streaky bacon, previously blanched,
¼ lb. of uncooked Bologna sausage,
1 faggot,
2 carrots, say 7 oz.,
2 onions, say 7 oz., with a clove stuck in one,
2 small pinches of pepper;

Moisten with enough broth to cover the cabbage, and 2 gills
of melted and strained dripping; put a round of doubled paper
over the cabbage; cover the stewpan closely; set boiling; then
simmer for an hour and a half;

When done, take out the partridges, sausage, and bacon, and
put them in the oven, to keep warm;

Drain the cabbage; put it in a stewpan, with a little salt and
pepper, on to a brisk fire; stirring, till all moisture is expelled;

Make a thick layer of the cabbage on a dish; untie the
partridges, and place them on it, as shown in woodcut, page
134.

Cut the bacon and sausage into slices; turn the carrots to the
shape of corks, and garnish the dish round with the bacon,
sausage, and carrots;

Prepare the sauce as follows :

Put, in a 2-quart stewpan, 1 oz. of butter, and 1 oz. of flour ; stir over the fire for three minutes ; moisten with a pint of Household Gravy ; reduce for ten minutes ; strain through the pointed gravy strainer ; put in a boat ; and serve, with the partridges.

LARKS

Take out the gizzards of 6 larks, singe them, and cut off the legs ; when they are singed, pick carefully any remaining feathers ;

Take a skewer, 1 foot long ; prepare six slices of fat bacon 2½ inches long, and 1½ inch wide ; cover the larks entirely with the bacon ; pass the skewer through each lark, so that the bacon be held on each side in its proper place ; avoid the larks touching one another ; tie each end of the skewer to the spit ; roast the larks, before a sharp fire, for eight minutes ; serve, with the gravy under ; and garnish with watercresses.

SALMI OF LARKS

Take out the gizzards of 12 larks ; singe, and pick them, leaving the legs. This number of birds will not much exceed the proportion required for four persons.

Cut ¼ lb. of streaky bacon, in pieces 1 inch long, ½ inch thick ; put 1 oz. of butter in a 2-quart stewpan ; fry the bacon—not previously blanched ; when sufficiently coloured, add the larks and half a pottle of mushrooms, picked, washed, and cut in slices —but not turned ;

Cook for eight minutes ; dredge over with 1 oz. of flour ; toss for one minute, to mix the contents of the stewpan ;

Boil, in a small stewpan, 3 gills of white French wine, seasoned with 1 pinch of pepper, and very little salt (to allow for the saltness of the bacon) ;

Pour the wine into the stewpan containing the larks ; stir (to prevent lumping), and add a tablespoonful of chopped parsley ; boil one minute ; dish up ; and serve.

LARKS ON THE SPIT

T 2

RAISED PIE

CHAPTER XII

POTTINGS AND PIES

POTTED TURKEY

FOR A potting pan of 7 inches diameter, draw, pick, singe, and bone a turkey, weighing 4 lbs., without the giblets; keep the bones to put in the *pot-au-feu*.

To make the forcemeat, take: the flesh of the thighs, removing the sinews; ½ lb. of fillet, or cushion, of veal; and 1 lb. of fat bacon; season with 1 oz. of spiced salt; chop the whole fine; pound it in the mortar, and take it out on to a dish;

Lard the breast of the turkey with strips of fat bacon, seasoned with 1 pinch of salt, and 1 small pinch of pepper; put a layer of forcemeat in the bottom of the pan; spread out the turkey, skin downwards, and sprinkle it with 2 pinches of spiced salt; put a layer of forcemeat all over the inside of the turkey; roll it round, and put it in the pan; cover with the remaining forcemeat, and on the top lay some thin slices of fat bacon, and a bay leaf; put the cover on the pan, and place it in a large stewpan. with 2 inches of water; cook in the oven for three hours;

ascertain if done by trying with the trussing needle; when cold, cover the potting entirely with a layer of poultry dripping, or lard.

Observation.—Pottings and pies should not be served within twenty-four hours of cooking.

POTTED GOOSE

Same process as for Potted Turkey (*vide* preceding recipe); melt the fat of the goose, and use it to cover the potting.

POTTING PAN

POTTED HARE

For the same sized pan as for Potted Turkey, take a hare, weighing about 5 lbs.; skin, empty, wash, and bone it; reserve the blood to mix with the forcemeat; take some of the meat from the shoulders, and half that of the legs, carefully removing all sinews and skin; add: ¾ lb. of fillet of veal, freed from skin and gristle, and 1 lb. of fat bacon; chop the whole, seasoning with 1 oz. of spiced salt; pound it, adding the blood whilst pounding.

Lard the fleshy part of the fillets with strips of fat bacon; cut the hare across in two pieces; sprinkle over with 2 pinches of spiced salt; fry for ten minutes in the *sauté*-pan, with 1 oz. of butter;—this operation is necessary, in order to expel the water contained in the hare;

Put a layer of the forcemeat, 1 inch thick, in the potting pan; then one half of the hare, with 1 small pinch of spiced salt; another layer of forcemeat; the other half of the hare, and the remaining forcemeat; cover the whole with a thin layer of fat bacon, and a bay leaf on the top; cook in the same way as potted turkey; and, when perfectly cold, cover with melted fat.

Observation.—Partridges, larks, rabbits, and pheasants, can be potted in the same way.

If the pottings are intended for keeping, the same quantities of pork should be substituted for the veal.

COLD CHICKEN PIE

Take an oval pie-mould, 8 inches long; make the paste in the following way: take:

1½ lb. of flour (best whites),	½ oz. of salt,
¾ lb. of butter,	½ pint of water.

PIE MOULD

Sift the flour on the board through a hair sieve; make a hole in the centre of the flour, to receive the butter, salt, and half the water; mix the flour and butter; add the remaining water at three different times, whilst working the whole to a smooth paste; sprinkle the table with flour, and gather up the paste in a lump. Paste, when properly mixed, does not adhere to the hands, table, or rolling pin. Let the paste rest for half an hour; take three parts of it; roll it of an oval shape, to the thickness of ⅓ inch; raise the edges all round, about 2 inches, and shape it in the form of the mould; butter the latter slightly, and put the paste in it, pressing it at the bottom, and round the sides of an even thickness; raise the paste ½ inch above the top of the mould, and roll out half the remaining paste for the cover.

Take a chicken, weighing about 2½ lbs.; draw, pick, singe, and bone it;

Make some forcemeat with 14 oz. of cushion of veal, freed of

skin and gristle, and 14 oz. of fat bacon; keep the rind to add
to the gravy; season the forcemeat with ½ oz. of spiced salt;
chop; pound it in the mortar; and put it in a basin;

Lard the chicken with some seasoned strips of fat bacon; put
a layer of forcemeat on the chicken, and roll it in the shape of
the mould; line the paste with forcemeat; lay the chicken in it,
skin upwards; put another thin layer of forcemeat on the top,
—keeping the edge of the paste clear, to receive the paste cover;
lay a thin slice of fat bacon over the forcemeat, and a bay leaf
on the top; moisten the paste at the top of the mould; lay the
paste cover on, and press the two together between the thumb
and the first finger, to form the edge; cut off the superfluous
paste even with the mould; pinch round the edge with the
pincers; roll out the remaining paste, and cut it in the shape of
the inside of the top of the pie, to make a second cover; moisten
the first, and lay this second cover over it; brush over the top
with an egg beaten as for omelet; cut a pattern on the cover
with a small knife, to half the thickness of the paste, and make
a hole in the centre, 1 inch wide;

Bake for two hours; if the oven be too fierce, cover the pie
with paper, to prevent its getting too brown; try, through the
hole in the top, with the trussing needle, to ascertain whether
the pie is cooked; if done, the needle should penetrate without
any resistance; take the pie out of the oven.

GRAVY JELLY FOR COLD CHICKEN PIE

Remove the gizzard and liver from the bones of the chicken
used for the pie; cut the neck and the bones in three pieces; put
them in a 3-quart stewpan, with the rind of the bacon, previously
soaked, well scraped, and cut in pieces; and

⅓ lb. of knuckle of veal,	1 faggot,
½ a calf's foot,	2 pinches of salt,
1 onion with a clove stuck in it,	2 small pinches of pepper,
	3 pints of broth;

Boil; skim; and simmer on the stove corner, until the bacon
rind is quite cooked; when done, strain the gravy through a
broth napkin;

Half an hour after the pie has been taken out of the oven,
pour this gravy into the pie, through the opening in the cover;
—close the hole with a piece of paste, to prevent evaporation.

COLD VEAL AND HAM PIE

Take 2 lbs. of boiled ham, with the rind and part of the fat cut off; and 3 lbs. of fillet, or cushion, of veal;

Free 1½ lb. of the best pieces of the veal from bone, skin, and gristle, and lard them through with seasoned strips of fat bacon.

To make the forcemeat: take the same quantity of fat bacon, freed from gristle and rind, as there remains of trimmings of veal, say, about 1½ lb.; season with ¾ oz. of spiced salt; chop fine; pound in the mortar; and put the forcemeat by in a basin;

Make the crust of the pie as directed for Cold Chicken Pie (*vide* page 142); put a layer of forcemeat at the bottom, on the paste; cut the ham in slices, and make a layer 2 inches thick; add another layer of forcemeat, then one of the larded veal, cut into large pieces; sprinkle over with 2 pinches of spiced salt; and make another layer of forcemeat, one of ham, and finish with the remaining forcemeat; cover the whole with thin slices of fat bacon, and a bay leaf on the top; finish the pie; and bake it in the same way as Cold Chicken Pie.

GRAVY JELLY FOR COLD VEAL AND HAM PIE

Cut the rind of bacon in pieces; put them in a 3-quart stewpan, with the bones and trimmings of veal; add:

½ a calf's foot, boned,	1 onion, with 2 cloves stuck
3 pints of broth,	in it,
1 faggot,	2 pinches of spiced salt;

Boil; skim; and simmer for two hours on the stove corner; when the calf's foot is done, strain the gravy through a broth napkin, and pour it in the pie, half an hour after it has been taken out of the oven.

COLD HARE PIE

Skin a hare; empty it, keeping the blood;

Cut it in two below the shoulders; keep the forepart for stewing, and bone the hind quarters, and lard them with small seasoned strips of fat bacon;

Take ¾ lb. of fillet, or cushion, of veal; trim off all skin;

bone, and gristle; ¾ lb. of fat bacon,—take off the rind, and keep it for the gravy; and 1 oz. of spiced salt;

Chop; pound in the mortar,—adding the blood whilst pounding, and put this forcemeat by in a basin;

Make the crust of the pie as directed for Cold Chicken Pie (*vide* page 142); fill it with alternate layers of forcemeat and hare; finish with a layer of forcemeat, and 2 pinches of spiced salt;

Cover the whole with thin slices of fat bacon and a bay leaf; finish the pie, and bake it in the same way as Cold Chicken Pie.

GRAVY JELLY FOR COLD HARE PIE

Put in a 3-quart stewpan:

3 pints of broth,	the trimmings of the veal,
the bones of the hare,	the rind of the bacon,
1 calf's foot, boned and cut in pieces,	1 faggot,
2 pinches of salt,	1 onion, with 2 cloves stuck in it;

Boil; skim; and simmer, till the calf's foot is tender; strain the gravy through a broth napkin; pour into the pie through the opening at the top, as indicated for Cold Chicken Pie (*vide* page 142).

Observation.—Partridge, pheasant, lark, rabbit—or other game—pies are made in the same way.

U

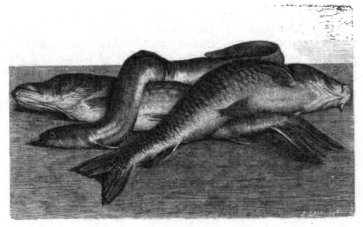

CARP—EEL—PIKE

CHAPTER XIII

FISH

I

SALT-WATER FISH

I SHALL continue to indicate approximate quantities sufficient for four persons; I therefore regulate all purchases on that principle.

TURBOT

Take a piece of turbot weighing about 3 lbs.; trim off the fins; steep it in cold water for two hours; drain; and cover the fish with a layer of salt, $\frac{1}{4}$ inch thick;

Put it in the oval stewpan (*vide* Kitchen Utensils, page 8), well covered with water; boil; skim; and simmer, for twenty-five minutes; drain, and put it on a hot napkin, on a dish, the white side uppermost; garnish with parsley; and serve.

Serve with it, in a boat, 1 pint of Melted Butter, or Dutch Sauce (*vide* page 62); (or Lobster, or Shrimp Sauce, made ·as follows : take a small lobster; cut the flesh into ¼ inch dice; pound the spawn in a mortar, with ½ oz. of butter, and pass it through a hair sieve; take 1 pint of melted butter; mix with it the pounded spawn, and put in the pieces of lobster to warm,— if preferred, picked shrimps may be substituted for the lobster;) and a dish of plain boiled potatoes.

BRILL

Brill is prepared in the same way as turbot, but requires scraping, to free it from scales;
Serve with the same sauces.

COD

Take a piece of cod, about 2 lbs.; wash, and steep it in cold water, for one hour; put it in boiling water, in the oval stewpan, with a good handful of salt; boil; skim; and simmer, for ten minutes; then drain it, and dish up on a hot napkin, and garnish with parsley; serve with Oyster Sauce, or Butter Melted (*vide* pages 66, 63), in a sauce boat.

GREY MULLET À LA MAÎTRE D'HÔTEL

Take a grey mullet, weighing about 2 lbs.; remove the gills, and cleanse the inside; scale; wash; wipe; and score the mullet on each side, with a dozen cuts, ¼ inch deep; lay it on a dish; sprinkle with 2 pinches of salt; and pour 3 tablespoonfuls of oil over it;
Broil, on an even moderate fire, for fifteen minutes, each side;
Place it on a dish; put ½ lb. of *Maître d'Hôtel* Butter on it; and serve.

GREY MULLET WITH DUTCH SAUCE

Grey mullet is also served with Dutch Sauce; in that case, it is boiled for twenty minutes, in salted water.

BOILED SALMON

Take about 2 lbs. of salmon,—in preference, a slice cut from the middle; put it in a gallon stewpan, with 3 quarts of water and 4 oz. of salt; boil; skim; and simmer till done; this will be, when the fish separates easily from the bone; drain immediately the salmon is sufficiently cooked; dish up on a napkin; and garnish with fresh parsley.

Serve with it, in a boat, 1 pint of Lobster Sauce (*vide* page 147), Dutch Sauce, or Melted Butter.

BROILED SALMON

Take about 2 lbs. of salmon; cut it in slices, about 1 inch thick; rub these over slightly with oil; sprinkle over 1 pinch of salt, and 1 small pinch of pepper; broil, on a clear and even fire, for half an hour; put on a dish; and serve, with 1 pint of Melted Butter, to which 2 tablespoonfuls of capers have been added.

LOBSTER WITH MAYONNAISE SAUCE

Choose a fresh and heavy boiled lobster; separate the tail from the body; break off and crack the claws; split both tail and body in two; dress, on a dish, with the body in the middle; garnish, with fresh parsley;

Serve 1 pint of *Mayonnaise* Sauce (*vide* page 67), in a boat.

SOLE AU GRATIN

Take a large sole; remove the gills; cleanse the inside; strip off the black skin; and scrape the other side; wash, and wipe it;

On the side which has been skinned, make an incision, $\frac{1}{4}$ inch deep, down each side of the backbone; and cut off the fins;

Spread 1 oz. of butter, in the oval *gratin*-pan; then add:

$\frac{1}{2}$ pint of French white wine,

2 pinches of salt,

2 small pinches of pepper;

Put in the sole, and pour over 3 gills of Italian Sauce (*vide* page 64); strew the top, thickly, with fine raspings; set boiling on the fire, for five minutes; then put in a moderate oven, for fifteen minutes; and serve, in the pan.

BAKED SOLE WITH WHITE WINE SAUCE

Prepare a large sole as in the preceding recipe; spread 1 oz. of butter in the *gratin*-pan; put in the sole; together with:

1 pint of French white wine,
2 pinches of salt,
2 small pinches of pepper;

Bake in the oven;

Put in a quart stewpan, 1 oz. of butter, and 1 oz. of flour; stir over the fire, for two minutes; then add: 1 pinch of salt, 1 small pinch of pepper; and 3 gills of water;

After twenty minutes' baking, pour the liquor from the sole into the sauce; boil one minute; add: 1 oz. of butter, and a tablespoonful of chopped parsley; stir the sauce off the fire, till the butter is melted;

Put the sole on a dish; pour over the sauce; and serve.

BAKED SOLE WITH FINES HERBES

Prepare a large sole as for Sole *au Gratin*; spread 1 oz. of butter in the *gratin*-pan;

Put in it, the sole; together with:

2 pinches of salt,   2 small pinches of pepper,
the juice of a lemon,   1 gill of water;

Bake in the oven;

Make some sauce in a stewpan, as in the preceding recipe;

After twenty minutes' baking, pour the liquor from the sole, into the sauce; add 2 oz. of butter, and a good tablespoonful of *fines herbes* (*vide* page 48); take the sauce off the fire; stir, till the butter is melted; put the sole on a dish; pour over the sauce; and serve.

FRIED SOLE

Take a large sole; remove the gills; cleanse the inside; strip off the black skin, and scrape the other side; wash, and wipe it; make an incision as directed for Sole *au Gratin* (*vide* page 148); steep it in milk, for ten minutes; then flour it well, on both sides, or else brush it over with egg, and bread-crumb it (*vide* Breading, page 74); put it in warm frying fat,—gradually acelerating the heat, till the sole is of an inviting golden colour; drain it on a cloth; sprinkle with salt; put it on a dish, on a napkin; garnish with fried parsley, and a lemon, cut in half

BURT, AU GRATIN, WITH FINES HERBES, WITH WHITE WINE, OR FRIED

Burt should be cleansed, scraped, the fins cut, washed, and prepared, in precisely the same way as Soles, either *au gratin*, with *fines herbes*, with white wine, or fried (*vide* pages 148 and 149).

BROILED MACKEREL À LA MAÎTRE D'HÔTEL

Remove the gills, and cleanse the inside, of a good-sized mackerel; cut off the end of the tail, and the fins; wipe, and clean it; split the back lengthwise to the bone; put it on a dish; season with 2 pinches of salt, 2 small pinches of pepper, and 2 tablespoonfuls of oil; put the mackerel on a gridiron, over a brisk fire for six minutes each side, and four minutes on the open back; place ½ lb. of *Maître d'Hôtel* Butter in the back; and serve, on a very hot dish.

SKATE WITH BROWN BUTTER

Take a white piece of skate; wash, and put it in a *sauté*-pan; cover it with water; add:

1 sliced onion, say 3 oz.,	2 gills of vinegar,
1 handful of parsley, say	1 oz. of salt,
1 oz.,	1 small pinch of pepper;

As soon as boiling commences, take off the fire, and simmer, very slowly, for ten minutes;

Put the liver of the skate into a quart stewpan; moisten, with some of the liquor of the skate; boil, for five minutes; and drain; drain also the skate; trim, and peel off the skin, from both sides; put the skate on a dish, with the liver; sprinkle with 2 pinches of salt, and 2 small pinches of pepper; garnish with a handful of fried parsley; pour over 1 pint of Brown Butter (*vide* page 63); and serve.

SKATE WITH CAPER SAUCE

Same preparation as for Skate with Brown Butter (*vide* preceding recipe); when boiled, and freed from skin, put it on a dish; pour over 1 pint of Melted Butter, with 2 tablespoonfuls of capers in it; and serve.

SALT COD WITH BUTTER AND POTATOES

Take a nice piece of salt fish, weighing about 2 lbs.; steep it, in tepid water, for six hours; and in cold water, for six hours more; changing the water four times;

Put the fish on the fire, in a 4-quart stewpan full of cold water, till it boils; then let it simmer, for five minutes; drain it well; put it on a dish; and pour over ½ lb. of butter melted, with the juice of a lemon in it; and garnish with 8 plain-boiled potatoes.

SALT COD WITH EGG SAUCE

Steep, and cook the salt fish, as in the preceding recipe;

Boil 2 eggs for ten minutes; cut them in large dice; mix them in a pint of Melted Butter (*vide* page 60);

Drain the fish; put it on a dish; pour over the sauce; and serve.

SALT COD À LA MAÎTRE D'HÔTEL

Prepare and cook the salt fish as before; when drained, put it on a dish, and pour over it ½ lb. of melted *Maître d'Hôtel* Butter; serve.

SALT COD WITH BROWN BUTTER

Steep, and cook the salt fish, as before; pour over 1 pint of Brown Butter, as directed for Skate (*vide* page 150); garnish with fried parsley; and serve.

WHITING AU GRATIN

Take 2 whiting, weighing about 1 lb. each; cleanse, scrape, wash, and wipe them; then score them on each side, to a depth of ¼ inch (*vide* woodcut, page 152).

Spread 4 oz. of butter in the *gratin*-pan; sprinkle in 2 pinches of salt, 2 small pinches of pepper, and 2 tablespoonfuls of raspings; put the whiting in; sprinkle again, with 1 pinch of salt, and 2 small pinches of pepper; add 1 gill of French white wine, and the liquor of a pottle of turned mushrooms; lay the mushrooms on the whiting; melt 1 oz. of butter, pour it on the mushrooms and whiting; sprinkle over with a tablespoonful of chopped parsley, and 2 tablespoonfuls of raspings; put in the oven, for fifteen minutes; they are then ready to serve.

SCORED WHITING

WHITING WITH CAPER SAUCE

Clean, and prepare 2 whiting, as in the preceding recipe; butter the *gratin*-pan; put in the whiting; season with 2 pinches of salt, 2 small pinches of pepper, and a gill of French white wine;

Bake in the oven for fifteen minutes;

Take 3 gills of Melted Butter; drain into it the liquor from the whiting; add 2 tablespoonfuls of capers; pour the sauce over the whiting; and serve.

FRIED WHITING

Clean, wash, and wipe 2 whiting; score them, as Whiting *au Gratin* (*vide* page 151); season with 1 pinch of salt, and 1 small pinch of pepper; dip them in a gill of milk; and flour them thickly; or brush over with egg, and bread-crumb them (*vide* Breading, page 74);

Fry the whiting in warm fat, for four minutes, and finish them in hot fat, for three minutes more.

By increasing the heat of the fat, fried things are rendered crisp, and of a good colour.

Drain the fish; sprinkle over them 2 pinches of salt; and dish them, on a napkin; garnish with fried parsley, and a lemon, cut in two; and serve.

WHITING WITH FINES HERBES, AND WHITING WITH WHITE WINE SAUCE

Same preparation as for Sole with *Fines Herbes*, and Sole with White Wine Sauce (*vide* page 149).

FRESH HERRINGS WITH MUSTARD SAUCE

Fresh herrings are only good when full of roe; when empty, they lose much of their quality.

Clean, scrape, cut off the fins, and wash 4 fresh herrings; score them in the same way as Whiting *au Gratin* (*vide* page 151); put them on a dish; and season them with 2 pinches of salt, 2 small pinches of pepper, and 2 tablespoonfuls of salad oil;

Broil them, on a brisk fire, for four minutes, each side; put on a dish; and serve.

Prepare 1 pint of Melted Butter; add 1 tablespoonful of mixed mustard with the finishing butter; stir; and serve in a boat.

FRIED HERRINGS

Prepare 4 herrings, as above; steep them in milk; and flour them thickly; or otherwise brush over with egg, and bread-crumb them (*vide* Breading, page 74); and fry as directed for Whiting (*vide* page 152).

Serve with them, in a boat, ½ lb. of *Maître d'Hôtel* Butter, slightly melted.

YARMOUTH BLOATERS

Take 2 bloaters; cut the heads and fins off; cut them open down the back; broil on a sharp fire for two minutes each side; and serve, on a very hot dish, with cold butter on a plate.

FRESH SARDINES

Clean, and wipe the sardines; put them on a gridiron; and broil, over a brisk fire, for two minutes, each side; sprinkle with salt; and serve, on a very hot dish, with a little butter melted.

SMELTS

Take 12 smelts; scrape, and wipe them; trim off the fins; pass a wooden or silver skewer through the cavity of the eyes, securing 6 smelts on one skewer; steep them in milk; and flour them well; or else brush over with egg and bread-crumb them (*vide* Breading, page 74).

Fry the smelts in the same way as whiting; when of a nice light brown colour, and crisp, they are done.

Drain, and sprinkle them with salt; dress them on a napkin, on a dish; garnish with fried parsley, and a lemon cut in two; and serve.

Smelts may also be fried singly, without skewers; in that case, pile them up on a dish, with fried parsley.

SMELTS AU GRATIN

Smelts are often served *au gratin*; the larger ones are preferable for this mode of dressing; proceed as for Sole *au Gratin* (*vide* page 148).

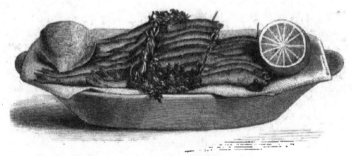

SMELTS ON SKEWERS

SHAD WITH SORREL, CAPER SAUCE, OR MAÎTRE D'HÔTEL BUTTER

Take a shad, weighing about 2 lbs.,—soft-roed, if possible;

Cleanse, scrape, wash, and score it, as directed for Herrings;

Steep it for an hour, in 4 tablespoonfuls of oil, seasoned with 4 pinches of salt, and 2 small pinches of pepper, turning the fish occasionally;

Broil, on a moderate fire, for eighteen minutes each side; and serve, either with 2 pints of *Purée* of Sorrel (*vide* page 57); 1½ pint of Caper Sauce, or ¾ lb. of *Maître d'Hôtel* Butter.

BOILED FLOUNDERS WITH DUTCH SAUCE, FLOUNDERS AU GRATIN OR FRIED

Take 2 good-sized flounders; remove the gills; cleanse, scrape, and wash them as said for Sole *au Gratin (vide* page 148);

Boil, in plenty of water, for fifteen minutes; adding 1½ oz. of salt to the water; drain, and serve, on a napkin, with 1 pint of Dutch Sauce, in a boat (*vide* page 62);

Flounders are also served *au gratin*; proceed as for Sole *au Gratin*.

For fried flounders, select the smallest, and fry them in the same way as Whiting (*vide* page 152); garnish with fried parsley, and a lemon cut in two.

BROILED RED MULLET À LA MAÎTRE D'HÔTEL

Take 4 red mullet; remove the gills only (red mullet are dressed with the inside left in); cut off the fins; scrape, and dip the fish in water, quickly, not to soak them; wipe, and score them in the same way as Whiting; put them on a dish, with: 3 tablespoonfuls of salad oil, 2 pinches of salt, 2 small pinches of pepper, 1 onion cut in thin slices, and a few sprigs of parsley, say 1 oz.; and steep them for half an hour; drain, and free them from onion and parsley; put them on the gridiron, over a sharp fire, for five minutes each side; serve, on a hot dish, with ½ lb. of *Maître d'Hôtel* Butter under them.

Red mullet are also served dressed with French white wine (*vide* Sole with French White Wine, page 149).

CONGER EEL WITH DUTCH SAUCE OR MELTED BUTTER

Take a piece of conger eel, weighing about 2 lbs.; cleanse it carefully; wash, and tie it together with string, in the same way as the meat for *pot-au-feu*; blanch in boiling water for ten minutes; drain, and put it in a 4-quart stewpan, covering the eel with water; add:

2 sliced onions, say 7 oz.,	2 gills of vinegar,
a handful of parsley, say 1 oz.,	1 clove of garlic,
	1 oz. of salt,
2 bay leaves,	½ oz. of whole pepper.;

Simmer, for half an hour; drain; and serve, on a napkin; garnish with fresh parsley.

Dutch Sauce, or Melted Butter, is served with it, in a boat.

BROILED SEA BREAM À LA MAÎTRE D'HÔTEL

Prepare similarly to Red Mullet; cleanse; broil; and serve, with *Maître d'Hôtel* Sauce, in a boat.

MUSSELS À LA POULETTE

Take 2 quarts of mussels,—the smallest are the most delicate; scrape the shells carefully, with a knife, and wash in water, changed several times, till perfectly free from grit;

Put 1 quart of the mussels in a *sauté*-pan; with:

1 sliced onion, say 4 oz.,
a few sprigs of parsley, say 1 oz.,
2 pinches of salt,
2 small pinches of pepper,
1 pint of French white wine;

Cover the *sauté*-pan; put it on the fire, and toss the mussels occasionally; when the shells open, the mussels are done; take them out of the *sauté*-pan, and take one shell off;

Put the second quart on the fire, and cook them in the same way.

I advise cooking only half the quantity at a time, as the mussels would not be done evenly, if too many were put in the pan at once.

Be careful not to let them be overdone, as this would shrink and harden them, and impair their quality.

Strain the liquor into a basin;

Put in a stewpan: 1 oz. of butter, and 1 oz. of flour; stir over the fire for three minutes; mix the liquor, and add enough water to produce a pint of sauce; thicken it with 2 yolks of egg, and $\frac{1}{2}$ oz. of butter; add 1 tablespoonful of chopped parsley;

Dip the mussels in plenty of hot water; drain them well, and wipe them.

Serve the mussels in their shells, pouring the sauce over them.

MUSSELS À LA MARINIÈRE

Prepare and cook the mussels, as in the preceding recipe; putting, however, ½ pint more wine for boiling them; that is, 1½ pint, instead of 1 pint. When the mussels are done, strain the liquor, through the pointed gravy strainer, into a stewpan;

Boil it; and add 3 oz. of butter, and a tablespoonful of chopped parsley; take off the fire, and stir till the butter is melted;

Drain, and wipe the mussels; put them on a dish, in their shells; pour the sauce over them; and serve;—½ oz. of well-washed and chopped shalot can also be added to the sauce, if the flavour is not objected to.

II

FRESH-WATER FISH

COURT BOUILLON, OR STOCK IN WHICH TO BOIL FISH

Court Bouillon is a highly seasoned stock, used to boil fresh-water fish, thereby redeeming its general tastelessness; it is prepared as follows:

Put in a gallon stewpan:

1 sliced carrot, say 4 oz.,	1 sprig of thyme,
1 sliced onion, say 4 oz.,	1 oz. of butter,
a handful of parsley, say 1 oz.,	1 oz. of salt,
	½ oz. of whole pepper;
2 bay leaves,	

Stir over the fire for ten minutes; add 2 quarts of water, and ½ pint of vinegar, and simmer for an hour on the stove corner; strain in a basin, and reserve till wanted.

Court Bouillon will keep a long time, if boiled every four days, adding 1 pint of water each time.

BOILED PIKE WITH CAPER SAUCE

Take a pike, weighing about 3 lbs.;—keeping it in the larder

for a couple of days will improve it; cleanse it, and cut off
the fins; tie the head with string;

Put the pike in the fish kettle, covered with *Court Bouillon*,
and simmer slowly for forty minutes.

If boiled the day before it is wanted, it will be much
improved; in any case, it should not be boiled later than the
morning of the day it is wanted.

Be sure that the kettle is well tinned, and after the pike is
cooked, let it still remain in the *Court Bouillon*; there is no
comparison in the quality of a pike thus left to soak for twenty-
four hours, and one which is only in the *Court Bouillon* for an
hour or two.

Before warming the pike, drain it, put the liquor in a basin,
and clean the kettle; then put the fish and liquor in again, and
warm for twenty minutes;

Dish up on a napkin, and garnish with fresh parsley; serve,
in a boat, 1 pint of Melted Butter, with 2 tablespoonfuls of capers
in it.

Observation.—Pike is also served cold, with *Mayonnaise* Sauce,
or oil and vinegar.

FRIED CARP

Take a carp, weighing about 1¾ lb.; remove the gills, and
scale it; slit the carp the whole length of the back, without
cutting quite through; remove the inside; reserve the roe.
Steep the carp and the roe in milk for five minutes; drain;
sprinkle with salt, and flour them well; fry in hot fat for eight
or ten minutes, till crisp, and of a pale brown colour; dish up
on a napkin; lay the roe on the carp; garnish with fried
parsley, and a lemon cut in two; and serve.

EEL WITH TARTAR SAUCE

Take an eel, weighing about 1½ lb.; skin, and clean it; steep
it in boiling water, for three minutes, to be able to rub off with
a cloth the second oily skin, which is indigestible; if this skin
does not come off easily, steep it a minute more; pare off
the fins from each side of the eel; cut it in pieces 3 inches long;
put them in a *sauté*-pan; cover with *Court Bouillon*, and simmer
for twenty minutes; when the eel is cooked, let it cool for
half an hour; then drain the pieces, on a cloth;

Break 2 eggs in a basin, with a tablespoonful of oil, and a tablespoonful of water; beat together with a fork, as for omelet; dip each piece of eel in the egg; bread-crumb them; and fry in hot fat, till of a nice light brown colour; dish up the pieces of eel on a napkin; garnish with fried parsley.

Serve with it 1 pint of Tartar Sauce (*vide* page 67), in a boat.

EEL AND CARP MATELOTE

Take an eel, and a carp, weighing about 1¼ lb. each; clean and scale the carp, and prepare the eel, as for Eel with Tartar Sauce (*vide* preceding recipe).

Cut both fish in pieces 2 inches long;

Put in a 3-quart stewpan: 2 oz. of butter, and 20 button onions, peeled and blanched; fry the onions till they are coloured; then dredge in 1½ oz. of flour; stir for ten minutes; and add:

1 quart of French red wine,	1 double faggot,
2 pinches of salt,	1 clove of garlic, whole;
2 small pinches of pepper,	

Simmer for ten minutes,—the stewpan closely covered; put in the pieces of eel, and boil gently for a quarter of an hour; then add the pieces of carp, and ½ gill of brandy, and simmer for ten minutes more; taste for seasoning, which should be full flavoured; take out the faggot, and garlic; put the pieces of fish on a dish; and garnish with the onions and sauce.

Observation.—This way of dressing a *matelote* appears to me the simplest and best; much superior to *Matelote à la Marinière*, in which the uncooked wine generally produces a disagreeable acid taste.

BROILED BARBEL WITH MAÎTRE D'HÔTEL BUTTER

Take two barbel, weighing about 1 lb. each; clean, scale, and wipe them carefully; score them in the same way as Whiting *au Gratin* (*vide* page 151); put them on a dish to steep, for half an hour, with 4 tablespoonfuls of oil, 3 pinches of salt, and 3 small pinches of pepper;

Broil them, on a moderate fire, for eight minutes each side; put them on a hot dish, with ½ lb. of *Maître d'Hôtel* Butter (*vide* page 62); and serve.

Barbel can also be dressed *en matelote*; proceed as for Eel and Carp *Matelote*.

STEWED TENCH WITH POULETTE SAUCE

Take about 1½ lb. of tench; remove the gills, and clean the tench; put them in boiling water, for three minutes, to facilitate skinning; wipe, and cut them in 2-inch pieces;

Put in a 3-quart stewpan: 2 oz. of butter, and 1½ oz. of flour; stir over the fire, for three minutes; add 1 quart of French white wine; boil for ten minutes, stirring all the time, with a wooden spoon;

Put the pieces of tench in the stewpan; add:

1 faggot,	3 pinches of salt,
1 clove of garlic, whole;	3 small pinches of pepper;

Simmer for fifteen minutes; thicken with 3 yolks of egg, and ½ oz. of butter (*vide Liaison* of Egg, page 59); take out the faggot, and garlic; taste the seasoning; add a tablespoonful of chopped parsley; pile the pieces of tench on a dish; pour the sauce over; and serve.

STEWED PERCH WITH WHITE WINE

Take 3 middle-sized perch; remove the gills; scale and clean them;

Put them in a *sauté*-pan; and cover them entirely, with 1 quart of French white wine; add:

2 pinches of salt,	1 faggot,
2 small pinches of pepper,	1 clove of garlic, whole;
1 sliced onion,	

Simmer for fifteen minutes; ascertain whether the fish is sufficiently cooked, by pressing it with the finger; if done, it will give way to the touch; drain it on a dish, and put the liquor in a basin;

Put in a *sauté*-pan 1 oz. of butter, and 1 oz. of flour; stir over the fire for three minutes; strain the liquor, through the pointed strainer, into the *sauté*-pan; put it on the fire; stir; and reduce for twenty minutes;

Skin the perch, reserving the fins; put the fish, side by side, on a dish; add 1 tablespoonful of chopped parsley, and $\frac{1}{2}$ oz. of butter to the sauce; stir till the butter is melted; pour the sauce over the fish, and replace the fins at each side of the perch, without the sauce covering them; and serve.

FRIED GUDGEON

Take 24 live gudgeon (indeed, all fresh-water fish should be used as soon as possible after taking out of the water); cut off the gills, and remove the inside by means of a small incision in the side; clean, and wipe them well; steep them in milk; flour them well, and fry in hot fat till they are crisp, and of a nice light brown colour; serve on a dish, on a napkin, with fried parsley.

CRAYFISH

There are several kinds of crayfish; those which are of a reddish tinge under the claws are considered the best.

STAND FOR DISHING CRAYFISH

Take 25 crayfish ; wash them well, and put them in a 3-quart stewpan, with :

1 sliced onion,	2 pinches of salt,
a handful of parsley (say 1 oz.),	4 small pinches of pepper,
	1 gill of French red wine

Cover the stewpan ; put it on a very brisk fire ; boil for ten minutes, tossing the crayfish three times ; when done, they should be of a bright red colour ; take out the onion and parsley ; drain the crayfish, and dish them up on a napkin in the shape of a pyramid ; garnish with fresh parsley.

CRAYFISH

VEGETABLES

CHAPTER XIV

VEGETABLES

As an invariable rule, vegetables intended for boiling should previously be well washed.

ASPARAGUS WITH MELTED BUTTER

Asparagus is in season in April and May; it should be chosen with fresh purple points, and white stalks.

Cut $\frac{1}{16}$ of an inch off the points, and scrape the asparagus all along, holding the knife in a slanting position; then throw the asparagus into cold water; tie in bundles of 8 or 10, according to size.

Have a large saucepan of boiling water; add $\frac{1}{4}$ oz. of salt for each quart of water; put the asparagus in, and boil for ten minutes; when done take it out; dip in cold water, and drain immediately; dish up on a napkin, keeping the points very even; serve with a boat of Melted Butter or Dutch Sauce.

Observation.—As soon as the asparagus is done, which is

Y 2

ascertained by pressing with the fingers, take it out of the water at once,—else it will become flabby and spongy.

All boiled vegetables allowed to remain in water after cooking will be spoilt in the same way.

ASPARAGUS WITH OIL AND VINEGAR

After boiling as above, let the asparagus get thoroughly cold; dish it up, on a napkin; and serve with it a seasoning of pepper and salt, oil and vinegar, in a boat.

ASPARAGUS PEAS

Take a bundle of green asparagus; when cut, it should produce 1½ pint of peas;

Clear the points and stalks of small leaves; break the asparagus, and cut it in pieces ¼ inch long; if very large, slit the asparagus in two;

Boil the peas in an untinned 2-quart stewpan, full of salted boiling water (¼ oz. of salt to a quart of water); when done, drain on a cloth; put the peas in a *sauté*-pan, with:

> 2 gills of Melted Butter,
> 1 teaspoonful of pounded sugar,
> 1 pinch of salt;

Thicken with 2 yolks of egg, 1 oz. of butter, and ½ gill of cream; toss over the fire till the butter is melted; put in a dish; and serve.

ARTICHOKES WITH MELTED BUTTER

Artichokes are in season from May to October.

Take 4 good artichokes, fresh cut and young; cut ½ inch off the top of each artichoke, and a few leaves off the bottom, and turn the latter with a knife, in the same way as directed for Turned Mushrooms (*vide* page 47).

Wash and boil the artichokes in plenty of salted water,—¼ oz. of salt to 1 quart of water.

To ascertain if done, try them with the trussing needle,—it should enter easily;

Drain the artichokes, and take the inside out with a spoon; dish on a napkin; and serve, with 1 pint of Melted Butter in a boat.

Artichokes are also served cold, with oil and vinegar, in the same way as asparagus.

ARTICHOKES À LA BARIGOULE

Prepare and blanch 4 artichokes, as in the preceding recipe; take out the inside; squeeze the water out; and season them with 1 pinch of salt, and 1 small pinch of pepper;

Put 6 tablespoonfuls of oil in the frying-pan, and fry the top of the leaves;

Prepare 1 gill of *fines herbes*, as for sauce (*vide* page 48).

Put in a quart stewpan:

4 oz. of grated bacon,	1 gill of broth,
½ oz. of butter,	the gill of *fines herbes*;
¼ oz. of flour,	

Stir over the fire for five minutes; put a fourth part of this stuffing in each artichoke; place a thin slice of bacon, 2 inches square, on the top of each; tie round with string, to keep them in shape; put them in a *sauté*-pan, with 2 gills of broth; bake in the oven for twenty minutes; ascertain if done; dish up; and serve.

FRIED ARTICHOKES

Take 2 artichokes, fresh cut, and young;

Cut off the top of the leaves; pare off the large leaves at the bottom; turn the artichokes in the same way as Artichokes with Melted Butter (*vide* page 164); cut them lengthwise, in slices ¼ inch thick; take out the inside, close to the bottom; throw the pieces in cold water, with a little vinegar in it, to keep them white; when all are cut, drain, and put them in a basin; sprinkle them with 1 pinch of salt, and 1 small pinch of pepper; break 3 eggs on to the artichokes, and add 3 tablespoonfuls of oil, and 3 oz. of flour; mix the whole with the hand, till all the pieces are well pasted over; if the batter be too thin, add a little flour; if too thick, sprinkle in a few drops of water, and mix as before, till the pieces of artichoke are evenly coated;

Warm the frying fat; ascertain the degree of heat with a piece of bread-crumb (*vide* Frying, page 74); it must only produce a slight fizzing; put each piece of artichoke into the fat, which must not be too hot, as the artichoke should not brown until it is cooked; drain on a wire sieve; sprinkle with salt; dish up on a napkin; garnish with fried parsley; and serve.

STEWED PEAS

Take 1 quart of fine peas, fresh shelled; put them in a 2-quart stewpan, with:

4 oz. of butter,	1 pinch of salt,
1 gill of water,	1 oz. of lump sugar;
3 green onions, say 2 oz.,	

Some add parsley, but I do not advise it, as its strong flavour destroys the fresh taste of the peas;

Close the stewpan, and boil the peas, on a slow fire, for thirty minutes; when done, add ¾ oz. of flour, mixed to a smooth paste, with 4 oz. of butter; toss the stewpan till the butter is melted, and the peas properly thickened; taste, and, if wanted, add a little salt or sugar; and serve.

When preserved peas are used, open the boxes; throw the peas in boiling water; drain, season, and finish, as with fresh peas.

BOILED PEAS

Put 2 quarts of water, with ¼ oz. of salt in it, in a 3-quart stewpan, on the fire; when it boils, pour in a quart of fresh shelled peas; boil quickly, and when done, drain, and put them in a *sauté*-pan with 3 oz. of butter; sprinkle with a little salt; toss them, till the butter is melted; and serve.

Observation.—1 oz. of green mint may be added to the water in which the peas are boiled.

STEWED PEAS WITH BACON

Take ¼ lb. of streaky bacon; remove the rind, and cut the bacon in pieces 1 inch long, ½ inch thick; blanch, for five minutes, in boiling water; drain, and put them in a 2-quart stewpan, with 1 oz. of butter; fry for five minutes; add ½ oz. of flour, and stir for four minutes; then add 1 pint of water, 1 quart of fine peas, and a green onion; when boiling, cover the stewpan, and simmer for half an hour;

Taste for seasoning; take out the onion; skim off the fat; and serve.

WHITE HARICOT BEANS À LA MAÎTRE D'HÔTEL

Haricot beans are in season from the beginning of July to the middle of October.

Take 1 quart of fresh shelled, white, haricot beans ;

Boil 3 quarts of water, with 3 pinches of salt, in a gallon stew-pan ; when boiling, throw in the beans, and boil gently till they are done, which can be ascertained by pressing one between the fingers ; drain, and put them back into the stewpan ; mix ½ oz. of flour with 1 oz. of butter, to a smooth paste ; divide it in small pieces, and add these to the beans, with :

2 pinches of salt,
1 small pinch of pepper,
1 tablespoonful of chopped parsley,
½ gill of the liquor in which the beans have been boiled ;

Toss the beans, till the thickening is well mixed ; and serve.

DRIED WHITE HARICOT BEANS

Wash 1 quart of dried, white, haricot beans ; put them in a stewpan, with 3 quarts of cold water, and a tablespoonful of salt ; set on the fire ; and, when boiling, put them to simmer, in the closed stewpan, on the stove corner, till tender ; drain, and put them back in the stewpan ; with :

4 oz. of butter,
1 tablespoonful of chopped parsley,
2 pinches of salt,
1 small pinch of pepper,
½ gill of the liquor of the beans ;

Toss the beans, till the butter is melted ; and serve.

Haricot beans are also served as a salad : let them get cold ; put them in salad bowl ; and season with oil, vinegar, pepper, and salt, and a tablespoonful of chervil and tarragon, chopped fine.

STEWED RED HARICOT BEANS

Take 1 quart of red haricot beans ; boil them, as in the preceding recipe ; take ½ lb. of streaky bacon ; remove the rind, and cut the bacon in pieces, 1 inch long, ½ inch thick ; blanch, for five minutes, in boiling water ; drain the bacon, and put it in a 2-quart stewpan ; stir over the fire, till of a light brown colour ; add ½ oz. of flour ; stir for three minutes more ; then add :

3 gills of French red wine,
2 gills of water,
2 small pinches of pepper ;

Simmer for twenty-five minutes; drain the beans, and put them in the stewpan; add 1 oz. of butter; toss, till the butter is melted; and serve.

FRENCH BEANS À LA POULETTE

Pick 1 lb. of French beans; put them in a gallon stewpan, with 3 quarts of boiling water, and 1 pinch of salt; and boil till tender;

Put in a 2-quart stewpan 1 oz. of butter, and ½ oz. of flour; stir over the fire, for three minutes; and add 3 gills of water, and 1 pinch of salt; boil for ten minutes; thicken with 2 yolks of egg, and ½ oz. of butter (*vide* Thickening with Egg, page 59); drain the beans; put them in the sauce, with half a table spoonful of chopped parsley; mix; and serve.

Observation.—To ensure beans retaining their colour, always boil them on a sharp fire, with plenty of water, in an uncovered stewpan, with the small quantity of salt indicated.

FRENCH BEANS SAUTÉS

Take 1 lb. of French beans; pick and boil them as in the preceding article;

Put in a *sauté*-pan 2 oz. of butter, and melt it over the fire; add the beans, well drained; and toss them, over a brisk fire, for eight minutes; add:

1 small pinch of salt,
½ tablespoonful of chopped parsley,
1 teaspoonful of lemon-juice;

Mix well; and serve.

PLAIN-BOILED FRENCH BEANS

Pick 1 lb. of French beans; cut them in pieces, lengthwise; and boil them, in the same way as French Beans *à la Poulette* (*vide* above);

Drain them; sprinkle with salt; put them on a dish; and serve.

LENTILS À LA MAÎTRE D'HÔTEL

Wash 1 quart of lentils; boil them gently, in 3 quarts of water, with a tablespoonful of salt; when done, drain, and put them in a *sauté*-pan, with ½ lb. of *Maître d'Hôtel* Butter, and ½ gill of the liquor in which they have been boiled; toss them well, till the butter is melted; and serve.

POTATOES WITH MILK

Wash, and boil, 2 lbs. of Dutch or French-kidney potatoes, in 2 quarts of water, with 1 pinch of salt;

Boil gently,—to prevent their breaking; when done, drain, peel, and cut them in slices, ¼ inch thick;

Put them in a 2-quart stewpan, with 1 pint of milk; simmer for ten minutes; then add 1½ oz. of butter, cut in six pieces; and 1 pinch of salt; toss, till the butter is well melted; and serve.

POTATOES À LA MAÎTRE D'HÔTEL

Boil, and cut the potatoes, as in the preceding recipe; put them in a stewpan, with ½ lb. of *Maître d'Hôtel* Butter; and ½ pint of broth, or water; mix well; and serve.

CAULIFLOWERS WITH MELTED BUTTER

Pick, wash, and boil, 2 cauliflowers, as directed for Cauliflowers for Garnish (*vide* page 54); drain; put on a dish; and pour over 1 pint of Melted Butter (*vide* page 60).

CAULIFLOWERS AU GRATIN

Prepare and boil the cauliflowers, as in the preceding recipe; make a sauce as follows:

Put in a 2-quart stewpan 1 oz. of butter, and 1¼ oz. of flour; stir over the fire to make a *roux*; add:

1½ pint of water,
2 pinches of salt,
3 small pinches of pepper;

Boil for ten minutes, stirring all the time; then put in the sauce, 1 oz. of grated Gruyère cheese, and 1 oz. of grated Parmesan cheese; reduce five minutes more;

Cut the cauliflowers in pieces, and put a layer of them, at the bottom of a vegetable dish; then, a layer of sauce; pile up the remaining cauliflowers on the top, and cover with the sauce;

z

sprinkle over 1 oz. of grated Parmesan cheese, and a tablespoonful of raspings; baste with ¾ oz. of butter, melted; put the
dish in the oven, for fifteen minutes; salamander the top to a
light brown colour; and serve.

BRUSSELS SPROUTS SAUTÉS WITH BUTTER

Pick, and boil, 1 lb. of Brussels sprouts, as directed at the
Chapter on Garnishes (*vide* page 55); drain them on a cloth;
put them in a *sauté*-pan, with 1½ oz. of butter, and 1 small pinch
of salt; toss them, over a sharp fire, for eight minutes; add a
tablespoonful of chopped parsley; mix; and serve.

MUSHROOMS AU GRATIN

Take 12 large mushrooms, about 2 inches diameter; pare the
stalks; wash, and drain the mushrooms on a cloth; cut off and
chop the stalks;

Put in a quart stewpan 1 oz. of butter, and ½ oz. of flour;
stir over the fire for two minutes; then add 1 pint of broth; stir,
till reduced to half the quantity;

Drain the chopped stalks of the mushrooms thoroughly in a
cloth; put them in the sauce with:

    3 tablespoonfuls of chopped, and washed, parsley,
    1 tablespoonful of chopped, and washed, shalot,
    2 pinches of salt,
    1 small pinch of pepper;

Reduce, on a brisk fire, for eight minutes;

Put 2 tablespoonfuls of oil in a *sauté*-pan; set the mushrooms
in, the hollow part upwards; fill them with the *fines herbes*; and
sprinkle over them, lightly, a tablespoonful of raspings; put in a
brisk oven, for ten minutes; and serve.

MUSHROOMS À LA POULETTE

Turn, and prepare 2 pottles of mushrooms, as described for
Garnish (*vide* page 47);

Mix ½ oz. of flour, with 1 gill of water; strain, through the
pointed gravy strainer, and pour into the stewpan containing the
mushrooms; stirring all the time,—to prevent lumping; thicken
with 2 yolks of egg, and ½ oz. of butter (*vide* Thickening with
Egg, page 59); mix well; and serve.

TOMATOES AU GRATIN

Take 8 tomatoes, 2 inches diameter; pare off the skin round the stalk, and make an opening, 1 inch diameter, in the tomatoes, to allow of taking out the seeds, with the handle of a teaspoon; season with 2 pinches of salt, and 2 small pinches of pepper;

Prepare some *fines herbes* stuffing, as for Mushrooms *au Gratin* (*vide* page 170); fill the hollow in each tomato with it;

Put 2 tablespoonfuls of oil in a *sauté*-pan; set the tomatoes in it; sprinkle over half a tablespoonful of raspings; put in a brisk oven, for eight minutes; dish up; and serve.

SPINACH

Pick, wash, blanch, and chop, 2 lbs. of spinach, as described for Garnish (*vide* page 55);

Put in a 3-quart stewpan:

    1 oz. of butter,
    $\frac{3}{4}$ oz. of flour,
    1 pinch of salt;

Stir over the fire for three minutes; put in the spinach, and stir well for five minutes; moisten with 1 gill of broth; stir for two minutes; then add 2 more gills of broth, stirring for five minutes more;

Take the spinach off the fire; add 1 oz. of butter; stir till it is well melted and mixed, and put the spinach on a dish;

Prepare some *croutons* in the following way:

Take a slice of crumb of bread $\frac{1}{2}$ inch thick; cut it in $1\frac{1}{2}$ inch triangular pieces; melt 1 oz. of butter in a small stewpan; skim it, when melted; put in the pieces of bread; fry and toss them, till of a light brown colour; drain, and place them round the spinach; and serve.

Milk may be used, instead of broth, in the preparation of spinach.

SPINACH WITH SUGAR

The spinach is prepared as above,—using milk instead of broth; and adding $\frac{1}{2}$ oz. of pounded sugar.

ENDIVE WITH GRAVY

Take 12 heads of endive; wash, blanch, and chop them, as directed for garnish (*vide* page 56);

Put in a 2-quart stewpan 1 oz. of butter, and ½ oz. of flour; stir over the fire for two minutes; put in the endive, and stir for five minutes; add 1 pint of Household Gravy (*vide* page 68); simmer for half an hour, stirring occasionally; take off the fire; add 1 oz. of butter; and, when it is melted, dish up the endive, and garnish with *croutons* in the same way as spinach.

Milk may also be substituted for Household Gravy, as in the preparation of spinach.

SALSIFY WITH MELTED BUTTER

Take 4 lbs. of salsify;—the leaves should be very fresh, and the root black and firm; cut off the roots, and scrape them to remove the black skin entirely; throw them in a large basin of cold water, with a little vinegar in it;

Put in a 3-quart stewpan ½ lb. of beef suet, chopped fine; melt it over a slow fire, without colouring it; add:

2 quarts of water,
2 pinches of salt,
2 tablespoonfuls of vinegar;

Stir over the fire till boiling takes place; add the salsify, previously cut in pieces 2½ inches long, and simmer for half an hour, —the stewpan not quite closed; drain them well, and put them in a 2-quart stewpan with 1 pint of Melted Butter; mix; and serve.

FRIED SALSIFY

Take 4 lbs. of salsify; prepare, boil, and cut it in pieces as above;

Make 1 pint of frying batter (*vide* Frying Batter, page 74);

Warm 2 lbs. of frying fat; drain the salsify; dip each piece in the batter; and fry them till they are crisp, and of a light brown colour; drain them on a cloth; sprinkle with salt; dish up on a napkin; garnish with fried parsley; and serve.

CUCUMBERS À LA POULETTE

Take 3 middle-sized cucumbers; cut them lengthwise into quarters; remove the seeds, and peel off the outside skin; then

cut them in pieces, 2 inches long, and 1 inch thick; put these in
a 3-quart stewpan, with :

    2 quarts of water,
    1 oz. of butter,
    2 pinches of salt;

Simmer till tender, which can be ascertained with the trussing
needle,—if done, it should enter easily ;

Drain on a cloth ;

Make a pint of *Poulette* Sauce ; put the cucumber in it ; and
serve.

CELERY WITH GRAVY

Take 6 heads of fresh celery ; cut off the tops, leaving each
head 6 inches long ; trim the outside leaves, and cut the roots to
a point ; wash, then blanch them for ten minutes, in boiling
water ; cool, and wash them again carefully ; tie the heads
together in two bundles ; and put them in a stewpan with :

3 gills of broth,	1 small carrot, say 2 oz.,
2 gills of water,	1 small onion, say 2 oz.,
1 gill of stock-pot fat, or	1 pinch of salt,
clean dripping,	1 small pinch of pepper ;
1 faggot,	

Put a round of paper over the whole, and close the stewpan ;
simmer for two hours ; when done, drain, and put the celery on
a dish,—3 heads at the bottom, then 2, then 1.

Prepare a sauce as follows : put 1 oz. of butter and 1 oz. of
flour in a stewpan ; stir over the fire for three minutes ; add $1\frac{1}{2}$
pint of Household Gravy (*vide* page 68) ; stir till reduced to 1
pint ; strain through the pointed strainer ; pour over the celery ;
and serve.

CABBAGE LETTUCES WITH GRAVY

Take 8 round and full cabbage-lettuces ; trim off all the
outside leaves ; wash and blanch for ten minutes ; cool them
well ; squeeze the water out ; cut them in two, lay them open
on a dish ; and season them with 3 pinches of salt ; tie the
halves together, and put in a 2-quart stewpan ; cover them with
broth ; and add 2 gills of stock-pot fat, 1 faggot, and 1 onion
with 2 cloves stuck in it ; place a round of paper on the top ;
and simmer for two hours ; when cooked, drain on a cloth ;
untie, and open the lettuces again ; cut the stalks out, and fold

the leaves round, giving to each piece an oval shape, about 3 inches by 2; and dish them up in a circle;

Reduce 1½ pint of Household Gravy to half the quantity; pour it over the lettuces; and serve.

Thin slices of crumb of bread, cut to the shape of the lettuces, and fried in butter, can be put between each lettuce.

CARROTS À LA FLAMANDE

Young carrots alone are prepared thus, say from May to September.

Blanch 1½ lb. of carrots, in boiling water, for five minutes; cool them; and rub off the skin with a cloth; cut them in slices ⅛ inch thick; and put them in a 2-quart stewpan, with:

½ gill of water,	1 pinch of salt,
1 oz. of butter,	1 small pinch of sugar;

Close the stewpan, and simmer for twenty minutes, tossing them occasionally, to ensure an even cooking; when the carrots are done, thicken with 2 yolks of egg, ½ gill of cream, and ½ oz. of butter (*vide* Thickening with Egg, page 59);

Add ½ a tablespoonful of chopped parsley; mix; and serve.

GLAZED TURNIPS WITH GRAVY

Turn 24 turnips to a ball-shape, about 2 inches diameter; blanch them, in boiling water, for five minutes; drain, and put them in the frying-pan with ½ oz. of butter; fry till of a brown colour; drain them from the butter, and put them in a *sauté*-pan with 1½ pint of Household Gravy (*vide* page 68); and 1 pinch of sugar; simmer till the turnips are quite done, which can be ascertained by trying them with the trussing needle; put them on a dish; and pour over the gravy.

CARDOONS

Cardoons will be treated of with full details in the Second Part of the book;—the richness of the seasoning they require renders them unsuitable for domestic cookery.

BROAD BEANS À LA POULETTE

Take 1 quart of small broad beans; pick, wash, and boil them in 3 quarts of boiling water, with a pinch of salt in it; when done, drain them;

Put in a 2-quart stewpan ¼ oz. of butter, and ½ oz. of flour; stir over the fire for three minutes; then thicken with 2 yolks of egg, ½ gill of cream, and ½ oz. of butter (*vide* Thickening with Egg, page 59);

Put the beans in the sauce; add a small pinch of pounded sugar, and a teaspoonful of chopped winter savory; mix; and serve.

MACÉDOINE OF VEGETABLES

Take :

　¼ lb. of carrots, cut in ¼ inch squares,
　3 oz. of turnips, cut in the same way,
　¼ lb. of asparagus peas,
　¼ lb. of peas, and
　¼ lb. of French beans, also cut in squares;

Blanch and boil all these vegetables separately, in plenty of water, with a little salt in it; when done, drain them on a cloth;

Make a *roux*, in a 2-quart stewpan, with 1 oz. of butter, and ½ oz. of flour; add ½ pint of broth, 2 pinches of salt, and 2 small pinches of sugar; boil for ten minutes; thicken with 2 yolks of egg, and 1 gill of cream;

Put all the vegetables in the sauce; mix carefully, so as not to mash them; and serve.

VEGETABLE SALAD

Cut, blanch, and boil the same vegetables, as in the preceding recipe;

When perfectly cold, put the French beans at the bottom of a deep vegetable dish; and arrange the other vegetables round the dish, according to colour, in the following regular order, and in equal quantities :

first, some of the carrots ;　　again, some of the carrots ;
then, some of the peas ;　　then, some of the peas ;
next, some of the turnips ;　　next, some of the turnips ;
and, some of the asparagus　　finishing, with some of the
　peas ;　　　　　　　　　　asparagus peas ;

Put the remainder of the vegetables in the centre, and sprinkle a tablespoonful of chopped *ravigote* on the top ; serve with the cruet.

ARTICHOKE

FANCY EGG DISH

CHAPTER XV

EGGS

BOILED EGGS

Take 6 new-laid eggs; put 3 pints of water in a 2-quart stewpan; when the water boils, put in the eggs; cover the stewpan; boil for one minute; take off the fire, and let the eggs remain in the water for five minutes; take them out of the water; and serve them in a napkin.

EGGS ON THE DISH

Spread 1 oz. of butter on a round tinned-iron dish; sprinkle with half a pinch of salt, and a small pinch of pepper;

Break 6 new-laid eggs in the dish; sprinkle over another half pinch of salt, and 2 small pinches of pepper; put on the stove with live coals on the glazing cover; cook for four minutes; —when the whites are set, the eggs are done;

Serve in the dish in which they have been cooked.

EGGS WITH BROWN BUTTER

Break 6 eggs in a plate; sprinkle over 1 pinch of salt, and 3 small pinches of pepper;

Put ¼ lb. of butter in the frying-pan; let it remain on the fire till the butter becomes brown; then pour it over the eggs in the plate, and pour the whole back into the pan; fry for two minutes; toss like a pancake; and fry for half a minute more; put the eggs on a dish;

Reduce 2 tablespoonfuls of vinegar to half the quantity; pour over the eggs; and serve.

EGGS BROUILLÉS AUX FINES HERBES

Put ¼ lb. of butter in a 2-quart stewpan; break in 6 new-laid eggs; add ½ gill of milk, 1 small pinch of salt, and 1 small pinch of pepper;

Put on the fire, and work briskly with a wire whisk; when the eggs begin to set, take the stewpan off the fire, and keep stirring for two minutes; then add half a tablespoonful of chopped parsley; put the eggs on a dish, and garnish with fried *croutons*, as for spinach (*vide* page 171).

Observation.—Complaints are sometimes made of non-success in this preparation; this arises either from the eggs being too much done, or from their not being properly worked; it is necessary to stir with the whisk in all parts of the stewpan, to avoid having the egg more set in some places than in others.

EGGS BROUILLÉS AU FROMAGE

Prepare the eggs as in the preceding recipe, adding with the butter 2 oz. of grated Parmesan cheese;

Cook as before; and serve.

Observation.—Peas and asparagus peas are also served with eggs *brouillés*; they are added when the eggs are set, before turning out on the dish.

FRIED EGGS WITH TOMATO SAUCE

Put 3 tablespoonfuls of oil in a *sauté*-pan; tilt it up, on the corner of the stove, to collect all the oil in one place, and hold the pan over a sharp fire; when the oil is hot, break 1 egg in it; season with a little salt, and pepper; with two spoons, gather the white of the egg over the yolk, so as to form a ball; turn over, and drain it immediately;

Fry separately, in the same way, as many eggs as may be required;—the yolks should not be set.

Sprinkle with pepper, and salt; put on a dish; and serve, with 3 gills of Tomato Sauce (*vide* page 66).

POACHED EGGS WITH GRAVY, SORREL, OR ENDIVE

Put 1 quart of water in a *sauté*-pan; add 1 pinch of salt, and ½ gill of vinegar; when boiling, break 6 new-laid eggs into the *sauté*-pan, and put the cover on;

Take the *sauté*-pan off the fire after a minute;

When the whites of the eggs are set round the yolks, take them out with a skimmer, and put them into a basin of luke-warm water, for ten minutes; drain them, and trim off any ragged pieces of white, so as to give them an oval shape; put the eggs on a dish;

Reduce 6 gills of Household Gravy (*vide* page 68) to 3 gills, and pour it over the eggs; sprinkle each with a small pinch of *mignonnette* pepper.

Poached eggs are also served on a layer of endive, spinach, or sorrel (*vide* Garnishes, pages 55, 56, 57).

HARD-BOILED EGGS WITH SORREL

Put 6 eggs in boiling water, and boil for ten minutes.

This time should not be exceeded, otherwise, the yolks would become of a bad colour.

Put the eggs in cold water; when cold, shell them; wash them clean, and cut each in two, lengthwise.

Put 1½ pint of sorrel, prepared for garnish (*vide* page 57), on a dish; lay the pieces of egg on it; and serve.

HARD-BOILED EGGS WITH ONIONS

Pick, and peel 3 onions, say 10 oz.; cut them in two, then lay each half on the board, and cut it in slices ⅛ inch thick; blanch in boiling water, for five minutes, and drain the onion on a cloth;

Put 1½ oz. of butter in a 2-quart stewpan ; put the onions in, and stir over the fire till they are brown ; add :

1 oz. of flour,	1 pinch of salt,
1½ pint of broth,	1 small pinch of pepper ;

Stir, over a slow fire, for twenty minutes ;

Take 6 hard-boiled eggs ; cut them in thin slices ; mix them with the onion ; taste for seasoning ; and serve.

OMELET WITH FINES HERBES

Omelet is another of those simple and elementary prepara-tions which often meet with failure, owing to carelessness, or want of knowledge of the exact principles which ensure success. It is a useful and pleasant dish, when prepared properly.

Break 6 eggs in a basin ; add 2 pinches of salt, 2 small pinches of pepper, and half a tablespoonful of chopped parsley ;

Beat the eggs with a fork, for about a minute, to mix them well, but not to render them too liquid,—as this would prevent making the omelet properly ;

Ascertain if the omelet-pan is perfectly free from rust or dirt. I will here remark again, that a pan should be reserved specially for omelets.

Put 3 oz. of butter in the omelet-pan, on a sharp fire ; stir, to melt the butter, without burning it ; when hot, pour in the eggs, and keep detaching the flakes of egg, from the sides of the pan, with a fork ; when half set, toss the omelet, and continue stirring over the fire, till all the egg is set ; then fold over both sides of the omelet, to give it an oval shape ; keep on the fire till it assumes a bright golden colour ; turn over, on to a dish ; and serve.

Remarks on Omelets.

Success in the preparation of omelet depends upon three points ;—should they not be attended to, failure will result :—

Firstly,—Never use more than 12 eggs for 1 omelet ; it is better, if a larger quantity be required, to make several small ones, rather than attempt a large one, which it would be most difficult to cook satisfactorily.

Secondly,—Never use any but the proper omelet-pan ; this is also an essential condition of success.

Lastly,—Never overbeat the eggs ; by so doing, nothing is

gained, and a watery mixture is produced, which would destroy the taste and appearance of the omelet.

OMELET WITH BACON

Blanch ¼ lb. of streaky bacon, for five minutes, in boiling water; cool, and wipe it, and take off the rind;

Cut the bacon in pieces 1 inch long, ½ inch thick; put ½ oz. of butter in a *sauté*-pan, and fry the pieces of bacon, till of a yellow colour; add them to 6 eggs, beaten in a basin, as for Omelet with *Fines Herbes* (*vide* preceding recipe); add 1 pinch of salt, and 1 small pinch of pepper; pour the eggs and bacon into the omelet-pan, and finish in the same way as Omelet with *Fines Herbes*.

OMELET WITH HAM

Take ¼ lb. of boiled ham; cut it in ¼ inch dice; add the ham to the eggs, together with 1 pinch of salt, and 2 small pinches of pepper; and finish the omelet as described before.

OMELET WITH MUSHROOMS

Take half a pottle of mushrooms, prepared as Stewed Mushrooms (*vide* Garnishes, page 49); proceed as for omelet with *fines herbes*; put the mushrooms in the centre of the omelet; enclose them, when folding over the sides; and serve.

OMELET WITH KIDNEY

Prepare three sheeps' kidneys, as directed for Kidneys *Sautés* (*vide* page 115); put them in the centre of the omelet; and finish it as above

OMELET WITH SORREL

Take ½ pint of sorrel; prepared and seasoned, as indicated for garnish (*vide* page 57); put the sorrel in the middle of the omelet; and serve.

OMELET WITH CHEESE

Take 1 oz. of Gruyère cheese, cut in ¼ inch dice, and 1 oz. of grated Parmesan cheese;

Prepare the eggs as for Omelet with *Fines Herbes*, omitting the parsley; season with 1 pinch of salt, and 3 small pinches of pepper; put the grated Parmesan cheese in the beaten eggs; fry the omelet; and, before folding it, strew the pieces of Gruyère cheese on it; fold over the sides; and serve.

BOILED EGGS

PASTES

CHAPTER XVI

PASTES

MACCARONI À L'ITALIENNE

PUT in a 2-quart stewpan, 3 pints of boiling water; add 6 oz. of good maccaroni,—its quality is shown by its smoothness, its transparent yellow colour, and by the fineness and closeness of its grain when broken; season with 1 pinch of salt, and 2 small pinches of pepper; simmer for twenty minutes; drain it well, and put it back into the stewpan, with ½ pint of broth; simmer again, till all the broth is absorbed;

Grate 2 oz. of Parmesan cheese, and 2 oz. of Gruyère cheese; put half of these quantities in the stewpan; mix with the maccaroni by shaking the stewpan, and tossing it; when mixed, add the remainder of the cheese, and 1 oz. of butter; keep tossing till the cheese is well melted, and the maccaroni stringy.

Should the cheese become oily, which it may do, from want of moisture, add 1 more gill of broth, and stir over the fire for one minute.

Milk may be substituted for broth, in the preparation of maccaroni.

MACCARONI AU GRATIN

Prepare the maccaroni as in the preceding recipe ; butter a *gratin*-pan ; dish up the maccaroni in it, in the shape of a dome ; sprinkle over 1 oz. of grated Parmesan cheese, and half a table-spoonful of raspings ; pour over ½ oz. of butter, melted ;

Put the maccaroni in the oven, till it assumes a nice golden colour ; and serve in the *gratin*-pan.

If the oven be not hot enough to colour the maccaroni properly, finish it with the salamander.

MACCARONI AU GRATIN

NOUILLES WITH HAM

To make *nouilles* paste, proceed as follows :

Take ½ lb. of sifted flour ; put it on the pasteboard ; make a hole in the centre of the flour ; break 3 eggs in it ; add ½ oz. of butter, and 1 pinch of salt ; mix all together to a firm smooth paste ;

Cut the paste in 3 pieces, and roll it very thin with the rolling pin, say to about $\frac{1}{16}$ of an inch ;

Let it dry ; and cut each piece in ribbons 1¼ inch broad ; put 5 of these ribbons above one another, sprinkling a little flour between each ; then, with a knife, cut them through crosswise into thin shreds, similar to vermicelli ; take them up in both hands, to loosen and shake them, and prevent their adhering to one another ; when all the paste is cut in this way, put 2 quarts of water, in a 3-quart stewpan, with 1 pinch of salt, and 1 small pinch of pepper ; when the water boils, drop the *nouilles* in with one hand, stirring with the other to prevent their getting lumpy ; boil gently for six minutes ; then drain them well, cool, and drain again on a sieve ;

Put in a stewpan :

    the *nouilles*,

    1 oz. of butter,

5 gills of Household Gravy reduced to 3 (*vide* page 68),
¼ lb. of boiled ham, cut into ¼ inch dice,
1½ oz. of grated Parmesan cheese ;

Mix lightly, not to bruise the *nouilles*; taste for seasoning ;
and serve, in a vegetable dish.

Nouilles are also prepared *au gratin*, in the same way as
Maccaroni *au Gratin* (*vide* page 186).

RICE À LA MÉNAGÈRE

Wash and blanch 6 oz. of rice, in boiling water, for five
minutes, in a 2-quart stewpan; cool, and drain it on a sieve ;

Take ¼ lb. of streaky bacon ; blanch, and cut it in 1-inch
dice ; fry it in a stewpan, till of a yellow colour ; add the rice,
1½ pint of broth, and 3 small pinches of pepper ;

Boil for twenty minutes,—taking care to stir the rice occasionally, to prevent its adhering to the stewpan ;

Take off the fire, and add ½ pint of Tomato Sauce ; mix
thoroughly, and put the rice on a dish; garnish, with some
small broiled sausages ; and serve.

GNIOCCHI

Put in a stewpan :

½ pint of water,	1 small pinch of salt,
1 oz. of butter,	2 small pinches of pepper ;

Boil, and take off the fire ; add ¼ lb. of sifted flour ; mix with
a wooden spoon; then add 2 oz. of grated Parmesan cheese;
stir over the fire for one minute ; take off the fire, and break in
3 eggs, one after the other, stirring all the time ;

Butter a *sauté*-pan slightly, and divide the paste into equal
quantities, and roll these into the shape of small walnuts ; put
these balls, or *gniocchi*, into the *sauté*-pan ; pour boiling milk
over them, and simmer for five minutes; drain carefully on a
sieve ;

For sauce, make a *roux* in a stewpan, with 1 oz. of butter,
and 2 oz. of flour ; then add 1 quart of milk; stir over the fire
for fifteen minutes, and strain through a tammy cloth ;

Put, in a vegetable dish, a layer of *gniocchi* ; sprinkle them
with grated Parmesan cheese ; then pour in a layer of sauce ;
continue the layers of *gniocchi*, grated cheese and sauce, till the
dish is full; finish with a layer of grated Parmesan cheese ;
colour in the oven : and serve.

SNOW EGGS

CHAPTER XVII

SWEETS

ORANGE CUSTARD PUDDING

BREAK 4 eggs in a basin ; add :

5 oz. of sugar,
1½ pint of milk, previously boiled,
½ a small pinch of salt,
the grated peel of an orange ;

Beat the whole together with a fork, as for Omelet, and strain, through the pointed strainer, into a pie-dish 2 inches deep ; put the dish containing the custard into a *sauté*-pan, with sufficient boiling water to reach the middle of the dish ; put in a moderate oven for twenty minutes. Should the custard not be sufficiently set at the end of that time, let it remain in the oven till quite firm ;

When cold, sprinkle some pounded sugar over it ; make a glazing iron red hot, and pass it lightly over the sugar to brown it, and form a kind of *caramel* on the surface of the custard.

LEMON CUSTARD PUDDING

This is prepared in the same way as the preceding custard, substituting the grated peel of a lemon for the orange.

COFFEE CUSTARD PUDDING

Put 2 oz. of ground coffee in a coffee filter; pour over 2 gills of boiling water; and strain it twice;

Prepare the eggs as for Orange Custard Pudding, but with only 1 pint of milk; add the coffee, and an extra ounce of sugar; strain into a dish; bake, and glaze, as for Orange Custard Pudding.

PLAIN APPLE CHARLOTTE

PLAIN APPLE CHARLOTTE

The apples best adapted for this preparation are, russet or Ribston pippins—as they are less watery than other kinds;

Take 18 apples; cut them in quarters; peel them; take out the cores, and cut them in slices ¼ inch thick;

Put in a *sauté*-pan:

 6 oz. of butter,
 the sliced apples,
 4 oz of pounded sugar;

Stir, on a brisk fire, for about fifteen minutes;

Cut twenty-four sippets of crumb of bread, 2 inches long, 1 inch wide, ¼ inch thick; fry them in butter, on both sides, in a *sauté*-pan; drain them, and spread a thin layer of apricot jam on each; dress them in a circle round a dish; fill the centre with the apples, and spread a little apricot jam on the top; serve hot.

Observation.—I have called this preparation *Plain* Apple Charlotte, because, without the trouble of moulding, a very good dish may be obtained by the simple means indicated.

APPLE FRITTERS

Take 4 good apples; cut each in 6 slices; take out the core with a vegetable cutter; peel and put them in a basin, with ½ gill of brandy, and 1 oz. of pounded sugar; toss gently, to impregnate the apples with the sugar and brandy;

When wanted, drain them well on a cloth, otherwise the batter would not adhere to them;

Make 1½ pint of frying batter (*vide* page 74).

Warm about 3 lbs. of fat in the frying kettle; when hot, place it on the stove corner;

Dip each piece of apple in the batter, and put them in the fat; accelerate the fire, when they are nearly cooked; when crisp and dry, and of a nice yellow colour, drain the fritters on a cloth, sprinkle some pounded sugar over both sides; pile them up on a napkin on a hot dish; and serve.

BEIGNETS SOUFFLÉS OR PLAIN FRITTERS

Put in a 2-quart stewpan:

    ½ pint of water,
    ¼ lb. of butter,
    ½ oz. of sugar;

Boil; then take off the fire, and add ½ lb. of sifted flour; mix, and stir over the fire, with a wooden spoon, for four minutes;

Take off the fire, and break in 3 eggs;—each egg should be thoroughly mixed before another is added; mix well, and if the paste be too stiff, add half or a whole egg;—the paste should be stiff enough not to spread out when dropped from the spoon;

Cut some strips of paper 2 inches wide; grease them slightly with cold frying fat; make the paste up into balls, about the size of a small walnut, and put them on the strips of paper;

Put 3 lbs. of frying fat on the fire, in the frying-kettle; try the heat with a piece of bread-crumb (*vide* page 74);—the bread should only produce a very slight fizzing; dip each strip of paper in the frying fat, till the balls of paste are detached from it; fry these gently, stirring with the skimmer; when of an even yellow colour, drain them, first on a sieve, then on a cloth; sprinkle with sugar; dish them up on a napkin; and serve.

OMELET SOUFFLÉE WITH LEMON

Break 6 eggs; separate the whites from the yolks; put 3 yolks in a basin, with 3 oz. of sugar, and half a grated lemon peel; stir, with a wooden spoon, for five minutes;

Put the 6 whites in a whipping bowl, and whip them until they are very firm; then mix them lightly with the yolks;—this should constitute a very solid paste;

Butter a round dish slightly; throw in the whole of the paste at once, as lightly as possible; smooth it over with a knife, and make an incision about 1 inch deep, with the handle of a silver spoon, all round the side of the omelet; put it in the oven for ten minutes, and serve immediately;

Should omelet *soufflée* be kept for a few minutes after it is taken out of the oven, it will be spoilt.

VANILLA SOUFFLÉ

Put in a 2-quart stewpan:

    6 oz. of flour,
    4 oz. of sugar,
    2 tablespoonfuls of vanilla sugar,
    1 small pinch of salt;

Mix these well with $1\frac{1}{2}$ pint of cold milk; put on the fire till boiling, and stir with a wooden spoon till smooth; then take off the fire;

Break 6 eggs; put the whites in the whipping bowl, and add the 6 yolks to the batter;

Whip the whites very firm, and mix with the batter, stirring very lightly; pour the whole in a buttered dish, and put in the oven;—twenty to twenty-five minutes should be sufficient to cook it;

When done, sprinkle with pounded sugar; and serve.

This *soufflé*, like omelet *soufflée*, must be served as soon as it is taken out of the oven.

RICE PUDDING WITH LEMON

Wash $\frac{1}{2}$ lb. of Carolina rice; blanch it in boiling water for five minutes; cool, and drain it on a sieve; put the rice in a 3-quart stewpan, with:

3 pints of milk,	$1\frac{1}{2}$ oz. of butter,
$\frac{1}{2}$ lb. of sugar,	the grated peel of a lemon;

Boil and simmer, on a very slow fire, for one hour; when cool, break 3 eggs in it, and mix well; butter a plain pudding mould, and strew as much bread-crumb in it as the butter will hold; then put the rice in the mould; bake in a moderate oven for half an hour; when nicely coloured, turn the pudding out of the mould on to a dish; and serve.

This pudding may be served plain, or with a custard sauce, made as follows:

Put 6 yolks of egg in a quart stewpan; add:

    3 oz. of sugar,
    the grated peel of a lemon,
    1 pint of milk;

Stir over the fire till the sauce begins to thicken, and forms a coating on the spoon; take off the fire, and stir for three minutes more; strain, through the pointed strainer; and serve, in a boat with the pudding.

RICE PUDDING WITH VANILLA

The preceding pudding can be made more quickly and easily, by baking it in a dish, instead of a buttered mould;

Prepare the rice in the same way, and, to vary, flavour it with vanilla sugar, instead of the grated lemon peel; put it in a pie-dish, slightly buttered; bake for half an hour; sprinkle some sugar over it; and serve.

SEMOLINA PUDDING WITH ORANGE FLOWERS

Boil 3 pints of milk in a 2-quart stewpan; when boiling, pour in ½ lb. of semolina with one hand, whilst stirring the milk with the other; add:

    2 oz. of sugar,
    ½ oz. of butter,
    a small pinch of salt;

Simmer on a very slow fire for twenty minutes; put the semolina in a basin, and mix 4 eggs in it,—being careful to mix each egg thoroughly before breaking in another; add a table-spoonful of candied orange flowers, previously crushed fine with the rolling-pin, and 2 oz. of sugar; mix all together, and put in a mould to bake, as for Rice Pudding with Lemon (*vide* page 189).

RICE CROQUETS

Prepare 6 oz. of rice, as for Rice Pudding (*vide* page 189); when the rice is cooked, spread it on a dish to a thickness of $1\frac{1}{2}$ inch; when cold, cut it up in portions $1\frac{1}{2}$ inch long, 1 inch wide; strew some bread-crumbs on the board, and put each portion of rice on it; then roll these to the shape of corks; break 3 eggs in a basin, and beat them as for omelet; dip each croquet in the egg, and bread-crumb them carefully (*vide* Breading, page 74).

Make some frying fat very hot; put the croquets in the wire frying basket; fry them quickly, till they are of a nice yellow colour; drain them; sprinkle them with sugar; dish them up on a napkin; and serve.

BAKED APPLES WITH BUTTER

Take 8 good apples; core them with a long cutter; and peel them whole;

Spread a thin layer of butter in a baking dish; put in the apples, with a small pinch of cinnamon; fill the holes in the apples with pounded sugar, and baste them with $1\frac{1}{2}$ oz. of butter, melted; put in the oven for twenty minutes; when done, serve hot.

APPLES MERINGUÉES

Prepare and cook 12 apples, as for Apple Charlotte (*vide* page 187); add 2 tablespoonfuls of apricot jam; put the apples on a round dish, raising them towards the centre;

Whip 3 whites of egg, and, when very firm, mix gently with 4 oz. of pounded sugar; cover the apples thickly with this mixture; sprinkle some sugar over, and put in a slow oven for ten minutes; when the top assumes a nice yellow colour, serve.

PEARS WITH RICE

Take 4 good stewing pears; cut them in half; peel and core them; put them in a 2-quart stewpan, with 3 pints of water, $\frac{1}{4}$ lb. of sugar, and the quarter of a stick of vanilla; boil gently for one hour or more, according to the nature of the pears;

Boil gently, for an hour, 6 oz. of rice, in 1½ pint of milk, with 4 oz. of sugar, and a quarter of a stick of vanilla; put the rice on a dish, and lay the pears on it; reduce the syrup, in which the pears have been boiled, till it registers 34° on the syrup gauge; pour it over the rice and pears; and serve.

OMELET WITH APRICOT JAM

Break 6 eggs in a basin; beat them with a fork; add 1 pinch of sugar, and 1 small pinch of salt; fry in the omelet-pan, in the same way as Omelet with *Fines Herbes* (*vide* page 182).

Before folding the omelet, put 3 tablespoonfuls of apricot jam in the centre; fold the sides of the omelet over the jam, and put it on a dish; sprinkle the omelet over with sugar, and glaze it with a red hot glazing iron.

Any kind of jam, or preserve, may be used, instead of apricot jam.

Observation.—These sweet omelets should be served rather underdone, and moist in the centre.

OMELET WITH RUM

Prepare an omelet as in the preceding recipe,—adding an extra pinch of sugar;

When cooked, put the omelet on a dish; pour over 1 gill of hot Jamaica rum; set fire to the rum; and serve burning.

PANCAKES

Put in a basin:
  ¼ lb. of sifted flour,
  1 egg,
  ¼ gill of milk;

PANCAKE PAN

Stir to a smooth paste; then add 1¾ gill of milk; 2 oz. of fresh butter, melted, and 1 small pinch of salt; mix well, and, if lumpy, strain this batter through the pointed strainer;

Put a small piece of butter in a pancake pan; when melted pour in 2 tablespoonfuls of the batter; spread it so as to cover the pan entirely; fry till coloured on one side; then toss it over, and cook the other side, and turn the pancake out on a dish;

When all the batter is cooked in this way, sprinkle the pancakes with sugar, and serve on a very hot dish, with a cut lemon.

Pancakes should be eaten as soon as fried.

SNOW EGGS FLAVOURED WITH LEMON

Boil, in a 2-quart stewpan, 1 quart of milk, with 2 oz. of sugar, and the grated peel of a lemon;

Break 6 eggs; put the whites in a whipping bowl, and reserve the yolks in a basin for the sauce;

Whip the whites, and, when very firm, mix in 4 oz. of pounded sugar;

Take a tablespoonful of the whipped whites, about the size of an egg, and drop it in the boiling milk; repeat the process,— bearing in mind, that about 6 spoonfuls will be enough in the stewpan at a time; put the stewpan on the stove corner, to simmer for four minutes; when the eggs are set on one side, turn them over with a spoon, or skimmer; when quite firm, drain them on a sieve; continue in the same way, till all the white of eggs is used.

Prepare a custard sauce, with the 6 yolks of egg, and some milk, as directed for Rice Pudding Sauce (*vide* page 190).

When cold, dish up the eggs in a pyramid; cover them with the cold custard sauce; and serve.

COFFEE CUSTARDS

For 6 cups, measure out 4 cupfuls of boiled milk; put it in a basin, with 1 cupful of very strong coffee; add 5 yolks of egg, and 1½ oz. of pounded sugar; mix well, and strain through the pointed strainer;

Fill the cups with the mixture; skim off, carefully, all froth from the surface; put them in a flat stewpan, with boiling water

to half the height of the cups ; put the stewpan, with live coals
on its cover, on a very slow fire, for fifteen minutes,—the water
should only bubble slightly ;

When set, let the custards cool in the water ; wipe the cups
clean ; and serve.

CARAMEL CUSTARDS

Prepare the custard as in the preceding recipe, adding, instead
of coffee, 1 cupful of *caramel*, prepared as follows :

Put in a small copper sugar-boiler, ½ oz. of pounded sugar ;
stir over the fire, till it becomes of a dark mahogany colour ;
then add 1 cupful of water ; boil one minute, till the sugar is
dissolved ; add this to the custard, instead of coffee, and finish
in cups, as described before.

VANILLA CUSTARDS

Boil 5 cupfuls of milk ; put half a stick of vanilla, cut in
small pieces, to soak in it for one hour ; make the custard ; pour
it in cups ; and cook as for Coffee Custards (*vide* page 193).

LEMON CUSTARDS

Take the same quantity of milk as in the preceding recipe ;
put in it the grated peel of one lemon, instead of the vanilla ;
and finish as before.

VANILLA CREAM

Boil 1½ pint of milk ; put in it half a stick of vanilla, cut in
small pieces ; cover the stewpan, and let the vanilla soak in the
milk for an hour;

Break 8 yolks of egg in a 2-quart stewpan, with ¾ lb. of
pounded sugar ; mix well; then add the milk, and stir over the
fire, with a wooden spoon, till the custard begins to thicken; avoid
boiling, and when it is thick enough to coat the spoon, take off
the fire, and stir a little longer.

Steep 1½ oz. of gelatine in cold water, for a quarter of an
hour ; drain it, and mix it in the hot custard, the heat of which
will be sufficient to melt the gelatine ; when melted, strain the
whole through the pointed strainer, into another stewpan ;

Get 6 lbs. of rough ice ; put the stewpan on the top, and stir all the time, till the contents begin to set ;

Then whip 5 gills of double cream ; take the stewpan off the ice, and mix in the whipped cream lightly ;

TURNING OUT OF THE CREAM

Fill a quart cylinder-mould with the mixture, and put it in a basin, with pounded ice round it ; cover the mould with a stewpan cover, with ice on the top of it ;—an hour and a half will be sufficient to set the cream.

When set, have a large basin of hot water,—as hot as the hand can bear it ; dip the mould entirely in the water ; take it out immediately, and wipe the top of the cream with a cloth ; put a dish over the mould ; reverse it ; remove the mould ; and serve.

Should the cream not come out freely, dip the mould in hot water again.

STRAWBERRY CREAM

Rub 2 lbs. of strawberries (preferably, small Alpine straw-berries, as having the most flavour) through a silk sieve, or tammy cloth ; put the pulp in a basin, with $\frac{3}{4}$ lb. of pounded sugar, and the juice of a lemon ;

c c 2

Steep 2 oz. of gelatine in cold water; dissolve it in a small stewpan; and strain it into the strawberries, through the pointed strainer;

Whip a quart of double cream, and finish as for Vanilla Cream.

Observation.—Never use tinned stewpans in any preparation of red fruit, as the tin would destroy the colour of the fruit.

APRICOT CREAM

Rub 18 good and ripe apricots through a tammy cloth;

Pound 12 of the apricot kernels; add them to the apricots in a basin, with $\frac{3}{4}$ lb. of pounded sugar, and 2 oz. of dissolved gelatine; mix, and finish, with whipped cream, as for Vanilla Cream.

The recipes for jellies, &c., will be found in the Second Part.

VANILLA CREAM

CHAPTER XVIII

PASTRY

SHORT PASTE CAKE

Put 1 lb. of sifted flour on the pasteboard; make a hole in the centre of the flour; and into this hole, put:

$\frac{1}{2}$ oz. of salt,	10 oz. of butter,
$\frac{1}{2}$ oz. of sugar,	2 gills of water;

Mix with the hands; and, when half mixed, sprinkle over the paste another gill of water, to mix all the flour to a smooth paste;

Rub off, with a little flour, any paste that may adhere to the hands; then work and press the paste between your hands, on the board; repeat this operation twice;

Gather all the paste into one smooth lump; and let it rest for one hour; then roll the paste, with a rolling pin, to a round shape about $1\frac{1}{4}$ inch thick; press the edge with the fingers; and score it round with a knife, with cuts $\frac{1}{4}$ inch apart, and $\frac{1}{4}$ inch deep;

Turn the cake on to a baking-sheet; break an egg in a basin, beat it as for Omelet; and egg the top of the cake with a paste brush dipped therein ; cut a pattern on the top, as shown in the woodcut (page 203) ;

Put in a brisk oven for half an hour ; and serve.

PUFF PASTE CAKE

Put 1 lb. of sifted flour on the pasteboard ; make a hollow in the centre of the flour, and fill it with ½ oz. of salt, and 1½ gill of water ; mix the flour gradually with the water, and, when this is done, and the paste about half mixed, sprinkle with another gill of water, to mix all the flour ; work to a smooth paste, and till it ceases to adhere to the board, or the hands, and roll it out to a round piece ;

ROLLING PIN

Take ¾ lb. of butter ; work it in a cloth to expel any water which may be in it ; lay the butter on the paste ; flatten both to a thickness of about 2 inches ; then fold the four sides of the paste to the centre, to enclose the butter, and form a square piece ;

Roll the paste to a length of about 3 feet ; then fold over one third of the length, and fold the other third over this.

This operation is called *giving one turn* ; and, as it constantly recurs in all recipes for making pastry, I have thought it necessary to explain its meaning ;

Let the paste rest for ten minutes ; then give it two turns ; and, ten minutes afterwards, two turns more, five turns in all ; then gather the paste to a lump ; roll it with the rolling pin ; and finish as for the preceding cake.

GÂTEAU DE PLOMB

Put 1 lb. of sifted flour on the pasteboard ; make a hole in the centre ; and put in :

½ oz. of sugar,	2 eggs,
1 pinch of salt,	10 oz. of butter ;
1 gill of cream,	

Mix the paste, adding another gill of cream ; and finish it, as for Short Paste Cake (*vide* page 197) ;

Let the paste rest for half an hour; then roll it to a round shape, 2 inches thick; score the edges; put the cake on a baking-sheet; egg, and cut a pattern on the top; cut some strips of paper of the thickness of the cake; butter them, and tie them round it, to prevent its spreading; put it in a hot oven to bake for one hour; then take it out, and press it, by putting a plate over it, with a 2 lbs. weight on the top, till cold; take off the paper; and serve on a dish.

GÂTEAU DE PLOMB

SMALL GÂTEAUX DE PLOMB FOR BREAKFAST

Make the same paste, as in the preceding recipe;

Divide it in 2-oz. portions, and make them up into small cakes of different shapes; and serve hot for breakfast.

BRIOCHE

Take 1 lb. of sifted flour; put a fourth part of it on the paste-board to make the sponge; make a hollow in the centre of the flour, and put in it ½ oz. of German yeast dissolved in ½ gill of warm water; mix as for puff paste, but rather softer;

When the paste is made, gather it in a lump, and put it to rise in a warm place, in a covered stewpan, with a little warm water in it;

Take the remaining three parts of flour; make a hollow in the centre; then add:

    1 pinch of salt,
    ½ oz. of sugar,
    2 tablespoonfuls of water, to melt the sugar and salt,
    10 oz. of butter,
    . 4 eggs;

Mix the paste lightly; then add another egg; mix again, adding another egg, till 7 eggs in all have been used in the paste,—which must be neither too soft, nor too hard.

When the sponge has risen to twice its original size, mix it lightly with the paste, and put the whole in a basin, in a warm place, for four hours; after which, put it on the board; roll and fold it, over and over again; put it back in the basin, to rise again, for two hours; and repeat the folding and pressing down; then put the paste in a very cold place, for two hours.

After that time, form it into a round lump, and put it on to a baking-sheet; make a hole in the centre, and pull out the paste till it forms a ring 12 inches in diameter; let it rest; egg it well with the paste brush; then make an incision all round the inside of the ring, and open it well, to prevent its closing; put in a brisk oven for half an hour.

I advise giving the *brioche* this shape, as it will make it easier to bake; it can, however, be made up into loaves, rolls, buns, or any fancy shape.

BRIOCHE WITH CHEESE

Add to the preceding quantity of paste :
  ¼ lb. of grated Parmesan cheese,
  ¼ lb. of Gruyère cheese, cut in ¼-inch dice ;
Mix the cheese well in with the paste; shape, and cook in the same way as plain *Brioche* (*vide* preceding recipe).

ALMOND CAKE

Take 6 oz. of Jordan almonds, and 10 bitter almonds; blanch

PESTLE AND MORTAR

them, in boiling water, for three minutes ; cool, peel, and wash them ; drain ; and wipe them in a cloth ;

Put them in a mortar, and pound to a paste with an egg, added in small quantities, to prevent the almonds turning oily ; when well pounded, add :

    6 oz. of pounded sugar,   1 tablespoonful of orange-flower
    6 oz. of butter,   water ;
    1 small pinch of salt,

Pound all well together, adding 3 eggs, broken in one after the other ; when well mixed, put the pounded almonds in a basin.

Make 1 lb. of puff paste, as described for Puff Paste Cake (*vide* page 198) ; give the paste five turns ; cut it into 2 pieces ; make a ball with each piece ; roll each flat with a rolling-pin, to the thickness of ½ inch ; put one on a baking-sheet ; spread the almond paste on it, leaving a margin of 1½ inch all round ; wet the edge of the paste, and lay the other piece over, and press with the thumb all round, to stick the two together ; trim off any superfluous paste ; egg the top, and cut a pattern with a knife, as for Short Paste Cake (*vide* page 197) ; bake in the oven for fifty minutes ; let the cake cool ; then sprinkle some sifted sugar over it ; and serve.

OPEN APPLE TART

Take ½ lb. of puff paste, at six turns (*vide* Puff Paste Cake, page 198) ; roll it to ¼ inch thickness ;

Butter an open tart mould, and put it on a baking-sheet ; then line it with the paste, and press it in, to take the shape ; cut the paste on a level with the top of the mould ; fill it with some apples, prepared as for Apple Charlotte (*vide* page 187) ; bake for half an hour ; when cold, spread over the apple 2 tablespoonfuls of apricot jam, or apple jelly.

OPEN TART MOULD

OPEN CHERRY TART

Line the mould with puff paste, as in the preceding recipe ; spread a little pounded sugar on the paste ; then lay some stoned

D D

cherries on the paste, side by side, till the whole surface is covered; bake for half an hour; sprinkle a little more sugar on the top; and serve.

OPEN APRICOT TART

Proceed as in the preceding recipe; garnish the paste with apricots, cut in halves and stoned, instead of cherries; sprinkle over with sugar; and serve.

OPEN PLUM TART

Proceed as for Cherry Tart; garnish the paste with stoned *mirabelles*, or greengage plums.

OPEN PEAR TART

Take 10 pears; cut them in two; peel, and put them in a 2-quart stewpan, with 1 quart of water, and ¼ lb. of sugar; simmer for about an hour; when done, drain the pears;

Line a mould with puff paste; upon it put a layer of apple, prepared as for Apple Charlotte, and place the pears on the top;

Strain, and reduce the syrup of the pears to 32°; pour it over the tart when cold; and serve.

CUSTARD TART MERINGUÉE

Put in a 2-quart stewpan:
    1 whole egg, and 3 yolks,—reserve the whites for whipping,
    1½ oz. of flour,
    1 gill of milk; .
Mix to a smooth paste; and add:
    6 gills of milk, in small quantities, to avoid lumping,
    1 oz. of butter,
    ¼ lb. of sugar,
    the grated peel of an orange;
Mix thoroughly, and stir over the fire till boiling; take the custard off the fire, and, when cold, pour it in the mould lined with paste, as for Open Apple Tart (*vide* page 201); bake the tart for half an hour, and let it cool;

Whip the 3 whites of egg very firm; add 3 oz. of pounded sugar, and spread the whipped egg over the tart; sprinkle over with sugar; bake in a slow oven, till of a nice yellow colour; and serve.

NOUGAT

Blanch ¾ lb. of almonds, in boiling water, for three minutes;
cool; drain, and peel them; wash, and dry them in a cloth;
cut each almond crosswise into 6 equal pieces; put them on a
baking-sheet, in a slack oven, to dry thoroughly;

Melt 6 oz. of pounded sugar, in a copper pan; add a teaspoonful of lemon juice;

When the sugar is well melted, and hot, pour the almonds in,
and mix with a wooden spoon.

The almonds should be very hot when added to the sugar, or
they would set it.

Oil a plain pudding-mould slightly; lay the *nougat* on a
baking-sheet, and commence, by lining the bottom of the mould
with *nougat* ¼ inch thick; then line the sides with some more
pieces, till the whole inside is covered with a coating ¼ inch
thick.

Nougat must be made quickly, or the pieces will not stick
together.

When cold turn the *nougat* out of the mould; and serve.

GENOESE CAKE

Put in a basin:

　　½ lb. of pounded sugar,　　the grated peel of a lemon,
　　½ lb. of sifted flour,　　4 eggs;
　　1 small pinch of salt,

Mix the whole, with a wooden spoon;

Melt ½ lb. of butter in a stewpan; pour it in the paste; and
mix thoroughly;

Slightly butter a plain-pudding mould; put the paste in it,
and bake for three quarters of an hour; ascertain if the cake is
done, by inserting the blade of a small knife;—if it comes out
damp, the cake is not quite done, and should be left in the oven
a few minutes longer;

Turn the cake out of the mould; let it cool; and serve.

SHORT PASTE CAKE

D D 2

CHAPTER XIX

DESSERT

FINGER BISCUITS

BREAK 6 eggs; put the whites in the whipping bowl, and the yolks in a basin;

To the latter add ½ lb. of pounded sugar, and stir for five minutes;

Whip the whites very firm; then put them in the basin containing the yolks, adding 5 oz. of sifted flour; mix thoroughly.

Take a sheet of stiff paper, and shape it into a funnel; secure it with sticking paste; and when dry, fill it with the biscuit paste; close the top, by folding over the paper, and cut off the end of the funnel, making an opening ¾ inch diameter;

Force some of the paste out of the funnel, on to a sheet of paper, in the shape of a finger 3 inches long, 1 inch wide; leaving an inch space between each biscuit; dredge some sifted sugar over them; put them on a baking-sheet, and bake in a moderate oven for ten minutes; let the biscuits cool on the paper; then take them off, and dress them on a dish;

The biscuits are flavoured by the addition of vanilla, lemon, or orange flower.

MACAROONS

Blanch and peel ½ lb. of almonds, including 8 bitter ones; wash, and dry them in a cloth; put in a mortar, and pound them to a fine paste, adding the white of an egg in two parts, to prevent the almonds turning oily; then add 6 oz. of pounded sugar, and the white of another egg; when well mixed, add 6 more ounces of pounded sugar, and another white of egg; when well mixed, put the whole in a basin;

Drop a teaspoonful of this paste on a sheet of paper, so as to form a small round cake, about 1 inch diameter, and $\frac{1}{2}$ inch thick; make as many of these macaroons as the quantity of paste will admit, placing them regularly on the paper, 2 inches apart; dredge a little fine sugar over them; put on a baking-sheet, and bake them in a moderate oven; when of an even yellow colour, the macaroons are done.

COMPOTE OF PEARS

Choose 7 middle-sized stewing pears; peel them whole, very smooth, and put them in a 2-quart stewpan; cover them with syrup, at 16°, a little prepared cochineal, and a quarter of a stick of vanilla; simmer for an hour and a half; let the pears cool in the syrup; drain them, and reduce the syrup quickly to 32°;

Dress six of the pears round a compote dish, and put the seventh in the centre; when the syrup is cold, pour it over the pears; and serve.

The syrup should only be added to compotes just before serving.

COMPOTE OF BAKING PEARS

Take 4 large baking pears; cut them in six pieces lengthwise; keep a whole half for the centre of the compote; core and peel the pears, and boil them in syrup at 16°, with a teaspoonful of prepared cochineal, and a lemon peel; when done, arrange the quarters in the compote dish, and put the half which has been reserved in the centre;

Reduce the syrup to 30°, and pour over the pears when cold.

COMPOTE OF BON CHRÉTIEN PEARS

Take 5 *Bon Chrétien* pears; cut them in halves; core and peel them; give one of the pieces a round shape;

Boil the pieces of pear quickly, in 3 pints of syrup, at 16°; when cooked, cool and dress them in a compote dish, putting the round piece in the centre; reduce the syrup to 30°, and pour it over the pears when cold.

The *Bon Chrétien* compote should always be white;—this is secured by boiling in plenty of syrup.

COMPOTE OF APPLES

Take 4 Colville apples; cut them in halves; core and peel them carefully;

Put 1 quart of syrup in a 2-quart stewpan, adding the juice of half a lemon; put the apples in to simmer very gently; turn them over when half cooked; when done, drain them on a sieve; and, when cold, put them in a compote dish;

Reduce the syrup; pour it over the apples; and serve.

APPLE MARMALADE

Take one dozen of russet or Ribston pippin apples; cut them in quarters; core, peel, and put them in a stewpan, with 2 tablespoonfuls of water, and 6 oz. of sugar; put them over a very slow fire till melted; then reduce, by stirring over a fiercer fire; cool, and dish up the apple in a compote dish; sprinkle some fine sugar over the top, and glaze with the red hot salamander; serve.

COMPOTE OF FRENCH PLUMS

Take 1 lb. of French plums; wash, and put them in a quart stewpan filled with water; add 1 oz. of lump sugar, and a piece of cinnamon; simmer very gently for three quarters of an hour; when done, drain them on a sieve; strain the liquor; add 2 oz. of sugar to it, and reduce it to 32°; put the plums in a compote dish; pour over the syrup when cold; and serve.

COMPOTE OF BRIGNOLES PLUMS

Take 1 lb. of Brignoles plums; put them in a copper sugar-boiler with ½ gill of French white wine, 1 gill of water, and 1 oz. of pounded sugar; simmer for ten minutes; drain the plums on a sieve; dress them in a compote dish; pour over the juice, when cold; and serve.

COMPOTE OF CHERRIES

Take 1 lb. of May-Duke or Kentish cherries; cut off all but $\frac{3}{4}$ inch of the stalks;

Put $\frac{1}{2}$ lb. of lump sugar in a copper sugar-boiler, with 2 quarts of water; boil for three minutes; put the cherries in this syrup; cover the pan, and simmer for five minutes; drain the cherries on a sieve; dish them up in a compote dish, the stalks upwards; reduce the syrup to 30°; let it cool; pour it over the cherries; and serve.

COMPOTE OF RED CURRANTS

Take 1 lb. of fine large red currants; pick them off the stalks, and put them in a basin, with $\frac{1}{2}$ lb. of pounded sugar; when it is melted, put the currants into a compote dish; after two hours, if properly mixed, the syrup should have set to a jelly. This will be found a very pleasant summer dish.

COMPOTE OF APRICOTS

Take 8 large apricots, not over ripe; cut them in two; take out the stones; break these, and blanch and peel the almonds;

Put $\frac{1}{2}$ lb. of lump sugar in a copper sugar-boiler, with 2 gills of water; when it boils, put in the apricots, and simmer very gently for five minutes; drain the apricots, and dress them in a compote dish; strain the syrup, and reduce it to 30°; when cold, pour it over the apricots; put half an almond, taken from the stones, upon each piece of apricot; and serve.

COMPOTE OF GREENGAGES

Take 20 fine greengages; put them in a copper sugar-boiler, with $\frac{1}{2}$ lb. of lump sugar, and 2 gills of water; when boiling, cover the pan, and simmer very gently for ten minutes; drain the greengages; strain the syrup, and reduce it to 30°;

Arrange the greengages in a compote dish; pour over the syrup; and serve.

COMPOTE OF MIRABELLE PLUMS

Take 40 nice *Mirabelle* plums; put them in a copper sugar-boiler, with 7 oz. of lump sugar, and 2 gills of water; boil, and finish in the same manner as Compote of Greengages.

COMPOTE OF ORANGES

Peel 4 oranges; pare off all the white skin; cut the oranges into eight pieces; then cut out the core; keep one half whole for the centre of the compote. Boil ¾ lb. of lump sugar in a copper sugar-boiler, with 2 gills of water; reduce this syrup to 36°; pour it, lukewarm, over the oranges in a basin; cover the basin, and let the orange steep in the syrup for two hours; then drain, and dress the pieces of orange in a compote dish, putting the whole half in the centre; reduce the syrup to 32°, and, when cold, pour it over the oranges; and serve.

ORANGE SALAD WITH LIQUEUR

Cut 4 good oranges in slices, about ¼ inch thick, without peeling them; dish the slices up in a compote dish, in a circle, overlapping one another; sprinkle over 3 oz. of pounded sugar, and add 1 gill of either rum, brandy, or kirschenwasser. When sweet liqueurs are used, such as Curaçoa, Maraschino, Anisette, or Eau-de-vie de Dantzic, sprinkle only 2 oz. of pounded sugar over the oranges.

COMPOTE OF CHESTNUTS, FLAVOURED WITH VANILLA, ORANGE, OR LEMON

Take 40 large chestnuts; peel the outer brown skin, and put them on the fire, in a 2-quart stewpan, with 3 pints of water; when getting hot, peel off the second skin, being careful not to break the chestnuts; put them in a large copper sugar-boiler, so that they may have plenty of room to lay at the bottom; cover them with syrup at 16°, and simmer gently for twenty minutes; when done, drain them; strain the syrup through the pointed strainer; reduce it to 30°; arrange the chestnuts in a compote dish; pour over the syrup; and serve.

Flavour the syrup, before it is reduced, according to taste, with either a quarter of a stick of vanilla, or half the rind of an orange or lemon, cut very thin; strain the syrup, and pour it over the chestnuts.

VERMICELLI CHESTNUTS

Prepare and cook the chestnuts as in the preceding recipe; drain them, and reduce the syrup;

Put back the chestnuts in the syrup; press them through a hair sieve, into a compote dish; the *purée* of chestnuts will fall into the dish like vermicelli;—this is its proper shape, and it should not be touched afterwards.

ORANGES GLACÉES AU CARAMEL

Peel 3 oranges very carefully; remove every particle of white skin; divide them into their quarters; have some very thin wooden skewers, about 5 inches long; put a skewer in the point of each piece of orange, about half way through; lay the skewers on a sieve, with the pieces of orange hanging outside, all round the sieve; let them dry thus for about two hours;

Put 1 lb. of lump sugar in a copper sugar-boiler, with 1 pint of water; when melted, put it over a brisk fire; boil, and skim it carefully;

Have a basin of cold water near the stove, and, when the sugar produces large air bubbles, skim off with the finger a small particle of the boiling sugar, and plunge your hand quickly into the cold water; if the sugar comes off the finger very easily, it will not, when eaten, stick to the teeth;—it is necessary to repeat this trial several times, to seize the right point of boiling, as a few seconds beyond it would make the sugar yellow;

Have a basin of pounded or brown sugar handy, to stick the skewers in, to drain the orange; dip each piece of orange into the boiled sugar, and stick the end of the skewer in the sugar in the basin, and let the piece of orange drain outside till it is cold; then take the pieces of orange off the skewers, and dish them up in a compote dish.

CHESTNUTS GLACÉS AU CARAMEL

Take 36 good sound chestnuts; slit the skin with a knife; roast them in a frying-pan, on a moderate fire, so that they do not get brown; peel, and pick off all skin; and, when quite cold, insert a skewer in each chestnut, as described above for Oranges *Glacées au Caramel*; dip the chestnuts in boiled sugar, and finish in the same way as directed for Oranges *Glacées* (*vide* recipe above).

GRAPES GLACÉS AU CARAMEL

Cut a bunch of grapes into small clusters of 4 or 5 grapes each; dip them in boiling sugar, and finish them as directed for Oranges *Glacées au Caramel.*

E E

CHERRIES GLACÉES AU CARAMEL

Either fresh or brandy cherries can be glazed in this way; cut off half the length of the stalk, and dip the cherries, singly, in the boiled sugar, in the same manner as with the Oranges *Glacées* (*vide* page 209).

CURRANTS GLACÉES AU CARAMEL

Take 20 bunches of red and 20 bunches of white currants, perfectly dry; dip each bunch in boiled sugar; let them dry; and, when cold, dish them up in a compote dish.

SUGARED CURRANTS

Beat the white of an egg in a plate with a fork; add a teaspoonful of maraschino or water, and mix well together;

Have about 1 lb. of hot pounded sugar in a basin; dip 40 bunches of white currants, one after the other, in the white of egg, and throw them in the sugar; shake them in it till they are well covered; then put them on a sieve, and, as soon as the sugar is dry, they are ready to serve.

CURRANT JELLY

Take 8 lbs. of currants, half red and half white, and 2 lbs. of raspberries; put them in a preserving pan with 1 quart of water,

PRESERVING PAN

to boil for eight minutes on a sharp fire, stirring with the skimmer to prevent the fruit adhering to the pan; put a hair sieve over a large basin, and pour the fruit in it; press it well, to make all the liquor pass through; then weigh the currant juice, and for every pound of juice add 10 oz. of lump sugar; put the juice and sugar back in the pan on the fire, and when the sugar is melted, strain the syrup through a silk sieve; then boil the syrup in two parts on a brisk fire; when it marks 28° on the syrup gauge, it is done; pour it in pots, and when cold, cover these, first, with a round of paper dipped in brandy, and laid on the top of the jelly, and, then, with a round of paper tied round the top of the pots with string.

Keep the preserve in a dry, cool place.

Observation.—Currant jelly is improved, both in colour and brilliancy, by being boiled in small quantities.

CHERRY PRESERVE

Take about 5 lbs. of May-Duke, or Kentish cherries, so that, after picking and stoning them, you may have 4 lbs. left; put 2 lbs. of lump sugar in the preserving pan, with 1 pint of water, and boil it for three minutes; then add the cherries, stirring lightly with the skimmer, so as not to break them; boil for eight minutes; then pour the whole into a large basin, and let the cherries soak for twenty-four hours; then drain them; boil the syrup, adding 1 lb. of lump sugar; throw in the cherries, and boil for eight minutes more;

When cold, put the preserve in pots and cover in the same way as directed for Currant Jelly (*vide* preceding recipe).

APRICOT JAM

Cut 8 lbs. of good apricots in slices; put them in a basin with 5 lbs. of pounded sugar; stir with a wooden spoon till the sugar is melted; and put the whole into the preserving pan, to boil for ten minutes, whilst stirring with the skimmer; take the skimmer out of the jam; cool what is on it, and if this feels greasy under the finger, the jam is done. Another way of ascertaining when the jam is done, is by pouring a little into a cold plate; if it shows little tendency to spread, it is done;

Pour the jam into pots, and cover with paper when cold, as previously directed.

E E 2

APPLE JELLY

Take 6 lbs. of sound apples,—Wellington or Colville apples are the best; peel, core, and slice them, and put them in the preserving pan to boil, with 2 quarts of water; when the apples are melted, drain them on a hair sieve over a basin; weigh the juice, and to every pound of juice add 10 oz. of lump sugar (the apple which remains on the sieve may be used for open tarts, apple Charlotte, or compotes, &c.).

Put the jelly and sugar in the pan over the fire; when the sugar is melted, pass the jelly through a napkin, and boil it in two parts; when it marks 28°, it will be done; pour the jelly into pots, and cover when cold.

QUINCE JELLY

Take 4 lbs. of quinces; cut them in quarters; peel, core, and slice them; put them in a preserving pan with 4 quarts of water; boil till the quinces are reduced to a pulp; drain them on a sieve over a basin, and to each pound of juice add 10 oz. of lump sugar; finish as for Apple Jelly (*vide* preceding recipe).

CHEESE AND FRUIT IN SEASON

It is unnecessary to give any special directions concerning cheese and fruit; the only recommendation I would make is, —always to buy the best obtainable. Another very important point to study, particularly with reference to fruit, is the art of dishing up with elegance and care; this greatly enhances its natural beauty.

COLVILLE APPLES

CONCLUSION OF THE FIRST PART

In this First Part, now come to its close, I think I have omitted nothing of any moment relating to domestic cookery; what I have given will, I feel confident, meet the daily requirements of any middle-class household. It would have been an easy matter to have inserted a greater number of recipes, but this I have purposely refrained from doing, convinced that it would have been at the risk of wandering beyond the limits of my subject, and of altering the character of that special order of cookery, which it has been my intention to define and explain clearly in this First Part.

Now it is evident, that the line which separates the First from the Second Part, is not of so absolute a character that it cannot, be passed at will; those who wish to go a little out of the usual routine, and to indulge now and then in a more *recherché* dinner, or even in a single dish of more elaborate preparation, will therefore always be able to have recourse to the Second Part; and there, I will venture to say, they will find quite enough to meet their requirements. I have sought, above all, to establish the broad distinction between the simple and tangible, and the elaborate and choice.

I have already, at the beginning, disclaimed any idea of giving instructions as to the proper way of serving. Everyone is acquainted with the daily table arrangements. In what part of the civilised world, may I ask, is the proper way of setting glasses, plates, knives and forks on a table, unknown? It will surely not be expected of me that, when writing upon cookery, I should remind my readers of the necessity of the table linen being white, or that the hands of those who wait at table should be perfectly clean, &c.

I have thought myself justified in not touching upon these matters, which are in reality the very rudiments of *savoir vivre*.

As to the mode of presenting a dinner in the regular course, it will always, in my opinion, be well served, if well dressed; the one follows the other, as daily experience will show. Any cook who has learnt to work properly will know, without requiring telling, that the best dishes, or those most highly seasoned, should succeed the simpler and less seasoned ones. The rules, therefore, to follow for the proper serving of meals in middle-class households, are implied by the very recipes; once these mastered and carried out in the manner directed, I see no reason to fear that the dishes themselves will not be judiciously introduced; and, if the matter be good, it will cover any slight mistake which may occur in the manner of serving. A cook, confident of her own ability to prepare a satisfactory meal, has therefore, in her own hands, the means of setting at rest any little cavilling upon this score.

SALAD

HIGH-CLASS COOKERY

DISH WARMER, DISH AND COVER

PRELIMINARY OBSERVATIONS

BEFORE entering upon the Second Part, I wish to put on record the ruling principle which has regulated all the recipes which follow; namely, that the very first and most important object of high-class cookery is the pleasant preparation of food. The processes are undoubtedly more intricate and complicated, and frequently more costly, than for domestic cookery; but the basis is the same. High-class cookery rests in the same way upon common sense, good taste, judgment, and a knowledge of the hygienic properties of the things to be served; it is by these that a cook should be constantly guided, and then he may rely upon not being led astray. Therefore, those who expect to find in what I call superior cookery anything suggestive of oddity, extravagance, or affectation, will be quite at fault. I would be the very last to countenance error, or that absurd *charlatanisme* against which culinary art is not always proof. In domestic cookery, I sought the approval of true housewives; in this high-class cookery, I must strive for the suffrages of culinary connoisseurs, in whose hands I unreservedly leave myself. I have tried, by uniting the good old rules with modern improvements, to convey what high-class cookery really is at the present day. Far from being an obsolete art, as some pessimists declare, it has merely undergone a transformation upon many points. Thus, while admitting that the number of large establishments has decreased; on the other hand, that of cookery connoisseurs has now become so considerable that this advantage more than compensates for the first-named loss; it is well to keep this fact in view when treating of cookery as a whole, and when explaining its details.

It is clear that it will be unnecessary to enter, in this Part, into such minutiæ as in the First Part. I shall no longer describe the most elementary operations; but, on the other hand, wherever I have thought it required, I have given precise data as to quantities, length of time of cooking, and execution; in order to adhere to my axiom that: 'In cookery nothing must be left to uncertainty or to chance.'

It will be evident, also, that I do not, as in household cookery, provide only for a limited number of people. High-class cookery has a wider range. Without falling into the other extreme of describing things on the gigantic scale which belongs to a bye-gone era, I have been anxious to give all the constituents of superior cookery: removes, *entrées*, hot *hors d'œuvre*, with the fullest development and perfection of detail of which they are capable. To have done otherwise would have been to destroy their distinctive character, and this I have been unwilling to do; in simple matters, my explanations have been as simple as possible; now that some of the most attractive subjects of culinary art come under consideration, I am desirous of giving them due importance. It does not follow, because the cookery which is treated of in the ensuing chapters is adapted for large banquets and numerous guests, that it is not available for smaller numbers; the contrary is the case, and where only a few have to be provided for, the very same attention is required as for a large party.

Those practitioners, to whom I shall now more specially address my remarks, will always be able to reduce the proportions given, to their requirements; more particularly from being able to appreciate the recipes in their entirety. That those who are equal to much will be equal to less, will be found to be the case in all culinary matters; and more especially if the progression in the study of the art has been upward—from the elementary to the complex. In this way alone is it possible to become a thorough cook; that is, one who, whilst he will be capable of showing fair results under any circumstances, will only call in the adventitious aid of taste, elegance, and decoration, when the perfect preparation of the things themselves will justify it.

I

MODE OF SERVING: À LA FRANÇAISE, À LA RUSSE.

Whilst, in the First Part, the question of table serving was, for the cook, one of but secondary consideration, it is not so in high-class cookery; and, in this part of a dinner specially concerning the *maître d'hôtel*, it is advisable that the cook should have his say. For it is very important that he should know how the dinner he is preparing will be put on the table, as the manner of doing this doubles its value, and determines its success.

There have been endless discussions as to the relative merits of the two systems of serving; named, rather arbitrarily, the one *à la Française*, the other *à la Russe*. The first consists in setting the whole of a course on the table at once, taking each dish off to carve it; in the second mode, the dishes are brought to table already cut up, which makes it difficult to present them otherwise than in fragments, set up together again in the best practicable way.

The differences of opinion as to which is the best of these two systems have now nearly been settled, as most questions of this kind are, by a compromise.

Both systems have their advantages and disadvantages; the mode of serving *à la Russe* is undeniably simpler and more expeditious than that *à la Française*, the complications and slowness of which have been justly criticised; but in the former system, the necessity of cutting up all the dishes before the guests see them, puts an end to the opportunities of decoration, which many cooks turned to so good account, and tends to destroy the tasteful and rich appearance which formerly characterised high-class cookery.

On the other hand, we must admit that it is very objectionable to keep such dishes waiting on the table as are likely to suffer thereby: dish warmers and covers are of little avail; for many of the most *recherché* dishes require to be eaten immediately they leave the kitchen. In such cases, there need be no uncertainty as to the right mode of serving; it would be folly to make a display of dishes of this kind, which cannot wait. The question of appearance must be made quite subordinate to that of consumption. Thus, when weighing the *pro* and *contra* of both modes of serving, there is little need to waver long between one or the other; the compromise is self-indicated by experience.

For instance: nothing is to prevent putting on the table, to dress and deck it as it should be: first, large cold pieces, capable of receiving such great richness of ornamentation; also, removes and hot *entrées*, which are generally equal to waiting on the dish-warmers, without deteriorating.

In this way the guests, when they sit down, will not be greeted by a table decked out merely with fruit, *compôtes*, bronze articles of *vertû*, vases of flowers, and similar objects, little nourishing in themselves, and unlikely to act as appetisers, so as to ensure justice being done to the dinner about to follow.

Neither will there be any objection to merely sending round the cut-up dishes which require immediate eating, without seeking to use them for show purposes. By these means, the dinner will be sooner and more evenly served, and ample time will be obtained to carve the large dishes properly.

I aver, that a dinner presented in this way, from the fusion of both systems, cannot fail to please the cook who has prepared it, and the guests who partake of it; the latter will not pause to consider whether they have been served more particularly *à la Française*, or *à la Russe*; but they will admit that the dinner has realised the essentials of gastronomy. The eyes, which it is often said do half the eating, will be satisfied by the appearance of the ornamented dishes, and, at the same time, connoisseurs will be able to enjoy, under the most favourable conditions, the delicacies of true cookery.

II

BILLS OF FARE

I shall give no lists of bills of fare, because I think it more useful for amateurs and cooks to know how the several dishes are made, than to be wearied with endless lists of them; the mere enumeration and arrangement of which are very simple matters, but become very different if they have to be realised. How many brilliant dinners, splendid on paper, have turned out, on execution, the most lamentable failures! I hold that all bills

of fare are good, as long as they are free from too glaring absurdities: such as the repetition of similar dishes, sauces, or
garnishes.   Far from conveying the idea that I consider lists of
bills of fare to be useless, I, on the contrary, hold them to be
very interesting; many people I know have regular collections
of them; but their value is, to me, of a rather negative character,
and I would sooner that a cook should rely upon his own knowledge and experience, in the composition and elaboration of a
dinner.

I, however, fully recognise the necessity of setting forth, for
the information of the guests, a detailed description of the dinner
to be put before them; such a bill of fare is a happy idea which
the service à la Russe has made almost indispensable.   Is it not
for the guest a real advantage to know beforehand how far his
appetite will be taxed, and to be able to prepare his plan of
campaign, upon the information thus obligingly vouchsafed him?

With reference to those bills of fare which emanate direct
from the cook, and represent nothing imaginary but are a bonâ
fide statement of a dinner, the preparation of which is about to
follow, I would wish to impress upon young practitioners the
following result of my personal experience: ' Never make out
your bills of fare too long beforehand, else you will be subjected
to numberless disappointments and difficulties; your pet scheme,
upon which you had built your expected success, may frequently
be overthrown by a superior will or caprice; this will necessitate
your setting to work again, with considerably damped ardour,
to remodel your plan in the best way you can.'

I would add: ' Never get your bills of fare printed, until you
have all your provisions together, and you are sure of what you
will be able to serve;' it is then only, when you have all you
require for your dinner at hand, that you should think of putting
forth the official and final programme of the dinner; otherwise,
you run the risk of not being able to carry out what you have
promised, on account of failure in procuring some particular
article which you had in view.   Nothing is more annoying than
a bill of fare which does not keep its promises, and deceives the
guests, by the delusive bait of the names of dishes, which they
wait for in vain, and which it will be impossible for the cook to
supply.

This evil will be guarded against, by taking the wise precau-
tions I recommend; by not making out the final bill of fare too
soon, one will be safe from laying on the table any other than
perfectly correct statements, true from beginning to end.

III

KITCHEN. STAFF

I do not wish to begin any description of high-class cookery—the practice of which is coupled with so much care, so many difficulties, and complicated minutiæ—without reminding those who really take pride in the way their table is supplied, of the advantage they will derive from being able to put at the disposal of their servants a kitchen laid out and fitted up as it should be. Is it so difficult a task, as we are led to believe, to realise a perfect kitchen, at the present day, when so many sumptuous mansions are being built? When will its importance be perceived, and the fact made clear, that half the art of gastronomy depends upon the proper arrangement of the kitchen, and the facilities it affords for working?

The best way when one is building, and space is not unreasonably limited, will of course be to put the architect in communication with the cook; the latter will be able to give all necessary hints with reference to the construction of the stoves; the need of ventilation, lighting, and water supply; the placing of the scullery, the sinks, and ice-bin, and more particularly of the larder.

A good cook will give on all these points the most valuable information, and will be far better able to say what is wanted than those who build haphazard, in perfect ignorance of special culinary requirements, and without first conferring with a practical man.

On the question of the proper composition of a household, and upon that more delicate one of the relation between masters and their cooks, I cannot touch. With reference to the latter, I will merely hint that these relations are not what they should be; all are agreed that there are here some very serious abuses to amend, and a great and wholesome reform to be worked; let us hope that the spirit of progress of the times will soon set these matters straight. That which is of more interest to us here, and is strictly within the limits of the subject, is the question of the kitchen staff, considered in its bearing upon the preparation of a dinner. If we say that a well-found and well-arranged kitchen is indispensable to a cook, more particularly to meet extra occasions, let us also add, that it is no less necessary that he should be efficiently seconded by a number of hands sufficient to carry through successfully the work he has undertaken to do.

However, when speaking of a sufficient culinary staff, I am not desirous of bringing matters back to what they were in byegone days. I do not mean to convey the idea, that it is possible or necessary to have, as was formerly the case, a head cook for each department, all working in the same kitchen; comptrollers, chief cooks, different cooks for soups, sauces, and *entremets*, roasting cooks, pastry cooks, confectioners, &c.; all these surrounded by assistants and apprentices working under them, and forming so many brigades, each under the control of its special *chef*. I know as well as anyone what are the requirements of the day, and what it is possible to expect from the present class of establishments: so, without falling back to the old proportions, which led undoubtedly to confusion and waste, I am still of opinion that one can, and should, allow the cook to have at least the number of subordinates that he judges necessary to second him.

If the cook be a good manager, he will know how to divide off the work of the different departments amongst his assistants, whose abilities should be known to him; and in this way he will be able to secure satisfactory results, at much less cost, and with fewer numbers, than in former days.

Let the cook have what assistance he may require according to circumstances; there will be positive advantage in it, both in the result, and the cost; for it is an indisputable fact, that, if he has all he requires, he will work better, and consequently more cheaply, than if he had to do so under the disadvantages of an unsuitable *locale*, and short-handed.

It will be money well applied that allows a cook to keep himself personally clear of too much work, so that at all times he may look after the whole of the business going on around him, and, always clear-headed, that he may give his whole attention to the details, to giving directions, and supervising generally,—matters which are amongst the important duties of his office.

IV

COOKERY TERMS

I will repeat here, what I said in the First Part, that there are not—or rather there should not be—any cookery terms; for cookery should be capable of being expressed in ordinary language. Nevertheless, there are some special operations which it is nearly impossible to express in this way, without tedious circumlocution. It is for these only that I have retained, for the sake of shortness and clearness, a few technical terms.

I annex a short list of them:

To *clouter* is to insert in poulards, fowls, veal cushions, and sweetbreads, nail-shaped pieces of either tongue, or truffle, into similarly shaped holes made to receive them.

To *contiser* is to insert pieces of truffle, tongue, &c., into fillets of poultry, game, or fish, prepared to receive them.

To *work*.—This expression is used to indicate that a sauce, or paste, is to be stirred briskly with a spoon, or the hands, until quite smooth. It is also used to convey the operation of freezing an ice by stirring it vigorously with the spatula, and detaching the ice from the side of the freezing pot as it forms.

SILVER CASSEROLE

CHAPTER I

SOUPS

INNUMERABLE absurdities have been written on the subject of soups—on their origin—their different kinds—and proper importance in cookery.

Some have even gone so far as to deny their merit, and to suggest their entire abolition.

I need not say that I shall not attempt any purposeless disquisition of this kind; what I think is the truest thing to be said of soups in general is, that, being intended to prepare for a dinner, they should not be of a nature to surfeit or satisfy the appetite. I have consequently omitted most of the rich soups of the old school, which, by the number of their ingredients, were a meal in themselves. I have wished that all the soups I give, even those having *purées* for basis, should keep to what I have given out above as their mission, so that they should not encroach in any way upon the dinner proper.

Soups are the branch of culinary art in which the wildest notions of nomenclature have given themselves play in the designation of would-be novelties.

It is ever an easy matter, by a mere addition of tarragon, sorrel, or of some *purée*, to invent a so-called new soup, to

G G

which the most peculiar name is at once given. I am certainly
a great advocate of novelties; I have ever been of opinion, that
search after variety and invention should be the cook's creed;
I have even set the example myself, in more than one part of
this work; but by novelties I mean really new things, and not
old things whose whole merit lies in the eccentricity of the
new names that are given them.

As in every other instance, I have described the soups by the
simplest and most explicit titles. I hold that the first require-
ment of the name of a dish is to convey to the guests some
idea of its composition. All are agreed that the usual culinary
nomenclature is sadly at fault in this respect, and if it had to be
re-made, we should doubtless arrive at a far more sensible result.
I do not pretend to work the desired transformation, or to break
through the old prejudice upon this score; but, where I have
been compelled to adhere to the peculiar notion of naming a
soup, or a dish, after some distinguished prince or statesman, I
have thought it wise to couple it with some indication of the
nature of the preparation so named.

If my *confrères* will but second me in this attempted reform,
I think it will be an easy task to get rid by degrees of all those
obsolete and purposeless names, which figure in a host of bills
of fare.

I have not wished to make a special enumeration of
the preparations added to soups, preceding the description of
the latter; I have preferred to follow the idea, that each soup
has its special garnish, and to include it in each recipe,—avoiding in this way the monotony which belongs to all generalisation.

GENERAL STOCK

General Stock, or *Grand Bouillon*, is the principle of all the
soups and sauces which follow; it is used instead of water,
to which it is much to be preferred.

General Stock is made with legs of beef, knuckles of veal,
and any fresh meat trimmings and bones.

Cut all the meat from the bones; break them; and put them,
together with the meat, in a stock-pot, with about 2½ pints of
cold water to each pound of bones and meat; add a little salt,
and put on the fire to boil; skim carefully; and put in some
carrots, onions, and leeks; simmer for five hours; strain the
Stock through a broth napkin, into a basin, and keep it in a
cold place, till wanted.

VEAL STOCK, OR BLOND DE VEAU

Take 4 lbs. of leg of veal, 2 lbs. of gravy beef, and 2 hens, previously removing their fillets;

Butter a 2-gallon stewpan; slice 3 onions; lay these at the bottom of the stewpan, and the meat and bones on the top; moisten with a pint of Stock, and put on the fire to boil down slowly to a glaze; when of a nice brown colour, add 5 quarts of General Stock, and 1 oz. of salt; boil; skim, and add some carrots and leeks; simmer for four hours on the stove corner; strain it through a broth napkin; take off the fat, very carefully; after cooling for half an hour, clarify the Stock in the following manner: take the fillets of the hens which have been kept; trim the fat off; then chop them fine, and pound them in the mortar to a pulp; put this in a large stewpan, and add a small quantity of the Veal Stock to it; when well mixed, pour in all the remaining Stock; put it on the fire, stirring with a skimmer till it boils; and simmer for ten minutes; the Stock should then be quite clear; strain it through a broth napkin into a basin, to keep till wanted.

Remarks on Blond de Veau

Blond de Veau, or Veal Stock, is generally used for *nouilles*, maccaroni, and all Italian Pastes' Soups, which, on account of their tastelessness, require a higher flavoured *consommé*; it is also used to darken any *consommé* which might be too light in colour.

Uninitiated persons will wonder that a white meat, such as veal, should be the basis and colouring principle of *consommés* and sauces; this is because veal, by its nutritive and gelatinous properties, is best adapted to draw to glaze, and thereby to impart to the Stock the golden colour which is the special characteristic of *Blond de Veau.*

BROTH, OR CONSOMMÉ

Take 6 lbs. of gravy beef, 4 lbs. of leg of veal, and 2 hens, removing their fillets;

Truss, and roast the hens before a brisk fire, so that they may be coloured before they are half cooked; in that state put them, together with the meat, in a stock-pot, with 7 quarts of

General Stock ; put the stock-pot on the fire to boil; skim; and
add some salt, carrots, and leeks ; simmer for four hours on
the stove corner; strain the broth ; take the fat off carefully,
and clarify the broth with the fillets of the hens, reserved for
the purpose. Strain the *consommé* again, through a broth
napkin into a basin, and keep it in a cold place till wanted.

CHICKEN CONSOMMÉ

Put 2 chickens, or hens, having first removed their fillets,
and 6 lbs. of fillet of veal, in a stock-pot, with 5 quarts of General
Stock, and ½ oz. of salt ; put on the fire to boil ; then skim, and
add 2 onions, with 2 cloves stuck in one, 4 leeks, and a head
of celery ; simmer on the stove corner for three hours ; strain the
broth ; take off the fat, and clarify the *consommé* with the
fillets of chicken, or hen, as previously described; and strain it
once more, through a broth napkin, into a basin.

Observation.—Chicken *Consommé* should be colourless; by
following the indications given, it will be obtained perfectly
white and clear.

GAME CONSOMMÉ

Put, in a stock-pot : a rabbit, and 2 partridges, having previously removed their fillets ; 2 lbs. of knuckle of veal; and
5 quarts of General Stock ;

Put on the fire to boil ; skim ; then add :

½ oz. of salt,	1 faggot,
2 onions, with 2 cloves stuck in one,	3 leeks,
2 carrots,	1 head of celery ;

Simmer on the stove corner for two hours ; strain ; skim off
the fat, and clarify the *consommé* with the fillets of rabbit and
partridges; then strain it, through a broth napkin, into a basin,
and keep it in a cold place, till wanted.

FISH CONSOMMÉ

Put, in a 2-gallon stewpan :

¾ lb. of butter,	1 clove of unpicked garlic,
5 sliced carrots,	3 cloves,
4 sliced onions,	2 bay leaves,
3 heads of celery, cut into small pieces,	1 sprig of thyme,
	12 sprigs of parsley ;
4 shalots, unpicked,	

Fry the whole till of a reddish brown colour; then pour in 1 bottle of Sauterne or Châblis, and 5 quarts of water; boil and skim; then add: 1½ oz. of salt, and 2 pinches of *mignonnette* pepper; 6 lbs. of gurnet, cut in pieces; and the heads and bones of 6 whiting (reserving the fillets to clarify the *consommé*); simmer for two hours; then strain, through a broth napkin; pound the fillets of whiting in the mortar, adding 2 whites of egg whilst pounding; mix this pulp in the *consommé*, to clarify it; boil for a few minutes; strain, through a broth napkin, into a basin, and put by for use.

FRESH VEGETABLE CONSOMMÉ

Cut 2 lbs. of carrots, and 2 lbs. of onions, in slices; put them in a stewpan, with 1 lb. of butter, some parsley, thyme, shalot, and celery; fry these vegetables till slightly coloured; then moisten with 5 quarts of water; boil, and skim; add:

1½ oz. of salt,	1 quart of green peas,
½ oz. of whole pepper,	1 quart of fresh white hari-
1 pinch of grated nutmeg,	cot beans;
3 cloves,	

Simmer on the stove corner for three hours; take off the fat, and strain the *consommé*, through a broth napkin, into a basin, to keep in a cool place till wanted.

When green peas and fresh haricot beans are not in season, this *consommé* may be made with dry vegetables:—

Boil 1 quart of white haricot beans, and 1 quart of lentils *à la reine*, in 1½ gallon of water, with 1 pinch of salt, 1 onion, and 1 faggot; simmer for three hours; strain, and add this liquor to the fried vegetables.

SOUP WITH CROUTES GRATINÉES

Take 2 large bun-shaped French rolls; cut out the bottom crust and the crumb; dip them in hot *consommé*, and put them on a silver dish, the round side uppermost; baste them with a little clarified chicken dripping; put them in the oven, till they are dry and crisp;

Blanch and cool a nice Savoy cabbage; open it; take out the core; season with a little pepper and salt; put it in a stewpan to boil, with 1 onion, having a clove stuck in it, 1 carrot, ½ pint of clarified chicken dripping, and sufficient General Stock to come up 2 inches over the cabbage; simmer for an hour and a half. When ready to serve, garnish round the prepared crusts with the cabbage, well drained, and with some leeks, carrots, and turnips, taken out of the *consommé*; and serve; sending up to table, with the *croutes gratinées*, 2 quarts of very hot *consommé*, in a soup tureen.

Observation.—The success of this soup depends on the bread being nice and crisp. Those who fancy that crusts of bread floating on greasy broth realise the character of this soup are much mistaken; the vegetables should be cooked in the *consommé*, except the cabbage, which requires to be cooked separately, so as not to spoil the flavour of the *consommé*.

CONSOMMÉ WITH POACHED EGGS

Poach 12 eggs, as directed in the First Part, page 181; dish up the eggs in a silver casserole, with enough *consommé* to cover them, and serve them, together with some more *consommé*, in a soup tureen.

RICE SOUP

Wash and blanch ½ lb. of rice; drain it, and put it in a stewpan with 3 pints of *consommé*; simmer for an hour; when about to serve, drain the rice in a colander; put it in a soup tureen, and pour over it 2 quarts of boiling clear *consommé*.

VERMICELLI SOUP

Blanch ½ lb. of vermicelli in boiling water for five minutes; drain; and cool it in plenty of cold water, and drain it again; put it in a stewpan with 1 quart of *consommé*; simmer for ten minutes on the stove corner; when ready, drain the vermicelli; put it in a soup tureen, and pour over it 5 pints of boiling clear *consommé*, and 1 pint of *Blond de Veau*.

TAPIOCA SOUP

Put 3 quarts of *consommé* in a stewpan, on the fire, and, when boiling, pour gently in ¼ lb. of prepared tapioca, stirring with a spoon; cover the stewpan, and let the soup simmer on the stove corner for twenty minutes; skim, and pour it into the soup tureen.

MACCARONI SOUP

Blanch ½ lb. of maccaroni in plenty of water, slightly salted; boil for ten minutes; drain, and cool it in water, and drain it again on a cloth; cut the maccaroni in 1-inch lengths, and put it in a stewpan with 1 quart of *consommé*; simmer till the maccaroni is cooked; then drain, and put it in a soup tureen with 1½ quart of clear *consommé*, and 1 pint of *Blond de Veau*.

Serve a plate of Parmesan cheese with it.

Observation.—It is often justly remarked, that the *consommé* is weakened by the addition of the blanched maccaroni, which always absorbs some water in the blanching process; and, on the other hand, if it be not previously blanched, and is cooked in the *consommé* itself, that it will make it thick and unpleasant; this is why I have thought it better to boil the maccaroni first in a small quantity of *consommé*, merely to cook it; and then, after draining it, to add it to a good clear *consommé*. By this means, a limpid and richly flavoured soup is obtained.

This observation applies to all Paste Soups.

NOUILLES SOUP

Prepare ½ lb. of *Nouilles* Paste, as directed for *Nouilles* with Ham (*vide* First Part, page 186); blanch the *nouilles*; drain, and put them in a stewpan with 1 quart of *consommé*; simmer by the side of the fire for fifteen minutes; then drain, and put them in a soup tureen, with 2 quarts of *consommé*, and 1 quart of *Blond de Veau*.

SEMOLINA SOUP

Put 3 quarts of *consommé* in a stewpan, and when it boils, pour in 5 oz. of semolina, stirring with a wooden spoon; cover the stewpan, and simmer on the stove corner for twenty-five minutes; then skim, and pour in the soup tureen.

PERSIAN SALEP SOUP

Put 3 quarts of *consommé* in a stewpan; when it boils, pour in 2 oz. of Persian salep, stirring with a spoon; simmer for forty minutes; skim; and serve.

SAGO SOUP

Proceed as above, substituting sago for salep.

ITALIAN PASTE SOUP

Blanch ½ lb. of Italian Paste; cool; drain, and put it in a stewpan, with 1 quart of *consommé*; simmer on the stove corner for fifteen minutes; drain the paste; and put it in a soup tureen with 2 quarts of *consommé*, and 1 quart of *Blond de Veau*.

Observation.—A plateful of grated Parmesan cheese should be served with this soup.

JULIENNE SOUP

Cut the red part of 4 carrots, the same quantity of turnips, the white of one head of celery, 3 onions, and 6 leeks, in thin shreds 1 inch long; put them in a stewpan, with ½ lb. of butter, and 1 pinch of pounded sugar; stir over the fire till of a nice light brown colour; moisten with 3 quarts of *consommé*; simmer on the stove corner for three hours;—avoid boiling fast, which would thicken the *consommé*. Ten minutes before serving, add a quantity of cabbage lettuce and sorrel, cut in the same way as the other vegetables, and previously blanched for one minute; simmer for a few minutes more; skim the fat off very carefully; and serve.

JULIENNE SOUP WITH POACHED EGGS

Prepare the *Julienne* as directed in the preceding recipe; put it in the tureen; and serve with it, in a casserole, 12 poached eggs, as described for *Consommé* with Poached Eggs (*vide* page 230).

JULIENNE WITH CONSOMMÉ CUSTARD À LA ROYALE

Put in a basin:

½ pint of strong *consommé*,	a very small pinch of salt,
8 yolks of egg,	a little grated nutmeg;

Beat well with a spoon, and strain through a tammy cloth; Butter a plain pudding mould; pour the custard in it, and set it in a stewpan, with boiling water to half the height of the mould; close the stewpan; and put some live coals on the cover; avoid boiling, and keep the custard on the fire till set very firm;[*] let it cool in the mould; when cold, turn the custard out, and cut it in ¼-inch dice; put them in a soup tureen, and pour over 3 quarts of *Julienne* Soup, prepared as directed page 232.

JULIENNE SOUP WITH VEGETABLE CONSOMMÉ

This soup is prepared in the same way as *Julienne* Soup; merely substituting Vegetable *Consommé* (*vide* page 229), for the ordinary *consommé*.

SPRING SOUP

Turn 60 pieces of carrots, and 60 pieces of turnips, with a round, or an oval, vegetable scoop; blanch them; and put them into two small stewpans; cover them with *consommé*, and put 1 pinch of sugar in each stewpan; draw the contents gently to a glaze, gradually reducing all the *consommé*;

Boil separately, in water, about the same quantities of asparagus peas, and French beans (the latter cut to a diamond shape), and ½ pint of peas; when blanched, put all these vegetables in a stewpan, with 1 quart of *consommé*;

Cut about 15 leaves of cabbage lettuce, and 15 leaves of sorrel, with a vegetable cutter ¼-inch diameter; put them in the *consommé*, with the rest of the vegetables; simmer for a few minutes; when done, drain the vegetables in a colander; put them in a soup tureen; pour in two quarts of boiling clear *consommé*; and serve.

Observation.—Great care should be taken, whilst boiling the vegetables, to preserve their shape and colour; but this is no reason, as is frequently done, to cook them insufficiently; if properly cooked, they will be perfect in shape and colour, besides being well done, and agreeable eating.

SPRING SOUP WITH CROUTONS

Prepare a Spring Soup, as in the preceding recipe; adding in the soup tureen, with the vegetables, the crust of 2 rasped French rolls, cut in ½-inch square pieces.

---

[*] This mode of cooking is known as poaching *au bain-marie.*

Observation on Quenelles for Soups

Quenelles for soups are made of chicken, game, or fish force-meat, which I shall describe in the Chapter upon Garnishes and Forcemeat (pages 305, 306). These *quenelles* must differ in this much from those for *entrées* and garnish of removes, that the forcemeat requires to be made lighter and more delicate, being intended for soups which must prepare, not satiate, the appetite. They should be small in shape, never bigger than a small olive ; under these conditions, they will not justify the complaint of being too substantial, and unfitted for the beginning of a dinner.

QUENELLES FOR SOUPS—QUENELLES FOR RAGOUTS—LARGE QUENELLES

SPRING SOUP WITH CHICKEN QUENELLES

Put some Chicken Forcemeat (*vide* page 305), in a paper funnel ; close the top by folding the paper down, so as to enclose the forcemeat ; cut the point of the funnel to the size required to shape the *quenelles* ; butter a *sauté*-pan slightly, and squeeze the forcemeat out of the paper upon it (*vide* woodcut).

Pour some boiling *consommé* over the *quenelles* ; simmer for five minutes ; drain ; and put them in a soup tureen ; pour over some soup, prepared as directed for Spring Soup (*vide* page 274), and serve.

SPRING SOUP WITH VEGETABLE CONSOMMÉ

Prepare the soup in the same way as Spring Soup (*vide* page 234), substituting Vegetable *Consommé* for that of Chicken.

SPRING SOUP WITH POACHED EGGS

Prepare the soup as in the preceding recipe; serve 12 poached eggs in a silver casserole separately.

SPRING SOUP WITH FISH QUENELLES

Prepare some Fish Forcemeat, as indicated in the Chapter on Forcemeats (*vide* page 306), and put it in a paper funnel; squeeze out about 60 small *quenelles*; poach them; drain, and put them in a soup tureen; pour over 2 quarts of Spring Soup, with Vegetable *Consommé* (*vide* page 229); and serve.

PURÉE OF VEGETABLES SOUP À LA ROYALE

Make 1 gill of Red Carrot *Purée*; press it through a fine hair sieve; break 2 eggs in a basin; beat them as for omelet; add:

the Carrot *Purée*,
½ pint of *consommé*,
a little grated nutmeg,

and a little prepared cochineal, to give it a nice red colour;

Press the *purée* through a tammy cloth with two wooden spoons;

Butter a plain pudding mould; put the above custard in it; put it in a stewpan, with boiling water, to poach it *au bain-marie*, without boiling; when set, let it cool; turn the custard out of the mould; trim it, and cut it in ¼-inch dice; reserve them till wanted.

Prepare, in the same way, another custard, with a gill of Asparagus *Purée*; add a little spinach greening, to give it a nice green colour, and finish in the same way as the carrot custard.

Prepare 6 oz. of white leaves of celery; cut in ¼-inch square pieces; blanch, drain, and boil them in Chicken *Consommé*; when done, drain the celery; put it in a soup tureen, with the dice of carrot and asparagus custard, and pour over 3 quarts of Chicken *Consommé*, slightly thickened with prepared tapioca; and serve.

SOUP WITH TRUFFLE AND CHICKEN PURÉES À LA ROYALE

Wash, trim, and cook enough truffles to produce a gill of purée (*vide* Truffle *Purée*, page 303); make a custard with the *purée*, in the same way as directed for Carrot Custard in the preceding recipe; prepare also a custard of Chicken *Purée* in the same way; when poached, and cold, cut the custards in dice; put them in a soup tureen, and pour over 3 quarts of Chicken *Consommé*, slightly thickened with Persian salep.

SOUP OF TRUFFLE PURÉE À LA PÉRIGORD

Prepare 2 gills of Truffle *Purée* to make a custard, as in the preceding recipe; when cold, cut it in dice; put them in a soup tureen, and pour over 3 quarts of thin Chicken *Purée*, with 1 gill of Almond Milk (*vide* Almond Milk with *Croutons*, page 252); and serve.

SOUP OF TURNIP PURÉE À LA CONDÉ

Prepare $\frac{1}{2}$ pint of Turnip *Purée*; pass it through a fine hair sieve;

Put 4 whites of egg in a basin; beat them as for omelet; then add:

    the Turnip *Purée*,
    a little grated nutmeg,
    1 pint of Chicken *Consommé*;

Press the mixture through a tammy cloth, with two wooden spoons; poach it *au bain-marie*, and when cold cut this custard in dice; put them in a soup tureen; pour over 3 quarts of red Haricot Beans *Purée*, diluted with *Consommé* of Game; and serve.

BRUNOISE SOUP

Cut in $\frac{1}{4}$-inch dice:

$\frac{1}{4}$ lb. of red carrots,	$\frac{1}{4}$ lb. of white celery,
$\frac{1}{4}$ lb. of turnips,	$\frac{1}{4}$ lb. of onions;
$\frac{1}{4}$ lb. of leeks,	

Blanch all these vegetables separately; drain, and put them in a stewpan, with $\frac{3}{4}$ lb. of butter; fry them for five minutes,

stirring all the time; add a teaspoonful of pounded sugar, and
1 pint of *consommé*; reduce to a glaze, and add 3 more quarts
of *consommé*, and simmer on the stove corner, skimming off the
fat as it rises to the surface;

Blanch, and cook ½ lb. of Italian Paste (*vide* page 232);
drain, and put it in a soup tureen; pour the *Brunoise* Soup
over; and serve.

SOUP À LA PAYSANNE

Remove the yellow core of 4 carrots, and cut the red part
in thin shreds; cut 4 turnips, ½ lb. of cabbage, and 3 onions in
the same way; put all these vegetables in a stewpan, with ¾ lb.
of butter, and a teaspoonful of pounded sugar; fry over the fire
till the vegetables assume a reddish brown colour; moisten with
3 gills of *Consommé*, and simmer for two hours; then add ¼ lb.
of cabbage lettuce, and ¼ lb. of sorrel, and simmer for one
hour more; put the crust of 3 French rolls, cut in pieces, in
the soup tureen; pour over the soup; and serve.

VEGETABLE SOUP WITH POACHED EGGS À LA COLBERT

Turn 20 balls of carrots, and 20 balls of turnips, with a
¾-inch vegetable scoop; blanch them separately, and put them
in two small stewpans, with enough Chicken *Consommé* to cover
them; add a pinch of sugar, and boil the *consommé* down to a
glaze; when both vegetables are glazed, put them together in
the same stewpan; add 1 pint of *consommé*; boil for a minute,
then drain, and put them in a soup tureen, with the same
quantity of small heads of cauliflowers, previously boiled in
salt water, and well drained; pour over 2 quarts of Vegetable
Consommé, and serve with 12 poached eggs separately.

SOUP WITH STUFFED CABBAGE LETTUCES

Pick, and wash 8 cabbage lettuces; blanch, drain, and cut
them in halves; remove the core; sprinkle them inside with a
little salt; put them together again, and bind them round with
string; butter a stewpan slightly, and cover the bottom with
slices of veal, to a thickness of about an inch; lay the lettuces
on the veal; cover them entirely with Stock, and add ½ pint of
clarified fat, 1 faggot, and 1 onion, with 2 cloves stuck in it.
Boil, cover the stewpan, and simmer for two hours; then drain

the lettuces; spread them open on a cloth, and lay a little Chicken Forcemeat on each half; flatten them with a knife, and fold over the ends and sides, to enclose the forcemeat, and form a long square; set them in a *sauté*-pan, and pour over 1½ pint of boiling *consommé*; simmer gently to poach the forcemeat, then drain the lettuces; lay them in the soup tureen; pour over 2 quarts of *consommé*; and serve.

Observation.—This soup is a particularly substantial one, and differs very much from those light soups which should prepare for a meal; I give it merely, in this instance, to meet the requirements of those who like a really tangible soup.

CONSOMMÉ SOUP WITH CABBAGE LETTUCES

Stew 6 cabbage lettuces, as in the preceding recipe; when done, drain and open them; remove the cores, and cut them crosswise, each in six pieces; put them in a soup tureen, and pour over 2 quarts of boiling *consommé*.

BLOND DE VEAU SOUP WITH CELERY

Trim, and wash, 6 heads of celery; cut all the white part in ¼-inch dice; blanch, drain, cool, and put them in a stewpan, with 1 quart of *consommé*; simmer for an hour and a half; then put on a sharper fire, to reduce the *consommé* to a glaze; put the celery in a soup tureen; add 2 quarts of boiling *Blond de Veau*; and serve.

VERTPRÉ SOUP

Boil ¼ lb. of prepared tapioca, in 3 quarts of *consommé*; prepare:

    ½ lb. of asparagus peas,
    ⅓ lb. of French beans, cut in diamonds,
    ½ lb. of green peas;

When all these vegetables are blanched, put them to boil, for a few minutes, in 1 pint of *consommé*; drain, and put them in a soup tureen; skim the tapioca; pour it over the vegetables in the soup tureen; and serve.

RAVIOLI SOUP

Make ½ lb. of *Nouilles* Paste, as directed for Nouilles with Ham (*vide* page 186);

Take ¾ lb. of Chicken Forcemeat; add to it a tablespoonful of grated Parmesan cheese, and either a tablespoonful of borage, blanched, pounded, and passed through a hair sieve, or a tablespoonful of spinach greening; roll out the *Nouilles* Paste as thin as possible, and cut it with a round fluted cutter, 2 inches in diameter; then moisten the edges of the rounds, with a brush dipped in water; lay a ball of the forcemeat, the size of a nut, upon each round of *Nouilles* Paste, folding over the side to enclose the forcemeat, and pressing the edges together to secure it; butter a *sauté*-pan; lay these *ravioli* in it; pour over a sufficient quantity of boiling Stock to poach them; simmer for five minutes; drain, and put the *ravioli* in a soup tureen; pour 3 quarts of boiling *Blond de Veau* over them; and serve, with a plate of grated Parmesan cheese, separately.

BARLEY SOUP À LA HOLLANDAISE

Blanch 6 oz. of pearl barley in 2 quarts of water; drain, cool, and put it in a stewpan, with 3 pints of General Stock; boil gently for two hours; when the barley is done, drain it, and put it in a stewpan, with 2 quarts of Chicken *Consommé*; and simmer for a quarter of an hour.

Make 50 small Chicken Forcemeat *Quenelles*, about the size of a large pea;

Cut 1 oz. of sorrel leaves in thin shreds; blanch, drain, and put them in a soup tureen with the *quenelles*; skim the Barley Soup; and pour it in the tureen.

QUENELLES SOUP WITH ESSENCE OF CHICKEN

Butter a *sauté*-pan slightly, into which press out 50 Chicken Forcemeat *Quenelles*, from a paper funnel, to the size of an olive, and pour 1 pint of Stock over them; simmer, till they are poached; drain, and put them in a soup tureen, with 3 quarts of boiling Essence of Chicken (*vide* page 268); and serve immediately.

GAME QUENELLES SOUP

Make 50 Game Forcemeat *Quenelles* as above (*vide* Game Forcemeat, page 304); poach, drain, and put them in a soup tureen, with 3 quarts of boiling Game *Consommé* (*vide* page 228); and serve.

FISH CONSOMMÉ SOUP WITH FISH QUENELLES

Make 50 Fish Forcemeat *Quenelles* (*vide* page 306); poach,
drain, and put them in a soup tureen, with 3 quarts of Fish
Consommé (*vide* page 228).

SOUP AUX TROIS RACINES

Cut, in thin shreds, 1 inch long:
    ¼ lb. of the red part of carrots,
    ¼ lb. of the white part of celery,
    ¼ lb. of parsley roots;
Blanch these vegetables for five minutes; drain, and fry them
in a stewpan, with ¼ lb. of butter, till they assume a reddish
brown colour; moisten, with 3 gills of *consommé*; and boil down
to a glaze;
Blanch ¼ lb. of *nouilles*, cut very fine; drain them; put them
in a soup tureen; add the vegetables; pour in 3 quarts of
boiling *Blond de Veau*; and serve.

PROFITEROLLES SOUP AU CHASSEUR

Take 40 *profiterolles*, that is, 40 small bun-shaped rolls, only
1 inch in diameter; cut the bottom crust, and remove all the
crumb; fill them with Game Forcemeat (*vide* page 304); put
them in a buttered *sauté*-pan in the oven, to poach the forcemeat; then arrange them in a soup tureen; pour 3 quarts of
Game *Consommé* (*vide* page 228) over them; and serve.
    Observation.—This soup must never be allowed to wait,—as,
if the *profiterolles* are left to soak too long, they will be spoilt.

SEMOLINA SOUP WITH SORREL À LA LÉOPOLD

Prepare some Semolina Soup, as described page 231; add
¼ lb. of sorrel, cut in thin shreds, and boiled in *consommé*; drain
the sorrel; put it in a soup tureen; pour the semolina over; mix,
and serve.

BARLEY SOUP WITH BLOND DE VEAU

Blanch ½ lb. of German barley; drain, cool, and put it in a
stewpan, with 1 quart of *consommé*; simmer for four hours;

drain, and put the barley in a soup tureen; pour over it 3 quarts of boiling *Blond de Veau*; and serve.

PAYSANNE SOUP WITH MACCARONI

Cut 1 lb. of the white part of some leeks, as for *Julienne*; blanch, drain, and put the shreds in a stewpan, with ¼ lb. of butter; fry over the fire till they are slightly coloured; moisten with 3 quarts of *consommé*, and simmer, on the stove corner, for three quarters of an hour;

Blanch ¼ lb. of small maccaroni; drain, and cut it in ½-inch lengths; put it in a stewpan, with 1 pint of *consommé*; boil for fifteen minutes; drain, and put the maccaroni in a soup tureen; skim the soup; pour it over the maccaroni; and serve.

Send some grated Parmesan cheese separately, on a plate.

SWALLOWS' NESTS SOUPS

This soup is in reality much simpler of preparation than its ambitious name would lead one to imagine. I give it here on account of its originality; and I think I may venture to say, that its principal merit, irrespective of its outlandish element, is due to the *consommé* employed in its preparation.

For soup for 12 persons, steep, say, 9 swallows' nests in water, for twenty-four hours; wash, and pick them very carefully; the nests will then be in shreds, very similar to *nouilles*; pick out any small feathers which may still adhere to the nests, and wash them again several times, until they are as white as snow; put them in a stewpan, with 1 quart of General Stock, and simmer for two hours very gently; drain, and put the nests in a soup tureen, and pour over 2½ quarts of boiling *consommé*, prepared as directed, page 227.

TAPIOCA SOUP, WITH CHICKEN, TONGUE, AND TRUFFLES

Boil ¼ lb. of prepared tapioca in 3 quarts of *consommé*; let it simmer for twenty minutes, in a covered stewpan; cut ¼ lb. of truffles, ¼ lb. of cooked fillets of fowl, and ¼ lb. of tongue, in thin shreds, ¾ inch long, ⅛ inch thick; put the whole in a soup tureen; skim the tapioca; pour it into the tureen; and serve.

I I

CRÉCY SOUP AU CONSOMMÉ

Slice off 1 lb. of the red outside part of some carrots; blanch it in plenty of water, for five minutes; and drain it.

Put in a stewpan:

½ lb. of butter,	1 sliced onion,
the white part of 4 leeks,	the sliced carrots;

Fry for five minutes; moisten with 1 quart of Chicken *Consommé*, and add ¼ lb. of crumb of French rolls.

I advise thickening with bread-crumb instead of rice, because I have noticed that the latter is liable to give the soup a starchy appearance; simmer till the carrot is quite done; press the whole through a tammy cloth; and moisten the *purée* with 2 quarts of Chicken *Consommé*; stir till boiling, and simmer for one hour in a closed stewpan; before serving, skim off all the fat, and pour in the soup tureen.

Serve on a plate some *croutons* made of crumb of bread cut in ⅛-inch dice, and fried yellow in clarified butter.

CRÉCY SOUP AU MAIGRE

Proceed exactly as in the preceding recipe, moistening with Vegetable *Consommé*, instead of with that of Chicken.

TURNIP PURÉE SOUP

Peel and slice sufficient turnips to produce about 1¾ lb.; blanch them in plenty of water, and let them steep in cold water for an hour;

Put in a stewpan 2 oz. of butter, and 1½ oz. of flour; stir over the fire for five minutes; then moisten with 1 quart of Chicken *Consommé*; add the turnips, well drained, 1 pinch of salt, and a small pinch of sugar; stir till boiling, and simmer on the stove corner, till the turnips are done; press them through a tammy cloth; then add another quart of Chicken *Consommé*; simmer again; and skim the fat off carefully.

Blanch, and boil ¼ lb. of rice in some General Stock for twenty-five minutes; drain the rice; put it in the soup tureen, and pour the *purée* over, adding ½ pint of double cream, and 1 oz. of butter; stir till the butter is melted; and serve.

POTATO PURÉE SOUP A LA PARMENTIER

Peel and slice 1½ lb. of mealy potatoes; put them in a stewpan, with 2 quarts of Chicken *Consommé*; boil them thoroughly;
press the potatoes twice through a tammy cloth; put the *purée*
in a stewpan, and add another quart of Chicken *Consommé*; stir
over the fire till boiling; simmer, and skim. Before serving,
thicken the *purée* with ½ pint of double cream, and 1 oz. of
butter; then add 2 tablespoonfuls of picked chervil leaves;
pour the soup into the tureen; and serve, with *croutons* of
bread, fried in butter, on a plate.

Observation.—Instead of *croutons* and chervil, a garnish of
asparagus points, and carrots, scooped into small balls, may be
added to the *purée*.

RED HARICOT BEANS PURÉE SOUP À LA CONDÉ

Wash 1 quart of red haricot beans; put them in a stewpan,
with:

1 gallon of water,	the green leaves of 1 head
1 onion with 2 cloves stuck	of celery,
in it,	2 pinches of salt;
1 carrot,	

Boil till the beans are well done; drain them in a colander;
pound them in a mortar; and press them through a hair sieve,
moistening with 1½ quart of Game *Consommé*;

When all the beans are passed through the sieve, put the *purée*
in a stewpan with another quart of *consommé*; stir till boiling
takes place; then put the stewpan on a very slow fire, to simmer
slightly for one hour; close the stewpan, and put some live coals
on the cover; by this slow simmering process, the *purée* will
acquire a nice red colour; put it to boil gently on the stove
corner, to facilitate skimming off the fat; skim the fat off, and
pour the *purée* in a soup tureen, and serve with some *croutons* of
fried bread, on a plate.

Boiled rice may be added to this soup, instead of serving it
with *croutons*.

Observation.—This simple method of cooking the beans de-
viates from that generally adopted of boiling them with ham,
old partridges, and *consommé*, which frequently impart to the
purée a strong acrid taste, difficult to get rid of.

I I 2

ASPARAGUS PURÉE SOUP

Break off all the tender parts of a bundle of green asparagus; reserve the points to add to the soup;

Blanch the pieces of asparagus in boiling water; drain, and put them in a stewpan with 2 oz. of butter, and 1½ oz. of flour; stir over the fire for five minutes; add 2 quarts of Chicken *Consommé*; simmer on the stove corner till the asparagus is cooked; then press it through a tammy cloth; put in a stewpan, and boil the *purée* gently for twenty minutes; pour it in a soup tureen; add 3 oz. of butter, and ½ pint of double cream; stir till the butter is melted; put in the asparagus points, previously boiled in salted water; and serve.

Observation.—Should the soup be too light in colour, a little spinach greening may be added.

ENDIVE PURÉE SOUP

Trim 18 endives, keeping only the white part; blanch, and cool them in plenty of cold water; drain, and squeeze the water well out, with the hands;

Make a *roux* in a stewpan, with 2 oz. of butter, and 2 oz. of flour; moisten with 2 quarts of Chicken *Consommé*; when it boils, add the endives; simmer very gently till they are done, and press them through a tammy cloth; put the *purée* in another stewpan; boil and simmer on the stove corner, to clarify it;

Boil ¼ lb. of rice in some *Consommé*, as indicated for Turnip *Purée* (*vide* page 242); put the rice in the soup tureen; skim the fat off the *purée*; mix ½ pint of double cream in it; taste for seasoning, and pour the soup on the rice in the tureen; and serve.

Observation.—It was formerly customary to finish Endive, Asparagus, Turnip, and other *purées*, with *Velouté* Sauce; I have purposely departed from this mode, because I have constantly found in practice, that, by boiling the vegetables with their thickening, the *purée* is obtained smoother, and with the flavour of the vegetables unimpaired.

LENTIL PURÉE SOUP À LA CONTI

Wash 3 pints of lentils *à la reine*; put them in a stewpan, with:

3 quarts of water,	1 onion with 2 cloves stuck
1 faggot,	in it,
1 carrot,	1 sprig of celery;

Boil till the lentils are done; then take out the faggot, onion, and carrot; drain, and pound the lentils in a mortar; press them through a tammy cloth, and put the *purée* in a stewpan, with 2 quarts of Game *Consommé*; stir over the fire till boiling, and simmer for one hour on the stove corner,—the stewpan three parts covered only;

Cut about ¼ lb. of celery leaves, in small bunches; boil them in some General Stock; drain, and put them in a soup tureen; skim the *purée*; pour it in the tureen, on the celery; and serve.

GREEN PEA PURÉE SOUP AU CONSOMME

Boil 3 pints of fresh green peas, in plenty of water, adding a carrot, an onion, and sufficient salt; when done, take out the onion and carrot; drain, and press the peas, through a tammy cloth; put the *purée* in a stewpan, on the fire, with 2 quarts of Chicken *Consommé*, and 1 pinch of sugar; stir till boiling commences; then simmer on the stove corner;

Blanch ¼ lb. of rice; drain, cool, and boil it in 1 pint of Chicken *Consommé*; when done, drain, and put the rice in a soup tureen; skim the *purée*; pour it over the rice; add 2 oz. of butter; stir till this is melted; and serve.

Observation.—If the *purée* of peas be too pale in colour, add a little spinach greening, passed through a silk sieve.

PEA SOUP À L'ALLEMANDE

Prepare a thickening, by gradually mixing in a stewpan 3 oz. of sifted flour with 1 quart of Chicken *Consommé*;

Boil 2 quarts of Chicken *Consommé* in another stewpan, and strain the prepared thickening into it, through the pointed strainer,—being careful to stir all the time, to prevent lumping; add ½ a pinch of salt, ½ a pinch of sugar, and 1 quart of fresh-shelled green peas, previously well washed; continue stirring with a spoon, till the soup boils, and simmer until the peas are cooked; then skim, and pour the soup in a tureen; add 1½ oz. of butter; stir till this is melted; and serve.

GREEN PEA PURÉE SOUP

Prepare the *purée* as directed for Green Pea *Purée* Soup *au Consommé* (*vide* page 245); moisten with the water in which the peas have been boiled, instead of *consommé*; boil the same quantity of rice in water, with a little butter and salt; and finish the soup in the same way as the *Purée au Consommé*.

Observation.—For these *purées* it is indispensable that the peas should be fresh-shelled.

SORREL SOUP WITH CREAM

Pick and wash ¾ lb. of fresh sorrel; cut it in thin shreds, and put it in a stewpan with ¼ lb. of butter; stir over the fire for five minutes; add rather less than 1 oz. of flour; stir again for a few minutes, and moisten with 2½ quarts of Chicken *Consommé*; stir till it boils; then simmer on the stove corner for twenty-five minutes; skim, and thicken the soup with 6 yolks of egg, and ½ pint of double cream;

Cut some crust of rasped French rolls in narrow strippets; put them in a soup tureen; pour the soup on to the bread; add ½ oz. of butter; stir till melted; and serve.

CHESTNUT PURÉE SOUP

Clean and prepare 60 chestnuts, as directed for *Purée* (*vide* page 302); boil them gently in 1 quart of General Stock; when done, press them through a tammy cloth; put the *purée* in a stewpan, with 2 quarts of *consommé*; stir till boiling, and simmer for one hour; skim, and pour the soup in a tureen, and serve with it some *croutons* of bread, fried in butter, on a plate.

WHITE HARICOT BEANS PURÉE SOUP

Boil 3 pints of white haricot beans, in a stewpan, with:

3 quarts of water,	1 carrot,
1 onion,	1 pinch of salt,
1 faggot,	1 small pinch of sugar;

When the beans are done, take out the onion, faggot, and carrot; drain the beans; pound them in a mortar, and press them through a tammy cloth;

Put the *purée* in a stewpan; moisten it with 2 quarts of Chicken *Consommé*, and simmer on the stove corner for half an hour;

Boil ¼ lb. of rice in some *consommé*; when done, drain, and put it in a soup tureen; pour the *purée* on it, adding a tablespoonful of picked leaves of chervil; thicken the soup with ½ pint of double cream, and 1 oz. of butter; mix thoroughly; taste; and serve.

LENTIL PURÉE SOUP WITH VEGETABLES À LA FAUBONNE

Prepare some Lentil *Purée*, as described for Lentil *Purée à la Conti* (*vide* page 244);

Add to it 1 pint of *Julienne* vegetables, previously blanched and glazed, as for *Julienne* Soup (*vide* page 232); boil for a few minutes; skim; pour the soup in the tureen; and serve.

This soup may be prepared with any other vegetable *purée*, with the *Julienne* vegetables added as above.

CHICKEN PUREE SOUP A LA REINE

Put 2 chickens in a stewpan, with :

5 quarts of General Stock,	2 small pinches of salt,
1 faggot,	2 small pinches of sugar ;
1 onion,	

Boil for half an hour; let the chickens cool in the broth for fifteen minutes; then drain them; strain the broth through a napkin; and skim off the fat very carefully;

Take all the meat off the chickens; free it of skin and fat, and chop and pound it in a mortar, together with the crumb of 2 French rolls, soaked in the broth; add the *purée* gradually to the remainder of the broth, and pass the whole through a tammy cloth; put it in a stewpan over the fire till very hot, without boiling; add a thickening prepared in the following manner :

Blanch, peel and wash 30 Jordan almonds; pound them in a mortar, adding ½ pint of cream whilst pounding; press through a cloth, and mix this *liaison* in the soup;

Put some Chicken Forcemeat *Quenelles*, prepared as directed for Spring Soup with Chicken *Quenelles* (*vide* page 234), in the soup tureen; pour the soup on to the *quenelles*; and serve.

CHICKEN PURÉE SOUP WITH CUCUMBERS

Prepare some Chicken *Purée* as above ;

Cut 2 cucumbers in slices, ½ inch thick ; then cut each slice with a round vegetable cutter, ⅓ inch in diameter ; boil the rounds of cucumber in some Chicken *Consommé* for twenty minutes ; drain, and put them in a soup tureen ; pour the *purée* over ; and serve.

GAME PURÉE SOUP

Take 3 partridges and 2 rabbits ; prepare them as for roasting ; put them in a stewpan to braize, with :

3 quarts of General Stock,	1 faggot,
1 onion, with 2 cloves stuck in it,	2 carrots ;

Boil, skim, and simmer till the rabbits are done ;

Let them get cool in the Stock ; then remove all the meat from the partridges and rabbits ; chop and pound it in a mortar with the crumb of 2 French rolls, soaked in 1 pint of the Stock ; add the remaining Stock gradually to the *purée* ; press the whole through a tammy cloth ; and put in a stewpan over the fire to get very hot, without boiling ;

Put some Game Forcemeat *Quenelles* in a soup tureen ; skim the soup ; pour it on them ; and serve.

GERMAN BARLEY SOUP

Put 10 oz. of German pearl barley in a stewpan with 3 quarts of water, 1 oz. of butter, and a pinch of salt ; simmer till the barley is well cooked ; then drain and put it in a stewpan with 2 quarts of Chicken *Consommé*, and 3 gills of Sorrel *Purée* ; stir over the fire till boiling commences, and simmer for fifteen minutes ;

Skim, and pour the soup in a tureen ; thicken it with ½ pint of double cream, and 1 oz. of butter ; mix well together ; and serve.

CRÈME DE RIZ SOUP WITH CHICKEN CONSOMMÉ

Wash and blanch ½ lb. of rice ; cool, and put it in a stewpan with 1 quart of Chicken *Consommé* ; boil gently till the rice is done, and press it through a tammy cloth ; put the *purée* in a stewpan with 2 more quarts of *consommé*; stir over the fire till boiling, and simmer for fifteen minutes;

Skim, and pour the soup in the tureen; thicken it with $1\frac{1}{2}$ oz. of butter, and $\frac{1}{2}$ pint of double cream; mix, and serve.

Observation.—Green asparagus points or green peas may be added to this soup.

CRÈME D'ORGE SOUP WITH CHICKEN CONSOMMÉ

Boil $\frac{3}{4}$ lb. of German pearl barley as directed for German Barley Soup (*vide* page 248); press it through a tammy-cloth; put the *purée* in a stewpan, with 2 quarts of Chicken *Consommé*; boil and simmer for fifteen minutes;

Skim, and pour into the soup tureen; thicken the soup with 3 gills of double cream, and 1 oz. of butter; stir till this is melted; and serve.

CRAYFISH SOUP, OR BISQUE

Put 40 crayfish in a stewpan, with:

1 bottle of Sauterne,	1 small sprig of thyme,
1 sliced onion,	1 bay leaf,
1 sliced carrot,	$\frac{1}{2}$ oz. of salt,
5 sprigs of parsley,	1 pinch of pepper,
1 small pinch of cayenne pepper;	

Boil for ten minutes; tossing the crayfish to cook them evenly; when done, take off the tails; free them of shell, and reserve them, to add to the soup;

Put by the shells and the claws, to make the crayfish butter.

Put the insides of the crayfish in the liquor in which they have been boiled; add 2 quarts of *consommé*, and 2 French rolls, previously cut in slices and dried in the oven, without being coloured; put the stewpan on the fire, and simmer for one hour; then pass the whole through a tammy-cloth, and pour the soup into another stewpan; stir over the fire till boiling takes place, and simmer for ten minutes;

Prepare some crayfish butter in the following manner:—

Put the shells and claws of the crayfish in a mortar; pound them well; add $\frac{1}{4}$ lb. of butter, and, when well mixed together, put in a closed *bain-marie*-pan placed in a stewpan half full of boiling water; boil thus for one hour; then press the butter through a broth napkin into a basin of cold water; when the butter is set, take it off the water ; drain, and dry it with a cloth, and pass it through a fine hair seive ; add a fourth part of this butter to ¼ lb. of Whiting Forcemeat and, with it, form some *quenelles* of the size of a pea ; poach them in some boiling broth ; drain, and put them in a soup tureen, together with the trimmed crayfish tails.

Boil up the soup ; skim ; and thicken it with the remaining crayfish butter ; pour it in the soup tureen ; and serve.

CRAYFISH SOUP, OR BISQUE, AU MAIGRE

Prepare 40 crayfish, as in the preceding recipe ; remove the tails ; pick, and put them by to add to the soup ;

Put all the shells and the bodies of the crayfish in a mortar ; pound them well ; put them in a stewpan with 3 quarts of Fish *Consommé* ; boil for half an hour, and strain through a broth napkin ; trim the tails ; put them in the soup tureen with some Fish Forcemeat *Quenelles*, made as above ; pour the soup over them ; and serve.

CRAYFISH SOUP WITH CREAM

Put 40 crayfish in a stewpan ; boil them with :

1 pint of *consommé*,	1 middle-sized sliced carrot,
10 sprigs of parsley,	2 middle-sized onions cut in slices ;

Boil for ten minutes,—tossing the crayfish occasionally ; when done, remove the tails ; pick them, and put them by ;

Pound the bodies, claws, and shells in a mortar ; put them in a stewpan, with 5 pints of Chicken *Consommé* ; boil ; and simmer for one hour ;

Make a *roux* in a stewpan, with ½ lb. of butter, and ¼ lb. of flour ; stir over the fire for five minutes ;

Strain the *consommé* from the pounded crayfish ; add it to the *roux* in the stewpan ; stir on the fire for twenty minutes ; add 1 pint of double cream, ½ pint at a time ; and, when the soup is sufficiently reduced, strain it through a tammy cloth, into a *bain-marie*-pan to keep warm ;

Five minutes before serving, boil up the soup, and add another ½ pint of double cream ; put the crayfish tails in the soup tureen ; pour the soup over ; and serve.

OYSTER SOUP

Blanch 5 dozen of Ostend or native oysters, by throwing them in boiling water, and stirring them with a spoon for one minute; drain; cool, and drain them a second time; and remove carefully every particle of shell;

Make a *roux* in a stewpan, with 2 oz. of butter, and 3 oz. of flour; stir it over the fire for three minutes; and moisten with $2\frac{1}{2}$ quarts of Fish *Consommé*; stir till boiling, and simmer for half an hour;

Put the oysters in a soup tureen, with a tablespoonful of picked leaves of parsley; skim the soup; thicken it with 6 yolks of egg, and 1 gill of cream; stir, till well mixed; pour it over the oysters; and serve.

MUSSEL SOUP

Take 60 small mussels, and put them in a stewpan, with :

1 sliced onion,	1 gill of water,
10 sprigs of parsley,	1 pinch of salt ;

Toss the mussels over the fire, till the shells open; remove the shells; wash the mussels in tepid water; drain, and put them by;

Make a *roux* to thicken $2\frac{1}{2}$ quarts of Fish *Consommé*; add the liquor in which the mussels have been cooked, and finish as for Oyster Soup.

BOUILLABAISSE

Put in a stewpan :

4 sliced onions,	2 bay leaves,
4 cloves,	1 sprig of thyme,
1 sliced carrot,	2 unpicked cloves of garlic,
1 oz. of parsley,	4 shalots ;

Cut in pieces about 5 lbs. of different fish, such as soles, flounders, small gurnet, red mullet, and whiting;

Put the pieces of fish in the stewpan, with the vegetables, and :

1 gill of olive oil,	$\frac{1}{2}$ oz. of capsicums,
1 oz. of salt,	2 quarts of water ;
2 small pinches of pepper,	

Boil for twenty-five minutes,—keeping the stewpan closely covered.

If whiting are used, they should not be added till the soup has boiled for fifteen minutes ;

Drain the fish carefully ; remove any pieces of vegetable, or spice, which might be adhering to it, and pile it up on a large dish ;

Add a teaspoonful of powdered saffron to the liquor ; strain it through the pointed gravy strainer, into the soup tureen ; and serve.

Hand the dish of fish round, and also some sippets of dry toast on a plate.

Observation.—Bouillabaisse, which is of Southern origin, requires to be highly flavoured. This soup can be prepared with fresh-water fish : proceed precisely in the same way, but, when practicable, give the preference to salt-water fish.

ALMOND MILK SOUP WITH RICE

Wash, and blanch ½ lb. of rice ; drain ; and put it in a stewpan, with 3 pints of milk, a small pinch of salt, and 1 oz. of sugar ; and simmer on a slow fire for an hour ;

Blanch, and peel ½ lb. of Jordan almonds, and 10 bitter ones ; pound them well in a mortar ; adding 1 pint of milk at different times, to prevent their turning oily ; when the almonds are well pounded, add them to 1 quart of milk, and strain through a broth napkin ;

Put the boiled rice in the soup tureen ; warm the almond milk, without boiling,—stirring it with a spoon to prevent its curdling ; and, when hot, pour it over the rice ; mix, and serve ; and add sugar to taste.

ALMOND MILK SOUP WITH CROUTONS

Blanch and peel 1 lb. of almonds, and 20 bitter ones ; pound them well ; moisten with 1 quart of milk, and press through a tammy cloth ;

Boil 3 pints of milk, with 2 oz. of sugar, and 1 pinch of salt ; pour the boiling milk in a soup tureen ; then stir in the almond milk, and serve with a plateful of *croutons*, prepared as follows :

Cut some thin slices of crumb of bread ; cut these out with a round cutter ¾ inch in diameter ; lay the rounds on a baking-sheet ; sprinkle some fine sugar over them ; put them in the oven, and glaze them with a red-hot glazing iron, so as to melt the sugar; turn them over, and glaze the other side in the same way.

RICE SOUP À L'ITALIENNE

Cut 2 onions in small dice; fry them in a stewpan, with ¼ lb. of lard, for four minutes; add 10 oz. of rice, previously well washed and dried in a cloth; 1 pinch of salt, 1 small pinch of pepper, and 1 small pinch of cayenne pepper; stir over the fire for four minutes; then moisten with 3 pints of water, and boil for twenty minutes; drain the rice; put it in the soup tureen, and pour over 1 quart of boiling *consommé*; and serve, with some grated Parmesan cheese on a plate.

RICE SOUP À LA TURQUE

Blanch 10 oz. of rice; drain, and put it in a stewpan, with 1½ pint of *consommé*, some salt, pepper, and a teaspoonful of powdered saffron, and boil the rice for twenty minutes;

Butter a plain pudding mould, and put the rice in it;

Boil 4 lbs. of breast of mutton in 2 quarts of water; skim, and add 2 carrots, 2 onions, and some pepper and salt;

When the meat is done, strain the broth through a napkin, and pour it in the soup tureen, without skimming off the fat;

Turn the rice out of the mould on to a plate, and serve it with the soup.

TURTLE SOUP *

Take a live turtle, between 90 and 100 lbs. weight,—under this weight they are not considered to be in perfection; have it the day before you intend dressing it.

Kill the turtle by cutting the head off, and put it over a pail to bleed all night; in the morning, lay the turtle on a table, on its back, and separate the shells, by cutting between the two, all round the edge of the belly shell; take this shell off, and, with a knife, detach all the intestines adhering to the back; remove all the inside, being careful, while so doing, not to lose any of the green fat which is mainly found round the inside of the shells; steep this fat in a basin of cold water.

Cut off the fins, and remove all the fleshy parts; then saw the

---

* The soups that follow are much too substantial to come up to my standard of what a soup should be; but as they are frequently in request, I have felt bound to describe them.

shells, each in six or eight pieces; put them in a large stock-pot full of boiling water, together with the fins and the head; after a few minutes' boiling, take each piece out, and remove the thin shell; take it off the fins and head also; put all the pieces in another stock-pot, with plenty of water, and boil them till they become tender, and separate easily from the bones; then take the pieces out; free them of all bones, and lay the pieces between two dishes to get cold; put the bones back in the stock-pot, and reduce the broth to add to the Turtle *Consommé* as directed further on.

For the *consommé*, put the following in a stock-pot:

 15 lbs. of leg of beef
 15 lbs. of knuckle of veal
 2 hens, having previously removed the fillets,
 the fleshy parts of the turtle,
 2 quarts of General Stock,
 ½ pottle of mushrooms,
 4 onions,
 1 large faggot, containing parsley, 6 bay leaves, and a
  good sprig of thyme,
 4 oz. of parsley roots,
 2 heads of celery,
 ½ oz. of whole pepper,
 ½ oz. of salt,
 8 cloves,
 1 bottle of sherry;

Put the stock-pot on a good fire, and boil till the liquor is reduced to a glaze; then pour in the broth in which the turtle has been boiled, and fill up with General Stock.

Boil, and skim the broth carefully; garnish it with onions and carrots, and simmer on the stove corner for five hours; then strain the broth through a napkin; skim off all the fat, and thicken with a *roux*, to the consistence of thin *Espagnole* Sauce; set the soup on the stove corner to clarify, and skim it till quite clear.   Take about:

 4 oz. of green basil,   1 handful of parsley,
 2 oz. of marjoram,   1 small sprig of thyme,
 2 oz. of lemon thyme;

Put these herbs in a stewpan, with 1½ pint of *consommé*, and simmer for one hour; then press them through a tammy cloth, and add the *purée* to the soup.

The turtle meat being cold, cut it in pieces about 1½ inch square, and put it in the soup to simmer for half an hour; taste

for seasoning, and add some salt, or pepper, if necessary; skim
the soup carefully, and put it in basins, in quantities sufficient
for twelve persons.

Blanch the green fat; drain, and divide it equally in each
basin.

When wanted, warm up the soup; add some Chicken *Quenelles*, two glasses of Madeira, a little lemon juice, and cayenne
pepper, according to taste.

Observation.—It is seldom that the requirements of even a
large household enable a cook to dress a whole turtle, unless
on very special occasions; therefore, in ordinary cases, some
consommé should be prepared, as directed above, and two or
more quarts of turtle meat should be procured from a wholesale
turtle dealer's, where it can always be had in perfection; thus
avoiding unnecessary expense, and producing as satisfactory a
result. Dressed turtle can only be kept a limited time.

MOCK TURTLE SOUP

Cut 3 lbs. of fillet of veal, and 3 lbs. of leg of beef, in 1½-inch
square pieces; put them in a stewpan, with:

¾ lb. of butter,	½ oz. of green basil,
6 oz. of onions,	¼ oz. of lemon thyme,
4 oz. of mushrooms,	¼ oz. of marjoram,
4 oz. of parsley roots,	2 bay leaves,
2 oz. of celery,	1 sprig of thyme;
1 oz. of parsley,	

Stir the whole over the fire, till it assumes a light brown
colour; then dredge in 6 oz. of flour, and stir over the fire for five
minutes longer; pour in 2 quarts of General Stock, 2 quarts of
consommé, and half a bottle of Madeira; add some salt, some
whole pepper, and a little cayenne pepper; stir till boiling, put
in half a calf's head, previously boned, and blanched, and boil
for three hours; when the head is done, take it out; clear it
of any vegetables or spice adhering to it, and press it between
two dishes till cold;

Strain the broth, through the pointed strainer, into a stewpan;
add 1 pint of *Blond de Veau*; and simmer on the stove corner
for one hour, skimming frequently;

When the head is cold, cut it in 1½-inch square pieces, previously paring off the meat and fat; put the pieces in a stewpan;
cover them with *consommé*; simmer for twenty minutes; drain,
and put them in the soup tureen; strain the soup through a

tammy cloth, and pour it over the pieces of head ; add half a
tablespoonful of lemon-juice, and 2 glasses of Madeira ; mix ; and
serve.

CLEAR MOCK TURTLE SOUP À LA DOUGLAS

Prepare the soup as above, omitting the flour ; strain the
broth, and clarify it with 1 lb. of veal, pounded in a mortar,
with 2 whites of egg ; and finish the soup, as in the preceding
recipe.

HARE SOUP

Take a young hare ; skin, and empty it (reserving the blood,
to thicken the soup) ; cut it in small equal pieces ; put these in
a stewpan, with :

  ½ lb. of butter,
  1 sliced onion,
  1 faggot ;

Season with salt and pepper ; and fry over a brisk fire, for
five minutes ;

Make a *roux*, in another stewpan, with ¼ lb. of butter, and
5 oz. of flour ; moisten it with a bottle of claret, and 2 quarts
of *consommé* ; pour this thickening into the stewpan, containing
the hare ; boil, and simmer, on the stove corner, till the hare
is cooked ;

Drain the whole in a colander ; trim, and clear each piece of
hare of all small bones or vegetables adhering to them ; and put
the pieces in a stewpan, to keep warm ;

Strain the broth, and put it in a stewpan, on the stove corner,
to clarify ; skim it thoroughly ; and thicken it with the hare's
blood (*vide* Thickening with Blood, page 59) ; taste for seasoning ; add a little cayenne pepper ;

Put all the pieces of the hare, excepting the head, in the soup
tureen ; pour the soup over ; and serve.

GIBLET SOUP

Take 2 sets of giblets ; scald, and pick them carefully, and
cut them in small equal pieces ; fry them in a stewpan, with some
butter, till slightly coloured ; then moisten with 1 gill of *consommé*, and 1 gill of sherry ; reduce these to a glaze, and add
3 quarts of *consommé*, and a faggot, made of turtle herbs (*vide*
Turtle Soup, page 254) ; when the giblets are cooked, drain

them in a colander; clean each piece; and put them in a
stewpan;

Make a *roux* in another stewpan, with 2 oz. of butter, and
2 oz. of flour; moisten it with the strained broth; stir till boiling,
and simmer on the stove corner for an hour; skim off the fat,
and strain the soup through a tammy cloth on to the giblets in
the stewpan; boil for five minutes, add a tablespoonful of turtle
herbs *purée*, a tablespoonful of lemon-juice, and a little cayenne
pepper; mix, and pour the whole in a soup tureen; and serve.

HOCHEPOT, OR OX-TAIL SOUP

Take 2 ox-tails, cut them at the joints, and then in small
pieces, as near of a size as possible;

Blanch, drain, and put them in a stewpan, with:
　　4 quarts of *consommé*,
　　1 onion, with 2 cloves stuck in it,
　　1 faggot;
Boil, then simmer, till the tails are cooked;

Turn 20 small new carrots to a pear shape; boil them in
consommé, and glaze them;

Boil, and glaze, 20 small button onions;

When the tails are cooked, drain in a colander; clean each
piece; put them in the soup tureen, together with the carrots and
onions; pour over 2 quarts of boiling *Blond de Veau*; and serve.

SCOTCH BROTH

Take 2 necks of mutton; trim them as for cutlets, rather
short, and remove the chine bone; tie them with string, and put
them in a small stock-pot, together with the breasts, bones and
trimmings, 4 quarts of water, 2 onions, with 2 cloves stuck in
one, some salt, and pepper;

Boil for three hours; after one hour and a half's boiling, take
out the two necks, and put them on a dish, to cool;

Blanch, and drain ¼ lb. of pearl barley; boil it in a stewpan,
with some water, a little butter, and some salt;

Prepare 1 gill of vegetables, cut as for *Brunoise* Soup (*vide*
page 236);

Strain the mutton broth; clarify it with some lean mutton
pounded in a mortar, with 2 whites of egg;

Cut the trimmed necks in small cutlets; warm them in a
stewpan, with some of the broth;

L L

Drain the barley, and put it in the soup tureen, together with the cutlets, the prepared vegetables, and a tablespoonful of parsley, coarsely chopped, and previously blanched; pour the mutton broth over; and serve.

DUCK SOUP À LA LIVONIENNE

Pick, draw, and singe, 2 ducks; truss them, as for braizing; put them in a stewpan, with:

4 quarts of *consommé*,	2 onions,
1 faggot,	2 carrots;

some salt and pepper; and boil gently till the ducks are done;

Cut ¼ lb. of parsley roots, and ¼ lb. of white celery, in thin shreds, as for *Julienne*; blanch, fry them in butter, moisten them with ½ pint of *consommé*, and boil it down to a glaze;

Drain the ducks, when they are done; strain the broth into another stewpan; and let it simmer on the stove corner, so as to facilitate skimming off all the fat; clarify the broth, with 1 lb. of lean beef, pounded in a mortar, and strain it through a broth napkin;

Remove the fillets of the ducks, and cut them into slices diagonally, cut the legs in two pieces, and put all the pieces in the soup tureen, together with the *Julienne* vegetables, and a tablespoonful of chopped fennel; pour the broth over; and serve.

GERMAN SOUP

Fry 1 oz. of cummin seed in a stewpan, with some butter; then moisten with 3 quarts of Chicken *Consommé*; and simmer on the stove corner, for three quarters of an hour;

Pour the soup in the tureen, and serve with it some sippets of toasted rye bread.

This soup is sometimes served as above, and at other times the *consommé* is first strained from the cummin seed and poured on to the sippets of toast in the soup tureen.

VEAL KIDNEY SOUP À LA RUSSE

Prepare 3 quarts of thin *Velouté* Sauce;
Cut 1½ oz. of gherkins in slices;
Turn 10 small mushrooms;
Cut 2 salted *ogourssis* in diamond-shaped pieces;

Cut a large onion in small dice; fry the latter in butter, till they assume a bright brown colour; then add 2 veal kidneys, also cut in small dice; toss them up for a few minutes only, to avoid overcooking them; drain them, and put them in a soup tureen, with all the other prepared garnishes; thicken the *Velouté* Sauce with 6 yolks of egg, and ½ pint of cream; add a little cayenne pepper; pour the soup in the tureen; and serve.

ONION PURÉE SOUP À LA RUSSE

Peel 1¼ lb. of onions; cut them in slices; blanch, cool, drain, and put them in a stewpan, with ¼ lb. of butter;

Stir over the fire for five minutes; add half a tablespoonful of flour; moisten with 1 gill of *consommé*, and 1 pint of cream, and stir over a moderate fire for twenty minutes; then add 1 pinch of salt, and 1 pinch of sugar;

Press through a tammy cloth, and put the *purée* in a stewpan;

Mix 6 tablespoonfuls of potato flour with 1 gill of water, in a basin; when it is smooth, add it to the *purée*;

Boil 1½ pint of milk; pour it in the *purée*; and stir, to mix the whole well together;

Take the soup off the fire; add 3 oz. of butter; stir till it is melted, and pour the soup in the tureen; and serve, on a plate, some Pike Forcemeat *Quenelles*, with crayfish tails added.

SET OF BAIN-MARIE PANS

CHAPTER II

SAUCES

Remarks upon the Use of Wine in Cookery and of Butter for Roux

I WILL preface this Chapter with a few remarks upon two of
the main constituents of Sauces and *Entrées*;—namely: Wine
and Butter; the ·use of which is constantly recurring in their
preparation.

It is sometimes assumed that, for the purposes of cookery,
wine of a very inferior quality may be used, and that the sauces
and stews will not suffer thereby.

I cannot protest too strongly against this mistaken idea.

What I have ever said with respect to provisions, I must
needs repeat, more emphatically still, with reference to wine.
With poor wine, successful cookery is impossible.

However, when I recommend the use of good wine for
cookery, I have in view none but fair average vintages of Red
and White Wine. I have no intention of following some im-
practical recipes in which the use of Château-Laffite, Château-
Yquem, Clos-Vougeot, Johannisberg, Tokay, Constance, and of
similar high-priced vintages, is continually prescribed; just as if
such wines were always at hand, in unlimited quantities, available to pour into the stewpans without measure or stint! On

the contrary, I hold that it would be unwarrantable waste to employ such wines for the ordinary preparation of sauces, whilst such excellent results are to be obtained by the use of an average Burgundy of good body and aroma, by a good dry claret, also of an average growth, or by using some Spanish wines, in moderation, in cases where the very nature of the dishes calls for them.

With such effective substitutes, it would be folly to use choice wines which, if they improve a preparation in any way, will certainly not do so proportionately to their cost; it would only be a way of increasing the expense without commensurate advantage, and would warrant the charge of extravagance,—one which has frequently been of much prejudice to the interests of culinary art.

Another wrong impression which has gained ground, and which I must protest against, is that butter used for *roux*, as it has to be cooked, need not be either particularly good or fresh; —nothing can be more contrary to fact: with bad butter it is impossible to make anything good.

The objections which are frequently brought against *roux* of being rich and indigestible, arise principally from its being too often prepared with inferior butter, and then, to make matters worse, kept for several days. This practice should be entirely condemned. *Roux* cannot be good unless the butter which constitutes it be perfectly fresh, and of the best quality. Nothing is gained by preparing it beforehand, as there will always be plenty of time to make it whilst the sauces are cooking; it will then be had under the most favourable conditions, so as to be employed immediately it is prepared.

On Sauces in general

The subject of the ensuing Chapter is one held in great estimation by epicures; and, while the preparation of sauces is one of those questions upon which few of the profession are agreed, when divested of the many complications of terms which render it obscure, it becomes, in practice, a very simple matter, of few operations, and easily describable in few words.

I hope to be able to show by the recipes, that such expressions as *Essences*, and *Espagnole*, *Allemande* and *Velouté Sauces*, which to most are unmeaning terms, refer in reality to very simple operations, resting in the same way, as most culinary preparations, upon the ordinary rules of common sense and taste.

The chief fact to bear in mind to understand what follows is this : that particular kinds of meat, found to be the most savoury, nourishing, and rich, have been selected to constitute a few main sauces, which themselves become the unvarying bases of numberless other sauces.

Some of these main sauces have received most extraordinary names, perfectly unintelligible in themselves, as they convey no idea of the constituents of the sauces ; such are the *Espagnole* and *Allemande* Sauces, named thus quite arbitrarily, and which have no apparent connection with either Spain or Germany.

I have called these main sauces, *Fundamental Sauces*, in order to define clearly the part they play in the preparation of the great number of special sauces. I have heard the following objected, by the uninitiated in culinary matters, with reference to these *Fundamental Sauces*, and notably of the *Espagnole Sauce* : ' If,' say they, ' you put some of this *Espagnole Sauce* in everything, a uniform cookery, of but one single flavour, will result.'

This notion, which the frequent use of *Espagnole Sauce* would seem to justify, is quite as unfounded as it would be to say of a painter that, with the limited number of colours at his command, he could only paint the same picture ; without taking into consideration the numberless combinations of tints and shades of which these few original colours are capable. I have made free to borrow this simile from an art far superior to mine, because I think it explains to some extent the part which the *Fundamental Sauces* play in cookery,—ever the same, they enter into the composition of that great variety of dishes, sauces, and seasonings, which constitute high-class cookery.

The results will be better appreciated when the particulars of the application of the above principle come under notice. The great improvement of modern cookery lies here : that, with these *Fundamental Sauces* always at hand, the preparation of a dinner is much simplified ; whereas, in former days, all the sauces were prepared separately, a few hours only before serving, at great cost of labour, and risk of failure.

I

FUNDAMENTAL SAUCES ·

ESPAGNOLE SAUCE

The quantities in this recipe are calculated to make 4 quarts of *Espagnole* Sauce, which will certainly not be too much when treating of high-class cooking operations. It must be borne in mind that *Espagnole* will keep perfectly good for three or four days; so that, in large establishments, even double the quantity I indicate may safely be prepared.

Butter a stewpan, and put in it 3 sliced onions; upon these place 6 lbs. of boned fillet of veal, and 2 lbs. of gravy-beef; moisten with 1 pint of General Stock, or *Grand Bouillon*, and set it boiling on a brisk fire; when the Stock is reduced one half, glaze the meat of a bright-brown and even colour, by simmering gently, and turning it frequently.

This process requires particular attention; for, if the glaze be over cooked, and of a dark-brown colour, the sauce will have an acrid taste, which no amount of sugar added to it would rectify.

When the meat is well glazed, take the stewpan off the fire; cover it, and let it stand five minutes before adding any more broth,—this will facilitate the dissolving of the glaze; then pour in 6 quarts of General Stock; boil; skim; and add:

1 faggot,	¼ oz. of *mignonnette* pepper,
2 carrots,	¼ oz. of sugar;
½ oz. of salt,	

Boil, and simmer; and, when the meat is done, take it out, and strain the Stock through a broth napkin.

Make a *roux* in a stewpan, with 14 oz. of clarified butter, and 14 oz. of flour; when this is cooked, moisten with the Stock; stir over the fire with a wooden spoon till boiling, and simmer for two hours on the stove corner, with the stewpan only three parts closed; skim, and take off the fat twice during that time; at the end of the two hours, skim, and free the sauce from fat once more; strain it through a tammy cloth; and put by for use.

Observation.—I do not advise adding a hen or any game to this sauce, as is so often done,—butcher's meat alone should constitute the basis of *Espagnole*, which, being intended to add to other preparations, any special flavouring given to it, either by poultry or game, would often be prejudicial.

ESPAGNOLE SAUCE MAIGRE (WITHOUT MEAT)

Butter a stewpan, and put in 3 sliced onions; place on these 6 lbs. of fish,—gurnet, pike, and whiting; pour in 1 pint of French white wine; boil to a glaze, and moisten with 5 quarts of Fish *Consommé*; add :

2 large carrots,	¼ oz. of salt,
1 faggot,	1 small pinch of *mignonnette* pepper;

Boil, and then simmer; and, when the fish is done, take it out.

Make a *roux*, in a stewpan, with ¾ lb. of clarified butter, and ¾ lb. of flour; moisten with the liquor; stir, till boiling, and let the sauce clarify on the stove corner; strain through a tammy cloth; and put by for use.

VELOUTÉ SAUCE

Take 6 lbs. of *noix*, or fillet of veal, and 2 hens, with the fillets cut off;

Butter a stewpan, and put in 2 sliced onions, the veal, and hens; pour in 1 pint of General Stock; simmer very gently, not to colour the meat; then moisten with 7 quarts of Stock; boil; skim; and add :

¼ oz. of salt,	1 small pinch of sugar,
1 small pinch of *mignonnette* pepper,	1 faggot,
	2 middle-sized carrots;

Simmer till the meat is cooked, and take out the veal, and the hens;

Strain the Stock through a broth napkin, and free it of all fat.

Make a *roux*, without browning, in a stewpan, with 14 oz. of clarified butter, and 14 oz. of flour; moisten with the Stock; stir over the fire till boiling, and simmer on the stove corner for two hours; skim off the fat twice during this time, and once more just before straining; strain through a tammy cloth; and put the sauce by for use.

VELOUTÉ SAUCE MAIGRE (WITHOUT MEAT)

Put 8 lbs. of fish,—gurnet, whiting, and pike,—in a stewpan, with :

2 middle-sized onions,	1 pint of French white wine,
2 cloves,	1 oz. of salt,
1 faggot,	2 oz. of *mignonnette* pepper ;
2 middle-sized carrots,	

Cover the stewpan, and simmer very gently for fifteen minutes ; then moisten with 1 bottle of French white wine, and 4 quarts of water ; boil ; skim, and simmer till the fish is done ; take it out, and strain the liquor through a broth napkin.

Make a white *roux*, with ¾ lb. of butter, and ¾ lb. of flour ; moisten with the liquor, reduce it by stirring over the fire for fifteen minutes ; strain through a tammy cloth ; and put by for use.

ALLEMANDE SAUCE

Prepare :

½ pint of Essence of Chicken (*vide* page 268),
1 gill of Essence of Mushrooms (*vide* page 268),
1 quart of *Velouté* Sauce (*vide* page 264) ;

Reduce these over the fire, till the sauce is of sufficient consistence to coat the spoon ; thicken with 4 yolks of egg, and ½ oz. of butter ; strain through a tammy cloth, into a *bain-marie*-pan ; put a tablespoonful of Chicken *Consommé* on the top of the sauce, to prevent a skin forming on the surface.

BÉCHAMEL SAUCE À L'ANCIENNE

Remove the *noir* from a fillet of veal, and cut up the remainder in 2-inch dice ; put these in a stewpan, with :

¾ lb. of butter,
2 middle-sized onions,
2 middle-sized carrots ;

Fry, without colouring, for ten minutes ; then add 6 oz. of flour ; stir over the fire for five minutes ; and put in :

3 quarts of General Stock,	1 faggot,
1 quart of double cream,	½ oz. of salt,
10 oz. of sliced mushrooms,	¼ oz. of *mignonnette* pepper ;

Stir over the fire till boiling, and simmer for one hour and a half, skimming off the fat occasionally ; strain through a tammy cloth; put the sauce in a large glazing stewpan, with 2 gills of cream to each quart of sauce; reduce it over the fire till it coats the spoon; then strain again through a tammy cloth, into a basin; and stir with a spoon till the sauce is cold, to prevent a skin forming on the top.

CHICKEN BÉCHAMEL SAUCE

Cut 2 lbs. of fillet of veal in 3-inch dice; take 2 hens, having previously removed the fillets; put the veal and hens in a stewpan, with:

1 oz. of butter,	½ oz. of salt,
2 middle-sized onions,	¼ oz. of *mignonnette* pepper;
cut in 8 pieces,	

Fry, without colouring, for five minutes; add ¾ lb. of flour; stir over the fire for five minutes; then add 5 quarts of General Stock, and 1 faggot; and stir till boiling;

Simmer for two hours, skimming off the fat frequently; strain the sauce, through a tammy cloth, into a large stewpan; reduce it, adding 1½ pint of double cream, in three parts; when the sauce coats the spoon, strain it through a tammy cloth into a basin; stir it till quite cold; and put by for use.

BÉCHAMEL SAUCE MAIGRE (WITHOUT MEAT)

Cut 3 onions, 1 carrot, and 2 shalots, in large dice; fry them in a stewpan, with ½ lb. of butter, for five minutes; add ½ lb. of flour; fry for five minutes more; and put in:

3 quarts of milk,	1 faggot,
½ oz. of salt,	¼ oz. of *mignonnette* pepper;

Stir, and reduce the sauce for fifteen minutes; strain it, through a tammy cloth, into a basin; cover it with a little butter, melted; and put by for use.

When the *Béchamel* is wanted, it should be boiled up, and thickened with ¼ lb. of butter, to each quart of sauce.

BROWN POIVRADE SAUCE

Cut 2 lbs. of *noix*, or fillet of veal, and 1 lb. of raw ham, in large dice; put them in a stewpan, with:

½ lb. of butter,	2 sliced carrots,
3 bay leaves,	4 cloves,
4 shalots,	½ oz. of *mignonnette* pepper,
3 sliced onions,	2 small pinches of grated nutmeg;

Fry, till the meat is slightly coloured ; then moisten with 1 pint of vinegar ; reduce it, without burning, and add :

2 quarts of *Espagnole* Sauce,
1 pint of *Blond de Veau* ;

Stir till it boils ; then simmer for half an hour, skimming it carefully ; strain, through a tammy cloth, into a basin ; and stir with a spoon, till cold.

WHITE POIVRADE SAUCE

Proceed as above, using the same quantities of *Velouté* Sauce, and White *Consommé*, instead of *Espagnole* Sauce, and *Blond de Veau.*

POIVRADE SAUCE MAIGRE (WITHOUT MEAT)

Put ½ lb. of butter in a stewpan, with :

3 bay leaves,	4 cloves,
4 shalots,	½ oz. of *mignonnette* pepper ;
3 sliced onions,	2 small pinches of grated
2 sliced carrots,	nutmeg ;

Fry slightly, and moisten with 1 pint of vinegar ; reduce it, without burning, and add 3 quarts of *Velouté* Sauce *Maigre* ; boil for ten minutes on a brisk fire ; and strain, through a tammy cloth, into a basin ; stir with a spoon, to prevent a skin forming on the surface ; and put by for use.

MARINADE

Take 1 lb. of raw ham, half lean, half fat ; cut it in pieces ; put these in a stewpan, with :

4 bay leaves,	2 oz. of parsley,
1 sprig of thyme,	2 unpicked cloves of garlic,
6 oz. of onions,	6 shalots,
6 oz. of carrots,	6 oz. of butter ;

Fry the whole together ; then moisten with 2 quarts of water, and 2 quarts of vinegar ; boil for two minutes ; add 3 oz. of salt, and 1 oz. of pepper ; and put by for use.

II

ESSENCES

ESSENCE OF CHICKEN

Remove the fillets, and legs, of 6 chickens; break up the
bones, and put them in a stewpan, with 2 lbs. of fillet of veal,
cut in 4 pieces; pour in 3 quarts of Chicken *Consommé*; add:

2 onions, with 2 cloves stuck in one,
1 middle-sized carrot,
1 faggot;

Boil, skim, and simmer till the meat is done; strain the
essence, through a broth napkin; free it of fat; and put by
for use.

ESSENCE OF TRUFFLES

Put 2 lbs. of well-washed and peeled truffles in a small
stock-pot, with :

1 bottle of Madeira,
1 quart of Chicken *Consommé*,
1 faggot,
½ oz. of salt,
1 small pinch of *mignonnette* pepper,
1 small pinch of grated nutmeg;

Close the pot, and boil on a very brisk fire for twenty
minutes;

When the truffles are cold, strain the essence through a broth
napkin, and keep the truffles for garnishes.

Observation.—It must not be thought that truffles are spoilt
when they have given out their essence; I have proved, that
when they are cooked as described above, they will retain
enough of their flavour to be added to dishes with advantage.

ESSENCE OF MUSHROOMS

Pick, and wash 2 lbs. of mushrooms; put them in a stewpan,
with ½ gill of lemon juice, and ½ oz. of salt; close the stewpan,
and put it on the fire for five minutes; then pour in 1 quart
of Chicken *Consommé*; boil for ten minutes; strain, through
a broth napkin; and put by for use.

ESSENCE OF FISH

Cut 1½ lb. of gurnet, and 1½ lb. of soles, in pieces ; put them in a stewpan, with :

2 onions,	4 shalots,
2 cloves,	½ oz. of salt,
1 carrot,	1 small pinch of pepper,
1 faggot,	1 pint of French white wine ;

Boil for five minutes, and add 2 quarts of Fish *Consommé* ; boil till the fish is done ; skim the essence, and strain it through a broth napkin ; and put by for use.

MIREPOIX, OR ESSENCE OF MEAT AND VEGETABLES

Observation.—*Mirepoix* is such a common term in cookery that I cannot help using it, although I have thought it well to indicate its composition in the title itself.

It is an extract of meat and vegetables ;—the word *mirepoix* alone would certainly not make this fact as clear as desirable.

To make *mirepoix* :

Cut 2 lbs. of fillet of veal, 1 lb. of fat bacon, and 2 lbs. of raw ham, half lean, half fat, in 1½-inch pieces, and put these in a stewpan, with :

4 sliced carrots,	1 sprig of thyme,
4 middle-sized onions,	4 shalots ;
4 bay leaves,	

Fry till the meat is of a light brown colour, and pour in 2 bottles of Madeira, and 5 quarts of General Stock ; add ½ oz. of *mignonnette* pepper ; boil ; then simmer gently for two hours ; strain through a broth napkin ; and put by for use,—without taking off the fat.

ESSENCE OF HAM

Put 1 lb. of lean raw ham, cut in pieces, in a stewpan, with :

1 oz. of parsley,	1 small sprig of thyme,
1 onion,	2 gills of French white
1 carrot,	wine (Châblis) ;
1 small bay leaf,	

Boil, till the wine is all reduced, and pour in 1 quart of *Blond de Veau* ; simmer for half an hour ; strain, through a broth napkin ; and put by for use.

ESSENCE OF PHEASANT

Remove the fillets and legs of 6 pheasants (reserving these parts for *entrées*); break up the bones, and put them in a stewpan, with :

1 middle-sized onion,	1 small pinch of grated nutmeg,
1 middle-sized carrot,	1 faggot,
2 cloves,	1 pint of Madeira ;

Boil to a glaze, and moisten with three quarts of *consommé*; boil, skim, and simmer for one hour and a half, on the stove corner ; strain through a broth napkin, and skim off the fat.

ESSENCE OF WOODCOCK

Take 6 woodcocks; remove the fillets, which put by for *entrées*;
Break up the bones, and proceed as in the preceding recipe.

ESSENCE OF PARTRIDGE

Remove the fillets of 6 partridges ;
Break up the bones, and proceed as directed for Essence of Pheasant (*vide* above).

ESSENCE OF LARKS

Remove the fillets of 36 larks, to be used for *entrées* ;
Break the bones, and prepare the essence as described for Essence of Pheasant (*vide* above).

ESSENCE OF LEVERET

Remove the fillets and legs of 5 leverets, which put by for *entrées* ;
Break up the bones, and put them in a stewpan, with the same vegetables and seasoning as for Essence of Pheasant (*vide* above); cook, and finish the essence in the same way.

ESSENCE OF RABBIT

Proceed as in the preceding recipe.

III

SEASONED BUTTER FOR SAUCES AND GARNISHES

MONTPELLIER BUTTER

Take 1 lb. of mixed chervil, tarragon, burnet, chives and cress; pick, wash and blanch the whole, for two minutes, in boiling water; drain, cool, and press the water out in a cloth;

Put these herbs in a mortar, with:

6 hard-boiled yolks of egg,
6 well-washed anchovies,
2 oz. of gherkins,
2 oz. of capers, previously pressed in a cloth, to free from vinegar;

A small piece of garlic (about the size of a pea); season with salt and pepper; pound the whole together, and pass it through a fine hair sieve;

Clean the mortar, and put in it:

2 lbs. of butter,
the pounded mixture,
2 tablespoonfuls of oil,
1 tablespoonful of tarragon vinegar;

Pound, and mix the whole well together; and put by for use.

Montpellier Butter should be of a bright green colour; if the herbs do not so colour it, a little spinach greening should be passed through a silk sieve, and added to the butter in the mortar.

RAVIGOTE BUTTER

Prepare the same herbs as described in the preceding recipe; pound them in a mortar, and add 2 lbs. of butter; pound, and mix thoroughly; pass it through a fine hair sieve; and put by for use.

LOBSTER BUTTER

Take the spawn of a lobster; pound it with ½ lb. of butter, and pass it through a silk sieve; season with salt and pepper; and put by for use.

Failing spawn or coral, the shell of the lobster should be pounded very fine, with 4 oz. of butter added; warmed in a *bain-marie*-pan, for one hour, and pressed through a cloth, into a basin full of cold water; the butter should then be skimmed off the water, drained in a cloth, passed through a silk sieve, and mixed to 4 oz. of fresh butter.

SHRIMP BUTTER

Take the shells of 500 shrimps;
Pound, and add them to the butter as described for Lobster Butter (*vide* page 271).

CRAYFISH BUTTER

Cook the shells of 40 crayfish as indicated for Crayfish *Bisque* (*vide* page 249);
Pound, and add them to the butter as directed for Lobster Butter (*vide* page 271).

Observation. — Should the Lobster, Shrimp, and Crayfish Butters not be sufficiently red, a few drops of prepared cochineal may be added.

All these butters should be used the same day as prepared.

ANCHOVY BUTTER

Wash 8 anchovies; wipe them well with a cloth, and pound them in a mortar, with 1 oz. of butter; pass through a silk sieve, and mix with 4 oz. of butter.

MAÎTRE D'HÔTEL BUTTER

Mix 1 tablespoonful of well-washed and coarsely-chopped parsley, with ½ lb. of butter; season with salt and pepper, and 1 tablespoonful of lemon juice; mix the whole thoroughly; and put by for use.

Observation.—This butter should not be worked too much, —else it would become oily.

IV

MEAT, POULTRY, GAME, AND FISH GLAZE

Remarks on Glaze

Meat, Game,. or Fish Glazes are added to certain sauces to finish them.

They are also used to glaze large joints and *entrées*, to which they impart that inviting appearance, justly prized by connoisseurs.

Glaze is also very useful to produce gravies and sauces whilst travelling, as it will take the place of butcher's meat, when the latter is not obtainable.

MEAT GLAZE

Bone, and bind with string:

6 lbs. of fillet of veal,
6 lbs. of knuckle of veal,
6 lbs. of gravy-beef;

Put the meat in a stock-pot, with 3 gallons of water, and 4 oz. of salt; boil; skim; and add:

1 lb. of leeks,	1 lb. of carrots,
1 lb. of onions,	1 faggot, weighing 3 oz.;

Simmer on the stove corner till the meat is cooked; take it out, and strain the broth through a napkin; put it in a large glazing stewpan; reduce it one-third; and pour it into a basin.

The next day, when the glaze is set, remove about ½ inch from the top, and also the thick deposit at the bottom of the basin; put the trimmed glaze in a stewpan; stir, over a very brisk fire, till it is reduced to the consistence of *Espagnole* Sauce, and pour it in a basin for use;

The trimmings of the glaze may be used when making General Stock (*vide* page 226).

Observation.—Glaze is often reduced in one operation, but I think it much preferable, both as regards success and economy, to proceed as indicated above;—to reduce it partially on one day, and to finish it the next.

I recommend this process with all confidence, having seen it practised by an experienced cook, M. Drouhat, at the Duchesse de Berry's Château at Rosny.

N N

CHICKEN GLAZE

Bone, and tie 6 lbs. of fillet of veal, and 6 lbs. of knuckle of veal; put this meat in a stock-pot, with 6 hens, and 2 gallons of General Stock; boil, and finish the glaze as in the preceding recipe.

GLAZING STEW-PAN

GAME GLAZE

Take:
  6 lbs. of fillet of veal,
  6 lbs. of knuckle of veal,
  6 lbs. of gravy beef;
Bone, and tie these with string, and put the whole in a stock-pot with 6 partridges, 4 wild rabbits, and 2½ gallons of General Stock; boil, reduce, and finish the glaze as directed for Meat Glaze (*vide* page 273).

FISH GLAZE

Put the following in a stock-pot:

6 lbs. of soles,	3 cloves of garlic, whole,
4 lbs. of gurnet,	2½ gallons of water,
4 lbs. of whiting,	
2 bottles of French white wine (Châblis);	

Boil, skim; and add:

1 lb. of leeks,	1 faggot, weighing 3 oz.,
1 lb. of onions,	4 oz. of salt;
1 lb. of carrots,	

Boil; and reduce as described for Meat Glaze (*vide* page 273.)

POIVRADE GLAZE

Put the following in a large stewpan :

1 lb. of onions,	$\frac{1}{2}$ oz. of bay leaves,
1 lb. of carrots,	$\frac{1}{3}$ oz. of thyme,
3 oz. of shalots,	8 cloves,
3 oz. of parsley,	4 cloves of garlic, whole,
3 oz. of celery,	2 quarts of vinegar ;
2 oz. of *mignonnette* pepper,	

Boil till the vinegar is all reduced, and pour in $2\frac{1}{2}$ gallons of General Stock; simmer for one hour and a half on the stove corner; strain through a broth napkin; and reduce as directed for Meat Glaze (*vide* page 273).

MEAT GRAVY

This gravy is generally served with roast or broiled meats.

Take 6 lbs. of fillet of veal, and 6 lbs. of gravy beef, and bind them with string; remove the rind from 1 lb. of lean raw ham; cut 4 onions, each in 4 pieces, and put them in a buttered stewpan, with the veal, beef, and ham; moisten with 1 pint of General Stock; reduce to a dark glaze, without burning; pour in 2 gallons of Stock; and add 1 hen, 1 faggot, and $\frac{1}{2}$ oz. of salt;

Boil; then simmer for three hours and a half; strain, through a broth napkin; and skim off the fat.

This gravy should be very clear,—if it be not so, clarify it with 1 lb. of pounded veal, and 2 whites of egg.

MEAT JELLY

Take :

6 lbs. of fillet of veal,
2 lbs. of boned knuckle of veal,
8 calf's feet, previously boned and blanched,
3 hens, previously removing the fillets,
4 lbs. of leg of beef, boned ;

Tie up the meat, and put the whole in a stock-pot, with $2\frac{1}{2}$ gallons of water, and 4 oz. of salt; boil; skim; cool, and add :

1 double faggot,	4 large carrots,
4 onions, with 4 cloves stuck in one,	4 leeks ;

Simmer on the stove corner, till the meat is done,—this will be before the calf's feet are cooked; take out the meat, and, when the feet are thoroughly cooked, strain the broth through a napkin into a stewpan; boil; skim; and simmer, so that the jelly may be perfectly clear; try it on the ice; if it be not firm enough, reduce it on the fire till it is.

When cold, clarify the jelly as follows: Pound the fillets of the hens, and put them in a stewpan, with 8 whites of egg, 1 pint of French white wine, and a little salt and pepper;

Add the jelly to the fillets in the stewpan, and stir quickly, with a wire whisk, over a brisk fire, till it boils; take off the fire, and let it rest for two minutes; then strain through a jelly bag; pour it back, and strain again; repeat the straining till the jelly is quite clear;—should it not be perfectly clear, it must be clarified again;

Pour the jelly in a basin, and, when cold, set it on the ice.

FISH JELLY

Put the following in a stock-pot :

4 lbs. of gurnet,	3 onions, with 4 cloves
2 lbs. of whiting,	stuck in one,
6 lbs. of turbot,—heads are	2 heads of celery;
preferable,	1 double faggot,
4 lbs. of soles,	2 cloves of garlic,
2 carrots,	2 gallons of water,

sufficient salt and *mignonnette* pepper for seasoning ;

Boil; skim; and simmer for two hours; try the strength of the jelly, as described in the preceding recipe; when firm enough, strain it through a broth napkin; taste for seasoning, and clarify the jelly with $1\frac{1}{2}$ pint of Madeira, 8 whites of egg, and 2 lbs. of pounded whiting; strain; let it cool, and set it on the ice, as indicated for Meat Jelly (*vide* page 275).

HALF GLAZE

This preparation is really the same as *Espagnole* Sauce, very slightly thickened.

Put 1 pint of *Espagnole* Sauce in a stewpan, with 1 pint of *Blond de Veau*, and 3 oz. of Meat Glaze ;

Reduce on the fire for five minutes; strain, through a tammy cloth; and put by in a basin.

V

SAUCES

D'UXELLES AND D'UXELLES SAUCE

Wash, chop, and press in a cloth :
  1 lb. of turned mushroom trimmings,
  1 lb. of parsley,
  6 oz. of shalots ;
Put the whole in a stewpan, with ¼ lb. of butter, and a
seasoning of salt and pepper ; fry on a brisk fire for five
minutes, stirring with a spoon, and put by the mixture, called
d'Uxelles, in a basin for use.

D'Uxelles Sauce is made by adding 1 gill of the above
mixture to each quart of *Espagnole* Sauce.

SHARP SAUCE

Put in a stewpan :
  3 gills of Brown *Poivrade* Sauce,
  1 gill of Veal Stock,
  1½ pint of *Espagnole* Sauce ;
Boil, till the sauce coats the spoon ; and add :
  1 gill of *d'Uxelles* (*vide* preceding recipe),
  1½ oz. of gherkins, previously chopped, and drained in a
    cloth,
  1 oz. of capers, also chopped and drained ;
Boil ; skim ; and put in a *bain-marie*-pan ; pour 1 tablespoonful of Veal Stock on the sauce, to prevent a skin forming
on the surface.

This is a very essential precaution to take with this, and all
other Brown Sauces.

POIVRADE SAUCE

Put 1½ pint of Brown *Poivrade* Sauce in a stewpan, with
1 pint of *Espagnole* Sauce, and ½ pint of *Blond de Veau* ;
Reduce these ; strain through a tammy cloth into a *bain-
marie*-pan, and pour 1 tablespoonful of *Blond de Veau* on the
top, to cover the sauce.

ITALIAN SAUCE

Reduce 1 pint of Châblis to half the quantity; add:
1 quart of *Espagnole* Sauce,
1 gill of Veal Stock,
1 gill of *d'Uxelles*;
Reduce for five minutes; skim, and put in a *bain-marie*-pan.

MATELOTE SAUCE

Put the following in a stewpan:

4 sliced onions,	1 small sprig of thyme,
4 shalots, whole,	3 gills of Burgundy;
1 small bay leaf,	

Simmer, till the onions are done: strain, through the pointed strainer, into a glazing stewpan; add 1 quart of *Espagnole* Sauce, and reduce till the sauce coats the spoon; then strain, through a tammy cloth, into a *bain-marie*-pan.

BORDELAISE SAUCE

Reduce 2 gills of Sauterne to half the quantity, with 1 pinch of *mignonnette* pepper, and 1 tablespoonful of shalots, previously blanched, and chopped; then add 1 pint of *Espagnole* Sauce; reduce for five minutes, and put in 1 tablespoonful of chopped parsley; skim; and pour into a *bain-marie*-pan.

ROBERT SAUCE

Put 1 oz. of butter in a stewpan, with 3 onions cut in squares; fry till of a reddish brown colour; add 3 gills of French white wine, and reduce to a glaze; pour in 1 quart of *Espagnole* Sauce; simmer for twenty minutes; skim; and put in a *bain-marie*-pan.

Before serving this sauce, it should be boiled up, and 1 oz. of Meat Glaze and 1 tablespoonful of French mustard added to it, mixed thoroughly; and then served.

MADEIRA SAUCE

Put 1 pint of Madeira in a stewpan, with 1½ oz. of Meat Glaze, and 1 small pinch of *mignonnette* pepper;

Reduce to half the quantity; add 1 quart of *Espagnole* Sauce, and continue the reducing till the sauce coats the spoon; strain, through a tammy cloth, into a *bain-marie*-pan.

THICKENED MAÎTRE D'HÔTEL SAUCE À LA CHÂTEAUBRIAND

Reduce 2 gills of French white wine, and 1 oz. of Meat Glaze; add 1 quart of *Espagnole* Sauce; continue reducing; then strain, through a tammy cloth, into a *bain-marie*-pan;

Before serving, boil up the sauce, and thicken it with ¼ lb. of *Maître d'Hôtel* Butter (*vide* page 272).

GENEVOISE SAUCE

Put 3 sliced onions in a stewpan, with:

3 shalots,	half a clove of garlic, un-
1 pinch of *mignonnette*	picked,
pepper,	¼ lb. of butter;

Fry till of a reddish brown colour; and add:

1 bottle of Burgundy,	1 faggot;

Simmer till the onions are done, then pour in 2 quarts of *Espagnole* Sauce, and ½ pint of Veal Stock; reduce the sauce, by stirring it over the fire, until it is thick enough to coat the spoon; skim; and strain, through a tammy cloth, into a *bain-marie*-pan.

Before serving, boil up the sauce, and add 2 tablespoonfuls of chopped truffles, boiled in Madeira, and ¼ lb. of Anchovy Butter.

PÉRIGUEUX SAUCE

Cut ¾ lb. of raw ham in large dice; put them in a stewpan, with:

1 oz. of butter,	1 sliced onion,
1 shalot,	1 pinch of *mignonnette* pepper;

Fry, till the onion is of a light brown colour, and pour in ½ pint of Madeira; reduce it one half; and add:

1½ pint of *Espagnole* Sauce,
½ pint of *Blond de Veau*,
½ pint of Essence of Truffles;

Simmer for twenty minutes; skim, and strain the sauce into another stewpan; reduce it till it coats the spoon, and put it in a *bain-marie*-pan;

Just before serving add 2 tablespoonfuls of chopped truffles, previously cooked in Madeira.

PÉRIGUEUX SAUCE MAIGRE (WITHOUT MEAT)

Put in a stewpan:

1½ pint of *Espagnole* Sauce *Maigre*,
½ pint of Essence of Truffles,
½ pint of Essence of Mushrooms;

Reduce till the sauce coats the spoon; strain, through a tammy cloth; add 2 tablespoonfuls of chopped truffles, as above; and serve.

ANCHOVY BUTTER SAUCE

Put in a stewpan:

1½ pint of *Espagnole* Sauce,
1 gill of Brown *Poivrade* Sauce,
2 gills of *Consommé*;

Reduce, until the sauce coats the spoon; and strain, through a tammy cloth, into a *bain-marie*-pan.

Before serving, boil up the sauce, and thicken it with 2 oz. of Anchovy Butter.

TOMATO SAUCE

Pick 3 lbs. of tomatoes; break them; and put the pieces in a stewpan, with:

2 onions, with 2 cloves stuck in one,
1 faggot,
½ pint of Châblis;

Season with salt and pepper;

Melt the tomatoes on a slow fire for forty minutes,—stirring occasionally, to prevent their burning; when they are melted, pour in:

½ pint of *Espagnole* Sauce,
½ pint of *Velouté* Sauce,
3 gills of Chicken *Consommé*;

Reduce for fifteen minutes; strain, through a tammy cloth; and put by for use.

Remarks on Tomato Sauce

This sauce is of greater consistence than most other sauces; it might, in fact, almost be numbered among thin *Purées*.

I have often had occasion to observe that Tomato Sauce is
spoilt by the number of different ingredients added to it.

In the above recipe, I have purposely given it in such a
way, that, while retaining its distinctive character, it will be of
sufficient richness to be suitable for the uses of High-Class
Cookery.

FINANCIÈRE SAUCE FOR POULTRY

Put in a stewpan:
    ½ pint of Essence of Truffles,
    ⅓ pint of Essence of Mushrooms,
    ⅓ pint of Essence of Chicken,
    1 quart of *Espagnole* Sauce;
Reduce, till the sauce coats the spoon; and strain, through a
tammy cloth, into a *bain-marie*-pan.

FINANCIÈRE SAUCE FOR GAME

Put in a stewpan:
    3 gills of Essence of Truffles,
    3 gills of Essence of Game,
    1½ pint of *Espagnole* Sauce;
Reduce, and strain the sauce through a tammy cloth; and put
it by for use.

FINANCIÈRE SAUCE FOR FISH

Put the following in a stewpan:
    3 gills of Essence of Truffles,
    3 gills of Essence of Mushrooms,
    2 gills of Madeira,
    1 oz. of Fish Glaze,
    1½ pint of *Espagnole* Sauce *Maigre*;
Reduce, and strain the sauce through a tammy cloth.

SAUCE À LA RÉGENCE

Cut ½ lb. of raw lean ham in pieces; put them in a stewpan,
with:
    2 onions,
    2 shalots,
    ¼ lb. of butter;

Fry, without browning, and pour in 1 pint of Essence of Chicken, and ½ pint of Sauterne;

Simmer gently till the onions are done; then strain, through a broth napkin, into a stewpan; and add:

    3 gills of Essence of Chicken,

    1½ pint of *Espagnole* Sauce;

Reduce, till the sauce coats the spoon; and strain, through a tammy cloth, into a *bain-marie*-pan.

SAUCE À LA DIABLE

Cut 3 shalots in pieces; put them in a stewpan, with:

1 gill of French red wine,	1 pinch of *mignonnette* pepper,
12 sprigs of parsley,	1 small pinch of cayenne
1 bay leaf,	pepper,
1 small sprig of thyme,	1½ pint of *Espagnole* Sauce,
1 clove of garlic,	½ pint of Veal Stock;

Simmer for twenty-five minutes, on the stove corner; skim carefully; and strain, through a tammy cloth.

SHALOT SAUCE

Put 8 sliced shalots in a stewpan, with:

1 small bay leaf,	1 sprig of parsley,
1 small sprig of thyme,	1 gill of *Blond de Veau*;

Reduce it to a glaze; then add 1½ pint of Meat Gravy (*vide* page 275); simmer for ten minutes; and strain, through a broth napkin, into a *bain-marie*-pan.

BIGARADE SAUCE

Reduce 1½ pint of *Espagnole* Sauce, and 3 gills of Veal Stock in a stewpan, and strain into a *bain-marie*-pan;

Cut the peel of 2 oranges in thin shreds; blanch, and add them to the sauce;

Before serving, add the juice of the oranges to the sauce; mix; and serve.

SAUCE À LA GODARD

Cut ½ lb. of raw lean ham in pieces; put them in a stewpan, with:

    ¼ lb. of butter,

    1 middle-sized sliced carrot,

    1 middle-sized sliced onion;

Fry to a light-brown colour, and pour in 1½ pint of dry Champagne; simmer gently for twenty-five minutes; skim carefully, and strain through a broth napkin into a glazing stew-pan; then add 1 quart of *Espagnole* Sauce, and ½ pint of Essence of Mushrooms; reduce, until the sauce coats the spoon; and strain it, through a tammy cloth, into a *bain-marie*-pan.

MELTED BUTTER

Put 2½ oz. of flour in a stewpan over the fire, with :
   1 quart of cold water,
   1½ oz. of butter;
Salt and pepper to season;
Stir over the fire for twenty minutes, and strain through a tammy cloth into a *bain-marie*-pan; pour a spoonful of butter, melted, on the sauce, to prevent a skin forming on the surface.

When about to serve, boil up the sauce, and put in it ! lb. of butter, cut in pieces;—the heat of the sauce will be sufficient to melt this without putting it on the fire;

Stir, and mix well together, and add ½ a tablespoonful of lemon juice.

If the sauce be too thick, mix in half a gill of water.

DUTCH SAUCE

Put 4 tablespoonfuls of vinegar in a stewpan on the fire, with :
   ¼ oz. of *mignonnette* pepper,
   ¼ oz. of salt;
Reduce to 1 tablespoonful; strain into another stewpan; and add :
   4 tablespoonfuls of water,
   8 yolks of egg,
   ¼ lb. of butter;
Stir with a wire whisk, over a slow fire, till the yolks begin to thicken;

Take off the fire, and add 2 oz. of butter, cut in pieces; take off the fire, and stir till the butter is melted;

Repeat this process, adding 2 oz. of butter each time, till ¾ lb. of butter has been used in the sauce;

Should the sauce thicken too much, add one or two table-spoonfuls of water.

Avoid boiling the sauce.

When finished, it should be of the consistence of Melted Butter ; taste for seasoning ; and serve.

OYSTER SAUCE

Blanch 36 oysters, as indicated at Oyster Soup (*vide* page 251).

Put 1 quart of *Allemande* Sauce in a stewpan on the fire ; when it boils, add 1 oz. of butter ; ½ a tablespoonful of lemon juice ; a little coarsely chopped parsley, and the oysters, well drained ; mix all together ; and serve.

LOBSTER SAUCE

Take a large lobster ;

Pick the flesh from the tail and claws ; cut it in large dice ;

Boil 1 pint of *Velouté* Sauce with 1 pint of White *Poivrade* Sauce ; thicken with ½ oz. of Lobster Butter, and 1½ oz. of fresh butter ; add the cut lobster, and half a tablespoonful of lemon juice ; and serve.

Observation.—Lobster Sauce, like all sauces thickened with butter, should not be put on the fire after the last quantity of butter has been added.

SHRIMP SAUCE

Pick 1 lb. of shrimp tails ;

Put 1 pint of Melted Butter and 1 pint of White *Poivrade* Sauce in a stewpan ; when boiling, thicken with 2 oz. of Shrimp Butter ; add the tails of the shrimps, and half a tablespoonful of lemon juice ; stir well together ; and serve.

FISH VELOUTÉ SAUCE

Put 1 pint of *Poivrade* Sauce and 1 pint of *Velouté* Sauce *Maigre* in a stewpan ; boil, and thicken with 2 oz. of butter ; add 1 tablespoonful of chopped tarragon ; and serve.

BÉARNAISE SAUCE

Put the following in a stewpan :

5 yolks of egg,	1 pinch of salt,
1 oz. of butter,	1 small pinch of pepper ;

Stir over the fire, till the yolks begin to thicken; take off the fire, and add 1 oz. of butter;

Stir over the fire for two minutes; then take off the fire, and add 1 oz. of butter;—this process should be repeated twice, using 5 oz. of butter in all;

Taste for seasoning, and put in 1 tablespoonful of chopped tarragon, and 1 teaspoonful of Tarragon Vinegar.

This sauce should be of about the same consistence as *Mayonnaise* Sauce.

VALOIS SAUCE

Boil 2 well-washed and chopped shalots, in 2 tablespoonfuls of vinegar; reduce it entirely, and take off the fire;

When the shalots are cold, add 5 yolks of egg, and 1 oz. of butter;

Stir over the fire for two minutes;

Take off the fire, and add 1 oz. of butter; mix it well with the sauce, and put on the fire again; add 1 oz. of Chicken Glaze cut in small pieces, and 1 oz. of butter; mix thoroughly, off the fire;

Put back on the fire; and add another ounce of butter, and 1 tablespoonful of chopped parsley; mix; and serve.

VENETIAN SAUCE

Put 1 quart of *Allemande* Sauce in a stewpan over the fire; when it boils, thicken it with 1 oz. of butter; add 1 tablespoonful of chopped parsley, and 1 tablespoonful of lemon juice; mix; and serve.

SAUCE À LA TORTUE

Put the following in a stewpan:

1 pint of Essence of Ham,	1 pint of Madeira,
1 pint of Essence of Truffles,	3 oz. of Meat Glaze;
1 pint of Essence of Mushrooms,	

Reduce to half the quantity, and pour in 2 quarts of *Espagnole* Sauce; reduce again, till the sauce coats the spoon;

Strain through a tammy cloth; and add 1 pinch of cayenne pepper.

SUPRÊME SAUCE

Few cooks agree as to the preparation of this sauce: some make it entirely with chicken; whilst others add parsley, and thicken it with egg; when thus thickened, it is, to my mind, nothing else but *Allemande* or *Velouté* Sauce;

On the other hand, if chicken alone be used, without the addition of a certain quantity of veal to strengthen it, a tasteless and colourless sauce, entirely without body, and very similar to starch, will be the result.

The recipe I give below is not of my own invention, but this, and many others, I have seen practised by such cooks as Dunant, Drouhat, Catu, Montmirel, and many others, whose example, in such matters, can always be safely followed.

These practical men have proved, by experience, that it is indispensable to add a certain quantity of veal to the chicken, and that, far from altering the flavour, this tends to bring it out, and gives the sauce that softness and mellowness to which it owes its name of *Suprème*, and which makes it rank amongst the very best examples of High-Class Cookery.

Moreover, as a convincing proof of the advantages derived by following the annexed recipe, it will only be necessary to compare Essence of Chicken, with a certain quantity of *Velouté* Sauce added to it; or Essence of Game, with *Espagnole* Sauce added; to sauces made of essences only, with no addition of butcher's meat.

To make *Suprème* Sauce, proceed as follows:

Put 1 pint of Essence of Chicken in a stewpan, with:

  1 quart of *Velouté* Sauce,
  1 gill of Essence of Mushrooms;

Boil; then simmer gently for half an hour; skim carefully; put in a glazing stewpan, and stir till the sauce coats the spoon; strain, through a tammy cloth, into a *bain-marie*-pan; and pour 1 tablespoonful of Chicken *Consommé* on the top.

Another Way of preparing Suprème Sauce

In the absence of *Velouté* Sauce to add to the *Suprème* Sauce, proceed as follows:

Put 2 lbs. of fillet of veal in a stewpan, with the bones of the chickens (having previously removed the fillets to make the *Suprème* itself), and 4 quarts of General Stock; boil; skim, and add:

1 faggot,	1 small pinch of salt,
2 onions, with 2 cloves stuck in one,	1 small pinch of grated nutmeg;

Simmer until the veal is cooked, and strain through a broth napkin ;

Make a white *roux* in a stewpan, with 7 oz. of clarified butter, and 7 oz. of flour; moisten with the strained broth; skim it till it boils; and simmer for one hour and a half on the stove corner; skim again; put it in a glazing stewpan, and reduce it till the sauce coats the spoon; strain, through a tammy cloth, into a *bain-marie*-pan, and pour a tablespoonful of *consommé* on the top.

Before serving, boil up the sauce, and thicken it with 1 oz. of butter, and 3 tablespoonfuls of milk of almonds.

FRENCH SAUCE

Make some *Béarnaise* Sauce (*vide* page 284), with 6 yolks of egg, 1 lb. of butter, and salt and pepper for seasoning; add, whilst mixing the sauce, 1 gill of Tomato *Purée*, previously passed through a silk sieve; finish the sauce with 1 oz. of Chicken Glaze, 1 tablespoonful of washed and chopped parsley, and 1 tablespoonful of reduced Chili vinegar.

RAVIGOTE SAUCE

Put 1 pint of White *Poivrade* Sauce in a stewpan, with :
   1 pint of *Velouté* Sauce,
   ½ pint of Chicken *Consommé* ;
Reduce, and thicken it with 1½ oz. of *Ravigote* Butter; strain through a tammy cloth; and serve.

BREAD SAUCE

Put 7 oz. of breadcrumbs in a stewpan, with :
   1½ pint of milk,
   1 onion ;
Boil for ten minutes; take out the onion; and serve.

MAYONNAISE JELLY

Put 1 quart of melted White Meat Jelly in a *sauté*-pan, with :
   1 tablespoonful of oil,
   1 tablespoonful of vinegar,
   1 pinch of *mignonnette* pepper ;

Whip briskly, with a wire whisk, for ten minutes, and put the *mayonnaise* on the ice; whip it well, till it sets; then melt the jelly, and repeat the whipping on the ice till it sets again; strain through a tammy cloth; it will then be ready for use.

I think it better to whip, and set the jelly on the ice twice, as this will make the *mayonnaise* smoother and whiter.

HORSERADISH SAUCE

Boil 1 pint of double cream; add 2 oz. of grated horseradish, and 1 pinch of salt; mix; and serve.

MINT SAUCE

Put 3 oz. of brown sugar in a sauce-boat, with 3 tablespoonfuls of green mint, chopped fine, and ½ pint of vinegar; mix thoroughly; and serve when the sugar is melted.

HOT MINT SAUCE

Reduce ½ pint of vinegar, with ½ oz. of brown sugar; moisten with 1 pint of water; boil for one minute; and add 1 tablespoonful of finely chopped mint; mix; and serve.

CHICKEN CHAUD-FROID SAUCE

Reduce 3 pints of *Velouté* Sauce with 3 gills of Essence of Chicken.

The sauce should be stiffly reduced.

Thicken with yolks of egg; strain through a tammy cloth, and add 4 tablespoonfuls of White Meat Jelly, cut in small pieces, stirring lightly, till melted, to keep it clear.

GAME CHAUD-FROID SAUCE

Reduce stiffly, 3 pints of *Espagnole* Sauce with 3 gills of Essence of Partridge; strain through a tammy cloth; add 4 tablespoonfuls of chopped Brown Meat Jelly; mix; and put by for use.

COLD BÉCHAMEL SAUCE

Reduce 3 pints of *Béchamel* Sauce; strain, through a tammy cloth; add 4 tablespoonfuls of chopped White Meat Jelly; mix; and put by for use.

VENISON SAUCE

Put 1 pint of Brown *Poivrade* Sauce in a stewpan, with :
 1 pint of *Espagnole* Sauce,
 2 oz. of Game Glaze,
 4 oz. of Red Currant Jelly ;
Boil for five minutes ;
 Reduce ½ pint of port wine to 1 gill; add it to the sauce ;
and strain, through a tammy cloth, into a *bain-marie*-pan.

BAIN-MARIE-PAN FOR GLAZE

CHAPTER III

GARNISHES AND FORCEMEATS

I

GARNISHES

WHOLE TRUFFLES FOR GARNISH

THE truffles should be chosen large and round; clean them well, and put them to boil in a small stock-pot, with some Chicken *Consommé*, and the same quantity of Sauterne, or Champagne; put some clarified chicken dripping, or fat, on the top; and add:

1 onion, with 2 cloves stuck in it,
1 faggot,
1 small unpicked clove of garlic;

Boil for fifteen minutes, keeping the pot closely shut; take off the fire; and let the truffles cool in the liquor.

CUT TRUFFLES FOR GARNISH

Clean the truffles; peel and boil them for ten minutes in Chicken *Consommé*, and Madeira; let them cool in the liquor;

then cut them to the shape of olives, and small balls, to be used as garnish for *entrées*.

These last trimmings of the truffles, but not the first *parings*, may be used for *Périgueux* Sauce.

The liquor in which the truffles have been boiled should be freed from fat, strained through a broth napkin, and used for sauces.

TURNED MUSHROOMS

Prepare the mushrooms, as described in the First Part, at Turned Mushrooms (*vide* page 47).

Patterns are sometimes cut on these turned mushrooms for garnish; I do not advise it, as, besides lessening their size, it does not, in my opinion, improve their appearance in any way.

STUFFED MUSHROOMS FOR GARNISH

Choose 24 white and firm mushrooms, about $1\frac{1}{2}$ inch in diameter, and as nearly of a size as possible; pick; wash, and remove the stalks, and set the mushrooms, hollow side uppermost, in a buttered *sauté*-pan.

Make a stuffing by reducing 3 gills of *Espagnole* Sauce, and adding to it 1 oz. of Meat Glaze, and 3 gills of *d'Uxelles*; fill the hollow part of each mushroom with this stuffing, which should be very firm; sprinkle some raspings over them; and bake, for ten minutes, in a hot oven.

STUFFED OLIVES FOR GARNISH

Take 1 lb. of large and round olives; remove the stones with a cutter, and blanch for three minutes in boiling water; drain, and fill the hollow in each olive with some Chicken Forcemeat, mixed with some *d'Uxelles*.

COCKS' COMBS

Take 1 lb. of cocks' combs; put them in a stewpan, with enough water to cover them entirely; put them on a brisk fire, and stir with a spoon, till the skin begins to rise; then pour in some cold water, to stop the cooking of the combs, and take them out; if allowed to cook after the skin rises, the blood would coagulate, and it would be impossible to whiten them.

Strip off the skin, and trim the part which has been cut off the head, so as to free it of all feathers; soak the combs in salted water for six hours; after which steep them in cold water, frequently changed, until they become perfectly white;

Then boil them in plenty of water, with some butter, salt, and lemon juice.

Cocks' combs should not be much cooked when required to garnish silver skewers.

COCKS' KERNELS

Choose these white, firm, and unbroken; wash them carefully, and put them in a stewpan, with water, salt, butter, and lemon juice; stir over the fire, without boiling, till they are firm; and take them out.

CRAYFISH FOR GARNISH

Choose 20 equal-sized crayfish; wash, and put them in a stewpan, with:

½ pint of vinegar,	1 small pinch of *mignonnette*
2 small pinches of salt,	pepper,
1 middle-sized onion, sliced,	2 sprigs of parsley;

Close the stewpan, and put it on the fire for ten minutes, tossing the fish occasionally, to cook them evenly; drain and put them by for use.

PRAWNS FOR GARNISH

Take 1 lb. of good prawns;
Pick the tails to use for garnishes; the shells can be pounded to mix with butter.

CARP SOFT-ROES

Cleanse the roes of all blood; steep them in cold water, till they are white; then drain, and boil them in water with a little salt, and vinegar; when they are done, drain, and put them in some General Stock, or in some Fish *Consommé*.

OYSTERS FOR GARNISH

Blanch some large oysters in boiling water, for two minutes; drain; cool, and free them carefully of any remaining particle of shell, and put them by for use.

MUSSELS FOR GARNISH

Clean the mussels, as directed for Mussels with *Poulette* Sauce (*vide* First Part, page 156); boil them in some French white wine, with an onion, and some parsley; when done, take them out of the shells; dip them in lukewarm water; drain; and put them by for use.

CHICKEN PURÉE

Braize 2 chickens in some Chicken *Consommé*; when they are done, let them cool; strain the *consommé*, through a silk sieve, or broth napkin, and free it carefully of fat; reduce it, and add double the quantity of *Velouté* Sauce; reduce both together, to the consistence of thick *Suprème* Sauce; when the chickens are cold, remove the meat from the bones; trim off all skin, and fat; then chop the meat, and pound it in a mortar, adding the sauce whilst pounding; press the *purée* through a tammy cloth, and put it in a *bain-marie*-pan.

PHEASANT PURÉE

Braize 2 pheasants in some Game *Consommé*; when they are done, make the *purée*, and the sauce, as described in the preceding recipe.

PARTRIDGE PURÉE

Braize 3 partridges in some Game *Consomme*, and proceed as directed for Chicken *Purée*.

WOODCOCK PURÉE

Braize 3 woodcocks in some Game *Consommé*, and make the *purée* as described for Chicken *Purée* (*vide* above).

LEVERET PURÉE

Cut a young hare in four pieces; fry these, in a stewpan, with some butter, and moisten with 1 pint of Burgundy, and 1 quart of Game *Consommé*; simmer on a slow fire, till the hare is done;

CARROTS À LA NIVERNAISE

Cut off the end of some small carrots, and turn them to the shape of olives, 1½ inch by ¾ inch; cook, and glaze them as directed in the preceding recipe.

TURNIPS FOR GARNISH

Turn the turnips to a pear shape; blanch them in boiling water for five minutes; cool; drain, and cook them in some Chicken *Consommé*, with a little salt and sugar added, and reduce the liquor to glaze them.

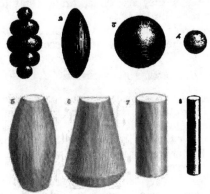

TURNED CARROTS AND TURNIPS FOR SOUPS AND GARNISH

ONIONS FOR GARNISH

Glaze the onions, as described in the First Part (*vide* page 52); substitute strong *consommé* for broth to glaze them.

FRENCH BEANS FOR GARNISH

Pick 2 oz. of French beans; cut them in diamond-shaped pieces, and boil them in salted water; when done, drain and put them in a *sauté*-pan with some butter.

Observation.—I think it preferable to put the beans in the butter as soon as they are drained, as, when they are allowed to cool first, they absorb a certain quantity of water, which would make the sauce to which they are added too thin.

CAULIFLOWERS FOR GARNISH

Cut the cauliflowers into small heads, about 2 inches in diameter; blanch them in boiling water; cool; drain, and boil them in water, with a little butter and salt added;

Cauliflowers for garnish should be rather underdone, so as not to break in the dishing up.

BRUSSELS SPROUTS

Pick, and wash some green Brussels sprouts; boil them in plenty of water; when they are done, drain; and toss them, in a stewpan, with some butter.

Observation.—Brussels sprouts for garnish should not be cooked as much as when intended for a second-course dish.

CABBAGE FOR GARNISH

Cut each cabbage in four pieces; pick; wash; blanch, and steep them in cold water for two hours; drain, and squeeze out the water in a cloth; cut out the stalks; season; tie, and put the pieces of cabbage in a stewpan, with some streaky bacon, previously blanched; moisten them with some General Stock, and cover them with clarified fat; close the stewpan, and simmer on a very slow fire for three hours; when the cabbages are done, drain them in a colander; put them in a stewpan, and stir over a brisk fire, to expel all moisture; season with pepper, and, if the bacon should not have sufficiently salted them, a little salt; when quite dry, roll the cabbage on a cloth into pieces 1½ inch thick;

Butter a *sauté*-pan; cut the rolls of cabbage in pieces 2 inches long; set them in the pan, and glaze them with some Meat Glaze, slightly diluted with water; warm in the oven, and put by for garnish.

ASPARAGUS PEAS FOR GARNISH

Pick off the small leaves, and cut up some green asparagus into peas; boil them in salted water; drain, and toss them in some butter in a *sauté*-pan.

Do not let the peas be overdone.

Q Q

PEAS FOR GARNISH

Boil the peas in salted water; drain, and toss them in butter, as directed for Asparagus Peas.

STUFFED TOMATOES

Choose some equal-sized tomatoes, about 2 inches in diameter; cut out the stalks, and the green parts round them, and take out the pips;

Reduce stiffly some *Espagnole* Sauce, and add some *d'Uxelles* to it, to make a stuffing, and fill the tomatoes with it.

Pour some oil in a *sauté*-pan, to a depth of a quarter of an inch; set the tomatoes in the pan; sprinkle them lightly with fine raspings, and bake in a sharp oven.

ARTICHOKE BOTTOMS FOR GARNISH

Trim off the under leaves, and cut off all the top ones; boil the bottoms in water, till the inside comes off easily; remove it; trim, and turn the artichoke bottoms; cook them in a white dressing, composed of flour, water, butter, salt, and some slices of peeled lemon, freed of pips; when done, let them cool in the liquor.

CARDOONS FOR GARNISH

Cut some white and perfectly sound cardoons, in 3-inch lengths; remove the prickles from the sides, and blanch in plenty of water for twenty minutes; then rub off the skin, and put them on a wire drainer, in an oval stewpan; cover them with thin slices of fat bacon, and pour in a white dressing made of flour, General Stock, and clarified poultry fat; add:

1 faggot,
1 onion,
2 cloves,

salt, and *mignonnette* pepper to season, and some slices of lemon, as described in the preceding recipe; simmer. till the cardoons are done; and put them in a basin for use.

WHITE CUCUMBER GARNISH

Peel, and remove the pips of the cucumbers, as directed in the First Part (*vide* page 172); then cut them in oval pieces, 2 inches long by 1½ inch, and ¾ inch thick;

Blanch them in water, and as soon as it comes to the boil, drain, and cook the cucumbers in a white dressing, as described in the preceding recipe; when done, let them cool in their liquor.

BROWN CUCUMBER GARNISH

Prepare, and cut some cucumbers as above; fry them in a *sauté*-pan, with some butter, and sugar, till they assume a bright brown colour; then put them in a stewpan, and finish their cooking in some *Blond de Veau*.

ENDIVE FOR GARNISH

Prepare some endives, as described in the First Part (*vide* page 172); put them in a stewpan; cover with Chicken *Consommé*, and put a round of buttered paper on the top; simmer slowly for two hours; then put the stewpan on a brisk fire; stir the endives, till the liquor is entirely reduced; and add some reduced *Béchamel* Sauce.

Before using, add some butter, and a pinch of grated nutmeg.

SPINACH FOR GARNISH

Prepare some spinach, as described in the First Part (*vide* page 171); stir it over a brisk fire with a little butter, to expel the moisture; and add some reduced *Béchamel* Sauce.

Before using, finish the spinach with some butter, and a pinch of grated nutmeg.

SORREL FOR GARNISH

Prepare some sorrel, as indicated in the First Part (*vide* page 57); reduce it with some *Allemande* Sauce; and add some butter, and a pinch of grated nutmeg.

CABBAGE LETTUCES FOR GARNISH

Cook the lettuces as directed for soups (*vide* Stuffed Lettuce Soup, page 237); drain them on a cloth; press them with the blade of a knife, and fold over the leaves, to give the pieces an oblong shape;

Butter a *sauté*-pan, and set the lettuces in it; glaze them with some Meat Glaze; and warm them in the oven when wanted.

CELERY FOR GARNISH

Prepare, and cook some celery, as directed in the First Part (*vide* page 173), substituting Chicken *Consommé* and clarified poultry fat for the broth and fat there indicated.

CELERY À LA FRANÇAISE

Blanch, and cut some heads of celery in ½-inch square pieces; cool; drain; and cook them as above.

GLAZED CHESTNUTS

Peel off the first skin of some chestnuts; throw them in boiling water, to facilitate removing the second skin, and put them in a buttered *sauté*-pan; cover them with equal quantities of *Blond de Veau* and *Consommé*; simmer gently, being careful that the chestnuts do not break; when done, glaze them with Meat Glaze.

CARDOON PURÉE

Cook some cardoons as directed page 298; cut them in pieces; add an equal quantity of *Béchamel* Sauce; reduce, and press the *purée* through a tammy cloth.

Before serving, add some butter and double cream to the *purée*.

WHITE ONION PURÉE À LA SOUBISE

Peel, and blanch some onions; cool them in water; drain, and put them in a stewpan, with sufficient Chicken *Consommé* to cover them; simmer gently, without colouring, till the onions are done; then reduce with the same quantity of *Béchamel* Sauce as there is of onion; press through a tammy cloth; and finish the *purée* with butter and Chicken Glaze.

BROWN ONION PURÉE À LA BRETONNE

Peel; blanch, and cool the onions in water; drain, and put them in a glazing stewpan, with some butter, salt, and sugar; fry them, till of a reddish brown colour, and reduce them with an equal quantity of *Espagnole* Sauce; press through a tammy cloth and add some butter and Meat Glaze to the *purée*.

ARTICHOKE PURÉE

Prepare and cook the artichoke bottoms as indicated for garnish (*vide* page 298).

Cook them till they become soft; drain, and cut them in pieces; and put them in a glazing stewpan, with an equal quantity of *Béchamel* Sauce; reduce, and press through a tammy cloth; and finish the *purée* with some double cream and butter.

ASPARAGUS PURÉE

Break off all the tender part of a bundle of green asparagus; wash; blanch; drain, and put the asparagus in a stewpan, with some butter; fry for four minutes; add the same quantity of *Béchamel* Sauce as there is of asparagus; reduce, and press through a tammy cloth; and finish the *purée* with butter and Chicken Glaze.

A little spinach greening should be added, if the *purée* be not sufficiently bright in colour.

CELERY PURÉE

Prepare and cook some celery as described for garnish (*vide* page 300); drain, and wipe it; cut it in small pieces, and put these in a glazing stewpan, with an equal quantity of *Béchamel* Sauce; reduce; press through a tammy cloth; and add some butter and double cream to the *purée*.

WHITE HARICOT BEANS PURÉE

Boil the beans in water, with some salt and butter, 1 faggot, and 1 onion; when the beans are done, take out the faggot, and press them through a hair sieve; put the *purée* in a stewpan, with half its quantity of *Béchamel* Sauce; reduce, and press through a tammy cloth; and finish the *purée* with butter and double cream.

LENTIL PURÉE À LA CONTI

Boil the lentils in water, with some salt, butter, a faggot, and an onion; drain; and press them through a hair sieve, and put the *purée* in a glazing stewpan, with half its quantity of *Espagnole* Sauce; reduce, and strain through a tammy cloth; and finish the *purée* with butter and Meat Glaze.

GREEN PEA PURÉE

Boil the peas in water; with 1 onion, and a seasoning of salt and sugar; when the peas are done, drain; and press them through a tammy cloth; put the *purée* in a stewpan, and mix it smooth with one-eighth of its quantity of *Béchamel* Sauce.

POTATO PURÉE

Cook the potatoes, as described for Potato Croquets (*vide* page 295); press them through a hair sieve; and finish the *purée* with butter and double cream.

TURNIP PURÉE

Peel, and blanch the turnips, and steep them in cold water; cook them in a stewpan, with some Chicken *Consommé*, some butter, and the crumb of a French roll;

When the turnips are done, drain, and reduce them with an equal quantity of *Béchamel* Sauce; pass through a tammy cloth; and finish the *purée* with butter and double cream.

CHESTNUT PURÉE

Pick, and peel some chestnuts, as described for Glazed Chestnuts (*vide* page 300);

Cook them in some Chicken *Consommé*, and when they are done, add half the quantity of *Espagnole* Sauce; reduce, and press through a tammy cloth; and finish the *purée* with butter, and Meat Glaze.

MUSHROOM PURÉE

Pick, and wash 1¼ lb. of mushrooms; cut them in pieces, and put them in a stewpan, with:

1 tablespoonful of water,
1 tablespoonful of lemon juice,
1 pinch of salt;

Boil for two minutes, and let the mushrooms cool in their liquor; drain, and wipe them on a cloth; pound them in a mortar, with 1 oz. of butter, and press the whole through a fine hair sieve;

Make 1 pint of *Béchamel* Sauce; reduce it, together with the liquor of the mushrooms; then add the *purée* to it.

Before serving, boil up the *purée*, and add 1 oz. of butter to it; mix; and serve.

TRUFFLE PURÉE

Take ½ lb. of well-cleaned and peeled truffles; pound them in a mortar, with 1 oz. of butter; and press them through a hair sieve;

Reduce 3 gills of *Espagnole* Sauce, with 1 gill of Essence of Truffles; and add the *purée* to it.

Before serving, boil up the *purée*, and thicken it with 1 oz. of butter and 1 oz. of Chicken Glaze.

TOMATO PURÉE

Pick 1 lb. of tomatoes; break them in pieces, and put them in a stewpan, with:

1 onion,
1 faggot,
and a seasoning of salt and pepper;

Stir over the fire, till the tomatoes are melted, and press them through a tammy cloth;

Make a *roux*, with 1 oz. of butter and 1 oz. of flour; cook it, for five minutes; add the *purée* to it, with 2 oz. of Meat Glaze; reduce the whole, for five minutes; and press, through a tammy cloth, into a *bain-marie*-pan.

CROUTONS FOR SOUPS

Cut some crumb of bread into ¼-inch dice; fry them in clarified butter, till of a light golden colour, tossing them to colour evenly.

CROUTONS FOR ENTRÉES

Cut some crumb of bread in heart-shaped pieces, 2 inches long, and ½ inch thick; fry them in clarified butter, till they assume a pale yellow tinge.

CROUTONS FOR VEGETABLE ENTREMÊTS

Cut some crumb of bread in 1½-inch triangular pieces, ½ inch thick; trim off the angles; and fry, of a light golden colour, in clarified butter.

II

FORCEMEATS

Remarks on Forcemeats

Forcemeats are very useful in cookery: they are turned to excellent account for *hors d'œuvre*, large dishes, *entrées*, &c. ; much care is required in their preparation; they should always be composed of meat and fish perfectly fresh, and with their nutritive properties unimpaired.

Forcemeat made with stale fish or meat will be of a very inferior description, and hardly likely to improve the dishes to which it may be added.

While recognising forcemeats as one of the elements of cookery, I would caution cooks against their too general use. It is unadvisable to introduce them constantly, and the art of a cook will lie principally in the discrimination with which he applies them.

Their too frequent recurrence in a dinner would satiate the guests, and would be deservedly censured by connoisseurs, who are unanimous that cookery should never be unnecessarily overloaded, and that it should, even in its most elaborate dishes, remain as simple and natural as possible.

GODIVEAU

Chop 1 lb. of *noix*, or fillet of veal, freed of skin and gristle; pick, and chop 1½ lb. of beef suet; mix it with the chopped veal; season with 1 oz. of spiced salt, and pound both together, in a mortar, to a smooth paste; adding 2 eggs, one at a time, whilst pounding.

No whole pieces of veal, or suet, should be visible in the forcemeat; put it on the ice, or in a cool place;

Mix in a stewpan:

2 eggs,	3 gills of milk,
1 oz. of butter,	1 pinch of salt;

Stir over the fire till boiling, and put the stewpan in a basin of water, to cool the contents; put the forcemeat back in the mortar, and pound it again, together with:

the above custard,

2 eggs,

¼ lb. of clean rough ice;

All the above should be added to the forcemeat in small quantities.

Try the forcemeat, by poaching a small *quenelle* of it in boiling water, and, should it prove too stiff, add a little more ice to it.

Godiveau Forcemeat should be made quickly, and in a cool place.

CHICKEN FORCEMEAT

Make some panada, with some crumb of bread, and General Stock; reduce it stiffly, by stirring over the fire, and put the panada on a plate to cool;

Pound sufficient fillets of chicken, or hen, to produce 1 lb. of *purée*, when pressed through a hair sieve; add 10 oz. of boiled udder of veal, also previously pounded and passed through a hair sieve, to the *purée*; pound, and mix both together; then add 10 oz. of the prepared panada; season with salt, pepper, and a small pinch of grated nutmeg; and mix the whole thoroughly, in the mortar, adding 1 gill of reduced *Allemande* Sauce;

Poach a small piece of the forcemeat, in water; should it be too stiff, add a little more *Allemande* Sauce, or double cream.

PHEASANT FORCEMEAT

Take 10 oz. of the flesh of a pheasant, and 7 oz. of that of a chicken, and make the forcemeat as directed in the preceding recipe, substituting *Espagnole* Sauce, reduced with Essence of Pheasant, for the *Allemande* Sauce.

PARTRIDGE FORCEMEAT

Take equal quantities of partridge and chicken; pound, and make the forcemeat as directed for Chicken Forcemeat; adding 1 gill of *Espagnole* Sauce, reduced with Essence of Partridge.

RABBIT FORCEMEAT

Take 1 lb. of the flesh of a rabbit;
Proceed as for Chicken Forcemeat (*vide* page 305); adding some *Espagnole* Sauce, reduced with Essence of Rabbit, instead of the *Allemande* Sauce, as there directed.

PIKE FORCEMEAT

Press 1 lb. of pike fillets through a hair sieve; add 10 oz. of butter, and 10 oz. of Bread Panada to the *purée*; season with salt and pepper, and moisten with 2 eggs, and some reduced *Velouté* Sauce *Maigre*, thickened with egg.
Finish as described for Chicken Forcemeat (*vide* page 305).

CARP FORCEMEAT

Proceed as above, using carp instead of pike.

WHITING FORCEMEAT

Make the forcemeat as directed for Pike Forcemeat, substituting whiting for the pike.

CONGER EEL FORCEMEAT

Proceed as described for Pike Forcemeat; substitute 1 lb. of conger eel for the pike fillets.

FOIE GRAS FORCEMEAT

Pound together in a mortar:
    1 lb. of firm and fresh *foie gras*,
    3 oz. of udder of veal, previously boiled, and allowed to get cold,
    7 oz. of Bread Panada, prepared as for Chicken Forcemeat (*vide* page 305);

Season with salt, pepper, and a small pinch of grated nutmeg; and press the forcemeat through a hair sieve; put it back in the mortar; pound it, and mix in 5 yolks of egg, one at a time; and put the forcemeat by for use.

Observation.—I must repeat, with reference to forcemeats, the remarks made on *Quenelles* for Soups (*vide* page 234); —namely, that they also should be delicate and light;

If too stiff, a little more sauce, or double cream, should be added.

ASPARAGUS FOR GARNISH

TIMBALES—BOUCHÉES—PATTIES—COCKS' COMBS À LA VILLEROY

CHAPTER IV

HOT HORS D'ŒUVRE

PATTIES

MAKE some puff paste, with 1 lb. of butter, and 1 lb. of flour, as directed for Puff Paste Cake (*vide* First Part, page 198); give the paste six turns, and roll it out to $\frac{1}{4}$-inch thickness;

Cut it into 24 rounds, with a plain $1\frac{3}{4}$-inch cutter;

Gather the trimmings of the paste into a lump; roll it out to the same thickness as the first, and cut it in 24 similar rounds; place these last cut rounds on a wet baking-sheet, and moisten the surface with a brush, dipped in water; put a small piece of Chicken Forcemeat on each; then take up one of the first cut rounds, and reverse it on to the forcemeat, so as to cover it; repeat this till all the patties are covered; press the two pieces of paste lightly together, with the top of a plain $1\frac{1}{4}$-inch cutter; brush them over with egg; and put to bake in a brisk oven.

FOIE GRAS PATTIES WITH TRUFFLES À LA MONGLAS

Make some paste with:

1 lb. of flour,	2 yolks of egg,
10 oz. of butter,	1 pinch of salt;

Mix the above with about ½ pint of water, to a softish paste; when it is quite smooth, gather it up in a lump, and let it rest for one hour on the ice; then roll it out, and line with it 18 small pie-moulds, 1¾-inch diameter, 2 inches deep; fill them with flour; put a paste cover on the top; press the two pastes together; cut the superfluous paste even with the mould, and pinch the edge round with the pincers; egg the top, and bake in a moderate oven; when the crusts are done, cut out the covers, inside the pinched edge; take out the flour, brush the inside, and take the crusts out of the moulds; egg them, inside and out, and dry them in the oven for two minutes;

Fill them with *foie gras* and truffles, cut in small dice, and mixed in some reduced *Espagnole* Sauce; pour a little sauce in each patty; and serve.

VEGETABLE PATTIES

Prepare 18 patty crusts as above; fill them with a *Macédoine* of vegetables, carrots, asparagus peas, and French beans; pour some thin *Béchamel* Sauce in each patty; and serve.

LARK PATTIES

Line 18 small pie-moulds with paste, as directed for Patties *à la Monglas* (*vide* recipe above);

Put 7 oz. of grated bacon in a *sauté*-pan, with 10 oz. of chicken livers;

Season with salt, pepper, and spice; fry for four minutes; and, when cold, pound in a mortar; and press the forcemeat through a hair sieve;

Bone 18 larks; open them, and season them slightly; spread a little of the forcemeat on each lark; place a piece of truffle, about the size of a nut, on the forcemeat, and roll the lark up into a ball, to enclose it;

Put a thin layer of forcemeat at the bottom of the lined moulds; place in each, one of the prepared larks, and spread another thin layer of forcemeat on the top; cover the patties with paste, as described for Patties *à la Monglas*; egg the tops, and lay on each a round of puff paste, cut with a 1¼-inch fluted cutter; egg the top, and bake the patties in a hot oven for twenty minutes;

Cut out the covers; pour in a spoonful of *Espagnole* Sauce, reduced with Essence of Larks; replace the covers; and serve.

MUTTON PATTIES

Chop, and pound in a mortar, equal quantities of fillet of mutton and fat bacon; season with spiced salt, and a small pinch of cayenne pepper;

Line some tartlet moulds with some trimmings of puff paste; put a round ball of the forcemeat, about 1 inch diameter, in the centre of each patty; flatten it slightly, and put a paste cover on the top; cut a hole in it, with a $\frac{1}{4}$-inch cutter;

Bake in a sharp oven; and, before serving, pour in some highly seasoned half glaze, through the opening in the top.

CROUSTADES À LA FINANCIÈRE

Line 18 *croustade* moulds with the same paste as for Patties *à la Monglas*; fill them with flour, and bake them; when the paste is done, take out the flour, brush the inside of the *croustades*; egg, and put them in the oven for two minutes;

Fill them with some *Financière Ragoût* (*vide* page 295), cut in small dice; pour some *Financière* Sauce in each *croustade*, and place some puff paste covers on the top.

To make the covers:

Take some puff paste at seven turns; roll it to $\frac{1}{4}$-inch thickness; cut out 18 rounds with a 2-inch fluted cutter, and 18 other rounds with a 1-inch fluted cutter;

Put the larger rounds on a wet baking-sheet; brush them over with egg, and place one of the smaller rounds on the centre of each large one; egg the tops, and bake them in a brisk oven.

CROUSTADES WITH TONGUE, TRUFFLES, AND CHICKEN, À LA BARAKIN

Prepare and bake the *croustades* as above;

Cut some fillets of chicken, some tongue, and truffles in shreds $\frac{3}{4}$ inch long, $\frac{1}{8}$ inch thick; warm these in some reduced *Espagnole* Sauce; fill the *croustades* with the mixture; place the puff paste covers on the top; and serve.

SALPICON BOUCHÉES, OR SMALL PATTIES

A mixture of chicken, game, or fish, with truffles, *foie gras*, and mushrooms, the whole cut in small dice, is known in cookery under the general name of *salpicon*.

Make some puff paste; give it six turns; cut out 18 *bouchées* with a fluted cutter 2 inches in diameter; put them on a baking-sheet, and let them rest on the ice for ten minutes; then brush them over with egg; dip a plain 1¼-inch cutter in hot water, place it on the centre of each *bouchée*, and cut through one-third of the thickness of the paste,—this will form the cover when baked; put the *bouchées* in a brisk oven; when they are done, take off the covers; trim off a little of the inside of the patties, and smooth it with the handle of a knife.

Prepare a *salpicon* of chicken, truffles, tongue, and mushrooms; put it in some *Allemande* Sauce; boil it up, and fill the *bouchées* with it; replace the covers; dish up on a napkin; and serve.

BOUCHÉES, OR SMALL PATTIES, À LA REINE

Prepare the *bouchées* as indicated in the preceding recipe; and fill them with some Chicken *Purée* (*vide* page 293).

GAME PURÉE BOUCHÉES, OR SMALL PATTIES

Prepare the *bouchées* as described for *Salpicon Bouchées*; fill them with any Game *Purée* (*vide* Pheasant, Partridge, Woodcock, and Hare *Purée*, page 293); and serve.

OYSTER BOUCHÉES, OR SMALL PATTIES

Make the *bouchées* as directed for *Salpicon Bouchées* (*vide* above).

Take 24 blanched oysters, and 10 turned mushrooms; cut the whole in dice, and warm them in some *Allemande* Sauce; fill the *bouchées*; replace the covers; and serve.

LOBSTER BOUCHÉES, OR SMALL PATTIES

Make the *bouchées* as described for *Salpicon Bouchées* (*vide* above).

Cut up the meat of a lobster in ¼-inch dice; warm some Lobster Sauce (*vide* page 284); add the pieces of lobster; fill the *bouchées* with the lobster and sauce; put on the covers; and serve.

SHRIMP BOUCHÉES, OR SMALL PATTIES

Take 18 *bouchées* prepared as for *Salpicon Bouchées* (*vide* page 311).

Pick, and cut in two pieces, the tails of 1 lb. of shrimps; warm them in some Shrimp Sauce (*vide* page 284); fill the *bouchées*; replace the covers; and serve.

Observation.—Lobster and Shrimp *Bouchées* are sometimes served without the paste covers; but then some fried bread-crumbs should be lightly sprinkled on the top.

SOLE BOUCHÉES, OR SMALL PATTIES

Make 18 *bouchées* as indicated page 311;

Take the fillets of a large sole, and cook them in a *sauté*-pan, with some butter, salt, and lemon juice; when done, press them between two dishes till cold; then cut them into small dice; warm some *Allemande* Sauce; put in it the pieces of sole, and, when warm, fill the *bouchées*; replace the covers; and serve.

CHICKEN CROQUETS

Take the fillets of some cold roast chickens; free them of all fat, gristle, and skin; and cut them in ⅛-inch dice;

Cut an equal quantity of truffles in the same way; mix both together in some stiffly reduced *Allemande* Sauce, and put on a dish to cool;

Strew a paste-board with bread-crumbs;

Divide the mixed chicken and truffles in equal-sized parts, and roll them to the shape of corks or balls; dip them in some eggs, beaten up with some oil, salt, and pepper, and roll them on the bread-crumbs;

Fry the croquets in hot fat, till they are crisp, and of a light-brown colour; drain on a cloth; sprinkle them with salt—(all croquets and fried things for Hors-d'œuvre should be similarly seasoned); put them on a napkin on a dish; and garnish with fried parsley.

Tomato, *Périgueux*, or *Poivrade* Sauces are served with these croquets.

SWEETBREAD CROQUETS

Take some blanched throat-sweetbreads; trim; and cut them in ¼-inch dice;

Cut an equal quantity of mushrooms in the same way, and mix both together in some stiffly reduced *Allemande* Sauce;

Make and fry the croquets as above.

PHEASANT CROQUETS

Take some fillets of cold roast pheasants; remove all skin, fat, and gristle; and cut them in small dice, with the same quantity of truffles; mix both in some *Espagnole* Sauce, stiffly reduced with some Essence of Truffles; and proceed to make and fry the croquets as directed for Chicken Croquets.

RABBIT CROQUETS

Remove the fillets of a cold roast rabbit; free them of skin and gristle;

Take an equal quantity of both truffles and mushrooms, and cut the whole in small dice; put these in some *Espagnole* Sauce, stiffly reduced with Essence of Rabbit; and finish the croquets as described for Chicken Croquets.

CROQUETS À LA MILANAISE

Cut equal quantities of cooked chicken, tongue, truffles, and maccaroni in small dice; mix the whole in some stiffly reduced *Allemande* Sauce; add some grated Parmesan Cheese, and make the croquets as directed page 312.

FOIE GRAS CROQUETS

Cut equal quantities of *foie gras* and truffles in small dice; mix them in some *Espagnole* Sauce, stiffly reduced with Essence of Truffles; and make the croquets as described before.

LOBSTER CROQUETS

Cut an equal quantity of lobster and mushrooms in small dice;

Reduce half as much as the above total quantity, of *Velouté* Sauce *Maigre* ; thicken it with egg and Lobster Butter ;

Mix the lobster and mushrooms in the sauce ; and, when cold, proceed as for Chicken Croquets.

TURBOT CROQUETS

Free some boiled turbot of bones and skin, and cut it in small dice ;

Reduce some *Velouté* Sauce *Maigre* ; thicken it with egg ; add some previously washed and chopped parsley ; mix the pieces of fish in the sauce ; and make and fry the croquets as aforesaid.

SOLE CROQUETS

Cut some previously cooked fillets of soles in small dice ;

Reduce some *Velouté* Sauce *Maigre*, together with the liquor in which the soles have been cooked ; thicken it with egg ; put the pieces of sole in it ; and, when cold, make the croquets as indicated page 312.

CHICKEN CROMESQUIS

Cromesquis are made of mixtures of chicken, game, truffles, mushrooms, or fish cut in small dice, mixed in reduced sauce, wrapped in udder of veal, dipped in frying batter, and fried.

Boil an udder of veal in a stock-pot ; cool, trim, and slice it as thin as possible, the whole length of the piece ;

Prepare a *salpicon* of chicken, tongue, truffles, and mushrooms, mixed in some reduced *Allemande* Sauce ;

When cold, place portions of this *salpicon*, 2 inches long by 1 inch, on the thin slices of udder ; wrap the udder round them, and roll the *cromesquis* to the shape of corks ; dip them in frying batter, and fry them in hot fat, till they are crisp, and of a light-brown colour ; drain, and dish them on a napkin ; garnish with fried parsley ; and serve.

GAME CROMESQUIS

Make a *salpicon* as directed for Pheasant Croquets (*vide* page 313) ; wrap equal portions of it in some thin slices of udder ; and finish the *cromesquis* as above.

SWEETBREAD CROMESQUIS

Prepare a *salpicon* as directed for Sweetbread Croquets (*vide* page 312); and make the *cromesquis* as indicated for Chicken *Cromesquis*.

SHRIMP CROMESQUIS

Pick some shrimp tails, and cut them in small dice;

Reduce some *Velouté* Sauce *Maigre*; thicken it with egg and butter; add the pieces of shrimp; and, when cold, wrap equal parts of this mixture in thin slices of udder; and finish as for Chicken *Cromesquis* (*vide* page 314).

SALMON CROMESQUIS

Cut some salmon in thin slices, about $\frac{1}{4}$ inch thick; cook them in a *sauté*-pan, with some butter, lemon-juice, salt, and pepper; when done, press them between two dishes till cold; then cut them into small dice, and mix these with half the quantity of truffles cut in the same way;

Reduce some *Velouté* Sauce *Maigre*; thicken it with egg and butter; add the mixed salmon and truffles to it, and, when cold, wrap portions of it in udder, and finish the *cromesquis* as aforesaid.

NOUILLES TIMBALES WITH GAME PURÉE

Make 1 lb. of *Nouilles* Paste; cut and blanch the *nouilles* in salted water; drain, and toss them in some butter in a *sauté*-pan, over the fire;

Put a layer of them, $1\frac{3}{4}$ inch thick, in a buttered *sauté*-pan; cover them with a round of buttered paper; and on this, place a baking-sheet, small enough to go inside the pan, and a 4-lbs. weight on the top.

When the *nouilles*, thus pressed, are cold, cut them through with a plain $1\frac{1}{2}$-inch cutter; brush these rounds over with egg, and bread-crumb them (*vide* Breading, First Part, page 74), and make an incision $\frac{1}{4}$-inch deep, on the tops, with a plain 1-inch cutter, to form the covers;

Fry these *timbales* in hot fat till they are crisp, and of a light-brown colour;

s s 2

Detach the covers, and cut out the inside of the *timbales*, leaving the crust only ¼ inch thick; fill them with Game *Purée* (*vide* Game *Purées*, page 293); put on the covers; and serve.

NOUILLES TIMBALES AU CHASSEUR

Make the *timbales* as above;

Remove the fillets of two young wild rabbits; fry them in butter in a *sauté*-pan; drain, and cut them in thin slices, and cut these again, with a plain ⅜-inch vegetable cutter;

Cut some truffles in the same way,—say one part of truffles to four of rabbit;

Mix the rounds of rabbit and truffles in some *Espagnole* Sauce, reduced with Essence of Rabbit; fill the *timbales* with this garnish; put the covers on; and serve.

OYSTERS À LA D'UXELLES

Blanch some large oysters; press them slightly between two dishes, till they are cold; then slit them open, without quite severing them;

Put a ¼-inch layer of reduced *d'Uxelles* Sauce inside, and fold the oysters together again; press them slightly, to enclose the *d'Uxelles*; dip them in some frying batter; and fry them in hot fat till they are crisp;

Pile the oysters up on a napkin, on a dish; garnish with fried parsley; and serve with a boat of *d'Uxelles* Sauce.

FRIED OYSTERS À LA VILLEROY

Blanch, and press the oysters as above   educe some *Velouté* Sauce *Maigre*; thicken it with egg and butter; dip each oyster in the sauce, and put them on a dish to cool; when the oysters are cold, egg and bread-crumb them; fry them in hot fat; drain, and pile them up on a napkin, on a dish; and serve with a boat of *Velouté* Sauce *Maigre*, thickened with egg and butter.

This sauce should not be reduced so much as that in which the oysters have been dipped.

ORLYS OF CHICKEN

Orly is a general name for fried Fillets of Chicken, Game, and Fish, and Fried Lobster Scollops, served with sauce, in a boat separately.

Remove the fillets of 2 chickens; trim, and cut each fillet in about five pieces, lengthwise; put them in a basin, with some salt, pepper, the juice of a lemon, a few sprigs of parsley, and half an onion, sliced; let them steep thus for two hours; then drain and wipe the pieces in a cloth; dip them in frying batter; fry in hot fat till crisp; drain, and pile them on a napkin, on a dish; garnish with fried parsley; and serve with a boat of Tomato or *Poivrade* Sauce.

Observation.—Fillets of Pheasants, Partridges, Rabbits, &c., are prepared as *Orlys,* in the same way.

ORLYS OF OYSTERS

Blanch, and press the oysters as directed for Oysters *à la d'Uxelles*;

Dip them in frying batter; fry them in hot fat; drain, and pile them on a napkin, on a dish; garnish with fried parsley; and serve with some Tomato Sauce, in a boat.

ORLYS OF SOLES

Remove the skin from some fillets of soles, and cut them first across, and then each piece lengthwise, in three strips; put them in a dish with some lemon-juice, a few sprigs of parsley, half an onion cut in slices, some salt, and pepper; let them marinade for two hours; drain, and wipe the pieces in a cloth; dip them in frying batter; fry them in hot fat; drain, and pile them on a napkin, on a dish; garnish with fried parsley; and serve with a boat of Tomato Sauce.

ORLYS OF ANCHOVIES

The best anchovies come from Nice,—they are easily recognised by their small size and plumpness, and by the redness of the pickle.

Steep the anchovies in cold water, till they are easily opened; cut off the heads; take out the middle bone, and scrape the scales off the outside; trim the anchovies to an even shape, and steep them in milk for one hour; drain, and flour them well; fry them in very hot fat; drain, and pile them up on a napkin, on a dish; garnish with fried parsley; and serve with some *Poivrade* Sauce, in a boat.

FILLETS OF SALMON À L'AMÉRICAINE

Cut some salmon in thin slices, and trim these to a pear shape; brush them over with egg, and bread-crumb them; fry in hot fat; drain, and dish the fillets up on a napkin; garnish with fried parsley; and serve with a boat of clear gravy, highly seasoned with cayenne pepper.

FOIE GRAS FRITTERS À LA CHEVREUSE

Boil some semolina in sufficient *consommé* to form a paste;

When cold, line some tartlet moulds with it, to a thickness of about ¼ inch.

Mix an equal quantity of *foie gras*, cut in dice, and of chopped truffles; season with salt and pepper, and fill the moulds with the mixture; cover with a layer of semolina; close the fritters thoroughly; take them out of the moulds; egg, bread-crumb, and fry them in hot fat; drain, and dish the fritters on a napkin; garnish with fried parsley; and serve.

CANNELONS À LA REINE

Chop some cooked fillets of chicken, some truffles, and mushrooms; and mix the whole in some stiffly reduced *Allemande* Sauce;

Roll out some seven-turns puff paste to about ⅛-inch thickness; moisten the surface with a brush dipped in water;

Place some equal-sized portions of the above mixture on the paste, about 2 inches long by 1 inch; enclose each portion with paste; press the edges of the paste together, and roll the *cannelons* on the board to a cork shape; fry them in warm fat; drain, and dish them on a napkin; garnish with fried parsley; and serve.

LAMB SWEETBREAD CASSOLETTES

Cook some rice in some *consommé*, 2½ gills of *consommé* to 1 gill of rice;

When the rice is thoroughly done, take it off the fire, and work it to a smooth paste with a wooden spoon; fill some small pie moulds (*vide* Patties à la Monglas, page 308) with the rice, and cut the tops ½ inch deep, with a plain 1¼-inch cutter, to form the covers;

When the rice is cold, take it out of the moulds; brush it over with butter, and put to colour in a brisk oven; then remove the covers; scoop out the inside, leaving the rice crust ¼ inch thick;

Fill the *cassolettes* with some Lamb Sweetbreads, cut in small dice, and mixed in some reduced *Allemande* Sauce; pour a spoonful of sauce in each *cassolette*; and serve.

Remarks on the Coquilles, or Shells used for Hors d'Œuvre

The natural shells of fish, which are still used in some establishments, are objectionable;

I would recommend their being superseded in all cases by light silver shells or *coquilles*, which are preferable for the preparation of these *hors d'œuvre*, and, moreover, always look well when brought to table.

CHICKEN EN COQUILLES

Cut the fillets of 3 chickens in small scollops; fry them slightly in some butter, in a *sauté*-pan;

Cut an equal quantity of truffles, previously cooked in Madeira, in the same way; mix both together in some reduced *Allemande* Sauce;

Fill some shells with this mixture; strew the top with fried bread-crumbs; put in the oven to warm; and serve.

Observation.—Proceed in the same way for any kind of game *en coquilles,*—only substitute reduced *Espagnole* Sauce for the *Allemande* Sauce.

OYSTERS EN COQUILLES

Blanch some oysters in boiling water; when they are done, cut them in ¼-inch dice;

Reduce some *Velouté* Sauce with some Essence of Mushrooms; thicken it with egg; mix the oysters and a quantity of sliced mushrooms in the sauce; fill the shells with this mixture; strew the tops with some fried bread-crumbs; warm in the oven; and serve.

LOBSTER EN COQUILLES

Cut in small dice equal quantities of lobster and mushrooms ;
Reduce some *Velouté* Sauce, with some Essence of Mushrooms;
thicken it with fresh butter and Lobster Butter ;
Mix the cut lobster and mushrooms in the sauce ; fill the
shells ; and bread-crumb and warm as above.

SHRIMPS EN COQUILLES

Pick, and cut the tails of some shrimps ;
Reduce some *Velouté* Sauce ; thicken it with fresh butter
and some Shrimp Butter ; mix the shrimps in the sauce ; fill
the shells ; sprinkle over some fried bread-crumbs ; warm in
the oven ; and serve.

MUSSELS EN COQUILLES

Cook the mussels as directed for Mussels with *Poulette* Sauce,
page 156.
Clean them thoroughly ; take them out of their shells ; and
cut them in two pieces ;
Reduce some *Velouté* Sauce, together with the liquor in which
the mussels have been cooked ; thicken with egg and butter ;
and mix some chopped parsley and the mussels in the sauce ;
fill the shells ; and finish as above.

CRAYFISH TAILS EN COQUILLES

Cut the flesh of some crayfish tails in three pieces, and slice
an equal quantity of mushrooms ;
Reduce some *Velouté* Sauce with some Essence of Mushrooms ;
thicken it with fresh butter and Crayfish Butter ; and add the cut
tails and mushrooms, a tablespoonful of chopped parsley, and a
few drops of lemon-juice ; mix the whole well together ; fill the
shells ; strew the tops with fried bread-crumbs ; warm in the
oven ; and serve.

CARP ROES EN COQUILLES

Prepare the soft roes as directed for Garnish (*vide* page 292) ;
and cut them in dice ;

Reduce some *Velouté* Sauce, together with some Essence of Mushrooms; thicken it with butter, and add the pieces of roe to it; fill the shells; and finish as above.

SOLE EN COQUILLES

Cook some fillets of sole in a *sauté*-pan, with some butter, lemon-juice, and salt; press them between two dishes till cold; and cut them in thin scollops ½ inch wide;

Reduce some *Velouté* Sauce with some Essence of Mushrooms; thicken it with butter; add the sole scollops to it; mix, and fill the shells with scollops and sauce; strew the top with fried bread-crumbs; warm in the oven; and serve.

TURBOT EN COQUILLES

Cut up some boiled turbot, freed from skin and bones, into small dice;

Prepare the sauce; and finish as above.

LARKS IN PAPER CASES

Take some paper cases, 2 inches in diameter (*vide* Woodcut page 325), and oil them slightly;

Prepare the larks and the forcemeat, as directed for Lark Patties (*vide* page 309);

Put a layer of the forcemeat, ½ inch thick, at the bottom of each case; place a lark on this; cover it with another layer of forcemeat; and bake in a moderate oven for fifteen minutes;

When done, wipe the top of the forcemeat very lightly with a cloth, to remove any fat; and pour in some *Périgueux* Sauce, reduced with Essence of Larks.

PARTRIDGE SCOLLOPS IN PAPER CASES

Oil some cases as above, and put them in a slack oven for five minutes;

Cut some fillets of partridges and some truffles in thin scollops; fry them in a *sauté*-pan in some clarified butter; drain, and fill the cases with them, and pour in some *Espagnole* Sauce, reduced with some Essence of Partridge.

T T

PHEASANT SCOLLOPS IN PAPER CASES

Proceed in the same way as in the preceding recipe,—reducing the *Espagnole* Sauce with Essence of Pheasant, instead of Essence of Partridge.

LAMB SWEETBREADS IN PAPER CASES

Steep some Lamb Sweetbreads in cold water; blanch; boil, and drain them; cut them crosswise in two pieces, and add them to some *Allemande* Sauce; fill the cases; and serve.

FOIES GRAS IN PAPER CASES

Cut some fresh and firm *foies gras* in slices, ½ inch thick; season with salt and pepper; fry them slightly in some butter in a *sauté*-pan, and let them cool;

Cut, in the same way, an equal quantity of truffles, previously cooked in Madeira;

Reduce some *Espagnole* Sauce with some Essence of Truffles; mix the *foies gras* and truffles in the sauce; fill some slightly oiled and dried paper cases; and serve.

FRIED COCKS' COMBS

Prepare the cocks' combs as directed at the Chapter on Garnishes (*vide* page 291);

Cut them open, without severing them; put in a small piece (the size of a nut) of Chicken Forcemeat (*vide* page 305), and fold the combs to enclose it; dip them in frying batter; and fry them in hot fat until they assume a nice golden colour; drain, and sprinkle them with salt; dish up on a napkin; and garnish with fried parsley.

PIG'S FEET CRÉPINETTES

Make some forcemeat, with equal quantities of *noix* of veal and fat bacon, and season with spiced salt;

Cook, and drain the pig's feet; cut them in slices ½ inch thick;

Steep some pig's caul in cold water; drain, and dry it with a cloth; and spread a layer of forcemeat on it, 3 inches long, by 1½ inch wide, and ¼ inch thick;

Cut some truffles, previously cooked in Madeira, in thin slices; place some of these on the forcemeat, then some pieces of pig's feet; cover with another layer of forcemeat, and wrap the whole round with the caul in such a way as to make an oval 3 inches long, by 2 inches wide;

When all the *crépinettes* are made, dip them in butter; bread-crumb and broil them over a slow fire for fifteen minutes; when nicely coloured, serve the *crépinettes* on a hot dish, with some *Périgueux* Sauce in a boat.

CHICKEN SAUSAGE

Take equal quantities of fillets of chicken, fat bacon, and crumb of bread; pound the whole in a mortar, and press through a hair sieve; add 2 eggs, and 2 gills of double cream to each pound of forcemeat; whip 2 whites of egg, and mix them in the forcemeat; and taste for seasoning;

Take some perfectly clean skins; fill them with the meat, and tie them in 5-inch lengths; put the sausages in hot water to set them; then take them out; dip them in cold water; drain them on a cloth; score, and broil them over a moderate fire; and serve.

CHICKEN SOUFFLÉS

Pound 1 lb. of roast chicken fillets, and press it through a fine hair sieve;

Reduce 1 pint of *Béchamel* Sauce to 3 gills; mix the pounded chicken in the sauce, and let it get cold; then add 5 yolks of egg, and a small pinch of grated nutmeg; whip the whites of egg very firm; add them to the *purée*, and fill some paper cases with it;

Bake in a hot oven for twelve or fifteen minutes; and serve.

GAME SOUFFLÉS

Game *Soufflés* are prepared as above,—substituting any kind of game for the chicken, and *Espagnole* Sauce, reduced with Essence of Game, for the *Béchamel* Sauce.

CHEESE SOUFFLÉS

Put 2¼ oz. of flour in a stewpan, with 1½ pint of milk; season with salt, and pepper; stir over the fire, till boiling,—and should there be any lumps, strain the *soufflé* paste through a tammy cloth;

Add 7 oz. of grated Parmesan cheese, and 7 yolks of egg; whip the whites till they are firm, and add them to the mixture; fill some paper cases with it, and bake in the oven for fifteen minutes.

Observation:—All these *soufflés* should be served immediately they are cooked.

HAM SCOLLOPS À LA MAÎTRE D'HÔTEL

Cut some ham in scollops, ¼ inch thick; fry them in butter for three minutes on each side; drain, and put them on a dish; pour over them some *Maître d'Hôtel* Butter, melted, with very little salt, and plenty of lemon-juice; and serve.

CHICKEN RISSOLES

Roll out some six-turns puff paste, to ⅓-inch thickness; cut out some rounds with a fluted 3-inch cutter; put a piece of Chicken Forcemeat, about the size of a walnut, on each round; fold one half over the other, and press the edges of the paste, so as to stick them together;

Fry the *rissoles* in warm fat; drain, and dress them on a dish, on a napkin; garnish with fried parsley; and serve.

GAME RISSOLES

Proceed as above,—substituting Pheasant, Partridge, or Leveret Forcemeat for the Chicken.

FISH RISSOLES

Prepare and make the *rissoles*, as directed for Chicken *Rissoles*;

Instead of the Chicken use Whiting, Carp, or Pike Forcemeat; and fry the *rissoles* in clarified butter.

CHEESE FRITTERS SOUFFLÉS À LA PIGNATELLI

Put 1 pint of water in a stewpan, with :
1½ oz. of butter ;
Season with salt, and pepper ; boil ; and add :
4½ oz. of flour,
1 oz. of grated Parmesan cheese ;
Stir over the fire for three minutes ; then moisten with some eggs, to make some paste as directed for *Beignets Soufflés* (*vide* First Part, page 188) ;

Add to the paste 1 oz. of lean cooked ham, cut in very small dice ; and fry the fritters in the same way as *Beignets Soufflés* ; drain ; dish on a napkin ; and garnish with fried parsley.

CHEESE PUFFS, OR RAMEQUINS

Put 2 oz. of butter in a stewpan, with ½ pint of water ; season with salt, and pepper ; boil ; and add ¼ lb. of flour ;

Stir over the fire for four minutes ; then mix in ¼ lb. of grated Parmesan cheese, and 3 eggs, one after the other ;

Put this paste on a baking-sheet, in lumps about the size of an egg ; flatten them slightly ; brush them over with egg ; and put a few small dice of Gruyère cheese on each ;

Bake in the oven ; and serve very hot.

PAPER CASES FOR SOUFFLÉS, QUAILS AND LARKS

ROAST SIRLOIN OF BEEF WITH POTATOES SAUTÉES

CHAPTER V

BEEF

REMOVES—ENTRÉES—ROASTS

REMOVES

BRAIZED RUMP OF BEEF À LA JARDINIÈRE

TAKE a rump of beef, weighing 16 lbs.,—this will be the smallest size for a good Remove;

Bone, and bind the meat with string, and boil it in a stock-pot for three hours; drain, and trim the beef, and put it in a braizing stewpan, on a drainer; pour in:

    1 bottle of Marsala,
    1 quart of *Mirepoix*;

Simmer for two hours, basting occasionally with the gravy, to glaze the meat; drain it; and strain the gravy, through a silk sieve, into a stewpan; reduce it, and add 1 pint of *Espagnole* Sauce; skim; and keep it warm, to serve in a boat with the meat;

Put the beef on a dish; garnish with a *jardinière*, consisting of 4 parts of cauliflowers, 8 of carrots, and 4 of Brussels sprouts; put a portion of the cauliflowers at each end, and on both sides of the dish; place some carrots on each side of the cauliflowers, and fill the spaces between with Brussels sprouts; glaze the beef, and the carrots; and serve with the gravy, in a boat.

BRAIZED RUMP OF BEEF WITH CARROT AND GLAZED ONION GARNISH

Prepare, and cook a rump as above; garnish it with 6 portions of carrots, turned to a pear shape, and 6 portions of glazed onions; put these portions alternately round the beef; glaze it and the vegetables; and serve, with the gravy, in a boat, as above.

BRAIZED RUMP OF BEEF WITH CAULIFLOWERS AND LETTUCE GARNISH

Boil, and braize a rump of beef, as directed for Rump *à la Jardinière* (*vide* page 326);

Make some Cauliflower, and Stuffed Cabbage-Lettuce Garnish (*vide* pages 297, 299);

Put the beef on a dish, and surround it with the garnish;

Glaze the meat, and the lettuces, and serve with a boat of the same gravy as for Rump *à la Jardinière*.

BRAIZED RUMP OF BEEF À LA FLAMANDE

Prepare, and cook the rump as aforesaid;

Make some Cabbage Garnish (*vide* page 297);

Turn 30 carrots to a pear shape, and glaze 30 onions;

Cut some Bologna Sausage in ¼-inch slices, and some streaky bacon in slices 2 inches square;

When the beef is glazed, put it on a dish; make a layer of the cabbage all round it, and place the carrots and onions on the cabbage at intervals; pile up the pieces of sausage and bacon, in the spaces between the carrots and onions; and serve, with some half glaze, in a boat.

BRAIZED RUMP OF BEEF WITH MACCARONI

Cook a rump of beef, as for Rump *à la Jardinière*;

Blanch some maccaroni; drain, and cook it in a stewpan, with some *Blond de Veau*, seasoned with *mignonnette* pepper;

when it is done, drain it, and add some reduced *Espagnole*
Sauce, and grated Parmesan cheese; mix thoroughly, and put
the maccaroni round the beef, on a dish; and serve with a
boat of Tomato Sauce.

BRAIZED RUMP OF BEEF WITH NOUILLES

Prepare a rump as before;

Blanch some *nouilles*; drain, and cook them in Chicken
Consommé; when done, drain the *nouilles* again, and mix them
with some Chicken Glaze, boiled cream, and grated Parmesan
cheese; add ½ lb. of lean cooked ham, cut in small dice;

Put the beef on a dish; glaze it; and garnish round with the
prepared *nouilles*; and serve with a boat of *Espagnole* Sauce,
reduced with Essence of Ham.

ROAST SIRLOIN À LA ST. FLORENTIN WITH ROBERT SAUCE

Saw off the chine bone of a sirloin of beef; remove the suety
fat; flatten the flap with the bat, and tie it under to the fillet;
trim the latter, and cover it with a layer of suet, 2 inches thick;
bind the meat round with string, and put it on the spit; tie
3 sheets of buttered paper over the top of the joint; and
roast it before an even fire;

Ten minutes before serving, remove the paper, and glaze the
sirloin; take it off the spit; put it on a dish, and serve with
a boat of *Robert* Sauce, adding a few tongue scollops to the
sauce.

ROAST SIRLOIN WITH POTATOES AND CHÂTEAUBRIAND SAUCE

Prepare, and roast a sirloin as above; put it on a dish, and
garnish each end with olive-shaped potatoes, *sautées* in butter;
pour some *Châteaubriand* Sauce over the potatoes; and serve,
with some of the same sauce in a boat (*vide Châteaubriand*
Sauce, page 279).

ROAST SIRLOIN GARNISHED WITH CHICKEN CROMESQUIS

Cook a sirloin, as indicated for Sirloin *à la St. Florentin*; put
it on a dish, and pile up some Chicken *Cromesquis* (*vide*
page 314) at each end;

Serve some *Espagnole* Sauce, reduced with Essence of Ham, in a boat.

ROAST SIRLOIN GARNISHED WITH CHICKEN RISSOLES

Prepare, and roast a sirloin as above; put it on a dish; garnish with Chicken *Rissoles* (*vide* page 324); and serve with a boat of *Espagnole* Sauce, reduced with Essence of Mushrooms.

ROAST SIRLOIN WITH POTATO CROQUETS AND BORDELAISE SAUCE

Prepare, and roast a sirloin as directed before; put it on a dish; garnish with Potato *Croquets* (*vide* page 295); and serve with *Bordelaise* Sauce, in a boat (*vide Bordelaise* Sauce, page 278).

Remarks on Braizes.

It will be noticed, that, in none of the braizes which follow, do I add any spices, or vegetables, whilst cooking.

By merely moistening with *Mirepoix*, containing, as it does, the essence of spices and vegetables, the addition of onions, carrots, cloves, &c., is rendered unnecessary; a limpid and stronger gravy will be thus obtained, without running the risk of any loss of savour, by cooking the meat with the vegetables.

BRAIZED SIRLOIN GARNISHED WITH STUFFED TOMATOES AND MUSHROOMS

Take a sirloin; saw off the chine bone; trim off some of the underneath fat; flatten the flap with the bat, and tie it under to the fillet; trim the latter, and cover it with a layer of suet;—when the sirloin is trimmed, and tied with string, it should be of an oblong shape;

Put it in a braizing stewpan, with 1 quart of *Mirepoix*, and 2 quarts of Stock;

Simmer till the meat is done; then drain, and untie it; put it on a dish, and glaze it; garnish round with stuffed mushrooms and tomatoes (*vide* Stuffed Mushrooms, page 291; Stuffed Tomatoes, page 298).

U U

Skim all fat off the gravy, and strain it through a hair sieve; add 1 pint of *Espagnole* Sauce; reduce both together for five minutes; and serve, in a boat.

BRAIZED SIRLOIN WITH CABBAGE À L'ALLEMANDE

Prepare, and braize a sirloin as above;

Blanch some Savoy cabbages in boiling water; drain, and press out the water; put them in a stewpan, with some salt, and pepper, 1 faggot, 1 onion, and some butter; simmer in the closed stewpan for three hours; then take out the faggot, and onion; drain the cabbages; put them in a stewpan, with some butter, and, when it is melted, put the beef on a dish; garnish both ends with the cabbage, and serve with some Half Glaze, in a boat.

BRAIZED SIRLOIN WITH STUFFED CUCUMBERS

Braize a sirloin, as directed for Braized Sirloin with Stuffed Mushrooms and Tomatoes;

Cut 3 middle-sized cucumbers in pieces 1½ inch long; peel, and take out the seeds, so as to form some rings; blanch these in boiling water for three minutes; drain, and cook them in some General Stock, with 1 faggot, and 1 onion;

When done, drain the pieces of cucumber on a cloth, and put them in a buttered *sauté*-pan; fill the centre of the rings with Chicken Forcemeat; smooth it even with the top; cover them with a round of buttered paper, and put in the oven, to set the forcemeat;

Put the sirloin on a dish; garnish each end with the pieces of cucumber, placed one above another; glaze the meat; and serve with some Half Glaze, in a boat.

BRAIZED SIRLOIN WITH ONIONS AND STUFFED LETTUCES

Braize a sirloin as above; put it on a dish, and glaze it; garnish round with Glazed Onions and Stuffed Cabbage-Lettuces (*vide* Garnishes, pages 296, 299);

Reduce the gravy of the meat, with some *Espagnole* Sauce; and serve it, in a boat, with the sirloin.

BRAIZED SIRLOIN WITH CELERY

Prepare, and cook a sirloin, as described for Sirloin with Stuffed Mushrooms and Tomatoes (*vide* page 329);

Prepare some heads of celery for garnish (*vide* page 300);

Put the meat on a dish, and garnish it with the celery;

Skim all the fat off the gravy; strain it through a hair sieve, and reduce it with some *Espagnole* Sauce; and serve in a boat with the meat.

BRAIZED SIRLOIN À LA CHIPOLATA

Braize a sirloin, as previously directed; put it on a dish, glaze it, and arrange round it some *Chipolata* Garnish (*vide* page 294).

BRAIZED SIRLOIN À LA NIVERNAISE

Prepare and cook a sirloin, as described for Braized Sirloin with Stuffed Mushrooms and Tomatoes (*vide* page 329); put it on a dish; glaze it, and garnish each end with Carrots *à la Nivernaise* (*vide* Garnishes, page 296).

FILLET OF BEEF À LA GODARD

Remarks on Removes known as à la Godard

All the large Removes bearing this name are highly ornamented and effective dishes, about which there is, unfortunately, much conflict of opinion, and diversity of preparation. For these, every cook has his own way of proceeding; and it becomes daily more difficult to know exactly to what special class of dishes the above name should be applied. From my own point of view, these preparations are merely Removes dressed with an abundance of large garnishes, such as truffles, cocks' combs, *quenelles*, and mushrooms, in connection with an appropriate sauce.

I fancy that by staying within this definition, which appears to me explicit, much confusion and misunderstanding will be avoided.

With a basis of this kind to start from, it will be easy to distinguish between those kindred preparations known as *à la Montmorency*, or *à la Régence*, which, although all very similar, still vary in some material points, which it is best to define, in

order to guard against the suspicion of presenting the same kind
of dishes under different names,—an expedient which has been
laid to the charge of several experienced practitioners, and
which is unworthy of the art.

FILLET OF BEEF À LA GODARD

Trim a fillet of beef, weighing from 8 to 10 pounds; lard it
with some small strips of fat bacon; put it in an oval pot or fish-
kettle, with 1 quart of *Mirepoix* and half a bottle of Marsala;
cook for two hours, basting the meat frequently with the gravy;
when the fillet is done, put it in the oven to keep warm; and
glaze it with some Meat Glaze.

Prepare the garnish as follows:

Make 8 Chicken Forcemeat *Quenelles*, 3 inches by 1½ inch;
roll them to an oval shape; and *contise* them (*vide* Cookery
Terms, Second Part, page 224) with thin slices of tongue;

Take 12 large truffles, carefully washed, but not pared;
and cooked in Marsala;

Wash and cook 12 cocks' combs;

Make some small Chicken *Quenelles*;

Slice some mushrooms and truffles, and mix them together
with the small *quenelles* in some *Godard* Sauce (*vide* page 282);

Take a dish, and, with some boiled rice, make a *socle*, or stand,
on it, of the same length and breadth as the fillet, and 3 inches
in height; brush it over with egg; and colour it in the oven.

I may mention, at once, that this *socle* is in no wise a part of
the dish itself; it is not intended for eating, and is only
introduced to raise the fillet, in order that the garnish may be
seen to advantage.

Drain the fillet, and put it on the rice *socle*; put the *ragoût*
of small *quenelles*, sliced mushrooms, and truffles all round the
socle on the dish; on the *ragoût*, place all round, alternately,
the large *quenelles* and the truffles, and put a cock's comb
on each truffle;

Garnish four silver skewers with some cocks' combs and truffles,
putting the cocks' combs at the top; stick these skewers in
the fillet; and serve with some *Godard* Sauce, in a boat.

FILLET OF BEEF À LA JARDINIÈRE

Trim, lard, and cook a fillet as above:

Make a rice *socle* on the dish, and put the fillet on it;

Fix a *Nouilles* Paste border, cut in a pattern, round the

inside edge of the dish; then, between this border and the rice *socle*, place a garnish of cauliflowers, turned carrots, cabbage-lettuces, turnips, artichoke-bottoms, French beans, or asparagus peas.

Put some vegetables on 3 silver skewers, and stick them in the fillet; and serve with some Half Glaze, in a boat.

FILLET OF BEEF À LA MILANAISE

Prepare, and cook a fillet as directed for Fillet *à la Godard*, and put it on a rice *socle*, on a dish;

Blanch some maccaroni in boiling water; drain, and cook it in some Chicken *Consommé*; when the maccaroni is done, add some *Espagnole* Sauce, some grated Parmesan cheese, and some finely sliced tongue, truffles, and mushrooms; mix the whole thoroughly in the maccaroni, and use it to garnish round the fillet; glaze the meat; and serve with it a boat of reduced *Espagnole* Sauce.

FILLET OF BEEF GARNISHED WITH ARTICHOKE-BOTTOMS AND A MACÉDOINE OF VEGETABLES

Trim, lard, and cook a fillet as above;

Put it on a rice *socle*, on a dish;

Make the garnish as follows:

Prepare 16 artichoke-bottoms, about 2 inches diameter;

Make some carrot rings $1\frac{1}{2}$ inch in diameter, $\frac{3}{4}$ inch thick, cutting out the centre with a $\frac{1}{2}$-inch vegetable cutter;

Prepare a *macédoine* with some carrots and turnips, cut with a small vegetable scoop, together with some peas and French beans; mix, in some *Béchamel* Sauce;

Put some Stuffed Cabbage-Lettuces (*vide* page 299) at the bottom of the dish round the rice *socle*; place the rings of carrot on the lettuce, the artichoke-bottoms on these, and pile up some of the *macédoine* on each artichoke-bottom;

Put some vegetables on 3 silver skewers; glaze the fillet; stick the skewers in it; and serve, with a boat of French Sauce (*vide* page 287).

FILLET OF BEEF WITH CROUSTADES À LA FINANCIÈRE

Cook a fillet as described for Fillet *à la Godard*; put it on a rice *socle*; garnish round with *Croustades à la Financière* (*vide* page 310);

Glaze the meat; and serve, with some *Financière* Sauce in a boat.

FILLET OF BEEF WITH SAUERKRAUT

Trim, lard, and cook a fillet as before directed; dish it on a rice *socle*; garnish round with Sauerkraut, and some pieces of streaky bacon and Bologna sausage; and serve, with some Half Glaze in a boat.

FILLET OF BEEF WITH MACCARONI À LA FRANÇAISE

Prepare and cook a fillet as for Fillet *à la Godard*; put it on a rice *socle* on a dish; and glaze it;

Blanch, and cool some maccaroni, and cut it in 1-inch lengths; put it in a stewpan with some Chicken *Consommé*;

When it is done, drain it, and put it back in the stewpan, adding some *Béchamel* Sauce, and grated Parmesan cheese;

Cut 1½ lb. of truffles to an olive shape, and toss them in a *sauté*-pan over the fire, in some Chicken Glaze diluted with *Consommé*;

Form a layer of maccaroni on the dish, round the *socle*; and, upon this layer, pile up, alternately, some little heaps of truffles and maccaroni;

Put some cocks' combs and truffles on three silver skewers; stick them in the fillet; and serve with some Half Glaze, in a boat.

FILLET OF BEEF À LA NAPOLITAINE

Trim and lard a fillet as directed for Fillet *à la Godard*;

Put it in an oval stewpan, with 1 quart of *Mirepoix*, and 1 quart of Malaga;

Simmer for two hours; half an hour before the fillet is done, put in ½ lb. of well washed and picked currants;

Glaze the meat; put it on a dish; skim the fat from the gravy; pour it in the dish; and serve.

ENTRÉES

BRAISED RIBS OF BEEF WITH GLAZED TURNIP GARNISH

Take 3 ribs of beef; saw off the chine bone, and remove the two outside rib-bones, leaving only the middle one; lard the

meat with some thin strips of lean ham ; tie it with string, and
put it in a braizing stewpan, with 1 quart of *Mirepoix*, and half
a bottle of Marsala ; simmer gently till the meat is done ; then
drain ; trim, and glaze it in the oven ;

Put it on a dish, and garnish with Glazed Turnips ; after
skimming the fat off the gravy, strain it through a silk sieve
into the dish ; put a paper frill round the end of the rib-bone ;
and serve.

BRAIZED RIBS OF BEEF WITH POTATO CROQUETS

Bone and tie 3 ribs of beef as above, and put to braize with
1 quart of *Mirepoix* ; when done, trim and glaze the meat ; put
it on a dish, and garnish round with Potato Croquets (*vide* page
295.) ;

Strain the gravy through a silk sieve ; free it of fat, and reduce
it together with ½ pint of *Espagnole* Sauce ; and serve in a boat
with the meat.

FILLET OF BEEF GRENADINS À LA FINANCIÈRE

Cut a piece of fillet of beef in slices ¾ inch thick, and trim
them to a pear shape, 3½ inches by 3 inches ;—these pieces are
called *Grenadins* (*vide* Woodcut, page 339).

Lard the tops with thin shreds of fat bacon, and put the
grenadins in a *sauté*-pan, with 1 pint of *Mirepoix*, and 1 gill of
Madeira ; put the pan over the fire, and, when the *grenadins* are
done, glaze them with Meat Glaze ;

Dress them in a circle, on a dish, and fill the centre with
Financière Ragoût (*vide* page 295).

FILLET OF BEEF GRENADINS WITH MUSHROOMS AND POIVRADE SAUCE

Prepare, and cook the *grenadins* as above ; dish them in a
circle ; and fill the centre with sliced mushrooms, mixed in
Poivrade Sauce (*vide* page 266) ; and serve, with some of the
same sauce in a boat.

FILLET OF BEEF GRENADINS WITH POTATOES AND VALOIS SAUCE

Prepare, cook, and dish up the *grenadins* as before ; fill the
centre with potatoes, turned to a ball shape, and *sautées* in

butter; pour some *Valois* Sauce (*vide* page 285) over them; and serve, with some more of the same sauce in a boat.

FILLET OF BEEF GRENADINS WITH OLIVES

Prepare, and cook the *grenadins* as directed for *Grenadins à la Financière*; glaze them, and dish them up in a circle; fill the centre with olives, previously blanched and stoned; pour some Half Glaze over them; and serve some Half Glaze in a boat.

FILLET OF BEEF SCOLLOPS À LA NIVERNAISE

Cut some fillet of beef into scollops, 2 inches wide, $\frac{3}{4}$ inch thick; flatten them slightly with the bat; trim them to a round shape, and of an equal size; season them with salt and pepper; and fry them in a *sauté*-pan with some clarified butter; drain, and dish them in a circle, and fill the centre with Carrots *à la Nivernaise* (*vide* page 296); pour some Half Glaze over; and serve.

FILLET OF BEEF SCOLLOPS WITH CHESTNUT PURÉE

Cut and fry the scollops as above;
Dish them in a circle; fill the middle with Chestnut *Purée*, and glaze the scollops;
Serve some reduced *Espagnole* Sauce, separately.

FILLET OF BEEF SCOLLOPS WITH TRUFFLES

Prepare, cook, and dish up the scollops as before; fill the centre with sliced truffles; pour over some Madeira Sauce (*vide* page 278); and serve some of the same sauce in a boat.

TOURNE-DOS

Cut and trim a piece of fillet of beef in slices as for *grenadins* (vide *Grenadins à la Financière*, page 335);
Steep them for twenty-four hours in some cooked marinade; drain, and fry them in a *sauté*-pan in some clarified butter; drain, and dish them in a circle, with a heart-shaped *crouton* between each slice of meat;
Prepare a sauce as follows, pour part of it over the meat, and serve the remainder in a boat:

Cut 2 onions in small dice; blanch, and fry them in butter till they assume a light brown colour; pour off the butter; and add 3 gills of *Poivrade* Sauce, and 2 gills of *Espagnole* Sauce; reduce for five minutes, and add a small pinch of cayenne pepper.

RIB STEAKS À LA BORDELAISE

Cut the steaks from between the rib-bones, $1\frac{1}{4}$ inch thick; flatten them slightly with the bat; trim and season them with salt and pepper; oil them slightly, and broil them over the fire for five minutes on each side;

Blanch some marrow; cut it in $\frac{1}{2}$-inch slices; pour some Meat Glaze over, and put it in the oven for one minute; put the steaks on a dish, the pieces of marrow on them; and pour over some *Bordelaise* Sauce (*vide* page 278); and serve, very hot.

RIB STEAKS À LA MAÎTRE D'HÔTEL

Prepare and cook the steaks as above; put some *Maître d'Hôtel* Butter on a dish; place the steaks on it; pour over some Meat Glaze; and serve.

FILLET STEAKS À LA CHÂTEAUBRIAND

Cut a fillet of beef crosswise, in $1\frac{3}{4}$-inch steaks; trim them; sprinkle them with salt and pepper, and oil them slightly; broil the steaks over the fire,—six minutes each side; put them on a dish; and garnish with potatoes *sautées*, and cut to an olive shape; pour some *Châteaubriand* Sauce (*vide* page 279)—over the steaks only; and serve.

Remarks on Steaks à la·Châteaubriand

These steaks should be cut in the best part of a fillet of beef. It frequently happens that they are cut too thick, which prevents their being cooked properly. Although requiring to be rather thicker than the ordinary run of steaks, this peculiarity should not be exaggerated; nothing will be gained thereby, and it will add to the difficulty of cooking.

X X

FILLET STEAKS À LA VALOIS

Cut and cook the steaks as above; put them on a dish; and spread on them a layer of *Valois* Sauce (*vide* page 285), 1 inch thick ; and serve.

FILLET STEAKS À LA BÉARNAISE

Prepare and cook the steaks as directed for Steaks *à la Châteaubriand*;

Substitute *Béarnaise* Sauce (*vide* page 285), for the *Châteaubriand* Sauce.

FILLET STEAKS SAUTÉS WITH TRUFFLES

Cut and trim the steaks as above ;

Fry them in a *sauté*-pan, with clarified butter ;

Put the steaks on a dish ; cover them with sliced truffles ; pour over some Madeira Sauce (*vide* page 278) ; and serve.

FILLET STEAKS SAUTÉS WITH MUSHROOM PURÉE

Proceed as for Steaks with Truffles ;

Put some Mushroom *Purée* in a dish ; place the steaks on it ; glaze them ; and serve.

FILLET STEAKS WITH TOMATO PURÉE

Cut, and broil the steaks, as described for Steaks *à la Châteaubriand*;

Put some Tomato *Purée* in a dish ; place the steaks on it ; glaze them ; and serve.

ROASTS

SIRLOIN

Take a piece of sirloin, comprising the best part of the fillet ; saw off the chine bone ; flatten the flap, and tie it under to the fillet ; trim the joint ; tie a layer of suet over the fillet, and cover the sirloin with buttered paper ; tie it up, and put it on the spit, to roast before an even fire ; ten minutes before the meat is done, take off the paper, and sprinkle the joint with salt ;

Take off the spit, and put on a dish ; glaze the sirloin ; and pour some Meat Gravy in the dish.

FILLET OF BEEF

Trim, and lard a fillet of beef with small shreds of fat bacon, and marinade it in 2 gills of Châblis, some oil, salt, pepper, sliced onions, and some sprigs of parsley.

The meat is generally allowed to marinade for twenty-four hours.

Clear the fillet of onion and parsley ; put it on the spit ; wrap it in buttered paper ; and put it to roast before an even fire ; five minutes before serving take off the paper, and glaze the fillet with Meat Glaze ; take it off the spit, and put it on a dish ; pour some Meat Gravy under it ; and serve, with Sharp Sauce, in a boat.

Observation.—Fillet of Beef is sometimes roasted without being marinaded ;—in that case, serve it with the gravy only, without the Sharp Sauce.

ROAST RIBS OF BEEF

Take a piece of ribs of beef, weighing about 10 lbs. ; saw off the chine bone ; wrap the joint in buttered paper ; roast ; and serve, as directed for Roast Sirloin.

FILLET OF BEEF GRENADIN

CALVES' EARS EN TORTUE

CHAPTER VI

VEAL

REMOVES—ENTRÉES—ROASTS

REMOVES

CALF'S HEAD EN TORTUE

BONE and blanch a calf's head; put the brains to steep in cold water, in a basin;

When the head has been cooled, cut off the ears, and the tongue; take 2 more ears, also blanched and cooled;

Cut the remainder of the head in 2-inch pieces; trim them to an even round shape;

Cook the tongue, and pieces of head, as directed for Calf's Head *au Naturel* (*vide* First Part, page 102);

Pick the brains, and cook them as indicated in the same recipe (*vide* First Part, page 103);

Prepare the following for garnish:

4 sweetbreads, larded,
8 crayfish,

24 large olives,

12 gherkins, cut to a ball shape, and previously steeped in water,

8 yolks of hard-boiled eggs,

10 large truffles,

24 large mushrooms,

5 fine cocks' combs;

Drain, and wipe the pieces of head; and put them in a glazing stewpan;

Score, and curl the ears;

Strip the skin off the tongue, and cut it in scollops 1½ inch in diameter; put these in a stewpan, with the olives, mushrooms, and 1 quart of Sauce *à la Tortue*;

Make a bread border round a dish; place a bread *croustade* in the centre; put the pieces of head round it; and pour over the *ragoût*, prepared with the tongue, olives, &c.; drain the brains, and put them on the top of the *croustade*.

Garnish round the *croustade* with the ears, sweetbreads, crayfish, gherkins, yolks of egg, &c.

Put some crayfish, truffles, and cocks' combs, on five silver skewers; stick them in, as shown in the coloured Plate; glaze the truffles; and serve, with some Sauce *à la Tortue* in a boat.

CALF'S HEAD À LA FINANCIÈRE

Prepare and cook a calf's head as above;

Make a *ragoût* of:

The tongue, cut in scollops 1½ inch in diameter,

Chicken *Quenelles*, with some chopped truffles mixed in the forcemeat,

Mushrooms,   Cocks'.combs,

Cocks' kernels,   Cooked truffles;

Scollops of *foie gras*,

Mix the whole in 1 quart of *Financière* Sauce;

Put some cocks' combs and truffles on five silver skewers;

Prepare:

6 large decorated Chicken *Quenelles*,

6 large truffles,

6 fine cocks' combs;

Dish up the head in the same way as *en Tortue* (*vide* page 340); pour the *ragoût* over it; and garnish round the *croustade* in the following manner:

Put :

   1 ear at each end,
   3 *quenelles* on each side,
   1 truffle, and 1 cock's comb between each *quenelle*,
   1 truffle in each ear,
   the brains on the *croustade*, and the skewers stuck in ;

Glaze the truffles ; and serve, with some *Financière* Sauce in a boat.

LOIN OF VEAL À LA JARDINIÈRE

Take a loin of veal, with two of the neck-bones attached ; bone it entirely ; flatten the flap ; cut out the kidney ; trim off some of the encircling fat, and put the kidney back in its place ; season with salt and pepper ; and fold the flap under, so as to cover the kidney and fillet ; tie the joint with string, to keep it in shape ; and put it in a braizing stewpan, with 1 quart of *Mirepoix*, and 1 quart of *Consommé* ; cover it with a doubled sheet of buttered paper ; simmer for two hours, basting the meat six times ; when done, drain the meat, and put it on a rice *socle* on a dish, as described for Fillet of Beef *à la Godard* (*vide* page 331) ; garnish round with a *jardinière* of cauliflowers, carrots, turnips, glazed onions, cabbage-lettuces, and asparagus peas, mingling the colours ;

Put some vegetables on three silver skewers, and stick them in the meat ; and serve, with some Half Glaze in a boat.

LOIN OF VEAL WITH STUFFED MUSHROOMS AND TOMATOES

Bone and prepare a loin of veal as above ;

Cook it in the same way ; put it on a dish ; and garnish one end with Stuffed Mushrooms, the other with Stuffed Tomatoes (*vide* Garnishes, pages 291, 298) ; glaze the meat ; and serve, with some Italian Sauce in a boat.

LOIN OF VEAL EN SURPRISE WITH BÉCHAMEL SAUCE

Bone ; and tie a loin of veal as before ; put it on the spit ; wrap it in a sheet of buttered paper ; and put it to roast before an even fire ;

Remove the paper ten minutes before taking the meat from the fire; sprinkle it with salt; and, when brown, take it off the spit;

Cut a square piece of the skin off the top of the loin; remove the lean part beneath it; mince this fine, and mix it with some *Béchamel* Sauce; put it back in its place, and replace the skin in such a way that the original shape of the joint be preserved; serve, with some *Béchamel* Sauce in a boat.

Observation.—The operation of raising and replacing the skin requires great care, as the fact of its having been touched should not be immediately perceptible.

LOIN OF VEAL WITH CARDOONS

Roast a loin of veal, previously boned and tied as directed for Loin *à la Jardinière* (*vide* page 342); when it is done, untie, and put it on a dish; garnish each end with cardoons, cut in slices; pour over some reduced *Espagnole* Sauce; and serve, with some of the same sauce in a boat.

LOIN OF VEAL À LA FINANCIÈRE

Braize a loin of veal as described for Loin *à la Jardinière*; Prepare a *ragoût* of:

truffles,	mushrooms,
chicken *quenelles*,	cocks' combs,
foie gras scollops,	onions,

mixed in 1 quart of *Financière* Sauce (*vide* page 281);
Prepare the following for garnish:

4 sweetbreads, larded with fat bacon,
6 large crayfish,
6 large Chicken Forcemeat *Quenelles*,
20 lamb sweetbreads, larded and glazed;

Put the loin on a rice *socle*, on a dish; pour the prepared *ragoût* in the dish, and, on this, garnish round with the sweetbreads, the *quenelles*, and crayfish;

Place the Lamb Sweetbreads in two lines on the top of the joint; between these two lines, and along the middle of the loin, stick four silver skewers, garnished with truffles and cocks' combs; and serve, with *Financière* Sauce in a boat.

LOIN OF VEAL À LA MACÉDOINE

Bone, and prepare a loin of veal as directed above (*vide* page 342); wrap it in buttered paper; and roast it before an even fire;

Prepare a *macédoine* of:

carrots,	asparagus,
turnips,	French beans;
peas,	

Put the meat on a dish; garnish each end with the *macédoine*; pour over some *Béchamel* Sauce (*vide* page 288); glaze the veal; and serve, with some of the same sauce in a boat.

LOIN OF VEAL GARNISHED WITH KIDNEYS

Prepare and roast a loin of veal as above;

Free 2 veal kidneys of all fat and skin;

Cut them in $\frac{3}{4}$-inch slices; flatten them with the bat, and season with pepper and salt; egg and bread-crumb the slices; and fry them for ten minutes in clarified butter;

Put the loin on a dish; glaze it; garnish both ends with the slices of kidney; and serve, with a boat of Tomato Sauce.

LOIN OF VEAL WITH CROQUETS À LA MILANAISE

Bone and roast a loin of veal, as directed for Loin of Veal *en Surprise* (*vide* page 342); put it on a dish, and garnish the ends with Croquets *à la Milanaise* (*vide* page 313); and serve, with it, in a boat, some *Velouté* Sauce reduced with Essence of Mushrooms.

ENTRÉES

NOIX OF VEAL WITH ENDIVE

Trim and lard a *noix*, or cushion of veal, with some shreds of fat bacon; put it in a glazing stewpan, with $\frac{1}{2}$ pint of *Mirepoix*; reduce this entirely; then moisten again with 1 pint of *Mirepoix*, and 3 gills of Veal Stock; cook for two hours, basting the meat frequently, and glaze it a quarter of an hour before it is done;

Prepare some endive as indicated for Garnish (*vide* page 299); put it in a dish, and place the veal on the top of it;

Skim the fat off the gravy; strain it through a silk sieve, into a sauce boat; and serve it with the meat.

NOIX OF VEAL WITH SORREL

Prepare and cook a *noix* as above;

Make some Sorrel Garnish, as directed page 299; put it on a dish; place the meat on it; and serve with the strained gravy in a boat.

NOIX OF VEAL WITH MUSHROOM PURÉE

Prepare a *noix* as directed for *Noix* of Veal with Endive; dish it on some Mushroom *Purée* (*vide* page 302); and serve.

NOIX OF VEAL À LA JARDINIÈRE

Take a *noix* of veal covered with the udder; cut the skin off the lean part, and lard it with thin shreds of fat bacon; lard the inside of the *noix* with larger strips of fat bacon and ham; put it in a stewpan with $\frac{1}{2}$ pint of Veal Stock; reduce this to a glaze, and moisten with 1 quart of *Mirepoix*; cover the meat with a double sheet of buttered paper; and simmer for four hours, glazing the *noix* fifteen minutes before it is done;

Strain, and reduce the gravy;

Put the *noix* on a dish; garnish round with a *jardinière* of cauliflowers, carrots, turnips, asparagus peas, French beans, and peas; pour the gravy over; and serve.

NOIX OF VEAL WITH CUCUMBERS

Prepare and cook a *noix*, as above; put it on a dish; garnish with some Cucumber Scollops, mixed in *Béchamel* Sauce; and serve with the same sauce, in a boat.

NOIX OF VEAL WITH CELERY À LA FRANÇAISE

Prepare a *noix* of veal as above; put it on a dish, and garnish with Celery *à la Française* (*vide* page 300).

CHUMP OF VEAL À LA NIVERNAISE

Bone a *quasi*, or chump of veal, and tie it up to its original shape;

Y Y

Put it in a stewpan with ½ pint of Veal Stock ; reduce this to a glaze, and add 1 quart of *Mirepoix* ; simmer until the veal is done ; and glaze it a quarter of an hour before serving ;

Put the meat on a dish ; garnish it with Carrots *à la Nivernaise* (*vide* page 296);

Pour over some reduced *Espagnole* Sauce ; and serve, with some Half Glaze in a boat.

CHUMP OF VEAL WITH CAULIFLOWERS

Prepare and cook a chump, or *quasi* of veal, as above ; put it on a dish ; and garnish with Cauliflowers (*vide* page 297) ; free the gravy of fat ; reduce ; and strain it into a boat ; and serve with the meat.

CHUMP OF VEAL WITH NOUILLES À L'ALLEMANDE

Prepare a *quasi*, or chump of veal, as directed above ; wrap it in buttered paper, and roast it before an even fire ; ten minutes before serving, take off the paper ; glaze the meat ; take it off the spit ; put it on a dish, and garnish with *Nouilles à l'Allemande* (*vide* First Part, page 186); and serve, with *Allemande* Sauce in a boat.

CHUMP OF VEAL WITH CARROTS À LA FLAMANDE

Prepare and braize a chump, or *quasi* of veal, as directed for Chump of Veal *à la Nivernaise* ; put it on a dish, and garnish with Carrots *à la Flamande* (*vide* First Part, page 174) ; strain, and reduce the gravy ; and serve it in a boat.

NECK OF VEAL WITH ENDIVE PURÉE

Take a whole neck of veal ; saw off the chine bone, and shorten the rib-bones to half their length ; trim the skin off the top ; and lard that part with fine shreds of fat bacon ; roll the flap underneath, and secure it with skewers ;

Put the joint on the spit ; wrap it in buttered paper ; and roast it before an even fire ; ten minutes before serving, take off the paper ; glaze the meat ; put it on a dish, and pour some Half Glaze under it ;

Make some Endive *Purée* by rubbing some Endive Garnish (*vide* page 299) through a hair sieve; mix it with Meat Glaze, and double cream; and serve it with the veal in a silver casserole.

NECK OF VEAL WITH GLAZED ONIONS

Prepare and cook a neck as above;

Put it on a dish; garnish it with Glazed Onions (*vide* page 296); and serve with some Half Glaze in a boat.

NECK OF VEAL À LA MACÉDOINE

Prepare and cook a neck as directed for Neck of Veal with Endive *Purée*;

Put it on a dish, and garnish round with a *macédoine* of:

carrots,   French beans,
turnips,   peas;
asparagus,

mixed in some *Allemande* Sauce; and serve with some of the same sauce in a boat.

NECK OF VEAL WITH SPINACH

Prepare and cook a neck as aforesaid;

Garnish it with Spinach (*vide* page 299);

Pour some *Velouté* Sauce over this; and serve with some Half Glaze in a boat.

VEAL SCOLLOPS WITH CELERY PURÉE

Cut a *noix*, or cushion of veal, into scollops 2 inches in diameter, ¾ inch thick; flatten them with the bat, and trim to a round and even shape; sprinkle them with salt, and fry in a *sauté*-pan with clarified butter, without colouring them;

Drain the scollops on a cloth; dress them in a circle on a dish, pour over some *Béchamel* Sauce, and fill the centre with Celery *Purée* (*vide* page 301).

VEAL SCOLLOPS WITH GLAZED TURNIPS

Cut and fry the scollops as above;

Put them on a dish, and garnish with Glazed Turnips (*vide* page 296), and serve with some reduced *Espagnole* Sauce in a boat.

VEAL SCOLLOPS WITH ARTICHOKE PURÉE

Cut the scollops as directed for 'Veal Scollops with Celery Purée';

Dip them in beaten egg, and fry them in clarified butter; dish them in a circle, and fill the centre with Artichoke Purée, (vide page 301); serve with some Half Glaze in a boat.

VEAL SCOLLOPS WITH CARDOON PURÉE

Cut and cook the scollops as indicated for 'Veal Scollops with Celery Purée';

Dish them in a circle, fill the centre with Cardoon Purée ; and pour some Béchamel Sauce over the whole.

VEAL SCOLLOPS WITH VENETIAN SAUCE

Prepare and cook the scollops as above;

Dish them in a circle, and pour over some Venetian Sauce (vide page 285), fill the centre with potatoes cut in small balls, and sautées in butter.

BLANQUETTE OF VEAL WITH MUSHROOMS IN A CROUSTADE

Roast a fillet of veal, and, when cold, cut it into scollops $1\frac{1}{2}$ inch in diameter, $\frac{1}{4}$ inch thick;

Slice a quantity of mushrooms equal to one fourth of that of veal, and mix both in some Allemande Sauce;

Make a paste croustade of the size of the dish, and 2 inches high;

Put the blanquette in it, raised towards the centre, and serve.

UNDER-FILLETS OF VEAL WITH ARTICHOKE-BOTTOMS EN BLANQUETTE

Cut 6 under-fillets in two pieces, in their thickness; flatten them with the bat, trim them to a pear shape, lard them with fine shreds of fat bacon, and put them in a sauté-pan with $\frac{1}{2}$ pint of Mirepoix; cook and glaze.

Put a paste croustade in the centre of a dish; dress the fillets round it, in a circle; fill it with artichokes en blanquette made by cutting some artichoke-bottoms, prepared as directed for garnish (page 298), in scollops, and mixing them in some *Allemande* Sauce;

After glazing the fillets, serve with some *Allemande* Sauce in a boat.

Observation.—I have adopted paste *croustades* in preference to those of rice or bread, as the former will hold better the garnish and sauce of the *entrées*.

UNDER-FILLETS OF VEAL BREAD-CRUMBED AND BROILED WITH ENDIVE PURÉE

Cut and trim the fillets as above; dip them in butter, bread-crumb and broil them;

Dish them in a circle round a *croustade* filled with Endive *Purée* (*vide* for the latter ' Neck of Veal with Endive *Purée*,' page 346).

UNDER-FILLETS OF VEAL EN GRENADINS À LA NIVERNAISE

Trim the fillets to a pear shape; lard them with some small strips of fat bacon; cook them in a *sauté*-pan with some *Mirepoix*; glaze and dish them in a circle round a *croustade*, filled with carrots *à la Nivernaise* (*vide* page 296); and serve with some reduced *Espagnole* Sauce.

VEAL CUTLETS WITH HAM À LA ZINGARA

Take a neck of veal, saw off the end of the rib-bones so as to make the cutlets 4 inches long, cut them of an even thickness, and trim them, without showing the bone; fry the cutlets in some clarified butter to colour them slightly, pour off the butter, and add 1 pint of *Blond de Veau*, and 3 gills of *Espagnole* Sauce;

Simmer till the cutlets are done.

Cut some lean ham in slices $\frac{1}{4}$ inch thick; trim them to the shape of the cutlets, and fry them in clarified butter for five minutes; drain the cutlets, and dish them in a circle, the fillets uppermost, with a slice of ham between each;

Skim the fat carefully off the gravy.

Strain the latter through a silk sieve, and serve it with the cutlets.

VEAL CUTLETS WITH SORREL PURÉE

Cut and trim the cutlets as above ;

Lard the lean part with thin shreds of fat bacon, and put them in a *sauté*-pan, with some clarified butter, and fry them, on one side only, for four minutes ; then add 1 pint of *Mirepoix*, and 1 pint of *Blond de Veau* ; cook and glaze the cutlets, and dish them in a circle, the lean part uppermost, round a *croustade* ; fill this with Sorrel *Purée* ; skim, and strain the gravy through a silk sieve ; pour it on the cutlets, and serve.

VEAL CUTLETS, LARDED WITH TONGUE, BACON, AND TRUFFLES À LA DREUX

Cut and trim the cutlets as before ; clear 1 inch of the end of the bone ; lard through the lean part with $\frac{1}{4}$ inch strips of tongue, fat bacon, and truffles, intermixing the colours (*vide* woodcut, page 355) ; put the cutlets in a *sauté*-pan with $\frac{1}{2}$ pint of *Mirepoix*, and 3 gills of Veal Stock ; cover them with a round of paper, close the pan, and put on the fire to simmer until the cutlets are done ; then drain, and press them between two dishes ; when the cutlets are cold, trim and put them in a *sauté*-pan ; strain the gravy through a silk sieve ; free it of fat, reduce it to a half glaze, and pour it on to the cutlets ; put them in the oven to warm, and dish them round a *croustade* ; pour the gravy over them ; fill the *croustade* with French beans (*vide* page 296), and serve.

These cutlets, prepared and dished in the same way, may be served with Mushroom, or Turnip *Purée*, in the *croustade*, in lieu of French beans.

SWEETBREADS À LA FINANCIÈRE

Prepare and lard 4 heart-sweetbreads, as directed in the First Part (*vide* page 102) ; cook and glaze them in the same way ;

Put a *croustade* in a dish ; place the sweetbreads against it ; put a large cock's comb and a truffle in each space between the sweetbreads ; fill the *croustade* with some *Financière Ragoût* (*vide* page 295) ; and, round the top of the *croustade*, place a circle of alternate cocks' kernels and truffles, turned to an olive shape ; and put a large cock's comb on the top in the centre ;

Glaze the sweetbreads just before serving, with a brush dipped in glaze.

SWEETBREADS WITH GREEN PEAS

Prepare and cook 4 heart-sweetbreads, as above; dish them round a *croustade*; fill it with green peas; and put some peas in the dish between the sweetbreads.

SWEETBREADS À LA MACÉDOINE

Prepare and dish the sweetbreads as above;
Fill the *croustade* with a *macédoine* of vegetables;
Put some round the dish with the sweetbreads; and serve with some reduced *Velouté* Sauce separately.

SWEETBREADS WITH ASPARAGUS PEAS

Lard and cook the sweetbreads as directed for Sweetbreads *à la Financière* (*vide* page 350); dish them round a *croustade* filled with asparagus peas; and put some in the dish with the sweetbreads

SWEETBREAD CLOUTÉ FOR GARNISH

SWEETBREADS À LA NIVERNAISE

Cook and dish the sweetbreads, as above;
Garnish with Carrots *à la Nivernaise* (*vide* page 296), both in the dish and in the *croustade*; serve with some Half Glaze in a boat.

centre of a dish ; place one ear against each side of the square ; Make a *ragoût* of *quenelles*, olives, mushrooms, truffles, and gherkins, the latter previously steeped in cold water, and turned to a ball shape ; mix the whole in some Sauce *Tortue* ;

Put a hard-boiled yolk of egg in each ear ; pile up the prepared *ragoût* in the spaces between the ears ; put 4 fine crayfish, claws downwards, on the *ragoût*, and put a larded heart-sweetbread on the top of the bread.

Serve with Sauce *Tortue* in a boat.

CALVES' EARS À LA FINANCIÈRE

Prepare, and dish the ears round a piece of fried bread, as above ; pile up some *Financière Ragoût* between each ear, placing a truffle and a cock's comb on each portion of *ragoût* ;

Finish with 4 fine cocks' combs on the top of the bread, and a large truffle in the centre ; and serve with some *Financière* Sauce, separately.

CALVES' TONGUES À LA SOUBISE

Steep, cool, and blanch 3 tongues, and cook them as directed for 'Calf's Head *au Naturel*' (*vide* First Part, page 102) ;

When the tongues are done, drain, and cut them in two lengthwise ; trim the pieces of an even size, and dress them in a circle on a dish ; glaze them, and fill the centre with Onion *Purée à la Soubise* (*vide* page 300).

CALVES' TONGUES À LA MAÎTRE D'HÔTEL

Prepare and cut the tongues as above ; dip the pieces in butter, bread-crumb, and broil them ; dish them up in a circle, and serve with some *Maître d'Hôtel* Sauce in a boat.

CALVES' BRAINS WITH RAVIGOTE SAUCE

Cook 3 sets of brains, as described for 'Calf's Head *au Naturel*' (*vide* First Part, page 103) ; cut the brains each in two pieces, and dress them on a dish ; pour over some *Ravigote* Sauce (*vide* page 287) ; and serve.

CALF'S HEAD WITH VENETIAN SAUCE

Prepare, cut, and cook half a calf's head, as described for ' Calf's Head *en Tortue*' (*vide* page 340); clean and score the ear; place the latter in the centre of a dish; put the pieces of head round it, and pour some Venetian Sauce over the whole.

ROASTS

ROAST LOIN OF VEAL

Saw off the chine-bone of a loin of veal; flatten the flap; place the kidney at the end of the fillet, and, after sprinkling with salt and pepper, cover both with the flap; tie the joint to keep it square and even; put it on the spit; wrap it in buttered paper, and roast before an even fire; take off the paper; put the meat on a dish; glaze it, and garnish each end with watercresses; and serve with some Meat Gravy in a boat.

ROAST NECK OF VEAL

Saw off the chine-bone, and the end of the rib-bones, leaving them only about 2 inches long; roll the flap, and secure it with small skewers;

Put the meat on the spit; wrap it in buttered paper, and put it to roast before an even fire; take off the paper; put the meat on a dish; glaze it, and garnish each end with watercresses;

Serve with some Meat Gravy in a boat.

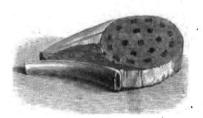

VEAL CUTLET À LA DREUX

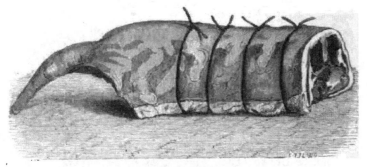

CHAPTER VII

MUTTON

REMOVES—ENTRÉES—ROASTS

REMOVES

LEGS OF MUTTON WITH VEGETABLE MACÉDOINE

TAKE 2 legs of mutton, a right and a left leg; bone them, leaving the knuckle-bone about 2 inches long; trim the joints; sprinkle them inside with salt and pepper, and tie each one up to a round shape; put them in a braizing stewpan with 1 quart of *Mirepoix* and 1 gill of brandy; simmer till the meat is done, and put the two legs on an oval dish, the thick part close together, and the knuckle-bones towards each end of the dish;

Place a pattern of turned carrots on the top of the legs where they meet; pile up some vegetable *macédoine* on the carrot, and garnish the sides of the dish with some more vegetable *macédoine*;

Put a paper frill on the knuckle-bones, and serve, with the skimmed and strained gravy in a boat.

HAUNCH OF MUTTON WITH CARROTS À LA FLAMANDE

Take a haunch of mutton; trim, and put it on the spit to roast before an even fire; when done, take it off the spit; put it on a dish; glaze it, and garnish round with carrots *à la Fla-mande* (*vide* First Part, page 174); and serve with some Meat Gravy in a boat.

HAUNCH OF MUTTON WITH HARICOT BEANS À LA BRETONNE

Trim, and roast a haunch of mutton, as above; put it on a dish; glaze it, and put a paper frill round the knuckle-bone;

Prepare 1½ pint of Brown Onion *Purée à la Bretonne* (*vide* page 300); add the same quantity of white haricot beans; mix, and put both together in a silver casserole, and serve with the meat.

BRAIZED LEGS OF WELSH MUTTON À LA JARDINIÈRE

Bone 4 small legs of mutton entirely; lard them inside with large strips of fat bacon and lean ham, and season them with salt and pepper; tie each leg to a round shape, and put them in a braizing stewpan with 1 gill of brandy, and sufficient *Mirepoix* to cover them entirely;

Simmer till the meat is done, then drain it;

Make a rice *socle* on a dish large enough to hold the 4 legs of mutton; place them on the *socle*; glaze them, and pile a *jardinière*, or garnish, of cauliflowers, carrots, asparagus peas, &c., in the spaces between them; dress the rice *socle* round with small heaps of the same garnish so as to hide it completely, and pile up some more *jardinière* on the top of the meat, in the centre; garnish 5 silver skewers with vegetables, and stick them in the meat;

Skim and strain the gravy; reduce it with some *Espagnole* Sauce, and serve it in a boat.

BRAIZED LEGS OF WELSH MUTTON À LA MILANAISE

Bone, lard, and cook 4 legs of mutton as above; dish them on a rice *socle* in the same way, and glaze them;

Prepare some maccaroni as directed for Fillet of Beef *à la Milanaise* (*vide* page 333); put it on the dish round the rice *socle*; pile up some maccaroni in the spaces between the meat, and also on the top in the centre, and serve, with some Half Glaze, separately.

BOILED LEG OF MUTTON

Take a good-sized leg of mutton; trim, and put it in a braizing stewpan nearly full of salted boiling water; add 12 equal-sized turnips; when the meat is done (reckon a quarter of an hour's cooking per lb. of meat), drain and put it on a dish; put a paper frill on the knuckle-bone; garnish round the dish with the turnips, and serve with a boat of Melted Butter, with some capers added.

SADDLE OF MUTTON WITH POTATO CROQUETS

Take a saddle of mutton; trim, and put it down to roast; when done, take it off the spit, put it on a dish, and garnish with Potato Croquets (*vide* page 295);

Serve with some Meat Gravy, in a boat.

Saddle of mutton is also served roasted, as above, and garnished with either Carrots and Cabbage-lettuces (*vide* pages 295, 299), or with Celery *Purée* (*vide* page 301).

ENTRÉES

CARBONADE, OR ROLLED LOIN OF MUTTON WITH SORREL PURÉE

Take 2 loins of mutton; bone them entirely, without separating the under-fillets; trim all the fat off the top of each, and lard that part with fine strips of fat bacon; cut off all but 1 inch of the flap; roll it to the under-fillet, and secure it with 2 small skewers; sprinkle the meat with salt, and put it in a stewpan, with 1 quart of *Mirepoix*, and 1 pint of Veal Stock;

Simmer till the mutton is cooked; then glaze the larded parts, and remove the skewers.

Put a layer of Sorrel *Purée* on a dish; place the rolled loins upon it; glaze them with Meat Glaze, and serve.

CARBONADE OF MUTTON À LA NIVERNAISE

Bone, lard, and cook 2 loins as above; put them on a dish; garnish round with Carrots *à la Nivernaise* (*vide* page 296); pour over some Half Glaze, and serve.

CARBONADE OF MUTTON WITH ARTICHOKE PURÉE

Prepare the loins as above; put them on a dish; garnish with Artichoke *Purée*; and pour over some Half Glaze.

CARBONADE OF MUTTON WITH ENDIVE

Proceed as directed for Carbonade of Mutton with Sorrel *Purée* (*vide* page 358), substituting Endive for Sorrel *Purée*.

CARBONADE OF MUTTON WITH MUSHROOMS AND POIVRADE SAUCE

Prepare and cook 2 loins as aforesaid; garnish round with Stuffed Mushrooms (*vide* page 291); and serve with *Poivrade* Sauce in a boat.

MUTTON CUTLETS À LA SOUBISE

Take a neck of mutton, and cut the cutlets 4 inches long; cut 2 bones for each cutlet; saw off the chine-bone, and remove one rib-bone;

Lard through the lean part of the cutlets with seasoned strips of fat bacon and tongue; the strips should be about $1\frac{1}{4}$ inch long, $\frac{1}{4}$ inch thick;

Put the cutlets in a glazing stewpan, with sufficient *Mirepoix* and *Blond de Veau* to cover them; simmer till the cutlets are done; then drain; and press them between two dishes till cold;

Skim the fat off the gravy; strain it through a silk sieve; and reduce it;

When the cutlets are cold, trim; and put them to warm in the reduced gravy; and dress them in a circle round a *croustade*; fill this with Onion *Purée à la Soubise* (*vide* page 300); pour the gravy over the cutlets; and serve.

Observation.—I do not advise dressing the cutlets with paper frills round the bones, as they are liable to come off into the sauce, or garnish, to which they are anything but a desirable addition.

BRAIZED MUTTON CUTLETS WITH CELERY

Cut, lard, and cook the cutlets as above; dish them in a circle, round a *croustade*, and fill it with Celery *à la Française* (*vide* page 300).

BRAIZED MUTTON CUTLETS WITH CARDOONS

Prepare and cook the cutlets as before ; and dish them round a *croustade* ;

Cut some cooked cardoons in scollops ; simmer these for five minutes in some *Espagnole* Sauce ; fill the *croustade* with them ; and serve with some of the same sauce in a boat.

BRAIZED MUTTON CUTLETS WITH CHESTNUT PURÉE

Proceed as directed for Cutlets *à la Soubise* (*vide* page 359) ; dish the cutlets round a *croustade* filled with Chestnut *Purée* (*vide* page 302) ; and serve with the gravy in a boat.

BRAIZED MUTTON CUTLETS À LA JARDINIÈRE

Cut the cutlets 3½ inches long, and cook them as above ; when they are done, trim them, without however clearing the end of the bones ;

Prepare as many Cabbage-lettuces (*vide* page 299) as there are cutlets ; and make a *Jardinière* of carrots and turnips, cut in ½-inch balls, and an equal quantity of small heads of cauliflowers and Brussels sprouts ;

Dish the cutlets, lean part uppermost, round a *croustade*, with a piece of lettuce between each cutlet ;

Mix the *Jardinière* in some *Béchamel* Sauce, and fill the *croustade* with it.

Serve with some Half Glaze, in a boat.

BRAIZED MUTTON CUTLETS WITH ARTICHOKE PURÉE

Prepare and cook the cutlets, as directed for Cutlets *à la Soubise* (*vide* page 359) ;

Dish them round a *croustade* filled with Artichoke *Purée* (*vide* page 301) ; and serve.

MUTTON CUTLETS SAUTÉES WITH POTATOES

Cut and trim 12 cutlets of an even size, and sprinkle them with salt;

Melt some clarified butter, in a *sauté*-pan; set the cutlets in it; put some butter over them, and cover them with a round of buttered paper; fry them; and when done, drain; glaze; and dish them in a circle; put some potatoes, turned to ½-inch balls, and *sautées* in butter, in the centre; pour over some *Châteaubriand* Sauce; and serve.

MUTTON CUTLETS SAUTÉES À LA FINANCIÈRE

Prepare and cook the cutlets as above; dish them round a *croustade* filled with *Financière Ragoût*; and serve.

MUTTON CUTLETS SAUTÉES WITH A MACÉDOINE OF VEGETABLES

Cut and cook the cutlets as directed for Mutton Cutlets *Sautées* with Potatoes;

Fill a *croustade* with a *Macédoine* of Vegetables; dish the cutlets round it; and serve.

BROILED MUTTON CUTLETS WITH POTATOES

Trim and broil the cutlets;

When done, dish them in a circle round a dish, and fill the centre with potatoes, cut to an olive-shape and *sautées* in butter; pour over some *Maître d'Hôtel* Sauce; and serve.

BROILED MUTTON CUTLETS WITH GREEN PEAS

Cook the cutlets as above; dish them in a circle, and fill the centre with Green Peas; and serve with some Half Glaze, in a boat.

BROILED MUTTON CUTLETS WITH TOMATO SAUCE

Trim and bread-crumb the cutlets; broil them; dish them in a circle; and serve with Tomato Sauce, in a boat.

BROILED MUTTON CUTLETS WITH ENDIVE

Trim, bread-crumb, and broil the cutlets; when they are done, dish them in a circle, and fill the centre with Endive (*vide* page 299); and serve with some Half Glaze, in a boat.

Remarks on Cutlets à la Maintenon

I have often been struck by the variety of ways in which this dish is prepared; another instance of the want of unanimity in our profession;

Some wrap the cutlets in pig's caul, others garnish them with cocks' combs and truffles, or serve them with Onions *à la Soubise*, or with *Financière* Garnish; in fact, every cook has his own mode of preparation. The recipe I indicate is, I think, the simplest; and I should like to see it adopted, not because I flatter myself that it is better than many others, but in order that it may be the means of ending the tedious controversy on the subject.

MUTTON CUTLETS À LA MAINTENON

Take a neck of mutton and cut it into cutlets, leaving 2 bones to each cutlet; remove one of them, and flatten and trim the cutlets; split them in two with a knife, without separating them at the bone; spread some reduced *d'Uxelles* Sauce inside; refold the cutlets, and broil them for four minutes on each side; put a layer of *d'Uxelles* on a dish; lay the cutlets on it; pour over some *d'Uxelles* Sauce; put the dish in a hot oven for four minutes; and serve.

BROILED BREASTS OF MUTTON WITH CELERY PURÉE

Cook the breasts of mutton in some General Stock; when done, take out the bones, sprinkle the meat with salt, and press it between two dishes till quite cold; then cut the mutton in pear-shaped pieces, 3 inches long; trim, and dip the pieces in butter; bread-crumb and broil them; dish them in a circle, and fill the centre with Celery *Purée* (*vide* page 301).

BROILED BREASTS OF MUTTON WITH BÉARNAISE SAUCE

Prepare, bread-crumb, and broil the breasts of mutton as above; dish them in a circle, and serve with some *Béarnaise* Sauce, in a boat.

BROILED BREASTS OF MUTTON WITH CHÂTEAUBRIAND SAUCE

Prepare the breasts of mutton as before ; dish them in a circle, and serve with some *Châteaubriand* Sauce in a boat.

GLAZED BREASTS OF MUTTON WITH ENDIVE

Braize, bone, and trim the breasts of mutton, as directed for Broiled Breasts of Mutton with Celery *Purée* (*vide* page 362); put the pieces in a *sauté*-pan with some *Blond de Veau* ; warm and glaze them, and dish them in a circle ; put some Endive (*vide* page 299) in the centre ; pour over some Half Glaze ; and serve.

GLAZED BREASTS OF MUTTON WITH CELERY À LA FRANÇAISE

Cook and glaze the breasts of mutton as above ; dress them in a circle on a dish ; fill the centre with Celery *à la Française* (*vide* page 300); pour over some Half Glaze ; and serve.

MARINADED UNDER-FILLETS OF MUTTON WITH MUSHROOMS

Take 12 under-fillets of mutton ; flatten them with the bat, and remove all skin and gristle ; trim them to a long pear-shape ; lard them with fine strips of fat bacon, and marinade them for twenty-four hours ;

Butter a *sauté*-pan ; drain the fillets on a cloth, and put them in the pan with some *Mirepoix* and Veal Stock, without covering them ; cook and glaze them ; dish them in a circle, and garnish the centre with sliced mushrooms ; pour some *Poivrade* Sauce over the mushrooms and serve with some of the same sauce, in a boat.

MARINADED UNDER-FILLETS OF MUTTON WITH SHARP SAUCE

Prepare, marinade, and cook the fillets as above ; dish them in a circle, and serve with some Sharp Sauce, in a boat.

3 A 2

BROILED UNDER-FILLETS OF MUTTON À LA MARÉCHALE

Cut and trim 12 under-fillets, as directed for 'Marinaded Under-fillets of Mutton with Mushrooms' (*vide* page 363);

Dip them in butter; bread-crumb and broil them; dish them in a circle, and serve with some Meat Gravy, in a boat.

BROILED UNDER-FILLETS OF MUTTON WITH TURNIP PURÉE

Cook and dish the fillets as above;

Fill the middle of the dish with Turnip *Purée* (*vide* page 302); and serve.

BROILED UNDER-FILLETS OF MUTTON WITH TRUFFLES

Prepare and cook the fillets as directed for Broiled Under-fillets of Mutton *à la Maréchale*; dish them round a *croustade* filled with sliced truffles, and serve with some Madeira Sauce, in a boat.

SHEEP'S TAILS WITH LENTIL PURÉE À LA CONTI

Blanch the tails, and put them in a braizing stewpan with equal quantities of *Mirepoix* and *Blond de Veau*; when they are done, drain and bone them; sprinkle them with salt, and press them between two dishes till cold;

Skim the fat off the gravy; strain it through a silk sieve, and reduce it one half; when the tails are thoroughly cold, cut off the ends, leaving them 4 inches long; warm them in the reduced gravy; dish them in a circle, and fill the centre with Lentil *Purée à la Conti* (*vide* page 302), and serve with some Half Glaze, separately.

SHEEP'S TAILS WITH ONION PURÉE À LA SOUBISE

Prepare and dish the tails as above; garnish the centre with Onion *Purée à la Soubise* (*vide* page 300); and serve with some Half Glaze, in a boat.

SHEEP'S TAILS WITH SORREL PURÉE

Cook the tails as aforesaid; dish them in a circle; and fill the centre with Sorrel *Purée* (*vide* page 299); serve with some Half Glaze, in a boat.

SHEEP'S TAILS WITH CUCUMBERS

Proceed as directed for Sheep's Tails with Lentil *Purée à la Conti*; when the tails are done, dish them in a circle; and fill the centre with Brown Cucumber Garnish (*vide* page 299), cut in slices; and serve with some Half Glaze, in a boat.

SHEEP'S TAILS À LA VALOIS

Blanch, cook, press, and trim the tails as above; brush them over with egg; bread-crumb and broil them; dress them in a circle round a dish; and serve with some *Valois* Sauce, in a boat.

ROASTS

ROAST HAUNCH OF WELSH MUTTON

Trim a haunch of mutton; saw off the bone 2 inches below the knuckle; put the joint on the spit to roast, before an even fire;

When done, put it on a dish; put a paper frill round the knuckle-bone; garnish round with watercresses; and serve with some Meat Gravy, in a boat.

ROAST SADDLE OF MUTTON

Trim; and put a saddle of mutton on the spit to roast, before an even fire; when done, take it off the spit; put it on a dish; and serve with some Meat Gravy, in a boat.

CARBONADE OF MUTTON

YORK HAM

CHAPTER VIII

PORK

REMOVES—ENTRÉES

REMOVES

MARINADED ROAST LEG OF PORK WITH ROBERT SAUCE

TAKE a leg of pork, weighing about 6 lbs.; saw off the chump-bone; and remove the leg-bone, sawing it off above the knuckle; put the meat in lukewarm marinade (*vide* page 267), let it remain in the marinade for ten days, or longer.

When about to cook the pork, drain it from the marinade; wrap it up entirely in 4 sheets of buttered paper, one above the other; put it on the spit to roast, before a moderate, but even fire, for three hours and a half; twenty minutes before serving, take the meat off the spit; remove the paper; put the pork on a baking-sheet; trim it; and glaze it in the oven; put it on a dish, with a paper frill round the knuckle-bone; and serve with *Robert* Sauce (*vide* page 278), in a boat.

BRAIZED HAM WITH VEGETABLES À LA MAILLOT

Trim and steep a ham in cold water for two days; then wrap it in a cloth, and put it in a braizing stewpan, with plenty of water; simmer till done; then drain, and trim the ham again; put it in another stewpan, with 1 bottle of Madeira; close the stewpan, and simmer for half an hour; take out, and glaze the ham.

Make a rice *socle*, not quite so large as the ham, on a dish; place the ham on it; and garnish round the rice with small heaps of carrots, cabbage-lettuces, onions, and French beans (*vide* Garnishes, pages 295, 296, 299);

Put some vegetables on 4 silver skewers, and stick them in the ham;

Serve with some Madeira Sauce, in a boat.

BRAIZED HAM WITH NOUILLES AND TOMATO SAUCE

Prepare and cook a ham as above;

Dish it on a rice *socle*; and garnish round the latter with *nouilles* mixed in some *Allemande* Sauce; and serve with some Tomato Sauce, in a boat.

BRAIZED HAM WITH SPINACH

Cook and dish a ham as aforesaid;

Garnish it round with Spinach (*vide* page 299); serve with some Half Glaze, in a boat, and some more spinach, in a silver casserole.

BRAIZED HAM À LA MILANAISE

Prepare and cook a ham as directed for Braized Ham *à la Maillot* (*vide* above); put it on a rice *socle*, on a dish; and garnish it round with small paste *croustades*, filled with a mixture of truffles, maccaroni, and mushrooms cut in small dice, grated Parmesan cheese, and reduced *Espagnole* Sauce;

Put some cocks' combs and truffles on 3 silver skewers; stick them in the ham; and serve with some Madeira Sauce, in a boat.

BRAIZED HAM À LA JARDINIÈRE

Prepare and dish a ham on a rice *socle* as above (*vide* Braized Ham *à la Maillot*, above); round it, pile up some portions of cauliflowers, turned carrots, and asparagus peas, sufficiently high to hide the rice ;

Serve with some Half Glaze, separately.

ENTRÉES

ROAST NECK OF PORK WITH STUFFED TOMATOES

Trim a neck of pork to the size of an *entrée*-dish ; put it to roast before a good clear fire ; when done, put it on a dish ; and garnish each side with Stuffed Tomatoes (*vide* page 298), and serve with a boat of *d'Uxelles* Sauce.

ROAST NECK OF PORK WITH POIVRADE SAUCE

Trim and roast a neck of pork as above ; put it on a dish ; and serve with some *Poivrade* Sauce, separately.

ROAST NECK OF PORK À LA SOUBISE

Prepare, roast, and dish a neck of pork as aforesaid ; garnish it round with Onion *Purée à la Soubise* (*vide* page 300) ; and serve with some Half Glaze, in a boat.

ROAST NECK OF PORK WITH CHESTNUT PURÉE

Proceed as above, substituting Chestnut *Purée* (*vide* page 302) for the Onion *Purée*, and serve with some Half Glaze, separately.

UNDER-FILLETS OF PORK WITH ENDIVE

Cut and lard 12 under-fillets of pork, as directed for ' Marinaded Under-Fillets of Mutton with Mushrooms' (*vide* page 363) ; put them in a *sauté*-pan with some *Mirepoix*, without covering them entirely, and simmer till they are done ; glaze the fillets ; dish them in a circle, and fill the centre with Endive (*vide* page 299).

UNDER-FILLETS OF PORK WITH CELERY À LA FRANÇAISE

Prepare, cook, and dish the fillets as above ; put some Celery *à la Française* (*vide* page 300), in the centre of the dish, and serve with some Half Glaze, separately.

UNDER-FILLETS OF PORK WITH MUSHROOM PURÉE

Cook and dish the fillets, as directed for Under-Fillets of Pork with Endive (*vide* page 368); fill the centre with Mushroom *Purée* (*vide* page 302); and serve, with some Half Glaze, separately.

UNDER-FILLETS OF PORK WITH CARDOON PURÉE

Proceed as above, substituting Cardoon *Purée* (*vide* page 300) for that of Mushrooms.

UNDER-FILLETS OF PORK WITH TOMATO PURÉE

Prepare and dish the fillets as aforesaid; garnish the centre with Tomato *Purée* (*vide* page 303), and serve with some Half Glaze, in a boat.

UNDER-FILLETS OF PORK À LA MARÉCHALE

Cut and trim the fillets, as directed for ' Marinaded Under-Fillets of Mutton' (*vide* page 363); dip them in butter; bread-crumb and broil them; dish them in a circle, and serve with some *Poivrade* Sauce, separately.

ROAST SUCKING-PIG

Put a sucking pig, as soon as it is killed, in a basin of hot, but not boiling, water, for two minutes; then rub off the hairs with a cloth; if they do not come off easily, put the pig in the water for one minute more; make a slit down the belly; take out the entrails; clean and singe the pig, and steep it in cold water for twenty-four hours; after which, drain and dry it thoroughly with a cloth.

Make some stuffing as follows:

Chop a large onion together with about a dozen sage-leaves; blanch the whole in boiling water for five minutes; drain, and put it in a stewpan with 2 oz. of butter; stir over the fire, and simmer for ten minutes; then add 3 oz. of bread-crumbs; season with salt and pepper; mix thoroughly, and fill the inside of the

3 B

pig with the stuffing; sew it up with fine twine; truss the legs back, and put the pig on the spit to roast, before a clear fire, basting it with salad oil;

When the pig is done, take it off the spit; put it on a dish, and serve with *Poivrade* Sauce, in a boat.

STUFFED PIG'S FEET

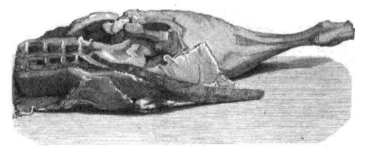

HIND-QUARTER OF LAMB

CHAPTER IX

LAMB

REMOVES—ENTRÉES—ROASTS

REMOVES

ROAST LAMB WITH POIVRADE SAUCE

Truss a whole lamb ; put it on the spit, and wrap it up in well-buttered paper ; put it to roast before a good fire, and five minutes before serving, untie and take off the paper ;

Put the lamb on a dish, with a paper frill round the knuckle of each leg, and serve with some *Poivrade* Sauce, in a boat.

HIND-QUARTERS OF LAMB WITH POTATO CROQUETS

Truss the hind-quarters of a lamb, and wrap the joint in buttered paper ; put it on the spit to roast before a good clear fire ; when done, take it off the spit ; put it on a dish, and glaze the meat ; garnish round with Potato Croquets (*vide* page 295), and serve with some Half Glaze, separately.

HIND-QUARTERS OF LAMB WITH CELERY

Prepare and roast the hind-quarters of a lamb as above ;

Place the joint on a dish ; surround it with some Celery for Garnish (*vide* page 300), and serve with a boat of Half Glaze.

HIND-QUARTERS OF LAMB WITH STUFFED TOMATOES

Roast the hind-quarters of a lamb as aforesaid; put it on a dish; garnish round with Stuffed Tomatoes (*vide* page 298), and serve with some *d'Uxelles* Sauce, in a boat.

HIND-QUARTERS OF LAMB WITH CROQUETS À LA MILANAISE

Truss and prepare the hind-quarters of a lamb as before; put down to roast before a good clear fire; when done, take the joint off the spit; put it on a dish and glaze it; garnish round with Croquets *à la Milanaise* (*vide* page 313), and serve with some Half Glaze, in a boat.

ÉPIGRAMMES OF LAMB WITH ASPARAGUS PEAS

Take 2 necks of lamb; saw off the breasts, and trim and cut the cutlets; remove the tendons of the two breasts; tie the latter together, and braize them in some General Stock with an onion (with 2 cloves stuck in it), and a faggot added;

When the meat is done, drain and take out all the bones; keep as many as there are cutlets, to add to the breasts when trimmed; sprinkle the meat with salt, and press it between two dishes till cold; then cut both the breasts of lamb in pieces, the size and shape of the cutlets; spread some reduced *Allemande* Sauce over these pieces, and bread-crumb them; then egg and bread-crumb them again;

Cut the bones, kept for that purpose, to a point at one end, and stick one in each piece of breast so as to represent a cutlet;

Fry them in hot fat, and drain them;

Dip the neck cutlets in clarified butter; set them in a *sauté*-pan; pour in a little more clarified butter, and fry them till they are done;

Dish the cutlets and the breast cutlets, alternately, round a *croustade* filled with Asparagus Peas (*vide* page 297), and serve, with a boat of *Béchamel* Sauce.

ÉPIGRAMMES OF LAMB WITH GREEN PEAS

Prepare and cook the *épigrammes* as above; dish them round a *croustade* filled with green peas, and serve them with *Béchamel* Sauce.

EPIGRAMMES OF LAMB À LA MACÉDOINE

Prepare, cook, and dish the *épigrammes* as before ; garnish the *croustade* with a *Macédoine* of Vegetables ; and serve with some Half Glaze, in a boat.

ÉPIGRAMMES OF LAMB WITH CUCUMBERS

Proceed as directed for *Épigrammes* of Lamb with Asparagus Peas (*vide* page 372) ; fill the *croustade* with White Cucumber Garnish (*vide* page 298) ; and serve with some *Allemande* Sauce, separately.

LAMB CUTLETS SAUTÉES WITH FRENCH BEANS

Trim and cut 2 necks of lamb into cutlets ; season them with salt and pepper ; dip them in clarified butter, and fry them in a *sauté*-pan ; drain ; and dish them round a *croustade* filled with French beans ; and serve with some *Béchamel* Sauce, in a boat.

LAMB CUTLETS SAUTÉES WITH COCKS' KERNELS AND TRUFFLES EN DEMI-DEUIL

Trim 2 necks of lamb into cutlets, without clearing the end of the bones ; season them with salt and pepper ; put them in a *sauté*-pan, and fry them in some clarified butter ; drain ; and dish them round a *croustade*, lean part uppermost, putting a slice of truffle, the same size and shape as the cutlet, between each ;

Fill the *croustade* with cocks' kernels ; pour some *Velouté* Sauce over them ; put a border of truffles, cut in 1-inch balls, round the top of the *croustade* ; and serve with some *Velouté* Sauce, in a boat.

LAMB CUTLETS SAUTÉES À LA FINANCIÈRE

Trim and cut 2 necks of lamb into cutlets ; season ; and put them in a *sauté*-pan ; fry them in some clarified butter ; drain, and glaze them ; dish them round a *croustade* ; fill it with *Financière Ragoût* ; and put a cock's comb on the top ;

Take some equal-sized mushrooms ; cut some truffles to the

same shape as the mushrooms; place them alternately round the cock's comb; and serve with some *Financière* Sauce, in a boat.

LAMB CUTLETS SAUTÉES WITH CHESTNUT PURÉE

Prepare, cook, and dish the cutlets as previous recipe; fill the *croustade* with Chestnut *Purée* (*vide* page 302); and serve.

LAMB CUTLETS SAUTÉES WITH LAMB SWEETBREADS EN BLANQUETTE

Cut and cook the cutlets as directed for Lamb Cutlets *Sautées à la Financière* (*vide* page 373);

Steep some equal-sized lamb sweetbreads in cold water; blanch, drain, and trim them; cook them in some white braize;

Drain, and cut the sweetbreads in scollops; and mix them in some *Allemande* Sauce;

Dish the cutlets in a circle, round a *croustade*; fill the latter with the *blanquette* of sweetbreads; and serve, with some *Allemande* Sauce.

LAMB CUTLETS SAUTÉES WITH SLICED MUSHROOMS AND TRUFFLES

Prepare, cook, and dish the cutlets as above;

Slice some mushrooms and truffles very fine; and mix both in some *Espagnole* Sauce, reduced with Essence of Truffles;

Fill the *croustade* with the mixture; and serve some of the same sauce in a boat.

BROILED LAMB CUTLETS WITH CARDOON PURÉE

Cut and trim 2 necks of lamb into cutlets; dip them in butter; bread-crumb, and broil them;

Dish them in a circle round a *croustade* filled with Cardoon *Purée* (*vide* page 300); and serve, with a boat of *Velouté* Sauce, reduced with Essence of Mushrooms.

BROILED LAMB CUTLETS AU SALPICON

Prepare, and cook the cutlets as above;

Cut some *foie gras*, truffles, and mushrooms, in $\frac{1}{2}$-inch dice;

mix them in some *Espagnole* Sauce, reduced with Essence of Truffles; fill a *croustade* with this *salpicon*; dish the cutlets round it; and serve with some of the same sauce, separately.

BROILED LAMB CUTLETS WITH CELERY PURÉE

Cut, bread-crumb, and broil the cutlets, as directed for 'Broiled Lamb Cutlets with Cardoon *Purée*;' dish them round a *croustade* filled with Celery *Purée* (*vide* page 301); and serve with some Half Glaze, in a boat.

BROILED LAMB CUTLETS À LA SOUBISE

Prepare and dish the cutlets round a *croustade* as before directed; garnish the *croustade* with Onion *Purée à la Soubise* (*vide* page 300); and serve with some *Béchamel* Sauce, in a boat.

BROILED LAMB CUTLETS WITH ARTICHOKE PURÉE

Proceed as above; fill the *croustade* with Artichoke *Purée* (*vide* page 301); and serve with some reduced *Velouté* Sauce, in a boat.

BROILED LAMB CUTLETS WITH MUSHROOM PURÉE

Prepare, cook, and dish the cutlets round a *croustade*, as directed before; fill it with Mushroom *Purée* (*vide* page 302); and serve with a boat of *Béchamel* Sauce.

BROILED LAMB CUTLETS WITH TRUFFLE PURÉE

Prepare the cutlets as directed for 'Broiled Lamb Cutlets with Cardoon *Purée*' (*vide* page 374);

Dish them round a *croustade*, filled with Truffle *Purée* (*vide* page 303); and serve with some Half Glaze, separately.

LAMBS' FEET À LA PÉRIGUEUX

Cook the lambs' feet, as directed for Sheep's Feet with *Poulette* Sauce (*vide* First Part, page 115).

Make some forcemeat with a *noix* of veal, and some fat

bacon, freed from rind and gristle; chop, and pound the veal and the bacon together, adding, whilst pounding, 1 gill of *Allemande* Sauce for each pound of forcemeat;

Drain the feet; bone; and cut them in two, lengthwise;

Spread out some well steeped pig's caul on a cloth; place on it a layer of the forcemeat, the same length as one of the half feet; put 2 slices of truffle on the forcemeat, and half a lamb's foot on these; then 2 more slices of truffle, and cover the whole with a layer of forcemeat; roll it in the caul to an oval shape, and, when all the feet are stuffed in this way, dip them in butter; bread-crumb, and broil them over a slow fire for fifteen minutes; and serve with some *Périgueux* Sauce (*vide* page 279), in a boat.

MARINADED LAMBS' FEET WITH TOMATO SAUCE

Cook the feet as before; cut them in two, and marinade them in lemon juice, salt, and pepper; drain the pieces, and dip them in frying batter, and fry them in hot fat till they are crisp; drain, and pile them up on a napkin on a dish; garnish with fried parsley, and serve with Tomato Sauce (*vide* page 280).

LAMBS' FEET À LA POULETTE

Cook the feet as aforesaid;

Put them in some hot *Allemande* Sauce, together with some sliced mushrooms and chopped parsley; mix; and serve.

BLANQUETTE OF LAMB SWEETBREADS WITH TRUFFLES

Steep, blanch, and cook some lamb sweetbreads; drain, trim, and cut them into scollops; put them to warm in some *Allemande* Sauce, together with some sliced truffles;

Make a potato border on a dish, as described for Potato Casserole (*vide* page 451);

Fill the centre with the *blanquette*; and serve;

BROILED BREASTS OF LAMB WITH POIVRADE SAUCE

Prepare the breasts of lamb as directed for *Épigrammes* of Lamb with Asparagus Peas (*vide* page 372); egg and bread-crumb them; broil, and dish them in a circle, and serve, with a boat of *Poivrade* Sauce.

BROILED BREASTS OF LAMB WITH VALOIS SAUCE

Prepare the breasts of lamb as before;
Dish them in a circle, and serve with *Valois* Sauce, separately.

BRAIZED SHOULDER OF LAMB À LA MACÉDOINE

Bone a shoulder of lamb, leaving only the knuckle-bone; saw
this off to 2 inches below the knuckle;
Sprinkle the lamb with salt, and tie it up into a ball shape;
put it in a braizing stewpan, with sufficient *Mirepoix* to cover it;
when done, glaze the meat;
Put a layer of Vegetable *Macédoine* on a dish; place the lamb
on this; put a paper frill round the knuckle-bone, and serve,
with the strained and reduced gravy, in a boat.

BRAIZED SHOULDER OF LAMB WITH ARTICHOKE PURÉE

Bone, cook, and dish up a shoulder of lamb as above, substituting Artichoke *Purée* (*vide* page 301) for the Vegetable
Macédoine.

BRAIZED SHOULDER OF LAMB WITH TOMATO PURÉE

Prepare and cook the shoulder as aforesaid; dish it up on
some Tomato *Purée* (*vide* page 307), instead of the Vegetable
Macédoine, and serve with the gravy, in a boat.

ROASTS

ROAST HIND-QUARTER OF LAMB

Take a hind-quarter of lamb; saw off the knuckle-bone, and
put the joint to roast before an even fire; when done, take it off
the spit; put it on a dish, and garnish round with watercresses,
and serve with some Horseradish or Mint Sauce (*vide* page
288), in a boat.

3 c

ROAST SADDLE OF LAMB

Trim, and put a saddle of lamb on the spit, to roast before an even fire ;

When done, take it off the spit ; put it on a dish ; garnish round with watercresses, and serve, with either Sharp, or Mint Sauce.

NECK OF LAMB

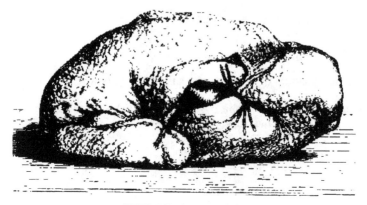

CHAPTER X

POULTRY

REMOVES—ENTRÉES—ROASTS

REMOVES

Remarks on Removes of Poultry

FOR removes of poultry I have indicated the use of 2 capons,
which will be about the proper quantity for these large second-
course dishes; but of course these removes can, when required,
be prepared as satisfactorily in lesser quantities, say by using
only one capon, or, in preference, 2 chickens; by such a sub-
stitution the character of the remove will be preserved; the bulk
alone will vary.

CAPONS WITH SWEETBREADS AND TRUFFLES À LA RÉGENCE

Pick, draw, and singe 2 capons; remove the forked part of
the breast-bone, and fill the crop skin with butter, seasoned with

3 c 2

salt and pepper; truss the capons for braizing (*vide* woodcut, page 379); lard the breasts with small strips of fat bacon, and tie some slices of fat bacon over the parts which are not larded;

Put the capons in a braizing stewpan, with sufficient *Mirepoix* to come above the pinions; place a round of buttered paper over the capons; close the stewpan, and simmer for one hour; then take off the paper and glaze the larded parts of the capons.

BLOCK OF FRIED BREAD

For garnish, take :

5 larded heart-sweetbreads,	12 fine cocks' combs,
12 large truffles,	8 large crayfish ;

Make a *ragoût* of chicken *quenelles* and cut mushrooms, mixed in Sauce *à la Régence*.

Cut a piece of crumb of bread to the shape of a block, 8 inches high, 6 inches square at the base, and $3\frac{1}{2}$ inches at the top (*vide* woodcut, above); fry it in hot fat; drain, and fix it in the centre of a dish; stick it on with a little paste made of flour and white of egg;

Drain the capons, and lean them against the block of bread, crop downwards, at each end of the dish;

Put the prepared *ragoût* in the dish, and place a sweetbread below each capon, another on the top of the bread, and the two remaining ones in the spaces between the capons; put a crayfish on each side of the sweetbreads, and a truffle on the latter;

Put some cocks' combs and truffles on 3 silver skewers, and stick them in the capons, and serve with some Sauce *à la Régence*, in a boat.

CAPONS À LA GODARD

Prepare 2 capons as before directed, without larding the breasts;
Cook them in the same way;
Make a *ragoût* of cocks' combs, truffles, and mushrooms, mixed
in Sauce *à la Godard*;
Dish the capons against a block of bread, as before;
Put a fried bread border round the dish; pour in the prepared
ragoût, and garnish with:

9 cocks' combs,	2 large *quenelles*, decorated
9 truffles,	with truffles and tongue;
3 larded heart-sweetbreads,	

Garnish 3 silver skewers, and stick them in the capons;
Serve with some Sauce *à la Godard*, separately.

CAPONS WITH VEGETABLES

Prepare and cook 2 capons as before, without larding them;
dish them against a block of bread in the same way; place a
trimmed tongue across the top of the bread, resting both ends on
the capons, and pile up a *jardinière* of:

cauliflowers,	asparagus,
carrots,	French beans,

between the capons, against the uncovered sides of the bread;
Garnish three silver skewers with vegetables, and stick them
in the tongue and capons; pour over some *Béchamel* Sauce, and
serve some of the same sauce in a boat.

CAPONS WITH QUENELLES AND TRUFFLES À LA MONTMORENCY

Prepare and cook the capons, without larding them, as directed
for Capons *à la Régence* (*vide* page 379);
Make a *ragoût* of cocks' kernels, truffles, mushrooms, and
chicken *quenelles*, mixed in some *Suprème* Sauce (*vide* page 285);
Put this *ragoût* in a dish, and dress the capons, crop upwards,
against the bread;
Put 2 large decorated *quenelles* in the spaces between the
capons; place a truffle on each *quenelle*, and another on both
sides of the *quenelles*;
Put a smaller decorated *quenelle* below each capon, with a

cocks' comb on each side, and a large *quenelle* on the top of the
bread ;

Garnish 3 silver skewers with cocks' combs and truffles, and
stick them in the capons as before ;

Serve with *Suprême* Sauce, separately. .

CAPONS À LA FINANCIÈRE

Prepare and cook the capons as before ;

Make a *ragoût* of *foie gras*, cut in scollops, mushrooms, and
small chicken *quenelles* mixed in *Financière* Sauce, and put it in
a dish, round a block of fried bread, as aforesaid ; place the
capons, crop downwards, against it, and put 2 *foies gras, cloutés*
with truffles, between the capons, one on each side of the bread ;
place a crayfish on each side of the *foies gras*, and a cocks' comb
on the top ;

Place a larded sweetbread on the top of the bread ;

Garnish 3 silver skewers with cocks' combs, crayfish, and
mushrooms ; stick them in the capons and sweetbreads, and
serve with some *Financière* Sauce.

CAPONS WITH RICE

Wash and blanch 10 oz. of rice, and cook it in some Chicken
Consommé ;

Prepare and cook 2 capons, without larding the breasts, as
directed for Capons *à la Régence* (*vide* page 379) ;

When the rice is done, taste it for seasoning, and strain into it
a little of the liquor in which the capons have been cooked ; stir
it, so as to mix both together, and make a layer of the rice on a
dish ;

Place the capons on it ;

Skim and strain the gravy, and serve it in a boat.

CAPONS WITH ROCK SALT

Prepare the capons, without larding the breasts, as directed
for Capons *à la Régence* (*vide* page 379) ; put them in a braizing
stewpan with some Chicken *Consommé* ;

When the capons are done, drain them ; strain and skim the
fat off the *consommé* ; add to it half its quantity of *Blond de
Veau*, and reduce both together ;

Put the capons on a dish : pour a part of the gravy over them, and strew them over with a little rock salt, and serve with the remaining gravy, in a boat.

CAPONS WITH NOUILLES

Remove the forked breast-bone, and truss 2 capons as directed for Capons *à la Régence* (*vide* page 379) ; cover the breasts with thin slices of fat bacon ; put the capons on the spit ; wrap them in buttered paper, and put them to roast before an even fire ; when done, take them off the spit and untie them ;

Mix some *nouilles* in some *Allemande* Sauce, together with some grated Parmesan cheese and Chicken Glaze ; make a layer of them, 2 inches thick, in a dish ; place the capons upon it, and serve with some *Allemande* Sauce.

CAPONS WITH STUFFED COCKS' COMBS AND SUPRÈME SAUCE

Prepare and truss the capons as above ; wrap them entirely in buttered paper, and roast them before a clear fire ; when done, take off the paper ; put the capons on a dish, and pour some *Suprème* Sauce over them ;

Garnish with some fried Stuffed Cocks' Combs (*vide* page 322), and serve with *Suprème* Sauce.

BRAIZED TURKEY STUFFED WITH TRUFFLES WITH PÉRIGUEUX SAUCE

Pick, draw, and singe a fat hen-turkey ; scald the feet to facilitate rubbing off the skin ; and cut off the neck, leaving the crop skin as large as possible ;

Clean and peel 3 lbs. of truffles ; cut them into $1\frac{1}{2}$ inch balls, reserving the trimmings ;

Put $1\frac{1}{2}$ lb. of grated fat bacon in a *sauté*-pan, with :

3 bay leaves,	2 shalots, whole,
1 sprig of thyme,	salt and pepper to season ;
1 unpicked clove of garlic,	

Melt the bacon on a slow fire, and let it cool ; then strain it through the pointed strainer, into a basin containing the truffles and part of the chopped truffle trimmings, the other part being reserved for the *Périgueux* Sauce ; when cold, fill the turkey with this stuffing, and truss it as for boiling; cover it with thin slices of fat bacon, and wrap it in a sheet of buttered paper;

Put it in a braizing stewpan; pour in 3 pints of *Mirepoix*, and half a bottle of Madeira;

When the turkey is done, drain, untie, and put it on a dish; pour some *Périgueux* Sauce (*vide* page 279) over it, and serve some in a boat.

Observation.—The turkey, prepared and trussed as above, may be roasted before an even fire, and served in the same way as when braized.

BRAIZED TURKEY À LA CHIPOLATA

Pick, draw, and singe a fat hen-turkey; scald the feet to facilitate removing the skin, and truss it as for braizing;

Cover it with thin slices of fat bacon, and wrap it in some buttered paper;

Put it in a braizing stewpan with 2 quarts of *Mirepoix*; when done, drain, and put the turkey on a dish; garnish with *Chipolata* Garnish (*vide* page 294), and serve with some *Espagnole* Sauce.

BRAIZED TURKEY À LA JARDINIÈRE

Prepare, truss, and cook a hen-turkey as above; when done, drain, untie, and put it on a rice *socle* on a dish;

Make a *jardinière* of carrots turned to a pear-shape, cabbage-lettuces, cauliflowers, turnips, and French beans;

Garnish round the rice so as to hide it completely;

Put some vegetables on 4 silver skewers; stick them in the turkey, and serve with *Béchamel* Sauce.

Observation.—Bear in mind that the rice *socle* should always be rather smaller than the joint.

ENTRÉES

FRICASSEE OF CHICKENS À LA ST. LAMBERT

Prepare and cut 2 chickens, as directed for Fricassee of Chicken (*vide* First Part, page 117); steep the pieces in cold water for half an hour; drain, and put them in a stewpan with some white *consommé*, 1 carrot, 1 onion, and 1 faggot; drain the pieces of chicken when they are done;

Strain the *consommé* through a broth napkin; reduce it one half; add 1½ pint of *Velouté* Sauce to it, and reduce both together until the sauce coats the spoon; thicken it with egg, and strain it through a tammy cloth into a *bain-marie*-pan;

Wipe and trim the pieces of chicken; put them in a stewpan; pour in enough sauce to cover them, and warm them without boiling; dress them on a dish; pour over some of the sauce out of the *bain-marie*-pan;

Garnish round with small portions of carrots cut to an olive-shape, button onions, previously boiled in white *consommé*, and asparagus peas; and serve with the remainder of the sauce, in a boat.

FRIED FRICASSEE OF CHICKENS À LA VILLEROY

Cut up 2 chickens as before;

Blanch the pieces, and cook them in some *Velouté* Sauce; when done, drain them; reduce and strain the sauce; thicken it with egg, and strain it again through a tammy cloth;

Dip the pieces of chicken in it, and let them get cold; then bread-crumb them; dip them in beaten eggs, and bread-crumb them again; fry them in hot fat; drain and dish them up on a napkin; garnish with fried parsley, and serve, with the remaining sauce, in a boat.

FRICASSEE OF CHICKENS À LA CHEVALIÈRE

Pick, draw, and singe 2 chickens; remove the skin from the breasts, and cut off the whole fillets with the pinion-bones attached; remove the legs and cut up, and cook the remainder of the chickens as for Fricassee of Chicken (*vide* First Part, page 117); take the minion fillets; flatten them slightly; trim, and turn them round so as to form a ring 3 inches in diameter; put this ring in a buttered *sauté*-pan, and, with a little white of egg, stick a thin ring of tongue, ½ inch wide, on the top of it;

Press the fillets on the table, smooth side downwards, and cut off the thin skin, by passing a very sharp knife between it and the flesh, so as to remove the skin without wasting too much of the fillet; then lard the fillets with thin strips of fat bacon; put them in a *sauté*-pan, and cover them with thin slices of fat bacon.

Bread-crumb the 4 legs as directed for Fricassee of Chickens *à la Villeroy* (*vide* preceding recipe).

When about serving, cook the minion fillets, and fillets in their

3 D

respective *sauté*-pans; glaze the latter in the oven, and fry the legs in hot fat;

Make a *croustade* border, 2½ inches high, in a dish;

Form a square in the centre with the backs and pinions of the fricasseed chickens; pour a little *Allemande* Sauce over them; lean the 4 legs against the sides of the square thus formed, and place a larded fillet between each leg; put the ring of minion fillets on the top, and a large truffle in the centre; glaze the larded fillets, and serve, with a boat of *Allemande* Sauce with mushrooms added.

FRICASSEE OF CHICKENS THICKENED WITH MILK OF ALMONDS

Cut up 2 chickens as directed for Fricassee of Chickens à la *St. Lambert* (*vide* page 384); blanch, drain, wipe, and trim the pieces; put them in a stewpan, with 1 quart of *Velouté* Sauce and 1 pint of Chicken *Consommé*;

When the chicken is done, pour the liquor out of the stewpan into another; skim off the fat, and reduce the sauce until it coats the spoon; then strain it on to the pieces of chicken in the stewpan; boil up together, and thicken the sauce with some Milk of Almonds, prepared as follows:

Blanch and peel 2 oz. of Jordan Almonds; wash and pound them in a mortar, moistening them with ⅓ pint of milk; when well pounded, press them through a broth napkin into a basin;

Take the fricassee off the fire; let it cool for a minute, and pour in the milk of almonds with one hand, whilst tossing the contents of the stewpan with the other, so as to mix and thicken the sauce;

Dress the fricassee on a dish; and serve.

CURRY OF CHICKENS

Cut up 2 chickens as above;

Put 1½ oz. of butter in a stewpan, with:

    2 onions cut in dice,

    1 oz. of curry powder;

Stir over the fire for five minutes; then put in the pieces of chicken, and fry them slightly;

Dredge in 1½ oz. of flour; season with salt and pepper, and stir over the fire for two minutes; pour in 3 pints of General Stock, and simmer till the chicken is done;

Pour the contents of the stewpan into a colander, over a basin; clean the pieces of chicken and put them in a stewpan;

Strain the sauce through a tammy cloth into a *bain-marie*-pan; pour a few spoonfuls of it over the pieces of chicken, and put them to warm; then dress them on a dish; pour over a little more sauce, and serve the remainder in a boat;

Put $\frac{1}{2}$ pint of rice in a stewpan, together with 1 pint of water; season with a little salt; boil for twenty minutes, and serve the rice in a silver casserole, with the chicken.

BRAIZED FOWLS À LA CHIVRY WITH RAVIGOTE SAUCE

Truss 2 fowls for boiling;

Cover them with thin slices of fat bacon; wrap them in buttered paper, and put them in a braizing stewpan, with 1 pint of *Mirepoix*, and simmer till the fowls are done; drain them; take off the paper and untie them; dress on a dish, and pour over some *Ravigote* Sauce (*vide* page 287).

BRAIZED FOWLS WITH OYSTERS

Prepare and cook 2 fowls as above;

Blanch and trim 4 doz. oysters; mix them in some *Allemande* Sauce, and put them in a dish round the fowls;

Serve with some *Allemande* Sauce, in a boat.

BRAIZED FOWLS À LA MACÉDOINE

Cook 2 fowls as directed above;

Make a *macédoine* of vegetables: of carrots, cut to a ball shape, French beans, green peas, and asparagus peas, mixed in some *Béchamel* Sauce;

Put the *macédoine* in a dish; place the fowls upon it; pour a little *Béchamel* Sauce over them, and serve some more separately.

BRAIZED FOWLS WITH CRAYFISH SAUCE

Prepare and cook 2 fowls as directed for Braized Fowls *à la Chivry* (*vide* above);

Thicken some *Poivrade* Sauce with Crayfish Butter;

Drain, and untie the fowls; put them on a dish; pour over part of the sauce, and serve the remainder separately.

FILLETS OF FOWLS EN SUPRÈME

Cut off the fillets of 6 fowls ; remove the minion fillets ; remove the thin skin of the large fillets, as directed for Fricassee of Chickens *à la Chevalière* (*vide* page 385), and trim them to a pear-shape, and of an even size ;

Butter a *sauté*-pan with clarified butter; lay the fillets in it, curving them slightly in one direction to facilitate dishing up; pour a little clarified butter over the fillets, and cover them with a round of buttered paper ;

Trim the minion fillets, and *contise* them with pieces of tongue; put them in a buttered *sauté*-pan, also curving them slightly ;

Cook the fillets in their respective *sauté*-pans; pour off the butter, and add 2 gills of *Suprème* Sauce, and 1 oz. of Chicken Glaze; move the fillets in the sauce till the glaze is melted, and dish them in a circle round a *croustade*; pour some *Suprème* Sauce over them ;

Cut 12 thin slices of tongue; cut these out with a round cutter to the same size as the top of the fillets, and insert one of these rounds between each fillet.

Fill the *croustade* with sliced truffles, cut with a ¾-inch cutter;

Put the minion fillets round the top of the *croustade* ;

Pour some Half Glaze over the truffles, and serve with *Suprème* Sauce, in a boat.

FILLETS OF FOWLS À LA TOULOUSE

Proceed exactly as above, merely putting cocks' kernels in the *croustade* instead of sliced truffles, and serve with *Suprème* Sauce.

FILLETS OF FOWLS WITH ASPARAGUS PEAS

Prepare and cook the fillets as before ;

Dish them with some slices of tongue, round a *croustade* filled with Asparagus Peas, and serve with *Suprème* Sauce.

FILLETS OF FOWLS WITH GREEN PEAS

Proceed as directed above ;

Fill the *croustade* with Green Peas, and serve with some *Allemande* Sauce, in a boat.

FILLETS OF FOWLS WITH FRENCH BEANS

Prepare and dish the fillets round a *croustade* as aforesaid ;
Garnish the *croustade* with French beans, and serve with
some *Allemande* Sauce, separately.

FILLETS OF FOWLS WITH CUCUMBERS

Proceed as for Fillets of Fowls *en Suprème* (*vide* page 388) ;
Fill the *croustade* with White Cucumber Garnish (*vide* page
298), mixed in *Allemande* Sauce, and serve some of the same
sauce in a boat.

FILLETS OF FOWLS À LA MACÉDOINE

Prepare and dish the fillets round a *croustade*, as above ; fill
the latter with a *macédoine* of vegetables, and serve with a boat
of *Béchamel* Sauce.

ÉPIGRAMMES OF FILLETS OF FOWLS WITH MUSHROOM PURÉE

Cut off the fillets of 3 fowls ; trim, and put them in a *sauté*-
pan, as directed for Fillets of Fowls *en suprème* (*vide* page
388 ;)
Cut off and bone the six legs ; braize them in some *Mirepoix*,
and, when done, press them between two dishes till cold ; then
trim, bread-crumb, and fry them as directed for *Épigrammes*
of Lamb with Asparagus Peas (*vide* page 372) ; stick in a
piece of bone, to represent the cutlet-bone ;
Cook the fillets, and dish them, alternately with the fried
legs, round a *croustade* ; fill this with Mushroom *Purée* (*vide*
page 302) ; and serve with *Allemande* Sauce.

FRITÒT OF FOWLS

Cut up 2 fowls as directed for Fricassee of Chicken (*vide*
First Part, page 117) ; marinade the pieces in oil seasoned with
lemon-juice, a sprig of parsley, a sliced onion, and salt and
pepper ;
Half an hour before serving, take out the onion and parsley ;

wipe the pieces of chicken on a cloth; dip them in milk, flour them well, and fry them in warm fat, gradually accelerating the heat;

When the fowl is cooked, and has attained a light brown colour, drain and dish it on a napkin; garnish with fried parsley, and serve with *Poivrade* or Tomato Sauce.

BRAIZED LEGS OF FOWLS WITH RAVIGOTE SAUCE

Remove the thigh-bones of 12 legs of fowls; braize them in some *Mirepoix*; when done, drain, and press them between two dishes till cold;

Trim them to a cutlet shape, and cut the end of the bones to an equal length;

Warm the pieces of fowl up in some Chicken *Consommé*; drain, and dish them in a circle; pour some *Ravigote* Sauce, (*vide* page 287) over them, and serve.

BRAIZED LEGS OF FOWLS À LA DIABLE

Prepare and braize 12 legs of fowls as above;

Press them between two dishes till cold; trim, and dip them in clarified butter; bread-crumb and broil them over a moderate fire;

Dish them up in a circle, and serve with Sauce *à la Diable* (*vide* page 282), in a boat.

BRAIZED LEGS OF FOWLS WITH TOMATO SAUCE

Remove the thigh-bones of 12 legs of fowls; trim, and shape them into cutlets; put them in a *sauté*-pan with a little clarified butter;

Season with salt and pepper, and moisten with some *Mirepoix*;

Simmer until the cutlets are done, without colouring them; drain, and dish them in a circle, and serve with Tomato Sauce.

LEGS OF FOWLS EN PAPILLOTES

Bone and braize the legs of fowls as directed for Braized Legs of Fowls with *Ravigote* Sauce (*vide* page 390);

Cut some stiff paper to form a *papillote* (*vide* Woodcut, page 100); place a thin slice of fat bacon on the paper; put a layer of reduced *d'Uxelles* Sauce on it; then a leg of fowl; another layer of *d'Uxelles* Sauce and, lastly, a thin slice of fat bacon; fold over the paper, and close the *papillote* as directed for Veal Cutlet *en Papillote* (*vide* page 100);

Wrap each leg in this way, and put them to warm on a gridiron over a slow fire for five minutes, turning them once; and serve.

BRAIZED LEGS OF FOWLS WITH ARTICHOKE PURÉE

Prepare and braize 12 legs of fowls, as directed for Braized Legs of Fowls with *Ravigote* Sauce (*vide* page 390);

Drain and dish them in a circle; glaze them, garnish the centre of the dish with Artichoke *Purée*; and serve with some Half Glaze, in a boat.

BRAIZED LEGS OF FOWLS WITH CELERY PURÉE

Proceed and dish up as above;

Fill the centre with Celery *Purée*; and serve with some Half Glaze separately.

BRAIZED LEGS OF FOWLS WITH CARDOON PURÉE

Prepare and cook the legs of fowls as above;

Dish them round a *croustade*; fill it with Cardoon *Purée*, and serve with a boat of Half Glaze.

BLANQUETTE OF POULARDS WITH ENDIVE À LA TALLEYRAND

Pick, draw, singe, and truss 2 poulards;

Put them on the spit; cover them with thin slices of fat bacon, and wrap them up in buttered paper, and put them to roast, without colouring them;

When done, untie the poulards; cut off the whole fillets; remove the skin; cut them into scollops, and mix them in some endive prepared as directed at page 299;

Put both together on a dish; garnish round with *croutons* of fried bread, or puff paste *fleurons*, and serve.

Observation.—I have seen this *blanquette* prepared, precisely as I have described, in the kitchen of the Prince de Talleyrand, by M. Louis Esbrat, many years *chef* in the Prince's establishment.

BLANQUETTE OF POULARDS WITH TRUFFLES

Prepare and roast 2 poulards as before;

Remove the fillets, and cut them into scollops;

Cut 1 pound of truffles in thin slices, previously cooked in Madeira, and mix them in 1 pint of reduced Madeira Sauce; warm both together; add the scollops; mix, and serve in a silver casserole.

TURKEY PINIONS WITH CHESTNUT PURÉE

Take some turkey pinions, all from the same side; remove the large wing-bone, and fold over the skin, at the end, where it has been boned;

Blanch, drain, and put the pinions in a stewpan with some *Mirepoix*;

When they are done, press them between two dishes till cold;

Strain and skim the fat off the gravy;

Reduce, and put it in a stewpan, with the pinions, to warm and glaze them;

Dish them in a circle, glaze them again, with a brush dipped in glaze;

Put some Chestnut *Purée* in the centre of the dish; and serve with some Half Glaze, in a boat.

TURKEY PINIONS AU CONSOMMÉ

Bone and blanch some pinions as above; cook them in Chicken *Consommé*;

Drain and dish them in a silver casserole; pour some *Blond de Veau* over them; and serve.

BOUDINS OF FOWL WITH SALPICON À LA RICHELIEU

Make some Chicken Forcemeat, rather stiffer than when required for small *quenelles*;

Cut an onion in small dice; blanch, cool, drain, and fry it in butter, without colouring; stir it over the fire for ten minutes, and add it to the forcemeat;

Butter some strips of paper, 4 inches by $2\frac{1}{2}$ inches; put a piece of forcemeat, $3\frac{1}{4}$ inches by $1\frac{3}{4}$, and $1\frac{1}{4}$ inch thick, on each strip of paper, and, with the handle of a spoon, remove part of the forcemeat in the centre of each *boudin*, so as to form a hollow ¾ inch deep, and ¾ inch wide; put some *salpicon*, made with truffles, cooked fillets of chicken and tongue mixed in stiffly reduced *Allemande* Sauce, in this hollow, without quite filling it, and cover the *salpicon* with some forcemeat, so as to hide it completely.

Fifteen minutes before serving, put the *boudins* in a *sauté*-pan in some General Stock, and simmer gently to set the forcemeat; drain the *boudins* on a cloth; dish them in a circle; pour over some reduced *Espagnole* Sauce; and serve.

BOUDINS OF FOWL WITH TRUFFLE PURÉE

Prepare the *boudins* as before, substituting Truffle *Purée* for the *salpicon*, and serve with Madeira Sauce.

BOUDINS OF FOWL WITH MUSHROOM PURÉE

Make the *boudins* as described for *Boudins à la Richelieu*;
Dish them in a circle, and fill the centre of the dish with Mushroom *Purée*; pour some *Allemande* Sauce over it, and serve some of the same sauce separately.

BOUDINS OF FOWL WITH ARTICHOKE PURÉE

Prepare and cook the *boudins* as before; dish them in a circle; garnish the centre with Artichoke *Purée*; pour some *Béchamel* Sauce over the *purée*, and serve some more sauce in a boat.

BOUDINS OF FOWL WITH PRAWNS

Make some forcemeat as described for *Boudins à la Richelieu* (*vide* page 392), adding some Shrimp Butter to it;
Shape the *boudins* in the same way, and put some prawn tails, cut in small dice, and mixed in reduced *Allemande* Sauce, in the inside of the *boudins*, instead of the *salpicon*;
Poach the forcemeat in some General Stock; drain, and dish the *boudins* in a circle; pour over some reduced *Allemande* Sauce; and serve.

FOIES GRAS SCOLLOPS WITH TRUFFLES

Cut some *foies gras* into scollops; put them in a *sauté*-pan with a little clarified butter; fry them slightly; season with salt
3 E

and pepper; drain and mix them in some Madeira Sauce, together with some sliced truffles, and serve them in a *croustade* on a dish.

FOIES GRAS CLOUTÉS WITH MADEIRA SAUCE

Cloutez some whole *foies gras* with pieces of truffle (*vide* To *Clouter*, page 224);

Put them in a stewpan with some *Mirepoix*; cover them with a round of buttered paper; close the stewpan, and simmer until the *foies gras* are done;

Drain and dish them in a *croustade*; pour over some Madeira Sauce; and serve.

FOIES GRAS WITH TRUFFLE PURÉE

Cook the *foies gras* as above;

Oil a paper *entrée*-case; fill it three-parts full with Truffle *Purée*;

Drain the *foies gras*; place them on the *purée*; and serve.

FILLETS OF DUCKLINGS À LA BIGARADE

Roast 5 ducklings;

Remove the fillets; score the skin slightly;

Dish them in a circle; pour over some *Bigarade* Sauce (*vide* page 282), and serve the same sauce separately.

FILLETS OF DUCKLINGS WITH GREEN PEAS

Remove the fillets of some roast ducklings, and score them as above; dish them up in a circle; garnish the centre with plain boiled green peas; and serve with some Half Glaze, in a boat.

FILLETS OF DUCKLINGS WITH OLIVES

Prepare and dish up the fillets as above;

Garnish the centre with turned olives, mixed in reduced *Espagnole* Sauce; and serve.

SALMI OF DUCKLINGS' LEGS

Cut off and trim the legs of the ducklings (from which the fillets have been removed for the above recipe); and put them in a buttered *sauté*-pan;

Break up the remaining bones of the birds; put them in a stewpan with:

    ½ pint of Burgundy,
    2 shalots whole,
    salt, pepper, and grated nutmeg to season;

Reduce the wine, and add 1 pint of *Espagnole* Sauce;

Simmer for twenty minutes, and strain through the pointed strainer into a stewpan, and simmer for five minutes more;

Warm the legs in the *sauté*-pan over a slow fire; put them on a dish;

Skim the sauce; pour it over the legs, and garnish round with 6 *croutons* of fried bread.

STEWED PIGEONS

Truss 4 pigeons, legs inward; put them in a stewpan; cover them with some thin slices of fat bacon; moisten with Chicken *Consommé*, and put a round of buttered paper on the top;

Close the stewpan, and simmer until the pigeons are done;

Fry a piece of crumb of bread 3 inches high, 2¼ inches square at the base, and 1¼ inch square at the top; drain, and stick it in the centre of a dish with some paste made of white of egg and flour;

STEWED PIGEONS

3 E 2

Drain the pigeons ; lean them against the sides of the block of fried bread ; pile up a *Jardinière* of cauliflowers, turnips, carrots and French beans, between the pigeons ;

Cut an artichoke-bottom to a bowl-shape ; place it on the top of the bread, and fill it with Brussels sprouts or French beans ;

Pour some *Béchamel* Sauce over the pigeons only ; and serve some of the same sauce in a boat.

PIGEONS À LA FINANCIÈRE

Truss and cook 4 pigeons as before ;

Prepare a *ragoût* of truffles, Chicken *Quenelles*, mushrooms, cocks' combs and kernels, mixed in *Financière* Sauce ;

Stick a block of fried bread in the centre of a dish, and place the pigeons against it as aforesaid ; put some of the *ragoût* round the dish, and pile some up between the birds ; lay a large crayfish, claws uppermost, on each heap of *ragoût*, and put a larded sweetbread on the top of the bread ; glaze the former, and pour some *Financière* Sauce over the pigeons, and serve the same sauce separately.

PIGEON CUTLETS WITH FRENCH BEANS

. Cut 4 pigeons in half, remove the wing-bones, and tuck the leg-bones inside ; fry them in a *sauté*-pan with a little butter, and season with salt and pepper ;

When the cutlets are done, press them between two dishes till cold ;

Dip them in butter, and bread-crumb them ;

Broil them over a slow fire to colour them ; dress them in a circle on a dish ; fill the centre with French beans (*vide* Garnishes, page 296) ; and serve with some Half Glaze, in a boat.

PIGEON CUTLETS WITH ASPARAGUS PEAS

Proceed as above, substituting asparagus peas for the French beans, and serve with some Half Glaze separately.

PIGEON CUTLETS WITH A MACÉDOINE OF VEGETABLES

Prepare and cook the cutlets as before ;

Dish them in a circle ;

Garnish the centre with a *Macédoine* of vegetables; and serve with some *Béchamel* Sauce in a boat.

PIGEON CUTLETS WITH SLICED MUSHROOMS

Prepare, cook, and dish the cutlets as directed for Pigeon Cutlets with French Beans;

Fill the centre with some sliced mushrooms; and serve some Half Glaze in a boat.

PAIN DE VOLAILLE, OR CHICKEN FORCEMEAT CAKE WITH TRUFFLES

Remove the fillets of 3 chickens;

Cut 4 fillets in two, lengthwise; trim, and lard them with thin strippets of fat bacon; put them in a *sauté*-pan, curving them slightly, as directed for Fillets of Fowls *en Suprême* (*vide* page 388).

Pound the meat of the legs together with the 2 remaining fillets, and the minion fillets; when well pounded, press the whole through a hair sieve, and put it back into the mortar; adding an equal quantity of boiled udder of veal, previously pounded and pressed through a hair sieve;

Pound, and mix both together; season with a pinch of salt and grated nutmeg, and moisten with some stiffly reduced *Suprême* Sauce;

Try a piece of the forcemeat by poaching it, when it should be delicate and light.

Butter a plain cylinder-mould; fill it with the forcemeat to a height of 3½ inches, and poach it *au bain-marie*.

Cook and glaze the larded fillets in the *sauté*-pan.

When the forcemeat is set, turn it out of the mould on to a dish; pour some *Suprême* Sauce over it; fill the centre with truffles cut to an olive-shape, and mixed in some Half Glaze; place the fillets in a circle round the top of the *pain*, and serve with *Suprême* Sauce in a boat.

Observation.—The quality of this dish depends entirely on the delicacy of the forcemeat; it should therefore be very carefully prepared.

ROASTS

ROAST CAPON

Prepare and truss a fine capon for roasting ;

Put it on the spit, to roast before a good clear fire ; when done, take it off the spit ; put it on a dish ; garnish round with watercresses ; and serve with some Meat Gravy in a boat.

ROAST HEN-TURKEY

Prepare and truss a turkey for roasting ;

Put it before an even fire ;

When done, take it off the spit ; put it on a dish ; garnish with watercresses ; and serve with a boat of Meat Gravy.

ROAST TURKEY STUFFED WITH TRUFFLES

Stuff a turkey as directed for Braized Turkey stuffed with Truffles with *Périgueux* Sauce (*vide* page 383);

Truss it for roasting ; put it on the spit, and wrap it in 4 sheets of stiff buttered paper, enclosing it completely ;

When done, untie the turkey ; put it on a dish ; and serve with some Meat Gravy or *Périgueux* Sauce.

HOUSE PIGEON

GAME

CHAPTER XI

GAME

REMOVES—ENTRÉES—ROASTS

REMOVES

ROAST HAUNCH OF ROEBUCK

TRIM and lard a haunch of roebuck with strips of fat bacon;

Put it in some marinade for two days; then drain and put the haunch on the spit, wrap it in buttered paper, and roast it before a good clear fire;

When done, take off the paper, put the joint on a dish with a paper frill round the knuckle-bone; glaze the larded parts; and serve with *Poivrade* Sauce and Currant Jelly separately.

Observation.—This joint is sometimes roasted without being marinaded; in that case it is served with Meat Gravy and Currant Jelly.

SADDLE OF ROEBUCK

Trim a saddle of roebuck, and, after larding it with fat bacon, steep it in some marinade for two days ;

When wanted, wrap it in buttered paper, and put it to roast ;

When the meat is done, remove the paper, and put the joint on a dish ; glaze it, and serve, with *Poivrade* Sauce and Currant Jelly.

BRAIZED PHEASANTS WITH FOIES GRAS AND TRUFFLES À LA BOHÉMIENNE

Make a *salpicon* with 1 lb. of *foies gras*, and 1 lb. of truffles cut in dice ; season with salt and pepper ;

Pick, draw, and singe 2 pheasants ; stuff them with the *salpicon ;* truss them as for braizing ; and tie some thin slices of fat bacon over them ;

Put the pheasants in a braizing stewpan, being careful to place the drainer in it ;

Pour in ½ pint of Madeira and three gills of *Mirepoix ;* close the stewpan ; put some live coals on the cover, and simmer on a slow fire for forty-five minutes ;

Prepare the following for garnish :

  2 *foies gras, cloutés* and braized ;
  18 large truffles ;
  12 large and white cocks' combs ;
  19 fine cocks' kernels ;

Cut a piece of bread-crumb, 3½ inches high, 4 inches long, by 2 inches ; cut it out at each end on the top, for the pheasants to rest against it ; fry the bread in hot fat, drain, and stick it in the centre of a dish, with a little white of egg and flour ;

When the pheasants are done, drain and untie them, place them at the ends of the dish, crop upwards, against the bread, cut to receive them ;

Garnish the sides with the truffles, *foies gras,* cocks' combs and kernels, so as to hide the bread completely ;

Put some truffles and cocks' combs on 3 silver skewers, and stick them in the pheasants ; pour over some *Espagnole* Sauce, reduced with Essence of Truffles ; and serve with some of the same sauce in a boat.

BRAIZED PHEASANTS À LA FINANCIÈRE

Prepare and cook 2 pheasants as before ;

Make some *Financière Ragoût*, with *foies gras*, cocks' combs, truffles, and Pheasant Forcemeat *quenelles*, mixed in *Financière* Sauce for Game (*vide* page 281) ;

For garnish take :

   3 larded and cooked heart-sweetbreads ;
   2 large *quenelles* ;
   12 cocks' combs ;
   9 fine crayfish ;

Lean the pheasants against each end of a block of fried bread as above ; put the *ragoût* in the dish ; place a large *quenelle*, below each pheasant, on the *ragoût* ; put a sweetbread on either side of the bread, and a truffle on each sweetbread ; fill up the intervals with 4 crayfish and some cocks' combs ; and put the remaining sweetbread on the top of the bread, over the pheasants ;

Garnish 5 silver skewers with cocks' combs, truffles, and crayfish, and stick them in the pheasants and sweetbreads ; and serve with some *Financière* Sauce, reduced with Essence of Pheasant.

WILD BOAR HAM WITH VENISON SAUCE

After singeing off all the bristles, wash the ham in hot water, and saw off the bone 2 inches below the knuckle ;

Put the ham in some marinade, and let it remain in it for eight days ;

When wanted, drain and wipe it with a cloth ; put it on the spit, and wrap it in buttered paper ; roast it before a good clear fire, basting it with the marinade every fifteen minutes ;

When the ham is done, take it off the spit, untie the paper, and strip off the skin ;

Brush the ham over with Meat Glaze, and put it in the oven to glaze ; place it on a dish, with a paper frill round the knuckle-bone ; and serve with a boat of Venison Sauce (*vide* page 289).

CROUSTADE OF PARTRIDGES

Pick, draw, singe, and truss 8 partridges as for braizing ; tie a thin slice of fat bacon on each bird ; put them in a stewpan with some *Mirepoix* ; and simmer till the partridges are done ;

3 F

Prepare 8 fine crayfish, 14 large truffles, and 8 cocks' combs, for garnish;

Make some *Financière Ragoût*, mixing it in *Espagnole* Sauce, reduced with Essence of Partridge;

Make an oval fried-bread *croustade*, in a dish; place a block of fried bread in the centre; drain and dress the partridges, crop downwards, against the block of bread, and place a crayfish between each bird;

Garnish 8 silver skewers with cocks' combs and truffles, and stick one in each bird, so as to form a circle; pile up the remaining 6 truffles inside this circle, and serve with the *Financière Ragoût*, in a silver casserole.

RED PARTRIDGES À LA RÉGENCE

Pick, draw, singe, and truss 6 red partridges;

Tie some slices of fat bacon on them, and cook them in a braizing stewpan with some *Mirepoix*;

Make a rice *socle* on a dish, and put a rice block on the centre of the *socle*;

When the partridges are done, drain and dress them against the rice block; put a large turned mushroom on the top, and a truffle at the bottom of each bird;

Garnish with 6 small larded heart-sweetbreads, and 6 similar sized Chicken Forcemeat *quenelles*: place these alternately round the rice *socle*, and fill up the spaces between with cocks' kernels and mushrooms;

Put some cocks' combs and crayfish on 6 silver skewers, stick them in the top of the block, and serve with Sauce *à la Régence* (*vide* page 281).

CROUSTADE OF ORTOLANS À LA PROVENÇALE

Take 24 ortolans, and 24 even-sized large truffles;

Make a hole in the centre of each truffle, large enough to contain one of the ortolans; line this hole with a little Chicken Forcemeat;

Cut off the necks and legs, and remove the gizzards of the ortolans, and season them slightly with salt, pepper, and grated nutmeg;

Put an ortolan, breast uppermost, in each truffle; place them in a glazing stewpan, and cover them with thin slices of fat bacon ; pour in a bottle of Madeira, and the same quantity of *Mirepoix* ; close the stewpan, and simmer for twenty-five minutes ; drain the truffles, and pile them up in a fried bread *croustade*, of the size of the dish ;

Strain the gravy ; free it of fat, and reduce it one half ; add 1 quart of *Espagnole* Sauce ; reduce both together until the sauce coats the spoon ; strain through a tammy cloth ; and serve it in a boat with the ortolans.

PAIN DE FAISAN, OR PHEASANT FORCEMEAT CAKE, WITH PHEASANT GRENADINS

Remove the fillets of 6 pheasants ;

Trim and lard the fillets with thin strippets of fat bacon ; place them in a buttered *sauté*-pan ; sprinkle them with salt, and put a round of buttered paper over them ;

Make some panada with some crumb of bread and Essence of Pheasant, and put it on a plate to cool ;

Cut the remaining flesh off the bones of the pheasants ; pound it in a mortar with the minion fillets and the fillets of 6 hens ; press the whole through a hair sieve ; put it back in the mortar, and add an equal quantity of boiled udder of veal, previously pounded and pressed through a hair sieve, and half the weight of the pheasant-meat of the panada ; season with salt, pepper, and grated nutmeg ; pound and mix the whole well together, adding 3 eggs, one at a time, and work the forcemeat to the proper consistence with some *Espagnole* Sauce, stiffly reduced with Essence of Pheasant ;

Butter a plain oval border-mould, 10 inches long, 2½ inches wide ; fill it with the forcemeat, and poach it *au bain-marie*, without boiling ; when the forcemeat is set, turn it out of the mould on to a *croustade*, on a dish ; glaze it, and put the pheasant fillets, previously cooked and glazed, in a circle round the top ;

Garnish 6 silver skewers with cocks' combs and truffles ; stick them into the forcemeat, and serve with a boat of *Espagnole* Sauce reduced with Essence of Pheasant.

Observation.—I will mention again that the success of this dish, like that of Chicken Forcemeat Cake, depends entirely on the delicacy and proper preparation of the forcemeat.

ENTRÉES

SADDLE OF ROEBUCK WITH POIVRADE SAUCE

Trim, and lard a saddle of roebuck with strips of fat bacon; put it on the spit to roast before a clear fire, basting it frequently; when done, take it off the spit, put it on a dish, and glaze it;

Pour some *Poivrade* Sauce (*vide* page 266) under the meat, and serve some of the same sauce in a boat.

FILLETS OF ROEBUCK WITH TRUFFLE PURÉE

Cut 2 loins of roebuck into 12 fillets;

Trim them to a long pear-shape, as directed for Fillets of Fowls *en Suprème* (*vide* page 388);

Lard them with strippets of fat bacon, and set them in a buttered *sauté*-pan;

Cook and glaze them; dish them in a circle round a *croustade* filled with Truffle *Purée*; glaze the fillets again, with a brush dipped in glaze; pour some Half Glaze in the dish, and serve.

FILLETS OF ROEBUCK WITH MADEIRA SAUCE

Prepare and dish the fillets round a *croustade* as above;

Garnish the *croustade* with some scollops of roebuck, mixed in some Madeira Sauce; and serve, with a boat of the same sauce.

ROEBUCK CUTLETS WITH GAME PURÉE

Trim, and cut 2 necks of roebuck into cutlets;

Put them in a buttered *sauté*-pan, and cover them with a round of buttered paper;

Fry the cutlets, and dish them round a *croustade*; fill it with Rabbit *Purée* (*vide* page 294); pour some *Espagnole* Sauce, reduced with Essence of Rabbit, over the cutlets; and serve.

ROEBUCK CUTLETS WITH POIVRADE SAUCE

Cut and cook the cutlets as above;

Dress them in a circle on a dish; pour over some *Poivrade* Sauce; and serve some more in a boat.

ROEBUCK CUTLETS WITH SLICED TRUFFLES

Prepare the cutlets as aforesaid ;

Dish them round a *croustade* filled with sliced truffles, and serve with a boat of *Espagnole* Sauce reduced with Essence of Truffles.

ROEBUCK CUTLETS À LA CHASSEUR

Cut and trim the cutlets as before;

Fry them in a *sauté*-pan in clarified butter ;

Put some sliced shalots fried in butter, and a piece of Meat Glaze in some *Poivrade* Sauce ; reduce it over the fire for five minutes ; and add a tablespoonful of chopped parsley ;

Dish the cutlets in a circle ; pour the sauce over them ; and serve.

ROEBUCK CUTLETS À LA MARÉCHALE

Cut the cutlets as directed for Roebuck Cutlets with Game *Purée* (*vide* page 404) ;

Dip them in butter ; bread-crumb, and broil them over a slow fire ; dish them in a circle ; and serve with a boat of Meat Gravy, with the juice of a lemon and a little cayenne pepper added.

FILLETS OF PHEASANTS À LA FINANCIÈRE

Trim the fillets of 6 pheasants ; put them in a buttered *sauté*-pan ; and cover them with a round of buttered paper ;

Trim the minion fillets ; place a dot of truffle on each end, and set them in a buttered *sauté*-pan, curving them to a crescent-shape ;

Make a *Financière Ragoût* of truffles, *foies gras*, cocks' combs, *quenelles*, and mushrooms, mixed in *Financière* Sauce for game ;

Fry the fillets ; dress them round a *croustade* on a dish ; put the prepared *ragoût* in the *croustade* ;

Cook, and place the minion fillets round the top, with a large cock's comb in the centre ;

Pour some *Financière* Sauce, reduced with Essence of Pheasant, over the fillets ; and serve with the same sauce separately.

FILLETS OF PHEASANTS WITH QUENELLES

Trim and cook some fillets of pheasants as above ;

Make some Pheasant Forcemeat *quenelles*, of the size of an olive ;

Dish the fillets round a *croustade* ;

Fill it with the *quenelles* ; pour some *Espagnole* Sauce, reduced with Essence of Pheasant, over the *quenelles* and fillets ; and serve with the same sauce in a boat.

FILLETS OF PHEASANTS WITH FOIES GRAS À LA PERIGUEUX

Prepare the fillets as before ;

Dish them round a *croustade* ; fill it with scollops of *foies gras* ; pour over some *Périgueux* Sauce ; and serve.

SALMI OF PHEASANTS

Roast 2 pheasants ; when they are cold, cut them up, trim, and put the pieces in a stewpan ;

Pound the bones and trimmings in a mortar ; put them in a stewpan with $\frac{1}{4}$ pint of Madeira, and $\frac{1}{2}$ pint of *Mirepoix* ; reduce one half, and add $1\frac{1}{2}$ pint of *Espagnole* Sauce ; simmer, and reduce further for an hour ; then skim off the fat ; strain the sauce through a tammy cloth, and pour half of it on the pieces of pheasant in the stewpan ; warm them, without boiling ; dress them on a dish ; garnish with fried, and glazed bread *croûtons* (*vide* Croûtons for Entrées, page 304) ; and serve with the remaining sauce in a boat.

PHEASANT PURÉE EN CROUSTADE GARNISHED WITH LARDED FILLETS

Remove the fillets of 3 pheasants ;

Cut them in two lengthwise ;

Trim them to a long pear-shape, as directed for Fillets of Fowls *en Suprème* (*vide* page 388) ;

Lard them with strippets of fat bacon, and put them· in a buttered *sauté*-pan, curving them slightly, to facilitate dishing up, and cover them with a round of buttered paper ;

Wrap the three pheasants in buttered paper, and put them

down to roast; when cooked and cold, cut off all the meat; chop, and pound it in a mortar with 1 oz. of butter.

FRIED BLOCKS OF BREAD FOR DISHING GAME AND POULTRY

Put the *purée* in a basin; mix and moisten it with some *Espagnole* Sauce, reduced with Essence of Pheasant;

Garnish a *croustade* with the *purée*; lay the fillets, cooked and glazed, in a circle on the top of the *croustade*; and pile up the remainder of the *purée* in the centre; glaze the fillets again with a brush dipped in glaze; and serve.

BOUDINS OF PHEASANT FORCEMEAT

Make some Pheasant Forcemeat (*vide* page 305); form some *boudins* with the forcemeat, as directed for *Boudins à la Richelieu* (*vide* page 392); poach them in the same way; drain, and dish them in a circle; pour over some *Espagnole* Sauce, reduced with Essence of Pheasant; and serve.

BRAIZED PARTRIDGES À LA PÉRIGUEUX

Truss 3 partridges as for boiling; tie some thin slices of fat bacon on them, and put them in a stewpan, with 1 gill of Essence of Truffles, and 3 gills of *Mirepoix*; cover them with a round of buttered paper, and simmer till the partridges are done;

Cut a three-sided block of bread 3 inches high, $2\frac{1}{2}$ inches at the base, and $1\frac{1}{4}$ inch at the top;

Fry it, and fix it in the centre of a dish with paste made of flour and white of egg;

Make three large Partridge Forcemeat *quenelles* of a long pear-shape;

When the partridges are cooked, drain, and place one on each side of the block of bread; put a *quenelle* between each bird, and pour over some *Périgueux* Sauce, mixed with some Essence of Partridge; put a large truffle on the top of the bread; and serve with some of the same sauce in a boat.

BRAISED PARTRIDGES À LA FINANCIÈRE

Prepare and cook 3 partridges as above;
Dish them against a similar block of bread;
Pile up some *Financière Ragoût* (*vide* page 295) in the spaces between the birds;
Put a crayfish, claws upwards, on each pile of *ragoût*; and place a larded and glazed sweetbread on the top of the bread;
Serve with *Financière* Sauce for Game in a boat.

SALMI OF PARTRIDGES

Roast 3 partridges; cut them up when cold, and finish as directed for *Salmi* of Pheasants (*vide* page 406).

CHARTREUSE OF PARTRIDGES

Roast 3 partridges
Prepare some cabbage as directed for Garnishes (*vide* page 297); add some Essence of Partridge to the cabbage, and stir it over the fire to expel all moisture;
Cut some pieces of carrot and turnip 2 inches long, with a long vegetable cutter, ½ inch in diameter; cook the carrots and turnips separately (*vide* Garnishes, pages 295, 296);
Butter a plain *entrée*-mould; place a round of paper at the bottom, and a sheet of paper all round the inside; garnish it with the pieces of carrot and turnip;
Put a layer of cabbage in the mould;
Cut up the partridges, and place 4 fillets on the cabbage; make another layer of cabbage;
Put a layer of partridge on this, and continue the alternate layers till the mould is full; warm the contents *au bain-marie*, and turn the *Chartreuse* out of the mould on to an *entrée* dish; garnish round the bottom with alternate rounds of carrot and turnip, with a French bean between each round;

Place some turnip rings round the top of the *Chartreuse*, and put a Brussels sprout in each ;

Fix a cup made of carrot in the centre, and fill it with French beans ;

Serve with a boat of *Espagnole* Sauce, reduced with Essence of Partridge.

FILLETS OF PARTRIDGE WITH PARTRIDGE PURÉE

Remove the fillets of 6 partridges ;

Trim them, and put them in a buttered *sauté*-pan ;

Trim the minion fillets ; curve them slightly in a buttered *sauté*-pan, and stick a dot of truffle on the round end of each minion fillet

Braize the partridges, and, when cold, make some *purée* as indicated in the chapter on Garnishes (*vide* page 293) ;

Reduce the gravy in which they have been braized, and add it to the *purée* ;

Fry the fillets, and dish them round a *croustade* ; make a second circle on these with the minion fillets ;

Fill the *croustade* with the *purée* ;

Pour some *Espagnole* Sauce, reduced with Essence of Partridge, over the fillets, and serve with some of the same sauce in a boat.

BOUDINS OF PARTRIDGE FORCEMEAT

Moisten some Partridge Forcemeat (*vide* page 306) with some Half Glaze and Essence of Partridge ;

Make the *boudins*, and dish them up as directed for *Boudins à la Richelieu* (*vide* page 392) ; pour over some *Espagnole* Sauce, reduced with Essence of Partridge ; and serve.

BRAIZED RED PARTRIDGES WITH FOIES GRAS

Pick, draw, and singe 3 red partridges ; lard them with strips of fat bacon ; put them in a stewpan with some *Mirepoix* ; simmer till they are done, and glaze them ;

Drain, and untie the partridges ; put them on a dish, so as to form a triangle ; fill the centre with some scollops of *foies gras* ;

Pour some *Espagnole* Sauce, reduced with Essence of Truffles, over the scollops ;

Glaze the partridges with a brush dipped in glaze, and serve with some *Espagnole* Sauce, reduced with Essence of Truffles, in a boat.

BRAISED RED PARTRIDGES WITH TRUFFLES

Pick, draw, singe, and truss 3 red partridges; cook them in a stewpan with some *Mirepoix*;

When the partridges are done, drain and put them on a dish so as to form a hollow triangle; fill the centre with sliced truffles, mixed in *Suprème* Sauce; and serve the same sauce separately.

RED PARTRIDGE PURÉE EN CROUSTADE WITH PLOVERS' EGGS

Take 4 red partridges; remove the fillets of 3, and put by the fourth whole to roast;

Cut each fillet in 3 pieces lengthwise, which will give 18 pieces; trim 14 of these pieces to be 3 inches long, ½ inch broad, ¼ inch thick;

Trim the remaining 4 pieces and the minion fillets to a pear-shape, 2 inches long—this will make 10 small fillets;

Cut a piece of crumb of bread, as shown in woodcut, 1½ inch wide, 3 inches high, and 8 inches long;

Put a thin slice of fat bacon on the bread;

CONTISED FILLETS

Contise the 14 pieces of fillet with some round slices of truffles; lay the fillets across the bread, and put another thin slice of fat bacon on the top;

Roast the 3 partridges and the whole one, which you have reserved; when they are done and cool, remove all skin and fat; chop and pound the meat in a mortar, and make the *purée* as directed page 293;

Boil 14 plovers' eggs;

Put the piece of bread, with the fillets on it, in a *sauté*-pan in the oven for a few minutes to cook the fillets;

Make a rice *croustade* on a dish;

Fill it partly with the *purée*; stand the plovers' eggs on the *purée*, all round the top of the *croustade*; putting one of the *contised* fillets between each egg;

Pile up the remainder of the *purée* in the centre, and lay the 10 small fillets on the top, with the points to the centre, forming a circle; put a small truffle in the middle; and serve.

FILLETS OF RED PARTRIDGES À LA TOULOUSE

Take the fillets of 6 red partridges;

Trim and put them in a buttered *sauté*-pan, curving them slightly;

Trim the minion fillets; put them, similarly curved, in another buttered *sauté*-pan, and, with a little white of egg, stick a dot of truffle on the round ends;

Fry the large fillets; drain and dish them in a circle round a *croustade*; fill it with cocks' kernels mixed in *Suprême* Sauce, and pour some sauce over the fillets;

Put the minion fillets in the oven, and, as soon as they are set, dress them in a circle on the other fillets; and serve with *Suprême* Sauce.

FILLETS OF RED PARTRIDGES À LA FINANCIÈRE

Cut and trim the fillets of 6 partridges;

Lard them with thin strips of fat bacon;

Cook and glaze them in a *sauté*-pan;

Make a paste *croustade* of the size of the dish, and 2 inches deep;

Cut the minion fillets into scollops, and put them in a *Financière Ragoût* made of *foies gras*, truffles, cocks' combs, cocks' kernels, mushrooms, and Chicken Forcemeat *quenelles*, mixed in *Financière* Sauce;

Put half this *ragoût* in the *croustade*;

Dish the fillets on it in a circle, and pile up the remaining *ragoût* in the centre ;

Serve with *Financière* Sauce.

FILLETS OF RED PARTRIDGES WITH TRUFFLES EN SUPRÈME

Trim the fillets and minion fillets of 6 partridges ;

Butter 2 *sauté*-pans ; put the fillets in one, and the minion fillets in the other, curving them both slightly ; stick a dot of tongue on the round end of each minion fillet ;

Fry the large fillets, and dish them in a circle round a *croustade* ; insert a thin slice of truffle, the same size as the fillets, between each ; set the minion fillets in the oven, and dress them on the fillets in a circle ;

Fill the *croustade* with truffles turned to an olive-shape, pour some Half Glaze on the truffles, and serve with *Suprème* Sauce in a boat.

Observation.—The use of *Suprème* Sauce in this *entrée* of game may appear strange, when it is remembered that this sauce is generally employed with poultry only ; however, the flesh of the red partridge being so similar to that of poultry, justifies the introduction of the *Suprème* Sauce.

WOODCOCKS À LA PÉRIGUEUX

Truss 3 woodcocks as for braizing ;

Put them in a stewpan ; cover them with thin slices of fat bacon, and pour in ½ pint of Madeira, and 1 pint of *Mirepoix*;

When the woodcocks are done, drain and untie them ; dress them on a dish, so as to form a triangle ; pour some *Périgueux* Sauce, reduced with Essence of Woodcock, over them; and serve.

FILLETS OF WOODCOCKS WITH FOIES GRAS À LA MANCELLE

Take the fillets of 5 woodcocks ; trim, and slit them open in the thickness ; spread a layer of *Foie gras* Forcemeat mixed with *d'Uxelles* inside the fillets, and fold the sides to again ; flatten them slightly with the handle of the knife, to stick the two pieces together ;

Butter a *sauté*-pan, and put the fillets in it; cover them with a round of buttered paper, and cook them over a slow fire;

Dish them round a *croustade* filled with *foie gras* scollops;

Reduce some *Espagnole* Sauce with some Essence of Woodcock; mix in a tablespoonful of chopped truffles cooked in Madeira, and a tablespoonful of *d'Uxelles*, and pour some of this sauce over the *foie gras* scollops and the fillets; and serve the remainder separately.

FILLETS OF WOODCOCKS WITH TRUFFLE PURÉE

Remove the fillets of 6 woodcocks; trim and put them in a buttered *sauté*-pan; sprinkle them with salt and pepper; pour a little clarified butter over them, and cover them with a round of buttered paper;

Trim the minion fillets; butter a *sauté*-pan; put them in it, and stick a dot of truffle on each fillet;

Cook the large fillets; dish them in a circle round a *croustade*; Set the minion fillets in the oven;

Fill the *croustade* with Truffle *Purée*; pour some Half Glaze and Essence of Woodcock over the fillets; place the minion fillets on them in a circle; and serve.

SALMI OF WOODCOCKS

Remove the trail of 3 woodcocks, and put them to roast; when done, and cold, cut them up, remove the skin, trim, and put the pieces in a buttered *sauté*-pan;

Pound the trimmings and bones in a mortar; then put them in a stewpan, with:

2 shalots,	1 faggot,
2 cloves,	½ a bottle of claret;

Reduce it one half, and add 1 quart of *Espagnole* Sauce; simmer on the stove corner for half an hour, skimming off the fat as it rises to the surface; strain the sauce through a tammy cloth into a stewpan, and reduce it again until it coats the spoon;

Pour a little of the sauce over the pieces of woodcock in the *sauté*-pan, and warm them, without boiling; put the pieces on a dish, pour the sauce over them, and garnish round with *croutons* spread with the woodcocks' trail, chopped and mixed with some *Foie gras* Forcemeat.

BOUDINS OF SNIPE FORCEMEAT WITH SALPICON

Make some forcemeat as directed for Partridge Forcemeat, (*vide* page 306), substituting snipe for the partridge;

Butter some *dariole* moulds; line them with the forcemeat to a thickness of ⅛ an inch; fill them with a *salpicon* of fillets of snipe, and truffles; pour in a little stiffly reduced *Espagnole* Sauce; put a layer of forcemeat on the top, so as to enclose the *salpicon* entirely;

Poach the *boudins, au bain-marie*; turn them out of the moulds, and dish them on a fried bread *socle*, cut so as to receive 3 tiers of the *boudins*, one above the other.

SALMI OF SNIPES

Roast 8 snipes; when they are done and cold, cut them in two, remove the neck, skin, and feet, and trim the pieces, and put them in a *sauté*-pan;

Pound the bones and trimmings; and finish as directed for *Salmi* of Woodcocks (*vide* page 413).

QUAILS À LA FINANCIÈRE

Truss 8 quails as for braizing;

Put them in a stewpan; cover them with thin slices of fat bacon; pour in 1 gill of Madeira, and ½ pint of *Mirepoix*; and simmer until the quails are cooked;

Fill a plain border-mould, 1¼ inch high, with Chicken Forcemeat; poach it *au bain-marie*, and turn the border out of the mould on to a dish, and fill the centre with a *Financière Ragoût* made of *foies gras*, truffles, cocks' combs, cocks' kernels, and Chicken Forcemeat *quenelles*, mixed in *Financière* Sauce;

Drain the quails, untie them, and place them half on the border, half on the *ragoût*, the legs towards the centre; put a cock's comb between each quail, and a large truffle in the centre; glaze the border, the quails and truffle with a brush dipped in glaze; and serve with *Financière* Sauce.

QUAILS À LA JARDINIÈRE

Prepare and cook 8 quails as above;

Butter a plain border-mould, and fill it with braized cabbage-lettuces; press them into the mould and turn the border out on to a dish; garnish the centre with a *Jardinière* of carrots, turnips, and French beans;

Place the quails on the border as above;

Put a small head of cauliflower between each, and place a circle of cauliflowers on the quails, just inside the border, and pile up some French beans in the centre;

Glaze the quails and the border; and serve with a boat of Half Glaze.

QUAILS EN CERISES WITH TRUFFLES

Bone 18 quails entirely; open them, sprinkle them with salt, and spread a layer of Chicken Forcemeat inside; put a truffle, turned to a ball shape, in each quail, and fold it to enclose the truffle;

Cut up an old broth napkin and tie up each quail, in pieces of it, like a pudding;

Braize them in Madeira and *Mirepoix*;

Put some Chicken Forcemeat in a border-mould; poach it, and turn the border out on to a dish, and fill the centre with sliced truffles;

Drain, and untie the quails; wipe, and place them all round the border, resting partly on it, and partly on the truffles; pile up some more truffles in the centre;

Glaze the quails and the border; and serve with a boat of *Espagnole* Sauce, reduced with Essence of Truffles.

QUAILS AU GRATIN

Bone 12 quails; sprinkle them with salt, and spread a layer of *Foie gras* Forcemeat inside; put a round truffle in each, and wrap the quail well round the truffle;

Take an *entrée croustade*-mould, 2 inches deep; line it with paste, and put a layer of *Foie gras* Forcemeat 1 inch thick at the bottom; set the quails all round the mould, on the forcemeat;

Cut a round piece of bread; cover it with a thin slice of fat bacon, and put it in the centre of the circle formed by the quails, on the forcemeat;

Place a paste cover on the top of the *croustade*, and pinch the edges together with the pincers; brush the top over with egg; and bake in the oven;

When done, take the *croustade* out of the mould; cut out the cover, inside the pinched edge; take out the piece of bread;

wipe the hollow with a cloth to absorb all the fat; and fill it with a *ragoût* of cocks' combs and truffles; pour in some Half Glaze; glaze the *croustade*, and serve.

SCOLLOPS OF QUAILS WITH TRUFFLES

Remove the fillets of 12 quails;

Cut each fillet in two, in the thickness, and trim them to a round shape;

Cook 1 lb. of truffles in Madeira, and cut them in slices;

Put the scollops in a *sauté*-pan, with some butter; toss them over the fire till they are done; drain and mix them with the sliced truffles;

Put a rice border on a dish; fill the centre with the scollops and truffles; pour in some *Espagnole* Sauce, reduced with Madeira; and serve.

BALLOTINES OF QUAILS WITH PÉRIGUEUX SAUCE

Bone 12 quails; fill them with Chicken Forcemeat; and fold and tie up the quails as directed for Quails *en Cerises* (*vide* page 415); cook them in the same way;

Make a potato border on a dish; dress the quails in it; pour over some *Périgueux* Sauce; and serve.

ORTOLANS IN CASES

Clean and singe 18 ortolans;

Take 18 small paper cases; oil them, and put them in the oven for a minute;

Put a tablespoonful of stiffly-reduced *Périgueux* Sauce in each case; place an ortolan on it; cook them in the oven; and pour over some *Périgueux* Sauce; dish them on a fried bread *socle*, as directed for *Boudins* of Snipe Forcemeat (*vide* page 414).

BALLOTINES OF LARKS

Proceed as for *Ballotines* of Quails;

Pour over some *Espagnole* Sauce, reduced with Essence of Larks; and serve.

LARKS AU GRATIN

Proceed as directed for Quails *au Gratin*;

Pour over some *Espagnole* Sauce, reduced with Essence of Larks; and serve.

FILLETS OF WILD DUCKS À LA BIGARADE

Roast 4 wild ducks, and remove the fillets; score the skin; dish them in a circle; and pour over some *Bigarade* Sauce (*vide* page 282); and serve.

FILLETS OF WILD DUCKS WITH POIVRADE SAUCE

Prepare the fillets as above;
Dish them in a circle; pour over some *Poivrade* Sauce; and serve.

FILLETS OF WILD DUCKS WITH OLIVES

Prepare and dish the fillets as above;
Garnish the centre with olives; and serve with some Half Glaze in a boat.

FILLETS OF WILD DUCKS WITH CELERY À LA FRANÇAISE

Proceed as directed for Fillets of Wild Ducks *à la Bigarade* (*vide* above);
Dish them in a circle; and fill the centre with Celery *à la Française* (*vide* page 300); and serve with some Half Glaze separately.

SALMI OF WILD DUCKS

Roast 2 wild ducks, and, when they are cold, cut them up; take off the skin; trim the pieces, and put them in a glazing stewpan;
Put in another stewpan:

2 onions,	½ a bottle of claret,
4 cloves,	4 shalots,
1 faggot,	the bones and trimmings;

Reduce the wine, and pour in 1½ pint of *Espagnole* Sauce;
Simmer for twenty minutes; skim and strain through the pointed strainer into a stewpan, and reduce till the sauce coats the spoon;
Pour one fourth of this sauce over the pieces of duck; warm them, without boiling; put them on a dish; pour over the remainder of the sauce; and garnish round with *croutons* of bread, fried and glazed.

3 H

UNDER-FILLETS OF WILD BOAR WITH ROBERT SAUCE

Take the under-fillets of a wild boar; cut and trim them as directed for Beef *Grenadins à la Financière* (*vide* page 335); lard them with thin strips of fat bacon; and marinade them for twenty-four hours;

When about to cook the fillets, drain and set them in a *sauté-*pan, with a little *Mirepoix*, not enough to cover them; cook and glaze them, and dish them in a circle; pour some *Robert* Sauce in the dish; glaze the fillets again; and serve.

HARE'S BACK WITH POIVRADE SAUCE

Take 2 hares' backs; lard them with strips of fat bacon; put them on the spit; wrap them in buttered paper; and put them to roast before a good clear fire; five minutes before serving, take off the paper, glaze the meat, put it on a dish; and serve with some Poivrade Sauce in a boat.

FILLETS OF HARE CONTISÉS

Remove the fillets of 6 hares; trim and *contise* them with slices of truffle; and roll the thin end round, as shown in the woodcut (*vide* page 410);

Put the fillets in a buttered *sauté*-pan; cover them with thin slices of fat bacon, and cook them in the oven;

When done, dish them in a circle round a *croustade* filled with Leveret Forcemeat *quenelles*; pour over some *Espagnole* Sauce, reduced with claret; and serve.

FILLETS OF HARE WITH FRENCH SAUCE

Take the fillets of 6 hares; lard them with thin strips of fat bacon, and turn the ends round as above; put them in a *sauté-*pan, and fry them in a little butter; glaze and dish them in a circle; and serve with French Sauce in a boat.

FILLETS OF HARE SCOLLOPS

Cut the fillets of 3 hares into scollops;

Set the scollops in a buttered *sauté*-pan; sprinkle with salt and pepper; put a little butter over them, and fry them slightly;

Pour off the butter ; pour in some *Espagnole* Sauce, reduced with Burgundy, and thicken it with the hare's blood (*vide* First Part, page 59).; put the scollops in a *croustade* on a dish ; pour over the sauce ; and serve.

FILLETS OF RABBIT CONTINUÉS

PAIN DE LIÈVRE, OR HARE FORCEMEAT CAKE, WITH VENISON SAUCE

Remove the fillets of 2 hares ; cut each fillet in two, and trim the pieces to a pear-shape ; lard them with thin strips of fat bacon, and put them in a buttered *sauté*-pan ;

Make some forcemeat with the remaining meat of the hares as directed for *Pain de Faisan* (*vide* page 403) ;

Butter a plain cylinder-mould ; fill it with the forcemeat, and poach the latter *au bain-marie* ;

Cook and glaze the fillets ;

Turn the forcemeat out of the mould on to a dish ; place the fillets on it in a circle ; glaze both with a brush dipped in glaze ; and serve with Venison Sauce.

PAIN DE LIÈVRE, OR HARE FORCEMEAT CAKE, WITH TRUFFLES

Prepare the forcemeat as above ;

Make a *salpicon* of truffles and fat bacon, previously boiled, and mix it with the forcemeat ;

Butter a plain cylinder-mould ; fill it with the forcemeat ;

poach and turn the latter out on a dish; glaze the *pain*, and serve with *Espagnole* Sauce, reduced with Essence of Hare.

BOUDINS OF HARE FORCEMEAT WITH SALPICON

Make some *boudins* of Hare Forcemeat and *salpicon* as described for *Boudins à la Richelieu* (*vide* page 392);

Dish them in a circle; pour over some *Espagnole* Sauce, reduced with Essence of Hare; and serve.

RABBITS' BACKS EN PAPILLOTES

Take the backs of 3 young rabbits; season them with salt and pepper; and fry them slightly in butter in a *sauté*-pan;

Oil a sheet of stiff paper; put a thin slice of fat bacon on it; spread, on the bacon, some stiffly-reduced *Espagnole* Sauce with some *d'Uxelles* added; place one of the backs on the sauce, then another layer of sauce, and finish with a thin slice of fat bacon on the top; fold the paper over, and close the edges; proceed in the same way for the two other backs, and put them on a gridiron over a slow fire for fifteen minutes, turning them once during that time; put the *papillotes* on a dish; and serve.

FILLETS OF RABBIT WITH TRUFFLE PURÉE

Take the fillets of 6 young rabbits; trim and lard them with thin strips of fat bacon; put them in a buttered *sauté*-pan, rolling the ends as shown in woodcut (*vide* page 410); fry the fillets, and dish them round a *croustade* filled with Truffle *Purée*;

Glaze the fillets; pour some Half Glaze in the dish; and serve.

FILLETS OF RABBIT WITH QUENELLES

Trim and *contise* 12 fillets of young rabbits; put them in a buttered *sauté*-pan, turning round the end as above;

Cook the fillets, and dish them round a *croustade* filled with Rabbit Forcemeat *quenelles*; pour some *Espagnole* Sauce, reduced with Essence of Rabbit, over the *quenelles*, and a little over the fillets; and serve some more of the same sauce in a boat.

RABBIT SCOLLOPS IN A FORCEMEAT BORDER

Cut the fillets of 6 young rabbits into scollops; put them in a *sauté*-pan with some clarified butter; season with salt and pepper, and put a little more butter on the top;

Trim the 12 minion fillets ; put them in a buttered *sauté*-pan, curving them slightly ; and, with a little white of egg, stick a dot of truffle on the thick end of each fillet ;

Fill a plain border-mould with Rabbit Forcemeat ; poach, and turn the latter out on to a dish ;

Toss the scollops over the fire in the butter, and cook the minion fillets ;

Glaze the forcemeat border ; place the minion fillets on it, in a circle ; drain the scollops ; mix them in *Espagnole* Sauce, reduced with Essence of Rabbit ; fill the border with the scollops ; and serve, with some of the same sauce separately.

BOUDINS OF RABBIT FORCEMEAT

Make the *boudins* with some Rabbit Forcemeat, in the same way as described for *Boudins à la Richelieu* (*vide* page 392) ; dish them in a circle ; pour over some Half Glaze, mixed with Essence of Rabbit ; and serve.

RABBIT GRENADINS À LA FINANCIÈRE

Trim 12 fillets of young rabbits ; lard them with thin strips of fat bacon ; and put them in a *sauté*-pan, with a little *Mirepoix*, not sufficient to cover them ;

Butter a plain border-mould ; fill it with Rabbit Forcemeat ; and poach the latter *au bain-marie* ;

Make a *Financière Ragoût* of *foies gras*, truffles, cocks' combs, cocks' kernels, and Rabbit Forcemeat *quenelles* ;

Cook and glaze the fillets ;

Turn the border out of the mould on to a dish ; dress the fillets in a circle on the border ; fill the centre with the *ragoût* ; pour over it some *Financière* Sauce, reduced with Essence of Rabbit ; and serve.

ROASTS

ROAST PHEASANTS

Pick, draw, and singe 2 cock pheasants ; truss them, and tie a thin slice of fat bacon on the breasts ; put them on the spit to roast, before a good fire ;

When the pheasants are done, untie, and put them on a dish ;

glaze them ; and garnish with bunches of watercresses at both ends, and on each side ; and serve, with the gravy in a boat.

ROAST BLACK-COCK

Pick, draw, and singe a black-cock ; truss it, and tie a thin slice of fat bacon on the breast ; put it to roast before a bright fire ; and, when done, put it on a dish ; garnish with water-cresses ; pour the gravy under ; and serve.

ROAST GROUSE

Pick, draw, and singe 3 grouse ; truss them, and tie a thin slice of fat bacon on each ; put them on the spit to roast ; and, when done, dish them on pieces of toast ; and serve.

ROAST PARTRIDGES

Pick, draw, and singe the partridges ; truss them, and tie a thin slice of fat bacon on the breasts ; put them to roast before a clear fire ; and, when done, put them on a dish ; and serve with Essence of Partridge in a boat.

ROAST WOODCOCKS AND SNIPES

Pick and draw the woodcocks or snipes, reserving the trail ; singe and truss them, and tie a thin slice of fat bacon on the breasts, and put them to roast before a clear fire ;
Chop the trail, spread it on pieces of buttered toast ; put them in the oven for two minutes ; and dish the birds on these pieces of toast.

ROAST ORTOLANS

Truss, and roast the ortolans before a very brisk fire ; put them on a dish ; garnish with watercresses ; and serve.

ROAST QUAILS

Truss the quails ; tie a slice of fat bacon and a vine-leaf on each bird ; roast them before a very brisk fire ; put them on a dish ; garnish with watercresses ; and serve with some gravy in a boat.

ROAST LARKS

Cut some thin pieces of toasted bread 1½ inch long by 1 inch, and put a thin slice of fat bacon on each side; place all the larks together, side by side, on a thin skewer, putting a piece of the toast between each ; tie the ends of the skewer to the spit; roast the larks before a very brisk fire ; and put them on a dish ; and serve with some gravy in a boat.

ROAST GUINEA-FOWLS

Truss and tie some thin slices of fat bacon on the fowls ; put them to roast before a clear fire ; place them on a dish ; garnish with watercresses ; and serve with some gravy separately.

ROAST WILD DUCKS, WIDGEON, AND TEAL

All the above should be roasted before a very brisk fire, and served with lemon-juice, and gravy, separately.

MIXED DISHES OF ROAST GAME

Various kinds of game are sometimes served together on one dish, such as :

A pheasant with plovers and larks ;

The pheasant should be put in the centre, the plovers on each side, and a row of larks all round the dish ; or

A pheasant surrounded with quails ; or

3 red partridges with ortolans ;

The partridges should be placed side by side, in the centre of the dish, with clusters of ortolans at each end, and at the sides ; or, again,

3 partridges and some larks ;

Placing the partridges side by side, and surrounding them with larks.

WILD BOAR'S HEAD

HADDOCK—BRILL—WHITING

CHAPTER XII

FISH AND SHELL-FISH

REMOVES — ENTRÉES

REMOVES

SALMON À LA CHAMBORD

CLEAN, wash, and wipe a salmon, and tie the head with string;

Put the salmon in the fish-kettle, on the drainer, cover it with *Mirepoix*, and put some sheets of buttered paper on the top;

Boil; and simmer on a slow fire for an hour;

Make a *ragoût* of Whiting Forcemeat *quenelles*, carp roes, mushrooms, and truffles mixed in *Espagnole* Sauce, reduced with Essence of Mushrooms and Truffles;

Prepare the following for garnish:

 24 carp roes,

 13 large truffles,

  6 large Whiting Forcemeat *quenelles*, decorated with fillets of sole *contisés*,

14 crayfish,

4 round Whiting Forcemeat *quenelles*, decorated with truffle,

8 large turned mushrooms;

Make a rice *socle*, 2 inches high, on a dish, and 1¾ inch smaller than the fish;

Drain the salmon, strip off the top skin; dry the fish with a cloth, and glaze it with a brush dipped in Fish Glaze;

Contise 4 fillets of sole, and stick them on the salmon with a little forcemeat; cover the *contised* fillets with buttered paper, and put the salmon in the oven to cook them; then take the paper off the fillets of sole, and put the salmon on the rice *socle*; pour the prepared *ragoût* round it, in the dish; and, on the top of the *ragoût* and in such a way as to hide the *socle*, garnish round with the carp roes, the 13 truffles, the 6 large *quenelles*, and 10 crayfish;

Put the round *quenelles*, the mushrooms, and 4 crayfish on 4 silver skewers; stick them in the salmon, and serve with *Espagnole* Sauce in a boat.

SALMON WITH LOBSTER EN COQUILLES

Cook a salmon as before;

Drain and put it on a dish on a napkin over a drainer;

Garnish round with Lobster *en Coquilles* (vide Hot *Hors d'œuvre*, page 320), and bunches of parsley, alternately; and serve, with Lobster Sauce (*vide* page 284) in a boat.

SALMON WITH ORLYS OF TROUT

Cook and dish a salmon on a napkin as above; garnish round with bunches of fried parsley, and *Orlys* of Trout prepared as directed for *Orlys* of Sole (*vide* page 317); and serve with *Genevoise* Sauce.

SALMON WITH SHRIMP CROQUETS

Cook a salmon as directed for Salmon *à la Chambord*; dish it on a napkin over a drainer;

Garnish round with bunches of fried parsley, and Shrimp Croquets, prepared as directed for Lobster Croquets (*vide* page 313); and serve with Shrimp Sauce (*vide* page 284).

3 I

BOILED TURBOT WITH FRIED SMELTS AND POTATOES

Clean a turbot; cut off the fins, and put it to steep in cold water for two hours; then wash it carefully in fresh water, and cover it with a layer of salt $\frac{1}{4}$ inch thick; put the fish in the turbot-kettle, with a napkin on the top ;

Put it on the fire, pour in some boiling water, and, when it boils up again, simmer for half an hour; as soon as the fish is done, dish it on a napkin over a drainer ;

Cut some plain-boiled potatoes to an olive shape, 2 inches long, and garnish round the fish with alternate heaps of these potatoes, and of fried smelts, and bunches of fried parsley ;

Serve with Lobster or Dutch Sauce (*vide* pages 283, 284).

Observation.—Turbot is frequently boiled in wine or milk; but I am no advocate of this method of cooking, as I consider salt water alone much to be preferred, for it will not impair in any way the delicate flavour of the fish, which wine or milk would be likely to do.

I do not think it necessary either to dress the turbot with decorated skewers; a fine white turbot will, in itself, constitute a most effective remove, when accompanied with the foregoing garnish.

BOILED TURBOT WITH FRIED OYSTERS AND CRAYFISH

Cook and dish a turbot as above ;

Garnish round with fried oysters, crayfish, and fried parsley, alternately, and serve with Dutch Sauce finished with Crayfish Butter.

BOILED TURBOT WITH CARP ROES EN COQUILLES

Prepare the turbot as directed above ;

Garnish round with Carp Roes *en Coquilles* (*vide* page 320), and bunches of fried parsley, and serve with Dutch Sauce finished with *Ravigote* Butter.

BOILED TURBOT WITH SOLE CROQUETS AND TRUFFLES

Cook and dish a turbot as directed for Boiled Turbot with Fried Smelts (*vide* above); ·

Garnish round with croquets (made of a *salpicon* of sole and truffles), and with fried parsley alternately; and serve with Dutch Sauce.

BRILL WITH ORLYS OF WHITING

Clean a brill; cut off the fins, and steep it in cold water for two hours; drain, cover it with salt, and cook it as directed for turbot (*vide* Boiled Turbot with Fried Smelts, page 426);

Dish it on a napkin over a drainer, and garnish round with fried parsley, and *Orlys* of Whiting, prepared in the same way as *Orlys* of Soles (*vide* page 317);

Serve with some Dutch Sauce finished with *Ravigote* Butter, and lemon juice.

BOILED BRILL WITH OYSTERS EN COQUILLES

Cook and dish a brill as above;

Garnish with Oysters *en Coquilles* (*vide* page 319), and parsley; and serve with some Dutch Sauce in a boat.

BOILED BRILL WITH POTATOES AND CRAYFISH

Prepare and cook a brill as directed for Turbot with Fried Smelts and Potatoes;

Dish it in the same way; and garnish round with plain-boiled potatoes cut to an olive-shape, and crayfish;

Serve with Lobster Sauce.

STURGEON WITH PAUPIETTES OF SOLES

Cut a piece, 10 inches long, from the middle of a sturgeon; clean, scale, and steep it in cold water; drain it, and tie some thin slices of fat bacon on it; put it in a fish-kettle, on the drainer; pour in an equal quantity of *Mirepoix* and French white wine, and put the fish on the fire to simmer;

Make 24 *paupiettes* of sole in the following way:

Take the fillets of 6 soles; strip off the skin, and trim the fillets; spread a layer of Whiting Forcemeat on the top of each fillet, the side which has been stripped of skin; roll each fillet round to form a *paupiette*; and wrap each one in a sheet of buttered paper;

Put them in a buttered *sauté*-pan;

3 1 2

Pour in sufficient *Mirepoix* to cover them one half; set them in the oven to poach the forcemeat; and take them out and remove the paper;

When done, drain the sturgeon; strip off the skin, and glaze the fish; put it on a dish, and garnish round with the *paupiettes*; put a turned mushroom on the top of each *paupiette*;

Strain the liquor in which the sturgeon has been cooked; free it of fat, and reduce it to a glaze; add 1 pint of *Espagnole* Sauce, and reduce again until the sauce coats the spoon; strain it through a tammy cloth; pour some over the *paupiettes*; and serve the remainder in a boat.

Observation.—I would always recommend cooking a piece of sturgeon in preference to a whole one; it is very difficult to prepare this gigantic fish satisfactorily otherwise.

As a case in point, I had, two years ago, on the occasion of a banquet at the Paris Jockey Club, to cook a sturgeon weighing no less than 150 pounds; I tried in vain in every direction to get a vessel large enough to cook the fish entire, but I was finally obliged to cut it in three pieces, and to cook them separately, re-uniting the severed pieces when serving.

Large sturgeon are always of better quality than small ones; —another reason why it is best to serve a slice of a large one rather than a small one whole.

STURGEON WITH CAPER SAUCE

Prepare and cook a piece of sturgeon as above;

Dish it on a napkin; garnish round with plain-boiled potatoes and parsley; and serve with a boat of Caper Sauce.

ROAST STURGEON WITH MATELOTE SAUCE

Remove the skin of a piece of sturgeon 10 inches long; sprinkle the fish with salt and pepper, and tie some thin slices of fat bacon on it;

Butter a sheet of stiff paper, sufficiently large to enclose the sturgeon;

Put some sliced onions and carrots on the paper, together with some thyme, bay leaf, and parsley; place the fish on these, and wrap it up in the paper; put it on the spit, and tie two more sheets of buttered paper round it; put it to roast before an even fire; and, when the fish is done, take it off the spit; untie it and put it on a dish ; glaze it ; pour over some *Matelote* Sauce ; and serve with some of the same sauce separately.

TROUT À LA CHAMBORD

Remove the inside of a trout through the gills, without cutting the fish open ;

Cut off the fins ; wash the trout, and cook it in an equal quantity of *Mirepoix* and claret;

Make a *ragoût* of Salmon Forcemeat *quenelles*, mushrooms, and crayfish tails ;

For garnish :

Cook and glaze 6 pieces of eel of an even size ; make and poach 6 large Salmon Forcemeat *quenelles* ; turn 24 large mushrooms, and cook 8 fine crayfish ;

When the trout is done, drain it and strip off the skin ; press some salmon forcemeat out of a paper funnel, in strips one inch wide, across the fish, beginning at the gills and putting the fourth strip about two inches from the tail ; insert some slices of truffle into the strips of forcemeat so as to *contise* them, and put the trout in the oven to poach the forcemeat ;

Strain the liquor in which the fish has been cooked ; remove all fat, and reduce it to a half glaze ; add one pint of *Espagnole* Sauce ; reduce it again until the sauce coats the spoon, and strain it through a tammy cloth into a *bain-marie*-pan ;

Make, on a dish, a rice *socle*, one inch shorter than the fish ; put the prepared *ragoût* round it, and pour some sauce over the *ragoût* ; place the trout on the *socle*, and garnish round with the pieces of eel, the crayfish, mushrooms, and *quenelles*, arranging these tastefully so as to hide the *socle* ;

Put some slices of *paupiettes* of sole (*vide* for the *paupiettes* page 427), some fried smelts, and mushrooms on 4 silver skewers ;

Stick them in the fish ; and serve with the sauce in a boat.

TROUT WITH POTATOES AND PRAWNS

Prepare and cook a trout as above ;

When done, drain and dish it on a napkin over a drainer ;

Garnish round with alternate heaps of prawns and potatoes, and serve with *Genevoise* Sauce (*vide* page 279).

TROUT WITH CRAYFISH TAILS EN COQUILLES

Cook a trout as before;

Put it on a dish on a napkin; and garnish round with Cray-fish Tails *en Coquilles* (*vide* page 320), and bunches of parsley;

Serve with Dutch Sauce finished with Crayfish Butter, and with lemon juice and chopped parsley added.

TROUT WITH FRIED ROES

Prepare a trout as directed for Trout *à la Chambord*; cook it in the same way; put it on a dish on a napkin; garnish with fried mackerel or carp roes; and serve with *Genevoise* Sauce.

COD WITH FRIED ANCHOVIES

Take a crimped cod; put it on a dish, and cover it with salt; place it on the drainer, and put it into a fish-kettle with suffi-cient boiling water to cover it entirely;

Boil for five minutes, then simmer for ten minutes; drain the fish, and dish it on a napkin over a drainer;

Garnish with fried anchovies, and fried parsley, alternately; and serve with a boat of butter, slightly melted, and a cut lemon on a plate.

COD WITH POTATOES

Cook and dish a cod as above;

Garnish round with plain-boiled potatoes, cut to an olive-shape, 2 inches long, and fried parsley; serve with Oyster Sauce (*vide* page 284).

PIKE À LA CHAMBORD

Remove the inside of a pike through the gills; scald it in boiling water to facilitate stripping off the skin; tie the head with string;

Wrap the pike in buttered paper; put it in a fish-kettle, and cover it entirely with *Mirepoix* and French white wine;

When done, drain the pike, and *clouter* it across with 4 double rows of nail-shaped pieces of truffle (*vide* to *Clouter*, 'Cookery Terms,' page 224); and, with a little Pike Forcemeat, stick a fillet of sole between each row, and put the pike into the oven, to cook the fillets ;

Make a *ragoût* of Pike Forcemeat *quenelles*, truffles, and mushrooms ;

Prepare the following for garnish :

    20 carp roes,

    16 fine crayfish,

     8 large pike forcemeat *quenelles*,

    10 mushrooms ;

Strain the liquor in which the fish has been cooked, skim off the fat, and reduce the liquor ;

Add 1 quart of *Espagnole* Sauce ; reduce again, and strain the sauce through a tammy cloth ;

Make a rice *socle* on a dish ; lay the pike on it ; put the *ragoût* in the dish ; pour some of the sauce over it, and garnish round with the large *quenelles*, the carp roes, crayfish, and mushrooms ; put some crayfish, truffles, and mushrooms on 4 silver skewers ; stick them in the fish ; and serve with the remaining sauce in a boat.

PIKE À LA FINANCIÈRE

Clean and cook a pike as before ;

Make a *ragoût* of Pike Forcemeat *quenelles*, mushrooms, crayfish tails, and truffles, mixed in *Financière* Sauce for Fish (*vide* page 281) ;

Prepare a garnish of :

truffles,	crayfish,
fried carp roes,	mushrooms ;
paupiettes of sole,	

Make a rice *socle* on a dish ; drain and glaze the pike ; lay it on the *socle* ; put the *ragoût* in the dish so as to hide the *socle*, and garnish round with the *paupiettes*, fried roes, mushrooms, truffles, and crayfish ;

Garnish 4 silver skewers with some crayfish, mushrooms, and smelts fried in a ring ; stick the skewers in the pike ; and serve with *Financière* Sauce for Fish.

PIKE WITH QUENELLES

Prepare a pike as above ;

Put it on a dish ;

Make some *quenelles* with Pike Forcemeat and Crayfish Butter:

Glaze the pike; garnish round with the *quenelles*; and serve with *Financière* Sauce for Fish.

PIKE À LA NORMANDE

Clean and cook a pike as directed for Pike *à la Chambord* (*vide* page 430); drain, and put the pike in a dish;

Make a *ragoût* of mushrooms, oysters, and mussels, mixed in *Allemande* Sauce;

Garnish round the pike with this *ragoût*; and serve with *Allemande* Sauce.

CARP À LA CHAMBORD

Scale and clean a large carp through the gills; tie the head with string; put the fish in the fish-kettle, and cover it with *Mirepoix* and claret;

Make a *ragoût* of eel scollops, mushrooms, crayfish tails, and truffles;

Prepare the following for garnish :

Carp Forcemeat *quenelles*,	truffles,
crayfish,	large mushrooms ;

Make a rice *socle* on a dish; drain the carp; glaze it in the oven; and put it on the *socle*;

Strain and skim off the fat from the liquor in which the carp has been cooked;

Reduce it, and add 1 quart of *Espagnole* Sauce; reduce again; strain through a tammy cloth, and mix the prepared *ragoût* in the reduced sauce; pour some of it in the dish, round the carp, and place the garnish round the *socle* so as to hide it;

Put some crayfish, truffles, and large mushrooms on 4 silver skewers; stick them in the carp; and serve with the remaining *ragoût* in a silver casserole.

Remarks on Fish dressed à la Chambord.

I would wish to make it plain with reference to my recipes of fish *à la Chambord*, that, whilst I have four times made use of the general name adopted for this kind of large fish dishes dressed with garnished skewers, those I thus describe constitute, by their different sauces and garnishes, four perfectly distinct removes, similar only in name and mode of dressing.

STUFFED CARP À L'ANCIENNE

The body of the carp in this recipe is entirely removed, and a similar-sized piece of Carp Forcemeat substituted;

Scale a carp; remove all the flesh, and make some forcemeat with it (*vide* page 306);

Cut the head and tail off the bone, leaving about 1 inch of it attached, to fix them in the forcemeat;

Cut a slice of bread ¼ inch thick, 4 inches wide, and of the length intended for the forcemeat carp;

Make a *ragoût* of carp roes, mushrooms, truffles, and crayfish tails, mixed in *Espagnole* Sauce stiffly reduced with Madeira;

Put the slice of bread on a dish; place the head and tail, previously cut off the carp, at each end; then form the carp with the forcemeat, on the bread; when it is of the right shape, scoop out, with a gravy spoon, a hollow in the centre of the forcemeat; fill it with some of the *ragoût;* cover it over with forcemeat 1 inch thick, and smooth the carp over with a wet knife; brush it over with egg; mark the forcemeat with the handle of a teaspoon to represent the scales, and poach it in the oven; put the remaining *ragoût* on the dish on each side of the carp; and serve.

GRANDE MATELOTE

Clean and scale 6 carp;

Clean 4 middle-sized pike;

Clean and skin 2 large eels;

Cut all the above fish in equal-sized pieces;

Slice 8 large onions; fry them in a stewpan with some butter till they are coloured;

Then add:

8 bottles of Burgundy,	4 cloves of garlic, whole,
2 quarts of *Mirepoix*,	6 shalots;
1 large faggot,	

Simmer for an hour, and season slightly with salt and pepper, and strain the liquor;

Put the pieces of carp in a glazing stewpan, and the pieces of pike and eel in another stewpan; pour half the liquor over

3 K

the carp, and the remainder over the pike and eel; and simmer until the fish is done;

Prepare a garnish of

100 small button onions, previously fried and glazed,
100 middle-sized mushrooms,
 18 large crayfish,
Sufficient hard roe to produce 4 portions, each of the size of an egg,
 12 carp soft roes,
 12 fried bread *croutons*;

Drain the pieces of carp, and put them in another stewpan; drain the pike and eel also, and put them in separate stewpans;

Strain, through a silk sieve, the liquor in which the carp, pike, and eel have been cooked; reduce it to a half glaze; add 3 quarts of *Espagnole* Sauce; and reduce again until the sauce coats the spoon;

Strain it through a tammy cloth into a *bain-marie*-pan; pour some of the sauce on the fish in the several stewpans, and warm it without boiling;

Stand all the heads of carp and pike in the centre of a dish to make a foundation; place the pieces of carp all round this to form a first row; on the centre of these, place the piéces of pike to make a second and smaller row; fill the centre with all the unshapely pieces, and place the pieces of eel on the pike to make a third and still smaller row; pour some sauce over the whole; put 12 crayfish and the *croutons* alternately round the dish, against the pieces of carp, and pile up small alternate heaps of onions and mushrooms on the pieces of carp, or first row;

Put, alternately, the four portions of hard roe, and four portions of soft roe on the pieces of pike, or second row;

Place 6 crayfish, claws uppermost, against the pieces of eel; put a circle of onions round the top, and crown the whole with some piled up soft roes;

Serve with the sauce in a boat.

Observation.—This fine dish has the great advantage of being dished without the help of garnished skewers or *croustades*; all its ornamentation is derived from the fish which constitutes it. I remember seeing it thus prepared many years ago by the elder Loyer at Rosny, the seat of the Duchesse de Berry. I was much struck by the handsome appearance of this dish as it left the kitchen. I do not believe that it is possible to produce a

more effective remove by such simple means.   I take this oppor-
tunity of paying a just tribute to the eminent practitioner I have
just mentioned; to a thorough knowledge of his art he joined
a manner so unassuming and kindly, that he was universally
respected by all those who came into contact with him.

ENTRÉES

SALMON WITH OYSTER SAUCE

Take a piece, about 6 inches long, from the middle of a
salmon; put it in a stewpan with some *Mirepoix*; when done,
drain and strip off the skin; glaze, and put the salmon on a
dish;
Garnish each side with some oysters, mixed in *Allemande*
Sauce, and serve with a boat of Oyster Sauce (*vide* page 284).

SALMON WITH FINANCIÈRE SAUCE

Cook a piece of salmon as above;
Take off the skin; glaze the fish, and put it on a dish;
garnish round with a *Financière Ragoût*, as directed for Pike
with *Financière* Sauce (*vide* page 431); and serve the same
sauce in a boat.

SALMON WITH GENEVOISE SAUCE

Cook a piece of salmon, about 6 inches long, in some *Mirepoix*; drain, and dish it on a napkin; garnish round with
bunches of parsley and plain-boiled potatoes, cut to a large
olive-shape; and serve with some *Genevoise* Sauce (*vide* page
279).

BROILED SALMON À LA MAÎTRE D'HÔTEL

Take 4 slices of salmon, $1\frac{1}{2}$ inch thick;
Clean, and dry them in a cloth; put them in a dish with some
oil, sliced onion, sprigs of parsley, salt and pepper; let them
marinade for half an hour;
Drain, and broil the slices over a moderate fire; dish them
on a napkin; garnish round with plain-boiled potatoes, and

bunches of parsley; and serve with some slightly melted *Maître d'Hôtel* Butter in a boat, or with a boat of Caper Sauce.

FILLETS OF SALMON WITH POTATOES À LA MONTREUIL

Trim some thin slices of salmon to the shape and size of fillets of fowl;

Butter a *sauté*-pan with clarified butter, and put the salmon fillets in it; sprinkle them with salt and pepper; put a little more butter over them, and cover with a round of buttered paper;

Cut some potatoes with a ¾-inch vegetable scoop; blanch them in boiling water; drain and toss them in some butter in a *sauté*-pan over the fire, without colouring them;

Make some *Allemande* Sauce; thicken half of it with Lobster Butter;

Cook the fillets in the *sauté*-pan; dish them in a circle round a *croustade*;

Mix the potatoes to that part of the sauce finished with Lobster Butter, and put them in the *croustade*; pour some of the plain sauce over the fillets; and serve the remainder in a boat.

FILLETS OF SALMON WITH VENETIAN SAUCE

Trim and cook some fillets of salmon as above; dish them in a circle; pour over some Venetian Sauce (*vide* page 285); and serve with some of the same sauce separately.

FILLETS OF SALMON WITH RAVIGOTE SAUCE

Prepare and cook some fillets of salmon as aforesaid; dish them in a circle; pour over some *Ravigote* Sauce (*vide* page 287); and serve some of the same sauce separately.

FILLETS OF SALMON WITH OYSTERS AND PRAWNS À LA PARISIENNE

Trim and cook some fillets of salmon as directed for Fillets of Salmon *à la Montreuil* (*vide* above);

Dish them round a *croustade*; fill it with oysters and picked prawns, mixed in Dutch Sauce, with some chopped parsley added; pour some of the same sauce over the fillets; and serve.

FILLETS OF SALMON WITH PÉRIGUEUX SAUCE

Cook some fillets of salmon as before ;

Dish them in a circle ; pour over some *Périgueux* Sauce *Maigre* (*vide* page 280) ; and serve the same sauce in a boat.

BOUDINS OF SALMON FORCEMEAT WITH CRAYFISH BUTTER

Make some Salmon Forcemeat in the same way as directed for Pike Forcemeat (*vide* page 306), and mix it with some Crayfish Butter ;

Make and poach the *boudins* as directed for *Boudins à la Richelieu* (*vide* page 392) ; dish them in a circle ; and pour over some *Allemande* Sauce, finished with Crayfish Butter.

SOLE À LA NORMANDE

Clean a large sole ; strip off the black skin, and make an incision, $\frac{1}{4}$ inch deep, on the skinned part, all along each side of the bone, so as to detach the flesh from the bone ;

Butter a silver dish ; strew it over with some onions, chopped very fine, and previously blanched ; season the sole with salt and pepper ; put it on the dish ; moisten with French white wine, and cook it in the oven ;

Prepare some oysters, mussels, mushrooms, smelts, and *croutons* for garnish ;

Make some *Velouté* Sauce *Maigre* ; add to it the liquor from the sole, and that in which the mussels have been cooked ; reduce it, and thicken it with yolks of egg ;

Place the oysters, mussels, and mushrooms on the sole ; pour over some sauce ; and put the dish in the oven for five minutes, —being careful not to colour the sauce ; garnish the top with the fried smelts and *croutons* ; and serve with the remaining sauce in a boat ;

The *croutons* for Sole *à la Normande* are cut from some rasped crust of French rolls, buttered on each side, and coloured in the oven.

Remarks on Sole à la Normande

·A similar dish, under the name of *Matelote Normande*, is frequently prepared with a sauce made of *Allemande* Sauce, and which then differs but little from the *Poulette* Sauce, so generally used for *Fricassée* of Chicken, Sheep's Trotters, &c.

The foregoing recipe has the advantage of having fish alone as its basis; I do not hesitate in giving it as genuine, as I hold it from M. Langlais, the *chef* of the *Rocher de Cancale*, where it was first prepared; my friend was good enough to communicate it to me in all its details, which are given literally above.

SOLE A LA COLBERT

Clean and strip the skin off a large sole;

Make an incision on each side of the bone down the whole length of the fish; break the bone in pieces with the handle of a knife, so as to facilitate removing it when cooked;

Brush the sole over with egg, and fry it in hot fat; when done, drain it, put it on a dish, and remove the pieces of bone; put some *Maître d'Hôtel* Butter in the cavity left by the bone;

Garnish with fried parsley, and a cut lemon; and serve.

GRATIN OF FILLETS OF SOLES

Trim 24 fillets of soles of an equal size;

Make some Whiting Forcemeat; mix it with some *d'Uxelles*, and spread a layer of it on each fillet, on the side which has been skinned;

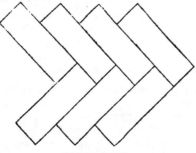

CROSS-SET FILLETS

Fold each fillet in two, and flatten it slightly, to stick the forcemeat together;

Put a layer of forcemeat on a silver dish; upon it place 12

fillets in a circle, the one overlapping the other, putting a little forcemeat between each, to keep the fillets together; then dress the 12 other fillets on these, also in a circle, but crosswise, that is, reversing them, as shown in woodcut (*vide* Cross-set Fillets, page 438).

Place a round piece of crumb of bread, covered with buttered paper, in the centre, to keep the shape of the circle of sole fillets whilst cooking; tie some buttered paper over the fillets, and cook them in the oven; when done, take off the paper, and remove the piece of bread from the centre; wipe the inner part of the ring gently with a cloth, to absorb any butter; pour some Italian Sauce (*vide* page 279) over the fillets; and serve.

FILLETS OF SOLES WITH VENETIAN SAUCE

Prepare 16 fillets of soles, in shape and size as directed for Fillets of Fowls *en Suprême* (*vide* page 388); put them in a buttered *sauté*-pan; sprinkle them with salt and pepper; cover them with a round of buttered paper; cook them, and dish them in a circle; pour over some Venetian Sauce (*vide* page 285); and serve.

FILLETS OF SOLES WITH CRAYFISH AND TRUFFLES À LA JOINVILLE

Trim 16 fillets of soles; fold them in two; and fix a crayfish claw in the top of each fillet;

Put the fillets in a buttered *sauté*-pan, and cover them with a round of buttered paper; cook them and dish them in a circle; fill the centre with picked prawns, and sliced truffles; pour some *Allemande* Sauce, finished with Crayfish Butter, over the garnish but not over the fillets; and serve with some of the sauce separately.

FILLETS OF SOLES WITH OYSTERS

Trim 16 fillets of soles, as directed for Fillets of Soles with Venetian Sauce (*vide* above);

Cook them in a buttered *sauté*-pan, and dish them round a *croustade* filled with oysters mixed in *Allemande* Sauce; pour some of the same sauce over the fillets; and serve with some more in a boat.

FILLETS OF SOLES WITH PRAWNS

Prepare and cook 16 fillets as above;

Dish them round a *croustade* filled with picked prawns; pour some *Allemande* Sauce finished with Shrimp Butter over the prawns and the fillets ; and serve the same sauce separately.

PAUPIETTES OF FILLETS OF SOLES

Trim 16 fillets of soles as before ;

Season them with salt and pepper, and spread a layer of Whiting Forcemeat on each fillet, and roll them round to make the *paupiettes* ; wrap them in buttered paper, and tie them with string to keep them in shape ; poach the *paupiettes* in the oven, take them out of the paper, and put them on a dish ;

Place a turned mushroom on the top of each *paupiette* ; pour over some *Allemande* Sauce, finished with Crayfish Butter ; and serve.

LOBSTER PILAU À LA TURQUE

Cut some lobster tails into scollops ; set them in a buttered *sauté*-pan ; warm them and dish a double row of the scollops in a circle ; fill the centre with rice prepared as directed for Rice Soup *à la Turque* (*vide* page 253) ; pour some thin *Espagnole* Sauce, with a little Cayenne pepper added, over the scollops only ;

Make some *Velouté* Sauce *Maigre* ; add some curry to it ; reduce, and strain it through a tammy cloth ; and serve it in a boat with the lobster.

CARP FORCEMEAT BOUDINS WITH SOFT ROES AND SUPRÊME SAUCE

Make some Carp Forcemeat, and shape it into *boudins*, as directed for *Boudins à la Richelieu* (*vide* page 392) ;

Prepare some carp roes for garnish ; poach the *boudins* ; drain and dish them in a circle ; put the roes in the centre ; pour over some *Velouté* Sauce *Maigre*, reduced with Essence of Mushrooms ; and serve.

FILLETS OF MACKEREL WITH DUTCH SAUCE

Remove the fillets of 4 mackerel ;

Cut them in two, and trim them to a long pear-shape ; put them in a buttered *sauté*-pan ; season them with salt and pepper ; pour over a little clarified butter ; and cover them with a round of buttered paper ;

Put the *sauté*-pan over a moderate fire ; and, when the fillets are done, drain and dish them in a circle ; pour over some Dutch Sauce ; and serve.

FILLETS OF MACKEREL WITH VENETIAN SAUCE

Prepare the fillets of 4 mackerel as before ; substitute Venetian Sauce for the Dutch Sauce ; and serve.

FILLETS OF MACKEREL WITH LOBSTER SAUCE

Trim and cook the fillets of 4 mackerel as before ; dish them in a circle ; fill the centre with some lobster tails, cut in large dice ; pour some Lobster Sauce over the pieces of lobster ; and serve.

FILLETS OF MACKEREL WITH SOFT ROES

Prepare and cook the fillets as directed for Fillets of Mackerel with Dutch Sauce (*vide* page 440); dish them in a circle round a *croustade*, filled with Carp roes; pour some *Ravigote* Sauce over the fillets ; and serve with *Ravigote* Sauce.

FILLETS OF MACKEREL WITH PRAWNS

Cook and dish the fillets round a *croustade* as before ; fill the *croustade* with picked prawn-tails; pour some Shrimp Sauce in the *croustade*, and over the fillets ; and serve.

ORLYS OF FILLETS OF MACKEREL

Take the fillets of 3 mackerel ; cut them lengthwise in three pieces ; put them in a basin with some oil, seasoned with sliced onions, sprigs of parsley, salt, and pepper ; let the fish marinade for half an hour ; then drain the pieces on a cloth, dip them in frying batter, and fry them in hot fat ; drain and pile the *orlys* on a napkin, on a dish ; garnish with fried parsley ; and serve with Tomato Sauce.

PIKE FORCEMEAT BOUDINS AU SALPICON

Make the *boudins* with some Pike Forcemeat, as directed for *Boudins à la Richelieu* (*vide* page 392),—introducing into each *boudin* a portion of *salpicon* made of truffles, carp roes, and

3 L

mushrooms, mixed in stiffly-reduced *Allemande* Sauce : cover the *salpicon* with forcemeat ; and poach the *boudins* as directed at page 392 ; dish them in a circle ; pour over some *Allemande* Sauce ; and serve.

RED MULLET EN PAPILLOTES

Wash 3 red mullet, and cut off the fins ;

Oil a sheet of stiff paper ; make a layer of reduced *d'Uxelles* Sauce on it, of the size of the mullet ; lay the fish on the sauce, and put another layer of sauce on it ; fold over the paper, and close the two edges together to make the *papillote* ; proceed in the same way for the other mullet ; then put them on a gridiron over a moderate fire ; when done, put the *papillotes* on a dish ; and serve.

RED MULLET À LA PROVENÇALE

Prepare 3 mullet as above ;

Make some stuffing with hard-boiled yolks of egg, chopped parsley, butter, and a little garlic ; moisten to a proper consistence with beaten eggs ; and fill the mullet with the stuffing ; wrap them in buttered paper, and broil them over a moderate fire ; when done, remove the paper, and put the fish on a dish ; pour over them some melted *Maître d'Hôtel* Butter, with a little garlic butter added ; and serve.

SALT COD BRANDADE

Steep some salt cod in water until nearly all the saltness has disappeared ; put it in a stewpan, with plenty of water, to boil ; then cover the stewpan, and simmer till the fish is done ; drain it, and remove all skin and bone very carefully ; put the fish in another stewpan, and stir it briskly over the fire for five minutes, adding some olive oil, in small quantities ; take it off the fire, and continue working with the spoon till the fish and oil form a smooth paste ; then add some double cream, and a little pounded garlic, still stirring to mix the whole well together ; taste for seasoning ;

Pile the *brandade* on a dish, and garnish round with *croûtons* of fried bread.

Observation.—The chief thing, in preparing this *brandade*, is to work it thoroughly with a spoon whilst adding the oil.

Fish that has been long in brine should never be used, as it will not work into a smooth enough paste to constitute a successful *brandade*.

GRATIN OF FILLETS OF WHITING

Take the fillets of 6 whiting;

Cook and dish them as directed for *Gratin* of Fillets of Soles (*vide* page 438); pour over some *Allemande* Sauce, finished with Lobster Butter; and serve.

PAUPIETTES OF FILLETS OF WHITING

Make and cook the *paupiettes* as directed for *Paupiettes* of Fillets of Soles (*vide* page 440);

Make a paste *croustade* of the size of the dish, and 2 inches high; place the *paupiettes* in it, leaving a space in the centre; fill this with oysters and mushrooms; pour over some *Allemande* Sauce, reduced with Essence of Mushrooms; and serve.

FRIED FILLETS OF WHITING

Cut and trim the fillets of 6 whiting; brush them over with egg, and bread-crumb them;

Fry the fillets in hot fat till crisp; drain, and dish them on a napkin, and garnish with fried parsley;

Add some butter, lemon-juice, and chopped parsley, to some reduced *Espagnole* Sauce; and serve it in a boat with the fish.

BOUDINS OF WHITING FORCEMEAT WITH RAVIGOTE SAUCE

Make some Whiting Forcemeat, and prepare the *boudins* as directed for *Boudins à la Richelieu* (*vide* page 392), inserting in each a portion of *salpicon* made of shrimp-tails, cut in small dice, and mixed in reduced *Allemande* Sauce;

Poach, and dish the *boudins* in a circle; pour over some *Ravigote* Sauce; and serve.

BOUDINS OF WHITING FORCEMEAT À LA MARINIÈRE

Make the *boudins* as above; put some mussels, cut in small dice and mixed in reduced *Allemande* Sauce, in each *boudin*;

enclose the *salpicon* with forcemeat; poach the *boudins*; and dish them in a circle;

Pour over some *Allemande* Sauce, reduced with the liquor in which the mussels have been cooked and with a little chopped parsley added; and serve.

BOUDINS OF WHITING FORCEMEAT À LA MARÉCHALE

Make the *boudins* as directed for *Boudins* of Whiting Forcemeat with *Ravigote* Sauce;

Brush them over with egg, and bread-crumb them; broil them over a moderate fire; dish them in a circle; and serve with a boat of Half Glaze, with a little lemon-juice added.

FILLETS OF EEL À LA BORDELAISE

Skin and clean an eel; slit it open, and take out the bone; cook the eel in some French white wine, seasoned with a slice of onion, a few sprigs of parsley, and salt and pepper; when the eel is done, press it between two dishes till cold;

Strain the liquor; reduce it, and add some Fish Glaze to it; strain it through the pointed strainer into a *bain-marie* pan;

Trim the eel into fillets similar to Fillets of Fowls *en Suprème* (*vide* page 388);

Put them in a *sauté*-pan; pour a little of the sauce over, and warm them;

Dish them in a circle, and fill the centre with some button onions, previously blanched and glazed; pour over some *Matelote* Sauce (*vide* page 278) with Anchovy Butter, and a little Cayenne pepper added; and serve.

FILLETS OF EEL À L'AMÉRICAINE

Prepare and trim an eel into fillets, as above;

Dip the fillets in butter, and bread-crumb them; broil them over a moderate fire; dish them in a circle; and serve with a boat of reduced *Espagnole* Sauce, with some chopped capsicums added.

FILLETS OF EEL WITH PIKE FORCEMEAT QUENELLES

Prepare and cook the fillets as directed for Fillets of Eel *à la Bordelaise*;

Dish them in a circle; fill the centre with Pike Forcemeat *Quenelles*; pour some *Espagnole* Sauce over the *quenelles*; and serve.

FILLETS OF EEL À LA TARTARE

Cut, trim, and cook an eel as directed for Fillets of Eel *à l'Américaine*;

Dish the fillets in a circle, and fill the centre with Tartar Sauce (*vide* First Part, page 67).

SHELL-FISH

CRAYFISH À LA BORDELAISE

Pick, and wash the crayfish; put them in a stewpan, with some French white wine, sliced onions, parsley, salt, pepper, and grated nutmeg; toss the fish over the fire till they are done; then drain, and keep them warm;

Cut some carrots and onions in very small dice; fry them in butter till they are coloured; moisten them with French white wine, and glaze them; then pour in some *Espagnole* Sauce, and strain in, through a silk sieve, the liquor in which the crayfish have been cooked; reduce the whole; and add some chopped parsley, and Cayenne pepper;

Pile the crayfish in a silver casserole; pour the sauce over them; and serve.

Observation.—Crayfish *à la Bordelaise* require to be highly seasoned, but they should not be made so hot as to become unpleasant to many.

LOBSTER À LA BORDELAISE

Take an unboiled lobster, break off the claws, and cut the tail and body in three or four pieces, according to size; saw the shell of the claws through in three places, without separating them, so as to facilitate removing the flesh when the lobster is cooked;

Put the lobster in a stewpan, and finish dressing and dishing up precisely as directed for Crayfish *à la Bordelaise*.

LOBSTER À LA PROVENÇALE

Cut an unboiled lobster in pieces as above; put them in a stewpan, with some oil, salt, pepper, a sprig of thyme, a bay leaf,

an onion, and a small clove of garlic; toss the lobster over the
fire, until it is done; take the pieces out of the stewpan; wipe off
any herbs adhering to them, and put them in another stewpan:

Add some *Espagnole* Sauce, French white wine, and brandy
to the herbs in the stewpan; reduce the sauce, and strain it
through a tammy cloth on to the lobster; warm and pile up
the pieces of lobster on a dish; pour the sauce over, without
skimming off the fat; and serve.

LOBSTER À L'AMÉRICAINE

Cut some boiled lobster tails into scollops $\frac{1}{4}$ inch thick; set
them in a circle in a silver *casserole*;

Make some sauce as follows:

Wash and chop some shalots; fry them in butter for two
minutes; moisten with French white wine; and cook them;

Then add equal quantities of *Espagnole* Sauce, and Tomato
Purée, and a little Cayenne pepper; and reduce the sauce for
five minutes;

Fill the centre of the *casserole* with the flesh of the claws cut
in small dice, and mixed in some of the sauce; pour the
remainder of the sauce over the scollops; put the *casserole* in
the oven for ten minutes, to warm the lobster; and serve.

COQUILLE FOR HOT HORS-D'ŒUVRE

POTATO CASSEROLE FILLED WITH RABBIT SCOLLOPS

CHAPTER XIII

ENTRÉES OF PASTRY

HOT RAISED PIE À LA FINANCIÈRE

MAKE some paste, with :

1 lb. of flour,	1 pinch of salt,
½ lb. of butter,	1 gill of water ;
3 yolks of egg,	

Work the paste till it is quite smooth, and roll it out ;

Butter an *entrée* pie-mould slightly, and line it of an even thickness, with the paste ; fill it with flour ; put a paste cover on the top, and pinch both together with the pincers ; brush over with egg, and put the crust to bake ;

When done, cut out the cover ½ inch inside the pinched edge ; take out the flour, and brush the inside ; take the crust out of the mould ; egg it inside and out ; and dry it in the oven for four minutes ;

Make some *Financière Ragoût* (*vide* page 295) ;

For garnish prepare :

5 fine crayfish,	5 turned mushrooms,
5 cocks' combs,	1 large truffle ;

Fill the crust with the *ragoût,* and arrange the garnish on the top ;

Glaze the crust with a brush dipped in thin glaze ; and serve.

HOT QUAIL RAISED PIE

Line an *entrée*-mould with paste, as before directed ;

Take 8 quails ; cut them in two, lengthwise ; put the pieces in a *sauté*-pan, with a little clarified butter ; season with salt and pepper, and put the *sauté*-pan on the fire for ten minutes ; when the quails are set, drain, and let them cool ;

Make some forcemeat with ½ lb. of calf's liver, and ½ lb. of fat bacon :

Cut the bacon in small dice ; put it in a *sauté*-pan over the fire, and, when the bacon begins to melt, add the liver, also cut in small pieces ; season with salt, pepper, a little thyme, and a bay leaf ; and fry till the bacon and liver are cooked ; take the pan off the fire, and, when cold, pound the liver and bacon together, in a mortar, and pass the forcemeat through a hair sieve ;

Put a layer of the forcemeat round the bottom of the mould, leaving a hollow in the centre ; upon the forcemeat lay 8 pieces of quail, selecting all those of the same size ; put a little forcemeat between each piece to keep them together ; then make another layer of forcemeat, and set in the 8 other pieces of quail in the same way, finishing with a layer of forcemeat ;

Cut a piece of crumb of bread to fit the hollow in the pie ; wrap a thin slice of fat bacon round the bread, and put it in the centre ; place a paste cover on the top ; pinch the edges together ; brush over with egg, and bake the pie in the oven ;

When done, remove the cover and the piece of bread from the centre ; put the pie on a dish, and fill the centre with sliced truffles, mixed in some *Espagnole* Sauce reduced with Essence of Truffles ; put a circle of cocks' kernels on the top of the forcemeat, and pile up some more sliced truffles in the centre ; and serve.

HOT WOODCOCK RAISED PIE

Line an *entrée*-mould with paste, as aforesaid ;

Take 4 woodcocks, and cut each one in 4 pieces ;

Make the forcemeat as described in the preceding recipe, adding the trail of the woodcocks whilst pounding ;

Fill the mould with layers of forcemeat, and pieces of woodcock as described for Quail Pie, putting all the legs on the bottom layer, and keeping the fillets for the top; put a paste cover on the top, and bake the pie in the oven;

When done, fill the centre with *foie gras* scollops; pour over some *Espagnole* Sauce, reduced with Essence of Woodcock; and serve.

HOT SNIPE RAISED PIE

Take 8 snipes and cut them in two, lengthwise;

Line a mould with paste; fill it with layers of forcemeat and snipe; and finish as directed for Quail Pie;

Fill the centre with sliced truffles; pour over some *Espagnole* Sauce, reduced with Essence of Snipe; and serve.

HOT PARTRIDGE RAISED PIE

Line an *entrée*-mould with paste, as directed for Hot Quail Raised Pie;

Cut 3 partridges in pieces, and fry them for five minutes in a *sauté*-pan with a little clarified butter;

Prepare the same forcemeat as directed for Quail Pie, adding some chopped truffles to it, and fill and finish the pie in the same way.

HOT LARK RAISED PIE

Line an *entrée*-mould with paste, and bake it as directed for Hot Raised Pie *à la Financière* (*vide* page 447);

Prepare 30 larks; remove the gizzards, and cut off the legs and necks; season the larks with salt and pepper, and cook them in a *sauté*-pan with a little butter; when done, drain and put them in the crust, finishing with a circle of the larks set close together, breast outwards, round the top of the pie; fill the centre with turned mushrooms; pour over some *Espagnole* Sauce, reduced with Essence of Larks; and serve.

HOT EEL RAISED PIE

Prepare a pie-crust as above;

Skin and clean a large eel; cut it in pieces $1\frac{1}{4}$ inch long; put them in a stewpan, with some French white wine, sliced onions, sprigs of parsley, thyme, bay leaf, and a very little garlic; boil and simmer till the eel is done; drain the pieces, and put them in a *sauté*-pan;

3 M

Strain the liquor through a silk sieve into a stewpan; add some *Espagnole* Sauce, and reduce it till the sauce coats the spoon; then strain it through a tammy cloth, and pour some of it on to the pieces of eel in the *sauté*-pan; boil for two minutes, and put the eel in the pie-crust; place a circle of turned mushrooms round the top, and pile up some carp soft roes in the centre; pour the remaining sauce over; and serve.

RICE CASSEROLE WITH LAMB SWEETBREADS

Wash 2 pounds of rice in water, twice; drain, and put it in a stewpan with double its quantity of water; season with salt and pepper, and put it on the fire; when the water boils, cover the rice with some thin slices of fat bacon, and put it on a slow fire with some live coals on the cover of the stewpan;

When the rice is cooked, pound it in a mortar; then gather it up in a ball; put it on a baking-sheet, and mould it with the hands to the shape of a *casserole*;

Brush the *casserole* over with a brush dipped in clarified butter, and put it in the oven until it assumes a nice yellow colour;

Trim and remove some of the rice from the inside, and fill the *casserole* with a *blanquette* of lamb sweetbreads, prepared as described for Lamb Sweetbreads in Cases (*vide* page 376); place a circle of larded and glazed lamb sweetbreads round the top, and finish with some cocks' combs in the centre; and serve.

RICE CASSEROLE WITH GAME PURÉE À LA POLONAISE

Make a rice *casserole* as above;

Prepare some Rabbit *Purée* (*vide* page 294), and 10 small fillets of rabbit, *contised* as described for Red Partridge *Purée* with Plovers' Eggs (*vide* page 410), and boil 10 eggs for six minutes;

Fill the *casserole* partially with the *purée*; stand the eggs in it round the top; put a *contised* fillet between each egg, and pile up the remaining *purée* in the centre.

RICE CASSEROLE WITH CHICKEN PINIONS À LA TOULOUSE

Make a rice *casserole* as described for Rice *Casserole* with Lamb Sweetbreads (*vide* above);

Prepare 12 chicken pinions (*vide* Garnishes, page 294); put them to warm in a stewpan with some *Allemande* Sauce; fill the *casserole* with them, and pour over some more *Allemande* Sauce;

Garnish the top with cocks' kernels and turned mushrooms; and serve.

POTATO CASSEROLE WITH BLANQUETTE OF CHICKEN

Make some Potato *Purée*, as described for Potato Croquets, (*vide* page 295); add 6 yolks of egg to it, and stir the *purée* in a stewpan over the fire to dry it; put it on a baking-sheet, and mould it, with the hands, to the shape shewn in the Woodcut (*vide* page 447); brush the *casserole* over with egg, and bake it in a sharp oven till of a nice golden colour;

Prepare a *blanquette*, without truffles, as directed for *Blanquette* of Poulards with Truffles (*vide* page 392); fill the *casserole* with the *blanquette*; and serve.

POTATO CASSEROLE WITH LARDED FILLETS OF CHICKEN

Make a potato *casserole* as above;

Remove the fillets of two chickens; cut each in two length-wise; trim them to a pear-shape, and lard them with thin strips of fat bacon; put them in a buttered *sauté*-pan; cook, and glaze them;

Make some Chicken *Purée* with the remainder of the two chickens; fill the *casserole* with part of the *purée*, and place the larded fillets in a circle round the top; pile up the remaining *purée* in the centre; pour over a little *Allemande* Sauce, reduced with Essence of Chicken; and serve.

POTATO CASSEROLE WITH RABBIT SCOLLOPS

Make a potato *casserole*, as described for Potato *Casserole* with *Blanquette* of Chicken;

Take the fillets of 2 young rabbits; cut each fillet in 3 equal-sized pieces; trim them to a pear-shape; *contise* them with pieces of truffle, and set them in a buttered *sauté*-pan;

Cut into scollops the remaining meat of the rabbits, besides that of 2 other rabbits; put the scollops in a buttered *sauté*-pan, and fry them slightly;

Slice 10 oz. of truffles, previously cooked in Madeira, and cook the fillets in the *sauté*-pan ;

Mix the rabbit scollops and truffles in some *Espagnole* Sauce, reduced with Essence of Rabbit; fill the *casserole* with the mixture, and place the *contised* fillets in a circle round the top ; pour over some more sauce ; and serve.

POTATO CASSEROLE WITH PHEASANT QUENELLES

Make a potato *casserole* as aforesaid ;

Take the fillets of 2 pheasants ; cut each fillet in two pieces, and trim them to the shape of the minion fillets ; making, with the 4 latter, 12 in all ;

Lard 6 of the fillets with fat bacon, and *contise* the other 6 with truffle, and put them in separate *sauté*-pans, slightly buttered ;

Make some forcemeat with the remaining flesh of the pheasants ; and, with two teaspoons, shape it into small *quenelles* ;

Cook the fillets in their respective *sauté*-pans, glazing those that are larded ; poach the *quenelles* ; drain and mix them in some *Espagnole* Sauce, reduced with Essence of Pheasant ; fill the *casserole* with the *quenelles*, and lay the larded and *contised* fillets in a circle alternately round the top; pour over some more sauce ; and serve.

POTATO CASSEROLE WITH FILLETS OF SOLES

Make a *casserole* as directed for Potato *Casserole* with *Blanquette* of Chicken (*vide* page 451) ;

Cut some cooked fillets of soles into round scollops ; put them to warm in a stewpan with some sliced mushrooms, and *Allemande* Sauce ; fill the *casserole* with the mixture ; and serve.

BREAD CROUSTADE WITH STUFFED LARKS

. Cut some crumb of bread to the shape of a *croustade*, and fry it in hot fat, till of an even golden colour; drain, and put it to dry in the oven for a few minutes ;

Bone 30 larks ; stuff them with some *Foie Gras* Forcemeat ; roll each lark to a round shape, and put each one in a *dariole*-mould ; put them to cook in the oven ; take them out of the moulds, and dish them in the *croustade* in the shape of a pyramid; pour over some *Espagnole* Sauce, reduced with Essence of Larks; and serve some more of the sauce, in a boat.

BREAD CROUSTADE WITH FOIES GRAS SCOLLOPS

Make a bread *croustade* as above;

Cut some *foies gras* into equal-sized scollops; put them in a *sauté*-pan, and fry them with clarified butter; drain them well, and mix them in some *Espagnole* Sauce, reduced with Madeira; fill the *croustade* with the scollops; and place a border of truffles, turned to a ball-shape, 1 inch in diameter, round the top; pour over a little sauce; and serve some more, in a boat.

BREAD CROUSTADE WITH LEVERET SCOLLOPS

Make a bread *croustade*, as directed for Bread *Croustade* with Stuffed Larks (*vide* page 452);

Cut some leveret fillets into scollops; fry them in a *sauté*-pan in some clarified butter; drain, and mix them in some *Espagnole* Sauce, reduced with Essence of Leveret, and thickened with the blood;

Fill the *croustade* with the scollops, and place a border of turned mushrooms round the top; pour a little sauce over; and serve some, in a boat.

MACCARONI TIMBALE À LA MILANAISE

Butter a plain *entrée*-mould;

Make some paste, with :

¼ lb. of flour,	3 yolks of egg,
1 oz. of butter,	1 pinch of fine sugar;

Mix all the above thoroughly to the consistence of *Nouilles* Paste; roll it very thin, and cut it out into different shapes with some fancy cutters; arrange these patterns round the buttered mould, and put it on the ice; when firm and cold, brush over the patterns with a wet brush, and line the mould with some thin seven-turns puff paste, made with 1 lb. of flour, to ¾ lb. of butter;

Boil some maccaroni in some broth or stock; drain and season it with salt, pepper, a little grated nutmeg, and some grated Parmesan cheese;

When the maccaroni is cold, fill the *timbale* with it; put a paste cover on the top; and bake in a moderate oven;

When done, turn the *timbale* out of the mould on to a dish ; cut out the top within one inch of the side ; remove half the maccaroni from the inside, and fill the hollow with some *Milanaise Ragoût* made of fillets . of chicken, tongue, and truffles, cut into scollops, sliced mushrooms, and some cocks' combs, the whole mixed in *Allemande* Sauce, and piled up 1½ inch above the top of the *timbale* ;

Place 12 small larded and glazed fillets of chicken in a circle on the top of the crust ; and finish with a large cock's comb on the centre of the *ragoût.*

MACCARONI TIMBALE À LA CHASSEUR

Make a maccaroni *timbale* as before ;

Cut some fillets of rabbits, and some truffles, boiled in Madeira, into scollops ;

Fry the rabbit scollops in a *sauté*-pan in some clarified butter ; drain, and add them to the truffles ; and mix together in some *Espagnole* Sauce, reduced with Essence of Rabbit ;

Take half the maccaroni out of the *timbale*, and fill it with the scollops ; place some even-sized turned mushrooms round the top of the crust ; and serve.

MACCARONI TIMBALE WITH STURGEON SCOLLOPS

Prepare a *timbale*, as directed for Maccaroni *Timbale à la Milanaise* (*vide* page 453) ;

Cut some cooked sturgeon into scollops ; mix them in some *Allemande* Sauce ; take half of the maccaroni out of the *timbale*, and fill it up with the scollops ; and serve.

MACCARONI TIMBALE WITH SALMON AND TRUFFLES

Make and bake a maccaroni *timbale* as before ;

Cut some salmon into equal-sized scollops ; fry them in a *sauté*-pan with a little clarified butter ; season with salt and pepper, and drain them ;

Cut some truffles, previously cooked in Madeira, into scollops ; add them to the salmon scollops, and mix both together in some *Espagnole* Sauce, reduced with Essence of Truffles ;

Turn the *timbale* out of the mould ; remove half the maccaroni from the inside ; fill it with the scollops ; and serve.

NOUILLES TIMBALE WITH HAM

Make 2 pounds of flour into *Nouilles* Paste (*vide* First Part, page 186); roll it very thin; cut it into *nouilles*; blanch, drain, and put them in a stewpan with a little butter, and 6 yolks of egg; season with salt and pepper, and stir the *nouilles* over the fire for three minutes, to dry them;

Butter a plain *entrée*-mould; put a round of paper at the bottom, and fill it with the *nouilles*; when cold, turn the *timbale* out of the mould; egg and bread-crumb it twice; put it on the drainer, and fry it in hot fat till of an even golden colour; drain it, and cut out the top within 1 inch of the side; remove the *nouilles* from the centre to within 1 inch of the bottom, and fill the *timbale* with some *nouilles* prepared separately, and tossed in a stewpan with some butter, *Allemande* Sauce, and grated Parmesan cheese, and with some boiled ham, cut in small dice, mixed with them.

NOUILLES TIMBALE AU SALPICON

Make a *nouilles* timbale as described in the preceding recipe;

Prepare a *salpicon* of fillets of chicken, tongue, and truffles, cut in small dice, and mixed in *Espagnole* Sauce, reduced with Madeira; add this *salpicon* to some *nouilles* prepared separately, and mixed in some *Allemande* Sauce, with some butter and grated Parmesan cheese; fill the *timbale* with the whole, well mixed together; and serve.

NOUILLES TIMBALE WITH PARTRIDGE SCOLLOPS

Prepare a *timbale* as directed for *Nouilles Timbale* with Ham, (*vide* above);

Cut some fillets of partridges into scollops; fry them with a little butter in a *sauté*-pan; drain, and mix them in some *Espagnole* Sauce, reduced with Essence of Partridge;

Add the scollops to some *nouilles*, tossed in a stewpan with some butter, reduced *Espagnole* Sauce, and grated Parmesan cheese; fill the *timbale* with the *nouilles* and scollops, well mixed together; and serve.

VOL-AU-VENT À LA FINANCIÈRE

Make some puff paste, with:
1 lb. of flour,

1 lb. of butter,
¼ oz. of salt ;

as directed for Puff Paste Cake (*vide* First Part, page 198); give the paste 6 turns, and roll it out to a ¾-inch thickness; lay a stewpan cover, of the size of the dish on which the *vol-au-vent* will be served, on the paste, and cut round it with a small plain or fluted knife ;

Turn the paste over on to a baking-sheet; brush over the top with egg, and make a circular incision, ¼ inch deep, with a knife, leaving a 1-inch margin all round ;

Put the paste in the oven; and, when it is cooked, remove the cover, which will have risen in the baking, and trim off the uncooked paste from the inside; brush the crust inside with egg, and put it back for five minutes in the oven ;

Put the *vol-au-vent* on a dish; fill it with *Financière Ragoût* (*vide* page 295) ;

Place 4 large crayfish on the top, with a cock's comb between each, and a large turned mushroom in the centre ; and serve.

VOL-AU-VENT WITH CHICKEN FORCEMEAT QUENELLES

Prepare a *vol-au-vent* crust as before ;
Butter a *sauté*-pan slightly ;

With two tablespoons, shape some Chicken Forcemeat *quenelles* of the size of an egg; set them in the *sauté*-pan; pour some boiling *consommé* over the *quenelles*; poach, drain, and mix them in some *Allemande* Sauce, and fill the *vol-au-vent* with the *quenelles* ;

Place some truffle scollops and turned mushrooms, in a circle, round the top, and pile up some sliced truffles in the centre ; and serve.

VOL-AU-VENT WITH RABBIT FORCEMEAT QUENELLES

Make a *vol-au-vent* crust as described for *Vol-au-vent à la Financière* (*vide* page 455); fill it with some Rabbit Forcemeat *quenelles*, mixed in some *Espagnole* Sauce, reduced with Essence of Rabbit; and serve.

VOL-AU-VENT WITH SALMON SCOLLOPS

Prepare a *vol-au-vent* crust as aforesaid ;
Cut some cooked salmon into equal-sized scollops ; mix them

in some *Allemande* Sauce ; fill the *vol-au-vent* with the scollops ; place 5 crayfish round the top to form a border, and pile up some sliced mushrooms in the centre ; and serve.

VOL-AU-VENT WITH TURBOT À LA BÉCHAMEL

Prepare a *vol-au-vent* crust as directed for *Vol-au-vent à la Financière* (*vide* page 455) ;

Cut some cooked turbot into scollops, and mix them in some *Béchamel* Sauce *Maigre* ;

Fill the crust with the scollops, and place 5 crayfish in a circle round the top ; and serve.

VOL-AU-VENT WITH SALT COD À LA BÉCHAMEL

Make and bake a *vol-au-vent* crust as above ; reserving the paste cover ;

Fill the *vol-au-vent* with some boiled salt cod scollops, mixed in *Béchamel* Sauce *Maigre* ; lay the paste cover on the top ; and serve.

VOL-AU-VENT WITH EGGS À LA BÉCHAMEL

Prepare a *vol-au-vent* crust as directed for *Vol-au-vent à la Financière*, reserving the paste cover ;

Boil some eggs for ten minutes ; cool, peel, and cut them in slices $\frac{1}{4}$ inch thick ; mix the slices lightly, so as not to break them, in some *Béchamel* Sauce *Maigre* ; fill the *vol-au-vent* with the eggs ; put on the paste cover ; and serve.

VOL-AU-VENT A LA NORMANDE

Prepare a *vol-au-vent* crust as above ;

Make a *Ragoût à la Normande* of fillets of soles, cut into scollops, oysters, mussels, and sliced mushrooms ;

Reduce some *Velouté* Sauce *Maigre* with the liquor in which the mussels have been cooked ; thicken it with yolks of egg ; add the *ragoût* to the sauce ; mix, and fill the *vol-au-vent* with it ; place the paste cover on the top ; and serve.

VOL-AU-VENT WITH FISH QUENELLES AND SOFT ROES

Prepare a *vol-au-vent* crust as aforesaid ;

With two teaspoons, mould some Pike Forcemeat *quenelles* to the size of a pigeon's egg ; poach and mix the *quenelles* in some *Périgueux* Sauce *Maigre* ; fill the *vol-au-vent* with them ; place some carp soft roes on the top ; and serve, with some more sauce in a boat.

VOL-AU-VENT

STUFFED EGGS

CHAPTER XIV

ENTREMETS, OR SECOND COURSE DISHES

OMELET WITH TRUFFLES

BREAK and beat 8 eggs in a basin; season them with salt, pepper, and a very little grated nutmeg;

Slice ¼ lb. of truffles, boiled in Madeira, and warm them in some *Espagnole* Sauce, reduced with Essence of Truffles; fry the omelet, and place the truffles on it, before folding the sides over to an oval shape; when the omelet is coloured, turn it on to a dish; pour round it some *Espagnole* Sauce, reduced with Essence of Truffles; and serve.

OMELET WITH ASPARAGUS PEAS

Make an omelet with 8 eggs, very slightly salted; garnish it, before folding, with asparagus peas, mixed in *Allemande* Sauce;

When coloured, turn the omelet on to a dish; pour some *Allemande* Sauce round it; and serve.

OMELET WITH CRAYFISH TAILS

Make an omelet as above; and, before folding it, garnish with some crayfish tails cut in dice, and mixed in *Allemande* Sauce thickened with Crayfish Butter; turn the omelet on to a dish; pour some sauce round it; and serve.

OMELET WITH MORILS

Pick and wash some morils (or small red mushrooms); cut them in pieces, and put them in a stewpan with some butter, lemon-juice, and salt; boil for five minutes, and drain the morils;

Reduce some *Velouté* Sauce, together with the liquor in which the morils have been cooked; mix them in some of the sauce, and put them in the centre of the omelet; fold it, and put it on a dish; pour the remainder of the sauce round it; and serve.

OMELET WITH SHRIMPS

Cut some shrimp tails in two, and mix them in some *Velouté* Sauce reduced with Shrimp Butter;

Fry an omelet; put the shrimps in it before folding it; turn the omelet on to a dish; pour some of the same sauce round it; and serve.

OMELET WITH CARDOON PURÉE

Prepare some Cardoon *Purée* (*vide* page 300);

Make an omelet, and put the *purée* in the centre before folding it; turn the omelet on to a dish; and serve.

OMELET WITH ARTICHOKE PURÉE

Proceed as directed in the preceding recipe,—substituting Artichoke *Purée* for the Cardoon *Purée*.

ENTREMET OF THREE DIFFERENT OMELETS

Make three omelets;

Garnish one with crayfish tails cut in pieces; another with asparagus peas; and the third with sliced truffles, as directed above;

Put the three omelets on the same dish, and serve with a boat of *Velouté* Sauce, reduced with Essence of Mushrooms.

Observation.—This dish may be served as a remove for luncheons.

EGGS BROUILLÉS WITH TRUFFLES

Break 8 new-laid eggs in a stewpan;
Add:

½ gill of double cream,
¼ lb. of butter,
a little salt, and grated nutmeg;

Stir briskly with a spoon over the fire, till the eggs begin to set, and add 3 tablespoonfuls of chopped truffles; mix, and put the whole on a dish; garnish with *croutons* of bread fried in butter; and serve.

EGGS BROUILLÉS WITH ASPARAGUS PEAS

Proceed as above,—substituting some asparagus peas for the chopped truffles.

STUFFED EGGS

Boil 12 new-laid eggs for ten minutes; cut them in two, lengthwise; remove the yolks; pass them through a hair sieve, and pound them in a mortar, together with an equal quantity of butter, adding 2 eggs, some salt, pepper, and grated nutmeg, and a tablespoonful of chopped parsley, whilst pounding; mix thoroughly, and put the whole in a basin;

Put a layer of the above stuffing on a silver dish:

Fill the cavity in the eggs with some more of the stuffing; smooth it over with a wet knife, and place the eggs in the dish; baste them with a little butter, and put them in a brisk oven for a few minutes to colour them; and serve with Tomato Sauce, separately.

CARDOONS WITH MARROW

Prepare some Cardoons as for Garnish (*vide* page 298);

Put them in a silver casserole, and pour over a little *Espagnole* Sauce;

Toast some slices of crumb of bread ¼ inch thick, and cut them in strips 2 inches by 1 inch;

Blanch some marrow in boiling water; drain and spread it thickly on the pieces of toast; sprinkle a little salt over them; glaze and put them in a very hot oven for four minutes; lay the *croutons* on the cardoons; and serve immediately.

CARDOONS EN BLANQUETTE

Prepare and cook the cardoons as directed page 298; cut them into scollops; mix them in some *Allemande* Sauce; put them in a silver casserole; and garnish with *croutons* of bread, fried in butter.

ARTICHOKES À LA LYONNAISE

Cut some artichokes in quarters; remove the outside leaves, and the stringy part inside, and trim the bottoms;

Blanch the pieces in boiling water; drain, and put them in a *sauté*-pan with some clarified butter, lemon-juice, and salt, and pepper; simmer till the artichokes are done, and put them in a moderate oven until they assume a light brown colour; drain, and put the pieces of artichoke in a silver casserole;

BLANCHING PAN

Cut an onion in small dice, and fry it in a small stewpan with a little butter till coloured;

Put 1 gill of *Blond de Veau* in the *sauté*-pan to melt the glaze left from the artichokes; strain it into the stewpan containing the onion; add some *Espagnole* Sauce, and reduce the whole for five minutes; add a tablespoonful of chopped parsley; pour the sauce over the artichokes; and serve.

ARTICHOKE-BOTTOMS À L'ITALIENNE

Prepare some artichoke-bottoms as directed for Garnish (*vide* page 298); dress them in a circle in a silver casserole, overlapping one another; pour over some Italian Sauce (*vide* page 278); and serve.

STUFFED ARTICHOKE-BOTTOMS

Prepare the artichoke-bottoms as before;

Fill the hollow part with some Chicken Forcemeat, with some *d'Uxelles* added;

Set them in a buttered *sauté*-pan, and put them in the oven to poach the forcemeat; dress them in a silver casserole; pour over some Half Glaze; and serve.

STUFFED CABBAGE LETTUCE WITH CROUTONS

Prepare some lettuces as directed for Stuffed Cabbage Lettuce Soup (*vide* page 237);

Cut some *croutons* of bread-crumb $\frac{1}{4}$ inch thick, and of the shape of the lettuces, and fry them in clarified butter;

Dress the lettuces and *croutons* alternately in a circle, in a silver casserole; pour over some Half Glaze; and serve.

TRUFFLES À LA SERVIETTE

Wash and clean the truffles very carefully; boil them in some *Mirepoix* and Madeira; dish them up inside a folded napkin; and serve, with some cold butter separately.

TRUFFLES STEWED IN CHAMPAGNE

Wash and clean the truffles; boil them in 1 bottle of dry Champagne, and an equal quantity of *Blond de Veau*, with salt and grated nutmeg to season;

Drain the truffles, and put them in a silver casserole;

Strain the liquor through a silk sieve into another stewpan; reduce it one half; pour it over the truffles; and serve.

TIMBALE OF TRUFFLES À LA TALLEYRAND

Observation.—This *timbale* has been named after the Prince de Talleyrand, because it was first prepared in the Prince's establishment by his celebrated *Chef* M. Louis Esbrat, whom I have already mentioned in these pages. I could not think of altering the name; for it has, by the great success of the dish, become an acknowledged culinary term.

Clean and wash thoroughly some fine equal-sized truffles; peel and cut them in slices ¼ inch thick;

Melt some butter in a *sauté*-pan; put in the slices of truffles; season with salt and grated nutmeg; and toss them well in the butter,—being careful not to break them;

Line a plain round mould with paste, as directed for Maccaroni *Timbale à la Milanaise* (*vide* page 453);

Fill it with the sliced truffles; put a paste cover on the top; make a small hole in the centre, to facilitate the cooking; and bake in a hot oven;

When the paste is done, stop up the hole with a piece of paste; turn the *timbale* out of the mould on to a dish; make a small opening in the top, and pour in some Half Glaze through a funnel; cover the hole with a slice of truffle; and serve.

TURNED MUSHROOMS WITH CROUTONS

Prepare the mushrooms as directed for Garnishes (*vide* page 291); drain, and mix them in some *Allemande* Sauce, reduced with Essence of Mushrooms, and put them in a silver casserole;

Cut the rasped crust of some French rolls in strips, 2 inches by 1 inch; dip them in butter, and put them on a baking-sheet in a hot oven for three minutes; place these *croutons* in a circle on the mushrooms; and serve.

VEGETABLE MACÉDOINE

Prepare a *macédoine* of carrots, turnips, cauliflowers, asparagus peas, French beans and peas; boil and glaze the vegetables as described in the Chapter on Garnishes (*vide* pages 295 to 298);

Put the whole in a *sauté*-pan with some *Velouté* Sauce, reduced with Essence of Vegetables; add a piece of butter; mix, and pour the *macédoine* in a silver casserole; and serve.

VEGETABLE MACÉDOINE MAIGRE

Proceed as before,—substituting some *Béchamel* Sauce *Maigre* for the *Velouté* Sauce.

CELERY

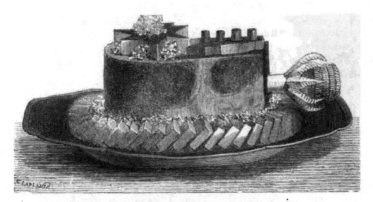

COLD RIB OF BEEF WITH JELLY

CHAPTER XV

COLD DISHES

PRELIMINARY REMARKS

Of Ornamentation in Cookery

I HAVE left to now what I had to say concerning decoration in Cookery, thinking that my remarks would find their proper place here, when treating of the preparation of Cold Dishes,— the part of Cookery in which ornamentation is most employed, and where it is most called for.

The differences of opinion are as numerous on this subject as they are upon most other culinary questions : some, who are great partisans of the mode of serving *à la Russe,* wish to do away with ornamentation altogether ; and it is a patent fact, that if dishes only reach the table carved ready for serving, it will be superfluous to lose time in their decoration or arrangement.

The decline of ornamentation is to be regretted. I have already stated my own opinion in the matter ; I am thoroughly convinced that true Cookery requires to be presented under

certain conditions of style and elegance, which are at once a
mark of its worth and genuineness. Those who will not admit
this consideration will be very liable to neglect the quality of
the preparations themselves, and will soon fall into a careless
habit of working, and of following their art in a mechanical
way, without taking any pride or interest in it.

On the other hand, I must own that in many instances this
love of ornamentation has been carried to unreasonable lengths;
and I have known cooks possessed by a perfect hobby for
decorating and beautifying everything; and who could not
serve the simplest dish without a profusion of puerile accessories
and would-be ornaments.

I have seen some employ to this end perfectly irrelevant
materials, which on no account should be introduced in things
which are made to be eaten. Thus, I have seen fat bacon
used as a substitute for Minion Fillets of Poultry for *Aspics en
Bellevue*; I have seen others make use, for the same purpose, of
a substance they called hard paste, but which was nothing else
but dried bread-crumb: in many instances it would break off,
and fall into and spoil the garnishes. Such delinquencies have
contributed, in a very marked manner, to render the practice of
decoration unpopular; as has also been the case where cooks
have attempted, with their cold dishes and sweet *entremets*, to
rivalise the architect and the sculptor, by trumpery lard or sugar
imitations of Greek temples, feudal castles, or martial trophies;
with reference to which they have been deservedly laughed at.

The very nature of the materials we use, and the particularly
ephemeral character of our productions, should certainly
convince us of the folly of attempting to match ourselves
against the higher arts, of which we can only reproduce clumsy
and ridiculous imitations.

I believe that the rule to lay down for all culinary decoration
(which is quite a *specialité* of itself, in the same way as stage
decoration) is this: that any ornament of a dish is either
intended for eating, or to make the thing it accompanies more
inviting to the eye and thence to the palate.

This rule, together with a man's natural talent and intelligence,
should keep him within the legitimate resources of his art, and
clear of pretentious attempts at monumental ornamentation.

I have endeavoured, in my recipes relating to Cold Dishes, to
specify this happy mean of decoration.

It is impossible to deny that large cold removes, dished up
with the proper style and richness, are calculated to grace a well-

decked table or sideboard ; and I do not fancy that any substitute for this mode of culinary ornamentation will ever be found.

But I cannot impress too much on my readers that I do not believe in a Cookery meant for the eye alone ; the crucial test is the palate, and the main consideration is, that after the guests have admired a dish prepared to please their sight, they may feel at least an equal pleasure in partaking of it.

REMARKS ON SOCLES AND ON THE MOULDING OF ASPIC JELLIES

On Socles in General

These *socles* or stands are used to raise the Removes and *Entrées*; to give them a better appearance; and to allow of more room for garnishing.

They have been made of all kinds of substances; but the best *socles* to use are the simplest, those entirely free from architectural pretensions, and composed of nothing which is likely to impair the dishes set upon them.

SOCLES OR STANDS FOR LARGE COLD DISHES

These *socles* are made of fat, prepared in the following manner :

Pick and chop some mutton-kidney suet; let it steep in cold water for several hours; drain it well, and put it in a stewpan over a slow fire; when thoroughly melted, without colouring, strain the fat through a cloth; mix it with an equal quantity of white and clean lard; and, when this is melted, strain the whole through a cloth into a large basin to cool; then whip it with a very clean whisk till quite cold and smooth;

Stick a block of wood, of the shape required for the *socle*, only smaller, on a baking-sheet with a little fat, and begin to lay the whipped fat gradually round the block, and shape it with a *profile* cut in wood to represent a vase or cup; when the first layer is quite cold, spread some more of the fat all round till the *socle* is completed;

By passing the *profile*, dipped in hot water, continually round the fat, a smooth surface, similar to that of parian, is obtained;

When the *socle* is completed, put the baking-sheet over the fire for a minute to melt the fat which holds the block of wood; remove the *socle*, and put it on a round of paper on another baking-sheet, ready to be decorated with coloured paste, or with flowers made of coloured fat, or, preferably, with natural flowers, which, when tastefully arranged, will always constitute the best ornamentation, one not to be equalled by artificial means.

FLAT SOCLES FOR RAISING REMOVES AND ENTRÉES

It used to be the fashion to make these stands or *socles* of fat. I consider the practice objectionable, as being likely to impart a disagreeable fatty taste to the preparations dished upon them; this risk is avoided by employing rice *socles*, coated with *Montpellier*, Lobster, or even plain butter.

I have adopted this plan, which I think the best of any.

The rice *socles* are made thus:

Wash 2 lbs. of rice; put it in a stewpan with one gallon of water, and a little salt; boil on a very slow fire; and, when the rice is done, pound it in a mortar, and mould it to the required shape.

For hot dishes, egg the *socle* over, and put it in the oven to colour it.

For cold dishes, spread the rice over very smoothly with either *Montpellier*, Lobster, or plain butter.

On the Moulding of Aspic *Jellies*

Prepare the *Aspic* Jelly as directed for Meat Jelly (*vide* page 275),—adding some lemon-juice when clarifying it.

The jelly should not be moulded until it is quite cold; as, should it retain any degree of heat, it would be liable to loosen the ornaments laid in the moulds, or on the minion fillets placed therein; on the other hand, avoid using the jelly too cold; for, if beginning to set, it would, when poured into the mould, fill it with air bubbles, and give the *aspic* a dull and misty appearance; it is also very necessary to pour the subsequent layers of jelly in a mould as soon as the preceding one is set, in order to guard against any dampness forming on the top, which would prevent the layers adhering to each other, and might possibly cause the *aspic* to break on its being turned out of the mould.

Fillets or other ornaments introduced in jellies must always be kept half an inch below the edge of the mould, so that, by completing the filling of the mould with a layer of plain jelly, a solid basis be secured when the *aspic* is turned out.

Moulds should always be well set in pounded ice.

These observations on moulding apply equally to second-course jellies garnished with fruit, &c.

- - - - - -

LARGE COLD DISHES—ENTRÉES—ENTREMETS— HORS D'ŒUVRE

LARGE COLD DISHES

TURKEY GALANTINE

Pick, draw, and singe a fat hen-turkey; cut off the legs, pinions, and neck, leaving the crop skin whole; bone it entirely, and remove almost all the meat from the fillets and legs, and free the leg parts of all sinew;

Make some forcemeat, with :

4 lbs. of fillet of veal, well freed from skin and gristle ;

4 lbs. of fat bacon, freed from rind and gristle :

Season with 2½ oz. of spiced salt ;

Chop and pound both together in a mortar ;

Make a *salpicon* of 1½ lb. of tongue, 1½ lb. of peeled truffles, and 1½ lb. of blanched fat bacon ;

Cut the whole in ¾-inch dice ;

Spread the turkey-skin on the board; on it make a 1-inch layer of the forcemeat; then a layer of the meat cut from the

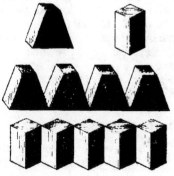

CROUTONS OF MEAT JELLY

turkey; sprinkle over some spiced salt, and make a layer of *salpicon*, another layer of forcemeat; spread on it the remainder of the turkey-meat; season with spiced salt; make another layer of *salpiçon*, and lastly a layer of forcemeat; fold over the skin to enclose the whole, and sew it together with a trussing needle and fine twine;

Wrap the *galantine* in a napkin, and tie each end securely; tie it across in two places, to keep the *galantine* of an oval shape with round ends; put it in a braizing stewpan; cover it well with *Mirepoix*;

Close the stewpan, and boil and simmer gently for four hours; when the *galantine* is done, take the stewpan off the fire; let the *galantine* cool in the liquor for an hour;

Drain and untie it; tie it up again in a clean napkin; and put it on a dish with a 7-lbs. weight on the top; when cold, take the *galantine* out of the napkin; put it on a baking-sheet in front of the open oven for two minutes to melt the fat; wipe it off with a cloth, and glaze the *galantine* with Chicken Glaze;

Make a rice *socle* 2 inches high, and of the size and shape of the *galantine*; spread some *Montpellier* Butter on it, and put it on a dish; place the *galantine* on it, and garnish the top of the *galantine* and round the bottom of the *socle* with *croutons* of Meat Jelly (*vide* Woodcut, page 470).

Three silver skewers, garnished with cocks' combs and truffles, may be stuck in the *galantine*, and will improve its appearance.

YORK HAM

Trim a ham weighing about 16lbs.; steep it in cold water over night; tie it in a cloth, and boil it gently for five hours in a large pan, with plenty of water; when done, drain, and put the ham, rind downwards, on a dish, to cool;

When cold, remove the rind, and trim the ham to a nice shape; glaze it, and dish it on a rice *socle*, covered with *Montpellier* Butter;

Garnish with *croutons* of jelly; and serve.

Silver skewers, garnished with cocks' combs and truffles, may be added.

NOIX OF BEEF WITH MEAT JELLY

Trim a *noix* of beef, leaving the fat on the top; lard through the fleshy part with large alternate strips of fat bacon, and of raw York ham;

Tie some slices of fat bacon on all the lean part; and put the meat in a braizing stewpan, with sufficient *Mirepoix* to cover it;

Boil and simmer gently for six hours; let the beef cool in the liquor; then drain, and trim the meat so as to show the strips of bacon and ham; trim the fat also, and cut a pattern on it; glaze the meat,—keeping the fat white;

Dish the beef on a rice *socle*, covered with *Montpellier* Butter; garnish with *croutons* of jelly; and serve.

STUFFED LOIN OF VEAL

Take a loin of veal, with three neck-bones attached, and bone it entirely;

Make some forcemeat, as directed for Turkey *Galantine* (*vide* page 470);

Cut 2 veal kidneys in 1-inch dice; cut, in the same way, an equal quantity of truffles and tongue; add the whole to the forcemeat; mix, and lay it on the veal; fold the sides over to enclose the forcemeat, and tie with string, to keep the meat of an oblong shape;

BRAIZING STEWPAN

Wrap it in a napkin as described for Turkey *Galantine*, and put it in a braizing stewpan, covering it with *Mirepoix*;

Boil and simmer gently for four hours; take the stewpan off

the fire, and, when cool, drain and untie the veal; wrap it up, in the same way, in a clean napkin, and put it on a dish, with a weight on the top;

When cold, untie the meat; trim, and glaze it with Meat Glaze; dish it on a rice *socle*, covered with *Montpellier* Butter; garnish with *croutons* of jelly; and serve.

FILLET OF BEEF WITH JELLY

For a remove, take 2 whole fillets of beef;

Trim, and lard them through with alternate strips of fat bacon and ham; roll each fillet round to form a ring, and tie them with string to keep them in shape; cover them with thin slices of fat bacon, and wrap each fillet in a napkin;

Put them in a braizing stewpan, with sufficient *Mirepoix* to cover them;

Boil and simmer for three hours; let the fillets cool, and drain them; untie, and glaze them; and put the two fillets on a rice *socle*, covered with *Montpellier* Butter;

Garnish with *croutons* of jelly; and stick 6 silver skewers, garnished with cocks' combs and truffles, in the fillets; and serve.

ASPIC WITH DECORATED FILLETS À LA BELLEVUE

Trim 24 fillets of chicken as for *Suprème*;

Put them in a buttered *sauté*-pan; fry them; drain, and put them on a plate to cool;

Cut 24 slices of truffle of the size and shape of the top of the chicken fillets;

Trim the minion fillets; cook, and drain them;

When cold, trim them again, and decorate them with patterns of truffle and tongue; stick the patterns on the minion fillets with a little white jelly, stiffened with clarified isinglass;

Pour some Chicken *Chaud-froid* Sauce (*vide* page 288) on the large fillets;

Take a large fluted oval cylinder-mould, and set it in the ice; put a small turned mushroom at the bottom of each rib of the mould;

Pour in a little *Aspic* Jelly, to cover the mushrooms; when this is set, place a decorated minion fillet in each rib, securing it at the top of the mould with a little piece of butter;

Pour some more jelly in the mould, to bring the thickness of

3 P

jelly to 1¼ inch; then place, alternately, 12 fillets of chicken, round side downwards, and 12 slices of truffle, in a circle in the mould; pour in a little jelly, and, when it is set, pour in some more, so as to cover the fillets; let this jelly set, and on it dress the remaining fillets and truffles in a circle, reversed to the first;

Remove the butter from the top of the minion fillets, and fill the mould with jelly;

Cover the mould with a baking-sheet, and put some ice on the top;

When the *aspic* has been in the ice for two hours, turn it out of the mould (by dipping it quickly in hot water), on to a rice *socle*, covered with butter; garnish round with *croutons* of jelly; and serve.

PAIN DE FOIE GRAS, OR FOIE GRAS FORCEMEAT CAKE

Cut 4 pounds of fat bacon in dice; put it in a *sauté*-pan on the fire, and fry it gently, seasoning with 1 sliced shalot, 4 sprigs of parsley, and some spiced salt; when the bacon is melted, add 4 pounds of white calf's liver, also cut in dice; fry briskly for four minutes, stirring with a wooden spoon; and put the whole on a dish to cool;

Take 4 lbs. of *foies gras*; cut it into 20 scollops, 2½ inches long, 1½ inch wide, and 1 inch thick;

When cold, put the fried liver and bacon in a mortar, together with the trimmings of the *foies gras* and 1 lb. of Bread Panada; pound the whole well together, adding 4 eggs; press the forcemeat through a hair sieve; taste for seasoning, and put it in a basin;

Make a *salpicon* with 1 lb. of boiled fat bacon, freed from skin and gristle, and 1 lb. of truffles,—both cut in large dice;

Butter a large plain oval mould, and also a smaller one; put a piece of buttered paper at the bottom of each mould; on the paper in each mould put a ¾-inch layer of the forcemeat; then a layer of the *foie gras* scollops and *salpicon*; and continue the layers of forcemeat, scollops, and *salpicon*, till the moulds are full; put them to cook *au bain-marie*—the large *pain* for an hour and a half, and the small one for three quarters of an hour;

When cold, warm the moulds on the stove, to enable you to turn out the *pains*; trim, and glaze them with Meat Glaze;

Dish the large *pain* on a rice *socle*, covered with *Montpellier*

Butter, and the small one on the top of the large one; garnish with *croutons* of Meat Jelly; and serve.

COLD STUFFED POULARDS WITH VEGETABLES

Take 2 poulards; bone them whole, leaving only the leg and wing bones; stuff the poulards with some forcemeat, prepared as directed for Turkey *Galantine* (*vide* page 470); truss them as for boiling, keeping them in shape; wrap each poulard in a napkin, and boil them gently for two hours, in some *Mirepoix*;

Drain, untie and retie the poulards in clean napkins; and put them on a dish to cool;

Make a rice *socle*; spread it over with Montpellier Butter; put it on a dish, and fix a block of fried bread on it (*vide* Woodcut, page 407);

Untie the poulards; wipe them, and pour over them some *Béchamel Chaud-froid* Sauce (*vide* page 288);—be particular that the sauce be of the right degree of cold, and in sufficient quantity to allow of coating the poulards of an even thickness in one operation;

Place them on the rice *socle*, resting the backs against the block of bread; and garnish between and round the poulards with:

Cauliflowers;	Turnips;
Carrots;	French beans;
. Brussels sprouts;	Peas;

mixed together in some of the *Chaud-froid* Sauce;

Place some *croutons* of jelly round the dish;

Garnish 3 silver skewers with small cups made of such vegetables as artichoke-bottoms, carrots, &c., and filled with peas mixed in jelly; stick a skewer in each poulard, and one in the centre of the bread; and serve.

WILD BOAR'S HEAD

Singe and clean a boar's head carefully;

Remove the ears;—which should be boiled separately, and not too much done, so that they may retain their shape;

Bone the head; sprinkle it with salt, and put it to pickle in a basin for four hours;

Take the fillets of 4 young rabbits; cut them in large dice, to make a *salpicon*, with:

2 lbs. of peeled truffles;

2 lbs. of tongue;

2 lbs. of boiled fat bacon;

all cut in 1-inch dice;

Free the remaining flesh of the rabbits from skin and gristle, and chop it coarsely, together with 4 lbs. of veal, and 4 lbs. of fat bacon, similarly freed of gristle and skin; season with 3 oz. of spiced salt; and put this forcemeat in a basin;

Drain the head; wipe it, and season it with a tablespoonful of prepared spices, without any salt; put a layer of the forcemeat on the head; then a layer of well-mixed *salpicon*, and continue alternating thus till the whole is used;

Wrap the head up in shape in a cloth, and boil it for five hours in some *Mirepoix* and a bottle of Madeira; ascertain if the head be done; let it cool; drain, and take it out of the cloth; and wrap it up again in a clean cloth, and bind it round very tightly with tape 1 ½ inch wide, beginning at the snout, and binding round and round the head; when quite cold, untie the head; put it in the oven for a minute, and wipe off the fat with a cloth;

Trim the back part of the head; put the ears in their places; fixing them in with some small wooden skewers and using a mixture of lard and mutton suet to hide the skewers;

Mix some clean soot with ¼ lb. of lard, and rub it all over the head, to produce a shiny black surface.

Some cooks use chocolate for this colouring, but I consider soot preferable, as it produces a smoother surface; moreover, I have seen Carême himself employ this very process to colour boar's head; and in this, as in most other instances, I think it well to follow the lead of this talented practitioner.

It should be borne in mind that all this skin is removed before beginning to carve the head.

When the head is coloured, cut out a piece of the skin, in the shape of a shield, between the eyes, 3 inches from the snout; fill this place with white lard, and decorate it with flowers made of fat, or natural flowers.

In some instances, I have seen coats of arms represented on these shields; and I have availed myself of them in many instances to display thereon the crests or monograms of those by whom I had the honour of being employed.

For wedding breakfasts, a boar's head, with an appropriate monogram of this kind, surmounted by a wreath of flowers, will look very well on the table; it is incredible how much these ornaments, very simple in themselves, but which demand care and nicety in their execution, contribute to give a pleasing appearance to a dish which of itself certainly lacks it.

The tusks and eyes are remodelled with fat, to complete the imitation; and then the head is dished on a rice *socle* covered with *Montpellier* Butter, garnished with *croutons* of jelly; and served.

COLD POULARD RAISED PIE WITH TRUFFLES

Bone a poulard;

Make some forcemeat, with 1½ lb. of fillet of veal, and 1½ lb. of fat bacon, freed from skin and gristle; season, chop, and pound both together in a mortar;

Peel and slice 1 lb. of truffles;

Take a pie-mould, large enough to hold the poulard and the forcemeat;

Line the mould with paste, and put a layer of forcemeat at the bottom, with some slices of truffle on the forcemeat;

Spread the poulard, skin downwards, on the board; season with spiced salt, and spread a layer of forcemeat on the poulard; put some slices of truffle on it, then another layer of forcemeat and truffles, and fold the skin over, and shape the poulard to fit the mould; put it in the mould, breast upwards; lay some more slices of truffle on it; and finish with a layer of forcemeat and some thin slices of fat bacon;

Cover the pie with paste; pinch the edges together, and lay another puff-paste cover on the top; egg it; and cut a pattern on it with a knife; make a hole in the centre, ½ inch in diameter, and bake the pie for two hours in a moderate oven; when done, take it out of the oven; let it cool for half an hour; and pour in, through the hole in the top, some melted Meat Jelly, mixed with some reduced Essence of Chicken, and close the hole with a little paste;

When quite cold, serve the pie, on a napkin, on a dish.

COLD FOIE GRAS RAISED PIE

Line a pie-mould with paste;

Make some forcemeat, as directed for *Pain de Foie Gras* (*vide* page 474);

Slice some truffles, and cut some *foies gras* in slices;

Put a layer of the forcemeat at the bottom of the mould; place some slices of truffle on it, and then a layer of the slices of *foie gras*; and continue the layers of forcemeat, truffles, and *foie gras* till the mould is full; cover the pie with a paste cover,

done, let the salmon cool in the liquor; drain, and dish it on a napkin on a decorated *socle*; garnish round with parsley and crayfish; and stick some silver skewers, garnished with prawns, parsley, and plain-boiled potatoes, in the salmon; and serve, with some *Mayonnaise* Sauce in a boat.

BUISSON OF SHELL-FISH

This *buisson* is made with lobsters, crayfish, and prawns;

Cut a square block of bread; put it on a folded napkin on a dish; place a lobster on each side of the block, hanging by the tail from the top of the bread, with the head resting on the dish; fill the spaces with parsley, so as to hide the bread; and lay some crayfish on the parsley between the lobsters;

Garnish 3 silver skewers with prawns and parsley.

BUISSON OF TRUFFLES

Boil 6 lbs. of large whole truffles, as directed for Garnish (*vide* page 290);

Cut a block of bread to an oval shape; put it on a dish, on a napkin;

Garnish 6 silver skewers, each with a large truffle; stick them in a circle round the top of the bread, one at each end, and two on the sides;

Hide the bread with parsley, and, on it, garnish round with some truffles; pile up the remaining truffles with parsley intermixed, on the top of the bread, in the centre of the six skewers.

SMALL ASPICS FOR GARNISH

Contise some minion fillets of chicken with slices of truffle;

Cut some carrots in cork-shaped pieces, 1 inch in diameter, $1\frac{1}{4}$ inch long; cover each piece of carrot with a thin slice of fat bacon, and fold a minion fillet round the bacon, pressing the two ends together so as to form a ring; wrap a piece of buttered paper round the fillets, and put them to cook in the oven; when done, take the paper off the fillets, and, when quite cold, take them off the pieces of carrot;

Pour a layer of *Aspic* Jelly, $\frac{1}{4}$ inch thick, in some *dariole*-moulds; when set, place a *contised* fillet on the jelly in each mould; pour in some more jelly, to come up ¼ inch over the fillets; and, when this is set, place another fillet on it; fill the moulds with *Aspic* Jelly; set them in the ice; and turn the *aspics* out of the moulds when wanted (*vide* Woodcut).

CONTISED FILLET AND SMALL ASPIC

COLD ENTRÉES

NOIX OF VEAL WITH MEAT JELLY

Take a large *noix* of veal, with the udder attached; lard through the meat with ¼-inch strips of truffle and ham; cover it with thin slices of fat bacon; wrap it in a napkin, and put it to cook in a braizing stewpan, with some *Mirepoix*;

When the veal is done, drain and let it cool; trim the meat so as to show the strips of truffle and ham, and cut a pattern on the udder;

Glaze the meat, but not the udder; dish it on a rice *socle*, covered with *Ravigote* Butter; garnish round with *croutons* of Meat Jelly; and serve.

RIBS OF BEEF WITH MEAT JELLY

Take 3 ribs of beef; saw off the chine-bone, and remove 2 rib-bones, leaving only one in the centre;

3 Q

Lard the meat through with ½-inch strips of fat bacon and
ham; tie it with string, and cook it in a braizing stewpan, with
some *Mirepoix*;

When done, let the meat cool in the liquor for half an hour;
drain, and put it on a dish, placing a baking-sheet, with a 4-lb.
weight on the top of the beef; when cold, trim the meat neatly,
and glaze it with Meat Glaze, and put a paper frill round the
rib-bone;

Dish it on a rice *socle*, covered with *Montpellier* Butter; garnish the top of the beef and the bottom of the *socle* with *croutons*
of Meat Jelly, as shown in Woodcut (*vide* page 466); and serve.

VEAL CUTLETS WITH MEAT JELLY

Trim 8 thick veal cutlets; cut the rib-bones short, so as to
leave the cutlets only 4 inches long; lard the meat through with
strips of bacon, truffle, and ham; and put the cutlets in a braizing
stewpan, with some *Mirepoix*; cook them, and, when they are
done, drain and press them between two dishes till cold; then
trim and glaze them;

Cut a block of crumb of bread, 2 inches in diameter, and 4
inches high; fry it; and, when cold, cover it with *Montpellier*
Butter, and fix it on a rice *socle*, also covered with *Montpellier*
Butter;

Place the cutlets upright against the bread, the bones in-
wards;

Make a small pat of *Montpellier* Butter, 3 inches in diameter;
fix it on the top of the bread, so as to hide the ends of the cutlet
bones; and put a small *aspic* (*vide* page 481) on the pat of
butter; place some chopped jelly between each cutlet, and on
the *aspic*; and garnish round the *socle* with *croutons* of Meat
Jelly.

CALVES' BRAINS WITH MONTPELLIER BUTTER

Pick 3 sets of brains, and blanch them in water with a little
salt and vinegar added; when set firm, drain and put the brains
in a stewpan with some General Stock; simmer for half an hour;
take the stewpan off the fire; and, when the brains are cold,
drain, cut them in half, and dish them in a circle on a rice *socle*,
covered with *Montpellier* Butter, putting a *crouton* of *Montpellier*
Butter, ½ inch thick, between each piece of brains; fill the centre
with thick Green *Mayonnaise* Sauce; garnish round with *croutons*
of Meat Jelly; and serve.

CHAUD-FROID OF CHICKENS

Wrap 3 chickens in buttered paper, and roast them, without colouring; when cold, cut them up, remove the skin, and cover each piece with Chicken *Chaud-froid* Sauce (*vide* page 288); and put them on a dish to cool;

Prepare a border of *Aspic* Jelly, putting a decorated fillet in each rib of the mould; when set, turn the border out of the mould on to a dish, and fix a block of fried bread, 1½ inch in diameter, 3 inches high, in the centre;

Dip each piece of chicken in the sauce again, and lean the 6 legs round the bottom of the block of bread; put the 3 right-hand wings on the legs, and let the sauce cool a little; then place the 3 other wings closely round the bread; and finish with the 3 pieces of breast;

Put a large cock's comb and truffle on a silver skewer, and stick it in the top.

Observation.—In a properly prepared *Chaud-froid*, no more sauce should be poured over the chicken when once it is dished up; the pieces should be evenly coated beforehand, so as to allow of the chicken being seen through the sauce.

BALLOTINES OF CHICKEN WITH JELLY

Bone 2 chickens;

Add a *salpicon* of tongue and truffles to some *Galantine* Forcemeat; stuff the chickens with it, and shape them into long rolls, 2½ inches in diameter;

Put each chicken in a napkin; secure it at each end, and divide each roll in three equal parts by tying it across in two places;

Boil the chickens in some *Mirepoix*; when done, let them cool for half an hour; then drain, untie them, and cut them across where they were tied;

Wash the napkins, and tie each *ballotine* up separately; when cold, untie, trim, and glaze the *ballotines*;

Make a round rice *socle* on a dish, and cover it with *Ravigote* Butter;

Stand five of the *ballotines*, on end, on the *socle*, and place the sixth on the top, in the centre; put a small decorated *aspic* (*vide* Woodcut, page 481) on this last *ballotine*, and decorate the top of the five others with a star of Meat Jelly; garnish the spaces between with chopped jelly; and make a border of *croutons* of jelly, round the *socle*.

FILLETS OF CHICKEN EN SUPRÈME WITH JELLY

Take the fillets of 6 chickens; trim and cook them as directed for Fillets of Fowls *en Suprème* (*vide* page 388);

Make a round rice *socle* on a dish; cover it with *Montpellier* Butter; and, on the centre, place a smaller rice *socle*, 2 inches in diameter, and 3½ inches high; cover this with *Montpellier* Butter also;

Drain the fillets of chicken; and, when cold, dip them in some Chicken *Chaud-froid* Sauce, as described for *Chaud-froid* of Chickens (*vide* page 483); and put them on a dish to cool;

Cut 12 slices of truffle of the size of the top of the fillets, and ¼ inch thick;

Dish the fillets, in a circle, on the *socle*, round the smaller *socle*, putting a slice of truffle between each fillet;

Place a small vase, made of prepared udder or fat, on the top of the small *socle*; garnish it with chopped Meat Jelly, and some *croutons* of jelly; and put some more *croutons* round the *socle*, on the dish.

CHAUD-FROID OF PARTRIDGES

Truss 4 partridges; wrap them in buttered paper; and roast, without colouring them;

When cold, cut them up; take off the skin; dip each piece in some Partridge *Chaud-froid* Sauce (*vide* page 288); and put them on a dish to cool;

Garnish a round border-mould with some decorated minion fillets of partridge; fill it with *Aspic* Jelly; and, when set, turn the border out on to a dish; place a block of bread in the centre; and dish the pieces of partridge, as described for *Chaud-froid* of Chickens (*vide* page 483).

PARTRIDGE GALANTINES À LA BELLEVUE

Prepare and bone 3 partridges; stuff and shape them into 3 small oval *galantines*, as directed for *Ballotines* of Chicken (*vide* page 483);

Take 3 partridge *galantine*-moulds (*vide* Woodcut, page 502);

coat them with *Aspic* Jelly, and decorate each rib with some hard-boiled white of egg and truffles, cut in patterns ;

Set the moulds in the ice ; pour in some *Aspic* Jelly, to a height of about 1½ inch ; and let it set ;

Trim the partridge *galantines* ; glaze them with Game Glaze ; place one in each mould, and fill it up gradually with *Aspic* Jelly ; when this is set, cover the moulds with a baking-sheet ; and put some ice on the top ;

Make a round rice *socle* on a dish, and cover it with *Ravigote* Butter ;

Turn the *galantines* out of the moulds on to the *socle* ; garnish round with *croutons* of Meat Jelly ; and serve.

FILLETS OF RED PARTRIDGES EN SUPRÈME

Take the fillets of 6 red partridges ; trim and fry them in a *sauté*-pan with a little clarified butter ; drain them ; and, when cold, dip each fillet in some Partridge *Chaud-froid* Sauce (*vide* page 288) ; and put them on a dish to cool ;

Make a round rice *socle* in a dish ; put a smaller one in the centre ; and cover both with *Montpellier* Butter ;

Dish the fillets in a circle on the large *socle* round the smaller one, putting between each fillet a slice of tongue cut to the size of the fillets ; and finish as directed for Fillets of Chickens *en Suprème* (*vide* page 484).

CHAUD-FROID OF WOODCOCKS

Truss 4 woodcocks ; wrap them in buttered paper ; and roast them, without colouring ; when cold, cut them up, and dip each piece in some *Chaud-froid* Sauce, reduced with Essence of Woodcock ; put them on a dish to cool, and, when cold, dish the pieces in a decorated border of *Aspic* Jelly, as directed for *Chaud-froid* of Partridges (*vide* page 484).

BALLOTINES OF PARTRIDGES

Bone 5 red partridges ; stuff them with *Galantine* forcemeat, with some tongue and truffles, cut in dice, mixed in it ; roll and wrap each partridge in a cloth, and boil them in some *Mirepoix* ; let them cool ; drain, and untie them, and tie them up again in clean cloths ;

When cold, untie the *ballotines*; trim each end, and glaze the *ballotines* with some Game Glaze;

Dish them on a round rice *socle*, covered with *Montpellier* Butter; and place a pat of the same butter, 2½ inches in dia-meter, ½ inch thick, on the top in the centre; on the pat of butter put a small vase or cup, made of prepared udder or fat; garnish the vase and the top of each *ballotine* with some *croutons* of *Aspic* Jelly and chopped jelly; and put some more *croutons* round the *socle* on the dish.

PAIN DE FOIE GRAS, OR FOIE GRAS FORCEMEAT CAKE WITH JELLY

Make some forcemeat, as directed for *Pain de Foie Gras* (*vide* page 474);

Butter a round *entrée* cylinder-mould; and also a small plain round mould; fill them with the forcemeat, and poach it *au bain-marie*;

When cold, turn the *pains* out of the moulds;

Trim, and glaze them with Chicken Glaze;

Dish the large *pain* on a round rice *socle*, covered with *Montpellier* Butter, and place the smaller one on it; put a small decorated *aspic* on the top, and garnish round the *socle*, on the dish, with *croutons* and chopped *Aspic* Jelly.

PAIN DE VOLAILLE, OR CHICKEN FORCEMEAT CAKE WITH JELLY

Take the fillets of 6 young hens, and cut them in small pieces; cut the same quantity of fat bacon in dice, and put the latter to melt, in a *sauté*-pan on the fire; when the bacon is melted, add the pieces of fillet, some thyme, a bay leaf, some parsley, pepper, and salt; fry for a few minutes on a brisk fire, stirring with a wooden spoon; then chop and pound the whole in a mortar; add half the quantity of Bread Panada; and, when well pounded, press the whole through a hair sieve, and moisten the forcemeat with ½ pint of reduced *Béchamel* Sauce and 3 eggs; when well mixed, add some truffles, cut in very small dice; and put the forcemeat in a basin;

Butter a plain round cylinder-mould, and also a small plain round mould;

Fill both with the forcemeat; and poach it *au bain-marie*;

When cold, turn the *pains* out of the moulds; trim, and glaze them with Chicken Glaze;

Make a round rice *socle* in a dish; cover it with *Montpellier* Butter; and place the large *pain* on it; put the smaller *pain* on the large one, with a small *aspic* on the top;

Garnish the top of the *pain* and round the *socle* with *croutons* of *Aspic* Jelly; and serve.

PAIN DE LEVRAUT, OR LEVERET FORCEMEAT CAKE WITH JELLY

Remove all the flesh of a leveret;

Melt an equal quantity of fat bacon, and proceed exactly as directed for *Pain de Volaille* (*vide* preceding recipe),—adding to the forcemeat some *Espagnole* Sauce, reduced with Essence of Leveret, instead of the *Béchamel* Sauce;

PAIN DE LAPREAUX, OR RABBIT FORCEMEAT CAKE

Remove the flesh of 3 young rabbits, and proceed to make the forcemeat; and finish the *pains* as directed in the preceding recipe,—merely reducing the *Espagnole* Sauce with Essence of Rabbit, instead of that of Leveret.

PAIN DE PERDREAUX, OR PARTRIDGE FORCEMEAT CAKE

Take the fillets of 6 partridges, and prepare the forcemeat as directed for *Pain de Volaille* (*vide* page 486),—substituting *Espagnole* Sauce, reduced with Essence of Partridge, for the *Béchamel* Sauce; poach and dish the *pains* in the same way.

LARK SCOLLOPS EN CROUSTADE

Take the fillets of 36 larks; set them in a buttered *sauté*-pan; season them with salt and pepper; fry and drain them; add them, when cold, to an equal quantity of sliced truffles; and mix both together in some Partridge *Chaud-froid* Sauce (*vide* page 288), which has been reduced with Essence of Larks, instead of that of Partridge;

Dish the scollops in a fried bread *croustade*, raising them towards the centre; and garnish round the *croustade* with *croutons* of jelly.

CHAUD-FROID OF LARK GALANTINES

Bone 30 larks; stuff each one with a small piece, the size of a nut, of Lark Forcemeat, with some chopped truffles mixed in it; and roll the larks round the forcemeat to a round shape;

Butter 30 *dariole*-moulds, and place a lark in each mould, breast downwards; put the moulds in a *sauté*-pan with a little water, and cook the larks in the oven; when cold, turn them out of the moulds; wipe them lightly with a cloth; and dip each one in some *Chaud-froid* Sauce, made of *Espagnole* Sauce reduced with Essence of Larks; and put them on a dish to cool;

Trim 30 small minion fillets of chickens; and *contise* them with truffles; and set them in the oven;

Prepare a *socle* of fried bread, cut so as to form three tiers; put some more sauce on the larks; and arrange them in rows one above another round the bread; place a small *contised* fillet between each lark; and garnish with chopped *Aspic* Jelly, and a border of *croutons* of jelly round the *socle* on the dish.

CHAUD-FROID OF QUAIL GALANTINES

Bone 10 quails; stuff them with *Galantine* Forcemeat, with some chopped truffles added; roll the quails to an oval shape, and tie them up in some pieces of broth napkins;

Cook them in some *Mirepoix*; let them cool, and drain them; and tie them up again in the same way in clean napkins;

Make a round rice *socle* on a dish; cover it with *Montpellier* Butter, and fix a piece of fried bread, 2 inches in diameter, in the centre;

Untie the quails; glaze them with Game Glaze; and dish them on the *socle*, resting nine of them against the bread, and putting the tenth on the top; garnish with chopped *Aspic* Jelly and *croutons* of jelly; and serve.

ASPIC OF FILLETS OF PARTRIDGE À LA BELLEVUE

Trim the fillets of 6 partridges in the same way as for *Suprème*;

Trim the minion fillets; put them in a buttered *sauté*-pan, and set them in the oven; when cold, decorate a round fluted cylinder-mould with one of the minion fillets in each rib; pour in a little *Aspic* Jelly, and on it place some hard-boiled white of egg and truffles, cut in patterns;

Fry the fillets in a *sauté*-pan with a little clarified butter; drain, and trim them small; dip each fillet in some Partridge *Chaud-froid* Sauce, and, when cold, lay them in a circle inside the decorated mould; fill it gradually with *Aspic* Jelly, and finish as described for *Aspic* with Decorated Fillets *à la Bellevue* (*vide* page 471);

When set, turn the *aspic* out of the mould on to a rice *socle* covered with *Ravigote* Butter; garnish with *croutons* and chopped *Aspic* Jelly; and serve.

ASPIC À LA FINANCIÈRE

Cut and cook some *Foie Gras* Scollops; dip them in some *Espagnole Chaud-froid* Sauce, and put them on a dish to cool;

Prepare some middle-sized cocks' combs, some cocks' kernels, truffles, and mushrooms; dip all in some Chicken *Chaud-froid* Sauce, and put them on a dish to cool;

Set a plain cylinder-mould in the ice; pour in a thin layer of *Aspic* Jelly; when it is set, decorate it with a pattern of truffles and hard-boiled white of egg;

Garnish the mould with some of the scollops, truffles, cocks' combs, mushrooms, and cocks' kernels, intermixing the whole, —being careful to put the cocks' combs in point downwards, so that they may not be upside down when the *aspic* is turned out of the mould;

Fill the mould up gradually with *Aspic* Jelly and the garnish; put a baking-sheet on it, with some ice on the top, and let it remain in the ice for two hours; then turn the *aspic* out of the mould on to a rice *socle* covered with *Montpellier* Butter; garnish with *croutons* of jelly and chopped *Aspic* Jelly; and serve.

ASPIC OF CHICKEN PURÉE À LA REINE

Put a layer of *Aspic* Jelly, $\frac{1}{8}$ inch thick, in a plain cylinder-mould; when set, put on it a $\frac{1}{2}$-inch layer of Chicken *Purée*, diluted with an equal quantity of *Aspic* Jelly; then another layer of *Aspic* Jelly, similar to the first, and a layer of diluted *purée*, and continue the alternate layers until the mould is full; cover the mould with a baking-sheet, with some ice on the top, and turn the *aspic* out, at the end of two hours, on to a

rice *socle* covered with *Montpellier* Butter; garnish with *croutons*
and chopped *Aspic* Jelly; and serve.

ASPIC OF CHICKEN AND TRUFFLE PURÉES

Put a thin layer of *Aspic* Jelly in a plain cylinder-mould;
when it is set, decorate it with a pattern cut in tongue and
truffles;
Make some Chicken *Purée* (*vide* page 293), and some Truffle
Purée (*vide* page 303);
Dilute each *purée* with an equal quantity of *Aspic* Jelly, and
fill the mould with alternate layers, ½ inch thick, of Chicken
Purée and Truffle *Purée*;
When well set, turn the *aspic* out of the mould on to a rice
socle covered with *Ravigote* Butter; garnish with chopped jelly
and *croutons* of *Aspic* Jelly; and serve.

ASPIC OF LOBSTER

Put a thin layer of *Aspic* Jelly in a plain cylinder-mould;
decorate it with hard-boiled white of egg and lobster spawn;
when set, cover this pattern with *Aspic* Jelly, ¼ inch thick;
Cut some lobster tails into scollops; marinade them in some
lemon-juice seasoned with pepper and salt;
Put a layer of *Montpellier* Butter, ¼ inch thick, on a baking-
sheet, and set it on the ice;
Put a ¼-inch layer of Lobster Butter on another baking-sheet,
and put it on the ice; when quite firm, cut both out, with a
round cutter, to the size of the lobster scollops;
Place a circle of alternate scollops of lobster and *Montpellier*
Butter in the mould; pour in sufficient *Aspic* Jelly to come ¼ inch
above them; when this is set, lay on it another circle of lobster
scollops, and Lobster Butter scollops, dressing them reversed to
the first circle; pour in some more *Aspic* Jelly, and, when set,
continue the alternate circles of lobster scollops and Lobster
Butter, and lobster scollops and *Montpellier* Butter, until the
mould is full;
Cover it with a baking-sheet with some ice on the top, and let
it remain in the ice for two hours; then turn the *aspic* out of
the mould on to a rice *socle* covered with Lobster Butter;
garnish with chopped jelly and *croutons* of jelly; and serve.

ASPIC OF FILLETS OF SOLE À LA RAVIGOTE

Remove the fillets of 4 large soles ; cut them in 2-inch lengths, and trim them to an oval shape ; put them on a buttered baking-sheet ; season with salt, pepper, and lemon-juice, and cook them in the oven ; when done, drain, and press them between two dishes till cold ; dip each piece in some Green *Mayonnaise* Sauce, diluted with white *Aspic* Jelly, and put them on a dish to cool ;

Put a thin layer of *Aspic* Jelly in a plain cylinder-mould ; decorate it with truffle and tongue ; and pour in some more *Aspic* Jelly to a ¼-inch thickness ; when it is set, dress some of the pieces of sole on it in a circle ; cover them with jelly ; and, when it is set, put in another reversed circle of pieces of sole ; continue in the same way till the mould is full ; and finish as above.

SALMON WITH MONTPELLIER BUTTER

Take a large slice of salmon, about 6 inches thick ; clean it ; and remove ½ inch of the bone at each end ; fill the hollow by inserting a large carrot, cut to its shape ;

Wrap the salmon in thin slices of fat bacon ; and bind it round with string ;

Put it in an oval stewpan on the drainer ; cover it with *Mirepoix*, and boil gently till the fish is done ;

Drain the salmon ; and, when cold, remove the carrot from the hollow part ; take off the skin very carefully ; glaze the salmon with Fish Glaze, and dish it on a rice *socle* covered with *Montpellier* Butter ;

Spread a layer of *Montpellier* Butter, ¼ inch thick, on a baking-sheet ; put it on the ice, to become very firm ; then cut a strip 1 inch wide, and lay it round the salmon, the edge resting on the rice *socle* ;

Cut another similar strip, and lay it round the top of the salmon ;

Trim 4 fillets of sole to the length of the space between the two strips of *Montpellier* Butter ; decorate them with truffles ; cook them in the oven ; and, when cold, stick them up with Fish Glaze, one at each end of the piece of salmon, and one on each side ;

Cover the top of the salmon with another slice of *Montpellier*

Butter, of the same shape as the salmon; and garnish it with *croutons* of jelly and chopped jelly.

GALANTINE OF EELS EN BASTION

Skin and·clean 2 large eels; slit them open down the belly, without severing them; and remove the bone entirely;

Make some *Galantine* forcemeat with a *salpicon* of truffles, fat bacon, and tongue added; (*vide* Turkey *Galantine*, page 470);

Spread a layer of this forcemeat inside the whole length of the eels, and refold them so as to enclose it; roll them up in separate napkins, and tie the ends with string; tie each eel across in three places, to keep them in shape whilst cooking;

Put them in a fish kettle; cover them with *Mirepoix*, and simmer till the eels are done; let them cool in the liquor for twenty minutes; then untie them, and tie them up again in clean napkins; when cold, untie and cut the eels into five pieces, 4 inches long; glaze four of the pieces with Fish Glaze; and cut a sixth piece, $3\frac{1}{2}$ inches long, and glaze it in the same way;

Make a round rice *socle* on a dish, and cover it with *Montpellier* Butter;

Stand four of the pieces of eel on end on the *socle*; put the fifth unglazed piece in the centre, sticking the pieces on with a little *Montpellier* Butter; spread a layer of *Montpellier* Butter over the top of the pieces, and stand the smaller one in the centre on the butter;

Spread a $\frac{1}{2}$-inch layer of *Montpellier* Butter on a baking-sheet; put it on the ice; and, when quite firm, cut four strips, 4 inches by $1\frac{1}{2}$ inch; stand one of these strips between each piece of eel; cut some more butter into 1-inch strips; fix them round the bottom of each piece of eel; and stick a $\frac{1}{2}$-inch strip of *Montpellier* Butter round the top of each piece;

Cook some fillets of sole in a *sauté*-pan with a little butter; when cold, trim and cut them out to represent battlements; and stick them round the top of each piece of eel above the $\frac{1}{2}$-inch strip of *Montpellier* Butter.

The pieces of eel will then present the appearance of a fort or bastion.

Decorate the bastion with some hard-boiled white of egg, to represent the loop-holes under the battlements; garnish with chopped *Aspic* Jelly and *croutons* of *Aspic* Jelly; and serve.

SALMON SALAD

Cut some salmon into scollops, $1\frac{1}{2}$ inch in diameter, and $\frac{1}{3}$ inch thick; put them in a buttered *sauté*-pan; season with salt and pepper, and fry them; when done, drain the scollops; and put them on a dish to cool; then season them slightly with salt, pepper, oil, and vinegar;

Pour a $\frac{1}{4}$-inch layer of white *Aspic* Jelly in a plain border-mould; when this is set, garnish the mould with some picked prawns, turned olives, cabbage-lettuces, cut in quarters, and hard-boiled eggs, arranging the whole tastefully; fill up the mould with *Aspic* Jelly, and, when the latter is set, turn the border out on to a dish;

Dish the salmon scollops in a circle inside the border; pour over some partly melted *Aspic* Jelly, seasoned with salt, pepper, vinegar, and chopped *Ravigote*; and, when this first row is set, fill up the centre with some of the unshapely pieces; and dish another and reversed circle of salmon scollops on the first; pour over some more seasoned jelly; and continue reversing and diminishing the circles until they come to a point; pour over some more jelly; put half a hard-boiled egg, with a cabbage-lettuce heart stuck in it, on the top; and serve.

TURBOT SALAD

Boil a piece of turbot; and, when cold, cut it into oval scollops, 2 inches by $1\frac{1}{2}$ inch;

Season them with salt, pepper, oil, and vinegar;

Prepare a decorated border of white *Aspic* Jelly; and finish as directed for Salmon Salad (*vide* preceding recipe).

FILLETS OF SOLES EN MAYONNAISE

Cook some fillets of soles, as directed for *Aspic* of Fillets of Soles (*vide* page 491);

Cut them in pieces 2 inches long; and, when cold, dip them in some *Mayonnaise* Sauce;

Prepare a border of white *Aspic* Jelly, garnished with crayfish tails, hard-boiled eggs, beetroot, and cabbage-lettuces;

Dish up the fillets, in reversed circles, inside the border, gradually diminishing to a point; pour over some *Mayonnaise* Sauce;

and place half a hard-boiled egg, with a cabbage-lettuce heart stuck in it, on the top.

LOBSTER SALAD

Cut the tails of 3 lobsters into scollops;

Season them with salt, pepper, and vinegar;

Prepare a border of white *Aspic* Jelly, decorated with a pattern cut in *Montpellier* Butter, and Lobster Butter; when set, turn the border out of the mould on to a dish;

Put a ring of Lobster Butter inside the border, and place a circle of lobster scollops on the butter; then another, smaller, ring of Lobster Butter on the scollops; and place another, reversed, circle of scollops on the butter; continue with alternate and decreasing rows of scollops and butter (filling the centre with the unshapely pieces mixed in *Mayonnaise* Sauce), until the salad finishes in a point; pour over some half-melted *Aspic* Jelly, seasoned with vinegar and chopped *Ravigote*; put a small round pat of Lobster Butter on the top; stick a cabbage-lettuce heart in it; encircle the latter with a ring of capers; and serve.

Instead of the border of *Aspic* Jelly, the bottom of the salad may be garnished round with some hard-boiled eggs, cut in quarters, and decorated with fillets of anchovies, with some olives, cabbage-lettuces, cut in quarters, and with a few sprigs of tarragon.

Observation.—Cold *Mayonnaise* Sauce is served in a boat, with all fish salads.

RUSSIAN SALAD

Cook some fillets of partridge and chicken in a *sauté*-pan, with a little butter; drain, and put them on a plate to cool;

Cook some thin slices of salmon in the same way;

Wash and trim 8 anchovies; and cut them into small dice, together with the partridge, chicken, and salmon;

Cut some carrots and turnips with a small round vegetable scoop; blanch, and cook them in water, with a little salt added;

Boil some asparagus peas, and some French beans, cut in diamond-shaped pieces;

Drain all the above vegetables; and, when cold, put them in a basin, with the fish, chicken, and partridge; season with salt, pepper, oil, vinegar, a little Cayenne pepper, and some chopped *Ravigote*;

Caviar may be added, according to taste;

Prepare a border of white *Aspic* Jelly, garnished with picked prawns, olives, and small Indian Pickle; when set, turn the border out on to a dish;

Add some partly-melted white *Aspic* Jelly to the salad, in the basin; mix, and dish it up in layers inside the border; pour a little jelly over each layer, and let it set completely before adding another; continue the layers, diminishing each one till the salad comes to a point; and serve.

VEGETABLE ENTREMETS

VEGETABLE MACÉDOINE

Prepare a *macédoine* of vegetables, as directed page 464;

Put the vegetables in a basin, and season them with salt, pepper, oil, vinegar, and chopped *Ravigote*; mix some half-melted white *Aspic* Jelly with the whole; and pile the *macédoine* up in a paste *croustade*, made to the size of the dish, and 1¼ inch high.

CAULIFLOWERS EN MAYONNAISE

Prepare some cauliflowers, as directed for Garnish (*vide* page 297); season them with a little salt, pepper, and vinegar; and pile them up, on a dish, to a point;

Arrange a border of carrots, turnips, and green vegetables, round the dish; pour over plenty of white *Mayonnaise* Sauce; and serve.

SALSIFY SALAD

Boil the salsify, and cut them in 2-inch lengths; season them with salt, pepper, oil, vinegar, and chopped *Ravigote*; and dish them in a paste *croustade*, as directed for Vegetable *Macédoine* (*vide* above).

ITALIAN SALAD

Cut some carrots and turnips through with a ¼-inch vegetable cutter; and cook them as described for Garnishes (*vide* pages 295, 296); when cold, cut them into slices ¼ inch thick;

Cut some boiled potatoes and beetroot in the same way, and put the whole in a basin; season with salt, pepper, oil, vinegar, and chopped *Ravigote*; and dish up the salad in a paste *croustade*.

GERMAN SALAD

Blanch 1 lb. of sauerkraut in boiling water for five minutes; cool, and drain it well;

Throw 1 lb. of red pickled cabbage in cold water; drain, and cut it, with the sauerkraut, in thin shreds, and put the whole in a basin;

Chop 2 onions very fine; blanch, drain, and add them to the sauerkraut, together with 1 oz. of grated and chopped horseradish, and a tablespoonful of chopped chervil;

Season with salt, pepper, 6 tablespoonfuls of oil, and 1 tablespoonful of vinegar;

Taste for seasoning; and dish the salad in a paste *croustade*.

SWEDISH SALAD

Wash and trim a pickled herring; cut it in small dice; and put it in a basin;

Take the same quantity of cold roast beef, boiled potatoes, and beetroot, russet apples, and 4 anchovies, previously steeped in water; cut the whole in small dice, and add it to the cut herring, with:

    1 tablespoonful of well-drained capers,
    1 tablespoonful of chopped gherkins,
    1 hard-boiled egg, chopped fine,
    2 tablespoonfuls of chopped chervil,
    1 tablespoonful of chopped tarragon,
    20 turned olives;

Season with salt, pepper, oil, and vinegar;

Mix, and put the whole in a salad bowl, and lay 24 fresh-opened oysters on the top.

This salad should be highly seasoned.

SUMMER SALAD

Peel about 6 oz. of cucumber, and slice it very thin;

Trim 6 oz. of raw artichoke-bottoms, and 2 oz. of white celery, and cut both in very thin slices; marinade the whole in salt for two hours; drain, and add 4 oz. of sliced red radishes;

Put the vegetables in a salad bowl, and season with a table-spoonful of mustard, mixed with 2 tablespoonfuls of Orleans vinegar, 8 tablespoonfuls of oil, 3 small pinches of pepper, and ½ oz. of picked chervil leaves; mix; and serve.

Observation.—Some red pickled cabbage may be substituted for the radishes.

WINTER SALAD

Cut 1 lb. of red cabbage in thin shreds; blanch it in boiling water for fifteen minutes;

Cool, drain, and put it in a basin with 1 oz. of salt, and let it pickle for four hours; then pour off the water; add ½ gill of vinegar; mix, and let the cabbage marinade for two hours;

Trim 1 lb. of celery; cut it in small dice, and blanch it in boiling water for ten minutes, and drain it;

Cut an equal quantity of cold boiled potatoes in the same way.

A quarter of an hour before serving, drain the cabbage, and mix the whole in a salad bowl, adding:

3 tablespoonfuls of oil,
1 tablespoonful of chopped tarragon,
2 small pinches of pepper;

Taste for seasoning; and serve.

POTATO AND TRUFFLE SALAD À LA DEMIDOFF

Peel and slice 1¼ lb. of truffles, previously boiled in Madeira, and an equal quantity of boiled French kidney potatoes;

Put them in a basin; and season with salt, pepper, oil, vinegar, and a tablespoonful of coarsely chopped *Ravigote*;

Make a border of carrots and turnips, cut, with a ½-inch vegetable cutter, into pieces 1 inch long; blanch; boil, and drain them; cut a little hole at the top of each piece, to receive an asparagus point in each; stand the pieces of carrot and turnip alternately round the dish, and pile up the potatoes and truffles in the centre.

MACÉDOINE SALAD

Cut the following vegetables in small dice:
2 artichoke-bottoms, and equal quantities of:

carrots,	celery roots,
turnips,	asparagus peas,
beetroot,	peas.
French beans,	

3 s

All the vegetables should be blanched, cooled, and drained on a cloth.

Put the whole in a salad bowl; season with some *Mayonnaise* Sauce *à la Ravigote*; and serve.

FRENCH BEANS SALAD

Cut some French beans into diamond-shaped pieces; blanch; cool, and drain them;

Season with salt, pepper, oil, vinegar, and chopped *Ravigote*; mix, and dish the salad in a paste *croustade*.

SMALL ROLLS À LA FRANÇAISE AU SALPICON

Make and bake some small French rolls of an oval shape, 2½ inches by 1¼ inch; rasp the rolls; cut out a piece of the crust on the top, and remove the crumb from the inside;

Prepare a *salpicon* of fillets of chicken, tongue, and truffles, mixed in *Mayonnaise* Sauce, with some chopped *Ravigote* added;

Fill the rolls with the *salpicon*; replace the covers; dish them on a napkin; and serve.

SMALL ROLLS À LA FRANÇAISE WITH LOBSTER

Prepare some rolls as directed in the preceding recipe;

Cut some lobster tails in small dice; mix them in some *Mayonnaise* Sauce, with some chopped *Ravigote* added;

Fill the rolls with the lobster; replace the covers; and serve.

SMALL ROLLS À LA FRANÇAISE WITH SOLES

Prepare some rolls as directed for Small Rolls *à la Française au Salpicon*;

Trim some fillets of soles, and cook them in a *sauté*-pan, with some butter and lemon-juice; when cold, cut them in small dice; season with salt, pepper, oil, vinegar, and chopped *Ravigote*; mix thoroughly; fill the rolls with the salad; replace the covers; and serve.

HAM SANDWICHES

Remove all the crust from a loaf of bread, baked in a tin;

Butter, and cut up the bread into slices ⅛ of an inch thick;

Cover one slice of bread, very evenly, with thin slices of boiled ham, laid on the buttered side; spread a little mustard on the ham, and reverse another slice of bread and butter on the top; proceed in the same way till all the bread is used; press the slices lightly together, and cut them through into pieces $2\frac{1}{2}$ inches by $1\frac{1}{2}$;

Dish the sandwiches on a napkin; and serve.

FOIE GRAS SANDWICHES

Prepare the sandwiches as before,—substituting some thickly-spread Potted *Foie Gras* for the butter and ham.

CHICKEN SANDWICHES

Cut some slices of bread and butter, as described for Ham Sandwiches;

Sprinkle some salt over, and garnish the sandwiches with fillets of cold roast chicken, cut very thin; press, and cut the sandwiches as above; dish them on a napkin; and serve.

ANCHOVY CANAPÉS

Cut some slices of crumb of bread, $\frac{1}{4}$ inch thick; cut these in pieces $2\frac{1}{2}$ inches long, $1\frac{1}{2}$ inch wide; and fry them in clarified butter, till of a nice golden colour;

When cold, spread the pieces with Anchovy Butter;

Steep some anchovies in cold water; drain, open, and trim them;

Place 4 fillets of anchovies, lengthwise, on each piece of bread, leaving three small spaces between the fillets; fill the first space with chopped hard-boiled white of egg; fill the middle space with chopped parsley, and the third with chopped hard-boiled yolk of egg;

Dress the *canapés* in a flat china boat, or small dish, generally used for all these cold *Hors d'œuvre*.

SHRIMP CANAPÉS

Cut some slices of crumb of bread $\frac{1}{4}$ inch thick; cut them out with a plain 2-inch cutter, and fry the rounds in a little clarified butter, till of a light golden colour; when cold, spread them over with Shrimp Butter; and place a *rosace*, or circular pattern, of trimmed shrimp tails on the top; put a little chopped parsley in the centre; and dish the *canapés* in a boat, overlapping one another.

CAVIAR CANAPÉS

Cut and fry the bread as described in the preceding recipe, and spread a layer of Caviar on the rounds; dish them in a boat; and serve.

CRAYFISH TAILS CANAPES

Cut and fry the bread as directed for Anchovy *Canapés*; spread the pieces with Crayfish Butter; lay some trimmed crayfish tails on the middle of the bread, and place a small border of chopped parsley on each side; dish the *canapés* in a boat; and serve.

LOBSTER CANAPÉS

Cut and fry the bread as described for Shrimp *Canapés* (*vide* page 499); spread the rounds with Lobster Butter, and put a large lobster scollop, previously marinaded in oil, vinegar, salt, and pepper, in the centre; place a row of capers round the lobster; and dish the *canapés* in a china boat.

SMOKED SALMON CANAPÉS

Cut and fry the bread as directed for Anchovy *Canapés* (*vide* page 499); spread the pieces with Anchovy Butter, and cover the butter with some very thin slices of smoked salmon; dish the *canapés* in a boat; and serve.

SMOKED HERRING

Cut off the head and tail of a smoked herring; trim off the skin, and remove the bones, and cut the fish lengthwise into fillets ¼ inch wide; steep the fillets in some salad oil for six hours; then drain, and set them in a china boat; pour some fresh oil over them; and serve.

FILLETS OF SOLE AND ANCHOVIES

Take the fillets of a small sole; trim, and fry them in a *sauté*-pan, with one tablespoonful of salad oil, some salt and pepper; drain, and press them between two dishes till cold;

Clean and prepare 4 anchovies; cut each half, lengthwise, into 4 fillets;

Cut the fillets of sole to the same size as the anchovy fillets; mix both together, and put them in a china boat;

Mix, in a basin:

4 tablespoonfuls of salad oil;
1 tablespoonful of tarragon vinegar;
1 chopped capsicum;

Pour the whole over the fish; and serve.

MARINADED TUNNY

Cut some marinaded tunny in thick slices; arrange them in a boat, overlapping one another; put a small heap of capers at each end, and at each side of the boat; pour over some fresh salad oil; and serve.

SMOKED SALMON

Trim a piece of smoked salmon, and cut it in very thin slices;

Put a sheet of oiled paper on a gridiron; lay the slices of salmon on the paper, and broil them, over a slow fire, for a minute on each side;

When cold, dish the slices in a china boat; pour over a little salad oil; and serve.

PRAWNS

Garnish the bottom of a china boat with fresh parsley, dishing some prawns closely on it, the heads outside and the tails to the centre; garnish with some more parsley; and serve.

MORTADELLE, OR ITALIAN SAUSAGE

Cut the sausage in very thin slices, and set them in a circle round a china boat.

PICKLED TONGUE

Trim a tongue, and cut it in thin slices; set them in a boat, overlapping one another, and garnish each side with a border of chopped parsley.

ANCHOVY SALAD

Steep and clean 7 anchovies; remove the scales and bones, and cut the anchovies into fillets ¼ of an inch wide ; lay them across in a china boat in a trellis pattern; garnish with a border made of small alternate portions of chopped hard-boiled yolk and white of egg, and chopped parsley.

Season with oil and vinegar just before serving.

PARTRIDGE GALANTINE MOULD

CHARLOTTE RUSSE

CHAPTER XVI

HOT AND COLD SWEET ENTREMETS

I

HOT ENTREMETS

SAVARIN

PUT 1 lb. of sifted flour in a basin;

Make a hole in the middle, and put in ½ oz. of German yeast, and ¼ gill of warm milk; mix it with the flour immediately surrounding it, about one quarter of the whole quantity, to make the sponge, and stand the basin in a warm place;

When the sponge has risen to twice its original size, add 1 gill of warm milk, and 2 eggs; work the contents of the basin with a spoon, and mix in another egg; then add ¾ lb. of worked butter, ¼ oz. of salt, ½ oz. of sugar, and ½ gill more warm milk; continue working with a spoon, and adding one egg at a time, until 5 eggs have been used;

Cut 2 oz. of candied orange peel in very small dice, and mix it in the paste;

Butter a fluted cylinder-mould; strew a tablespoonful of chopped almonds on the butter, and half fill the mould with the paste; let it stand, and, when it has risen to the top of the mould, put the *savarin* to bake in a moderate oven;

When done, turn it out of the mould; let it cool for twenty minutes; pour over it some syrup, flavoured with *Anisette*; and serve.

BISCUITS À LA CRÈME, FLAVOURED WITH LEMON

Break 6 eggs; put the whites in a whipping bowl and the yolks in a basin; add ½ lb. of pounded sugar, and the grated peel of a lemon to the latter; and work the whole for a few minutes, with a wooden spoon;

Whip the whites, and mix them with the yolks; add 3 oz. of flour, and 1 gill of whipped cream; put the paste in some paper cases (*vide* Woodcut, page 544); sprinkle some fine sugar on the top; bake in the oven; and serve.

BISCUITS À LA CRÈME, FLAVOURED WITH ORANGE

Make the *biscuits* as above,—substituting the grated peel of an orange, for the lemon.

BISCUITS À LA CRÈME, FLAVOURED WITH VANILLA

Proceed precisely as directed for *Biscuits à la Crème*, flavoured with lemon,—substituting vanilla sugar, for the grated lemon peel.

RICE CAKE WITH APRICOTS

Wash and blanch 1 lb. of rice; drain, and put it in a stew-pan, with 1½ quart of boiled milk, ¼ lb. of pounded sugar, and 2 oz. of butter;

Simmer gently for an hour; and, when partly cold, mix in 3 eggs;

Take 18 preserved apricots; separate them in halves; put them in a sugar-boiler, with some syrup at 20°; simmer for five minutes; and drain the apricots on a sieve;

Butter a plain pudding-mould; strew the butter with bread-crumbs, and put in a layer of rice, 1 inch thick; then a layer of pieces of apricot; and continue the alternate layers till the mould is full; bake in the oven; and, when done, turn the cake out of the mould; and serve with a custard sauce, made as follows:

Put 8 yolks of egg in a stewpan, with ¼ lb. of pounded sugar, and 1 pint of milk; stir over the fire, without boiling, until the sauce coats the spoon; add ½ gill of Noyeau; strain the sauce through a tammy cloth; put it in a boat; and serve.

RICE CAKE WITH PINE-APPLE

Prepare the rice as above;

Cut ½ lb. of pine-apple in large dice; cook them in syrup; drain, and mix them in the rice;

Butter a plain pudding-mould; strew it with bread-crumbs; fill it with the rice and pine-apple, and put it to bake in the oven; when done, turn the cake on to a napkin, on a dish; and serve, with the following sauce:

Peel and core 3 large Wellington apples; cook them in 1 pint of syrup at 16°; when the apples have melted down, strain through a silk sieve, and mix this syrup with that in which the pine-apple has been cooked; reduce it until it coats the spoon; and serve it in a boat, with the cake.

CROÛTES AU MADÈRE

Make some *Savarin* Paste, as directed at page 503; put it in a plain cylinder-mould, 8 inches in diameter; bake in the oven; and, when cold, cut the cake in slices; lay these on a baking-sheet; sprinkle them over with fine sugar, and glaze them in the oven; spread each slice over with some apricot jam; and dish them in a circle;

Make a *salpicon* of pears, cooked in syrup, preserved cherries, and angelica; put all the above in a stewpan, with ½ gill of Madeira, and ½ gill of syrup at 30°; warm, and fill the centre of the dish with this *salpicon*;

Boil 1 gill of Madeira, and 1 gill of syrup at 36°; pour it over the *croûtes*; and serve.

CROÛTES WITH PINE-APPLE

Prepare some *croûtes* as above;

Cut some pine-apple into slices, ¼ inch thick, and 2 inches in diameter, and cook them in syrup at 24°;

3 T

Pound the trimmings of pine-apple in a mortar ; press them through a silk sieve ; and put the *purée* in a basin ;

Drain the pine-apple ; and dish the *croûtes*, and pieces of pine-apple, alternately, in a circle ;

Strain the syrup in which the pine-apple has been cooked : reduce it to 32°, and mix it to the Pine-Apple *Purée* ; pour it over the *croûtes* ; and serve.

MAZARIN CAKE WITH RUM

Sift 1 lb. of flour on to a pasteboard ;

Make some sponge with a fourth part of the flour, ½ oz. of German yeast, and warm water ; and put it in a warm place to rise ;

Gather the remainder of the flour together ; make a hole in the centre, and put in :

¼ lb. of butter ;	⅓ oz. of sugar ;
1 gill of warm milk ;	1 pinch of salt ;

Work the whole into a paste ; and add 7 eggs, one after the other, beating and working the paste all the time ;

When the sponge has risen to double its size, mix it with the paste ;

Butter a plain pudding-mould ; strew it with almonds, cut in very thin strips ; half fill the mould with the paste ; and, when it has risen so as to fill it entirely, bake it in the oven ;

Make a sauce as follows :

Put ½ pint of syrup at 30° in a stewpan, with 1 gill of rum and 2 oz. of finely chopped candied citron ; boil, and thicken the sauce with 3 oz. of butter ;

Turn the cake out of the mould ; cut it in two in the thickness ; pour half the above sauce on each piece, and, when the cake has absorbed it all, replace one piece above the other ; dish the cake on a napkin ; and serve.

BRIOCHE À L'ALLEMANDE WITH MADEIRA SAUCE

Make some *Brioche* Paste as directed in the First Part (*vide* page 199).

Butter a plain pudding-mould ; half fill it with the paste, and, when it has risen to the top of the mould, bake the *brioche* in the oven ;

Rub ½ lb. of Apricot Jam through a hair sieve ; put it in a

stewpan with ½ pint of Madeira; boil for three minutes, stirring with a spoon;

When the *brioche* is done, turn it out of the mould; cut it into four equal rounds; spread each slice over with some of the apricot, and replace them one above the other; glaze the outside of the cake with some more of the apricot, and serve the remainder in a boat.

CAKE A LA MONTMORENCY

Sift 1 lb. of flour on to a pasteboard; take a fourth part of it and mix it with ½ oz. of German yeast and warm water, to make the sponge, and put it to rise in a warm place;

Gather the remainder of the flour together; make a hole in the middle; and put in:

½ oz. of pounded sugar,	10 eggs,
½ gill of water,	¾ lb. of butter;

Mix the whole together; work and beat the paste, adding 5 more eggs, one after the other;

When the sponge has risen to twice its original size, mix it with the paste, together with ¼ lb. of dried cherries, cut in four pieces;

Butter a plain pudding-mould; half fill it with the paste; and, when it has risen to the top of the mould, bake the cake in a moderate oven;

When the cake is done, turn it out of the mould, and dish it on a napkin;

Boil 1 pint of syrup at 36°, with 1 pint of Kirschenwasser; and serve the sauce in a boat with the cake.

PLUM PUDDING WITH RUM

Take:

¾ lb. of picked and finely chopped suet;

¼ lb. of stoned raisins;

¾ lb. of well washed and picked currants;

¼ lb. of candied orange peel and citron, cut in small dice;

¾ lb. of pounded sugar;

¾ lb. of bread-crumbs;

2 peeled russet apples, cut in small dice;

the grated peel of a lemon;

Mix the whole thoroughly in a basin, with 3 pounded cloves, a pinch of salt, 6 eggs, one at a time, and ½ gill of rum;

Butter a pudding-mould; fill it with the mixture, and tie a cloth over the top;

Reverse a small baking-sheet at the bottom of a stock-pot, three parts full of boiling water; put the pudding in it, and boil for four hours, keeping the pot replenished with boiling water;

Turn the pudding out of the mould on to a hot dish; sprinkle the dish with pounded sugar; pour in ½ pint of warm rum, and light it when putting the pudding on the table

PLUM PUDDING WITH MADEIRA SAUCE

Prepare and cook a pudding as before;
For the sauce:

Put 8 yolks of egg in a stewpan, with ¼ lb. of pounded sugar; 3 gills of Madeira, and half the grated peel of a lemon; stir over the fire, until the sauce coats the spoon; strain through a tammy-cloth; and serve the sauce in a boat with the pudding.

CABINET PUDDING

Break 10 yolks of egg in a basin; beat them for a minute, and add, whilst stirring:

¼ lb. of pounded sugar;
1½ pint of boiled milk;
½ gill of Kirschenwasser;

and strain the custard through a tammy-cloth into a basin;

Stone 3 oz. of raisins;

Pick, wash, and dry 2 oz. of currants;

Cut 3 preserved apricots, and 2 oz. of dried cherries, into small dice;

Butter a plain pudding-mould; put a round of paper at the bottom, and set in a ¼-inch layer of the mixed fruit; on this place a layer of finger biscuits or of slices of sponge cake; continue the alternate layers till the mould is two-thirds full; pour in the custard slowly; let it stand for a few minutes, and cook the pudding *au bain-marie*, without boiling; turn it out of the mould on to a dish; and serve with a sauce, made as follows:

Put 8 yolks of egg in a stewpan, with ½ pint of syrup; stir over the fire until the sauce coats the spoon; add 1 gill of Kirschenwasser; strain the sauce through a tammy-cloth; and serve it in a boat, with the pudding.

APPLE CHARLOTTE

Peel and core 20 Ribston or Orange Blenheim Pippin apples; cut them in thin slices; put them in a *sauté*-pan, with some butter and pounded sugar, and toss them over the fire till they are done;

Line a plain round mould with bread, as follows :

Cut some thin slices of crumb of bread ; cut out a round, with a 1.-inch cutter, to put in the centre; then cut some heart-shaped pieces, and dip them in butter, together with the round piece ; put the latter at the bottom of the mould, in the centre; and place the heart-shaped pieces round it, overlapping one another, and with the points resting on the round piece ;

Cut the remainder of the slices of bread into strips 1½ inch wide, and of the height of the mould ; dip them in butter, and stand them all round the mould, also overlapping one another ; fill the centre with the cooked apples, and put the Charlotte in the oven until the bread is well coloured ;

Turn the Charlotte out of the mould on to a dish ; glaze it over with some boiled apricot jam ; and serve.

CHARLOTTE MOULD.

PEAR CHARLOTTE

Line a mould with bread as above ;

Peel 15 *Bon Chrétien* pears ; cut them in quarters, and cook them in a *sauté*-pan, with some butter and vanilla sugar ;

Fill the mould with the pears ; put the Charlotte to colour in the oven ; turn it out, and glaze it as above.

PANCAKES WITH APRICOT JAM

When making a quantity of pancakes it is better to use two or three frying-pans, so that they may be prepared more quickly.

Put ½ lb. of flour in a basin, with :
   5 eggs,
   1 oz. of pounded sugar,
   1 small pinch of salt ;

Mix the above well together, and mix in ¼ lb. of butter melted ; then add 5 gills of milk, stirring all the time ;

Cut a piece of crumb of bread to a flattened dome shape, 4½ inches diameter ; sprinkle it with fine sugar, and glaze it in the oven ;

Put three pancake pans on the fire ; butter them slightly with some clarified butter, and put about two tablespoonfuls of the batter in each pan ; as soon as one side of the pancake is coloured, turn it on the dome-shaped piece of bread ; spread the top with apricot jam, and continue putting the pancakes one above the other, spreading some jam on each,—except the top one ; sprinkle this with fine sugar ; glaze it with a hot salamander ; and serve.

SUGAR DREDGER

APPLES WITH A SALPICON OF FRUIT À LA PARISIENNE

Make and bake a *savarin* in a cylinder-mould 8 inches diameter (vide *Savarin*, page 503) ; when done, turn it out of the mould, and trim it so as to form a *socle*, or stand, 1¼ inch high, and put it on a dish ;

Peel and cut 2 Colville apples into small dice, and cook them in some syrup ;

Cut some *Bon Chrétien* pears in the same way, and cook them in syrup, with a little prepared cochineal added ;

Peel and core 7 other Colville apples ; cut them in two, and cook them in syrup ;

Cut 14 slices of preserved pine-apple to the size of the pieces of apple, and warm them in some syrup ;

Dish the slices of pine-apple and apple, alternately, in a circle on the *savarin*;

Cut some preserved apricots, greengages, and cherries in small dice; add them to the apples and pears cut in dice; and put the whole in a sugar-boiler, with 1 gill of syrup at 32°, and ½ gill of Kirschenwasser; boil for a minute, and fill the centre of the circle with this *salpicon*; garnish with preserved cherries and angelica; and serve.

APPLES WITH RICE

Core 12 small Colville apples, with a long cutter;

Peel them very smooth, and cook them in some syrup at 18°;

Make a rice *croustade* to fit the dish, and 2 inches high;

Boil ½ pint of rice in 1 quart of milk, with some sugar; when the rice is done, put it in the *croustade*;

Drain the apples, and pile them up on the rice, putting a well-drained preserved cherry on the top of each apple, and a diamond-shaped piece of angelica between each apple; and serve;

Strain the syrup in which the apples have been cooked; reduce it, and pour it over the apples; and serve.

PEARS WITH RICE

Turn 15 Rousselet pears; remove the cores, and cook the pears in some syrup, adding a little prepared cochineal;

Make a rice *croustade* to the size of the dish, and 2 inches high;

Boil some rice; finish, and dish the pears as directed for Apples with Rice (*vide* preceding recipe).

APRICOTS WITH RICE

Cut 18 apricots in halves; remove the stones; and cook them in some syrup;

Make a rice *croustade* to the size of the dish, and 2 inches high;

Boil ½ pint of rice in 1 quart of milk, with some sugar, and half a stick of vanilla;

Simmer gently for an hour; and put the rice in the *croustade*, raising it towards the centre; place the apricots on it in circles; pour over them the strained and reduced syrup; and serve.

PEACHES WITH RICE

Cut 12 peaches in halves; take out the stones; and blanch the fruit in syrup at 20°;

Drain the peaches on a sieve, and remove the skin;

Make a rice *croustade* to the size of the dish, and 2 inches high;

Boil some rice to fill it; and finish as before.

APRICOTS À LA CONDÉ

Cut 18 apricots in halves; stone; and cook them in some syrup;

Mix 4 tablespoonfuls of Indian-Corn Flour with 1½ pint of cold milk, 3 oz. of pounded sugar, and 1 stick of vanilla; and stir over the fire until it thickens to a paste;

Take half of this paste; spread it on a dish; and, when cold, shape it into croquets about the size of a cork; dip them in egg, and bread-crumb them;

Make a *savarin socle,* as directed for Apples *à la Parisienne* (*vide* page 510), and put it on a dish;

Drain the apricots; and strain and reduce the syrup;

Fry the croquets in hot fat;

Dish 18 pieces of apricot in a circle on the *savarin*; and on these place the other 18 pieces in a reversed circle; garnish round the *socle* with the croquets;

Add some hot cream to the remainder of the paste, till it forms a thick *bouillie*; put it in the centre of the circle of apricots; glaze the latter with the reduced syrup; and serve.

PEACHES À LA CONDÉ

Cut 12 peaches in halves; remove the stones, and put the pieces in some boiling syrup for a few minutes; drain them on a sieve, and take off the skin;

Make the croquets; dish the peaches, and finish as directed for Apricots *à la Condé* (*vide* preceding recipe).

HOT MACÉDOINE OF FRUIT

Cut 5 *Bon Chrétien* pears in quarters; trim them smooth; and cook them in some syrup at 18°, with a teaspoonful of Maraschino added;

Cut 5 Colville apples in quarters; trim; and cook them in some syrup at 16°;

Cut 6 slices of pine-apple in half, and cook them in some syrup at 16°;

Cut 8 preserved apricots, and 8 preserved greengages, each in two pieces, and warm the whole in some syrup;

Drain all the above fruit, and dish it in a silver casserole, intermixing the colours;

Boil 3 gills of syrup at 30°, and ½ pint of Maraschino together; pour over the fruit; and serve.

BRIOCHE TIMBALE WITH FRUIT

Line a plain mould with *Brioche* Paste, ¼ inch thick;

Butter a *sauté*-pan with clarified butter;

Peel and cut 5 *Bon Chrétien* pears in quarters; set them in the *sauté*-pan; sprinkle over some fine sugar; cover the pan; put some live coals on the top, and cook the pears on a very slow fire;

Peel and cut 5 Colville apples in quarters, and cook them in the same way as the pears;

Cut 24 preserved Mirabelle plums in two; stone, and boil them in syrup for two minutes;

Drain the apples, pears, and plums; mix the whole together, and fill the *brioche timbale* with them;

Put a *Brioche* Paste cover on the top; make a hole in the cover, and bake the *timbale* in a moderate oven; when done, close the hole in the cover with a piece of paste; turn the *timbale* out of the mould on to a dish; make a hole in the top, ¼ inch in diameter, and pour in 1 pint of syrup, mixed with ½ pint of Noyeau; put a preserved cherry on the hole; and serve.

BRIOCHE TIMBALE WITH A MACÉDOINE OF FRUIT

Prepare a *brioche timbale* as above;

Cut and cook some *Bon Chrétien* pears, and some Colville apples, as described in the preceding recipe;

Cut some slices of pine-apple in two pieces, and some preserved apricots and greengages in halves; and stone them;

Fill the *timbale* with all the above fruit, adding some preserved cherries; put a *Brioche* Paste cover on the top; and finish as directed in the preceding recipe, pouring in, through the

3 U

hole in the top, 1 pint of syrup at 30°, with $\frac{1}{2}$ pint of Maraschino added.

ALMOND CUSTARD FRITTERS

Put 5 eggs in a stewpan, with 1 lb. of flour; mix; and pour in, by degrees, 1 quart of milk, and stir over the fire for twenty minutes, when the custard should be very smooth; take it off the fire; and add :

$\frac{1}{4}$ lb. of pounded sugar,
1 oz. of blanched and pounded bitter almonds,
6 yolks of egg,
1 small pinch of salt;

Mix; and spread the custard to a 1-inch thickness on a slightly buttered baking-sheet; when cold, cut it in pieces, 2 inches by $1\frac{1}{4}$ inch; dip the pieces in egg; bread-crumb, and fry them in very hot fat till slightly coloured; drain; sprinkle them with sugar, and pile them up on a napkin, on a dish; and serve.

ORANGE CUSTARD FRITTERS

Prepare a custard as above, substituting some grated orange-peel for the bitter almonds; fry, and finish the fritters in the same way.

Observation.—The custard fritters may be flavoured with chocolate, coffee, vanilla, &c.

CUSTARD FRITTERS FLAVOURED WITH CARAMEL AND ORANGE FLOWER

Put 1 oz. of pounded sugar in a small sugar-boiler; stir over the fire until the sugar acquires a dark brown colour, without burning, and pour in $\frac{1}{2}$ gill of water to melt the *caramel*, and 1 tablespoonful of Orange Flower Water;

Butter 8 *dariole*-moulds;

Put 10 yolks of egg in a basin, with $\frac{1}{4}$ lb. of pounded sugar, the dissolved *caramel*, and some boiled milk (measuring out 6 *dariole*-moulds full of the latter);

Mix the whole well together, and strain through a tammy cloth;

Fill the above moulds with the custard; poach it *au bain-marie*, putting some live coals on the cover; and, when cold, turn the custards out of the moulds; cut each one across, in three equal-sized pieces; dip the pieces in frying batter; fry them in hot fat; drain; and sprinkle them over with fine sugar; glaze them in the oven; pile them up on a napkin, on a dish; and serve.

APRICOT FRITTERS À LA DAUPHINE

Make 1 lb. of *Brioche* Paste, using only ¼ lb. of butter; moisten it with equal quantities of milk, and eggs, and put it in a basin to rise for three hours; then put the paste on the board, and fold it over and over; repeat this twice, and put the paste in a lump on a baking-sheet, on the ice, or in a cool place; when it has become firm, roll it out to ⅛-inch thickness, and cut it out with a 2-inch round cutter;

Moisten the top edge of the rounds with a little water, and put a portion of apricot jam (about the size of a nut) in the centre of each; cover the jam with a second round of paste, as directed for Patties; and press the two rounds together with the top of a 2-inch cutter;

Fry the fritters in warm fat; drain, and sprinkle some fine sugar over them; pile them on a napkin, on a dish; and serve.

BOX OF PASTE CUTTERS

CANNELONS WITH ALMOND PASTE

Blanch and peel ½ lb. of Jordan almonds; pound them in a mortar, moistening them with white of egg; when well pounded, add ½ lb. of pounded sugar, and 2 eggs, one at a time; mix, and put the paste in a basin;

Make some six-turns puff paste, and shape the *cannelons* as directed for *Cannelons à la Reine* (*vide* page 318), putting some of the almond paste inside; fry them in warm fat; drain, and sprinkle them with sugar; pile them up on a napkin, on a dish; and serve.

CANNELONS WITH APRICOT JAM

Proceed as before,—substituting apricot jam for the almond paste.

OMELETS À LA CELESTINE

Break 10 eggs in a basin; beat them up with 1 oz. of sugar, and a small pinch of salt; butter a small pancake-pan; pour in 2 tablespoonfuls of the egg, letting it spread in the pan like a pancake; fry it for a few minutes, and fold one side to the centre; put a little apricot jam on the centre; fold the two ends to the middle, over the jam, and roll the omelet round. Make 6 of these small omelets; put them on a dish; sprinkle over some fine sugar, and glaze them with a hot salamander; and serve.

Observation.—These small Omelets *à la Celestine* are in reality nothing more than egg pancakes, and should always be made very thin and light.

SMALL VANILLA SOUFFLÉS IN CASES

Make some *Soufflé* Paste as directed in the First Part (*vide* Vanilla *Soufflé*, page 189);

Fill some paper cases with the paste; bake them in the oven; sprinkle over some fine sugar; and serve.

SMALL ORANGE FLOWER SOUFFLÉS IN CASES

Proceed as above,—substituting some crushed candied orange flowers for the vanilla.

SMALL COFFEE SOUFFLÉS IN CASES

Roast ½ lb. of coffee, without browning it, in a sugar-boiler over the fire;

Boil 1 quart of milk; put the roasted coffee in it, and let it steep for an hour; strain, and make the *Soufflé* Paste with this milk;

Fill some paper cases with the *Soufflé* Paste; bake them in the oven; sprinkle over some fine sugar; and serve.

II

COLD SWEET ENTREMETS

MERINGUES

Put 10 whites of egg in a whipping bowl, and whip them very firm; add 1 lb. of pounded sugar; mix; and, with a spoon, set the mixture at intervals on sheets of paper, in portions of the shape and size of an egg; dredge some pounded sugar over the *meringues*, and, after a minute, shake off the superfluous sugar;

Cook the *meringues* in the oven on some baking boards; and, when they assume a pale yellow tinge, take them off the paper;

WHIPPING BOWL AND WHISK

Remove some of the inside with a spoon,—being careful not to spoil the shape of the *meringues*; dredge a little sugar over, and put them on a baking-sheet, in a slack oven, to dry;

Reduce ½ pint of very strong coffee with ¾ lb. of sugar, to obtain a syrup registering 38° on the syrup gauge; when cold, mix this syrup to some well-whipped double cream;

Fill the *meringues* with the cream, reversing one *meringue* over the other, and pile them up on a napkin on a dish.

ALMOND BLANC-MANGER

Blanch and peel ¾ lb. of Jordan almonds, and ½ oz. of bitter almonds;

Pound them in a mortar, and add 1 quart of water: strain through a broth napkin, and put the almond milk in a basin;

Put 2 oz. of gelatine, ⅓ lb. of sugar, and 1¾ pint of water in a stewpan; stir over the fire till the gelatine is melted, and strain it through a silk sieve; when cold, add the strained almond milk and 1 teaspoonful of orange flower water, and mix the whole thoroughly;

Put a cylinder-mould in the ice; fill it with the *blanc-manger*, and let it remain in the ice for two hours; turn it out of the mould; and serve.

PAIN D'ANANAS, OR COLD PINE-APPLE PUDDING

Make 1½ pint of Pine-Apple *Purée* by pounding some pine-apple, previously boiled in 1½ pint of syrup, and pressing it through a silk sieve;

Steep 2 oz. of gelatine in water for a quarter of an hour; drain, and put it in the hot syrup, in which the pine-apple has been boiled, and stir over the fire till the gelatine is melted; strain it through a silk sieve; let it cool, and add it to the *purée*;

Decorate a plain cylinder-mould with almonds, angelica, and dried cherries; sticking them on the mould with a little melted and sweetened gelatine;

Set the mould in some pounded ice; fill it with the Pine-Apple *Purée*; put a baking-sheet on the top, with some ice on it, and let the mould remain in the ice for two hours; then turn out the *pain*; and serve.

PLAIN CYLINDER-MOULD

PAIN DE FRAISE, OR COLD STRAWBERRY PUDDING

Make 2½ pints of Strawberry *Purée*, and mix it with ¾ lb. of pounded sugar;

Melt 1¾ oz. of gelatine in ½ pint of water; when cold, strain it, through a silk sieve, into the *purée*, stirring all the time;

Decorate a plain cylinder-mould with almonds;

Put it on the ice, and fill it with the *purée*, placing a baking-sheet, covered with ice, on the top; let the pudding remain in the ice for two hours; turn it out of the mould; and serve.

CALF'S FOOT JELLY À L'ANGLAISE

Put 12 boned calves' feet in a 2-gallon stock-pot; fill it with cold water, and put it on the fire; when the water boils, skim it very carefully, and simmer for ten hours,—being careful to add some more boiling water to keep the pot replenished;

At the end of the ten hours there should be about 5 quarts of stock; strain it through a hair sieve into basins, and put them in a cold place till the next day; then remove all the fat from the top of the jelly, wash it with boiling water, and wipe it with a cloth;

Put the jelly to clarify in a stewpan over the fire, with:

3 lbs. of lump sugar,
1½ oz. of whole cinnamon,
12 cloves,
1 tablespoonful of coriander seeds,
the juice of 12 lemons,
1 bottle of sherry or Madeira;

Put 8 whites of egg and 2 whole eggs in a basin;

Whip them, adding a few drops of water; then pour in about 1 quart of the jelly, and mix it with the whipped egg, working it with the whisk; pour the whole into the stewpan containing the remainder of the jelly, and whip it till it boils; simmer for five minutes; close the stewpan; put some live coals on the cover, and simmer for fifteen minutes more;

Put the yellow peel of 3 lemons in the jelly-bag; pour the jelly through it;

Pour it back again two or three times until it is perfectly clear; then put the jelly in basins, and keep it in a cold place till wanted.

Observation.—This jelly may be used for Fruit or Liqueur Jellies, in which case the cinnamon, cloves, coriander seeds, and wine should be omitted when clarifying it, and more lemon-juice should be added.

FRUIT JELLY WITH CHAMPAGNE

Put 2 oz. of gelatine in a stewpan, with ¾ lb. of lump sugar :

Beat 3 whites of egg ; moisten them with 1 quart of water and the juice of a lemon; pour the whole into the stewpan containing the gelatine, and put it on the fire, stirring with a wire whisk till it boils ;

Take the jelly off the fire ; let it cool for a few minutes, and strain it through a jelly-bag; pour it back, and strain again until it is perfectly clear ;

When quite cold, add 1 pint of Champagne to the jelly ;

Prepare a *macédoine* of pears and apples, cut to an olive shape and boiled in syrup at 38°, dried cherries, preserved apricots and greengages ;

Put a plain cylinder-mould in the ice ;

Pour in ⅛-inch thickness of jelly ; arrange some of the fruit at the bottom of the mould on the jelly ; pour in sufficient jelly to cover it, and continue the layers of fruit and jelly until the mould is nearly full ; then let it set a little, and finish with jelly only ; cover the mould with a baking sheet, with ice on the top ; let it remain in the ice for two hours ; turn the jelly out of the mould ; and serve.

Observation.—In the fruit season this jelly may be garnished with fresh strawberries, apricots, grapes, peaches, currants, &c.

Remarks on Coloured Jellies.

For all coloured jellies I would recommend the exclusive use of copper sugar-boilers and silver spoons ; otherwise, if tinned utensils be used, the colour and limpidity of the jellies would be likely to be impaired, and their pleasing appearance entirely destroyed.

BARBERRY JELLY WITH APPLES

Clarify 2 oz. of gelatine with 3 whites of egg, 1½ pint of water, and the juice of a lemon ;

Boil 1 quart of syrup in a copper sugar-boiler, and throw in it ¼ lb. of picked barberries ; pour the whole into a basin ; cover it, and let it stand for two hours ; then strain the barberries through a broth napkin, and mix the syrup with the gelatine.

Should the jelly be too pale in colour, add a few drops of prepared cochineal.

Cut 5 Colville apples each in 8 pieces ; cook them in some syrup, and drain them on a sieve ;

Put a plain cylinder-mould in the ice ; pour in some of the jelly to a depth of ¼ inch ; when it is set, arrange on it a layer of the pieces of apple ; cover them with jelly ; let it set ; continue in the same way till the mould is nearly full ; and finish as directed for Fruit Jelly with Champagne.

NOYEAU JELLY WITH APRICOTS

Clarify some gelatine as directed for Fruit Jelly with Champagne, and add 2 gills of Noyeau to the jelly ;

Cut some apricots in halves ; cook them in some syrup, and drain them on a sieve :

Break the stones of the apricots ; blanch and peel the almonds, and separate them in two ;

Put a plain cylinder-mould in the ice, and fill it with alternate layers of jelly and apricot, strewing the almonds round the inside of the mould ; cover it with a baking-sheet, with ice on the top, and turn the jelly out after it has remained two hours in the ice.

STRAWBERRY JELLY

Boil 1 quart of syrup at 30°, and put it by to cool a little ;

Put 1½ lb. of picked Alpine strawberries in a basin ; pour the warm syrup over them, and let them steep for an hour ;

Clarify 2 oz. of gelatine with 1¼ pint of water, 3 whites of egg, and the juice of a lemon, as directed for Barberry Jelly (*vide* page 520) ;

Strain the strawberries through a jelly-bag, and add the syrup to the gelatine ;

Put a mould in the ice ; pour the jelly into the mould, and let it remain in the ice for two hours ; turn out the jelly on to a dish ; and serve.

PUNCH JELLY

Clarify 2 oz. of gelatine with ¾ lb. of sugar, the juice of 4 lemons, the peel of half a one, and 2½ pints of water, as directed for Fruit Jelly with Champagne (*vide* page 520) ; when cold, add 1 gill of rum ;

Set a cylinder-mould in the ice ; pour the jelly into it, and finish as aforesaid.

KIRSCHENWASSER JELLY WITH CHERRIES

Pick and stone 1 lb. of May-Duke cherries ;

Boil some syrup at 30° ; put the cherries in it ; boil for five minutes, and pour the whole into a basin ;

Clarify 2 oz. of gelatine with ¾ lb. of sugar, the juice of a lemon, 3 whites of egg, and 2½ pints of water, as directed for Fruit Jelly with Champagne (*vide* page 520) ; and add 1½ gill of Kirschenwasser to the jelly, when cold ;

Break 50 cherry-stones ; blanch and peel the kernels ;

Drain the cherries, first on a sieve, then on a cloth ;

Put a cylinder-mould in the ice ; pour in a little jelly ; put a row of cherries on this, and fill the mould with alternate layers of jelly and cherries, strewing in some of the kernels whilst filling it ;

Cover the mould with a baking-sheet ; put some ice on the top ; leave the jelly in the ice for two hours ; then turn it out ; and serve.

MARASCHINO JELLY WITH PEACHES

Cut 12 peaches in halves ; blanch them in boiling water for five minutes ; peel, and put them in some syrup in a basin ;

Clarify 2 oz. of gelatine, as directed for Fruit Jelly with Champagne (*vide* page 520), and add ½ pint of Maraschino to the jelly ;

Drain the peaches on a sieve, and cut each piece in two ;

Put a mould in some pounded ice ; pour a little jelly in it, and, when this is set, fill the mould with alternate layers of peach and jelly ;

Let the jelly remain in the ice for two hours ; turn it out of the mould ; and serve.

ORANGE JELLY WITH ORANGES

Cut off the peel of 8 oranges ; divide them in quarters with a knife ; remove the pips, and put the pieces of orange in a basin, with 1 pint of syrup at 30° ;

Press out the juice of 6 other oranges into a basin, and filter it as follows :

Reduce some paper to a pulp, by washing it in plenty of

water; add this pulp to the orange juice in the basin, and strain both together through a jelly-bag;

Clarify 2 oz. of gelatine with ½ lb. of sugar, and 3 whites of egg, as indicated above;

Drain the oranges, and pour the syrup through the jelly-bag in which the orange juice is filtering;

When the clarified gelatine is cold, add it to the strained syrup; mix the whole, and add a few drops of prepared cochineal;

Put a mould in the ice; fill it with the pieces of orange and jelly, as directed for Maraschino Jelly with Peaches (*vide* preceding page), finishing in the same way.

WHITE CURRANT JELLY WITH RASPBERRIES

Pick 1½ lb. of white currants;

Boil 1½ pint of syrup at 30°; put the currants in it, and let them remain on the fire for two minutes, tossing the sugar-boiler to cook the currants evenly; pour the whole into a basin, and, when cold, pass through a jelly-bag;

Clarify 2 oz. of gelatine with ⅓ lb. of sugar, and 3 whites of egg, as directed for Fruit Jelly with Champagne (*vide* page 520); add it to the currant syrup; pour the jelly in a mould set in the ice, garnishing it with 1½ lb. of picked raspberries; and finish as aforesaid.

ANISETTE JELLY WITH PEARS

Cut 6 *Bon Chrétien* pears, each in 6 pieces; trim them, and cook them in some syrup, adding a few drops of prepared cochineal;

Clarify 2 oz. of gelatine, with:

¾ lb. of lump sugar,	2¼ pints of water,
3 whites of egg,	the juice of a lemon;

As described for Fruit Jelly with Champagne (*vide* page 520);

When cold, add ½ pint of *Anisette* to the jelly;

Drain the pears;

Put a mould in the ice, and fill it with alternate layers of jelly and pears, as directed for Maraschino Jelly with Peaches (*vide* page 522).

CRÈME DE MOKA JELLY

Put 2 oz. of gelatine and ¾ lb. of lump sugar in a stewpan ;

Beat 3 whites of egg; add 2½ pints of water, and the juice of a lemon ; pour this mixture on the gelatine, and stir with a wire whisk over the fire until it boils; then strain the jelly through a jelly-bag, until it becomes perfectly clear ; when it is cold, add ½ pint of *Crème de Moka*, or Coffee Liqueur ;

Put a mould in the ice ; fill it with the jelly, and turn the latter out at the end of two hours.

CRÈME DE THÉ JELLY

Proceed as above,—substituting a flavouring of *Crème de Thé* for that of *Crème de Moka*.

WHIPPED MADEIRA JELLY À LA RUSSE

Put 1½ oz. of gelatine in a stewpan, with ¾ lb. of lump sugar, and 1 pint of water ; melt it over the fire; strain it through a silk sieve, and add 3 gills of Madeira ;

Put a tinned copper whipping-bowl on the ice; pour in the jelly, and whip it with a wire whisk ; take it off the ice, and whip it for ten minutes more ;—should the jelly become too firm, dip the bowl in warm water for a few seconds ;—continue whipping until the jelly is all a thick froth ; then pour it into a mould, set in the ice ; let it remain therein for three quarters of an hour ;

Turn the jelly out ; and serve.

CHAUD-FROID OF FRUIT

Make some Orange Jelly, as described at page 522 ; pour a little of it in a plain border-mould set in the ice ; when it is set, garnish the mould with :

Some preserved greengages, cut in halves,

Some preserved apricots, cut in quarters,

Some slices of pine-apple, cooked in syrup ;

And fill the mould up with the jelly ;

Cut 8 Colville apples in quarters ; peel and core them ; and cook them in some syrup ;

Drain, and let them cool ;

Turn the border out of the mould on to a dish ; pile up the pieces of apple in the shape of a pyramid ; pouring some partly set *Blanc-manger* (*vide* page 517) over each row, and letting it set before beginning another ;

Take 4 large French plums ; remove the stones, and put the four plums together, so as to imitate a truffle ;

Cut half an apple to represent a cock's comb ;

Make a garnishing skewer with some sugar (prepared as directed for that used for Oranges *Glacées au Caramel, vide* First Part, page 209) ;

Put the cut apple and the plums on this skewer ; coat the apple with some *Blanc-manger*, stick in the skewer on the top of the pyramid ; and serve.

Observation.—It will be observed that this dish is intended as an imitation of the *Chaud-froid* of Chicken ; I do not give it for any intrinsic merit of its own, but merely as a pleasant fancy dish.

COFFEE BAVAROIS À LA MODERNE

Melt, in a stewpan over the fire, $\frac{3}{4}$ oz. of gelatine, and 10 oz. of lump sugar, in 1 pint of water ; strain the jelly through a silk sieve ; and, when cold, add to it 1 gill of *Crême de Moka* ;

Put a cylinder-mould in the ice, and coat it with the jelly ;

Make a cream, as directed for Vanilla Cream (*vide* First Part, page 194),—flavouring it with strong coffee, instead of vanilla ; and finishing the cream with some whipped cream, in the same way ;

Pour the coffee cream into the mould ; let it remain in the ice for an hour and a half ; then turn the *Bavarois* out ; and serve.

COCOA BAVAROIS À LA MODERNE

Melt $\frac{3}{4}$ oz. of gelatine, in a stewpan, over the fire ; with :

    10 oz. of lump sugar ;

    1 pint of water ;

    1 stick of vanilla ;

Strain the jelly, through a silk sieve, into a basin, to cool ;

Take $\frac{1}{2}$ lb. of cocoa-nibs ; roast them in a copper sugar-boiler, over a slow fire ; and put them, hot, in $1\frac{1}{2}$ pint of boiling milk, and let them steep for an hour ;

Put 8 yolks of egg in a stewpan, with 10 oz. of sugar and the milk and cocoa-nibs; stir over the fire, without boiling; add 1½ oz. of gelatine, previously steeped in water; and press the whole through a tammy cloth;

Stir the above custard on the ice, till it begins to set; and add 1½ pint of whipped cream;

Put a cylinder-mould in the ice; take it out, and coat it with the vanilla jelly; put it back in the ice; and, when the jelly is set, fill the mould with the cocoa cream; let it remain in the ice for two hours; turn the *Bavarois* out of the mould; and serve.

LEMON BAVAROIS À LA MODERNE

Coat a cylinder-mould with some Lemon Jelly;

Steep the peel of 2 lemons in 1½ pint of boiling milk, for an hour;

Put 8 yolks of egg, in a stewpan, with 10 oz. of pounded sugar, and the lemon milk; stir over the fire, till the egg begins to thicken; add 1½ oz. of gelatine, previously steeped in water; and, when this is melted, strain the whole, through a tammy cloth, into a stewpan;

Put the stewpan on the ice, and stir the custard till it begins to thicken; then add 1 pint of whipped double cream;

Fill the coated mould with the Lemon Cream; let it remain in the ice for two hours;

Turn the *Bavarois* out of the mould; and serve.

ORANGE BAVAROIS À LA MODERNE

Coat a mould with some Orange Jelly; and set it in the ice;

Make a cream as above,—substituting the peel of 2 oranges, for the lemon peel; and finish the *Bavarois* in the same way.

APRICOT CREAM À LA MUSCOVITE

Observation.—This cream can only be prepared in a hermetically closing ice-mould.

Rub sufficient apricots through a hair sieve to make 1 quart of *purée*; put it in a basin, and add 10 oz. of pounded sugar, and ¾ oz. of gelatine, dissolved in ½ pint of water; put the basin on the ice, and work the contents as directed for Vanilla Cream (*vide* First Part, page 194), adding 1 pint of whipped double cream ;

When the apricot cream begins to thicken, put it in an ice mould ; close the mould, and spread some butter over the opening, so that no water may penetrate inside ; imbed it in some pounded ice and saltpetre, or bay salt, so that it be surrounded by, at least, a 3-inch thickness of ice ;

At the end of two hours and a half, turn the cream out of the mould ; and serve.

All creams *à la Muscovite* should be thoroughly iced.

STRAWBERRY CREAM À LA MUSCOVITE

Make a cream as before,—substituting some Strawberry *Purée* for the Apricot *Purée* ; and finish the cream in the same way.

PEACH CREAM À LA MUSCOVITE

Prepare a cream as before,—using Peach *Purée*, instead of Strawberry *Purée* ;

Finish and freeze the cream in the same way.

PINE-APPLE CREAM À LA MUSCOVITE

Boil some slices of peeled pine-apple in syrup ;

When cold, drain, pound, and press the pine-apple through a tammy-cloth ;

Make the cream as described for Apricot Cream (*vide* page 526),—substituting 1 quart of the Pine-Apple *Purée* for that of Apricot ; and finish the cream as aforesaid.

RASPBERRY CREAM À LA MUSCOVITE

Make and freeze a cream as above,—substituting Raspberry *Purée* for Pine-Apple *Purée*.

TIMBALE DE GÉNOISE WITH ORANGE JELLY AND PINE-APPLE

Make some *Génoise* Paste in a basin, with :
 ½ lb. of flour,
 ¼ lb. of sugar,
 4 eggs ;

Work the above briskly with a wooden spoon for five minutes, and add ¼ lb. of butter, melted;

Butter a square baking-sheet; spread the paste on it, and bake it in a moderate oven until it acquires a light yellow tinge;

Take a plain pudding-mould, and put a round of paper at the bottom;

Cut a round of the paste to fit it, and place it on the paper; then cut a strip of the paste of the height of the mould; and, whilst it is hot, line the mould round with it, securing the *génoise* together at the edges with *Glace Royale* (a paste made of white of egg and finely sifted sugar);

Put the *timbale* on the ice;

Make some Orange Jelly, as directed for Orange Jelly with Oranges (*vide* page 522);

Add to it ¼ lb. of pine-apple, cooked in syrup, and cut in small dice; put the jelly in a *sauté*-pan on the ice, and, when it is partly set, fill the *timbale* with it;

Let it remain on the ice for two hours; then turn the *timbale* out of the mould, and glaze it with some Apricot Jam diluted with a little syrup; and serve.

TIMBALE DE GÉNOISE WITH FRUIT JELLY

Prepare a *timbale* as above;

Make some jelly and a fruit *macédoine*, as directed for Fruit Jelly with Champagne (*vide* page 520); mix the fruit and jelly in a *sauté*-pan on the ice; when partly set, fill the *timbale*; and finish as above.

TIMBALE DE GÉNOISE WITH KIRSCHENWASSER JELLY, APPLES, AND CHERRIES

Make a *timbale* as directed for *Timbale de Génoise* with Orange Jelly and Pine-Apple;

Cut 4 Colville apples each in 8 pieces; cook them in syrup, and drain them; when they are cold, add them to some Kirschenwasser Jelly, garnished with Cherries (*vide* page 522); when the jelly is partly set, fill the *timbale* with it, and finish as described for *Timbale de Génoise* with Orange Jelly and Pine-Apple, glazing it with some reduced Cherry Syrup, instead of with apricot.

MERINGUE WITH COFFEE CREAM

Whip 6 whites of egg, and, when very firm, mix in ½ lb. of pounded sugar;

Cut 5 rounds of paper, 6½ inches diameter;

Put the *meringue* in a paper funnel, and press it out on each round of paper into rings 5½ inches in diameter; sprinkle some sifted sugar over the rings, and put them on baking boards in the oven;

When they are of a nice yellow colour, turn the rings over on to a baking-sheet, and dry them in a slack oven;

Make some *Génoise* Paste, as directed for *Timbale de Génoise* with Orange Jelly (*vide* page 527);

When the paste is done and cold, cut out a round, 5½ inches diameter, and put the 5 rings of *meringue* on it, one above the other;

Reduce 1 gill of strong coffee and ¼ lb. of sugar to a syrup registering 36°; when cold, add it to 1 quart of well-whipped double cream;

Fill the centre of the *meringue* with this cream, piling it up 2 inches above the *meringue*; and serve.

MERINGUE WITH CHOCOLATE CREAM

Prepare the *meringue* as above;

Melt ½ lb. of chocolate in 1 gill of syrup at 20°;

When cold, add it to some whipped cream, and finish as above.

MERINGUE WITH STRAWBERRY CREAM

Prepare the *meringue* as aforesaid;

Make 1 pint of Strawberry *Purée*; mix it with ½ lb. of pounded sugar, and add a few drops of prepared cochineal;

Mix the *purée* to some whipped cream, and finish as described for *Meringue* with Coffee Cream.

MERINGUE WITH VANILLA CREAM

Prepare and dish some *meringue* rings, as directed for *Meringue* with Coffee Cream;

Sweeten 1 quart of well-whipped cream with some vanilla sugar, and plain sifted sugar;

3 Y

Fill the *meringue* with the cream, heaping it up 2 inches above the edge ; and serve.

VACHERIN WITH VANILLA CREAM

Blanch and peel 7 oz. of Jordan almonds ;

Wash, and dry them in a cloth, and pound them in a mortar with some white of egg ; when well pounded, mix the almonds, with 7 oz. of pounded sugar, to a stiffish paste ;

Roll out a piece of the paste ¼ inch thick, and cut out a round 6½ inches in diameter, and put it on a round baking-sheet sprinkled with sugar ;

Roll out the remainder of the almond paste to a ¼-inch thickness, and cut it in a band 2 inches wide, and long enough to line round a plain mould 5½ inches in diameter ; stick both ends together with a little of the same paste, moistened with white of egg ;

Put both the mould and round baking-sheet in a slack oven, to dry the paste ;

Take the paste ring out of the mould, and stick it on to the round piece of almond paste, and put it in the oven to colour slightly ;

When cold, fill the *vacherin* with whipped cream, flavoured with vanilla sugar, heaping it up 1 inch above the top of the *vacherin* ; and serve.

Observation.—These *vacherins* may be filled in the same way with either whipped Coffee or Chocolate Cream.

TIMBALE OF ALMOND GAUFRES WITH FILBERT ICE

Blanch, peel, wash, and dry 7 oz. of Jordan almonds ; pound them in a mortar with some white of egg ; add ¼ lb. of pounded sugar, and mix both together to a paste, which should not be too stiff ;

Warm some untinned baking-sheets ;

Rub them over with pure white wax, and, when cold, spread the paste on them, in strips 4 inches wide and ⅛ inch thick ;

Cook them in the oven ; when nearly done, trim the edges of the strips ; cut them across into pieces 1½ inch wide ; put them back in the oven, to finish cooking ; and roll each piece quickly, lengthwise, round some sticks, so as to make the *gaufres* ½ inch in diameter ;

With a little *Glace Royale* stick these *gaufres* upright together round a plain mould ;

Make a round of *Gênoise* Paste, the same size as the mould, and ¼ inch thick ;

Take the ring of *gaufres* out of the mould ; stick it on the round of paste ; put the *timbale* in a slack oven to dry ; and, when cold, fill it with some iced cream, made as follows :

Roast 10 oz. of filberts in a copper sugar-boiler, to remove the skin ; when cold, pound them in a mortar, adding 1 quart of boiled cream whilst pounding, and press the whole through a broth napkin into a basin ;

Put 10 yolks of egg in a stewpan, with 10 oz. of pounded sugar and the strained filbert cream ; stir over the fire, without boiling, till the yolks begin to thicken ; strain through a silk sieve into a freezing pot, set in pounded ice, and work the cream with the spatula ; when it is partly frozen, mix in 1 pint of well-whipped cream ; let it freeze, and fill the *timbale* with the ice 2 inches above the edge ;

Place a large preserved cherry on the top of each *gaufre* ; dish the *timbale* on a napkin ; and serve.

TIMBALE OF ALMOND GAUFRES WITH MARASCHINO ICE

Make a *gaufre timbale* as before ;

Fill it with some iced cream, prepared as above,—flavouring the cream with ½ pint of Maraschino, instead of the filberts ; and place a large strawberry on the top of each *gaufre* ;

Dish the *timbale* on a napkin ; and serve.

CHARTREUSE OF FRUIT

Peel 16 Colville apples, and, with a ¼-inch vegetable cutter, cut them into 1½-inch lengths ; boil the pieces in syrup at 16°, and drain them on a sieve ;

Peel 8 *Bon Chrétien* pears ; cut them in the same way as the apples ; boil the pieces in some syrup, adding a teaspoonful of prepared cochineal ; and drain them also on a sieve ;

Remove the cores and pips of the trimmings of the apples and pears, and put this fruit, with ½ pint of water, in a stewpan, over the fire ; when melted, press the whole through a hair sieve ;

Boil ¾ lb. of sugar, as indicated for Oranges *Glacées au*

Caramel (*vide* First Part, page 209); add the *purée* to it, and 1 gill of Maraschino, and reduce the whole to a very stiff marmalade;

Stone :

    10 preserved apricots,
    10 preserved greengages,
    10 preserved Mirabelle plums;

Boil the whole, with 2 oz. of dried cherries, in some syrup for a minute; let the fruit cool, and drain it on a sieve;

Wet a round of paper; put it at the bottom of a plain mould, and line round the mould with a strip of wet paper;

Arrange the strippets of apple and pear in the mould; fill the garnished mould with the preserved fruits, mixed in the apple marmalade;

Turn the *chartreuse* out of the mould on to a dish; pour some white orange jelly round, and, when this is set, garnish round, on the white jelly, with *croutons* of red orange jelly, and chopped jelly;

Put a pattern of red jelly on the top of the *chartreuse*; pile up some chopped jelly in the centre; and serve.

NEAPOLITAN CAKE

Blanch, peel, wash, and dry 1 lb. of Jordan almonds; pound them in a mortar, moistening them with white of egg, to prevent their turning oily; when well pounded, add :

1 lb. of pounded sugar,	1 small pinch of salt,
$\frac{1}{2}$ lb. of butter,	the grated peel of an orange ;
$1\frac{1}{4}$ lb. of flour,	

Mix the whole to a stiffish paste, with 12 yolks of egg, and let it rest for an hour;

Roll out the paste to $\frac{3}{16}$ inch thickness; cut it out with a plain round $5\frac{1}{2}$-inch cutter; put the rounds obtained on baking-sheets, in the oven;

When of a light golden tinge, take the rounds out of the oven, and trim them with the same cutter;

When the rounds are cold, lay them one above the other, spreading them over alternately with apricot jam, and red currant jelly;

All the pieces being stuck together, trim the outside of the cake with a knife, and spread it over with apricot jam;

Roll out some twelve-turns puff paste, $\frac{1}{8}$ inch thick; cut it into patterns with some fancy cutters; lay these patterns on a baking-sheet ; dredge some fine sugar over them, and bake them in the oven, without colouring them ;

Decorate the top and round the cake with these puff paste patterns ; and serve.

BABA WITH RAISINS

Sift 1 lb. of flour on to a pasteboard ; mix a quarter of it with ½ oz. of German yeast, and some warm water, to a softish paste, and put this sponge to rise in a warm place ;

Gather the remainder of the flour together ; make a hole in the centre, and put in :

10 oz. of butter,	½ oz. of pounded sugar,
3 eggs,	1 pinch of salt ;

Work the whole together ; then add 5 eggs, one at a time, whilst beating and working the paste, until it becomes quite smooth ;

When the sponge has risen to double its original size, work it with the paste ; then mix in ; 1½ oz. of finely chopped candied citron, 1½ oz. of well washed and dried currants, and 3 oz. of stoned raisins ;

Butter a *baba*-mould, 6 inches diameter ; half fill it with the paste, and put it in a warm place until it rises to the top of the mould ; bake in a moderate oven, and turn the *baba* out on to a napkin on a dish ;

Serve the following sauce in a boat :

Put half a pot of apricot jam in a stewpan, with ½ pint of syrup at 32°, and 1 gill of rum ;

Boil and strain the sauce through a hair sieve.

GLAZED VANILLA CAKE À LA CUSSY

Put 1 lb. of pounded sugar in a whipping bowl ; break 14 eggs on to it, and whip both together, over a very slow fire, for ten minutes ; then add 6 oz. of ground rice, ¼ lb. of butter, melted ; and 1 tablespoonful of vanilla sugar ;

Butter and flour a plain mould, 3 inches high, 9 inches diameter ; put the paste in it, and bake in a very moderate oven ;

Turn the cake out of the mould, and, when cold, glaze it with some icing, made as follows :

Put in a copper sugar boiler :

1 pint of syrup at 36°, and 1 stick of vanilla cut in pieces ; boil the syrup until it registers 38°, and take it off the fire ; when

cool, take out the pieces of vanilla, and work the syrup with a spatula till the icing thickens and becomes perfectly smooth.

GROUND RICE CAKE GLAZED WITH APRICOT JAM

Put 1 lb. of pounded sugar in a whipping bowl with 16 eggs, and whip both together over a very slow fire for fifteen minutes; then add ½ lb. of ground rice, ¾ lb. of butter, slightly melted, and ½ gill of Maraschino, and mix the whole lightly together;

Butter and flour a fluted cylinder-mould, 3 inches high; put the paste in it, and bake in a moderate oven; when done, turn the cake out of the mould; glaze it by pouring over a coating of apricot jam reduced with syrup, and sprinkle over the hot jam with chopped almonds and pistachios; let the cake cool; and serve.

NOUGAT À LA PARISIENNE

Blanch, cool, and peel 1 lb. of Jordan almonds; wash them and dry them in a cloth; slit them in halves, and put them to dry on a baking-sheet in a hot-closet;

Blanch and peel 2 oz. of pistachios; wash and dry them in a cloth, and cut them in small dice;

Break up some lump sugar and sift it through a coarse sieve so as to obtain 2 oz. of small pieces of the same size as the pistachio dice;

Put 7 oz. of pounded sugar in a copper sugar-boiler, with 1 tablespoonful of lemon-juice, and stir over a slow fire till it is melted;

Make the almonds very hot, and mix them in the melted sugar to make the *nougat*;

Oil a *nougat*-mould slightly;

Spread a small portion of the *nougat* on a baking-sheet; strew over it some of the pieces of sugar and pistachios, and lay it at the bottom of the mould; continue in the same way until the inside of the mould is completely coated with *nougat*, pressing it slightly with a lemon against the sides, to give it the shape of the mould;

When cold, turn the *nougat* out of the mould; and serve.

SULTANE À LA CHANTILLY

Prepare some *meringue* rings, as directed for *Meringue* with Coffee Cream (*vide* page 529);

Put ½ lb. of lump sugar in two small copper sugar-boilers, with a little water; and boil it as directed for Oranges *Glacées au Caramel* (*vide* First Part, page 209);

Oil the outside of a *nougat*-mould;

When the sugar has attained the right degree of boiling, let it cool for a few minutes; then put the left hand inside the mould; hold it up before you, and pour a ring of sugar, ¼ inch thick, out of the pan, all round the bottom of the mould; then pour the sugar out of the pan very slowly, moving it up and down the mould, so as to cover it with fine threads of spun sugar;

When the contents of the first sugar-boiler have become too cold, take the second, containing some more hot sugar, and continue pouring out the sugar in the same way until the mould is coated with threads of sugar to an even thickness; then warm the *sultane* by the side of the stove, to facilitate pressing the threads together without breaking them;

Put the *meringue timbale* on a napkin, on a dish, and fill the centre with whipped cream, flavoured with coffee;

When cold, take the *sultane* off the mould; place it over the *meringue*; and serve.

CROQUENBOUCHE OF FRUIT

Prepare and glaze some oranges, plums, and apricots, as directed in the First Part for Oranges *Glacées au Caramel* (*vide* page 209);

Oil a plain mould, and line it with the fruit, sticking them together with some of the sugar in which they have been glazed;

Make a tuft or plume of spun sugar;

Turn the *croquenbouche* out of the mould; put the spun sugar tuft on the top; and serve.

CROQUENBOUCHE DE GÊNOISE

Spread some *Gênoise* Paste on a baking-sheet, as directed for *Timbale de Gênoise* (*vide* page 527); bake it in the oven, and cut it out into rounds with a 1-inch plain cutter;

Boil some sugar with a little water, until it begins to form large air-bubbles; then skim a little off with the finger, and instantly plunge your hand into some cold water; if the sugar comes off easily and is brittle, it has attained the right degree of boiling;

Colour part of this sugar with a little prepared cochineal, and glaze half the rounds of *génoise* with this pink sugar; and glaze the remainder with the uncoloured sugar;

Oil a plain mould; line it with the rounds of glazed *génoise*, arranging the colours in patterns, and sticking the rounds together with a little of the white sugar;

Turn the *croquenbouche* out of the mould on to a napkin, on a dish; place a plume of spun sugar on the top; and serve.

CROQUENBOUCHE OF CHOUX GARNIS

Make some paste as directed for *Beignets Soufflés* (*vide* First Part, page 188);

Put the paste in a paper funnel; cut the point off, leaving an opening ¼ inch in diameter; squeeze out the paste on to a baking-sheet, in portions of the size of a large nut; brush them over with egg, flattening the point at the top;

Put the baking-sheet in the oven, and, when the puffs or *choux* are done, make a very small hole in each; put some Apricot Jam in a paper funnel; insert the point in the hole made in the puffs, and fill them with the jam;

Oil a plain mould;

Boil some sugar as described in the preceding recipe; dip the puffs in the sugar, and line the mould with the puffs placed side by side; when cold, turn the *croquenbouche* out of the mould on to a napkin on a dish; and serve.

VENETIAN BISCUIT

Break 6 eggs;

Put the whites in a whipping-bowl, and the yolks in a basin; add ½ lb. of pounded sugar to the latter, and beat them with a spoon for twenty minutes;

Butter a plain mould, and sprinkle some fine sugar over the butter;

Whip the whites, and when they are firm mix them with the yolks, adding ¼ lb. of flour; put the paste in the mould, and bake it in the oven;

When done, turn the *biscuit* out of the mould on to a sieve, and when it is cold glaze it with chocolate icing, made as follows:

Put 1 lb. of lump sugar in a sugar-boiler with ¾ lb. of chocolate broken in pieces, and 1½ pint of water;

Stir over the fire till the chocolate is melted, and strain the whole, through a hair sieve, into a clean sugar-boiler, and stir over the fire until the syrup registers 38° on the syrup gauge;

Take it off the fire, and work it with the spatula till the icing thickens, and, when cool, pour it over the cake; put it in the oven for a few minutes to dry it; and serve the *biscuit* when cold.

VENETIAN BISCUIT WITH ICED CREAM EN SURPRISE

Make a *biscuit* as before;

When it is cold, remove all the inside from the bottom, leaving only a ¾-inch thickness all round;

When about to serve, dish some Vanilla-cream ice on a napkin, in such a way that the *biscuit* crust will cover it entirely;

Put the *biscuit* over; and serve.

CHARLOTTE À LA CHATEAUBRIAND

Make 1 lb. of Neapolitan Cake Paste (*vide* page 532);

Roll out part of it in two strips, ⅛ inch thick and as wide as the height of the mould; put them on a square baking-sheet, and bake the paste in a slow oven;

When it is of a light golden colour, take 'it out of the oven; trim the edges very smooth, and cut the strips across in pieces ¾ inch wide;

Roll out the remainder of the paste to the same thickness, and bake it in the same way; when of a light golden colour, cut it out into rounds with a plain ¾-inch cutter;

Put a round of paper at the bottom of a Charlotte-mould;

Make some stiff *Glace Royale* with some white of egg and fine sugar, and with it stick the rounds of paste together at the bottom of the mould, overlapping one another, and in reversed circles;

WOODEN STAND FOR DISHING ENTREMETS OF PASTRY

3 z

When the bottom of the mould is covered in this way, put some of the *Glace Royale* in a paper funnel, and squeeze out some dots of it at intervals, between each circle of rounds of paste, so as to stick them together;

Put a little *Glace Royale* on one edge of each of the narrow strips of paste, and stick them together round the mould, overlapping one another, and being careful that the *Glace Royale* does not show outside;

Squeeze out a circle of *Glace Royale* inside the Charlotte, in the angle where the strips of paste join the rounds, so as to stick both together, and put the Charlotte in the hot-closet, to dry;

Put 10 yolks of egg in a stewpan, with ½ lb. of pounded sugar and 1 quart of boiled cream flavoured with vanilla;

Stir over the fire until the egg begins to thicken; take it off the fire, and stir for three minutes more, and strain the whole through a silk sieve;

Cut in dice:

6 preserved pears,	5 preserved greengages,
5 preserved apricots,	¼ lb. of dried cherries;

Put all the above fruit in separate sugar-boilers, with some syrup flavoured with Maraschino; boil up the syrup; let the fruit cool therein, and drain it;

Set a freezing-pot in the ice;

Put the cream in it, adding ½ gill of Maraschino, and 1 gill of Milk of Almonds;

Work the cream with the spatula, and, when it is partly frozen, mix in 1 pint of whipped cream; continue working until the cream is frozen, and add the prepared fruit; mix and fill an ice-mould small enough to go under the Charlotte, with the cream; close the mould; spread some butter on the opening so that no water may penetrate into the cream; and imbed it in the ice for two hours; then turn the iced cream out of the mould on to a napkin on a dish, and cover it with the Charlotte, having previously glazed the latter with Apricot Jam, diluted with syrup.

CHARLOTTE À LA SICILIENNE

Prepare a Charlotte as before; when it is quite cold, turn it out of the mould, and glaze it with a coating of thin *Glace Royale*, and strew over some coarsely chopped pistachios, and similar-sized pieces of lump sugar;

Put 1 lb. of chocolate in a stewpan, with 1 quart of cream, and stir over the fire until it is melted ;

In another stewpan, put: 8 yolks of egg, and ½ lb. of pounded sugar; add the melted chocolate, and stir over the fire without boiling, till the egg begins to thicken; take off the fire; stir for three minutes more, and strain the whole through a silk sieve;

Put the cream in a freezing-pot set in the ice; work it with the spatula, and add 1 pint of whipped cream; continue working until the cream is frozen; mould, and dish it as directed in the preceding recipe; place the Charlotte over the iced cream; and serve.

Remarks on Charlottes à la Chateaubriand and à la Sicilienne

Both these *entremets* are due to the inventive talent of M. Montmirel, known, at least in name, to all those who study the culinary art.

I have given the recipes exactly as I hold them from him; *Chateaubriands* and *Siciliennes* can be made in many other ways, but they will not then be in accordance with the dishes so named by their inventor.

MARQUISE PUDDING

Peel and core 10 *Bon Chrétien* pears; cook them in 3 pints of syrup at 12° ;

Simmer slowly, so as not to reduce the syrup; when the pears are done, press them through a silk sieve, and add ½ pint of syrup at 30° to the *purée* ;

Cut ½ lb. of pine-apple into dice, and cook it in syrup at 18° ;

Cut ½ lb. of dried cherries in two; boil them up in some syrup at 16°, and let them cool in it;

When the pine-apple is cooked and cold, strain the syrup through a silk sieve into the Pear *Purée*, and put the whole into a freezing-pot set in ice; work the *purée* with the spatula till it is partly frozen, and add 3 whites of egg of Italian *meringue*, made thus :

Put ¼ lb. of sugar in a sugar-boiler, with a little water, and boil it till it registers 40° ;

Whip 3 whites of egg, and add the boiling sugar to them,

whipping all the time; when cold, add this mixture to the *purée*, as directed above;

Continue working with the spatula, until the *purée* is completely frozen; then add the drained cherries and pine-apple; put the whole in an ice-pudding mould, of a dome shape, 6 inches diameter, and 5 inches high; close the mould, and spread some butter over the opening, to prevent any water penetrating into the ice;

Imbed the mould in some pounded ice and bay-salt for two hours;

Turn the pudding out on to a napkin, on a dish, and serve with the following sauce :

Pour half a bottle of Champagne, and 1 gill of syrup at 30°, in a small freezing-pot set in ice; let it freeze, and add 1 white of egg of Italian *meringue*, prepared as above; mix thoroughly; and serve the sauce in a boat.

NESSELRODE PUDDING

Peel 40 chestnuts; blanch them in boiling water for five minutes; peel off the second skin, and put them in a stewpan with 1 quart of syrup at 16°, and 1 stick of vanilla;

Simmer gently till the chestnuts are done; drain, and press them through a fine hair sieve;

Put 8 yolks of egg in a stewpan, with ½ lb. of pounded sugar, and 1 quart of boiled cream;

Stir over the fire, without boiling, till the egg begins to thicken; add the Chestnut *Purée*, and press the whole, through a tammy cloth, into a basin, and add 1 gill of Maraschino;

Stone ¼ lb. of raisins, and wash and pick ¼ lb. of currants; cook both together, in ½ gill of syrup at 30°, and 1 gill of water; drain, and let them cool;

Put a freezing-pot in the ice; pour in the chestnut cream, and work it with the spatula; when it is partly frozen, add 3 gills of whipped cream, and continue working with the spatula until the cream is frozen; then add the currants and raisins, and put the pudding into an ice-mould; close it, and put some butter on the opening, to prevent any salt or water penetrating inside; imbed the mould in ice, and let it remain therein for two hours;

Make the sauce as follows :

Put 3 gills of boiled cream in a stewpan, with 8 yolks of

egg, and ¼ lb. of pounded sugar; stir over the fire, without boiling, till the egg begins to thicken; take off the fire, and stir for three minutes more; strain the custard through a tammy cloth, and add ½ gill of Maraschino;

Put the sauce on the ice until it is very cold, without freezing;

Turn the pudding out of the mould on to a napkin, on a dish; and serve with the sauce in a boat.

Remarks on Marquise and Nesselrode Puddings

I have been favoured with the recipes of both these puddings by one of my old friends, M. Mony, many years *chef* at Count Nesselrode's; I can, therefore, in this case, as in that of the Charlottes *à la Chateaubriand* and *à la Sicilienne*, guarantee the authenticity of my recipes, as I receive them direct from their inventors, to whom I am happy to convey here my tribute of thanks and good fellowship.

PLOMBIÈRES

Blanch and peel ¾ lb. of Jordan almonds, and 20 bitter almonds; wash, and dry them in a cloth, and pound them in a mortar, mixing them to a softish paste with some milk; add 3 pints of boiled cream, and press the whole through a tammy cloth; put it in a stewpan with 10 yolks of eggs, and ¾ lb. of pounded sugar;

Stir over the fire without boiling, till the egg begins to thicken; take off the fire, and stir for three minutes more; strain the cream through a tammy cloth, and put it in a freezing pot set in the ice; work it with the spatula, and, when it is partly frozen, add 1½ pint of whipped cream; and continue working the cream;

Draw off any water that might be in the ice-pail, and refill it with pounded ice and bay salt, covering the freezing-pot entirely;

At the end of two hours uncover the freezing-pot, and form three decreasing rings of the iced cream, one above the other, on a napkin on a dish; coat each ring with apricot jam; and serve.

ICED RICE À L'IMPÉRATRICE

Blanch ½ lb. of rice in boiling water; drain, and put it in a stewpan with 3 pints of boiled cream, and ¾ lb. of sugar;

Simmer gently for an hour;

Make a *salpicon* of preserved fruits:

pears,	greengages,
pine-apple,	cherries;
apricots,	

Set a freezing-pot in the ice; put the rice in it, and work it with the spatula until it is partly frozen; then add 2 whites of egg of Italian *meringue*, prepared as directed for Marquise Pudding (*vide* page 539);

Continue working with the spatula, and, when the rice is frozen, add the *salpicon*; mix, and put the whole in an ice-mould; close it, and cover the joints with butter, so that no water may penetrate into the mould; and imbed it in the ice for two hours;

Make some sauce as follows:

Put half a bottle of Champagne and 1 gill of syrup at 30° in a freezing-pot set in ice;

When partly frozen, mix in 1 white of egg of Italian *meringue* prepared as described for Marquise Pudding (*vide* page 539);

Turn the rice out of the mould on to a napkin on to a dish; and serve, with the above sauce in a boat.

APRICOT CHARLOTTE RUSSE

Line a plain mould with some finger biscuits, and put it in the ice;

Make 1 pint of Apricot *Purée*; put it in a basin, and add ¾ lb. of pounded sugar and 1 oz. of gelatine, previously dissolved in 1 gill of water; put the basin on the ice, and work the contents with a spoon until the *purée* begins to freeze; then add 1 quart of well-whipped cream; mix, and fill the mould with the apricot cream, and cover it with a baking-sheet with some ice on the top; let it remain in the ice for an hour; then turn the Charlotte out of the mould on to a napkin on a dish; and serve (*vide* Woodcut, page 503).

COFFEE CHARLOTTE RUSSE

Line a mould with finger biscuits, as above;

Roast ½ lb. of green coffee in a copper pan;

Boil 1 quart of cream; put the coffee in it, and let it stand in a warm place for an hour;

Put 8 yolks of egg in a stewpan with ¾ lb. of pounded sugar;

strain in the coffee cream, and stir over the fire until the egg begins to thicken;

Steep 1 oz. of gelatine in cold water; drain, and add it to the cream; stir till the gelatine is melted; strain through a hair sieve into a basin, and stir the cream on the ice until it begins to thicken; add 1 quart of well-whipped cream, and finish the Charlotte as directed in the preceding recipe.

BURNT ALMOND CHARLOTTE RUSSE

Line a plain mould with finger biscuits, as aforesaid;

Chop ½ lb. of Jordan almonds;

Put ¼ lb. of pounded sugar in a copper pan; melt it until it becomes red hot; then pour in the chopped almonds, and stir them over the fire for a few minutes;

Spread them out on a baking-sheet, and, when they are cold, pound them in a mortar, adding 1 quart of boiling cream, and press the whole through a broth napkin;

Steep 1 oz. of gelatine in cold water;

Put the almond cream in a stewpan with 8 yolks of egg and ¾ lb. of sugar, and stir over the fire until the yolks begin to thicken;

Drain the gelatine, add it to the cream, and finish as directed for Apricot Charlotte *Russe* (*vide* page 542);

PROFITEROLLES PUDDING

Make and fill 50 small puffs or *profiterolles* with Apricot Jam, as directed for *Croquenbouche* of *Choux Garnis* (*vide* page 536);

Stone ¼ lb. of raisins, and cook them in some syrup at 20°;

Put 1 oz. of gelatine to steep in cold water;

Put 10 yolks of egg in a stewpan with ¾ lb. of pounded sugar and 1 quart of boiled cream;

Stir over the fire, without boiling, until the custard thickens; take it off the fire, and stir for three minutes more;

Drain the gelatine, add it to the custard, and, when it is dissolved, strain the whole, through a tammy-cloth, into a basin;

Put a cylinder-mould in the ice;

Add 1 gill of Kirschenwasser to the cream, and, when it is quite cold, put a layer of it, 1 inch thick, at the bottom of the mould;

Place a circle of the *profiterolles* on it, and strew some raisins in the intervals; then make some more similar layers of cream and *profiterolles*, until the mould is full;

Cover it with a baking-sheet with some ice on the top, and let it remain thus for an hour;

Turn the pudding out of the mould on to a dish; and serve.

ORLEANS PUDDING

Steep 1 oz. of gelatine in cold water;

Put 10 yolks of egg in a stewpan with ¾ lb. of pounded sugar and 1 quart of boiled cream, and stir over the fire until the egg begins to thicken;

Drain the gelatine; add it to the cream; stir till it is dissolved, and strain the whole, through a tammy-cloth, into a basin;

Cut 1 oz. of candied orange peel, and 1 oz. of candied citron in small dice;

Stone 1 oz. of raisins;

Wash and pick 1 oz. of currants;

Put all the above in a stewpan on a slow fire, with 1 gill of rum; when the rum is reduced, take the stewpan off the fire;

Set a cylinder-mould in the ice;

Put a layer of the cream at the bottom, and strew some of the fruit on it; then put a layer of slices of sponge cake and crushed ratafias; then another layer of cream, with some fruit; some more slices of sponge cake and ratafias; continue in the same way till the mould is full; and cover it with a baking-sheet, with some ice on the top;

Let the pudding remain in the ice for an hour; then turn it out of the mould on to a dish; and serve.

BISCUIT À LA CRÈME

FRUIT

CHAPTER XVII

DESSERT

Remarks on Dessert

UNDER this heading I have given a limited number of recipes of *Petits-Fours*, of Bonbons and Ices, without attempting an elaborate treatise of confectionery,—a course which would have required far more space than I have left.

However, as this special department appears to be losing its distinctive features, and merging towards final amalgamation with the other parts of a cook's business, I have thought it necessary to give sufficient indications to carry any cook successfully through the preparation of an ordinary dessert.

In this part of the work particularly, I should have needed but little inducement to increase the number of my descriptions, as, in all matters relating to dessert, a very unimportant modification will suffice to alter the character of a dish, and multiply the recipes; but I have preferred indicating only the main preparations, and if these be supplemented and diversified by the cook's

4 A

own ingenuity, I think he will find here all he requires, not merely for ordinary dinners, but for the more arduous elaboration of suppers for balls and parties.

I

PETITS-FOURS

FILBERT MACAROONS

Roast ½ lb. of filberts in a copper pan, to remove the skins: when the filberts are cold, pound them in a mortar, adding the white of an egg, in small portions; add ¼ lb. of pounded sugar. and continue pounding and mixing the whole, with some whites of egg, to a softish paste,—which, however, should not spread ;

With a teaspoon, form the paste into round balls, ¾ inch in diameter; and put them on some sheets of paper, leaving a 2-inch space between each macaroon; sprinkle over some fine sugar, and bake in a slow oven;

When of a light golden colour, take the macaroons out of the oven, and turn the sheets of paper over, so that the macaroons may rest on the table; moisten the paper at the back with a brush, dipped in water, to facilitate taking off the macaroons; and put them on a sieve till wanted.

PISTACHIO MACAROONS

Blanch and peel 7 oz. of pistachios, and 7 oz. of Jordan almonds; pound both together in a mortar, moistening with a white of egg; add ¼ lb. of pounded sugar, 1 tablespoonful of Kirschenwasser, and a small teaspoonful of green vegetable colouring ;

Shape and finish the macaroons as directed in the preceding recipe.

CHOCOLATE MACAROONS

Blanch and peel ½ lb. of Jordan almonds; pound them in a mortar; and add ¼ lb. of pounded sugar, and ¼ lb. of chocolate. slightly warmed in the hot-closet ;

Mix the above to a softish paste, with some whites of egg: and shape and finish the macaroons as directed for Filbert Macaroons.

MACAROONS SOUFFLÉS

Blanch and peel ½ lb. of Jordan almonds; cut each almond, lengthwise, in thin shreds, and put these in a basin, with 1 lb. of pounded sugar, sifted through a silk sieve; and moisten to a softish paste, with some whites of egg;

Mix the paste thoroughly; and put portions of it, of the size of a small nut, at regular intervals, on some sheets of paper; bake the macaroons in a slow oven; and take them off the paper, as described for Filbert Macaroons (*vide* page 546).

LEMON MASSEPAINS

Blanch, peel, and pound 10 oz. of Jordan almonds; add 10 oz. of pounded sugar, and moisten, to a stiff paste, with some white of egg, adding the grated peel of a lemon;

Force the paste on to some sheets of paper, sprinkled with fine sugar, through a syringe, with a ½-inch star at the end;

Cut the paste into 3-inch lengths, and turn each strip round into a ring;

Put some sheets of paper on a baking-sheet; sprinkle them with fine sugar; place the rings on the paper, and bake them in a very brisk oven, so that they may be coloured in three minutes;

Take the *massepains* out of the oven; take them off the paper, and put them on a sieve till wanted.

ALMOND PASTE LOAVES FLAVOURED WITH ORANGE

Blanch, peel, and pound 10 oz. of almonds; add 10 oz. of pounded sugar, and the grated peel of an orange; mix the whole with some white of egg, to a stiffish paste;

Divide the paste into small portions, about the size of a walnut; shape them into small oval loaves; brush them over with egg, and place them on a buttered baking-sheet; make an incision, ¼ inch deep, along the middle of the loaves, and bake them in a slow oven;

When done, take them out of the oven; and put them by till wanted.

ALMOND PASTE LOAVES WITH APRICOT JAM

Blanch, peel, and pound ¼ lb. of almonds; add ½ lb. of flour, ¼ lb. of pounded sugar, and mix the whole to a paste, with 4 yolks of egg;

Shape, and bake the loaves as before;

When they are cold, fill the opening with some stiffly reduced Apricot Jam.

ALMOND PASTE CRESCENTS

Blanch, peel, and pound 10 oz. of almonds; add 10 oz. of pounded sugar, and moisten, to a stiffish paste, with some white of egg;

Sprinkle a pasteboard with fine sugar; roll the paste on it to a ¼-inch thickness, and cut it out, with a 1½-inch round cutter, into crescent-shaped pieces, ¾ inch wide;

Bake the crescents in a slack oven; and, when cold, glaze them with some *Glace Royale*, flavoured with Kirschenwasser; strew some coarsely sifted sugar on the top, and dry them in the oven for two minutes.

ALMOND PASTE CAKES

Blanch, peel, and pound ½ lb. of almonds; add ½ lb. of pounded sugar, ½ lb. of flour, and the grated peel of a lemon; moisten with an egg, and mix the whole to a stiffish paste;

Cut the paste into olive-shaped pieces, 2 inches long, 1 inch wide; brush them over with some sweetened egg, and put them on a buttered baking-sheet, and bake them in a slack oven;

When the paste is done, fold each piece on a rolling pin, to give them the shape of quarters of lemon peel.

ALMOND PASTE RINGS

Make some paste, as directed for Almond Paste Loaves Flavoured with Orange (*vide* page 547);

Shape it into rolls, ¼ inch thick; cut these into 4-inch lengths, and turn them round to form a ring;

Chop some peeled almonds very fine; put them in a basin, with a little white of egg; add some pounded sugar, and mix the almonds thoroughly in it;

Egg the almond paste rings, and strew them over with some of the chopped almonds, and sugar; put them on a slightly buttered baking-sheet, to bake in the oven;

When the paste is partly done, place a well-drained preserved cherry in the centre of each ring, and put them back in the oven to finish cooking;

When coloured, take the rings out of the oven, and set them on a wire drainer to cool.

ALMOND PASTE TARTLETS WITH PINE-APPLE

Blanch, peel, and pound ½ lb. almonds; add ½ lb. of flour, ½ lb. of pounded sugar; and mix together, with some egg, to a stiff paste;

Roll the paste out as thin as possible, and cut it out with a 1¾-inch fluted cutter;

Butter some tartlet-moulds, slightly;

Line each mould with one of the rounds of paste; fill them with some preserved pine-apple, cut in small dice, and mixed in Apricot Jam;

Bake the tartlets in the oven; when done, take them out of the moulds, and put them to cool on a wire drainer.

ICE WAFERS

Put ½ lb. of flour in a basin, with:

   ½ lb. of pounded sugar,
   1 teaspoonful of vanilla sugar,
   3 eggs;

Mix well together, and add ½ oz. of butter, melted, and work the whole to a smooth paste; then mix in 1 quart of milk, in small quantities at first;

Heat a wafer-iron over a moderate fire; turn it over, to heat both sides equally, and pour in a spoonful of the wafer paste on one side, close the iron, and put it over the fire;

When the wafer is cooked on one side, turn the iron over, and cook the other side; cut off the superfluous paste round the iron; open it, and place a stick on one end of the wafer, and roll it quickly round the stick;

Cook all the paste in the same way; and put the wafers in a tin box, in a dry place, till wanted.

DUTCH WAFERS

Put 7 oz. of sifted flour on a pasteboard;
Add:

   5 oz. of pounded sugar,
   3 oz. of butter,
   the grated peel of an orange;

Mix the whole with 1 egg; and work it to a smooth, stiff paste;

Divide the paste into pieces, of the size of a walnut, and give them an olive-shape;

Heat an oval wafer-iron; place one of the pieces of paste in it; close the iron tightly, so as to spread the paste, and cook it on both sides; take the wafer out of the iron, and put it flat on a sieve;

When all the paste is cooked in this way, put the wafers by till wanted.

ALMOND WAFERS À L'ALLEMANDE

Blanch, peel, and pound ½ lb. of almonds; add ¼ lb. of pounded sugar, and moisten the paste with 2 whites of egg;

Warm some untinned baking-sheets; rub them over with pure white wax; and, when cold, place on them small portions of the paste, of the size of a small walnut, at regular intervals;

Flatten each portion, with a knife, to a round, 2 inches in diameter; strew the top with chopped almonds, mixed in white of egg and pounded sugar;

Bake the wafers in a slack oven; and, when done, press them on a rolling pin to curve them; and put them by for use.

RASPBERRY BOUCHÉES DE DAMES

Break 6 eggs;

Put the whites in a whipping bowl, and the yolks in a basin; add ½ lb. of pounded sugar to the latter, and work them with a wooden spoon for five minutes;

Whip the whites very firm, and add them to the yolks with ¼ lb. of flour; mix, and put the paste in a paper funnel, and press it out in rounds, 1½-inch diameter, on to some sheets of paper; dredge a little fine sugar over; and bake them in the oven;

When done, trim the rounds with the same round cutter; spread the flat surface of a round with Raspberry Jam, and place another round on it to make the *bouchée*;

Proceed in the same manner for the remainder of the rounds; and glaze the *bouchées* with some raspberry icing, made as follows:

Boil some syrup registering 36°, as directed for Oranges *Glacées au Caramel* (*vide* page 209); just previous to the syrup's reaching the breaking point, add some raspberry juice in sufficient quantity to bring the syrup down to 38°; take it off the fire; and, when it is cool, work it with the spatula until it is quite smooth, and put the icing in a basin;

Melt part of it, adding a few drops of prepared cochineal, should it not be sufficiently deep in colour;

Stick one of the *bouchées* on the point of a skewer; dip it entirely in the icing, and put it on a wire drainer;

When all the *bouchées* are glazed, put them on the drainer, in the oven to dry for two minutes;

Trim the *bouchées*, and put them on a sieve to cool.

CHOCOLATE BOUCHÉES DE DAMES

Prepare the *bouchées* as before,—spreading them with Apricot Jam instead of Raspberry Jam;

Glaze them in the same way with some chocolate icing, made as directed for Venetian *Biscuit* (*vide* page 536).

Observation.—Should the icing be too thick, dilute it with a little syrup at 32°.

COFFEE GLACÉS

Make some *biscuit* paste as directed for Raspberry *Bouchées de Dames* (*vide* page 550);

Put the paste in a paper funnel, and press it out on to some sheets of paper, in rounds, 3 inches in diameter and ¾ inch thick; bake them in the oven, and, when done, take them off the paper;

Glaze the rounds with coffee icing prepared as directed for Raspberry *Bouchées de Dames*, substituting some strong coffee for the raspberry juice.

KIRSCHENWASSER GLACÉS

Prepare some *biscuit* rounds as above;

Glaze them with Kirschenwasser icing, made with some syrup boiled until it registers 40°, and brought back to 38° by the addition of Kirschenwasser.

MARASCHINO GLACÉS

Proceed as above,—substituting an equal quantity of Maraschino for the Kirschenwasser.

STRAWBERRY GLACÉS

Prepare some rounds of *biscuit* as directed for Coffee *Glacés*;

Glaze them with strawberry icing, prepared as described for Raspberry *Bouchées de Dames* (*vide* page 550),—substituting some strawberries, pressed through a silk sieve, for the raspberry juice.

SMALL SOUFFLÉS WITH ORANGE FLOWERS

Sift ½ lb. of pounded sugar, through a silk sieve, into a basin, and moisten it to a stiffish paste with some white of egg, adding 2 oz. of candied orange flowers;

Put some nut-sized portions of this paste in some small paper cases, and cook them in a slack oven.

SMALL SOUFFLÉS WITH FILBERTS

Proceed as above,—substituting some finely chopped filberts for the orange flowers.

SMALL MERINGUES WITH CHERRIES

Boil ¾ lb. of sugar to a syrup registering 40°;

Whip 4 whites of egg;

When the sugar has partly cooled, add it to the eggs, whipping all the time; shape the *meringues*, with a teaspoon, to an oval shape, 2 inches long by 1½ inch, and put them at intervals on some sheets of paper; sprinkle over some fine sugar, and cook the *meringues* in the oven on some baking boards.

When they are done take them off the paper, and, with a teaspoon, remove some of the inside, filling it with preserved cherries; cover the cherries with a reversed *meringue*, and, when all are filled, put them on a sieve to dry in the hot-closet.

SMALL MERINGUES WITH PINE-APPLE

Make the *meringues* as above,—substituting some reduced Pine-Apple *Purée* for the cherries.

SMALL FINGER BISCUITS WITH ALMONDS PRALINÉES

Make some *biscuit* paste as directed for Raspberry *Bouchées de Dames* (*vide* page 550);

Put the paste in a paper funnel, and press it out on to some sheets of paper in oval-shaped strips, $1\frac{1}{4}$ inch long and $\frac{3}{4}$ inch wide; strew them over with finely chopped almonds, mixed in pounded sugar and Kirschenwasser;

Bake the biscuits in the oven, and, when they are done, take them off the paper; spread the flat surface of one biscuit with Apricot Jam, and reverse another biscuit on it;

Proceed in the same way for all the biscuits, and put them by for use.

SMALL FINGER BISCUITS WITH PISTACHIOS

Make and bake some finger biscuits as above, without strewing the tops with almonds;

Glaze the tops with some Italian *Meringue* (*vide* Marquise Pudding, page 539); strew over some chopped pistachios; and put the biscuits on a sieve, to dry in the hot-closet.

II

BONBONS FOR DESSERT

CANDIED PISTACHIO PASTE

Pound $\frac{1}{4}$ lb. of blanched almonds and $\frac{1}{4}$ lb. of blanched pistachios in a mortar; moisten them with a little white of egg, to prevent their turning oily; and add:

$\frac{1}{2}$ lb. of syrup at 40°,
1 tablespoonful of Kirschenwasser,
a little prepared green vegetable colouring;

Mix the whole together, and let the paste cool; take it out of the mortar, and divide, and shape it in small pieces, of the size and shape of an olive;

Put these pieces on a sieve, to dry in the hot-closet for four hours;

Set them in a candy-tin; pour over some syrup at 36°, slightly cooled, coming 1 inch above the olives; cover the tin with a sheet of paper, and allow the bonbons to candy for fifteen hours in a drying hot-closet;

Break the top of the sugar; drain off the syrup; place the bonbons on a wire drainer, and dry them in the hot-closet.

4 B

CANDIED FILBERT PASTE

Proceed exactly as before,—making the paste with pounded filberts, instead of the almonds and pistachios.

CANDIED ALMOND PASTE

Blanch, peel, and pound ½ lb. of almonds in a mortar, moistening them with a little white of egg; add:

½ lb. of syrup at 40°,
2 tablespoonfuls of Kirschenwasser,
a little prepared cochineal;

Mix the whole, and, when the paste is cold, shape, and candy the bonbons as directed for Candied Pistachio Paste.

CANDIED BONBONS À L'ANISETTE

Have a wooden case, 15 inches square and 2 inches deep; fill it with some dry starch powder, sifted through a silk sieve;

Take a plaster of Paris star or rose-shaped ornament; press it into the starch, so as to leave a hollow of the same shape;

Cover the surface of the starch with these impressions, leaving a ¼-inch space between each;

Boil 1 lb. of sugar until it registers 40°, and bring it back to 38°, by the addition of *Anisette*; let it cool, and work it with a wooden spoon until it forms a paste, and put it in a basin;

Melt part of the above paste in a small sugar-boiler, used for *pastilles*; rub some whiting on the under part of the spout, and fill the patterns in the starch with the sugar; let it dry for two hours; then take the bonbons out of the starch; brush them lightly with a soft brush; place them in a candy-pan; cover them with syrup at 36°, and finish as directed for Candied Pistachio Paste (*vide* page 553).

CANDIED BONBONS WITH MARASCHINO

Prepare a wooden case of starch powder as above; imprint the starch with a plaster of Paris mould, cut to a fluted diamond-shape;

Boil and work the sugar, as described in the preceding recipe,—substituting Maraschino for the *Anisette*; and finish the bonbons in the same way.

CANDIED BONBONS WITH KIRSCHENWASSER

Proceed as before,—using a fluted ring-shaped mould, 1¼-inch diameter;

Boil and work the sugar, as directed for Candied Bonbons *à l'Anisette*, flavouring it with Kirschenwasser;

Pour the sugar into the impressions left in the starch, and, after two hours, take the rings out; brush them with a soft brush; place a well-drained preserved cherry in the centre of each ring; set them in a candy-pan; and finish as directed for Candied Bonbons *à l'Anisette*.

VARIEGATED BONBONS

Prepare three different coloured Bonbon-pastes, by boiling and working some sugar, as described for Candied Bonbons *à l'Anisette*.

Flavouring:

The white paste, with Kirschenwasser;

The pink, with Maraschino, adding a few drops of prepared cochineal;

The third, with chocolate;

When cold, roll out the pastes to a ¼-inch thickness; place the three thicknesses one above the other, putting the pink paste in the centre; cut the bonbons in pieces 1¼ inch by ¾ inch; and put them on a baking-sheet to dry, for two hours;

Set them in a candy-pan; and finish as directed for Candied Bonbons *à l'Anisette* (*vide* page 554).

TANGERINES GLACÉES

Peel some Tangerine oranges; divide them into their quarters, and stick a thin wooden skewer through the point of each quarter;

Make some icing as described for Raspberry *Bouchées de Dames*,—substituting some orange juice, and a little of the grated orange peel, for the raspberry juice; add a few drops of prepared cochineal to the icing, and dip each piece of orange in it, and put them to dry in the hot-closet, sticking the ends of the skewers into a basinful of pounded sugar, as described for Oranges *Glacées au Caramel* (*vide* First Part, page 209);

CHERRIES GLACÉES

Dry some brandy cherries in the hot-closet, and glaze them
with icing, flavoured with Kirschenwasser, prepared as directed
for Candied Bonbons with Kirschenwasser.

RASPBERRIES GLACÉES

Drain some preserved raspberries; dry them in the hot-closet,
and glaze them with some raspberry icing, prepared as directed
for Raspberry *Bouchées de Dames*.

CHESTNUT BONBONS GLAZED WITH CHOCOLATE

Make some Chestnut *Purée*, as directed for Vermicelli Chestnuts (*vide* First Part, page 208);

Divide it into portions about the size of a chestnut, and press
ach portion in the corner of a cloth, to shape the chestnut;

Stick a small skewer in each bonbon, and let them dry for
an hour;

Glaze them with some chocolate icing, made as directed for
Venetian *Biscuit* (*vide* page 536); and dry them in the hot-
closet.

TEA CARAMEL TABLETS WITH CREAM

Boil ½ lb. of sugar to the breaking point, when tried in
cold water, as directed for *Croquenbouche de Gênoise* (*vide* page
535);

Add 1 tablespoonful of *Crème de Thé*, and 4 tablespoonfuls
of double cream; and boil the whole up again to the breaking
point;

Let the sugar cool, and pour it on to a slightly oiled marble
slab;

When nearly cold, cut it into tablets, with a 1-inch square
sugar-cutter, and put the tablets on a sieve in a dry place.

WHITE CHOCOLATE CARAMEL TABLETS

Boil ½ lb. of sugar as above; add 1 oz. of Cocoa Butter; and
finish the tablets as described in the preceding recipe.

CHERRY CARAMEL TABLETS

Boil ⅛ lb. of sugar as directed for Tea *Caramel* Tablets ; just before the sugar has attained the breaking point, add 1 table-spoonful of cherry juice, and 8 drops of Pyroligneous Acid ;

Finish boiling the sugar and making the tablets as aforesaid.

WHITE COFFEE CARAMEL TABLETS WITH CREAM

Proceed as directed for Tea *Caramel* Tablets,—substituting *Crême de Moka* for the *Crême de Thé.*

CHOCOLATE CREAMS

Boil ¼ lb. of sugar with 1 stick of vanilla, until it registers 40° on the syrup gauge ;

Add 2 tablespoonfuls of double cream, and pour the whole into a basin ;

When partly cold, take out the vanilla, and work the sugar with a wooden spoon until it forms a paste, and divide this in portions of the size of a small nut ;

Melt some chocolate in a sugar-boiler, adding sufficient syrup at 20° to bring it to the consistence of thick *bouillie* ;

Dip each ball of cream in the chocolate ; take it out with a fork, and put them on a baking-sheet till cold ; then take them off, and put them on a sieve to dry ;

Observation.—These Chocolate Creams may be flavoured with Coffee, *Caramel*, Kirschenwasser, Pistachios, &c. ; instead of the Vanilla.

CHOCOLATE CREAMS AU NOUGAT

Chop 1 oz. of blanched almonds ;

Melt 2 tablespoonfuls of pounded sugar in a sugar boiler ; add the chopped almonds ; and stir over the fire till they acquire a brown tinge ;

Spread the *nougat* on a baking-sheet, and, when cold, chop it very fine, and mix it with an equal quantity of Vanilla Cream, prepared as described in the preceding recipe ; roll the mixture into small balls, and dip them in the chocolate, as described above.

STRAWBERRY DROPS

Put ¾ lb. of coarsely sifted sugar,—having previously sifted all the fine sugar away,—into a basin; and mix it to a stiff paste, with some Strawberry *Purée*;

Put the paste in a *pastille* sugar-boiler, and stir it over the fire till it boils; then let the drops fall slowly out of the pan on to a baking-sheet; and, when cold, put them on a sieve to dry in the hot-closet.

PINE-APPLE DROPS

Make the drops as above,—mixing the sugar with Pine-Apple *Purée*, instead of the Strawberry *Purée*.

PUNCH DROPS

Put ¾ lb. of coarsely-sifted sugar in a basin; mix it to a stiff paste, with some rum and lemon-juice;

Put the paste in a *pastille* sugar-boiler; boil it, and make the drops as described for Strawberry Drops.

RED CURRANT DROPS

Make the drops as aforesaid, mixing the sugar to a stiff paste with equal quantities of red currant-juice and water.

ORANGE FLOWER BONBONS IN CASES

Boil ¾ lb. of sugar to 38°; let it cool, and work it with the spatula until it becomes white; add 1 oz. of candied orange-flowers; fill some small paper cases with the sugar; and put them in the hot-closet to dry.

PINE-APPLE BONBONS IN CASES

Boil and work some sugar, as above;

Substitute some chopped preserved pine-apple for the orange flowers; and finish the bonbons in the same way.

III

COMPOTES AND FRUIT

CHESTNUT COMPOTE

Make some Chestnut *Purée*, as directed for Vermicelli Chestnuts (*vide* First Part, page 208);

Shape the *purée* into balls, about the size of a chestnut, and set them on a slightly-buttered baking-sheet; cover them thickly with fine sugar; glaze them with a hot salamander; and dish them in a compote glass;

Mix 1 gill of Noyeau with 1 gill of syrup at 29°; and, just before serving, pour it in the compote glass,—but not over the chestnuts.

PINE-APPLE COMPOTE

Cut all the peel off a pine-apple; cut it into slices $\frac{1}{4}$ inch thick; keep one of the middle slices whole, and cut the remainder in two;

Put all the pine-apple in a sugar-boiler, with some syrup at 20°;

Boil, and simmer for an hour on the stove corner, and pour the whole into a basin; let the pine-apple steep thus for twenty-four hours;

Put the pieces on a wire drainer;

Strain the syrup, through a silk sieve, into a sugar-boiler; and reduce it to 32°;

Dress the half slices of pine-apple in a circle, in a compote glass; put the whole slice in the centre; pour the syrup over; and serve.

MIXED FRUIT COMPOTE WITH ICED CHAMPAGNE

Cut 2 *Bon Chrétien* pears in quarters; peel and trim them very smooth; cook them in a sugar-boiler, with some syrup at 16°, and sufficient prepared cochineal to make the pears of a nice pink colour;

Cut 2 Colville apples in quarters; peel, trim, and cook them in a sugar-boiler, with some syrup at 16°;

Cut 2 slices of pine-apple in two pieces, and cook them in some syrup;

Stone 5 greengages, and cook them in syrup;

When cold, drain all the fruit, and arrange it, tastefully, in a compote-glass, and put it in a very cold place ;

Set a small freezing-pot in some pounded ice and bay salt ; pour in half a bottle of Champagne, and ½ gill of syrup at 30° ;

Let it freeze to icicles, and pour it over the fruit before serving.

ICED CHERRY COMPOTE

Remove the stalks and stones of 2 lbs. of May-Duke cherries ;

Cook them in 3 gills of syrup at 32° ;

When cold, drain the cherries, and strain the syrup, through a silk sieve, into a freezing-pot set in ice ; add 3 tablespoonfuls of Kirschenwasser ; and, when it is frozen to icicles, add the cherries ;

Let them remain in the ice for a quarter of an hour ;

Pour the whole into a compote-glass ; and serve.

ICED STRAWBERRY COMPOTE

Arrange some fine picked strawberries in a compote-glass ;

Set a small freezing-pot in the ice ; pour in 1 pint of Marsala, and 1 gill of syrup at 32° ; when the wine is frozen to icicles, pour it over the strawberries ; and serve.

CORBEILLES OF FRUIT

These *corbeilles* should be filled with fruit in season, arranged in a tasteful manner ;

Say, in Summer, with :

peaches,	nectarines,
strawberries,	plums,
apricots,	pine-apple, &c. ;
grapes,	

And in Winter, with :

apples,	raisins,
pears,	pine-apple, &c.
oranges,	

IV

ICES AND SORBETS

VANILLA AND STRAWBERRY ICE

Boil 1½ pint of double cream with a stick of vanilla ;

Put 6 yolks of egg in a stewpan, with ¼ lb. of pounded

sugar; add the boiled cream, and stir over the fire, without boiling, and, when the egg begins to thicken, strain the whole, through a silk sieve, into a basin;

Make 1 pint of Strawberry *Purée*; add 1 pint of syrup at 35°; mix both thoroughly, and strain through a silk sieve;

Set 2 freezing-pots and an ice-mould in some pounded ice and bay salt;

Put the vanilla cream in one pot, and the strawberry syrup in the other;

Freeze, and work both ices with the spatula, until they are very smooth;

Cut a piece of cardboard to fit the centre of the ice-mould; place it in perpendicularly, dividing the mould in two equal parts; fill each side completely, one with the vanilla ice, and the other with the strawberry ice, and remove the piece of cardboard; close the mould, and imbed it in the ice for two hours;

Take the mould out of the ice; dip it in water; turn the ice out on to a napkin, on a dish; and serve.

APRICOT AND PISTACHIO ICE

Blanch, peel, and pound ¼ lb. of pistachios;
Boil 1½ pint of milk;
Put 6 yolks of egg in a stewpan, with ¼ lb. of pounded sugar, and the boiled milk;

SUGAR BOILER

Stir over the fire, till the egg begins to thicken, and, when cool, add the pounded pistachios, and a little green vegetable colouring, and strain the whole through a tammy cloth into a basin;

Make 1 pint of Apricot *Purée*; mix it with 1 pint of syrup at 35°, and strain through a silk sieve;

Freeze the ices, and mould them together, as directed in the preceding recipe.

4 c

BURNT ALMOND AND ORANGE ICE

Chop 2 oz. of blanched almonds;

Melt 2 tablespoonfuls of pounded sugar, in a sugar-boiler; add the chopped almonds, and stir over the fire until they assume a red-brown colour, and spread them on a baking-sheet;

Boil 1½ pint of double cream;

Put 6 yolks of egg in a stewpan, with ¼ lb. of pounded sugar; add the boiled cream, and stir over the fire until the egg thickens;

Pound the burnt almonds in a mortar; add them to the cream; and strain the whole, through a tammy cloth, into a basin;

Mix 1 pint of orange juice with 1 pint of syrup at 35°, in which some orange peel has been steeping, and strain through a silk sieve;

Freeze the ices, and mould them together, as described for Vanilla and Strawberry Ice.

ALMOND AND RASPBERRY ICE

Blanch, peel, and pound ½ lb. of Jordan almonds, and ½ oz. of bitter almonds;

Boil 3 pints of double cream; when cool, add ½ lb. of pounded sugar, and 12 yolks of egg;

Stir over the fire, without boiling, until the egg thickens; add the pounded almonds, and 1 tablespoonful of Kirschen-wasser; and strain the whole, through a tammy cloth, into a basin;

Mix 1 quart of raspberry juice, and 1 quart of syrup at 35°, and strain through a silk sieve;

Set two freezing-pots in the ice;

Put the almond cream in one pot, and the raspberry syrup in the other; freeze, and work the ices; draw the water out of the pails; replenish them with fresh ice and bay salt; close the freezing-pots; cover them with ice, and put a wet cloth on the top;

Pile the ices up on a napkin, on a dish, in irregular layers, mingling the colours; and serve.

PARFAIT AU CAFÉ

Roast ½ lb. of coffee in a copper pan;

Boil 3 pints of double cream; put the coffee in it; cover the stewpan, and let the coffee steep for an hour:

Put 12 yolks of egg in a stewpan, with ½ lb. of pounded sugar;

Strain the cream; add it to the egg, in the stewpan; stir over the fire, without boiling, until it thickens, and strain it through a tammy cloth;

Set a freezing-pot and a *parfait*-mould in some pounded ice, and bay salt;

Put the cream in the freezing-pot, and work it with the spatula;

When the cream is partly frozen, add ½ gill of syrup at 32°; continue working the cream, and, when the syrup is well mixed, add another ½ gill of syrup, and 1 quart of well-whipped cream;

Fill the mould with the iced cream; close it hermetically, and imbed it in the ice for two hours;

Turn the *parfait* out of the mould on to a napkin, on a dish; and serve.

CURRANT AND VANILLA BOMBE

Mix 1½ pint of red currant juice, and 1½ pint of syrup at 30°, and strain the syrup through a silk sieve into a basin;

Put 18 yolks of egg in a stewpan, with 1 pint of syrup at 32°, 1 quart of double cream, and 1 stick of vanilla;

Stir over the fire, without boiling, till the egg begins to thicken, and strain the whole, through a silk sieve, into a basin;

Set two freezing-pots and a *bombe*-mould in some pounded ice and bay salt;

Put the currant syrup in one pot, and the vanilla cream in the other; freeze, and work both the ices;

Line the mould with an inch thickness of the currant ice, and fill the centre with the vanilla ice;

Close the mould, and imbed it in the ice for two hours;

Turn the *bombe* out of the mould on to a sheet of paper;

Cut it in slices ¾ inch thick, and cut each slice in half; dish the pieces on a napkin; and serve.

APRICOT AND MARASCHINO BOMBE

Make 1 quart of Apricot *Purée*; mix it with 1 quart of syrup at 30°; and strain it, through a silk sieve, into a basin;

Put 14 yolks of eggs in a stewpan, with:

    3 gills of syrup at 32°;

    3 gills of cream;

    3 tablespoonfuls of Maraschino;

Stir over the fire until the egg begins to thicken ; strain the cream, through a silk sieve, into a basin, and whip it until it becomes of the consistence of *biscuit* paste ;

Set 2 freezing-pots and a *bombe*-mould in some pounded ice and bay salt ;

Put the apricot syrup in one freezing-pot ; freeze, and work it with the spatula ;

Put the cream in the other pot, and work it with the spatula, adding 3 gills of whipped cream ;

Line the mould with a coating of apricot ice 1 inch thick ; fill the centre with the Maraschino ice ; close the mould, and imbed it in the ice for two hours ;

Turn the *bombe* out on to a sheet of paper ; cut it in slices ¾ inch thick ; cut each slice across ; dish the pieces on a napkin ; and serve.

ROMAN PUNCH

Put 1 quart of Châblis in a basin, with :

   1 quart of syrup at 35°,

   ½ pint of lemon-juice ;

Strain the whole, through a silk sieve, into a freezing-pot set in pounded ice and bay salt ;

Work the syrup with the spatula, and, when it is frozen, add 2 whites of egg of Italian *meringue* (*vide* Marquise Pudding, page 539) ;

Close the freezing-pot, and cover the pail with a wet cloth ;

When about serving add ½ gill of rum and half a bottle of Champagne to the iced syrup ; mix and ladle the punch out into glasses ; and serve.

Observation.—This punch and the following *sorbets* are served at dinner with the roasts.

SORBET AU RHUM

Put 1 quart of Châblis in a basin, with :

   1 quart of syrup at 35°,

   ½ pint of lemon-juice ;

Mix the whole well together, and strain it, through a silk sieve, into a freezing-pot set in some pounded ice and bay salt ;

Work the ice with the spatula, and, when it is frozen, add ½ gill of rum ; mix, and serve the *sorbet* in glasses.

KIRSCHENWASSER SORBET

Make some ice as before, omitting the lemon-juice ;

Flavour the *sorbet* with an equal quantity of Kirschenwasser, instead of rum, when about serving.

ICED CHAMPAGNE GRANITE WITH STRAWBERRIES

Set a freezing-pot in some pounded ice and bay salt ;

Pour in 1 quart of syrup at 25° and 2 bottles of Champagne ;

Let it freeze to icicles, and add 1 lb. of picked strawberries, and serve the granite in glasses.

Observation.—The above quantity is calculated for 20 to 24 persons.

ICED LEMON GRANITE

Set a freezing-pot in the ice, and pour in 3 pints of syrup at 28°, and 1 gill of filtered lemon-juice ; freeze it into icicles ; and serve the granite in glasses.

ICED ORANGE GRANITE

Pare the peel off 6 oranges ; cut them into quarters, removing all the white skin and pips ;

Put the pieces of orange in a basin, with 3 pints of syrup at 20° ; let them steep for two hours ; then drain them, and strain the syrup, through a silk sieve, into a freezing-pot set in ice ;

When the syrup is frozen to icicles, put in the pieces of orange ;

Cover the freezing-pot for twenty minutes ; and serve the granite in glasses.

ICED COFFEE

Mix ½ pint of strong coffee in a basin, with 3 pints of scalded double cream, and 1 pint of syrup at 35° ;

Strain the coffee, through a silk sieve, into a freezing-pot set in ice ;

Let it freeze for an hour ; detach the frozen cream adhering to the pot ; and serve the coffee in *sorbet* glasses.

ICED CHOCOLATE

Melt 1 lb. of Vanilla Chocolate with 3 gills of water ; add 3 pints of double cream, and ½ gill of syrup at 35° ; strain the whole, through a silk sieve, into a freezing-pot, and finish as directed for Iced Coffee (*vide* preceding recipe).

Remarks on Ices

All the foregoing ices were wont to be prepared in this way, and with very great success, by my old friend M. Etienne, sometime confectioner to the Princess de Bragation, and so well known by his exhaustive Treatise on Confectionery, a work which will well repay perusal.

He excelled in all that relates to his art, and, where nearly all is perfect, it would be invidious to praise any particular part. I merely wish to add my testimony of his great talent to that of all those who have known him.

V

REFRESHING DRINKS

Remarks on Refreshing Drinks

I have purposely given the good old-fashioned way of preparation, in my recipes of the following refreshing drinks. I think it is to be regretted that this method should not be more general, as there is nothing to equal the pleasant freshness of these simple beverages. I consider them immeasurably superior to those prepared with iced water and fruit syrup, in which the flavour of the fruit is always impaired.

ORANGEADE

Steep the peel of 6 oranges in 1 quart of syrup at 35° ;

Press out all the juice of the oranges; mix it with the juice of 3 lemons, and filter it through a jelly-bag, with some paper (*vide* Orange Jelly, page 522) ;

Strain the syrup through a silk sieve into a basin; add the filtered juice and 2 quarts of water; mix, and pour the Orangeade into glass jugs.

CURRANT WATER

Press 1 quart of red currants and $\frac{1}{2}$ pint of raspberries in a basin ; add 2 quarts of water ; and filter the juice through a jelly-bag with some paper (*vide* preceding recipe) ;

Add 1 quart of syrup at 35° to the filtered juice; mix, and pour the Currant Water into glass jugs.

Observation.—In winter, substitute some preserved currant-juice, which will still be preferable to currant syrup, so seldom obtained with the full flavour of the fruit.

CHERRY WATER

Pick 2 lbs. of May-Duke cherries; put them in a basin, and pour 3 quarts of boiling water on them; cover the basin, and let the cherries steep for two hours;

Filter the juice through a jelly-bag with some paper;

Add 1 quart of syrup at 38° to the filtered juice; mix, and pour the Cherry Water into glass jugs.

LEMONADE

Steep the peel of 6 lemons in 1 quart of syrup at 35°;

Press out the juice of the lemons; add 2 quarts of water, and filter the whole through a jelly-bag with some paper;

Strain the syrup through a silk sieve; mix it with the filtered juice, and pour the Lemonade into glass jugs.

ORGEAT

Blanch and peel ½ lb. of Jordan almonds;

Pound them in a mortar, adding 3 pints of water; press through a broth napkin, and add 1 quart of syrup at 30° and a teaspoonful of orange-flower water; mix, and pour the *Orgeat* into glass jugs.

Observation.—When the jugs are filled with either of the above drinks, they should be put in the ice for two hours before they are served.

PEAR COMPOTE

APPENDIX

I

MODE OF FOLDING A NAPKIN FOR DISHING, ETC.

THE FOLLOWING is the most usual and elegant way of folding a napkin, either to set before each guest, or to lay in a dish under fried preparations :—

Take a damask napkin folded in three lengthwise (*vide* fig. 1) A B C D.

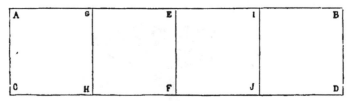

FIG. 1.

Fold it then into four equal squares : A H, G F, E J and I D; and, reopening the napkin, bring it back to the shape A B C D.

Fold across from e to h and from e to j (*vide* fig. 2).

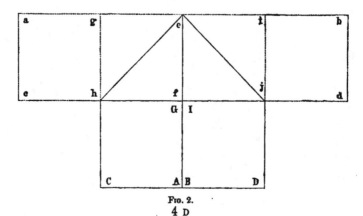

FIG. 2.

4 D

Following the line F X in the middle of E h (fig. 3), refold the napkin, so that h may fall on E.

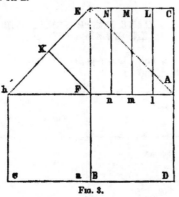

FIG. 3.

Fold over the square E C F A at the three points L M and N; namely, C A on M m; L l on N n; M m on E F; and then give one more fold over from N n to o p (*vide* fig. 4).

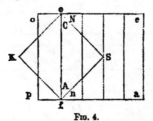

FIG. 4.

Repeat the same process for the part e B D j (fig. 2), folding it over

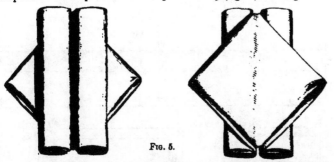

FIG. 5.

from j to e, and folding round the part I B D j (fig. 2) in the same way as E C F A (fig. 3). The folded napkin will then present the appearance indicated in fig. 4; S N e o K p f n; or, to put it more clearly, that illustrated in fig. 5.

II

DIRECTIONS TO MAKE PAPER FRILLS FOR GARNISHING KNUCKLE BONES, ETC.

Cut out a piece of white letter-paper, 18 inches long, 5 inches wide (*vide* A B C D, plate I, fig. 1).

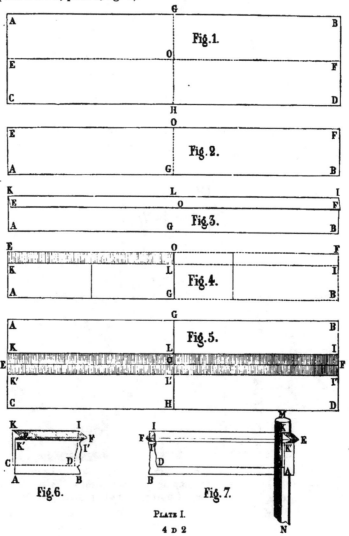

PLATE I.

4 D 2

Fold it in two lengthwise, following the line ʙ ꜰ (*vide* figs. 1 and 2).

Fold down ʙ ꜰ about ½ an inch (*vide* ᴋ ʙ ɪ ꜰ, fig. 3).

Re-open this last fold, and double over the paper at ᴏ ɢ (fig. 4), so that ꜰ may fall on ʙ and ʙ on ᴀ. Then with scissors or a sharp pen-knife, snip from ʙ ᴋ to ᴏ ʟ, in a series of very regular parallel cuts, ⅛ inch apart, and perpendicular to ʙ ᴏ.

Then unfold the whole paper (*vide* fig. 5).

Refold the paper as shown in fig. 6; that is:—Taking ᴋ ɪ as the main fold, draw down the part ɪ′ ᴋ′ ʙ ᴀ from ɪ ᴋ ᴅ ᴄ, so as to form the small triangles ᴋ ʙ ᴋ′ and ɪ ꜰ ɪ′ and the space ᴄ ᴀ, ᴅ ʙ; then, following

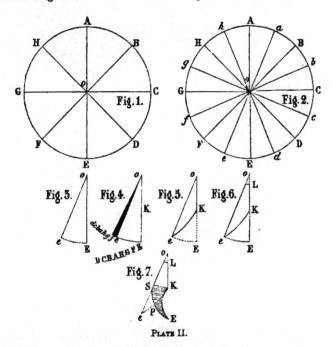

Pʟᴀᴛᴇ II.

the indications given in fig. 7, roll the paper round the handle of a wooden spoon, keeping the small triangle ᴋ ʙ ᴋ′ in shape, so as to form a close spiral (*vide* plate 3, fig. 1).

For the rosette or lower part of the frill, cut a round of paper about 7 inches diameter; fold it over 3 times on one side (*vide* fig. 1, plate 2), and three times on the other side (*vide* fig. 2).

Fold all these divisions one over the other into a triangle (fig. 3), of which the centre *o* will be the apex, and the circumference ʙ *e* the base. In fig. 4 the left side represents the folds indicated in fig. 2, and the right side those indicated in fig. 1.

Keeping the sixteen thicknesses close together with the thumb and forefinger, cut through the whole with scissors in a curved line κ e (fig. 5), removing the portion κ ε e; the point κ should be the middle of the line o ε.

Keeping the whole still close together, set the paper with the point e outwards, in the corner of a napkin on the edge of a table; fold the napkin tightly round it, and press the whole down firmly with the left hand, whilst with the right you give the napkin a series of sharp downward pulls, so that at each pull the folded paper may be drawn gradually

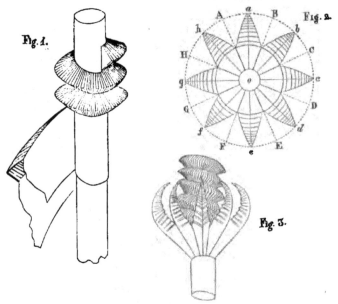

PLATE III.

out, and that the points between κ e s (fig. 7) may be gauffered; a little practice will make this operation very easy.

There will only remain to cut through the point at L, about ½ an inch from the apex o (figs. 6 and 7) and to unfold the paper; it will then have the shape of an eight-pointed star or tulip-like rosette, which should be slipped on the above frill (*vide* plate III. fig. 1), which it will hold together.

Fig. 3 of the above plate shows the frill complete.

Fig. 2 is the rosette before it is added to the frill, and shows all the folds, the cut-out portions, and the gauffering.

INDEX

---

4 E

4 F

4 G

INDEX TO WOODCUTS

The 'Edition de Luxe,' with the Coloured Plates and Woodcuts, handsomely bound for the drawing-room, price Two Guineas, may still be obtained at all Booksellers.

THE

ROYAL COOKERY BOOK

(LE LIVRE DE CUISINE),

By JULES GOUFFÉ,

CHEF DE CUISINE OF THE PARIS JOCKEY CLUB.

TRANSLATED AND ADAPTED FOR ENGLISH USE BY

ALPHONSE GOUFFÉ,

HEAD PASTRY COOK TO HER MAJESTY THE QUEEN.

ILLUSTRATED WITH

SIXTEEN large PLATES, beautifully PRINTED in COLOURS,

AND

ONE HUNDRED AND SIXTY-ONE WOODCUTS.

The **PALL MALL GAZETTE**, in reviewing the original French work, says:—'JULES GOUFFÉ, the most renowned *officier de bouche* of the present day, has written, and Messrs. Hachette have published, by far the ablest and most complete work on Cookery that has ever been submitted to the gastronomic world. It is difficult to say which is most admirable, the eminent good sense and thorough knowledge of his subject displayed by the great French cook, or the liberality, skill, and taste with which his compositions have been typified and illustrated by the great French publishers. . . . . The receipts contained in M. GOUFFÉ's work must be studied and performed in order to be appreciated as they deserve. In performing his task, M. GOUFFÉ acknowledges with gratitude the assistance he has received from many eminent artists of the day, and more especially from his distinguished brothers, ALPHONSE and HIPPOLITE, the elder of whom has for the last twenty-five years filled a high position at the Court of Queen VICTORIA, whilst the younger has for a like period directed the 'Interior' of Count ANDREW SCHOUVALOFF. Every assistance that can be rendered from pencil as well as pen, the student of "*Le Livre de Cuisine*" enjoys. It is impossible to speak too highly of the clearness of M. GOUFFÉ's language, of the minuteness and exactitude of his directions, or of the marvellous *luxe* and beauty of the wood-engravings and chromolithographs, by which he on all occasions illustrates his theory and his practice.'

The **SATURDAY REVIEW** says:—'M. JULES GOUFFÉ is the Author of this sumptuous volume. He has been moved to compose it by the sight of the unutterable platitudes into which the notabilities of culinary literature are constantly falling. It seems that the *servum pecus* of imitators have found their way even as far as the kitchen, and have *ravalé la profession* so as to degrade it in the esteem of all true judges. M. GOUFFÉ is an excellent guide, and we can trust him thoroughly. Nor should the humble housekeeper be frightened at the sight of an octavo which seems only fit for the luxuries of a West-end Club; *la cuisine de ménage* receives its due share of attention, and if transcendental dinners can be prepared from the formulæ therein contained, so may the simple repasts of Government clerks and commercial travellers. The whole realm of the kitchen will find in M. GOUFFÉ's "*Livre de Cuisine*" an irrefragable authority; and numerous illustrations in the way of chromolithographs, woodcuts, and even geometrical figures, enable the novice, not only to distinguish between good and bad meat, but to lay the cloth tastefully and to fold a napkin *comme il faut*.'

London: SAMPSON LOW, SON, & MARSTON, Crown Buildings, 188 Fleet Street.

4 H

NEW ILLUSTRATED WORKS.

AN ELEGY IN A COUNTRY CHURCHYARD.

By THOMAS GRAY.

WITH SIXTEEN WATER-COLOUR DRAWINGS BY EMINENT ARTISTS, PRINTED IN COLOURS
IN FACSIMILE OF THE ORIGINALS.

Uniform with the Illustrated 'Story Without an End.'

Royal 8vo. cloth, 12s. 6d.; or in morocco, 25s.

'Another edition of the immortal "Elegy," charmingly printed and gracefully bound, but with a new
feature. The illustrations are woodcuts in colours, and they are admirable specimens of the art.'
ART JOURNAL.

'Remarkable for thoughtful conception and all that artistic finish of which this newly-born art is
capable.'—MORNING POST.

'Beauty and care visible throughout.'—STANDARD.

THE STORY WITHOUT AN END.

FROM THE GERMAN OF CAROVÉ.

By SARAH AUSTIN.

ILLUSTRATED WITH SIXTEEN ORIGINAL WATER-COLOUR DRAWINGS BY E. V. B.,
PRINTED IN FACSIMILE,

AND NUMEROUS ILLUSTRATIONS ON WOOD.

Small 4to. cloth extra, 12s.; or in morocco, 21s.

*** Also a Large Paper Edition, with the Plates mounted (only 250 copies printed), morocco,
ivory inlaid, 31s. 6d.

'Nowhere will he find the Book of Nature more freshly and beautifully opened for him than in "The
Story Without and End," of its kind one of the best that was ever written.'—QUARTERLY REVIEW.

ALSO, ILLUSTRATED BY THE SAME ARTIST.

CHILD'S PLAY. Printed in Facsimile from Water-Colour
Drawings, 7s. 6d.

TENNYSON'S MAY QUEEN. Illustrated on Wood. Large
Paper Edition, 7s. 6d.

PEAKS AND VALLEYS OF THE ALPS.

FROM WATER-COLOUR DRAWINGS BY ELIJAH WALTON,

Chromolithographed by J. H. LOWES, with Descriptive Text by the Rev. T. G. BONNEY,
M.A., F.G.S.

Folio, half morocco, with Twenty-one large Plates. Original subscription, Eight Guineas.
A very limited edition only now issued at £4 14s. 6d.

London: SAMPSON LOW, SON, & MARSTON, Crown Buildings, 188 Fleet Street.

CPSIA information can be obtained
at www.ICGtesting.com
Printed in the USA
LVHW010423150720
660226LV00007B/277